OLD TESTAMENT HISTORY

The Bible Study Textbook Series

NEW TESTAMENT

The Bible Study New Testament Ed. By Rhoderick Ice	**The Gospel of Matthew** In Four Volumes By Harold Fowler (Vol. IV not yet available)	**The Gospel of Mark** By B. W. Johnson and Don DeWelt
The Gospel of Luke By T. R. Applebury	**The Gospel of John** By Paul T. Butler	**Acts Made Actual** By Don DeWelt
Romans Realized By Don DeWelt	**Studies in Corinthians** By T. R. Applebury	**Guidance From Galatians** By Don Earl Boatman
The Glorious Church (Ephesians) By Wilbur Fields	**Philippians - Colossians Philemon** By Wilbur Fields	**Thinking Through Thessalonians** By Wilbur Fields
Paul's Letters To Timothy & Titus By Don DeWelt	**Helps From Hebrews** By Don Earl Boatman	**James & Jude** By Don Fream
Letters From Peter By Bruce Oberst	**Hereby We Know (I-II-III John)** By Clinton Gill	**The Seer, The Saviour, and The Saved (Revelation)** By James Strauss

OLD TESTAMENT

O.T. History By William Smith and Wilbur Fields	**Genesis** In Four Volumes By C. C. Crawford	**Exploring Exodus** By Wilbur Fields	**Leviticus** By Don DeWelt
Numbers By Brant Lee Doty	**Deuteronomy** By Bruce Oberst	**Joshua - Judges Ruth** By W. W. Winter	**I & II Samuel** By W. W. Winter
I & II Kings By James E. Smith	**I & II Chronicles** By Robert E. Black	**Ezra, Nehemiah & Esther** By Ruben Ratzlaff & Paul T. Butler	**The Shattering of Silence (Job)** By James Strauss
Psalms In Two Volumes By J. B. Rotherham	**Proverbs** By Donald Hunt		**Ecclesiastes and Song of Solomon** — By R. J. Kidwell and Don DeWelt
Isaiah In Three Volumes By Paul T. Butler	**Jeremiah and Lamentations** By James E. Smith		**Ezekiel** By James E. Smith
Daniel By Paul T. Butler	**Hosea - Joel - Amos Obadiah - Jonah** By Paul T. Butler		**Micah - Nahum - Habakkuk Zephaniah - Haggai - Zechariah Malachi** — By Clinton Gill

SPECIAL STUDIES

The Church In The Bible By Don DeWelt	**The Eternal Spirit** By C. C. Crawford	**World & Literature of the Old Testament** Ed. By John Willis	**Survey Course In Christian Doctrine** Two Bks. of Four Vols. By C. C. Crawford
New Testament History — Acts By Gareth Reese	**Learning From Jesus** By Seth Wilson		**You Can Understand The Bible** By Grayson H. Ensign

OLD TESTAMENT HISTORY

FROM CREATION TO THE RETURN OF THE JEWS FROM CAPTIVITY

by

William Smith, LL.D
Author of *SMITH'S BIBLE DICTIONARY*

REVISED BY
Wilbur Fields

College Press, Joplin, Missouri

First Printing — August 1967
Second Printing — August 1970

Major Revision
Third Printing — August 1971
Fourth Printing — April 1973
Fifth Printing — October 1974
Sixth Printing — March 1976
Seventh Printing — September 1978

Revised Edition, 1979
Ninth Printing — 1980
Revised Edition — 1983

Art by Robert E. Huffman

ISBN 0-89900-000-2
ISBN 0-89900-001-0

Dedicated to

JESUS, THE MESSIAH

"of whom Moses in the law,
and the prophets did write"
(John 1:45).

(Christ Jesus is the theme of the Old Testament as well as the New. The drawings inside the covers illustrate some of the great prophecies in Old Testament History which foretold His coming.)

Contents

CHARTS AND PICTURES

MAPS

ix

SPECIAL STUDIES

Preface

This book has been prepared with only one goal in mind — to help you know the history related in the Old Testament. We believe that this history is God's Word, true and essential. We want you to know it thoroughly.

The core of this book is Professor William Smith's *Old Testament History*. Smith is famous for his *Bible Dictionary*, recently revised and reissued. Now in this book we have extensively revised his *Old Testament History*. While its scholarly and spiritual qualities have been retained, it has been brought thoroughly up-to-date in the light of recent studies of archaeology, chronology and geography.

A familiar and helpful outline of Old Testament history by periods is followed in this book. Information concerning each period is discussed in a number of smaller sections and a thorough set of review questions follows each section.

Many maps and charts, professionally prepared by Robert E. Huffman, are included. These will be most valuable for memorization and comprehension. Many of these maps are adapted from *Sacred History and Geography* by Don DeWelt. This book is the successor to *Sacred History and Geography*.

Many years of teaching Old Testament History to freshman students in Bible colleges lie behind this work. The knowledge and experience of many minds have contributed to make it helpful and effective. The principal participants in its production have been professors at Ozark Bible College, Joplin, Missouri.

Old Testament History

Introduction

1. Why study Old Testament History. 2. The books of
the Old Testament. 3. Sacred history by periods.

1. *Why is the study of Old Testament history important?*
   a. It is important because the holy Scriptures are able to make
      us wise unto salvation (II Timothy 3:15). The apostle Paul
      had reference to the Old Testament scriptures when he
      spoke of the holy scriptures.
   b. *The Old Testament is the background for the New Testament.*
      From the *Old Testament* historical books alone there are
      over 450 quotations or allusions in the New Testament.
      The New Testament cannot be understood without some
      knowledge of the Old Testament.
   c. *All parts of the Old Testament contain prophecies and other
      writings that predict and point toward Christ.* Jesus said,
      "Search the scriptures; . . . for they are they which testify of
      me" (John 5:39; Luke 24:26). We can begin at any point in
      the O.T. and preach Jesus, for Christ is the theme of the
      whole Bible (Acts 8:35).
   d. *The Old Testament history is completely true.* Jesus our Lord
      said that the O.T. scriptures could not be broken, but were
      true in every detail (John 10:35; Matthew 22:29; Matthew
      19:4; et al).

The holy men who wrote the Old Testament did not speak the words themselves, but were moved by the Holy Spirit (II Peter 1:21). The scriptures are inspired, that is, breathed of God (II Timothy 3:16).

The Old Testament history is our only reliable source of knowledge about creation, the early history of humanity, and God's ancient dealings with mankind.

e. *The events in the Old Testament were written for our learning.* They are examples to us (I Corinthians 10:6, 11; Romans 15:4). In the Old Testament we have examples of God's dealings with His people that should warn, instruct and comfort us.

2. *The books of the Old Testament.*

a. Every disciple of Christ should learn the books of the Old Testament, and the divisions of the books. Surely this is the first step in taking up the sword of the Spirit, which is the word of God (Ephesians 6:17).

(1) *5 books of Law:* Genesis, Exodus, Leviticus, Numbers, Deuteronomy (Books often called *Torah,* or *Pentateuch*).

(2) *12 books of History:* Joshua, Judges, Ruth, I & II Samuel, I & II Kings, I & II Chronicles, Ezra, Nehemiah, Esther.

(3) *5 books of Poetry* (or devotion): Job, Psalms, Proverbs, Ecclesiastes, Song of Solomon.

(4) *5 major prophets:* Isaiah, Jeremiah, Lamentations, Ezekiel, Daniel.

(5) *12 minor prophets:* Hosea, Joel, Amos, Obadiah, Jonah, Micah, Nahum, Habakkuk, Zephaniah, Haggai, Zechariah, Malachi.

(The Hebrew Bible divides the books into three parts — Law, Prophets, and Writings. The books are also arranged in a different order.)

b. The historical portion of the Old Testament is contained in the books Genesis through Esther. The poetic and prophetic books fit into the history at points that will be indicated later.

3. *Sacred history by periods.* All of sacred history, both in the Old and New Testaments, can be summarized in fourteen periods. See the chart. Old Testament history can be outlined by the first eleven of the periods. This book follows the outline of history contained on the chart.

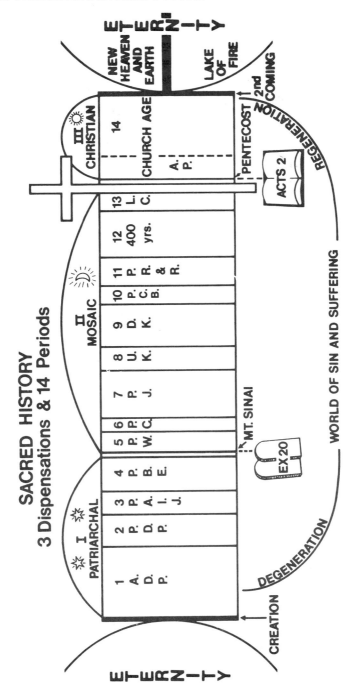

SACRED HISTORY
3 Dispensations & 14 Periods

Explanation of the Chart

A. The three large arches across the top are the three great dispensations in God's program between creation and Christ's second coming.

B. The periods of sacred history within the dispensations are indicated by abbreviations. The Scriptures given below are the sections of scripture written during or pertaining to each period.

1. A.D.P. (Antediluvian period, or period before flood). Mankind went rapidly into sin (Gen. 1-8). Because of the wickedness of men, God destroyed the world by the flood. This period lasted over 1600 years.

2. P.D.P. (Postdiluvian period, or period after flood). Man went back into sin after the flood (Gen. 9-11).

3. P.A.I.J. (Period of Abraham, Isaac and Jacob). God called Abraham and his family. In them all nations were to be blessed (Gen. 12-50; Book of Job).

4. P.B.E. (Period of bondage). 400 years in Egypt (Exodus 1-12).

5. P.W. (Period of wandering). 40 years in the desert (Exodus 13-40; Lev.; Num.; and Deut.).

6. P.C. (Period of conquest). (Joshua).

7. P.J. (Period of judges). (Judges, Ruth and I Samuel 1-7).

8. U.K. (United kingdom). Reigns of Saul, David and Solomon (I Sam. 8-31; II Sam.; I Kings 1-11; I Chron. 10-29; II Chron. 1-9).

   Poetic books of Psalms, Proverbs, Ecclesiastes and Song of Solomon are from this period.

9. D.K. (Divided kingdom). Kingdoms of Judah and Israel (I Kings 12-22; II Kings; II Chron. 10-36).

   Prophetic books of Isaiah, Jeremiah, Lamentations, Hosea, Joel, Amos, Obadiah, Jonah, Micah, Nahum, Habakkuk and Zephaniah are from this period.

10. P.C.B. Period of Captivity in Babylon. 70 years in Babylon (Books of Daniel and Ezekiel; Psalm 137).

11. P.R.&R. (Period of Return and Restoration). (Ezra, Nehemiah, Esther, Haggai, Zechariah, Malachi).

12. 400 years between O.T. and N.T.

13. L.C. (Life of Christ). (Matthew, Mark, Luke, John).

14. Church age. (Acts, Epistles, Romans through Jude, and part of Revelation). During this age men can receive Christ,

Christ, and be saved from the world. The first part of the church age (to about 100 A.D.) was the A.P., Apostolic period.

Questions

1. Give five reasons why the study of Old Testament history is important.
2. Recite the books of the Old Testament in order, and give the divisions of the books.
3. What books of the O.T. contain its historical portion?
4. Into how many periods can sacred history be outlined?

Period I —
Antediluvian Period

From creation to the flood (Genesis 1-8)

Section I
The Book of Genesis

While the book of Genesis deals with the first three periods of sacred history, an overall view of the book is necessary to introduce the antediluvian period (period before the flood). 1. The name Genesis. 2. Author. 3. Extent of its history. 4. Its scientific accuracy. 5. Its ten divisions. 6. Outline. 7. Messianic prophecies in Genesis.

1. *The name Genesis means "origin," "source" or "beginning."* This name is taken from the Greek Old Testament. The Hebrew name for the book is *Bereshith,* which means "In the beginning." The Old Testament was almost all written in Hebrew, and *Bereshith* is the first word in Genesis.
2. *Moses is the author of Genesis.* "Did not Moses give you the law?" (John 7:19). "If they hear not Moses and the prophets . . ." (Luke 16:31). Moses was fully capable of doing this task, as he was educated in all the great learning of the Egyptians (Acts 7:22).

Certainly God is the ultimate author of Genesis and all the other books of the Bible. God inspired Moses for his task. This means that God breathed into the mind of Moses the thoughts and words that he should write. Thus Moses knew information that no man could have known without revelation, such as the details of creation. Also Moses was thus enabled to write about the things with which he was familiar without error. See II Tim. 3:16; II Pet. 1:21.

3. *Genesis deals with history from the creation to the death of Joseph.*
4. *Genesis is scientifically and archaeologically accurate.*
   a. All the oceans on earth are actually "in one place," or literally, "in one bed" (Gen. 1:9). They are actually just one ocean. How did Moses, who had never circled the globe, know this, unless God revealed it?
   b. Creatures reproduce "after their kind," as Genesis says (Gen. 1:11, 21). Cows always give birth to cows, and corn seeds always produce corn. This is a proven law of genetics.
   c. The most ancient cities that have been dug up and studied show that the earliest peoples on earth had the fewest gods. Instead of man evolving from the worship of many gods to one God, Genesis and the Bible are true in indicating that man started with one God, and soon added many gods. (See Sir Charles Marston, *The Bible Comes Alive*, Joplin, Mo.: College Press, 1969, pp. 17-19.)
5. Genesis divides itself into ten parts. Each of these divisions begins with some such words as "These are the generations (or history) of . . ."
   Introduction—The creation account; 1:1-2:3.
   (1) The generations of heaven and earth; 2:4-4:26.
   (2) The generations of Adam; 5:1-6:8.
   (3) The generations of Noah; 6:9-9:29.
   (4) The generations of the sons of Noah; 10:1-11:9.
   (5) The generations of Shem; 11:10-26.
   (6) The generations of Terah; 11:27-25:11.
   (7) The generations of Ishmael; 25:12-18.
   (8) The generations of Isaac; 25:19-35:39.
   (9) The generations of Esau; Ch. 36. Note 36:1,9.
   (10) The generations of Jacob; Chs. 37-50.
6. Outline of Genesis. (Memorize)
   Part I—The earliest history; Chapters 1-11.
   (1) Creation; Chs. 1-2.
   (2) The fall; Ch. 3.

(3) The two lines of humanity; Chs. 4-5.
(4) The flood; Chs. 6-9.
(5) Noah's descendants; Chs. 10-11.
Part II—History of the patriarchs; Chs. 12-50.
(1) Abraham; 12:1-25:11.
(2) Isaac; 25:12-28:9.
(3) Jacob; 28:10-ch. 36.
(4) Joseph (and Jacob's other sons); Chs. 37-50.
7. Genesis contains several wonderful Messianic prophecies
   (prophecies of Christ).
   a. *Genesis 3:15*. The first promise of the Savior is here given. It
      declares that the seed of the woman (Christ) will bruise the
      head of the serpent (Satan), and the serpent will bruise the
      heel of the woman's seed.
   b. *Genesis 12:3* and *22:18*. God promised to bless all peoples
      through Abraham and through his "seed" (who is Christ).
      See Acts 3:25-26 and Galatians 3:8,16.
   c. *Genesis 49:10*. The tribe of Judah will be the ruling tribe in
      Israel until "Shiloh" comes. "Shiloh" means "peaceful," or
      "rest-giver," or "he to whom it (the scepter) belongs." The
      name *Shiloh* refers here to Christ.

Questions on Section I
The Book of Genesis

1. What does the name *Genesis* mean?
2. In what language was the Old Testament written?
3. Who was the author (or writer) of Genesis? Who was its
   ultimate author?
4. What are the first and last events in Genesis?
5. Is Genesis a scientifically and archaeologically accurate book?
6. How many divisions does Genesis divide itself into?
7. How does each of these divisions begin?
8. Write from memory the outline of Genesis including
   Scripture references.
9. Give Scripture references for four Messianic prophecies in
   Genesis.

Section II
The Creation (Genesis 1-2)

1. Purpose and scope of Scripture history. 2. The
universe created by God only. 3. At a definite time.

1. *The purpose and scope of Scripture history.* The purpose of Scripture history is to set forth the steps by which God built up for Himself a people, a *church.* God had an "eternal purpose" in mind when He made heaven and earth, namely that He would finally send Christ Jesus into the world to die for and redeem (purchase and rescue) mankind (Eph. 3:11; 1:4; I Peter 1:20; Rev. 13:8).

The scope of Scripture history spans from the *beginning,* from the commencement of creation. Thus we begin where the Bible itself begins: "In the beginning God created."

The Bible then shows us the successive offers of grace which God made: first, to all mankind, then to the family of Abraham, then to the nation of the Jews, and lastly again to all mankind in Jesus Christ. Thus it exhibits the result of these several offers, to make us know our own impotence and our total dependence upon His mercy in Christ Jesus.

2. *The universe created by God only.* Without preface or argument on the being of God, the sacred writer speaks of Him as the Creator of the universe: "In the beginning God created the heaven and the earth."[1] The purpose of this declaration was practical. It is designed to guard believers against the first steps in unbelief. There is in it a tacit reference to all the forms of error respecting the origin of the universe. The world was created by God, not by *chance,* not by *self-generation,* not by impersonal *powers of nature,* not by *many agents,* whether acting in harmony, or in antagonism, like the good and evil principles of the Persian religion. Above all, the sacred story reveals the *love* which was the ruling principle of the whole work, for at each stage God pronounces it *good.* And if we take this first statement in connection with other passages of the Bible, we learn that the

---

1. Gen. 1:1. On the *Names of God,* see *Special Studies,* p. 15-16.

agent in creation was the *Son*, the *Word* (John 1:1-3; Heb. 1:2; Col. 1:16).

3. *This work of creation was performed at a definite time.* "*In the beginning* God created the heaven and the earth." They did not exist, therefore, from eternity; nor are we permitted to trace them backward from age to age, till we lose all idea of their having had a beginning. The scripture links the creation of heaven and earth with God's making of all things on earth (Ex. 20:11). We should therefore believe that the universe and the earth are "young" rather than billions of years old.

4. *The objects created* by God are declared to be the heavens and the earth. The *heavens* which God created are those which we see, whether at once, by unaided vision, or gradually by the discoveries of the astronomer. The *earth* is the whole structure which forms our portion of the great Cosmos, manifested to us in like manner. These phenomena are so spoken of in the plain language of common sense, as to leave the reader's judgment open for the reception of scientific facts and laws; but whatever wonders science may reveal in heaven and earth, the simple truth remains, that *God created them all.*

5. *The order of creation* as a whole can often only be appreciated by knowing its parts. We are further taught the *order* in which the various portions of the created universe were produced; and that this order was *progressive*, with each step being necessary for the next. From the first simple fact of *creation by God at a definite time* we are led on to a second point of time, when the *earth* (for the *heaven* is not now mentioned, Gen. 1:2) existed indeed, but in a state of *disorder* and *emptiness*. Its materials were not yet arranged in order, and it was void of the forms of being that were to cover its surface. There were then no sedimentary deposits such as now cover most of the earth. Water in both the forms of vapor and liquid shrouded the inky blackness of Earth. It was impossible to distinguish sky from solid earth. This *watery chaos* is the stage from which the more detailed narrative begins: "The earth was *without form and void,* and *darkness* was upon the face of the deep. And the spirit of God moved upon the face of the waters." ("Spirit" should not here be translated "wind.")

6. *Duration of the chaos and the days of creation.* It is often proposed that there was a long time gap between the creation of Genesis 1:1 and the chaos of 1:2. This is contrary to the plain

statement of Ex. 20:11 and to the grammar of the Hebrew statement.[1] The chaos seems to have been the condition immediately after creation.

While the word *day* (Hebrew, *yom*) occasionally in scripture refers to a long period of time (as in John 8:56 and Heb. 3:15), in the creation account it appears to refer simply to twenty-four hour periods immediately following one another.

a. The days are divided into evenings and mornings, according to the Hebrew custom. This terminology is applicable to ordinary days, but hardly to periods of time.

b. On the third day plants were made. The sun did not appear till the fourth day. Could plants have survived a "day" millions of years long without sunlight?

c. The Hebrew word *day* when used with numbers always refers to days of twenty-four hours.

d. Adam was created on the sixth day. He lived through the sixth and seventh days in the garden of Eden. Some time after the seventh day he was expelled from the garden. His wife bore Cain and Abel. They grew up, and Cain killed Abel. At the birth of a third son Adam was only 130 years old (Gen. 5:3). Therefore the sixth and seventh days cannot refer to periods of time thousands of years in duration.

e. Gen. 1:14 clearly distinguishes days from years and seasons.

f. The Sabbath day of the Jews was a twenty-four hour period, and was observed as a memorial of the seventh day of creation (Exodus 20:11).

7. *The following are the works assigned to each day.*

a. On the FIRST DAY went forth the Word of God — the *creative* FIAT, as it has been well called, for "He *spake* and it was *done*" — "Let there be LIGHT, and *Light was.*" Light broke over the face of chaos. It shone upon each part of the earth's surface that was exposed to it in turn, and so "God *divided* the light from the darkness; and God called the light *Day,* and the darkness he called *Night.* And the evening and the morning were the *First Day*" (Gen. 1:3; Comp. II Cor. 4:6).

b. As yet the watery vapors formed an envelop of mist around the earth. They were now parted into two divisions, those which lie upon and hang about the surface of the earth, and those which float high above it. The blue heavens became visible, like a crystal vault, called the *firmament* (literally

---

1. The position of the *and* at the start of 1:2 before the noun *earth* rather than with the verb indicates simultaneous rather than consecutive actions. See John J. Davis, *Paradise to Prison* (Baker, 1975), pp. 42-45; and Kautzsch and Cowley, *Gesenius' Hebrew Grammar* (Oxford, 1949), pp. 453-454.

expanse), because its appearance is that of an outspread covering, elsewhere likened to a *tent* (Isa. 40:22). But the word chosen no more implies that the sky is really a solid vault than it is a canvas tent. It forms, to the eye, the partition between the upper and lower heavens, between "the waters under the firmament and the waters above the firmament." Such was the work of the SECOND DAY.

c. Next began the tremendous upheavings and sinkings of the earth's crust, by the forces at work within it, which formed it into mountains and valleys, and provided channels and basins for the waters on its surface. These were now gathered into one bed which was called *Seas*. A view of a world map or globe will show that all the seas are joined, and actually in one bed even though continents separate the waters into various oceans. The name of *Earth* was applied, in a narrower sense than before, to the portions exposed above the waters. On these portions vegetation began at once to burst into life, forming grass and fruit trees. These had *their seed in themselves, after their kind.* Here is the great law of *reproduction according to species,* on which depends the order of the vegetable and animal kingdoms. This was the work of the THIRD DAY (Gen. 1:9-13).

d. On the FOURTH DAY, the *Sun* and *Moon* were set in the firmament of heaven. It is sometimes argued that the sun and moon were created at the very beginning, but were not made visible through the water vapors until the fourth day. Gen. 1:14 seems to say that the sun and moon came into existence on the fourth day. The heat and light originally upon the earth must therefore have been like that which shall be in the new heaven and earth, where we shall need no light of sun or moon (Rev. 21:23). Stress is laid on their *ruling* as well as *lighting* the day and night. God said: "Let them be for *signs,* and for *seasons,* and for *days* and *years.*" They were designed, as they have ever since been used, to mark out the periods of human life; to inculcate the great lesson that "to every thing there is a *season,* and a *time* to every purpose under the heaven" (Gen. 1:14-19; Eccl. 3:1).

e. The existence of plant life was essential if animal life was to survive. Therefore, following the appearance of plant life animal life was created. First the waters teemed with the "creeping things" and the "great sea-monsters," with fishes and reptiles. Birds were produced at the same time, and might

and reptiles. Birds were produced at the same time, and might have been seen flying over the waters and in the open firmament of heaven. This was the work of the FIFTH DAY (Gen. 1:20-23).

Summary of the Seven Days of Creation

First day — Light and dark
Second day — Firmament
Third day — Dry land and plants
Fourth day — Sun, moon and stars
Fifth day — Water and air creatures
Sixth day — Land animals and man
Seventh day — Rest

---

f. The SIXTH DAY witnessed the creation of the *higher animals and* MAN. These were formed out of the earth, the chemical constituents of which are the same as those of animal bodies.

MAN, the last created, for whom all the previous work was but a preparation, differed from all other creatures in being made *in the image of God.* The depth of meaning contained in this statement, though partly revealed in the Son of God, the true head of our race, remains to be revealed in the world to come. But at least it includes *intellectual* and *spiritual* likeness, intelligence, moral power and holiness. To man was given dominion over all other animals; and both to him and them the plants were given for food. All were appointed to continue their species according to their own likeness, and all were blessed with fertility; but on the human race was pronounced the special blessing: "Be fruitful, and multiply, and replenish the earth, and *subdue* it" — so that Man's lordship of the creation is a part of his original constitution (Gen. 1:24-31; Comp. Psalm 8).[1]

On each of the works of the last four days God pronounced the blessing that *it was very good;* perfect in its kind, useful in its purpose, and entirely subject to His holy laws.

8. On the SEVENTH DAY God ceased from his finished work, rested, and blessed the day. His rest, however, was not an entire cessation from activity. He was done *creating,* but he continued to

---

1. The name *Adam,* which is used in a threefold sense — *generic,* for the human creature, both male and female (see Gen. 4. 2); *specific,* for the male; and hence as a *proper name* for the first man — is derived from the *ground (Adamah)* out of which he was formed. The root sense is the same as that of *Edom, red.* The name applied to man in the nobler aspect of his nature is *Ish (a man of worth,* Gen. 2:23).

sustain and *bless* his creatures. "My Father worketh hitherto, and I work" (John 5:17), said Christ; and thus this seventh day finds its perfect analogy in the day for which he also gave the law, "to *do good* on the Sabbath-day."

The fact that God's creative work was *finished* by the seventh day precludes subsequent evolutionary development of new species. Since the completion of creation many types of creatures have become extinct, and a great amount of variation has developed within the limits of the "kinds" of animals. But the range of the variations has definite limits beyond which creatures cannot reproduce.

9. The account of the Creation in *Genesis 1-2:3,* is followed by a more particular account of the *creation and primeval state of man* (Gen. 2:4-25). His frame was made from the dust (or clay) of the ground; his life was breathed into his nostrils by God. The female, created to be "a help meet (that is, corresponding to or suitable) for him," was made out of the substance of his own body, whence she was called *woman (Ishah,* the feminine of *Ish,* man) (Gen. 2:21-25). This is given now, and long afterward used by Christ, as a reason for the *law of marriage,* which is a divine institution, plainly involved in the fact that *one woman* was created for *one man.* "Therefore shall a man leave his father and his mother, and shall cleave unto his wife, and they shall be one flesh" (Gen. 2:24; Matt. 19:5). From these words, coupled with the circumstances attendant on the formation of the first woman, we may evolve the following principles: (a) The unity of man and wife, as implied in her being formed out of man, and as expressed in the words "one flesh"; (b) the indissolubleness of the marriage bond, except on the strongest grounds, (c) monogamy, as the original law of marriage, resulting from there having been but one original couple, as is forcibly expressed in the subsequent references to this passage by our Lord (Matt. 19:5) and apostle Paul (I Cor. 6:16); (d) the social equality of man and wife, as implied in the terms *ish* and *ishah,* the one being the exact correlative of the other, as well as in the words "help meet for him"; (e) the subordination of the wife to the husband, consequent upon her subsequent formation (I Cor. 11:8-9; I Tim. 2:13); and (f) the respective duties of man and wife, as implied in the words "help meet for him."

To this pair God gave an abode and an occupation. He placed them in a Garden in Eden, an Eastern region, the name of which survived in historic times, and at least two of its four rivers are identified with the Tigris and Euphrates.[1] Their easy and pleasant occupation was to keep and dress the garden, or as the Septuagint calls it, *Paradise*. This word, of Persian origin, describes an extensive tract of pleasure land, somewhat like an English *park;* and the use of it suggests a wider view of man's first abode than a *garden*. Perfect as he was in physical constitution, man might roam over a very extensive region, such as that which lies between the highlands of Armenia and the Persian Gulf. Here he might find occupation for his mind in the study of the creatures made subject to him, and so be qualified to *name* them, as he did when God brought them before him.

Many lines of evidence point toward the lower Tigris-Euphrates valley as the location of Eden. A possible alternate location would be the Armenian highlands south of the Ararat mountains.

The fact of Adam's naming the animals proves that he was endowed from his first creation with the power of *language*. The narrative of his fall bears indirect but certain testimony to his close fellowship with God. All else is speculation; but we may dwell with delight on Milton's pictures of unfallen man, and believe with South that "Aristotle was but the rubbish of an Adam, and Athens the rudiments of Paradise." More perfectly, however, does Christ, "the second Adam," reveal to us the perfection of the first.

The last stroke in the description indicates the perfection of man's innocence by the absence of the sense of shame which sin alone has introduced into the original moral harmony of man's constitution: "They were both naked, the man and his wife, and were not ashamed" (Gen. 2:25).

Special Study
The Hebrew Names of God

Throughout the Hebrew Scriptures three chief names are used for the one true divine Being — ELOHIM, commonly translated *God* in our version; and JEHOVAH (or YAHWEH), translated LORD, and ADONAI, translated *Lord*.

---

1. The Hiddekel is the Tigris; but with regard to the Pison and Gihon, a great variety of opinion exists. Many ancient writers, as Josephus, identified the Pison with the Ganges, and the Gihon with the Nile. We must keep in mind that the topography of the earth was greatly altered by the flood of Noah.

1. ELOHIM is the plural of ELOAH (in Arabic *Allah*), a form which occurs only in poetry and a few passages of later Hebrew (Neh. 9:17; II Chr. 32:15). It is also formed with the pronominal suffixes, as ELOI, *my God,* and in compound names, in which it is often used in the short form, EL (a word signifying *strength*), as in EL-SHADDAI, *God Almighty,* the name by which God was specially known to the patriarchs (Gen. 17:1; 18:3; Ex. 6:3). The etymology is uncertain, but it is generally agreed that the primary idea is that of *strength, power to effect;* and that it properly describes God in that character in which He is exhibited to all men in His works, as the creator, sustainer and supreme governor of the world. Hence it is used to denote any being believed in and worshiped as God. But in the sense of a heathen deity, or a divine being spoken of indefinitely, the singular is most often used, and the plural is employed, with the strict idea of number, for the collective objects of polytheistic worship, *the gods, the gods of the heathen.* It is also used for any being that strikes an observer as godlike (I Sam. 28:13), and for kings, judges and others endowed with authority from God (Psalm 82:1,6; 13:6; 97:7, etc.; Ex. 21:6; 22:7,8). The short form *El* is used for a *hero,* or *mighty man,* as Nebuchadnezzar (Ezek. 31:11), a sense derived at once from the meaning of strength. The plural form of ELOHIM has given rise to much discussion. It is either what grammarians call the *plural of majesty,* or it denotes the fullness of divine strength, the *sum of the powers* displayed by God.

2. JEHOVAH denotes specifically the one true God, whose people the Jews were, and who made them the guardians of His truth. The name is never applied to a false god, nor to any other being, except ONE, the ANGEL-JEHOVAH, who is thereby marked as one with God, and who appears again in the New Covenant as "God manifested in the flesh." This much is clear, but all else is beset with difficulties. At a time too early to be traced, the Jews abstained from pronouncing the name, for fear of its irreverent use. The Rabbis use the phrase THE NAME (Lev. 24:16) for the unutterable word. They also call it "the name of four letters" (YHWH, or the tetragammaton), "the great and terrible name," "the peculiar name," "the separate name." In reading the Scriptures, they substituted for it the word ADONAI (Lord). From this it was rendered in the Septuagint (Greek O.T.) as *Kurios,* or *Lord,* and in the Latin Vulgate as *Dominus,* from whence we obtained the term LORD in the King James Version. The King James version does use JEHOVAH in four passages (Ex. 6:3; Psalm

83:18; Is. 12:2; 26:4), and in the compounds *Jehovah-Jireh*, *Jehovah-Nissi*, and *Jehovah Shalom* (*Jehovah shall see*, *Jehovah* is *my Banner, Jehovah* is *peace*, Gen. 22:14; Ex. 17:15; Judges 6:24); while the similar phrases *Jehovah-Tsidkenu* and *Jehovah-Shammah* are translated, "the LORD our righteousness," and "the LORD *is there*" (Jer. 23:6; 33:16; Ezek. 48:35). In one passage the abbreviated form JAH is retained (Psalm 68:4). This form JAH (or YAH) occurs about forty-four times in the Hebrew Bible. The substitution of the word LORD is most unhappy; for, while it in no way represents the meaning of the sacred name, the mind has constantly to guard against a confusion with its lower uses, and, above all, the direct personal bearing of the name on the revelation of God through the whole course of Jewish history is kept injuriously out of sight. For these reasons, we have restored the name in the following pages, in the common form, its true pronunciation (possibly YAHWEH) having been completely lost.

The key to the *meaning* of the name is unquestionably given in God's revelation of Himself to Moses by the phrase "I AM THAT I AM," in connection with the statement, that He was now first revealed by his name JEHOVAH (Ex. 3:14; 6:3). The name JEHOVAH appears to be related to the Hebrew verb *hayah*, which means *to be* or *become*. Thus the name JEHOVAH indicates that JEHOVAH is the existing one, the eternal one; or, perhaps even better, the becoming one, the one who causes things to become and exist. People could know his name JEHOVAH, and not know the true significance of that name. And here we find the solution of a difficulty raised by Ex. 6:3, as if it meant that the name *Jehovah* had not been known to the patriarchs. There is abundant evidence to the contrary. As early as the time of Seth, "men began to call on the name of Jehovah" (Gen. 4:25). The name is used by the patriarchs themselves (Gen. 18:14; 24:40; 26:28; 28:21). It is the basis of titles, like *Jehovah-Jireh*, and of proper names, like *Moriah*, and *Jochebed*. Indeed, the same reasoning would prove that the patriarchs did not know God as *Elohim*, but exclusively as *El-Shaddai*. But, in fact, the word *name* is used here, as elsewhere, for the attributes of God. He was about, for the first time, to reveal that aspect of His character which the name implied.

3. ADONAI, translated *Lord*, and literally meaning *my lord*, from *adon*, or *lord*, is used several hundred times as the name of God, most often in combination with the name ELOHIM, and translated together as *Lord God* (Gen. 15:2,8; 18:3). *Adon* (or lord) is often applied to people (Gen. 18:12; 23:6).

Questions on Section II
The Creation (Gen. 1-2)

1. What was the condition of the earth after its creation?

2. What moved upon the face of the waters?

3. Give a summary of the things done or made on the seven days of creation.

4. Give three reasons for arguing that the days of creation were successive periods of twenty-four hours.

5. Why do the days of creation have evenings first, then mornings?

6. What does the word *firmament* mean, and to what does it refer? See Gen. 1:14,20.

7. What did the firmament divide?

8. What did God call the firmament?

9. Where were the waters under heaven gathered?

10. What did God call the dry land?

11. What did God cause the earth to put forth or yield?

12. In what manner did the trees and plants bear fruit and seed?

13. What were the lights in the firmament of heaven for?

14. With what words did God bless the birds and the sea-monsters?

15. In what likeness and image was man made?

16. Over what was man given dominion?

17. Was man told to reproduce before his first sin?

18. What was originally given to man for food? What was given to the beasts?

19. What descriptive word describes everything God made?

20. How completely was God's creative work finished?

21. What did God do with the seventh day?

22. How did God water the ground before rain fell on earth?

23. From what did God form man?

24. What did God breathe into man?

25. Where did God put the man?

26. In what two ways are the trees of Eden described (2:9)?

27. What two trees in the garden were named?

28. How did the river from Eden divide?

29. What were the names of the four rivers out of Eden?

30. What work was given to man?

31. What was man prohibited from eating, and what was the penalty if he ate?

32. What did God determine to make for man?

33. How did the animals get their names?
34. From what was the woman made?
35. Why was the woman called Woman?
36. Whom is the man to leave when he marries?
37. What are the man and wife to be?

Section III
Man's Probation and Fall (Gen. 3)

1. The trees of life and knowledge. 2. The law and its penalty. 3. The temptation and fall. 4. Eyes opened to evil. 5. God's judgments — (a) on the serpent — (b) on the woman — (c) on the man. 6. Promise of a Redeemer — The name of Eve. 7. Institution of sacrifice — Dispensation of mercy. 8. Traditions of heathen nations.

1. *The happiness of Paradise was granted to the first human pair on one simple condition.* A restraint was to be placed upon their appetite and self-will. Abundant scope was given for gratifying every lawful taste: "The Lord God caused to grow every tree that is pleasant to the sight and good for food" (Gen. 2:9). But two trees are distinguished from the rest, as having special properties. The *tree of life* had, in some mysterious way, the power of making man immortal (Gen. 3:22). The *tree of the knowledge of good and evil* revealed to those who ate its fruit secrets of which they had better have remained ignorant; for the purity of man's happiness consisted in doing and loving good without even knowing evil.

2. *The use of these trees was not left to man's unaided judgment.* God gave him the plain command: "Of every tree of the garden thou mayest freely eat: but of the fruit of the tree of the knowledge of good and evil, thou shalt not eat of it: for in the day that thou eatest thereof thou shalt surely die" (Gen. 2:16,17). The vast freedom granted to him proved the goodness of the Creator; the one exception taught him that he was to live under a *law;* and that law was enforced by a practical penalty, of which he was mercifully warned. We must not regard the prohibition merely as a test of obedience, nor the penalty as arbitrary. The knowledge forbidden to him was of a kind which would corrupt his nature — so corrupt it, as to make him unfit, as well as unworthy, to live forever.

3. *The trial of man's obedience was completed by a temptation from without.* The tempter is simply called in *Genesis* the *Serpent* (Gen. 3:1; Comp. 2 Cor. 11:3); but that creature was a well-known type of the chief of the fallen angels, the Evil Spirit, whose constant effort is to drag down man to share his own ruin. From this enmity to God and man, he is called SATAN (the *adversary),* and the DEVIL (the *accuser* or *slanderer).* He slandered God to our first parents, teaching them to doubt his truth, and to ascribe his law to jealousy. *"Ye shall not surely die:* for God doth know that, in the day ye eat thereof, then your eyes shall be opened, and *ye shall be as gods,* knowing good and evil" (Gen. 3:4-5). He addressed the temptation first to the woman, who fell into the threefold sin of *sensuality, pleasure* and *ambition,* "the lust of the flesh, the lust of the eyes, and the pride of life" (I John 2:16). She "saw that the tree was *good for food,* and that it was *pleasant to the eyes,* and a tree to be desired *to make one wise"* (Gen. 3:6); and she ate the fruit, and gave it to her husband. The threefold appeal of the tempter to the infirmities of our nature may be traced also in the temptation of Christ, the second Adam, who "was in all points likewise tempted, but *without* SIN."

4. *In one point the devil had truly described the effect of eating the forbidden fruit.* "Their eyes were opened" (Gen. 3:7). They had "become as gods" in respect of that knowledge of evil, as well as good, which God had reserved to himself and mercifully denied to them. They became conscious of the working of lawless pleasure in place of purity, in the very constitution given them by God to perpetuate their race; and they were ashamed because they were naked. Toward God they felt fear in place of love, and they fled to hide themselves from His presence among the trees of the garden (Gen. 3:8).

5. *Thus they were already self-condemned before God called them forth to judgment.* Then the man cast the blame upon the woman, and the woman upon the serpent; and God proceeded to award a righteous sentence to each (Gen. 3:9-19).
a. The judgment passed upon the serpent is symbolical of the condemnation of the devil. The creature, as Satan's instrument and type, is doomed to an accursed and degraded life; and the enmity that has ever since existed between him and man is the symbol of the conflict between the powers of hell and all that is good in the human race.
b. The woman is condemned to subjection to her husband, and sorrow and suffering in giving birth to her children; but she

had the consolation of hearing that *her seed* was to conquer in the battle with the serpent, crushing its head, after the reptile had inflicted a deadly wound upon his heel (Gen. 3:15; Compare Rom. 16:20).

c. The man is shut up to a life of toil, and the earth is cursed for his sake, to bring forth, like himself, evil weeds, that require all his exertions to keep them down. But, as before, a promise is added; his labors shall not be without its reward — "in the sweat of thy brow, *thou shalt eat bread.*"

Reminded of the doom they had incurred, though its execution was postponed — "dust thou art, and unto dust shalt thou return" — and clothed by God's goodness with the skins of beasts, they were driven out of Paradise. Angelic guards called cherubim, with a flaming sword, debarred them from returning to taste the tree of life; for it would have perpetuated their suffering (Gen. 3:21-24).

6. *But yet they had received the revelation of eternal life.* The curse upon the serpent and the promise to the woman pointed clearly to a Redeemer, who should be born of a woman, and, by his own suffering, should destroy the power of the devil; and here we have the *first prophecy of the Messiah.* Henceforth the woman lived in the expectation of the promised seed, which should make her the mother of a truly *living* race; and, to signify this hope, Adam gave her the name of EVE *(Chavah,* that is, *living).* Thus already life began to spring from death (Gen. 3:20).

7. *There can be no reasonable doubt that the sacrifice of living animals was now instituted as a prophetic figure of the great sacrifice which should fulfill this promise.* Animals must have been slain to provide the skins that clothed Adam and Eve; and wherefore slain, except in sacrifice? This might not seem conclusive in itself; but the whole reason for sacrifice began to exist now: its use is taken for granted in the next chapter (Gen. 4); and it continues throughout the patriarchal age without the record of any other beginning. Thus early, then, man learned that, "without shedding of blood, there is no remission of sin"; that his own forfeited life was redeemed, and to be restored by the sacrifice of the coming "seed of the woman"; and that he was placed by God under a new *dispensation of mercy.* Nay, even his punishment was a mercy; for his suffering was a discipline to train him in submission to God's will. The repentance of our first parents is nowhere expressly stated: but it is implied here and in the subsequent narrative.

8. We must not omit to notice the traces of these truths, which

are found among many nations. The Greek legend of Pandora traces the entrance of evil to a woman; the Babylonian myth of Adapa[1] tells how man forfeited the chance of eternal life. Delitzsch well says, "The story of the Fall, like that of the Creation, has wandered over the world. Heathen nations have transplanted and mixed it up with their geography, their history, their mythology, although it has never so completely changed form, and color, and spirit, that you cannot recognize it. Here, however, in the Law, it preserves the character of a universal, human, world-wide fact: and the groans of Creation, the Redemption that is in Christ Jesus, and the heart of every man unite in their testimony to the literal truth of the narrative of the fall."

Questions on Section III
The Fall (Gen. 3)

1. How did the serpent differ from other beasts?
2. What question did the serpent ask Eve?
3. Who actually spoke through the serpent (Cf. Rev. 12:9)?
4. Had God forbidden Eve to *touch* the fruit of the tree in the midst of the garden as Eve indicated (Cf. Gen. 2:16-17)?
5. What statement of God did the serpent bluntly deny?
6. Why did the serpent say that God did not want them to eat the fruit?
7. What three things about the tree tempted Eve? How do these temptations compare to the worldly temptations listed in I John 2:16?
8. Where was Adam when Eve ate the fruit?
9. What was the first thing they became aware of after eating?
10. What was used to make aprons?
11. What was God's question when he called for Adam?
12. Whom did Adam blame for his eating the forbidden fruit?
13. Whom did the woman blame for her eating it?
14. What punishment was pronounced on the serpent?
15. What was the serpent's seed to do to the woman's seed, and the woman's seed to the serpent?
16. What were the punishments pronounced on the woman?
17. What were the punishments pronounced on the man?
18. What effect did Adam's sin have on the whole subsequent human race (I Cor. 15:21-22)? What effect on the whole material creation (Rom. 8:20-22)?

---

1. M.F. Unger, *Archaeology and the O.T.* p. 40-41.

19. Does God approve of nudity now? How do you know?
20. Why did God drive man from Eden?
21. What blocked man's way back into Eden?

Section IV
The Old Testament World

Thirty-two places are marked on the following map. The names and locations of all of these are to be memorized. Memorizing them in groups will be a big help. Do not start on another group until you have conquered the first. Remember Phil. 4:13.

A. *Rivers*
   1. Araxes — The border between Armenia and Media.
   2. Orontes — An important location during the time of the kingdom of Israel.
   3. Tigris — The wicked city of Nineveh lay by this river.
   4. Euphrates — Ezekiel and Abram looked upon its waters.
   5. Nile — The lifestream of Egypt. Once it became blood.
   6. Jordan — Naaman dipped himself seven times here.

B. *Bodies of Water*
   1. Caspian Sea
   2. Persian Gulf — This receives the waters of the Tigris and Euphrates rivers.
   3. Red Sea — Has two arms: the Gulf of Suez and the Gulf of Akabah.
   4. Dead Sea — The lowest place on earth's surface.
   5. The Great Sea — The Mediterranean.
   6-7. Lake Van and Lake Urumiah — Not mentioned in the Bible, but they are near the place where the ark landed.

C. *Mountains*
   1. Ararat Mountains — The high mountains where the ark rested.
   2. Zagros Mountains — The key to the ancient Babylonian language was discovered in these mountains. (See "Behistun" in any encyclopedia.) Lie between Media and Assyria.
   3. Lebanon Mountains — These have two sections: (a) Lebanon range on west of Jordan; (b) Anti-Lebanon range on the east of the Jordan and Orontes rivers.
   4. Mt. Sinai — Moses received the law here.

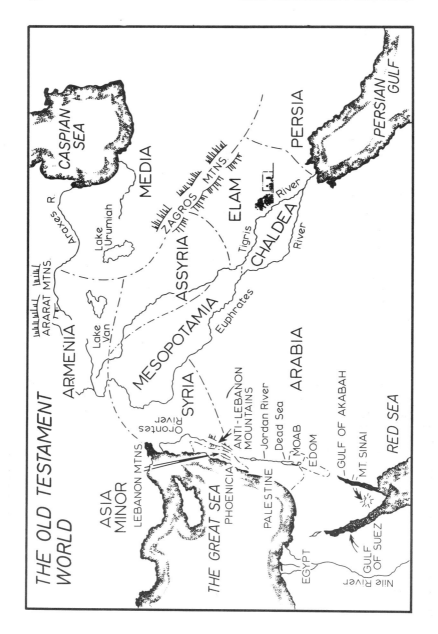

D. *Lands* (Memorize in groups of 2-3, 2-3, 2-3, as listed)
  1. Armenia — Noah's residence for a time.
  2. Media — The people who helped God fulfill the handwriting on the wall.
  3. Assyria — A cruel empire that captured the kingdom of Israel.
  4. Elam — People of this country captured Abraham's nephew.
  5. Persia — A Jewish girl became queen of Persia.
  6. Mesopotamia — This name means "between the rivers."
  7. Chaldea — Abram's home was in Ur of the Chaldees. Also called Babylonia.
  8. Asia Minor — This was the main center of the Hittites.
  9. Syria — Jacob worked for Rachel seven years in Syria (or Aram).
 10. Arabia — This land is mostly desert, inhabited by nomads.
 11. Phoenicia — Wicked queen Jezebel came from this seafaring kingdom.
 12. Palestine — Also called Canaan and Israel.
 13. Moab — Homeland of Ruth.
 14. Edom — Mountainous home of Esau's descendants.
 15. Egypt — Israel lived in Egypt 400 years.

Review

On the blank map below write in Key numbers for the names of the thirty-two locations in their proper places. Use Key numbers here and write the thirty-two facts on a separate list.

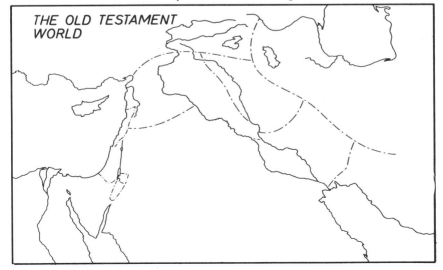

THE OLD TESTAMENT WORLD

Section V
The Two Lines of Humanity
(Gen. 4-5)

1. Births of Cain and Abel. 2. Their different occupations and characters — Two types of men. 3. Their respective offerings. 4. The murder of Abel. 5. The punishment of Cain. 6. His descendants. 7. The race of Seth. 8. Character of Enoch — His translation. 9. Methuselah — Epoch of his death. 10. Longevity of the patriarchs.

1. *After the expulsion of man from Paradise, Eve bore her first-born son, and named him Cain* (i.e., *possession,* or *acquisition*), saying "I have gotten a man from the Lord." The name itself, and the reason given for its choice, indicate her belief that this man-child was the promised "seed of the woman." Her mistake seems to have been soon revealed to her, for on the birth of her second son, she gave him a name expressive of disappointment, ABEL (Heb. *Hebel,* i.e., *breath, vapor, transitoriness:* some, however, take it to refer to the shortness of his life).

2. *In the occupation of these two sons of Adam, we trace the two great branches of productive industry pursued by men in an early stage of society.* "Abel was a *keeper* (or feeder) *of sheep,* but Cain was a *tiller of the ground."* Here are the beginnings of the *pastoral* and *agricultural* modes of life; and in this respect, as in others, the two first sons of Adam are representatives of his posterity. For we must avoid the error of thinking of Cain and Abel as the only progeny of Adam and Eve. The mention of Cain's wife, as well as his fear that men would slay him (v. 14), are indications that the "filling of the earth" had made considerable progress before the murder of Abel. Cain and Abel are to be viewed as *types* of the two classes of character, which appeared from the first among men: the good and the wicked, the "children of God" and the "children of the devil." This is clearly recognized by Jude, who uses "the way of Cain" for a type of wickedness (Jude 11), and by the apostle John, who says that "Cain was *of that wicked one* (the devil), and slew his brother. And wherefore slew he him? Because *his own works were evil,* and *his brother's righteous"* (I John 3:12). We see here, not ony the distinction itself, but the jealousy and hatred with which wicked men regard the virtue that condemns them,

and which vents itself in persecution. Accordingly Abel is named by our Saviour as the first of the noble army of martyrs (Matt. 23:35).

3. *This difference of character was made evident when they were called to observe the services of religion.* Cain and Abel brought their several offerings according to their several possessions. "Cain brought of the fruit of the ground: Abel the firstlings of his flock, and of the fat thereof": that is, the choicest of the firstborn lambs or kids (Gen. 4:3-5). Abel presented his offering in a spirit of faith (Heb. 11:4), and was therefore accepted, but Cain's was rejected on account of the state of mind in which it was brought. This is implied in God's rebuke to Cain, who "was very wroth, and whose countenance fell," though it is obscured by the language of the English version. The passage may be rendered thus: "Why art thou wroth, and why is thy countenance fallen?" If thou doest well, is there not an elevation of the countenance (i.e., *"cheerfulness, happiness");* but if thou doest not well, *there is a sinking of the countenance;* sin lurketh (as a wild beast) at the door, "and to thee is its desire" — it seeks the mastery over you; "but thou art to rule over it" — to resist and subdue it.

4. *Cain scorned the remonstrance, and his anger advanced to its natural result in the murder of his brother* (Gen. 4:8). It is uncertain whether the words "Cain talked with Abel" imply a treacherous snare, or a quarrel which led on to the fatal deed. In any case, Cain's rage at his brother's being preferred to him was its true cause. For, fearful as is the truth that the first overt act of sin after the fall was a brother's murder, he who knew what was in man has testified that "whosoever is angry with his brother without a cause" has already broken the spirit of the Sixth Commandment (Matt. 5:22), and that "whosoever hateth his brother is a murderer" (I John 3:15). This truth is confirmed by all history; and Christ does not hesitate to tell the Jews, who were enraged at him for the purity of His doctrine: "Ye are of your father the devil, and the lusts of your father ye will do; he was a murderer from the beginning" (John 8:44).

5. *This first crime was promptly punished.* The sullen indifference of Cain's reply to God's demand, "Where is Abel thy brother?" was probably affected, to conceal the remorse which has ever haunted the murderer (Gen. 4:9). The blood of the victim seems always to have that power, which is ascribed to the blood of Abel, of "crying to God from the ground" (Gen. 4:10). The cry implied is clearly that for vengeance; and the same cry proceeds from the

blood of all the martyrs (Rev. 6:10). Cain was doomed to a new infliction of the primal curse. To Adam the earth yielded its fruit, though with toil and sweat; but to Cain, as if indignant at the outrage done her by his brother's blood, the earth was cursed for him again, refusing to yield her strength under his tillage, or even to grant him an abode at the scene of his crime (Gen. 4:12). But even in this aggravation of the curse, we still see the mercy which turns the curse into a blessing; for it was no doubt an incentive to those mechanical arts which were first practiced by the family of Cain.

Cain received his doom in the same hardened spirit of impenitence, filling up the measure of his unbelief by the cry, "My iniquity is too great to be forgiven" (Gen. 4:13). While lamenting his expulsion from the abodes of men and from the face of God, his great fear is for his life, lest men should slay him. To quiet this fear, God gave him a special sign that he should not be slain (for such seems to be the true meaning of the "mark set on Cain"), and pronounced a sevenfold punishment on any one who should kill him. With his person thus protected, he was driven from his home, as "a fugitive and a vagabond in the earth" (Gen. 4:14).

6. *Cain directed his steps to the east of Eden, and settled in the land of Nod, that is, wandering.* He became the ancestor of a race, whose history is recorded in a very striking contrast with that of the chosen race of Seth. The two genealogies, when placed side by side, are as follows:

The Two Lines of Humanity
(Genesis 4-5)

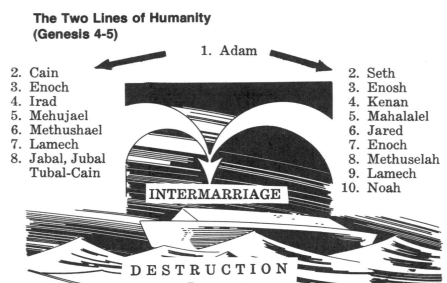

1. Adam

2. Cain	2. Seth
3. Enoch	3. Enosh
4. Irad	4. Kenan
5. Mehujael	5. Mahalalel
6. Methushael	6. Jared
7. Lamech	7. Enoch
8. Jabal, Jubal	8. Methuselah
Tubal-Cain	9. Lamech
	10. Noah

INTERMARRIAGE

DESTRUCTION

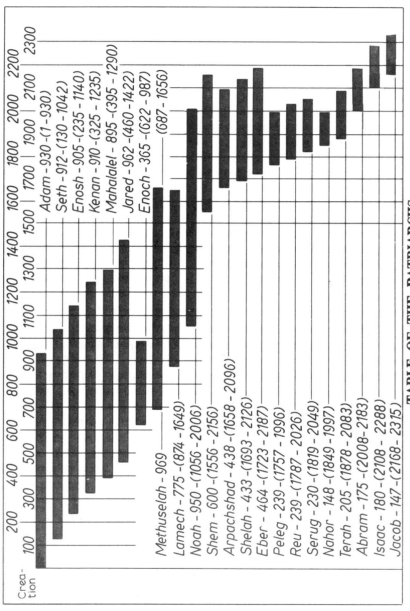

TABLE OF THE PATRIARCHS

Adam – 930 –(1 – 930)
Seth – 912 –(130 – 1042)
Enosh – 905 –(235 – 1140)
Kenan – 910 –(325 – 1235)
Mahalalel – 895 –(395 – 1290)
Jared – 962 –(460 – 1422)
Enoch – 365 –(622 – 987)
(687 – 1656)
Methuselah – 969
Lamech – 775 –(874 – 1649)
Noah – 950 –(1056 – 2006)
Shem – 600 –(1556 – 2156)
Arpachshad – 438 –(1658 – 2096)
Shelah – 433 –(1693 – 2126)
Eber – 464 –(1723 – 2187)
Peleg – 239 –(1757 – 1996)
Reu – 239 –(1787 – 2026)
Serug – 230 –(1819 – 2049)
Nahor – 148 –(1849 – 1997)
Terah – 205 –(1878 – 2083)
Abram – 175 –(2008 – 2183)
Isaac – 180 –(2108 – 2288)
Jacob – 147 –(2168 – 2315)

Table of the Patriarchs

This chart vividly pictures the great overlapping in the lives of the patriarchs. Adam was still living when Lamech, Noah's father, was born. And Shem, Noah's son, outlived Abraham!

Any history or information that Adam (and God!) wanted to hand down could have come through only two generations of the human race when the flood came. And it was only in the third generation by the time of Abraham. This makes the history in Genesis most trustworthy.

What a power for godliness, and what a warning against evil were the venerable and aged saints such as Adam! Their very presence and words through so many generations constantly reminded people about the way God had dealt with sin even way back at the beginning.

Methuselah died in the year of the flood (1656 from creation), but he probably did not perish in the flood.

This chart shows also the life span of people has progressively shortened since sin entered into the world. Sin has caused degeneration.

The resemblances in the names of the two families seem a natural consequence of the use of significant names at a time when language had acquired no great variety. The only personal facts of their history are: the foundation by Cain of the first city, which he named after his son *Enoch;* the polygamy of Lamech; and the occupations of his sons, of whom Jabal was the first nomad herdsman, Jubal the inventor of musical instruments, both stringed and wind, and Tubal-Cain the first smith. It deserves notice also, that Lamech's address to his wives is the earliest example of poetry; it forms three couplets of parallel clauses. The great contrast, however, between the two races, is in their social and moral condition.

7. *Dismissing the family of Cain, the narrative traces the line of the chosen race.* The new son, who was given to Eve "instead of Abel, whom Cain slew," was hence named SETH (properly *Sheth* [Gen. 4:25], i.e., *appointed).* The list of his race is headed with a remarkable phrase. Adam was made *in the likeness of God;* and he begat a son *in his own likeness,* after his image (Gen. 5:1-3). Adam handed down to Seth and his descendents the promise of mercy, faith in which became the distinction of God's children. This seems to be the meaning of the statement that, in the days and in

the family of Seth, "men began to call upon the name of Jehovah." For the *"name"* of any great personage is the symbol of allegiance to him — "jurare in *nomen*" — and so it is used repeatedly in the Old Testament of the name of God, and in the New continually of the name of Christ, "the name which is above every name," at which "every knee shall bow and every tongue confess." From the very beginning, then, of the race whose history is traced in Scripture, God was never without the public recognition of His name and cause by true worshipers, and such we find first in the family of Seth, in contrast to that of Cain. Public worship thus began in the time of Seth.

8. *Of Enosh (man or multitude), Kenan (possession), Mahalalel (praise of God), and Jared (or Jered, descent), no particulars are recorded* (Gen. 5:9-20). But "ENOCH, the seventh from Adam," stands conspicuous among the race of Seth. After the statement, emphatically repeated, that he "walked with God," we are told, "he was not, for God took him" (Gen. 5:22-24). The former phrase is also applied to Noah, among the antediluvian patriarchs (Gen. 6:9), and is often used to describe a life of close communion with God, or in one word, godliness. The apostle explains it, that "he pleased God," and traces Enoch's piety to his faith in God, as the only true God and the hearer of prayer, for "without faith it is impossible to please Him: for he that cometh to God must believe that He is, and that he is a rewarder of them that diligently seek him" (Heb. 11:5,6).

But Enoch's life was not all spent in quiet meditation; he "walked with God" in the path of active duty and the courageous maintenance of the cause of God amid an ungodly race. This we learn from the Apostle Jude, who describes the antediluvian world as already infected with those vices which came to a head in the days of Noah, which are ever the curse of advanced civilization, and which will again mark the last age of the world. Against these sins Enoch prophesied, and warned their perpetrators of the coming of the Lord to execute judgment upon them. He stands conspicuous, therefore, as the FIRST OF THE PROPHETS (Jude 14-15).

Enoch's faith was rewarded by a special favor in the mode of his departure from the world. "He walked with God" till "he was not, for God had taken him." The men to whom he prophesied missed him, perhaps at the very moment they were planning his death: "he was not found, because God had translated him" (Heb. 11:5). The apostle who uses this phrase leaves no doubt as to its meaning: "by faith Enoch was translated *that he should not see death.*" This distinction was shared by Elijah alone of all the human race; and we may probably infer that, as in his case, so in Enoch's, the miracle was a testimony to the divine mission of the prophet, as well as a reward of the piety of the man.

9. *Methuselah (a man of arms), the son of Enoch, is noted as having reached the greatest age of any man.* He was contemporary with Adam for 243 years, and with Noah for 600. It is interesting to observe that he died in the very year of the Deluge. Was he "a righteous man taken away from the coming evil," or having lapsed into wickedness, did he perish with them that believed not? We are allowed to suppose the former, from the probability that he would have been saved in the ark, with the rest of Noah's family, had he been still alive. His son LAMECH (properly *Lemech),* the father of Noah, died five years before the deluge.

10. *Did the patriarchs actually live as long as Genesis 5 indicates?* The answer must be affirmative. This need not astound us. God apparently created man with sufficient vitality to live forever. Sin has caused degeneration of the race. After sin entered the world the life span of man dropped steadily until man's time shrunk to "three score and ten" (Psalm 90:10). (See Table of Patriarchs, p. 29.)

A very ancient clay prism has been found at Kish in Mesopotamia, listing the ten "kings" who ruled before the flood. The life spans of these kings (obviously exaggerated and distorted) extends from 10,800 years upward, making the lives of Adam and Methuselah appear brief! While this material is legendary and exaggerated, it does indicate that the fact of long life spans before the flood was known even outside the Biblical record.[1]

Special Studies

The Poem of Lamech (Genesis 4:23-24)

The remarkable poem which Lamech uttered is the only extant specimen of antediluvian poetry; it came down, perhaps as a popular song, to the generation for whom Moses wrote, and he inserts it in its proper place in his history. It may be rendered:

1. See D.J. Wiseman, *Illustrations from Biblical Archaeology,* pp. 8,9.

> Adah and Zillah! hear my voice,
>> Ye wives of Lamech! give ear unto my speech;
> For a man had I slain for smiting me,
>> And a youth for wounding me,
> Surely sevenfold shall Cain be avenged,
>> But Lamech seventy and seven.

Lamech shamelessly boasts about having killed a young man. He has no fear of punishment, either from God or man. Scorning all divine protection, such as God offered even to Cain, he himself threatens much severer vengeance on any who harm him. It is easy to imagine Lemech brandishing a new brass sword made by his son Tubal-Cain, as he utters these boasts and threats.

Seven generations on Adam's godly line through Seth produced an Enoch. Seven generations in the line through Cain produced Lemech!

The Cainite Race

The social condition of the Cainites is prominently brought forward in the history. Cain himself was an agriculturalist, Abel a shepherd: the successors of the latter are represented by the Sethites and the progenitors of the Hebrew race in later times, among whom a pastoral life was always held in high honor, from the simplicity and devotional habits which it engendered; the successes of the former are depicted as the reverse in all these respects. Cain founded the first city; Lamech instituted polygamy; Jabal introduced the nomadic life; Jubal invented musical instruments; Tubal-Cain was the first smith; Lamech's language takes the stately tone of poetry; and even the names of the women, Naamah *(pleasant)*, Zillah *(shadow)*, Adah *(ornamental)*, seem to bespeak an advanced state of civilization. But along with this, there was violence and godlessness; Cain and Lamech furnish proof of the former, while the concluding words of Gen. 4:26 imply the latter.

The contrast established between the Cainites and the Sethites appears to have reference solely to the social and religious condition of the two races. On the one side there is pictured a high state of civilization, unsanctified by religion, and productive of luxury and violence; on the other side, a state of simplicity which afforded no material for history beyond the declaration "then began men to call upon the name of the Lord." The historian thus accounts for the progressive degeneration of the religious condition of man, the evil gaining a predominance over the good by its alliance with worldly power and knowledge, and producing the state of things which necessitated the flood.

Questions on Section V
The Two Lines of Humanity (Gen. 4-5)

1. Who was Adam's first son? His second?
2. What were the sons' occupations?
3. What did the sons bring as offerings to Jehovah? How did Jehovah regard the offerings?
4. What was Cain's reaction to God's rejection of his offering?
5. What warning did God give Cain?
6. What did Cain do to Abel? Where?
7. What question did God ask Cain after his crime, and what was Cain's answer?
8. What was Cain's punishment?
9. What was Cain's reaction to his punishment?
10. How did God protect Cain from being killed?
11. Into what land did Cain go after his crime?
12. Who built the first city?
13. Who was the first bigamist, and what were his wives' names?
14. What was the occupation of Jabal? Jubal? Tubal-Cain?
15. What did Lamech brag about doing? To what degree did Lamech threaten vengeance on anyone who harmed him?
16. Who was Adam and Eve's next son?
17. What did men begin to do in Seth's time?
18. What name did God call upon the first couple?
19. How long did Adam live?
20. Name the people in the generations from Adam to Noah.
21. How did Enoch's life on earth end (Cf. Heb. 11:5)?
22. How long did Methuselah live?
23. What does the name Noah mean?
24. Who were Noah's three sons?

Section VI
Noah and the Flood (Gen. 6-8)

1. Significance of Noah's name. 2. State of the antediluvian world — The Sethite and Cainite races

intermixed — Their progeny and the Nephilim.
3. Interval of divine forbearance: God's resolve to
destroy the world. 4. Also to preserve the race of man
for a new dispensation — Noah and his family — The
ark prepared. 5. Noah enters the ark. 6. The flood: its
duration and subsidence. 7. Questions of a universal or
partial flood. 8. Noah leaves the ark — His sacrifice.

1. *The name of Noah is very significant.* It means *rest,* or *comfort,*
and his father gave it by prophetic inspiration, saying: "This shall
comfort us concerning our work and toil of our hands, because of
the ground which the Lord hath cursed" (Gen. 5:29). These
words seem to express a deeper weariness than that arising from
the primal curse, from which indeed the age of Noah brought no
deliverance. But it did bring the comfort of rest from the
wickedness which had now reached its greatest height.

2. *The brief history of the world before the flood may fairly be filled up,
to some extent, from our knowledge of human nature.* We have seen the
race of Cain inventing the implements of industry and art; and we
can have no doubt that their inventions were adopted by the
progeny of Seth. During the years before the flood, vast strides
were· made in knowledge and civilization. Arts and sciences
reached a ripeness, of which the record, from its scantiness,
conveys no adequate conception. The destruction caused by the
flood must have obliterated a thousand discoveries, and left men
to recover again by slow and patient steps the ground they had
lost. But the race of Seth also became infected with the vices of the
Cainites. This seems to be the only reasonable sense of the
intermarriage between "the sons of God" *(sons of the Elohim)* and
"the daughters of men" (Gen. 6:1-2, *daughters of the Adam).* We
may put aside all fancies borrowed from heathen mythology
respecting the union of superhuman beings with mortal women,
and assume that both parties were of the human race. The family
of Seth, who preserved their faith in God, and the family of Cain,
who lived only for this world, had hitherto kept distinct; but now a
mingling of the two races took place which resulted in the
thorough corruption of the former, who falling away, plunged
into the deepest abyss of wickedness. We are also told that this
union produced a stock conspicuous for physical strength and
courage; and this is a well-known result of the intermixture of
different races. Here it is a frequent mistake to confound these

"mighty men of old, men of renown," with the "giants" (Heb. *Nephilim*), from whom they are expressly distinguished.[1]

On the whole, it seems that the antediluvian world had reached a desperate pitch of wickedness, the climax of which was attained by the fusion of the two races. The marked features of this wickedness were lust and brutal outrage. The fearful picture of depravity drawn by Peter and Jude evidently refers to the antediluvian age as a pattern of the wickedness of the last days which shall again make the world ripe for destruction (II Pet. 2,3; Jude 14,15).

3. *An interval of divine forbearance only brought this wickedness to its height.* "Jehovah said, My spirit shall not always strive with (or *remain* or *rule in*) man (the *Adam*); for that they are but flesh, and their days shall be an hundred and twenty years" (Gen. 6:3). In the somewhat obscure brevity of this speech, it is difficult to determine the force of each word; but the general sense seems to be: "I will take away from man the life I at first gave him, since he has corrupted himself to mere flesh, and I will limit his time on earth to one hundred and twenty years." That the period thus defined was a space for repentance, seems clear from the context. The opinion, that it marks out the future length of human life, does not at all agree with the duration of the lives of the post-diluvian patriarchs.

Meanwhile "God saw that the wickedness of man was great in the earth, and that every imagination (or purpose) of the thoughts of his heart was only evil continually. *And it repented Jehovah that he had made man on the earth, and it grieved Him at His heart*" (Gen. 6:7). He resolved to destroy the existing race of living creatures. "The earth was corrupt before God, and the earth was filled with violence. And God looked upon the earth, and behold it was corrupt, for all flesh had corrupted his way upon the earth" (Gen. 6:11,12). Measures of amelioration would not meet the case. It was necessary (to use an expressive phrase) "to make a clean sweep" of the existing race, if there were to be any hope of better things among another. For the destruction contemplated was neither total nor final; and in these respects the Deluge is distinguished from the last conflagration.

4. *The family chosen for this experiment was that of Noah.* "Noah

---

1. Gen. 6:4. The word *Nephilim* is used in one other passage (Num. 13:33) as the name of a tribe of Canaanites; and as these were men of vast stature, the LXX made the *Nephilim* of Noah's days giants also. But the word itself has no such meaning. It signifies either *fallen ones*, or *those who fall on others*, apostates or men of violence; and we cannot be far wrong in believing the *Nephilim* to have been both.

found grace in the eyes of the Lord" (Gen. 6:8). He is described as "a just man, and perfect (upright or sincere) in his generation" (*i.e.,* among his contemporaries); and, like Enoch, he "walked with God" (Gen. 6:9). Like Enoch, too, he testified against the prevailing wickedness, for he is called "a preacher of righteousness" (II Pet. 1:5). He had three sons — Shem, Ham and Japheth, as they are named in order of precedence (Gen. 5:32; 6:10); but Japheth seems to have been the eldest, and Ham the youngest (Gen. 9:24; 10:21). Their birth is placed at the 500th year of Noah's life (Gen. 5:32). This seems to refer to the eldest son; for Shem was born two years later (Gen. 11:10). About this time, perhaps at the beginning of the 120 years of delay, God revealed His design to Noah, bidding him to prepare an "ark" to save his family from the coming flood, with the races of animals needful for them, and promising to establish a new covenant with his race (Gen. 6:13-21).

Like Abel and Enoch, Noah believed God, and so acted. "By *faith* Noah, being warned of God of things not seen as yet, moved with fear, prepared an ark to the saving of his house; whereby he condemned the world, and became heir of the righteousness which is by faith" (Heb. 11:7). Doubtless Noah continued his "preaching of righteousness," especially as occasions arose from the scoffing curiosity of those who watched his work; but that work preached louder still. And so "the long suffering of God waited in the days of Noah, while the ark was preparing" (I Pet. 3:20). But it waited in vain. The unheeded warning, as is usual, only plunged men into greater carelessness. They went on, "eating and drinking, marrying and giving in marriage, until the day that Noah entered into the ark; and knew not till the flood came and took them all away" (Matt. 24:38-39).

5. *At the beginning of the six hundredth year of Noah's life the ark was completed; and on the tenth day of the second month of that year he entered into it, by God's command, with his wife, his three sons and their wives –* eight persons in all — who were saved from the flood, and, in a figure, baptized by its waters to a separation from the polluted life of the old world and the beginning of a new course (I Pet. 3:21). They took with them the food they would require, which was as yet of a vegetable nature. They also took two (a pair) of every animal; but of clean animals (for the use of sacrifice had already established this distinction) they took seven; by which is generally understood three pairs to continue the race, and one male for

sacrifice. They took seven days to enter the ark, and then "Jehovah shut Noah in" (Gen. 7:16).

6. *On the same day, namely, the seventeenth day of the second month of the 600th year of Noah's life, the flood began.* The physical causes of the flood were twofold: (1) "The fountains of the great deep were broken up, and (2) the windows of heaven were opened" (Gen. 7:11-12).

By this we are to understand that great fissures opened at the bottom of the seas, and subterranean waters poured forth from the earth's interior. No doubt this produced indescribable shocks, earthquakes, upheavals, tidal waves and volcanic phenomena. Many of the geologic formations on earth today doubtless came into being as a result of this rupture of the fountains of the deep and the subsequent flood that overwhelmed the earth under many feet of water.

The opening of the windows of heaven to produce rainfall for forty days indicates that much more water was suspended above the antediluvian firmament than now exists in the atmosphere (Gen. 1:7). There is now in the atmosphere only enough water to cover the entire earth about two inches deep, insufficient water to fall continuously over the earth for forty days.

The antediluvian canopy of water above the firmament doubtless served to make its climate more uniform and warm. The existence of tropical plant fossils in earth's cold regions indicates that a warm climate once prevailed overall. This uniform climate was probably reinforced by the fact that antediluvian mountains were not as high as the mountains after the flood. See Ps. 104:8-9.[1]

The Biblical narrative of the flood is vivid and forcible, though entirely wanting in that sort of description which in a modern historian or poet would have occupied the largest space. We see nothing of the death-struggle; we hear not the cry of despair; we are not called upon to witness the frantic agony of husband and wife, and parent and child, as they fled in terror before the rising waters. Nor is a word said of the sadness of the one righteous man who, safe himself, looked upon the destruction which he could not avert. But one impression is left upon the mind with peculiar vividness, from the very simplicity of the narrative, and it is that of utter desolation. "All flesh died that moveth upon the earth, both

---

1. For an excellent discussion of the antediluvian earth, and the geologic effects of the worldwide flood, see Whitcomb and Morris, *The Genesis Flood.*

of fowl, and of cattle, and of beast, and of every creeping thing that creepeth upon the earth, and every man. . . . They were destroyed from the earth, and Noah only remained alive, and they that were with him in the ark" (Gen. 7:21-23). The vast expanse of water appeared unbroken, save by that floating home of all that were left alive, for 150 days or five months.

Meanwhile God had not forgotten Noah and those that were with him in the ark (Gen. 8:1). On the seventeenth day of the seventh month of the 600th year of Noah's life, the subsiding waters left the ark aground upon the mountains of Ararat. More than two months were still required to uncover the tops of the mountains, which appeared on the 1st day of the tenth month. Noah waited still forty days (to the eleventh day of the eleventh month) before he opened the window of the ark. He sent out a raven, which flew to and fro, probably on the mountain-tops, but did not return into the ark. After seven days more (the eighteenth day) he sent forth a dove, which found no resting-place and returned to the ark. In another seven days (the twenty-fifth) she was sent out again, and returned with an olive-leaf in her bill, the sign that even the low trees were uncovered. After seven days more (the second of the twelfth month), the dove was sent out again, and proved by not returning that the waters had finally subsided. These periods of seven days clearly point to the division of time into weeks.

7. *The question as to whether the flood was universal or partial has caused much controversy.* However, it is impossible to read the Scripture narrative and not gain the impression that the Bible intended for us to understand that the flood covered all the earth. If the author had intended that his readers should regard the flood as universal, he could not have conveyed that impression more definitely than the Bible description does.

If the flood had been a local inundation there was no need to build an ark to preserve life on earth. There was no cause to enter the ark; flight to higher ground could have saved Noah's family.

In the New Testament our Lord gives the sanction of His own authority to the historical truth of the narrative, declaring that the state of the world at His second coming shall be such as it was in the days of Noah. Peter speaks of the "long suffering of God," which "waited in the days of Noah while the ark was a preparing, wherein few, that is, eight souls, were saved by water," and sees in the waters of the flood by which the ark was borne up a type of baptism, by which the Church is separated from the world. And again, in his Second Epistle (II Pet. 2:5), he cites it as an instance of the righteous judgment of God who spared not the old world. The truth of the Biblical narrative is confirmed by the many traditions of the flood preserved by peoples in all parts of the earth. These traditions preserve the memory of the great and destructive flood, from which only a small part of mankind escaped. Nearly a hundred such traditions of primitive peoples have been recorded.[1] They seem to point back to a common center, whence they were carried by the different families of man, as they wandered east and west.

8. *Noah goes forth from the ark.* Noah at length removed the covering of the ark, and beheld the newly-uncovered earth, on the first day of the 601st year of his age (Gen. 8:13). On the twenty-seventh day of the second month the earth was dry, and Noah went out of the ark by the command of God, with all the creatures (Gen. 8:14-19). His first act was to build an altar and offer a sacrifice of every clean beast and bird. This act of piety called forth the promise from God that He would not again curse the earth on account of man, nor destroy it as He had done; but that He would forbear with man's innate tendency to evil, and continue the existing course of nature until the appointed end of the world (Gen. 8:20-22).

Special Studies

Noah's Ark

The precise meaning of the Hebrew word *(tebah)*, translated *ark,* is uncertain. The word occurs only in Gen. 6-8 and in Ex. 2:3. In all probability it is to the old Egyptian that we are to look for its original form. Bunsen, in his vocabulary, gives *tba,* "a chest," *tpt,* "a boat," and in the Copt. Vers. of Ex. 2:3,5, *thebi* is the rendering of *tebah.* This "chest" or "boat" was to be made of gopher *(i.e.,* cypress) wood, a kind of timber which, both for its lightness and its durability, was employed by the Phoenicians for building their vessels. The planks of the ark, after being put together, were to be protected by a coating of pitch, or rather bitumen, which was to be laid on both inside and outside, as the most effectual means of making it water-tight. The ark was to consist of a number of "nests" or small compartments, with a view no doubt to the

1. See Alfred Rehwinkel, *The Flood,* Chs. 9-10.

convenient distribution of the different animals and their food. These were to be arranged in three tiers, one above another; "with lower, second, and third (stories) shalt thou make it." Means were also to be provided for letting light into the ark. In the A.V. we read, "A *window* shalt thou make to the ark, and in a cubit shalt thou finish it above" — words, which it must be confessed, convey no very intelligible idea. The original, however, is obscure, and has been differently interpreted. What the "window" or "light-hole" was, is very puzzling. It was to be at the top of the ark apparently. If the words "unto a cubit shalt thou finish it *above*," refer to the window and not to the ark itself, they seem to imply that this aperture or skylight extended to the breadth of a cubit the whole length of the roof. But if so, it could not have been merely an open slit, for that would have admitted the rain. Are we, then, to suppose that some transparent, or at least translucent, substance was employed? It would almost seem so. A different word is used in chapter 8:6, where it is said that Noah opened the window of the ark. There the word is *challon,* which frequently occurs elsewhere in the same sense. Supposing, then, the *tsohar* to be, as we have said, a skylight, or series of skylights running the whole length of the ark, the *challon* might very well be a single compartment of the larger window which could be opened at will. But besides the window there was to be a door. This was to be placed in the side of the ark. Of the shape of the ark nothing is said; but its dimensions are given. It was to be 300 cubits in length, 50 in breadth, and 30 in height. Taking 18 inches for the cubit, the ark would be 450 feet in length, 75 in breadth, and 45 feet in height. This would give a cubic capacity of 1,400,000 cubic feet, the equivalent of 500 ordinary railway box cars. There was abundant room on the ark for all living types of animals and their food.[1] It should be remembered that this huge structure was only intended to float on the water, and was not in the proper sense of the word a ship. It had neither mast, sail nor rudder; it was in fact nothing but an enormous floating house, or rather oblong box. Two objects only were aimed at in its construction: the one that it should have ample stowage, and the other that is should be able to keep steady upon the water.

Mount Ararat

We are told that the ark "rested upon the mountains of Ararat"

---

1. See Whitcomb and Morris, *The Genesis Flood,* pp. 10-11, 65-70.

(Gen. 8:4), meaning the mountains of Armenia, for Ararat in Biblical geography (II Kings 19:37; Jer. 60:27) is not the name of a mountain, but of a district — the central region, to which the name of Araratia is assigned by the native geographer Moses of Chorene. This being the case, we are not called upon to decide a point which the sacred writer himself leaves undecided, namely, the particular mountain on which the ark rested. But nothing is more natural than that the scene of the event should in due course of time be transferred to the loftiest of the mountains of Armenia, and that the name of Ararat should be specially affixed to that one: accordingly all the associations connected with the ark now center in the magnificent mountain which the native Armenians name *Macis,* and the Turks *Aghri-Dagh.* This is the culminating point of the central range of Armenia, the Abus of the ancients. It rises majestically out of the valley of the Araxes to the elevation of 17,260 feet above the level of the sea, and about 14,350 above the valley, and terminates in a double conical peak, the lower or Lesser Ararat being about 4000 feet below the other. The mountain is very steep, as implied in the Turkish name, and the summit is covered with eternal snow.

Questions on Section VI
Noah and the Flood (Gen. 6-8)

1. Who are the "sons of God" and the "daughters of men" of Genesis 6:1?
2. What did the sons of God observe about the daughters of men?
3. Whom did the sons of God take as wives? Was monogamy practiced?
4. What had been striving with men?
5. How many years of probation did God grant the world before the flood (6:3)?
6. What sort of people were the offspring of the sons of God and the daughters of men?
7. What did men have on their minds before the flood?
8. What did God determine to do with man and other living things?
9. Who found grace in the eyes of the Lord?
10. How is Noah's character described?
11. Of what wood was the ark made?
12. Give the length, breadth and height of the ark.
13. What was the ark coated with to make it watertight?

14. How many stories were there in the ark?
15. What was Noah doing during the years before the flood (II Pet. 2:5)?
16. What did God promise to establish with Noah?
17. How were the animals brought to the ark (Gen. 6:20)?
18. How fully did Noah obey God's commands?
19. How many of each type of clean beast were taken on the ark? How many unclean?
20. How many days elapsed between the command to board the ark and the start of the rainfall?
21. How old was Noah when the flood began?
22. How many people were saved in the ark?
23. What were the two sources of the waters of the flood?
24. How long did it rain?
25. How high upward above the mountains did the waters prevail?
26. What died in the flood?
27. How long did the waters prevail upon the earth?
28. What did God cause to pass over the earth that made the waters subside?
29. Where did the ark come to rest?
30. How many times were birds sent forth from the ark before it was opened? What birds were sent each time? What were the results each time?
31. How long was Noah in the ark altogether (Cf. Gen 7:11 and 8:14)?
32. What did God tell Noah and the animals to do when they left the ark (Gen. 8:17)?
33. What did Noah build right after leaving the ark?
34. What did Noah offer upon his altar?
35. What did God say he would never do again?
36. What seasons are not to cease as long as the earth remains?

Period II
Postdiluvian Period
(From the Flood to the
Call of Abram;
Gen. 9:1-11:26)

During the postdiluvian period (period after flood) mankind rapidly multiplied in number and rapidly went back into sin. Civilization advanced rapidly[1] but idolatry became rampant (Rom 1:21-24).

Section I
Noah After the Flood
(Gen. 9)

1. God's blessing and precepts to Noah. 2. The covenant with Noah: God's covenant of forbearance. 3. The curse upon Canaan and prophecy of Noah's sons. 4. Noah's death.

1. *God's blessing and precepts to Noah.* After Noah's sacrifice God repeated to Noah and his sons the blessing pronounced on Adam

---

1. See J.A. Thompson, *The Bible and Archaeology*, pp. 15-36.

and Eve, that they should "be fruitful and multiply and replenish the earth," and that the inferior creatures should be subject to them. To this He added the use of animals for food (Gen. 9:3-4). But the eating of their blood was forbidden, because the blood is the life; and lest the needful shedding of their blood should lead to deeds of blood, a new law was enacted against murder. The horror of the crime was clearly stated on the two grounds of the common brotherhood of man, which makes every murder a fratricide, and of the creation of man in God's image. The first murderer had been driven out as a vagabond and fugitive; but his life was sacred. Now, however, the penalty was changed and the law laid down — "He that sheddeth man's blood, by man shall his blood be shed" (Gen. 9:5-6). This law amounts to giving the civil magistrate the "power of the sword" (Rom. 13:4); and hence we may consider *three new precepts* to have been given to Noah, namely, the abstinence from blood, the prohibition of murder, and the recognition of the civil authority (Rom. 13:4). These precepts have survived the Jewish (Mosaic) dispensation. The law of abstinence from blood was imposed by the apostles upon the Gentile converts to Christianity (Acts 15:29).

2. In addition to these promises and precepts, God made with Noah a COVENANT (Gen. 9:8-11), that is, one of these *agreements* by which He has condescended again and again to bind Himself toward man. Of these covenants, that made with Noah on behalf of his descendents is the first; and it may be called the *Covenant of God's forbearance,* under which man lives to the end of time. It repeated the promise that the world should not be again destroyed by a flood; and it was ratified by the beautiful sign of the rainbow in the cloud, a *natural* phenomenon suited to the *natural laws* of whose permanence it was the token.

3. *Noah soon gave proof that his new race was still a fallen one, by yielding to a degrading vice.* Intoxication was doubtless practiced by the profligate race who "ate and *drank*" before the flood; but it would seem to have been a new thing with Noah. He began his new life as a husbandman; and living in a land (Armenia) which is still most favorable for the vine, he planted a vineyard, made himself drunk in his tent, and suffered the degrading consequences which always, in some shape or other, attend the quenching of reason in wine, by a shameful exposure of himself in the presence of his sons (Gen. 9:20-21). And now they began to show those differences of character, which have severed even the families chosen by God in every age. Ham told his father's shame

to Shem and Japheth, who hastened to conceal it even from their own eyes (Gen. 9:22-23). On coming to himself, Noah vented his feelings in words which are unquestionably prophetic of the destinies of the races that descended from his sons. For in the primitive state of society, the government was strictly *patriarchal.* The patriarch — that is, the head of the race for the time being — had over his children and theirs the full power of the later *king;* he was their *priest;* and thus we have seen Noah offering sacrifices; and, among those who preserved the true religion, he was a *prophet* also. Thus with the inspiration of the Holy Spirit guiding him as a prophet and with the authority of a patriarch over his family, Noah pronounced a curse upon the descendants of Canaan (Ham's son) and a blessing upon Shem and Japheth. Canaan was to become a slave race to his brethren.

Noah gave to Shem and Japheth the respective blessings already symbolized by their names, *Shem* (the *name,* chosen above all others) and Japheth *(enlargement)* — to the former that Jehovah should be his God in some special sense; to the latter that he should (1) be "enlarged" with worldly power, and (2) should ultimately share the blessings of the family of Shem. Japheth would "dwell in the tents of Shem."

Thus early in the world's history was the lesson taught practically, which the law afterward expressly enunciated, that God visits the sins of the fathers upon the children.

With leering gaze Ham had looked upon the nakedness of his father. The immoral quality in Ham's nature demonstrated by his action seems to have been most conspicuously perpetuated in his son Canaan's descendants. By the time the children of Israel occupied the land of Canaan both the lives and the religion of the Canaanites were thoroughly obsessed with sex.

The subsequent history of Canaan shows in the clearest manner possible the fulfillment of the curse. When Israel took possession of Canaan's land, Canaan became the slave of Shem (Judges 1:28,31,33). When Tyre fell before the arms of Alexander and Carthage succumbed to her Roman conquerors, Canaan became the slave of Japheth.

To argue that the curse upon Canaan was a curse upon all the descendents of Ham, and the Negro races in particular, is a cruel wresting of Scripture. Only Canaan was cursed, not all the Hamites, and Canaan's descendents were not Negroes. To defend slavery or segregation from the curse of Canaan is monstrous.

The blessing on Shem was fulfilled in the history of the Jews. Jehovah God was their God in a unique sense; they were the chosen people. Because the Jews have been the most notable of the Semites (or Shemites), the term Semite has come to be associated with the Jews almost exclusively in many people's minds, even though other peoples are also Semites.

The blessing on Japheth, the ancestor of the great European nations, is illustrated by every age of their history and especially by religious history. Japheth was to be "enlarged," and the territory occupied by the descendents of Japheth is much larger than that of Shem or Ham.

Japheth has come to dwell in the tents of Shem as a result of the Semitic Jews' rejection of their Messiah, Jesus. When this occurred, the Japhetic Gentiles were given the gospel of God and entered into the spiritual relationship with God that the Jews (except for a believing remnant) forfeited (Romans 11:11, 20-24).

4. *Noah lived for 350 years after the flood, and died at the age of 950.* He survived the fifth and eighth of his descendants, *Peleg* and *Nahor;* he was for 128 years contemporary with *Terah,* the father of *Abraham;* and died only 58 years before the birth of Abraham himself (A.M. 1948, 2166 B.C.). Looking backward, we find that he was born only 126 years after the death of *Adam,* and fourteen years after that of *Seth.* He was contemporary with *Enos* for 84 years, and with the remaining six antediluvian patriarchs (except Enoch) for centuries. We give these computations not as a matter of curiosity, but to show by how few steps, and yet by how many contemporary teachers, the traditions of primeval history may have been handed down — from Adam to Noah, and from Noah to Abraham, and, we might add, from Abraham to Moses. (See the Table of the Patriarchs.)

Questions on Section I
Noah After the Flood (Gen. 9)

1. What feeling toward people did the beasts have after the flood?
2. What was given to man for food after the flood?
3. What part of living creatures is not to be eaten by mankind?
4. What law was given about men or beasts that killed people?
5. What provision did God's covenant contain about future floods?
6. What was the token of God's covenant with Noah?
7. Who was the father of Canaan?

8. Of what people was the whole earth overspread?
9. What did Noah plant after the flood?
10. What degrading thing happened to Noah?
11. What did Ham do that suggests that he had a very evil nature?
12. Who covered Noah as he lay in his tent?
13. What did Noah say would happen to Canaan?
14. In what respect was Shem to be blessed?
15. What future did Noah prophesy for Japheth (two things)?

Section II
The Table of Nations (Gen. 10)

1. The peopling of the earth. 2. Tripartite division of the nations from a centre in Armenia. 3. Interpretation of the record in Genesis 10. 4. The three great families — (a) of Japheth — (b) of Shem — (c) of Ham.

1. *The history of Noah's children divides itself into two parts:* the general peopling of the earth by the descendents of his three sons, and the particular line of the chosen family. The former subject is briefly dismissed, but with notices full of interest (Gen. 10), and the latter is pursued down to Abraham, on whose migration to Canaan we again come in contact with the other races of men.

2. *Two facts are prominent in the outline of the population of the world, which is given in Genesis 10:* the tripartite division of the nations into the descendents of Japheth, Shem and Ham; and the original centre of all these races in the mountains of Armenia, where Noah came forth from the ark. That the record is meant to include all the peoples of the known world is clear from the concluding words: "These are the families of the sons of Noah, after their generations in their *nations,* and *by these were the nations divided in the earth* after the flood" (Gen. 10:32). Now if we turn to the results of ethnological science, remembering that the science itself is quite recent, we must be struck with the points of agreement.

First, as to the locality. The highlands of Armenia are admirably adapted to be the central spot whence the streams of population should pour forth on all sides of the world. They are equidistant from the Caspian and Black seas in the north, and from the Mediterranean and the Persian Gulf in the south. Around those seas the earliest settlements of civilized man were made, and they became the high roads of commerce and colonization. Physiologists are now generally agreed on the common origin of the human race, and they find its noblest type in the regions south of the Caucasus. Again, the safest guide to the affinities of nations is found in the comparative study of their languages: and two great families of these have been clearly established, with a general correspondence to the races of Japheth and of Shem.

3. *The identification of the names mentioned in Genesis 10 is attended with considerable difficulties.*[1] First, there is a question respecting the extent of the world over which these nations must be looked for; but as the account is one of the *first* peopling of the earth after the flood (Gen. 10:32), the space to which it refers must be comparatively small; and it belongs to later history to trace the further diffusion of the nations. Again, some names, which would be well known in their native or classical forms, seem unfamiliar to us in the Hebrew. The same names, too, appear among different races, as will be seen by comparing the Hamite and Shemite peoples of Arabia with each other and with the descendents of Abraham by Keturah (Gen. 25). Such cases are satisfactorily explained by assuming that, when a people of one race settled in a country previously occupied by another, either expelling or subduing or coalescing with the former inhabitants, the new race are called by the already established *geographical* name of the older, just as the English received the name of Britons.

The chief stumbling-block, however, is found in the mixture of individual with national names. Now this is really of little consequence, since, with a few exceptions, as that of Nimrod (Gen. 10:8,9), the purpose is clearly to exhibit the affinities of *nations*. The record is *ethnographical* rather than *genealogical*. This is clear from the *plural* forms of some of the names (for example, all the descendents of *Mizraim),* and from the ethnic form of others, as those of the children of *Canaan,* nearly all of which are simply *geographical.* The genealogical form is preserved in the first generation after the sons of Noah, and is then virtually abandoned for a mere list of the nations descended from each of these progenitors. But in the line of the patriarchs from Shem to

---

1. See M.F. Unger, *Archaeology and the Old Testament,* Chs. 6, 7, 8.

Abraham the genealogical form is strictly preserved, since the object is to trace a *personal* descent.

On the other hand, the identification is greatly aided, first, by the geographical explanations given in the record itself (Gen. 10:5, 10-12, 19, 30); next, by the well-known names occurring among the less known; while on these latter much light is thrown by subsequent allusions in the prophetical as well as the historical books of the Old Testament.

4. *The annexed map exhibits a probable view of the leading peoples.* The three great races extend over three nearly parallel zones inclining from north-west to south-east; but they were also intermingled in a way which the map could not conveniently represent.

a. The territories of JAPHETH lie chiefly on the coasts of the Mediterranean, in Europe and Asia Minor, "the isles of the Gentiles" (Gen. 10:5); but they also reach across Armenia and along the north-eastern edge of the Tigris and Euphrates valley over Media and Persia. The race spread westward and northward over Europe, and at the other end as far as India embracing the great Indo-European family of languages. This wide diffusion was prophetically indicated by the very name, Japheth *(enlarged),* and by the blessing of his father Noah.
Japheth (Aryans)
1. Gomer — The *Cimmerians,* a people that dwelt in the "uttermost parts of the North" (Ezekiel 38:6).
2. Magog — Probably a comprehensive term for northern barbarians. Josephus said that Magog was ancestor of the *Scythians.*
3. Madai — *Medes.*
4. Javan — *Greeks.*
5. Tubal — Probably the people called *Tabali* mentioned in Assyrian records. In Assyrian times they lived northeast of Cilicia.
6. Meshech — Probably the people called *Mushki* in Assyrian records. They migrated to an area near the Black Sea.
7. Tiras — A people dwelling along the shores of Greece. *Thracians.*

b. The race of SHEM occupied the south-western corner of Asia, including the peninsula of Arabia.
Shem (Semites)
1. Elam — *Elamites.*
2. Asshur — *Assyrians.*

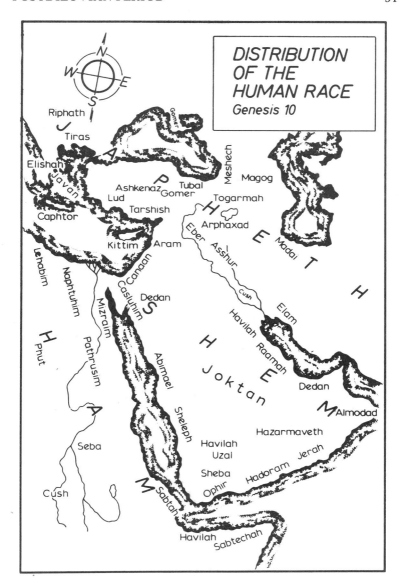

DISTRIBUTION OF THE HUMAN RACE
Genesis 10

3. Arphaxad – *Chaldeans* (or Babylonians) and Jews.
4. Lud — *Lydians* (in Asia Minor).
5. Aram — *Arameans* (or Syrians).

Arphaxad was ancestor of both the Hebrews and of the Arabs.

c. The race of HAM presents very difficult but interesting problems. Their chief seat was in Africa, but they are also found mingled with the Semitic races on the shores of Arabia, and on the Tigris and Euphrates, while on the north they extended into Palestine (the land of the *Philistines*), Asia Minor and the larger islands, as Crete and Cyprus.

Ham (Hamites)

1. Cush – *Ethiopians*. Cush was first associated with Babylonia (Gen. 10:8-12). Later the Cushites were in Ethiopia (or Nubia), the area south of Egypt.
2. Mizraim – *Egyptians*.
3. Put (or Phut) – *Libyians*. Land of Cyrenaica.
4. Canaan – *Palestine* (Canaanites).

   Among the sons of Mizraim, the *Ludim* correspond to Libya; and those of Cush represent tribes which crossed the Red Sea and spread along the southern and easter shores of Arabia, up the Persian Gulf and the valley of the Tigris and Euphrates.

(Students should memorize the names of the sons of Shem, Ham, and Japheth and the peoples descending from each.)

Questions on Section II
The Table of Nations (Gen. 10)

1. In what general areas did the descendents of Japheth settle?
2. Where was the chief seat of the Hamites?
3. Which of Noah's sons was the ancestor of Jews and Arabs?
4. Who was a mighty hunter in the earth?

Section III
The Tower of Babel and the
Descendants of Shem (Genesis 11)

1. The city and tower of Babel. 2. The confusion of tongues and dispensation from Babel. 3. Nimrod's empire. 4. The postdiluvian patriarchs.

1. *The city and tower of Babel.* The dispersion of these nations to their several abodes only began a considerable time after the Deluge. It was in the days of Peleg, the fifth from Noah, that the earth was divided (Gen. 10:25). Men never leave their abodes in masses except under the pressure of necessity or compulsion; and that pressure was supplied by the interposition of God to defeat a

daring scheme, by which men aimed to make themselves independent of Him. "The whole earth was as yet of one language and of one speech" when "as they journeyed eastward they found a plain in the land of Shinar, and they dwelt there." That Shinar means Babylonia, admits of no doubt; but who were the people that journeyed eastward to it? Were they one of the three races of Noah's sons, and if so, which? Or was it a migration of the great body of Noah's offspring from the rugged highlands of Armenia in search of a better soil and climate? The latter seems the more probable, though there is a difficulty about bringing the Japhetic race into this region. They discovered the art of making brick from the soil, and cementing it with the mineral bitumen, or asphalt. Soon that idea sprang up in their minds, which has been the dream of man in every age — a universal empire, with a mighty city for its capital. In the blindness of their pride, they fancied that, when thus banded together, they might defy God himself and defeat His wise design of dispersing them over the earth. "Come," said they, "let us build us a *city,* and a citadel with its top (reaching) to heaven; and let us make us a *name,* lest we be scattered abroad upon the face of the whole earth" (Gen. 11:4).

2. *The means by which the design was defeated was a "confusion of speech" among the builders,* caused by the direct power of God, "that they might not understand one another's speech" (Gen. 11:7). This confusion of speech accounts for the origin of the different languages of men.[1] The Scripture narrative says that the confusion was such as to make them leave off working together, and that then "Jehovah scattered them abroad from thence upon the face of all the earth: and they left off to build the city" (Gen. 11:7-9). It seems to be implied that some of the most striking differences which mark the various families of languages were then suddenly caused by God's immediate act, and that the builders separated because they could no longer understand each other.

From the *confusion (Babel) of tongues,* the city received the name of *Babel,* and is renowned under the Greek form of *Babylon.* It is supposed that the tower was afterward completed. Similar edifices were used in other cities of the region as citadels, temples, and observatories, and the ruins at Borsippa, called *Birs-Nimrud,* (Nimrod's mound), may be taken as a type of such structures.

3. *The early importance of Babylonia and Assyria is testified by the*

---

[1]. See J.M. Free, *Archaeology and Bible History,* pp. 46-47.

notice of their capitals, and in the account of the division of the nations, *Nimrod,* the son of Cush, founded the first great military despotism on record. The "mighty hunter" (Gen. 10:9) made men his game; for the phrase, in its connection, seems a great symbol of violence and rapine. His capital was Babylon, but he founded also three other cities in the plain of Shinar, namely, Erech, Accad and Calneh. Thence he extended his empire northward along the course of the Tigris over Assyria (Gen. 10:11), where he founded a second group of capitals, Nineveh,[1] Rehoboth, Calah and Resen.

Our present information does not permit us to identify Nimrod with any personage known to us either from inscriptions or from classical writers. We have no reason on this account to doubt the personal existence of Nimrod, for the events with which he is connected fall within the shadows of a remote antiquity. His name still survives in tradition, and to him the modern Arabs ascribe all the great works of ancient times, such as the *Birs-Nimrud* near Babylon, *Tel Nimrud* near *Baghdad,* the dam of *Suhr el Nimrud* across the Tigris below *Mosul,* and the well-known mound of *Nimrud* in the same neighborhood.

Special Study

The Tower of Babel

When the Jews were carried captive into Babylonia, they were struck with the vast magnitude and peculiar character of certain of the Babylonian temples, in one or other of which they thought to recognize the very tower itself. The predominant opinion was in favor of the great temple of Nebo at Borsippa, the modern *Birs-Nimrud,* although the distance of that place from Babylon is an insuperable difficulty in the way of the identification. There are in reality no real grounds either for identifying the tower with the Temple of Belus, or for supposing that any remains of it long survived the check which the builders received (Gen. 11:8). But the *Birs-Nimrud,* though it can not be the tower of Babel itself, may well be taken to show the probable shape and character of the edifice. This building appears to have been a sort of oblique pyramid, built in seven receding stages. "Upon a platform of crude brick, raised a few feet above the level of the alluvial plain, was built of burnt brick the first or basement stage — an exact

---

1. The cities are discussed in M.F. Unger, *Archaeology and the Old Testament,* pp. 86-90.

square, 272 feet each way, and 26 feet in perpendicular height. Upon this stage was erected a second, 230 feet each way, and likewise 26 feet high; which, however, was not placed exactly in the middle of the first, but considerably nearer to the south-western end, which constituted the back of the building. The other stages were arranged similarly — the third being 188 feet square, and again 26 feet high; the fourth 146 feet square, and 15 feet high; the fifth 104 feet square, and the same height as the fourth; the sixth 62 feet square, and again the same height; and the seventh 20 feet square, and once more the same height. On the seventh stage there was probably placed the ark or tabernacle, which seems to have been again 15 feet high, and must have nearly, if not entirely, covered the top of the seventh story. The entire original height, allowing three feet for the platform, would thus have been 156 feet, or without the platform, 153 feet. The whole formed a sort of oblique pyramid, the gentler slope facing the N.E. and the steeper inclining to the S.W. On the N.E. side was the grand entrance, and here stood the vestibule, a separate building, the debris from which, having joined those from the temple itself, fill up the intermediate space, and very remarkably prolong the mound in this direction" (Rawlinson's *Herodotus,* vol. 1, pp. 582-3). The *Birs* temple, which was called the "Temple of the Seven Spheres," was ornamented with the planetary colors, but this was most likely a pecularity.

4. *From this general account of the origin of the nations, the sacred narrative turns to the genealogy of the Postdiluvian Patriarchs,* in ten generations from Shem to Abraham. The only remaining point requiring notice is the decrease in the duration of life after Eber, the common head of the Hebrew and Arab races.

Questions on Section III
The Tower of Babel (Gen. 11)

1. How did human speech immediately after the flood differ from speech now?
2. Where was the plain where Noah's descendants at first settled?
3. What materials were used for building?
4. What were the two purposes for building a tower?
5. How was the tower project stopped?
6. Name the city where the tower was built.
7. How many generations from Shem to Abram inclusive? Name them.

Period III
The Patriarchal Period[1]
(From the Birth of Abraham to the Death of Joseph; Gen. 11:27-Ch. 50, and the book of Job)

During the patriarchal period God began to work out His program through one family and nation, the family of Abraham, the nation of Israel. Other nations were allowed to walk in their own ways (Acts 14:16) until the Christ should come through the seed of Abraham. Then all nations would be blessed in turning away from their iniquities (Acts 3:25-26).

Section I
The Land of Promise

1. Facts about the land. 2. Names of the land.
3. Divisions of the land: (a) Geopolitical, (b) Natural.
4. Brooks and rivers. 5. Mountains.

---

1. The patriarchs of this period are Abraham, Isaac, Jacob and Joseph. The earlier saints from Adam to Abraham may also be called patriarchs, or "father-rulers," but the patriarchs under consideration are given much more attention in Scripture than the earlier patriarchs.

During the life of Abraham the land of Palestine became the main center of events in sacred history, and it continued to be such afterwards. We should learn certain facts about the land.

1. *Facts about the land of promise.*
a. Palestine is about 5200 miles from America, and is located on the east of the Mediterranean Sea.
b. Palestine is part of the "fertile crescent," a land area stretching in an arch around the desert, from Egypt, through Palestine and Syria, and downward through Mesopotamia. Palestine is the natural bridge between Egypt, Arabia and Africa on the South, and Syria, Mesopotamia and Asia Minor to the north. See map on p. 62.
c. Palestine is a small land. It is only about 150 miles from Dan to Beersheba (I Sam 3:20). Dan and Beersheba were cities in the northern and southern areas of the land. See map on page 59.

2. *Names of the land.* At various times the land of promise has been divided up differently and called by different names.
a. *Canaan.* This name applies to the area west of the Jordan river, about 6000 square miles, an area slightly smaller than Massachusetts. It was named after Ham's son Canaan. Its name also means "Land of the red-purple," possibly from the purple dye used by Phoenician Canaanites.
b. *Palestine.* A larger area, including Canaan and the land east of the Jordan, about 12,000 square miles. The name Palestine is derived from the Philistines who inhabited its lower coastal area.
c. *Israel.* Same territory as Palestine. Named for Jacob, or Israel.
d. *Judah* (or Judea). This name applies only to the southern part of Canaan. Judah was for a time separated from the rest of Israel.
e. The *Holy Land.* This name is given to it because God's holy son lived, died and rose again there.
f. The *promised land.* God promised this land to Abraham and his descendants. For the boundaries of the land as promised by God, see map on page 58.

3. *Divisions of the land.*
a. Geopolitical divisions. See map on page 60.
   (1) Upper Galilee — Northwest of Sea of Galilee.
   (2) Lower Galilee — Plain of Esdraelon and hills just north.
   (3) Samaria — Central area.
   (4) Judah — Dominant political area.
   (5) Negeb — Semi-desert area, extending south of Judah to

the Gulf of Akabah. The word Negeb (or Negev) means South.

b. Four natural divisions. See map on page 61.

    (1) Coastal plain.

    (2) Mountain region.

    (3) Jordan valley.

    (4) Eastern tableland.

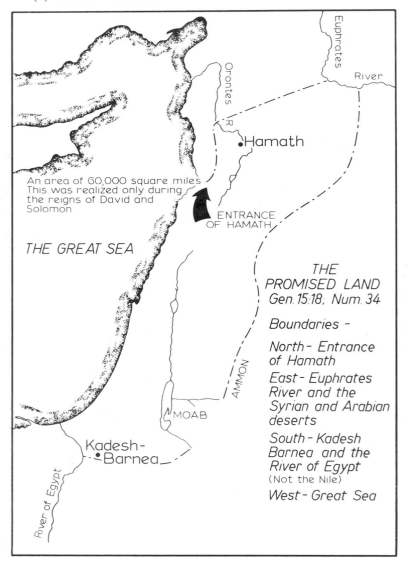

An area of 60,000 square miles. This was realized only during the reigns of David and Solomon

THE GREAT SEA

ENTRANCE OF HAMATH

•Hamath

THE PROMISED LAND
Gen. 15:18; Num. 34

Boundaries –

North – Entrance of Hamath

East – Euphrates River and the Syrian and Arabian deserts

South – Kadesh Barnea and the River of Egypt (Not the Nile)

West – Great Sea

Kadesh-•Barnea

River of Egypt

MOAB

AMMON

Orontes R.

Euphrates River

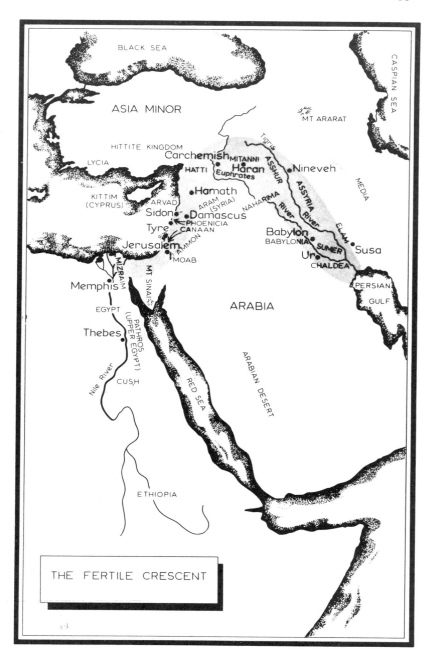

THE FERTILE CRESCENT

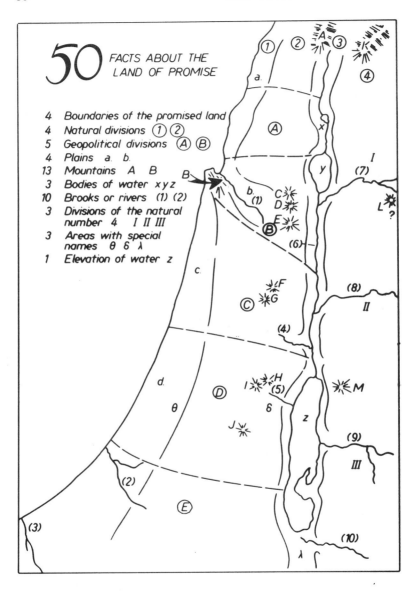

50 FACTS ABOUT THE
LAND OF PROMISE

4   Boundaries of the promised land
4   Natural divisions ① ②
5   Geopolitical divisions Ⓐ Ⓑ
4   Plains a. b.
13 Mountains A B
3   Bodies of water x y z
10 Brooks or rivers (1) (2)
3   Divisions of the natural
    number 4   I II III
3   Areas with special
    names θ δ λ
1   Elevation of water z

Four Boundaries of the Promised Land
N — Entrance of Hamath and the Euphrates river.
E — Syrian and Arabian deserts.
S — The River of Egypt and Kadesh-Barnea.
W — The Great Sea.

Four Natural Divisions
① Coastal (or maritime) Plain
② Central Mountain region
③ The Jordan Valley
④ The Eastern Tableland

Five Geopolitical Divisions
Ⓐ— Upper Galilee   Ⓑ — Lower Galilee
Ⓒ— Samaria   Ⓓ — Judea
Ⓔ— Negev (Negeb)

Four Plains
a — Asher (also called Acre, Akko, Zebulun)
b — Esdraelon (or Jezreel)
c — Sharon   d — Philistia

Thirteen Mountains

A — Lebanon	E — Gilboa	I — Zion
B — Carmel	F — Ebal	J — Hebron
C — Tabor	G — Gerizim	K — Hermon
D — Moreh	H — Olives	L — Gilead (?)
		M — Nebo

Three Bodies of Water
x — Lake Huleh (or Waters of Merom?)
y — Sea of Galilee
z — Dead Sea (or Salt Sea)

Four Brooks or Rivers

1. Kishon	6. Jordan
2. Besor	7. Yarmuk
3. River of Egypt (≠Wady el-Arish)	8. Jabbok
4. Wady Kelt (Cherith?)	9. Arnon
5. Kidron	10. Zered

Three Divisions of Natural Division
I. Bashan   II. Gilead   III. Moab

Three Areas with Special Names
θ The Shephelah (foothills)
ς Wilderness of Judea (Jeshimon)
λ The Arabah

Elevation of Water z, the Dead Sea ≑ 1296 feet below sea level.

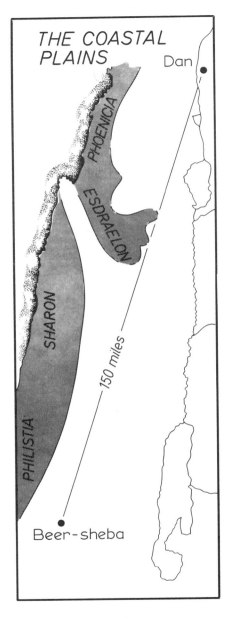

The Coastal Plains

Four plains — Phoenicia (or Asher), Esdraelon (or Jezreel), Sharon and Philistia — occupy the coastal areas of Palestine. These areas receive the most abundant rains of the land. Note that the plain of Esdraelon goes inland for considerable distance along the Kishon river.

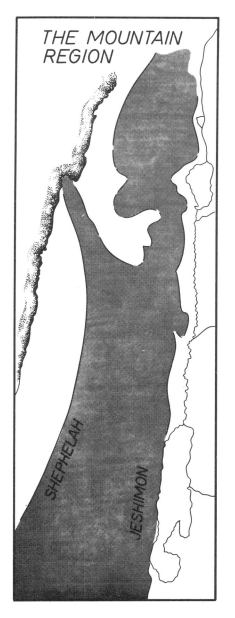

The Mountain Region

The Lebanon mountains extend down into Palestine west of the Jordan river. The mountain region is the backbone of the land. The mountains are generally higher in the north and become lower in the south.

The plain of Esdraelon breaks into the mountain chain in lower Galilee.

A line of low foothills called the *Shephelah* lies to the west of the mountains of Judea.

The rugged wasteland west of the Dead Sea is called the *Jeshimon* (or *Wilderness of Judah*) (Number 21:20; 23:28). It is a badlands without verdure, penetrated with deep ravines and caves.

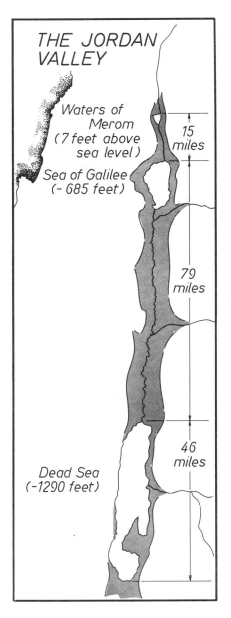

THE JORDAN VALLEY

Waters of Merom (7 feet above sea level)

Sea of Galilee (- 685 feet)

15 miles

79 miles

46 miles

Dead Sea (-1290 feet)

The Jordan Valley

Three bodies of water connected by the Jordan river lie in the great depression of the Jordan valley.

1. Waters of Merom — A swampy lake three miles across, seven feet above sea level. Also called Lake Huleh.

2. Sea of Galilee — This is called Chinneroth or Chinnereth in the Old Testament. It is 9 mi. x 13 mi. and 685 feet below sea level.

3. Dead Sea — Also called the Salt Sea or the Sea of the Plain. It is 46 miles long and 1,290 feet below sea level. It is the lowest surface on earth. Water can escape only by evaporation.

The Jordan originates at several springs on or near Mt. Hermon. From its source it is 40 miles to the Waters of Merom, 15 miles more to the Sea of Galilee, and 70 miles to the Dead Sea. While the river extends 134 miles in a line, its wanderings make it 200 miles long.

"The Jordan falls over 3,000 feet from its source, an average fall of over 22 feet to the mile. It varies in width from 80 to 180 feet and in depth from five to twelve feet (Hurlbut's *Bible Atlas*).

The deep depression of the Jordan valley extends on south of the Dead Sea to the Gulf of Akabah. This depression is called the *Arabah*. The Jordan valley north of the Dead Sea is also called Arabah.

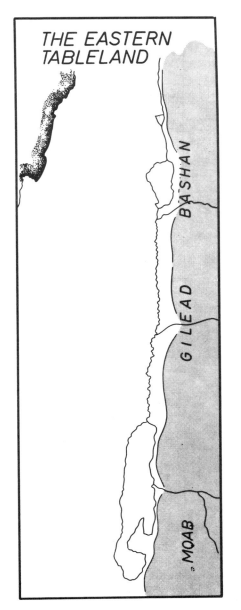

THE EASTERN TABLELAND

BASHAN

GILEAD

MOAB

The Eastern Tableland

East of Jordan steep cliffs rise, and from their summits high plains stretch away into the great desert eastward. Much of the area is fertile and productive.

The area is divided into three sections: (1) Bashan in the north; (2) Gilead in the center; (3) Moab below the Arnon river.

Bashan is a fertile area, famous for its fat livestock (Ezek. 39:18).

Gilead is famous for the "balm of Gilead," a healing resin produced by a type of tree (Jer. 8:22).

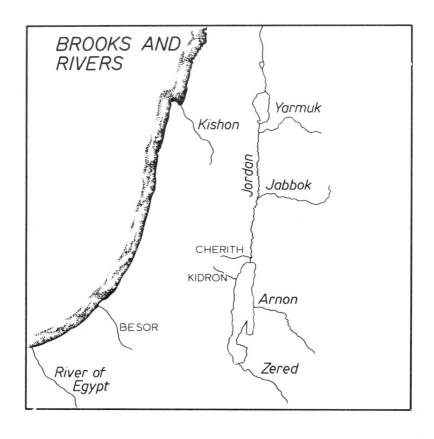

Brooks and Rivers of the Old Testament

 (1) Yarmuk.
 (2) Jabbok. Jacob wrestled here (Gen. 32:22).
 (3) Arnon. The border of Moab (Num. 21:13).
 (4) Zered. Israel and Moses camped here (Num. 21:12).
 (5) Kishon. This swept away God's enemies (Judges 5:21).
 (6) Besor. David pursued enemies across this (I Sam. 30:9,.
 (7) River of Egypt. The southern limit (Gen. 15:18).
 (8) Cherith. Ravens fed Elijah here (I Kings 17:5).
 (9) Kidron. David crossed this in sorrow (II Sam. 15:23).
(10) Jordan.

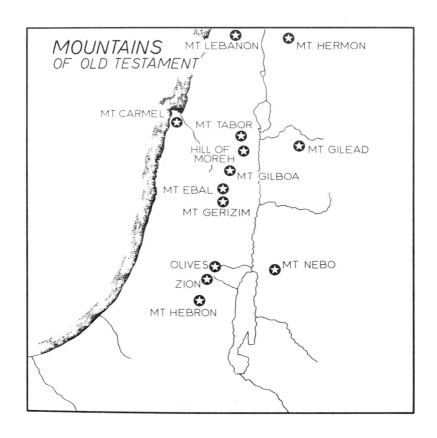

Mountains of the Old Testament

1. Mt. Lebanon, a range. Highest peak is 10,200 ft.
2. Mt. Carmel. 1,750 ft.
3. Mt. Tabor. 1,843 ft.
4. Hill of Moreh. 1,815 ft.
5. Mt. Gilboa. 1,715 ft.
6. Mt. Ebal. 3,075 ft.
7. Mt. Gerizim. 2,850 ft.
8. Mt. of Olives. 2,665 ft.
9. Mt. Zion. 2,550 ft.
10. Mt. Hebron. 3,030 ft.
11. Mt. Hermon. 9,200 ft.
12. Mt. Gilead. 3,000 ft.
13. Mt. Nebo (Pisgah). 2,670 ft.

Section II
Life of Abraham to Age 99
(Gen. 11:27-19:38)

1. God's choice of a family. 2. Genealogy of Terah — Birth of Abram. 3. First call of Abram at Ur — Removal to Haran — Death of Terah. 4. Abram's second call — His journey to Canaan and abode at Shechem. 5. His removal to Bethel — Retreat to Egypt, and return to Bethel. 6. His separation from Lot, and abode at Mamre, near Hebron — The third giving of the promise. 7. The War of Sodom — Abram's rescue of Lot — Melchizedek. 8. The promise of a son — The faith of Abraham — The Covenant made with him — Promise respecting his descendants and their land. 9. Hagar, the Egyptian — Birth of Ishmael. 10. Completion of the promise — The names of Abram and Sarai changed — Covenant of Circumcision — The birth of Isaac foretold. 11. New relation of Abraham to God — Divine visit to him at Mamre. 12. Destruction of the cities of the plain — Rescue of Lot — Moab and Ammon.

1. In the course of God's dealing with man which is traced in the sacred narrative, a new step was taken by *the choice of a family* from which the promised seed of the woman was to spring, and which should meanwhile preserve the knowledge and worship of the true God. Jehovah, in the revelation of himself to man, retires, so to speak, from the whole compass of the race of Noah into the inner circle of the family of Abraham. It was a step required by the state of the world, which had relapsed into idolatry and wickedness before the death of Noah. This is clear from the story of the building of Babel, and it is implied in the subsequent history. Joshua expressly says that the family of Terah were idolaters (Josh. 24:2).

2. The patriarch Abraham, who was the head of the chosen family, was born about 2166 B.C. and died 1991 B.C.

His father was TERAH, the ninth of the patriarchs from Shem and the nineteenth from Adam (inclusive). His genealogy, which the subsequent history requires to be most clearly understood, is exhibited in the following chart. It is important to include the whole family of Terah in our view, as the call of God came to

Abram while he was still living in the house of his father. The call was in some way addressed to the whole family, and was in some degree obeyed by all of them.

In the list of the postdiluvian patriarchs it is stated that Terah, at the age of 70, begat three sons: Abram, Nahor and Haran (Gen. 11:26). This is the order of dignity, but there can be little doubt that Haran was the eldest of the three, since Nahor married Haran's daughter; and Abram seems to have been the youngest. He was born when his father was 130 years old, for he was seventy-five years old when his father died in Haran at the age of 205. His name AB-RAM (meaning *exalted father*) was prophetic of his calling to be the ancestor of a race chosen for an exalted destiny; but it was afterward changed into the more significant name of AB-RAHAM *(father of a multitude)*.

3. Terah had already lost his eldest son, Haran, whose son LOT became his heir, when God called Abram to depart into a land that he would show him (Gen. 12:1). This first call came to him while the family still dwelt in the very ancient city of "UR of the Chaldees." This is expressly stated by Stephen (Acts 7:2), whose speech before the Sanhedrin is of the highest authority, were it only for his profound scriptural learning. Ur was located by the Euphrates river near the Persian Gulf. Terah left this city in the time of its greatest culture and power, the third Dynasty of Ur (2135-2025 B.C.). While its culture was amazing, its religion had degenerated into the deepest idolatry and superstition. It was necessary that the chosen family should separate themselves from this contaminating environment until God's provisions for the salvation of the whole world were ready to be proclaimed.

Therefore the chosen family left Ur at the command of God, and migrated northwestward about 600 miles, and took up residence at Haran, a city located by the river Balikh, a branch of the Euphrates in the land of Aram (or Syria). Here Terah died after a residence of some years (as is clear from Gen. 12:5); and here, charmed probably by the fertility of the country, and claiming the right of a first choice, Nahor settled. We shall find his family here in the next two generations, bearing a character suited to the motive thus suggested.

4. Meanwhile, and, as it seems, immediately on his father's death, and probably in consequence of a repetition of the Divine call, Abram proceeded on his journey with his wife Sarai and his nephew Lot. The "separation from his kindred" (Gen. 12:1) may

refer to Nahor, or even to other branches of his father's house left
behind in Ur; for Terah may have had other children besides the
three who are specially mentioned on account of the subsequent
relations of their descendants.

FAMILY OF TERAH

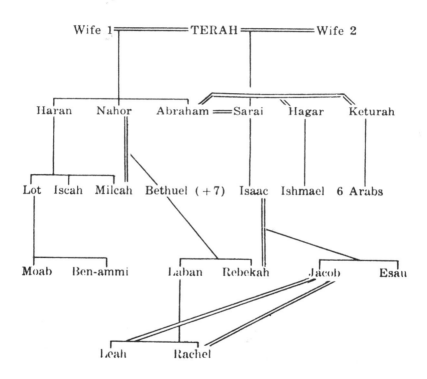

NOTES

a. The above information is taken from Gen. 11:27,29; 19:37-38; 20:12;
22:20-24; 24:15; 28:2,5.

b. A double line indicates a marriage.

c. Gen. 20:12 indicates that Sarai was half-sister to Abram. The language of this
verse could indicate that she was Abram's niece, but the fact that there was but ten
years difference between his age and hers (Gen. 17:17) renders this hypothesis
less probable.

d. Tradition has identified Iscah with Sarai, Abram's wife, but there is no real
basis for such a supposition.

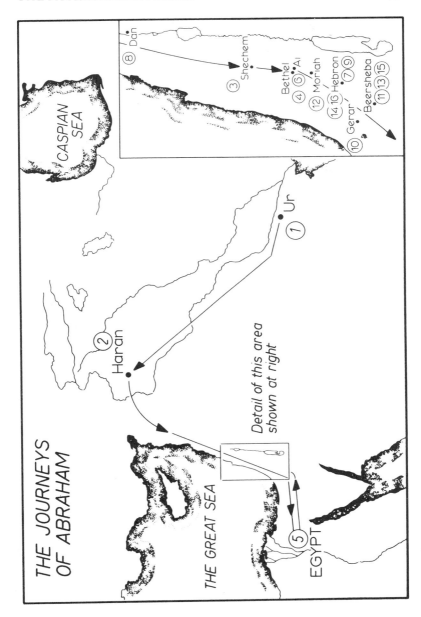

The Life and Journeys of Abraham

1. *Ur* of the Chaldees; Gen. 11:27-31.
   a. Original call to Abram; Acts 7:2-3.
   b. Terah's migration; Gen. 11:27-31.
2. *Haran;* Gen. 11:32-12:3.
   a. Death of Terah; 11:32.
   b. Second call to Abram; 12:1-3.
3. *Shechem;* Gen. 12:4-7.
   a. First promise of land.
4. Between *Bethel* and *Ai;* 12:8-9.
   a. Altar built.
5. *Egypt;* 12:10-20.
   a. Lie about Sarai.
6. Back at *Bethel;* 13:1-17.
   a. Separation from Lot.
7. *Hebron;* 13:18-14:12.
   a. Invasion from the East.
8. *Dan;* 14:13-16.
   a. Rescue of Lot.
9. Returning to *Hebron* and at Hebron; 14:17-19:38.
   a. Meeting with King of Sodom and Melshizedek; 14:17-24.
   b. God's covenant with Abram; Ch. 15.
   c. Hagar and Ishmael; Ch. 16.
   d. Covenant of circumcision; 17:1-14.
   e. Promise of Isaac; 17:15-21.
   f. Circumcision of household; 17:22-27.
   g. Destruction of Sodom and Gomorrah; Chs. 18-19.
10. *Gerar;* Gen. 20:1-21:20.
    a. Lie about Sarah to Abimelech; Ch. 20.
    b. Birth of Isaac; 21:1-7.
    c. Removal of Hagar and Ishmael; 21:8-21.
11. *Beersheba;* 21:22-34.
    a. Covenant of Abraham and Abimelech.
12. Land of *Moriah;* 22:1-18.
    a. Offering of Isaac.
13. *Beersheba;* 22:19-24.
    a. Abraham learns of Nahor's family.
14. *Hebron;* Ch. 23.
    a. Death and burial of Sarah.
15. *Beersheba;* 24:1-25:8.
    a. Wife for Isaac; Ch. 24.

    b. Marriage to Keturah; 25:1-4.
    c. Last days of Abraham; 25:5-8.
16. *Hebron;* 25:9-10.
    a. Burial of Abraham.

Abram's future abode was described by Jehovah simply as "a land that I will show thee"; and so "he went out, not knowing whither he went." This was the first great proof of that unwavering *faith* which added to his two other names of *Father* the title of *Father of the Faithful* (Heb. 11:8; Rom. 4:11,12,16; Gal. 3:7,9). He was now seventy-five years old; and this is the period usually assigned to the CALL OF ABRAHAM; though it was, in fact, the *second step* of his career. In tracing these stages, it is important to observe the special form of *promise* and *blessing* of which each was the occasion. The *first* of these involves the germ of all the rest, though as yet but vaguely stated: "I will make of thee *a great nation,* and *I will bless thee,* and make thy *name great,* and *thou shalt be a blessing* [to others]: and *I will bless them that bless thee,* and curse him that curseth thee, and *in thee shall all families of the earth be blessed*" (Gen. 12:2-3). The last words already involve the crowning blessing of the Old Covenant, the *Promise of the Messiah,* and that to *the Gentiles,* "all families of the earth" (Acts 3:25; Gal. 3:8).

Abram now left Mesopotamia and crossed the Great River, the Euphrates (called the *flood* in Josh. 24:2). This separated him entirely from his old home, and possibly accounts for the title *Hebrew* which he came to wear (Gen. 14:13). While some think that the name Hebrew came from the patriarch Eber (Gen. 11:16), it may come from the Hebrew verb meaning to "cross over."

Abram now passed through the great Syrian desert; and, though his route is not mentioned in the sacred narrative, we may credit the tradition that he tarried at Damascus, since Eliezer, "the steward of his house," was a native of that place. Leaving Damascus, Abram crossed the Jordan, and entering the HOLY LAND, passed into the *valley of Shechem* (or *Sichem*). His resting-place was marked, like other memorable localities, by an oak or a grove of oaks ("The oak or oaks of Moreh," rather than "the *plain* of Moreh," as in the King James version), near "the place of Shechem," between Mounts Ebal and Gerizim. Here God appeared to him again, and gave him the *second promise,* of the possession of the land by his seed; and here Abram built the first

The Blessing of Abraham
(Gen. 12:1-3; 22:18; Gal. 3:14,16)

Abraham and his *seed* became the funnel through which God's blessings are channeled to a needy world.

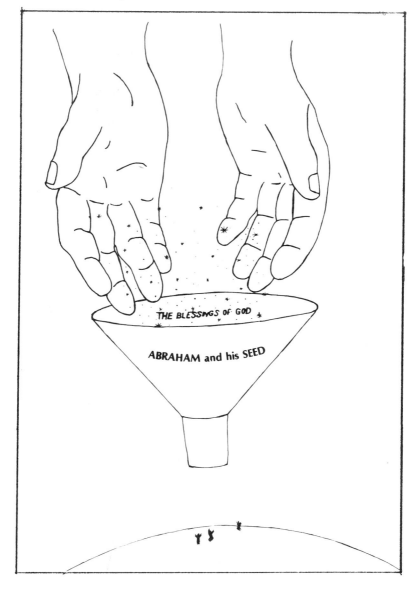

The Blessing of Abraham

(See chart on preceding page)

Mankind fell far short of doing God's will both before and after the flood. After the flood man attempted to build the tower to heaven.

God therefore selected one man of great faith, Abram (later called Abraham), and promised to *bless* every nation through Abraham and through his seed (or offspring). (Gen. 12:1-3; 22:18. Learn where these references are.)

In the years that followed the promise to Abraham, God allowed all other nations to walk in their own ways (Acts 14:16). In those centuries, up until the time of Christ, God concentrated His efforts upon the nation of Israel, to prepare it and perfect it, so that the promised seed of Abraham might deliver the blessing promised to Abraham.

Who is (or are) the *seed* of Abraham, through whom the blessing of Abraham was to come?

1. The *Hebrew* (Jewish) *people.* The Jewish people (the fleshly seed of Abraham) were to be God's instruments of bringing blessing to the world (John 4:22).

2. *Jesus,* the Messiah. Jesus is *the* special seed of Abraham, through whom God's blessings are given (Galatians 3:16). This is the reason for the statement in Matthew 1:1 that Jesus is the son of *Abraham.* If he were not the offspring of Abraham, he could not be the channel for God's blessings.

3. *Christians.* "If ye are Christ's, then are ye Abraham's seed" (Galatians 3:29). We Christians are to be channels for God's blessings to reach humankind.

Exactly what is this blessing of Abraham which is extended to all mankind?

1. Righteousness (or justification) by faith (Galatians 3:6-7; Romans 4:9,23-24).

2. The Holy Spirit (Galatians 3:14).

---

of those altars to JEHOVAH, which the patriarchs erected wherever they pitched their tents. Thus Shechem became his *first stopping place* in the Holy Land.

5. It is uncertain whether "the place of Shechem" was yet marked by the city which afterward took its name from the Amorite Shechem, the contemporary of Jacob. But it is distinctly stated that "the Canaanite was then (*i.e.,* already) in the land,"

having probably driven out an earlier population. They would view with no friendly eye the tents of the patriarch, surrounded by his flocks and herds; and Abram seems neither to have had the power nor the inclination to resort, like Jacob, to "his sword and his bow" (Gen. 48:22). He removed southward to a place which lay afterward on the northern border of the kingdom of Judah, on the heights which skirt the Jordan, between BETHEL (then called Luz) on the west, and AI[1] on the east, where he built another altar, and called on the name of Jehovah. This was his *second stopping place* in the Holy Land.

Abram's abode in this mountain region secured him from the Canaanites, who occupied the more fertile plains below, but it afforded only scanty pasture for his cattle. He therefore went on continually southward, till the pressure of famine drove him out of the promised land into Egypt (Gen. 12:9-10). The great subject of the history of Egypt, in relation to the family of Abraham, will be considered later. It is enough here to observe that the mighty kingdom of the Pharaohs had already been long established in Lower Egypt. In this crisis the faith of Abram failed. To protect himself from the license of a despot, he stooped to that mean form of deceit, which is true in word but false in fact. He caused Sarai to pass as his sister. The trick defeated itself. Sarai, as an unmarried woman, was taken to the house of the king, who heaped wealth and honors upon Abram. Warned of his mistake by plagues sent upon him and his household, the king restored Sarai to her husband, with a rebuke for his deceit, and sent him out of Egypt with all the wealth he had acquired, for he was now "very rich in cattle, in silver, and in gold" (Gen. 12:11-13:4). Abram travelled back through the south of Palestine to his old encampment near Bethel, where he again established the worship of Jehovah.

6. He now began to feel the evils of prosperity. The land could not support his own cattle and Lot's. Their herdsmen quarreled. Abraham's faith did not fail this time. Remembering that he was "the heir of better promises," he gave the choice of present good to Lot. Their encampment looked westward on the rugged hills of Judaea and eastward on the fertile plain of the Jordan about Sodom, "well watered everywhere, as the garden of the Lord, like the land of Egypt" he had only lately left. Even from that distance,

---

1. This is the well-known city whose fall is related by Joshua. Bethel is the place so conspicuous in the history of Jacob, who gave it the name Beth-el, or "House of God."

through the clear air of Palestine can be distinctly seen the long and thick masses of vegetation which fringe the numerous streams that descend from the hills on either side to meet the central stream in its tropical depths. It was exactly the prospect to tempt a man who had no fixed purpose of his own, who had not, like Abram, obeyed a stern call of duty. So Lot left his uncle on the barren hills of Bethel, and chose all the precinct of the Jordan, and journeyed east. Abram received his reward in a *third blessing and promise* from Jehovah, who bade him lift up his eyes and scan the whole land on every side, for it should be the possession of his seed, and they should be unnumbered as the dust of the earth. Abram now removed to the *oaks of Mamre*,[1] near HEBRON, in the centre of the hills of the south, and there built an altar. This was his *third resting-place* in the Holy Land, and Mamre became his usual abode.[2]

7. Lot had meanwhile pitched his tent in a memorable spot. The land S.E. of the Dead Sea was then occupied by the five "cities of the plain." Sodom, Gomorrah, Admah, Zeboiim and Bela (afterward called Zoar), formed a *Pentapolis,* each with its own king, Sodom being the chief. Their wickedness was such that Sodom has given its name to a sin of which "it is a shame even to speak," but which was committed not "in secret."[3] Lot's worldliness had not quite stifled his piety, and "his righteous soul was vexed with their filthy conversation" (II Pet. 2:7-8).

While thus tempted, he became involved in another danger. The confederacy of the five cities was tributary to a great empire, which had already been established in Western Asia under Chedorlaomer, king of Elam. Elam was primarily the mountainous region on the eastern margin of the plain of Chaldea, but in a wider sense it included some adjoining territory.

In the thirteenth year of the subjection of Sodom and the other four cities they revolted, and Chedorlaomer marched against them with three allied kings. After conquering the nations to the east and south, the four kings invaded the territories of the five, and joined battle with them in the vale of Siddim, which was full

---

1. Named after an Amorite prince, with whom, and his brothers Eschol and Aner, Abram formed a league (Gen. 14:13).
2. Gen. 13:5-18. Hebron was originally called Kirjath-Arba (Gen. 23), that is, "the city of Arba," from Arba, the father of Anak, and progenitor of the giant Anakim (Josh. 21:11, 15:13,14). It is situated about twenty miles south of Jerusalem, and thirty miles north of Beersheba. It became the burialplace of Abraham and his family in the cave of Machpelah (see below, p. 88); and from this circumstance it is revered by the Mohammedans, who call the city *El-Khalil,* "the Friend," i.e., of God, the name which they give to Abraham.
3. Gen. 13:13, 18:20, 19:5; Deut. 23:17; Rom. 1:27; 2 Pet. 2:7,8.

of pits of bitumen. Among these the forces of the cities were entangled and defeated; the kings of Sodom and Gomorrah fell; and the rest fled to the mountains, while Sodom and Gomorrah were spoiled, and Lot and his goods were carried off (Gen. 14:5-12). The news was brought to Abraham, who, with his Amorite allies, and 318 men of his own household, sallied forth from Mamre, and overtook the victors at the sources of the Jordan, where Laish (Dan) afterward stood.[1] Dividing his band, he fell upon them by night, disordered no doubt after their success, pursued their routed forces to Hobah, north (the "left hand") of Damascus (Gen. 14:13-16), and rescued Lot, with all the spoil, but refused to accept any part of it from the new king of Sodom, who came out to meet him at SHAVEH, or the KING'S DALE.[2]

The return of this expedition was marked by one of the most memorable prophetic incidents in Abram's career. MELCHIZEDEK, king of Salem, the priest of the "Most High God," also came to meet him, bringing bread and wine, and blessed him in the name of the Most High God, and Abram gave him tithes of all the spoil (Gen. 14:18-20). There is something surprising and mysterious in the first appearance of Melchizedek, and in the subsequent references to him. He bore a title which Jews in after ages would recognize as designating their own sovereign, and bore gifts which recall to Christians the Lord's Supper. This Canaanite crosses for a moment the path of Abram, and is unhesitatingly recognized as a person of higher spiritual rank than the friend of God. Disappearing as suddenly as he came in, he is lost to the sacred writings for a thousand years; and then a few emphatic words for another moment bring him into sight as a type of the coming Lord of David. Once more, after another thousand years, the Hebrew Christians are taught to see in him a proof that it was the consistent purpose of God to abolish the Levitical priesthood. His person, his office, his relation to Christ, and the seat of his sovereignty, have given rise to innumerable discussions, which even now can scarcely be considered as settled (Ps. 110:4; Heb. 6:20-7:17).

That Melchizedek was both a king and priest, is quite in

---

1. The Dan referred to may be the Dan-Jaan in Gilead, mentioned in II Sam. 24:6, rather than Dan-Laish near the sources of Jordan.
2. Shaveh is located near Jerusalem, according to Josephus *(Ant.* VII, 10, 3) and Jewish tradition. *Salem,* associated with Shaveh in Gen. 14:17-18, is an ancient name for Jerusalem. See Psalm 76:2. The name *Salem* is preserved in the word Jerusalem, and means *peace* (Heb. 7:2).

accordance with the patriarchal state of society; but his priesthood seems to have a dignity above that of the ordinary head of a family. That he was "the priest of the Most High God," implies a relic of the true worship outside of the chosen family, such as we find long after in the story of the prophet Balaam.

The extraordinary reverence paid to him by Abram, and apparently by the king of Sodom, completes all our positive knowledge respecting his person and office. Tradition and fancy have found in him Shem or some other patriarch, an angel, and even a personification of the Son of God, a view which is a gross confusion of type and antitype.[1]

8. Following the encounter with Melchizedek, the word of Jehovah came to Abram in a vision to assure him of His blessing and protection. His faith had begun again to waver. With unbounded promises of the number and blessedness of his offspring, he was yet childless; with vast wealth, he had no heir but his steward and slave, Eliezer of Damascus. And now God unfolded to him a plainer and more solemn revelation, which was made the more emphatic by the threefold form of a *promise,* a *sign* and a *covenant.* The *promise* was that his own son should be his heir. The *sign* was given by a view of the clear sky of an Eastern night, studded with stars, which Jehovah bade Abram count, if he would tell the number of his posterity. And then "ABRAM BELIEVED JEHOVAH; AND IT WAS COUNTED TO HIM FOR RIGHTEOUSNESS" (Gen. 15:6). This was the crisis of his religious life, and of that of his spiritual children. With the moral submission of the will, which is the essence of faith, he *trusted God for what was beyond the scope of his reason* (Gen. 15:1-6). The test of his faith was as simple as that of Adam's obedience; the belief of God's word that he would have a son after the natural limit of age; but the principle was the same as in faith's highest flights. "He *staggered not* at the promise of God through unbelief, but was strong in faith, giving glory to God, and being fully persuaded that what He had promised He was able also to perform. And *therefore* it was imputed to him for righteousness" (Rom. 4:20-21; Heb. 11:11,12).

This promise was ratified by a new COVENANT, in which Abram

1. The "order of Melchizedek," in Ps. 110:4, is explained by some to mean "manner" — likeness in official dignity — a king and priest. The relation between Melchizedek and Christ as type and antitype is made in the Epistle to the Hebrews to consist in the following particulars. Each was a priest (1), not of the Levitical tribe; (2) superior to Abraham; (3) whose beginning and end are unknown; (4) who is not only a priest, but also a king of righteousness *(melchi-zedek)* and peace *(salem).*

stood to God in the relation of the Father of the Faithful, just as Noah, in the covenant made with him, stood for all his race. The forms with which this new covenant was made are minutely related; and they seem to agree with the customs then observed in covenants between man and man.

Those forms are alluded to in the phrase, "Jehovah made a covenant with Abram" (Gen. 15:18). A victim (or more) was slain in sacrifice, and equally divided, and the parts being placed over against each other, the contracting parties passed down between them. The ceremony clearly signifies the equality of the contract, its religious character and the penalty due to its violation. Each part of the ceremony was observed in this case. God's presence was indicated by the fire that passed between the pieces of the victims sacrificed, and Abram had already passed between them.

The promise was as specific as it was solemn. It included:
a. The bondage of the Hebrews in a strange land for 400 years (Gen. 15:13).
b. Their delivery, with great wealth, and amid judgments on their oppressors (Gen. 15:14).
c. Their return to the promised land in the fourth generation, when the iniquity of its inhabitants should be full (Gen. 15:17).

The boundaries of their possessions in that land were strictly defined, "from the river of Egypt unto the great river, the river Euphrates," to which the kingdom of David and Solomon actually reached (Gen. 15:18; I Kings 4:21). The definition is still more clearly made by the enumeration of the Canaanitish tribes that occupied the land (Gen. 15:19-21).

At a later period, when the covenant was renewed, the sign of *circumcision* was added to it.

9. To wait patiently for the fulfillment of the promise, in spite of natural obstacles, was too much, if not for the faith of Abram, at least for that of Sarai. Being herself barren, she gave Abram her handmaid Hagar, an Egyptian, for his concubine; and Hagar bore him a son (Gen. 16:1-3). But, before the child was born, the insolence of Hagar provoked the jealousy of Sarai, whose ill-treatment of her handmaiden drove her to flee into the wilderness of Kadesh, southeast of Abram's abode. Here the "angel of the Lord" appeared to her, and, while bidding her to return and submit to her mistress, he encouraged her by the promise of a numerous offspring. In memory of God's hearing her cry of distress, He bade her name the coming child ISHMAEL (that is, *God shall hear),* and he foretold his character and destiny

in words which to this day describe the Bedouin Arabs who are descended from him: "He will be a wild man; his hand will be against every man, and every man's hand against him: and he shall dwell *in the face of all his brethren,*" that is, to the *east* of the kindred tribes sprung from Abraham.[1]

On this occasion we have the first of those distinctive names which were given to Jehovah in remembrance of special divine interpositions. Hagar said, *"Thou God seest me,"* and she named the well by which she had sat *Beer-lahai-roi,* that is *The Well of him that liveth and seeth me* (Gen. 16:7-14).

The practice of a slave woman bearing a child for a childless wife seems strange to us. However, this was a common practice in the society of the patriarchal world, as the Nuzu tablets and the Code of Hammurabi have shown.[2] If the couple later had a child of their own, they could not thrust out the slave woman's offspring. This explains Abraham's reticence about thrusting out Ishmael (Gen. 21:11-12). Abraham probably would never have done this without God's direct approval.

10. The birth of Ishmael took place when Abram was eighty-six years old (Gen. 16:15-16); but he had to wait fourteen years more for the true fulfillment of the promise of an heir. The event was preceded by new revelations. In Abram's ninety-ninth year, Jehovah, appearing to him by the name of EL-SHADDAI *(God Almighty),* renewed the covenant with him in the new character of *"Father of many Nations,"* in sign thereof he changed his name from AB-RAM *(exalted father)* to AB-RAHAM *(father of a multitude).* The promise was now repeated to Abraham, more clearly than ever, *on behalf of his posterity:* "I will be a God unto thee, and to thy seed after thee" (Gen. 17:7-8). As a sign of this inclusion of children in the covenant, God enjoined the rite of *circumcision,* which became henceforth the *condition* of the covenant on the part of those with whom God made it (Gen. 17:9-14). The uncircumcised was cut off from all its benefits, "he hath broken my covenant," while the stranger who received circumcision was admitted to them; and the head of the family was commanded to extend the rite to every male in his household, servants as well as children. It was to be performed on children the eighth day after

1. The Hebrews and Arabs named the cardinal points from the position of the body when the *face* was turned to the east; the *back,* therefore denoted the *west,* the *right hand* the *south,* and the *left hand* the *north.* Thus the Mediterranean was called the *hinder* sea, and to the present day Syria is *Esh-sham,* the *left hand;* and North-western Arabia *El-Yemen,* the *right hand.*

2. *See* Unger, *Arch. and O.T.* 122; Free, *Arch.* and *Bible Hist.* 59.

birth, and on slaves when they were purchased; and all the family of Abraham were at once thus brought within the covenant.

The dignity of Sarai, as the mother of the promised seed, was marked by the change of her name to SARAH *(princess),* and it was declared that she should "become nations; and kings of the people should be of her" (Gen. 17:16). Her son was to be named ISAAC *(laughter),* from the utterance of his father's feelings on the announcement (Gen. 17:17). With him and his seed the covenant was to be continued in the new character of an *"everlasting* covenant," thus marking the distinction between its eternal and temporal blessings. The latter blessings were assured to Ishmael, in answer to Abraham's earnest prayer; but the covenant was *"established"* with Isaac." He is emphatically called the *child of the promise* and Ishmael the *child of the flesh* by the Apostle Paul, who carries out the contrast in a very remarkable passage (Gen. 17:18,21; Gal. 4:21-31).

Ishmael's share in the temporal promise was confirmed by his circumcision (Gen. 17:25), and the rite is still observed by the Arabs and other Semitic races. It was also practiced by the ancient Egyptians, who affirmed that "the Syrians in Palestine" had learned it from them. They used it for physical reasons only, and it is consistent with God's manner of symbolic teaching that a rite already existing should have been adopted in a new religious sense; but we must not hastily accept the statement that it was thus borrowed.

11. ABRAHAM, from the time when by this new name he received the full divine revelation and covenant, is presented to us in a higher character than before. The more open and familiar intercourse which he enjoys with Jehovah marks him as peculiarly "the friend of God." Of this we have an example in Genesis 18. As Abraham sat at his tent door, under the oak of Mamre, he became aware of the presence of "three *men*" (Gen. 18:2), for such they seemed to him; and the same language is continually employed for the appearances of celestial beings in human form.[1]

Afterward the chief speaker is denoted, first by the mere pronoun, which is often used when God is meant (Gen. 18:10), and then by the name of JEHOVAH. Doubtless he was the "Angel Jehovah," the "Word of God," through whom God spake to the fathers, and who, when dwelling upon earth in the actual incarnation which such appearances prefigured, declared, "Your

---

1. See, for example, Judges 13:10,11; Acts 1:10; Rev. 21:17.

father Abraham rejoiced to see my day: and he saw it, and was glad" (John 8:56). It is simplest to regard the other two as attendant angels; and it appears, from the sequel, that while the chief of the three (Jehovah himself) remained behind in converse with Abraham, and then "went his way" to execute judgment upon Sodom,[1] the other two were sent forward to rescue Lot.

Abraham offered to the "three men" that hospitality which is commemorated in the apostolic precept: "Be not forgetful to entertain strangers, for thereby some have entertained angels unawares.[2] He soon learned the dignity of his visitors, when they inquired after Sarah, and rebuked her incredulity by repeating the promise that she should bear Abraham a son, and fixing the time for its fulfillment. They then departed, with their faces toward Sodom; and as Abraham brought them on the way, he was favored — in consideration of his character as the head of the chosen family, to whom he was to teach God's righteous ways — with a revelation of the judgment coming upon Sodom and Gomorrah for their sins. Thus was the truth revealed to the believing children of Abraham in every age, that God does execute judgment upon sinners, even in this life. But the patriarch's faith grasped at another truth, the privilege of intercession for such sinners.

Then follows that wondrous pleading, in which he who was "but dust and ashes," taking on himself to speak with God, obtained the pardon of the guilty cities, if but fifty, then if forty-five, and so on down to only ten, righteous men were found in them, and might have prevailed if he had continued to plead, for the sake of the *one* really there; for such seems the necessary complement of this great lesson that "men ought always to pray, and not to faint" (Luke 18:1; James 5:16).

12. Meanwhile the two angels went on their mission to Sodom, whose people gave them a reception which filled up the measure of their sins (Gen. 19:4-11). Even the sons-in-law of Lot despised their warning; and Lot himself was reluctantly dragged, with his wife and two daughters, from the condemned city. Even then, he could not quite tear himself from the scene where his worldly prosperity had been purchased by constant vexation of spirit, and he pleaded that one of the five cities might be preserved as his abode, because it was but a little one, whence the city, before named *Bela*, was called *Zoar,* that is, *little.*[3] The sun was risen when

---

1. See Gen. 18:17-23, compared with 19:1,24.
2. Heb. 13:2; compare Gen. 19:1-3.
3. Gen. 19:17-22; comp. 13:10, 14:2.

Lot entered Zoar, and the people of Sodom and Gomorrah, with the two smaller cities of Admah and Zeboiim, which shared their fate,[1] had begun another day of wanton revelry (Luke 17:29), when the heavens were overcast, and "Jehovah rained down upon them brimstone and fire from Jehovah out of heaven; and he overthrew those cities, and that which grew upon the ground."[2]

The plain in which the cities stood, hitherto fruitful "as the garden of Jehovah," became henceforth a scene of perfect desolation. Our Lord himself, and the apostles Peter and Jude, have clearly taught the lasting lesson which is involved in the judgment; that it is a type of the final destruction by fire of a world which will have reached a wickedness like that of Sodom and Gomorrah.[3] A more special warning to those who, when once separated from an ungodly world, desire to turn back, is enforced by the fate of Lot's wife, who when she looked back from behind him, became *a pillar of salt* (Gen. 19:26; Luke 17:32). Lot himself, though saved from Sodom, fell, like Noah after the Deluge, into vile intoxication, of which his own daughters took advantage to indulge the incestuous passion, from which sprang the races of *Moab* and *Ammon.*[4]

Questions Over Section II
Life of Abraham to Age 99

(Note — *Students should memorize all of the places in the journeys of Abraham from the map, and learn at least one event connected with each place.*)

1. Why did God choose one family through which to work out his program?
2. Whose family was chosen (Gen. 11:31; 12:1)?
3. Who were Terah's three children (11:27)?
4. Who was Lot's father (11:27)?
5. Where did Terah first live, and to what place did he go (11:31)?
6. What do the names *Abram* and *Abraham* mean?
7. Where did Abram receive his first call (Acts 7:2)?

1. Gen. 19:25; comp. Gen. 13:10; 14:2; Deut. 29:23.
2. Gen. 19:24,25; comp. Deut. 29:23; Isaiah 13:19; Jer. 20:16, 1. 40; Ezek. 16:49, 50; Hos. 11:8; Amos 4:11; Zeph. 2:9.
3. Luke 17:29; 2 Peter 2:6; Jude 7.
4. Gen. 19:30-38. On Moab and Ammon see *Neighbors of Israel and Judah.* pp. 535, 545.

8. Where did he receive his second call (Gen. 11:32)?
9. Where did Terah die (11:32)?
10. Tell four things God promised to Abram when he called him the second time (12:2-3).
11. How old was Abram when he left Haran (12:4)?
12. Into what land did Abram come, and what was his first stopping-place there (12:5-6)?
13. Why did Abram go into Egypt (12:10)?
14. What deceitful thing did Abram do in Egypt (12:11 13)?
15. Why did Abram and Lot separate? Where did the separation take place (13:2, 6)?
16. Where did Lot go to live (13:12)?
17. What blessing was announced to Abram after his separation from Lot (13:14-16)?
18. Where did Abram then go to dwell (13:18)?
19. Who invaded the city where Lot lived (14:1-2, 12)?
20. Who told Abram of Lot's capture (14:13)?
21. How many men did Abram have (14:14)?
22. Where did Abram rescue Lot (14:14)?
23. What would Abram not accept from the king of Sodom (14:17, 21-23)?
24. Who was Melchizedek (14:18)?
25. What did Abram give Melchizedek (14:20)?
26. Who did Abram assume would be his heir and possessor of his house (15:2)?
27. How many seed (descendants) did God promise Abram (15:5)?
28. What did God reckon (or account) as righteousness unto Abram (15:6)?
29. How long did God foretell that Abram's seed would sojourn in a strange land (15:13)?
30. What were the limits of the land God promised to Abram (15:18)?
31. Who was Sarai's handmaid (16:1)?
32. What was the attitude of the handmaid when she conceived (16:4)?
33. Who called a well *Beerlahairoi,* and why (16:7, 13-14)?
34. What was Hagar's son's name, and Abram's age at his birth (16:16)?
35. How old was Abram when his name was changed (17:1, 5)?
36. What did the change of names indicate about the change of Abraham's status (17:5-6)?

37. What was the token of God's covenant with Abraham (17:11)?
38. To what was Sarai's name changed, and what does the new name mean (17:15)?
39. What caused Abraham to laugh (17:17)?
40. How many princes (or tribes) were to come from Ishmael (17:20)?
41. Who were the three visitors who came to Abraham at Mamre (18:1; 19:1)?
42. What did Abraham feed his guests (18:8)?
43. What promise was given concerning Abraham's son by his visitors (18:10)?
44. Why did Sarah laugh (18:12)?
45. What plans did Jehovah reveal to Abraham about Sodom (18:20, 23)?
46. How many righteous people could have saved Sodom (18:32)?
47. Where did the angels stay in Sodom (19:2-3)?
48. How was an assault on Lot's house stopped (19:11)?
49. What members of Lot's family got out of Sodom (19:15)?
50. To what small city did God permit Lot to flee (19:23)?
51. What was the fate of Sodom and Gomorrah (19:24)?
52. What was the fate of Lot's wife (19:26)?
53. Give the names of the sons of Lot's two daughters, and the people descended from each (19:37-38).

Section III
Life of Abraham (Gen. 20:1-25:18)
From birth of Isaac to Abraham's Death

1. Abraham at Gerar — His lie about Sarah. 2. Birth of Isaac — Expulsion of Hagar and Ishmael. 3. Abraham at Beersheba — Covenant with Abimelech. 4. Offering of Isaac on the mountain of Moriah. 5. Death of Sarah. 6. Marriage of Isaac and Rebekah. 7. Death and burial of Abraham — Death of Ishmael.

1. After a long residence at Mamre, Abraham once more set forth upon his wanderings, turning toward "the south country, and dwelled between Kadesh and Shur, and sojourned in Gerar."

This was a settlement about nine miles from Gaza. In this district the Philistines had already begun to form settlements, and a warlike king of this race, whose hereditary name was ABIMELECH *(Father-King)*, reigned in the valley of Gerar. Here the deceit which Abraham had put upon Pharaoh, by calling Sarah his sister, was acted again, and with the like result. The repeated occurrence of such an event, which will meet us again in the history of Isaac, can surprise no one acquainted with Oriental manners; but it would have been indeed surprising if the author of any but a genuine narrative had exposed himself to a charge so obvious as that which has been founded on its repetition. The independent truth of each story is confirmed by the natural touches of variety; such as, in the case before us, Abimelech's keen but gentle satire in recommending Sarah to buy a veil with the thousand pieces of silver which he gave to her husband. We may also observe the traces of the knowledge of the true God among Abimelech and his servants (Gen. 20:9-11).

2. It was during Abraham's abode around Gerar that his hopes were crowned by the birth of his son ISAAC, when he himself was a hundred years old (Gen. 21:1-7). At the "great feast" made in celebration of the weaning, "Sarah saw the son of Hagar the Egyptian, which she had born unto Abraham, mocking," and urged Abraham to cast out him and his mother. The patriarch was deeply grieved, but being reassured by God that of Ishmael He would make a nation, sent them both away, and they departed and wandered in the wilderness of Beersheba. Here the water being spent in the bottle, Hagar cast her son under one of the desert shrubs, and went away a little distance, "for she said, Let me not see the death of the child," and wept. "And God heard the voice of the lad, and the angel of the Lord called to Hagar out of heaven," renewed the promise already thrice given, "I will make him a great nation," and "opened her eyes, and she saw a well of water." Thus miraculously saved from perishing by thirst, "God was with the lad; and he grew, and dwelt in the wilderness; and became an archer." It is doubtful whether the wanderers halted by the well, or at once continued their way to "the wilderness of Paran," where he dwelt, and where "his mother took him a wife out of the land of Egypt" (Gen. 21:9-21).

3. Abraham seems to have moved his flocks gradually south and east to the area of Beersheba. Here Abimelech, the king of Gerar, came to Abraham, desiring to make a covenant of peace. Abraham swore an oath of peace. Abimelech had nothing to fear

from Abraham, but as a sinner he was incapable of comprehending that the man of God did not have the treachery in his heart that he himself would have practiced.

A dispute arose between Abraham and Abimelech respecting a well in the neighborhood, marking "the importance which, in the migratory land of the East, was and is always attached to the possession of water." This dispute led to a treaty between Abraham and Abimelech, which gave to the well the name of "Beersheba," or *the well of the oath*, "because there they sware both of them." Here also "Abraham planted a grove, and called on the name of Jehovah, the *everlasting God*"; in opposition doubtless to the deified heroes of the surrounding heathen.[1]

Abraham and his descendants dwelt for a long time at BEERSHEBA, at the southwestern extremity of the maritime plain, upon the borders of the desert. It continued till the latest times to be the southern boundary of the Holy Land, so that "from Dan to Beersheba" became the established formula to indicate the whole country.

4. Henceforward the story of Abraham is intertwined with that of Isaac, of whom it was said, "In Isaac shall thy seed be called."[2] The plan of the sacred narrative passes over every detail that does not bear upon the history of the covenant itself, and carries us on to a period when Isaac had reached the age of intelligence. A tradition preserved by Josephus makes Isaac twenty-five years old at the time of the crowning trial of Abraham's faith,[3] and we certainly gather from the Scripture narrative that he was an intelligent and willing party to the sacrifice of his life at the command of God. It is impossible to repeat this story, the most perfect specimen of simple and pathetic narrative, in any other words than those of the sacred writer. "And it came to pass after these things, that God did tempt Abraham, and said unto him, Abraham. And he said, Behold, there I am. And he said, Take now thy son, thine only son Isaac,

---

1. Gen. 21:22-23. There are at present on the spot two principal wells and five smaller ones. They are among the first objects encountered on the entrance into Palestine from the south, and being highly characteristic of the life of the Bible, never fail to call forth the enthusiasm of the traveller. The two principal wells lie just a hundred yards apart. The larger of the two, which lies to the east, is 12½ feet diam., and at the time of Dr. Robinson's visit was 55½ feet to the surface of the water. The other well is 5 feet diam, and was 42 feet to the water. The curb-stones around the mouth of both wells are worn into deep grooves by the action of the ropes of so many centuries. Round the larger well there are nine, and round the smaller five large stone troughs — some much worn and broken, others nearly entire, lying at a distance of 10 or 12 feet from the edge of the well.

2. Gen. 21:12; comp. Rom. 9:7,8; Heb. 11:18.

3. Josephus, *Ant.* I, 13, 2.

whom thou lovest, and get thee into the land of Moriah; and offer him there for a burnt-offering upon one of the mountains which I will tell thee of. And Abraham rose up early in the morning, and saddled his ass, and took two of his young men with him, and Isaac his son, and clave the wood for the burnt-offering, and rose up, and went unto the place of which God had told him. Then on the third day Abraham lifted up his eyes, and saw the place afar off. And Abraham said unto his young men, Abide ye here with the ass; and I and the lad will go yonder and worship, and come again to you. And Abraham took the wood of the burnt-offering, and laid it upon Isaac his son; and he took the fire in his hand, and a knife; and they went both of them together. And Isaac spake unto Abraham his father, and said, My father: and he said, Here am I, my son. And he said, Behold the fire and the wood; but where is the lamb for a burnt-offering? And Abraham said, My son, God will provide himself a lamb for a burnt-offering: so they went both of them together. And they came to the place which God had told him of; and Abraham built an altar there, and laid the wood in order; and bound Isaac his son, and laid him on the altar upon the wood. And Abraham stretched forth his hand, and took the knife to slay his son. And the angel of the LORD called unto him out of heaven, and said, Abraham, Abraham. And he said, Here am I. And he said, Lay not thine hand upon the lad, neither do thou any thing unto him: for now I know that thou fearest God, seeing thou hast not withheld thy son, thine only son, from me. And Abraham lifted up his eyes, and looked, and, behold, behind him a ram caught in a thicket by his horns: and Abraham went and took the ram, and offered him up for a burnt-offering in the stead of his son. And Abraham called the name of that place Jehovah-jireh: as it is said to this day, In the mount of the LORD it shall be seen" (Gen. 22:1-14).

The *primary doctrines* taught are those of *sacrifice* and *substitution,* as the means appointed by God for taking away sin; and, as co-ordinate with these, the need of the *obedience of faith* on the part of man to receive the benefit (Heb. 11:17). A confusion is often made between Isaac and the victim actually offered. Isaac himself is generally viewed as a type of the Son of God, offered for the sins of men; but Isaac, himself one of the sinful race for whom atonement was to be made — Isaac, who did not actually suffer death — was no fit type of Him who *"was slain,* the *just* for the unjust."* But the animal, not of the human race, which God provided and Abraham offered, was, in the whole history of sacrifice, the recognized type of "the Lamb of God, that taketh away the sins of the world." Isaac is the type of *humanity itself*, devoted to death for sin, and submitting to the sentence. Once more the covenant is renewed in its special blessing to the descendants of Abraham, and in its full spiritual extension to all families of the earth, as the reward of his obedience; and now, for the first time, God confirmed it with an oath.[1]

Special Study
The Canaanites and the Rephaim

In the life of Abraham we find references to various peoples who lived in or around Canaan. Among these were seven tribes of Canaanites (Gen. 12:6; 15:19-21), and groups of giants called Rephraim (Gen. 15:5-6).

These peoples also appear later in the sacred narrative, in the records of Moses and the children of Israel (Ex. 3:8; Deut. 7:1; Joshua 3:10; etc.).

A. THE CANAANITES (Code word: CHAP-JHG)

The Canaanites were descendants of Ham's fourth son (Gen. 9:18; 10:15-20). While the etymology of the name Canaan is uncertain, some have thought it means *low,* or lowlanders. In Numbers 13:29 the Canaanites are described as dwelling by the sea and along by the side of the Jordan, i.e. in the lowlands of Palestine. See Josh. 11:3.

In its narrow sense the name Canaanite is applied only to the tribe which inhabited a particular area west of Jordan, as in Numbers 13:29.

In a broad sense the name Canaanite is applied to all the people who inhabited the whole country west of Jordan. Thus Jerusalem, which had Amorite and Hittite founders, is stated to be the land of the Canaanite (Ezekiel 16:3).

In this broader meaning seven nations are usually indicated by the term *Canaanite:*

1. The *Canaanites* proper. The lowlands inhabited by the Canaanites were the richest and most important parts of the country, and it is not unlikely that this was one of the

---

1. Gen. 22:15-18; Psalm 105:9; Luke 1:73; and especially Heb. 6:13,14. The sacrifice is said to have taken place upon a mountain in "the land of Moriah"; but whether this was the hill in Jerusalem on which the Temple afterward stood, or Mount Gerizim, is uncertain.

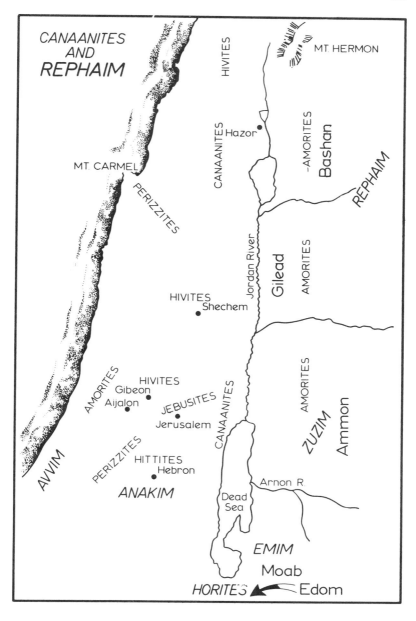

reasons for the name Canaanite being applied as a general name to the inhabitants of the land. Jabin, King of Hazor, was a Canaanite (Judges 4:2). See also Judges 1:27-33.

2. The *Hittites* were descendants of Ham's grandson, Heth (Gen. 10:15). They settled in Asia Minor and north Syria where they became rulers of a great empire, 1850-1200 B.C. (See *Neighbors of Israel and Judah.*) Many Hittites dwelt in Canaan. In fact Abraham spoke of them as "the people of the land" around Hebron (Gen. 23:7; 26:34; Num. 13:29; etc.). In Genesis they are represented as a peaceful people, and thus Abraham, though he chose his allies from the Amorites, goes to the Hittites to obtain a grave.

3. The *Amorites* ("mountain dwellers") were a warlike people who swarmed out of the desert areas east of Canaan about 2000 B.C. (near the time of Abraham). They settled in Mesopotamia, Syria, Canaan and even Egypt. Although the Amorites were originally Hamites (Gen. 10:15), they seem to have been absorbed by Semites who took the name "Amorites." These Semitic Amorites took over Mesopotamia under Hammurabi about 1728 B.C. A tomb painting at Beni Hassan in Egypt shows a group of 37 Amorites entering that land about 2000 B.C.

They were a very wicked people. God told Abraham that his descendants would mete out His vengeance on this people when their iniquity was full (Gen. 15:16).

The Amorites overran a large portion of the land of Moab, all that lay north of the Arnon river, under King Sihon (Num. 21:25-26; Judges 11:21). Genesis speaks of their abode as being on the western shores of the Dead Sea (Gen. 14:7), and in the plain of Mamre (Gen. 14:13). Compare Judges 1:34-35. They also dwelt around Mt. Hermon, and southward in all of Gilead and Bashan (Deut. 3:8; 4:48; 3:10). This area east of Jordan came to be spoken of as the land of the two kings of the Amorites, Sihon and Og (Deut. 31:4; Josh. 2:10; 9:10; 24:12).

4. The *Perizzites* seem, next to the Canaanites, to have been the most important tribe, as the "Canaanite and the Perizzite" are frequently mentioned together, to the exclusion of the other tribes, as the inhabitants of the land (Gen. 13:7; 34:30; Judges 1:4,5). In Judges 1:4,5 they are placed in the southern part of the Holy Land, and in Josh.

16:15-18 they occupy, with the Rephraim, or giants, the "forest country" in the western flanks of Mt. Carmel.

5. The *Jebusites,* a mountain tribe, descending from Ham (Gen. 10:15), inhabited Jerusalem when the Israelites conquered the land. They were finally conquered by King David, but continued to dwell with the children of Judah and Benjamin to a late date (Num. 13:29; Josh. 11:3; 15:8; Judges 1:21; 19:11; II Sam. 5:6-7; 24:18).

6. The *Hivites* were also descendants of Ham through Canaan (Gen. 10:15-16). At the time Jacob returned to the Holy Land they occupied Shechem (Gen. 34:2). Their morals were typically Canaanite. At the time of the conquest by Joshua they were living on the northern confines of Palestine — "Under Hermon, in the land of Mizpah," east of the Sea of Galilee (Josh. 11:3). In Josh. 9:7 we read that the village of Gibeon just a few miles north of Jerusalem was a Hivite settlement. Hivites also dwelt in the north (Judges 3:3).

The Hivites may have been the same people as the Horites, or Hurrians. The name *Hivite* may mean "village of nomads" and they seem to have been scattered through the area in various villages.

7. The *Girgashites* are a people about whom little is known. They were descendants of Ham (Gen. 10:15-16). They were conquered by Israel in the time of Joshua (Deut. 7:1). Their land was promised to Abraham (Gen. 15:21; Joseh. 3:10). Tradition says they fled to Africa.

Questions about the Canaanites

1. Name the seven groups of Canaanites.
2. Where was the center of the Hittite empire? (See p. 25.)
3. About when did the Amorites settle into various countries?
4. Name two cities controlled by Hivites at some time in their history.
5. What city did the Jebusites occupy?

B. THE REPHAIM
1. Deut. 2:10-11, 20-21; 3:11, and Genesis 14:5-6 mention a race of giants (Heb. REPHAIM). These were called by various names in the areas where they lived.
2. Before the children of Israel entered Canaan, various

peoples had occupied the areas once inhabited by these giants. By the time of the conquest of Canaan, there was only a remnant, a few, of these Rephaim remaining. The children of Israel destroyed most of these remaining giants during the period of conquest.

3. A few of these continued down to the time of King David (II Sam. 21:16-22; I Chron. 20:4-8). These passages mention several giants among the Philistines who fought with King David. Goliath himself apparently was one of these Rephaim.

4. Where did these giants come from? No one really knows much about them except the facts given in the Scripture. Gen. 6:4 speaks of giants (Nephilim, not Rephaim) that lived in the earth before the flood. Some archaeological evidences of a large race of men have been found. But these pre-flood giants were all destroyed in the flood; therefore the giants (Rephaim) of Deut. 2 were some freakish descendants of Noah.

5. It is interesting to note that the plural of the word "giants" (Rephaim) is used several times in the O.T. to refer to the dead (e.g. Ps. 88:10; Isa. 14:9; Prov. 9:18). This is not, however, sufficient evidence to conclude that these giants were some type of ghosts of men walking about in gigantic form.

6. Groups of Rephaim: (Code word: R-E-Z-A)
   a. *Rephaim in Bashan.* Og, the giant with the big bed, was the last of the remnant of Rephaim in Bashan in the time of Moses (Deut. 3:11; Josh. 12:4, 13:12).
   b. *Emim.* Deut. 2:10-11; Gen. 14:5. These were the Rephaim who dwelt in *Moab* before it was Moab, before the Moabites took over that land. They were a people great, many and tall. Chedorlaomer also smote them.
   c. *Zamzummim* (probably the same people called Zuzim in Gen. 14:5).
      1. These were the Rephaim who dwelt in the land of *Ammon* before the Ammonites took it over. Jehovah helped Ammon displace them (Deut. 2:20-21).
      2. Chedorlaomer smote the Zuzim during the time of Abraham (Gen. 14:5).
   d. *Anakim.* Deut. 2:10-11.
      1. These were the Rephaim who dwelt in the south part of Canaan around Hebron (Josh. 15:13-14) and

south of Jerusalem (Josh. 15:8). They were the people who made the Israelites look like grasshoppers (Num. 13:33). Some authors say the name Anakim means "the long-necked ones."

2. The *Israelites* displaced the Anakim. Caleb drove out the Anakim from Hebron (Josh. 15:14; 11:21-22).

7. *Peoples associated with the Rephaim.* (These peoples are not called Rephaim, or giants, but are spoken of in connection with the Rephaim.)

a. *Horites* (or Horim, or Hurrians).

1. These were the aboriginal inhabitants of Mt. Seir (Deut. 2:12). They were displaced by Esau and the *Edomites* (Deut. 2:22).

2. Chedorlaomer smote the Horites in Mt. Seir (Gen. 14:6).

3. If the Horites and Hurrians are the same people (as many scholars think), they came from the highlands of Media sometime after the time of Abraham, and overspread the region from Media to the Mediterranean before finally being subdued by the Hittites. The Horites of Palestine and Edom, were remnants of a once-conquering race, later themselves conquered.

b. *Avvim* (or Avim). Deut. 2:23

1. These were the early inhabitants of the southern part of the coastal plain of Canaan. They were displaced by the *Philistines*.

2. The Philistines who displaced the Avvim are called the Caphtorim (Jer. 47:4; Amos 9:7). Caphtor seems to be a name for the isle of Crete. Philistines lived in Canaan in the time of Abraham (Gen. 21:32). However, the main immigration of Philistines came later, during the time of the judges. (See *The Neighbors of Israel and Judah,* p. 560.)

Questions About the Rephaim

1. What does the name Rephaim mean?
2. How many Rephaim remained by the time Israel conquered Canaan?
3. In what area was Og, the last of the remnant of Rephaim?
4. What were the Rephaim called in Ammon, Moab and

southern Canaan? What peoples displaced the Rephaim in each of these areas?

5. Where did the Horites live, and who displaced them?

6. Where did the Avvim live, and who displaced them?

5. The next event recorded in Abraham's life is the *death of Sarah* at the age of 127 at Hebron. The fact that Sarah died at Hebron indicates either that Abraham had returned from Beersheba to his old home at Hebron, or that Sarah was away from Beersheba, possibly visiting, when she died (Gen. 23:1-2). Her death led to an interesting transaction between the patriarch and the people of the land in which he was a sojourner. God had "given him none inheritance in the land, no not so much as to set his foot on" (Acts 7:5). He had used it to pitch his tent and feed his flocks on, but not a foot of it was actually his *property*. But now the sanctity of the sepulchre demanded that his burying-place should be his own; and he makes a bargain with Ephron the Hittite, in the presence of all the people of the city, in the course of which he behaves, and is treated by them, like a generous and mighty prince. Courteously refusing both the use of their sepulchres, and the offer of a place for his own as a gift, he buys for its full value of four hundred shekels' weight of silver, "current money with the merchant,"[1] the *Cave of Machpelah* (or the *Double Cave),* close to the oak of Mamre, with the field in which it stood. Here he buried Sarah; here he was buried by his sons Isaac and Ishmael; there they buried Isaac and Rebekah his wife, Jacob and his wife Leah.[2] The sepulchre still exists under the Mosque of Hebron, and was first permitted to be seen by Europeans since the Crusades, when it was visited by the Prince of Wales in 1862.[3]

6. After the burial of Sarah, Abraham returned to Beersheba. His last care was for the marriage of his son Isaac to a wife of his own kindred, and not to one of the daughters of the Canaanites. His oldest servant undertook the journey to Haran, in Mesopotamia, where Nahor, the brother of Abraham, had settled, and a sign from God indicated the person he sought in Rebekah, the daughter of Bethuel, son of Nahor.[4] The whole

---

1. This is the first mention of money in the history of the world, but it was uncoined.
2. Gen. 25:9,10; 35:29; 49:31; 50:13.
3. For an account of this visit, see Stanley's *Lectures on the Jewish Church,* part I, App. II. Hebron is held by the Moslems to be the fourth of the Holy Places, Mecca, Medina and Jerusalem being the other three.
4. Gen. 24. See *The Family of Terah,* p. 65.

narrative is a vivid picture of pastoral life, and of the simple customs then used in making a marriage contract, not without characteristic touches of the tendency to avarice in the family of Bethuel, and particularly in his son Laban (Gen. 24:30). The scene of Isaac's meeting with Rebekah seems to exhibit his character as that of quiet pious contemplation (Gen. 24:63). He was 40 years old when he married, and his residence was by *Beer-la-hai-roi,* the well of *La-hai-roi)* in the extreme south of Palestine (Gen. 25:62; 26:11,20).

7. It was after the marriage of Isaac that Abraham formed a new union with *Keturah,* by whom he became the father of the *Keturaite Arabs.* Keturah seems to have been only a concubine, and her sons were sent away eastward, enriched with presents, as Ishmael had been during Abraham's life, lest the inheritance of Isaac should be disputed. To him Abraham gave all his great wealth, and died apparently at Beersheba "in a good old age, an old man, and full of years," his age being 175. His sons Isaac and Ishmael met at his funeral, and buried him in the Cave of Machpelah (Gen. 25:1-10). Ishmael survived him just 50 years; and died at the age of 137 (Gen. 25:17).

Questions Over Sec. III
Life of Abraham, from Birth of Isaac to Death

1. Who was Abimelech (Gen. 20:2)?
2. What lie did Abraham tell Abimelech (20:2)?
3. How did Abimelech discover the deception (20:6)?
4. What was the name of Abraham's son, and the meaning of his name (21:3; 17:19)?
5. What was the age of Abraham at the birth of his son (21:5)?
6. What was done to Hagar and Ishmael when Isaac was weaned? Why (21:9-10)?
7. How did God save Hagar and Ishmael (21:19)?
8. Where did Ishmael's wife come from (21:21)?
9. In (or through) what person was Abraham's seed to be called (or accounted) (21:12)?
10. Why did Abimelech seek to make a covenant with Abraham? (21:22-23)
11. Concerning what did Abraham reprove Abimelech (21:25)?
12. Why was a well called *Beersheba* (21:31)?
13. How did God test Abraham (22:1-2)?
14. Where did the test take place (22:2)?

15. What question of Isaac surely pained Abraham deeply (22:7-8)?
16. Was Abraham willing to do everything God commanded (22:10)?
17. What animal was provided as a substitute offering (22:13)?
18. What does the name *Jehovah-jireh* mean (22:14)?
19. What blessings were promised to Abraham because he was willing to offer Isaac (22:17-18)?
20. Who was to be blessed in Abraham's seed (22:18)?
21. How many children did Milcah bear to Nahor (22:23)?
22. Where did Sarah die (23:2)?
23. From whom did Abraham purchase a burial ground (23:8-10)?
24. What sort of property did he buy (23:17)?
25. Who was sent to find a wife for Isaac (24:2-3)?
26. Where was he sent (24:4,10)?
27. What sign did the servant ask God to show him to identify the right woman (24:14)?
28. What woman was found as a wife for Isaac (24:15)?
29. Who was her father, and who was her brother (24:15, 29)?
30. How was Isaac related to his wife (24:24; 11:27-29)?
31. How long did the servant stay at the damsel's house (24:54-56)?
32. Where was Isaac when he met his bride (24:62)?
33. Why did Isaac take the woman to Sarah's tent (24:67)?
34. Who became Abraham's wife in his old age (25:1)?
35. How many children did Abraham have by this wife (25:2)?
36. How were this woman's children treated differently from Isaac (25:5-6)?
37. How long did Abraham live (25:7)?
38. Where was Abraham buried? By whom (25:9)?

Section IV
Family of Isaac (Gen. 25:19-28:9)

1. Isaac at Lahai-roi. 2. Esau sells his birthright. 3. Isaac and Abimelech at Gerar. 4. The blessings of Jacob and Esau. 5. Moral aspect of the transaction. 6. Jacob's danger from Esau.

1. After his marriage Isaac continued to dwell at

Beer-la-hai-roi. It was not till twenty years later that Rebekah, whose barrenness was removed through the prayers of Isaac, bore twin sons,[1] ESAU *(hairy)* or EDOM (the *Red), and J*ACOB the *Supplanter),* whose future destiny was prophetically signified by the strange incidents which accompanied their birth. Their struggle in the womb portended the deadly animosity of the two nations that were to spring from them; and the grasp of the younger on the elder's heel foreshadowed the way that Jacob would take hold of his brother's birthright and blessing, and supplant him as the main family heir. Their physical appearance was as different as their characters afterward proved: the ruddy and hairy Esau became a rough, wild hunter; the smooth Jacob a quiet denizen of the tent. These differences of character were fostered by the foolish partiality of their parents, the great curse of all family life: "Isaac loved Esau, because he did eat of his venison: but Rebekah loved Jacob" (Gen. 25:21-28).

It is important to observe that God chose Jacob, the younger, to be over his brother Esau before they were born. Before the children were born, neither having done anything good or bad, it was God's declared purpose that the older should serve the younger (Rom. 9:10-13; Gen. 25:23). Subsequent events may lead us to condemn Jacob for his fraudulent methods of obtaining the family blessing. But that which Jacob sought was his by God's decree. Certainly God was within His sovereign right to make this choice. And assuredly the characters of Jacob and of Esau that subsequently emerged showed God's wisdom and foreknowledge in choosing Jacob.

2. After the death of Abraham an event occurred which fixed the destinies of Jacob and Esau. Esau, returning from hunting in a famished state, saw Jacob preparing some red pottage of lentils, and quickly asked for "some of that red, red" (Gen. 25:30).[1] His impatience was natural, for food is not readily procured in an Eastern tent, and takes time to prepare. Jacob seized the occasion to obtain Esau's birthright as the price of the meal; and Esau consented with a levity which is marked by the closing words of the narrative: "thus Esau *despised* his birthright." For this the Apostle calls him "a *profane* person, who for one morsel of food sold his birthright," and marks him as the pattern of those who sacrifice eternity for a moment's sensual enjoyment (Heb. 12:16). The justice of this judgment appears from considering what the

---

1. The birth of Jacob and Esau took place before Abraham died. Abraham was 160 years old at their birth (Gen. 21:5; 25:26).

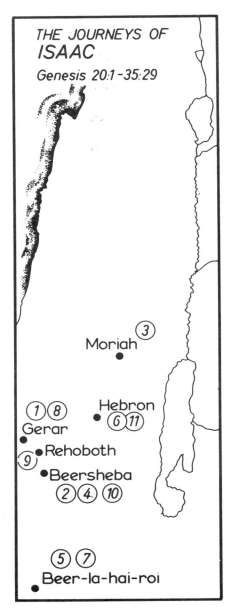

THE JOURNEYS OF
ISAAC
Genesis 20:1-35:29

Moriah ③
●

①⑧ Hebron
Gerar ⑥⑪
● ●Rehoboth
⑨
●Beersheba
②④⑩

⑤⑦
Beer-la-hai-roi
●

Life of Isaac

1. *Gerar*
   a. Birth; Gen. 20:1;
      21:1-22.
   b. Rejection of Ishmael;
      21:8-21.
2. *Beersheba*
   a. Boyhood home;
      21:32-34.
3. *Moriah*
   a. Sacrifice of Isaac;
      22:1-20.
4. *Beersheba*
   a. Death of mother;
      23:1-20.
5. *Beerlahairoi*
   a. Marriage to Rebekah;
      Ch. 24.
6. Trip to *Hebron* and back
   a. Death and burial of
      Abraham; 25:7-10.
7. *Beerlahairoi*
   a. Birth of twin sons;
      25:11,19-26.
   b. Birthright sold; 25:27-34.
8. *Gerar*
   a. Lie about Rebekah;
      26:1-11.
   b. Great crops and herds;
      26:12-17.
   c. Disputed wells; 26:18-
      21.
9. *Rehoboth*
   a. Undisputed well;
      26:22
10. *Beersheba*
    a. Covenant with Abi-
       melech; 26:26-33.
    b. Esau's wives;
       26:34-35.
    c. Blessing given to
       Jacob; Gen. 27.
    d. Jacob sent away
       28:1-5.
11. *Hebron*
    a. Reunion with Jacob;
       35:27.
    b. Death and burial of
       Isaac; 35:28-29.

birthright was, which he sold at such a price. If he had received the birthright, he would have been the head of the family — its prophet, priest and king; and no man can renounce such privileges, except as a sacrifice required by God, without "despising" God who gave them. But more than this: he would have been the head of the *chosen* family; on him devolved the blessing of Abraham, that "in his seed all families of the earth should be blessed"; and, in despising his birthright, he put himself out of the sacred family, and so became a "*profane* person." His sin must not be overlooked in our indignation at the fraud of Jacob, which, as we shall see presently, brought its own retribution as well as its own gain.

3. Driven from Lahai-roi by a famine, Isaac was forbidden by God to go down to Egypt, and was commanded to remain in the land. At the same time the promise was renewed to him. He betook himself to his father's old residence at Gerar; and here he practiced the same deceit of which his father had been guilty, by giving out that his wife was his sister. The falsehood was discovered; but the remonstrance of Abimelech (apparently a descendant of Abraham's contemporary) was followed by special protection and respect both from king and people. Isaac now made an advance beyond the pastoral life — "He sowed in that land, and received in the same year an hundred-fold: and Jehovah blessed him." His prosperity roused the envy of the Philistines, who had filled up the wells dug by Abraham, as a precaution (it would seem) against his return (Gen. 26:18). At length Abimelech desired Isaac to leave his country; and he retired along the valley of Gerar, digging his father's wells anew, and restoring their former names. Two wells so dug were disputed with him by the herdsmen of Abimelech, and at once yielded by Isaac, who gave the wells the names of *Esek (contention)* and *Sitnah (enmity)*. His peaceful conduct not only secured him the quiet possession of a third well, which he named *Rehoboth (room)*, but brought him a visit from Abimelech, who made a treaty with Isaac at a newly-discovered well, which was hence called *Shebah (the oath)*, and which gave its name a second time to Beersheba *(the*

---

1. "Therefore was his name called EDOM,"*i.e., Red.* The red lentil is still a favorite article of food in the East; it is a small kind, the seeds of which, after being decorticated, are commonly sold in the bazaars of India. Dr. Robinson, who partook of lentils, says he "found them very palatable, and could well conceive that to a weary hunter, faint with hunger, they would be quite a dainty *(Bib. Res.* 1:246). Dr. Kitto also says that he has often partaken of red pottage, prepared by seething the lentils in water, and then adding a little suet to give them a flavor; and that he found it better food than a stranger would imagine; "the mess," he adds, "had the redness which gained for it the name of *adom*" *(Pict. Bib.,* Gen. 25:30,34).

well of the oath). There is no reason to consider this as different from Abraham's Beersheba.

4. This tranquil course of Isaac's life, which presents a marked contrast to the varied incidents of Abraham's career, was vexed by the disobedience of Esau, who, at the age of forty married two Hittite wives, thus introducing heathen alliances into the chosen family. But a greater family trial was in store for Isaac. The approach of his hundreth year and the infirmity of his sight[1] warned him to perform the solemn act by which, as prophet as well as father, he was to hand down the blessing of Abraham to another generation. Of course, he designed for Esau the blessing which, once given, was the authoritative and irrevocable act of the patriarchal power; and he desired Esau to prepare a feast of venison for the occasion. Esau was not likely to confess the sale of his birthright, nor could Jacob venture openly to claim the benefit of his trick. Whether Rebekah knew of that transaction, or whether moved by partiality only, she came to the aid of her favorite son, and devised the strategem by which Jacob obtained his father's blessing.

It must be observed that Isaac was in the wrong when he attempted to give Esau the blessing. He could not have been ignorant of God's decree about the sons before they were born. However much we deplore the acts of Rebekah and Jacob, the greater fault was with Isaac and Esau.

This chapter gives another example of the matchless power and beauty of the sacred narrative, in the quiet statement of the facts; the preparation of the scheme step by step; the suspicious scrutiny of Isaac; the persistent fraud with which Jacob baffles the passionate appeal made even after the blessing has been given — 'Art thou my very son Esau?" — the horror of Isaac and the despair of Esau when his return discovers the fraud; the weeping of the strong man, and his passionate demand — "Hast thou not reserved a blessing for me?" Like Ishmael, he received a temporal blessing, the fatness of the earth and the dew of heaven, the warrior's sword, qualified by subjection to his brother, whose yoke, however, he was at some time to break. The prophecy was fulfilled in the prosperity of the Idumaeans, their martial prowess, and their constant conflicts with the Israelites, by whom they were subdued under David, over whom they triumphed at

---

1. We mark here the shortening of life: this is the first example of the infirmities of old age.

the Babylonian Captivity, and to whom they at last gave a king in the person of Herod the Great.[1] But all this was no compensation for the loss of the higher and spiritual blessing which fell to the lot of Jacob, and which involved, in addition to all temporal prosperity, a dominion so universal that it could only be fulfilled by the kingdom of Messiah (Gen. 27:28,29,37).

5. The *moral aspect* of the transaction is plain to those who are willing to see that the Bible represents the patriarchs as "men compassed with infirmity," favored by the grace of God, but not at all endowed with sinless perfection. It is just this, in fact, that makes their lives a moral lesson for us. Examples have occurred in the lives of Abraham and Isaac; but the whole career of Jacob is the history of a growing moral discipline. God is not honored by glossing over the patriarch's great faults of character, which were corrected by the discipline of severe suffering. We need not withhold indignant censure from Rebekah's cupidity on behalf of her favorite son — so like her family — and the mean deceit to which she tempts him. Nor is Isaac free from the blame of that foolish fondness, which, as is usual with moral weakness, gives occasion to crime in others. What, then, is the difference between them and Esau? Simply this — that they, in their hearts, honored the God whom he despised, though their piety was corrupted by their selfish passions. Jacob valued the blessing which he purchased wrongfully, and sought more wrongfully to secure. But Esau, whose conduct was equally unprincipled in desiring to receive the blessing which was no longer his, was rightly "rejected, when he would have inherited the blessing" (Heb. 12:17). His selfish sorrow and resentment could not recall the choice he had made, or stand in the place of genuine repentance. "He found no place for repentance, though he sought for it with tears," and he is held forth as a great example of unavailing regret for spiritual blessings wantonly thrown away.

6. The true state of Esau's spirit is shown by his resolve to kill his brother as soon as his father should die. To avert the danger, Rebekah sent away Jacob to her family at Haran. Isaac approved the plan, as securing a proper marriage for his son, to whom he repeated the blessing of Abraham, and sent him away to Pandanaram (Gen. 32:10)[2]

---

1. For the history of Edom, see *Neighbors of Israel and Judah*, p.
2. Gen. 27:41-28:9. It is here incidentally mentioned that Esau tried to please his father by marrying the daughter of Ishmael.

Questions Over Sec. IV
The Family of Isaac

True or False? Correct all false statements.

1. Isaac was forty years old when he married Rebekah (Gen. 25:20).
2. Rebekah was barren thirty years after marriage (25:20,26).
3. Rebekah had twin sons (25:24).
4. God said the younger son would serve the older (25:23).
5. Esau was a quiet man, dwelling at home in tents (25:27).
6. The name *Edom* means *red,* and was given to Esau (25:30).
7. Jacob sold his birthright for some red pottage (25:33).
8. Jacob despised his birthright (25:34).
9. Abimelech was king of Philistines at Gerar (26:1).
10. Isaac went into Egypt because of famine (26:7).
11. Isaac told a lie similar to one told by Abraham (26:7).
12. Isaac suffered famine around Gerar (26:12).
13. The Philistines and Isaac got along well (26:15-16, 27).
14. Esek and Sitnah were Isaac's sons (26:20-21).
15. *Rehoboth* means *room* (26:22).
16. God appeared to Isaac in Beersheba (26:23-24).
17. Abimelech made a covenant with Isaac (26:28,31).
18. Esau married two Amalekite women (26:34).
19. Esau sent Isaac to take venison (27:1-3).
20. Rebekah desired that Jacob get the blessing (27:5-10).
21. Rebekah put Esau's clothing on Jacob (27:15).
22. Isaac heard the voice of Esau, but felt the hands of Jacob (27:22).
23. Isaac made Jacob lord over his brethren (27:29).
24. Esau came in soon after Jacob left (27:30).
25. Isaac took back the blessing pronounced on Jacob (27:33,37).
26. Esau soon forgave Jacob (27:41).
27. Rebekah planned to send Jacob to her brother Laban (27:43).
28. Isaac agreed with Rebekah's plan to send Jacob away (28:1-2).
29. Esau married the daughter of Israel (28:9).

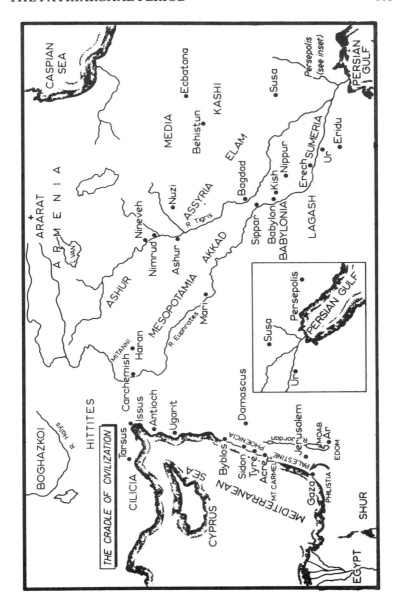

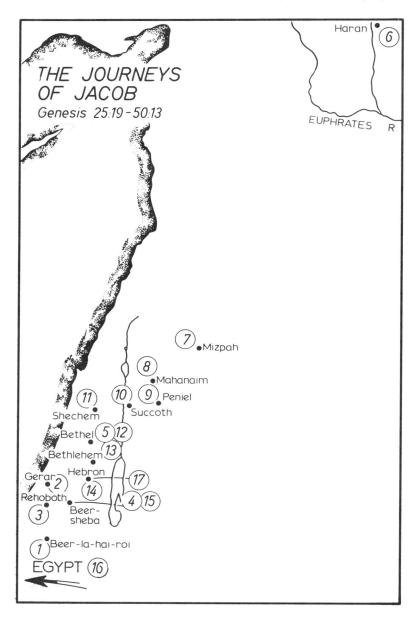

THE JOURNEYS
OF JACOB
Genesis 25:19 - 50:13

Life and Journeys of Jacob

1. *Beer-la-hai-roi;* Gen. 25:19-34
    a. Birth of Jacob and Esau.
    b. Birthright sold.
2. *Gerar* (26:1-21)
    a. Accompanies parents.
3. *Rehoboth* (26:22)
    a. Accompanies parents.
4. *Beersheba* (26:23-28:9)
    a. (Jehovah's appearance to Isaac; The covenant with Abimelech)
    b. (Esau's two wives)
    c. Jacob obtains the blessing (27:1-45).
    d. Jacob sent away (28:1-9).
5. *Bethel* (28:10-22)
    a. Jacob's dream.
6. *Haran* (29:1-31:21)
    a. Jacob's dealings with Laban.
    b. Jacob's wives and children.
7. *Mizpah* (31:22-25)
    a. Final meeting and covenant of Laban and Jacob.
8. *Mahanaim* (32:1-21)
    a. Meeting with the angels.
    b. Preparations to meet Esau.
9. *Peniel* (32:22-33:16)
    a. Wrestling with angel (32:22-32).
    b. Meeting with Esau (33:1-16).
10. *Succoth* (33:17)
    a. House and booths built.
11. *Shechem* (33:18-35:5)
    a. Purchase of ground (33:18-20)
    b. Sin of Shechem (34:1-31)
    c. Command to go to Bethel (35:1-5)
12. *Bethel* (35:6-15)
    a. Altar built
    b. Deborah dies
    c. The blessing of God
13. *Bethlehem* (35:16-20)
    a. Death of Rachel and birth of Benjamin
14. *Hebron* (35:21-45:28)
    a. Sin of Reuben (35:21-22)
    b. Death of Isaac
    c. Descendants of Esau (Ch. 36)
    d. The story of Joseph (37:1-45:28)
15. *Beersheba* (46:1-7)
    a. God appears as Jacob goes to Egypt
16. *Egypt* (46:8-50:6)
    a. Jacob's family sojourns in Egypt
17. *Hebron* (50:7-13)
    a. Burial of Jacob

Section V
The Family of Jacob
(Gen. 28:10-36:43; 38)

1. Jacob's flight to Padan-aram. 2. His marriage to Leah and Rachel — His family. 3. His service with Laban — His prosperity and departure — Mahanaim. 4. His prayer and wrestling at Peniel. 5. His meeting with Esau — Abode at Shechem, and removal southward. 6. Death of Rachel — Jacob at Mamre — Death and burial of Isaac. 7. Judah and Tamar.

1. Leaving his parents' abode at Beersheba with nothing but the staff he carried (Gen. 32:10), Jacob, the heir of the promises, retraced the path by which Abraham had traversed Canaan. Proceeding northward, he lighted on a place, the site doubtless of Abraham's encampment near Bethel, where he found some stones, which possibly belonged to the altar set up by Abraham, one of which he made his pillow. Thus forlorn, amid the memorials of the covenant, he was visited by God in a dream, which showed him a flight of stairs leading up from earth to the gates of heaven, and trodden by angels, some descending on their errands as "ministering spirits" upon earth, and others ascending to carry their reports to Him, whose "face they ever watch" in dutiful service. This symbol of God's providence was crowned by a vision of Jehovah, and his voice added to the renewal of the covenant a special promise of protection. Jacob awoke, to acknowledge the awful presence of Jehovah, of which he had lain down unconscious, and to dedicate to Him himself and all that God should give him. As a memorial of his vow, he set up his pillow for a monument, consecrating it with oil, and called the place BETH-EL, the *House of God*. The date of this, the turning-point in Jacob's religious life, is fixed by subsequent computations to his 77th year. (See Chronology of Patriarchs, pp. 136-138.)

2. Jacob's arrival at Padan-aram presents us with a repetition of the pastoral scene, which Abraham's servant had witnessed at the same place (Gen. 29:1-9). Rachel, the daughter of his uncle Laban, comes with her sheep to the well, like her aunt Rebekah just a century before, and brings him to the house. He engages to serve Laban as a shepherd for wages; for it is not the custom with

Orientals for even a relative to eat the bread of idleness. Laban had two daughters, Leah and Rachel, the former with some dullness or weakness of the eyes, but the latter of perfect beauty. Jacob loved Rachel, and engaged to serve for her seven years, which "seemed unto him but a few days, for the love he had to her." When he claimed his reward, Laban, by a trick rendered easy by the forms of an Eastern wedding, where the bride is closely veiled, gave him Leah in place of Rachel, and excused the deceit by the impropriety of marrying the younger sister before the elder; but he gave Jacob Rachel also, on the condition of another seven years' service. During these seven years, Jacob had eleven sons and a daughter, whose births are recorded at length, with the reasons for their significant names, in Gen. 29 and 30.

The account of the jealousy and contention between Leah and Rachel (Gen. 29:31, 30:21), and the subsequent sinfulness and jealousy of the sons of Jacob (Gen. 34:25,30; 35:22; 37:8,18; 49:5-6) shows vividly the fruits of polygamy. For the one man, Adam, God made the one woman Eve. And why only one? Because He sought a godly seed (Malachi 2:15). Broken and divided homes produce ungodly offspring.

The following is the list of Jacob's twelve sons, in their order of precedence, those of his wives ranking before those of their handmaids, with the significance of their names (Gen. 35:23-26):

a. The *sons of Leah:* Reuben *(see! a son)*, Simeon *(hearing)*, Levi *(joined)*, Judah *(praise)*, Issachar *(hire)*, Zebulun *(dwelling)*. Also Dinah, a daughter.

b. The *sons of Rachel:* Joseph *(adding)*, Benjamin *(son of the right hand)*.

c. The *sons of Bilhah*, Rachel's handmaid: Dan *(judging)*, Naphtali *(my wrestling)*.

d. The *sons of Zilpah*, Leah's handmaid. Gad *(fortunate)*, Asher *(happy)*.

(Students should memorize the names of the wives and handmaids, and the children born of each one.)

3. After the birth of Joseph, Jacob wished to become his own master; but Laban prevailed on him to serve him still, for a part of the produce of his flocks, to be distinguished by certain marks. Jacob's artifice to make the most of his bargain may be regarded as another example of the defective morality of those times; but, as far as Laban was concerned, it was a fair retribution for his attempt to secure a contrary result. Jacob was now commanded in a vision by "the God of Bethel" to return to the land of his birth;

and he fled secretly from Laban, who had not concealed his envy, to go back to his father Isaac, after twenty years spent in Laban's service — fourteen for his wives, and six for his cattle. Jacob, having passed the Euphrates, struck across the desert by the great fountain at Palmyra; then traversed the eastern part of the plain of Damascus and the plateau of Bashan, and entered Gilead, which is the range of mountains east of the Jordan, forming the frontier between Palestine and the Syrian desert.

Laban called his kindred to the pursuit, and overtook Jacob on the seventh day in Mount Gilead, his anger being increased by the loss of his household gods *(teraphim),*[1] which Rachel had secretly stolen. The theft, which might have caused Jacob to be carried captive, was ingeniously concealed by Rachel, and the interview ended peaceably. Laban, forewarned by God not to injure Jacob, made a covenant with his son-in-law; and a heap of stones was erected as a boundary between them, and called Galeed *(the heap of witness)* and Mizpah *(watch-tower).* As in later times, the fortress on these heights of Gilead became the frontier post of Israel against the Aramaic tribe that occupied Damascus, so now the same line of heights became the frontier between the nation in its youth and the older Aramaic tribe of Mesopotamia. As now, the confines of two Arab tribes are marked by the rude cairn or pile of stones erected at the boundary of their respective territories, so the pile of stones and the tower of pillar, erected by the two tribes of Jacob and Laban, marked that the natural limit of the range of Gilead should be their actual limit also. Jacob now received a divine encouragement to meet the new dangers of the land he was entering. His eyes were opened to see a troop of angels, "the host of God," sent for his protection, and forming a second camp beside his own; and he called the name of the place Mahanaim[2] *(the two camps* or *hosts)* (Gen. 32:1-2).

4. His first danger was from the revenge of Esau, who had now become powerful in Mount Seir, the land of Edom. In reply to his conciliatory message, Esau came to meet him with four hundred armed men. Well might Jacob dread his purpose; for though such a retinue might be meant to do him honor, it might also be designed to insure revenge. "Jacob was greatly afraid and distressed" (Gen. 32:7). He had now reached the valley of the

---

1. The teraphim were household idols. They were most important, because their ownership involved the inheritance of the property of Laban, as is illustrated by the Nuzi tablets. See M.F. Unger, *Arch. & O.T.* p. 123.
2. A town of this name was afterward built on the spot, and became a place of importance in the time of the monarchy (2 Sam. 2:9; 17:24). Its position is uncertain.

Jabbok. He divided his people and herds into two bands, that if the first were smitten, the second might escape. Then he turned to God in prayer (Gen. 32:9-12). This prayer is the first on record; for the intercession of Abraham for Sodom was more of a remonstrance or argument than a prayer. Many prayers had been offered before the time of Jacob; but this is the first of which we have any knowledge. It does not seem that there could be a finer model for a special prayer than this, the most ancient of all. To prayer he adds prudence, and sends forward present after present that their reiteration might win his brother's heart. This done, he rested for the night; but rising up before the day, he sent forward his wives and children across the ford of the Jabbok, remaining for a while in solitude to prepare his mind for the trial of the day. It was then that "a man" appeared and wrestled with him till the morning rose. This "man" was the "Angel Jehovah," and the conflict was a repetition in *act* of the prayer which we have already seen Jacob offering in *words*. This is clearly stated by the prophet Hosea: "By his strength he had power with God: yea, he had power over the angel, and prevailed: he wept, and made supplication unto him" (Hosea 12:3-4). Though taught his own weakness by the dislocation of his thigh at the angel's touch, he gained the victory by his importunity — "I will not let thee go except thou bless me" — and he received the new name of ISRAEL *(he who strives with God, and prevails)*, as a sign that "he had prevailed with God, and should therefore prevail with man" (Gen. 32:28). Well knowing with whom he had dealt, he called the place Peniel *(the face of God)*, "for I have seen God face to face, and my life is preserved." The memory of his lameness, which he seems to have carried with him to his grave (Gen. 32:31), was preserved by the custom of the Israelites not to eat of the sinew in the hollow of the thigh. Its moral significance is beautifully expressed by Wesley:

> "Contented now, upon my thigh
> I halt till life's short journey end;
> All helplessness, all weakness, I
> On Thee alone for strength depend;
> Nor have I power from Thee to move,
> Thy nature and thy name is Love."

5. Jacob had descended into the valley of the Jabbok at sunrise, when he saw Esau and his troops. He divided his last and most precious band, placing first the handmaids and their children, then Leah and her children, and Rachel and Joseph last.

Advancing before them all, he made his obeisance to Esau, who "ran to meet him, and fell on his neck and kissed him: and they wept." After a cordial interview, Jacob prudently declined his brother's offer to march with him as a guard; and Esau returned to Mount Seir, and we hear little more of him except the genealogy of the descendants, the Edomites (Gen. 36).[1]

Jacob pursued his journey westward and halted at Succoth, so called from his having there put up "booths" *(Succoth)* for his cattle, as well as a house for himself. He then crossed the Jordan, and arrived at Shechem, which had grown since the time of Abraham into a powerful city, and was named after Shechem, the son of Hamor, prince of the Amorites. From them he bought a piece of land, *the first possession of the family in Canaan,* on which he pitched his tent, and built an altar to God, as the giver of his new name, and the God of the race who were ever to bear it — "God, the God of Israel" *(El-elohe-Israel).* The memory of his abode there is still preserved by "Jacob's Well," on the margin of which his divine Son taught the woman of Sychar (Shechem) a better worship than that of sacred places.

He was soon involved in a conflict with the Shechemites, through their violence to Dinah, and the treacherous revenge of Simeon and Levi, which afterward brought on them their father's curse (Gen. 34; 49:6). The city of Shechem was taken; but Jacob deemed it prudent to avoid the revenge of the Canaanites by retiring from the neighborhood. It seems probable that he returned afterward and rescued "from the Amorites with his sword and his bow" the piece of land he had before purchased, and which he left, as a special inheritance, to Joseph (Gen. 48:22; Josh. 17:14).

6. Meanwhile Jacob returned, by the command of God, to Bethel, and performed the vows which he had there made when he fled from home, and received from God a renewal of the covenant (Gen. 35). There Rebekah's nurse, Deborah, died, and was buried beneath "the oak of weeping" *(Allon-bachuth).* As he journeyed southward, and was near Ephrath or Ephratah, the ancient name of Bethlehem, Rachel died in giving birth to Jacob's youngest son. The dying mother called him *Ben-oni (son of my sorrow);* but the fond father changed his name to BEN-JAMIN *(son of the right hand).* The grave of Rachel was long marked by the pillar which Jacob erected over it; and her memory was associated with

---

1. See *Neighbors of Israel and Judah,* p. 548, for information about the Edomites.

the town of Bethlehem (Jer. 31:15; Matt. 2:18). Jacob's next resting-place, near the tower of Edar, was marked by the incest of Reuben, which forfeited his birthright (Gen. 35:22; 49:4). At length he reached the encampment of his father Isaac, at the old station of Mamre, beside Hebron. Here Isaac died at the age of 180, "old and full of days, and his sons Esau and Jacob buried him" (Gen. 35:27-29). This was thirteen years after Joseph was carried to Egypt; but the whole course of that narrative is reserved for the next section.

7. One notable incident in Jacob's family must yet be noted, the matter of *Judah and Tamar* (Gen. 38). This occurred after Joseph was sold into Egypt and interrupts that narrative.

Judah, Jacob's fourth son, through whom the chosen line of descendants was carried on, begat three sons of a Canaanite woman. A wife named Tamar was taken for the oldest son, Er, who was wicked. The Lord slew him, and he died childless. A younger brother, Onan, would not then take Tamar to raise up seed to continue his brother's family. The Lord also slew Onan, whose name has come to be applied to the wickedness (onanism) he practiced.

We observe here the first instance of that custom wherein a brother was to beget children of his brother's widow when the brother died childless (Levirate marriage). This practice was later prescribed by God in the law of Moses (Deut. 25:5-10), but had been practiced in the patriarchal age either by unknown divine instructions or by approved custom.

Because Judah delayed too long in giving Tamar to the third son, Shelah, Tamar deceived her father-in-law, Judah, and conceived seed by him.

This record is notable because one of the twin sons of Judah and Tamar *(Perez,* or Pharez) carried on the chosen line that culminated in Christ Jesus (Matt. 1:3). The grace of God is vividly demonstrated by His use of these abominable events to accomplish His own purposes.

Questions Over Section V
The Family of Jacob

1. Write from memory the places on the map of the journeys of Jacob, and at least one event at each place.
2. What was Jacob's dream at Bethel (Gen. 28:12)?
3. What does the name *Bethel* mean (28:19)? What was the place previously called?

4. What were three promises God made to Jacob in the dream (28:13-15)?
5. What did Jacob promise God (28:22)?
6. Where did Jacob meet Rachel (29:2,6)?
7. How was Jacob related to Rachel?
8. Who was Rachel's father? Her sister (29:16)?
9. How did Jacob obtain Rachel (29:20,30)?
10. What deception did Laban practice on Jacob (29:23)?
11. Write from memory the names of Jacob's thirteen children, and the mothers of all.
12. How did Jacob acquire great flocks (30:31-43)?
13. How did Jacob and Laban get along together (31:7)?
14. What was Laban doing when Jacob left (31:19-20)?
15. What did Rachel steal (31:19)?
16. What did God tell Laban as he pursued Jacob (31:24)?
17. What made Jacob angry with Laban (31:36)?
18. What two names were given to the heap of stones set up between Jacob's and Laban's territories (31:48-49)?
19. What does the name Mahanaim mean, and why was it employed by Jacob (32:1-2)?
20. How did Jacob prepare to placate Esau before they met (32:1-20)?
21. At what brook did Jacob wrestle (32:22-24)?
22. What were two results of Jacob's wrestling (32:25-28)?
23. What does the name *Israel* mean?
24. Did Esau harm Jacob (33:15-16)?
25. What does the name *Succoth* mean (33:17)?
26. Where did Jacob first buy property in Canaan (33:18-19)?
27. Who took Dinah (34:1-2)?
28. Who massacred the Shechemites (34:25-26)?
29. How did Jacob react to the massacre (34:30)?
30. Who called Jacob to Bethel (35:1)?
31. Who died at Bethel (35:8)?
32. What was said of Jacob's name at Bethel (35:10)?
33. Where was Benjamin born (35:16,19)?
34. What did Rachel call Benjamin? Why? What does the name mean (35:18)?
35. How did Reuben lose his right as firstborn son (35:22; 49:3-4)?
36. Where did Isaac die (35:27-29)?
37. Who was Shuah (38:2)?
38. Who were Judah's first three sons (38:3-5)?

39. Who was Tamar (38:6)?
40. Who was Judah's son who carried on the chosen line (Matt. 1:3)?

Section VI
Egypt

1. Names of Egypt. 2. Divisions of the land. 3. The Nile River. 4. Important cities. 5. History of Egypt. 6. Religion of Egypt.

Beginning with the story of Joseph, the history of God's people Israel becomes inseparably involved with the land of Egypt. It is therefore necessary to present here some information about Egypt.

1. NAMES OF EGYPT
    A. *Kem* (or Kemet)
        1. Most ancient name.
        2. Means black land.
        3. Evidently the name given the land by the people themselves.
    B. The *Land of Ham*
        1. Cf. Ps. 78:51; 105:23; 106:22.
        2. Called "the land of Ham" because Mizraim, the son of Ham, moved here.
    C. *Mizraim*
        1. Plural (or dual) form, because of Egypt's division into Upper and Lower Egypt, or the Nile Valley and the Delta.
        2. Cf. Genesis 12:10,11,13; 13:1.
        3. Used over eighty times. Name of Ham's son (Gen. 10:6).
    D. *Rahab*
        1. Poetic name for the land.
        2. Cf. Ps. 87:4, 89:10; Isa. 51:9.
    E. *Egypt*
        1. Greek name for the land.
        2. This name was never used by the inhabitants themselves during ancient times.
2. DIVISIONS OF THE LAND OF EGYPT (see Pfeiffer, *Egypt and Exodus,* pp. 11-19)

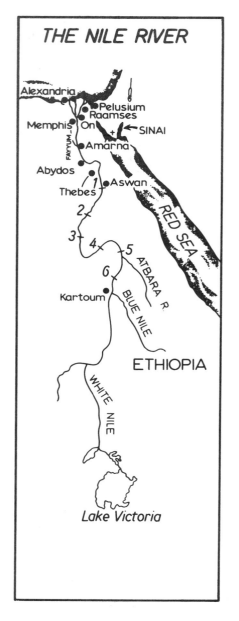

THE NILE RIVER

Egypt and the Nile

> "Egypt is the gift of the Nile."
> (Herodotus)

The Nile is 4,200 miles long from its origin at Lake Victoria in central Africa to the Mediterranean.

Numbers on the map indicate the cataracts of the Nile.

The first cataract at Aswan marks the southern limits of Egypt.

A. According to location (direction)
   1. Southern Egypt from the first cataract (at Aswan) to the Delta is called *Upper Egypt.*
      a. Tableland from one to twenty-four miles in width, hugging the shores of the Nile.
      b. From this fertile valley the Egyptian could look to the east or the west and see barren desert cliffs as high as 1800 feet rimming the valley.
   2. Northern Egypt (the Delta area) is called Lower Egypt.
      a. As the Nile waters entered the Delta they were diverted into a number of branches, only two of which have persisted into modern times; the others having largely dried up.
      b. At its widest extent the Delta extends about 125 miles. The Delta is in the shape of a huge triangle with the point at the bottom.
      c. In the Delta grew the papyrus plants, which provided the writing material of ancient Egypt. Papyrus was the forerunner of our paper.
B. According to the character of the land
   1. Desert
      a. 96% of the land is desert.
      b. If not for the Nile, all would be barren desert.
      c. Rainfall is almost zero.
   2. Nile Valley
      a. This is the northern portion of Nile, from Aswan to Mediterranean Sea.
      b. It is only two to twelve miles wide, with steep cliffs on both sides.
      c. In Lower Egypt, land of Goshen occupied eastern portion of Delta and was very suitable for raising flocks.
      d. A branch of the Nile goes west through a break in the cliffs near Amarna, and produces a fertile area called the *Fayyum.*
3. THE NILE RIVER
   A. Three sources of the Nile
      1. White Nile
         a. Flows from Lake Victoria in Central Africa.
         b. Land from which it flows is tropical.
         c. Provides steady source of water throughout the year.

        d. Flows over grassy land and rocky bottom and thus it
           is relatively clean and clear.
        e. The rise in the White Nile from April to November
           is six feet annually.
    2. Blue Nile
        a. Flows from Lake Tana in the Abyssinian plateau
           (Ethiopian plateau). Joins White Nile at Khartoum.
        b. Very tempestuous; muddy stream.
        c. Rises 26 feet from April to August; causes Nile
           flooding.
    3. Atbara River (200 miles downstream from Blue Nile)
        a. Only other significant tributary of Nile.
        b. Brings additional flood waters from highlands of
           Ethiopia.
  B. Annual overflow of the Nile
    1. Begins at Aswan at the end of May or the beginning of
        June.
    2. Continues to rise until early in September.
    3. Remains stationary twelve days at a height of about 36
        feet above its ordinary level at Thebes, 25 feet at Cairo,
        and four feet at its mouth.
    4. Keeps the land fertile as it brings with it new soil.
  C. Two principal mouths of the Nile at the Delta.
    1. The west mouth: Rosetta (Canopic).
    2. The east mouth: Damietta (Pelusiac).
  D. Cataracts of the Nile
    1. Six in all. (These are not falls, but rocky rapids which
        prevent navigation.)
    2. First cataract at Aswan.
    3. Sixth cataract at Khartoum, where Blue Nile runs into
        White Nile.
  E. Miscellaneous information regarding Nile and Nile Valley
    1. Second longest river valley on earth.
    2. Nile is approximately 4200 miles long.
    3. Nile valley provides Egypt with about 13,300 square
        miles of cultivable land (about area of Massachusetts
        and Connecticut). (Total area of Egypt is about 350,000
        square miles.)
4. IMPORTANT CITIES OF EGYPT
  A. Lower Egypt
    1. *Memphis* (Noph — cf. Isa. 19:13): one of ancient
        capitals.

2. *Heliopolis* (city of Sun) — called *On* in Bible (cf. Gen. 41:45). It was a priestly city.
3. *Rameses* in land of Goshen.
   a. Starting point of Exodus.
   b. Also called Zoan, or Tanis or Avaris.
4. *Pelusium*
   a. Also called Sin (cf. Ezek. 30:15,16).
   b. Very obscure as far as history goes.
   c. Alexander the Great fought a battle here.
5. *Alexandria*
   a. Founded by Alexander the Great around 331 B.C.
   b. Most prominent city in later history.
B. Upper Egypt
   1. *Thebes*
      a. Most important city in upper Egypt.
      b. In Bible is called No or No-Ammon (cf. Jer. 46:25).
      c. Long the capital of Egypt.
   2. *Amarna*
      a. Capital of Egypt during the brief time of Akhenaton (1376-1362 B.C.).

5. HISTORY OF EGYPT
   A. Predynastic period (about 3500-2800 B.C. The flood is most often dated at 3500 B.C.).
      1. Local lords ruled small areas.
      2. Hieroglyphic writing developed.
         a. Picture writing.
         b. Used throughout the history of Egypt.
      3. Earliest settlers domesticated cattle and finally became cultivators of the soil.
   B. Early dynasties, I and II (2800-2600 B.C.)
      1. Local lords in upper and lower Egypt were united into one kingdom under King Menes (or Narmer).
      2. Capital at Abydos.
   C. Old Kingdom (Dynasties III-IV, 2600-2150 B.C.)
      1. Capital at Memphis (Noph).
      2. Great material progress:
         a. Step Pyramid at Saqqara.
         b. Great Pyramid at Giza (481 feet high, from a thirteen-acre base).
         c. Gigantic Sphinx representing King Khafre of the Fourth Dynasty.

   d. Approximately seventy pyramids built during this
    period.
  3. Breakup of the kingdom near end of 6th century.
(Intermediate period of decline and recovery, Dynasties
VII-X, with minor kings at Memphis and Thebes.)
 D. Middle Kingdom (Dynasties XI-XII, 2050-1720 B.C.)
  1. Reappearance of a powerful centralized government.
  2. Although native to Thebes, the Twelfth Dynasty
   established its capital near Memphis.
  3. Conquests into Palestine.
  4. Literature dealing with religious matters developed.
  5. Burials in Valley of the Kings (tombs in cliffs).
  6. Abraham visited Egypt 2090 B.C.
  7. Joseph became ruler about 1883 B.C.
 E. Hyksos Period (Asiatic domination; Dynasties XIII-XVII,
  1750-1570 B.C.)
  1. Following the Middle Kingdom, there were two
   centuries of disintegration, decline and invasion.
   (History very obscure.)
  2. "The febble Thirteenth and Fourteenth Dynasties were
   terminated by an invasion of Hyksos warriors. The
   intruders, who possibly came from Asia Minor,
   overpowered the Egyptians by means of horse-drawn
   chariotry and the composite bow, both of which were
   unknown to the Egyptian troops. The Hyksos
   established Avaris in the Delta as their capital.
   However, the Egyptians were allowed to maintain a
   semblance of authority at Thebes. Shortly after 1600
   B.C. the Theban rulers became powerful enough to
   expel this foreign power and to establish the
   Eighteenth Dynasty, introducing the New Kingdom."
   (S.J. Schultz, *The O.T. Speaks* (New York: Harper &
   Row, 1960, p. 16).
 F. New Kingdom (Dynasties XVIII-XXI, 1580-935 B.C.)
  1. Capital at Thebes.
  2. The 18th and 19th dynasties constitute the period of
   Egypt's greatest glory.
  3. A woman, Hatshepsut, was ruler of Egypt from
   1501-1479.
  4. Thutmose III (1490-1447) made seventeen
   campaigns into Palestine and Syria; considered
   possible Pharaoh of oppression.

5. Amenhotep II (1447-1421); possible Pharaoh of Exodus.
6. Exodus of Israelites — 1446 B.C. (Memorize this date.)
7. Thutmose IV — non-firstborn ruler, successor of Amehotep II.
8. Akhenaton (1376-1362); monotheistic reformer; capital at Amarna.
9. Tutankamon (1360-1350); King "Tut."
10. Seti I (1320-1300); 19th dynasty conqueror.
11. Rameses II (1300-1234); conqueror and builder; thought by some to be the Pharaoh of the oppression.
   a. Under Rameses IV-XII, the power of the Egyptian kings declined considerably (1167-1085).
   b. At the time of decline, the rule was wrested from the political leaders and placed in the hands of the priestly class.
G. Foreign dynasties (Dynasties, XXII-XXV, 935-663)
   1. Shishak (a Lybyian) (947-925); I Kings 14:25-26.
      a. In Shishak's time (contemporary with King Rehoboam) Egypt became again powerful enough to invade Palestine (926 B.C.).
   2. Tirkahah (a Nubian, or Ethiopian) (689-663); II Kings 19:9.
H. Native Egyptian dynasties, XXVI-XXVIII, 662-525)
   1. Pharaoh Necho (609-593).
      a. King Josiah was slain by Necho as he was going to help Assyria against Babylon, 608 B.C. (II Kings 23:29-30).
      b. Necho made Jehoiakim king of Judah (II Chron. 36:4).
   2. Pharaoh Hophra (588-567) tried to aid Zedekiah (Jer. 37:5-7).
I. Persian rule (525-406, 343-332; interrupted by three Egyptian dynasties). Alexander the Great conquered Egypt in 331 B.C. (Hellenistic)
J. Period of Ptolemies (323-31 B.C.). The Ptolemies were Greek rulers descended from one of Alexander's generals.

6. RELIGION OF EGYPT
   A. Egypt was a land of many gods.
      1. There was never one religion in Egypt.

    2. "With local deities as the basis of religion, Egyptian gods became numerous" (Schultz, p. 46).

    3. The religion was a conglomeration of many ideas about life, death, nature and the gods.

B. Some of the earliest gods were animal gods.

    1. Baboon, cat, cow, hippo, ichneumon fly, cobra, et cetera.

    2. In later times many of the gods "took" the forms of these animals, or these animals became sacred to them.

C. The Egyptians did believe in the immortality of the soul (called Ba).

    1. Some thought the dead wandered in the cemeteries seeking food.

    2. Some thought the dead went to Osiris for judgment and eternal life.

    3. Some thought the dead joined the gods who floated in the heavenly ocean on boats of the sun.

    4. Some thought the dead were carried off by a Hathor cow or bull to wait for the bodily resurrection.

D. The Egyptians had at least three types of gods, but these were often confused in the people's thinking, and the names of gods in one place were taken by residents of other areas.

    1. Gods of places:

        a. At Memphis: Ptah (creator god, who was incarnate in the sacred Apis bull).

        b. At Thebes: Amon (often confused or combined with the sun god, Re).

        c. At Abydos: Osiris (god of the underworld); his wife, Isia; their son, Horus.

    2. Cosmic gods:

        a. Sun god, Re (national deity of Egypt).

        b. Sky goddess, Nut.

        c. Earth god, Geb.

    3. Gods responsible for functions of life:

        a. Sekhmet, lion-headed goddess of war and disease.

        b. Hathor, cow-goddess of love.

        c. Thoth, Ibis-headed god of wisdom; recorder of gods.

E. A popular religious legend: *Osiris* and *Horus*. Osiris was slain by his brother, Seth. Isis found his body, and embalmed, and buried it; Osiris revived and became *king of the underworld.* Isis bore Horus to Osiris. Egyptians associated the rising and the falling of the Nile with Osiris legend. Egyptians desired to be buried at Abydos where Osiris was buried.

For detailed bibliographies on Egypt: See pages 54-55 of *The Old Testament Speaks* by Samuel J. Schultz, Harper and Row, Publishers, New York, 1960. See pages 89-91 of *Egypt and the Exodus* by Charles F. Pfeiffer, Baker Book House, Grand Rapids, Michigan, 1964.

Questions Over Section VI — Egypt

1. Give five names of Egypt.
2. Which parts of Egypt are called Upper and Lower Egypt?
3. What is the Delta of the Nile?
4. What is the character of most of the land of Egypt?
5. How wide is the Nile Valley?
6. What are the three sources of the Nile?
7. When does the Nile overflow each year?
8. What are the cataracts of the Nile, and how many of them are there?
9. What was the ancient capital in Lower Egypt?
10. What was the most important city in Upper Egypt?
11. Who were the Hyksos?
12. What woman ruled Egypt for a time during the New Kingdom?
13. What is the date suggested for the Exodus?
14. What Egyptian god was regarded as king of the underworld?

Section VII
Joseph and Jacob in Egypt
(Genesis 37, 39-50)

1. Joseph's early life — His two dreams — Hatred of his brethren. 2. They sell him into Egypt. 3. Joseph in Potiphar's house. 4. Imprisonment of Joseph — Pharoah's cup-bearer and chief cook — Their dreams interpreted by Joseph. 5. Pharaoh's two dreams — Joseph made ruler of Egypt — His name Zaphnath-paaneah — His marriage, and his two sons. 6. His government in Egypt — The seven years of plenty and the seven years of famine. 7. Joseph's

brethren in Egypt. 8. God's purpose in Israel's removal
to Canaan. 9. Jacob and his family go down to Egypt —
Their numbers. 10. Their interviews with Pharaoh and
settlement in Goshen. 11. Jacob's last years — His
desire to be buried with his fathers. 12. His blessing on
Joseph and his sons. 13. His prophetic address to his
twelve sons, and their blessings — i. Reuben — ii.,
iii. Simeon and Levi — iv. Judah — Messianic sense —
v. Zebulun — vi. Issachar — vii. Dan — viii. Gad —
ix. Asher — x. Naphtali — xi. Joseph — Messianic
sense — xii. Benjamin — The twelve tribes now
constituted. 14. Death, embalmment and burial of
Jacob. 15. Joseph's kindness to his brethren.
16. Joseph's last prophecy and injunction — His death
and burial. 17. Death and burial of the other patriarchs.
18. Interval between Joseph and Moses.
19. Chronology of the pilgrimage in Canaan and Egypt.

1. We go back over a period of thirteen years from the death of
Isaac to the beginning of that narrative of Joseph's life, which may
safely be called the most charming in all history. It will guard us
against much confusion to bear in mind that the birth of
Benjamin and Rachel's death occurred only five or six years
before Joseph was sold into Egypt. Almost up to this time,
therefore, he had been his father's youngest son, and he was now
doubly dear to him as the son of his old age and the child of his
newly-lost Rachel (Gen. 37:3). Parental partiality, however, was as
injurious in Jacob's family as in any other; and though the
character of Joseph is one of the purest that we meet in Scripture,
his father's preference tempted him to assume toward his
brethren the part of a censor and informer — a course of which
the modesty was questionable, and the prudence more so, in a
youth of seventeen.

It is worthy of notice that the sons of the handmaids, Bilhah
and Zilpah, were those whose misconduct Joseph reported to his
father. Their lower birth seems to have diminished their
self-respect and to have stimulated their envy. When Jacob made
for Joseph a special dress,[1] "his brethren hated him, and could

---

1. This appears to have been a long tunic with sleeves, worn by youths and maidens of the richer class. It was a
token of rank, indicating that Jacob intended to make Joseph the head of the tribe. There seems no reason for
the LXX rendering "a coat of colors," except that it is very likely that such a tunic would be ornamented with
colored stripes or embroidered.

not speak peaceably unto him." To increase their hatred, Joseph dreamed two dreams. His father, who seems to have discerned their prophetic character (Gen. 36:11), censured his imprudence in repeating these. In the first dream his brothers' sheaves of corn bowed down to his, which stood upright in their midst; a most fit type, not only of their submission to him, but of their beseeching him for grain in Egypt. The second dream was of wider and higher import. It included his father and his mother, as well as his brethren (now specified as *eleven),* in the reverence done to him[1] and the emblems chosen leave little doubt that the dream prefigured the homage of all nature to Him whose sign was the *star* of Bethlehem, and of whom Joseph was one of the clearest types. Joseph's brothers were determined to prevent any such humiliation, even if this meant killing Joseph (Gen. 37:18).

2. It seems that Jacob was now at Hebron, with his father Isaac, while his sons fed his flocks where they could find pasture, Joseph being sometimes with his brethren, and sometimes acting as a messenger between them and his father (Gen. 37:2,13). Thus he was sent from Hebron to Shechem, where the piece of land purchased by Jacob of the Amorites had probably been recovered; but his brethren had gone farther north to Dothan, a place about 13 miles north of Shechem. Thither he followed them on his father's errand of kindness; but the very sight of him at a distance prompted them to conspire to kill him. His life was saved by Reuben, who persuaded them to avoid the actual shedding of Joseph's blood by casting him into an empty pit, whence Reuben intended to take him and restore him to his father. When he came to them, they stripped him of his tunic, cast him into the pit, and coolly sat down to eat bread. Just then an Arab caravan[2] was seen on the high road which leads from Mount Gilead through Dothan to Egypt, carrying to the latter country the spices and gums of the Syrian desert. Judah suggested (Reuben having left them, v. 29) that they might now get rid of their prisoner without the guilt of murder; and so, when the Midianites came near (v. 28), they took Joseph out of the pit and sold him for twenty shekels of silver, the very sum which was, under the Law, the value of a male from five

1. From Joseph's second dream, and his father's rebuke, it might be inferred that Rachel was living at the time that he dreamt it. The dream, however, indicates eleven brethren besides the father and mother of Joseph. If therefore Benjamin were already born, Rachel must have been dead: the reference is therefore more probably to Leah, who may have been living when Jacob went into Egypt.
2. In Gen. 37:25,28 they are called *Ishmaelites;* in vss. 28 & 36 *Midianites.* Apparently the term *Ishmaelite* is used in the O.T. in a wide sense to refer to nomadic Arabic tribes generally. See Judges 8:22-24. Strictly speaking, the Midianites were descendants of Keturah, not Hagar and Ishmael (Gen. 25:1-2).

to twenty years old — a type of the sale of Him "whom the children of Israel did value" (Lev. 27:5; Matt. 27:9). They carried back his tunic to Jacob dipped in a kid's blood; and though he seems to have had his suspicions, which afterward broke out into reproaches,[1] they imposed on their father the tale that a wild beast had devoured Joseph; and their guilty consciences had to bear the trial of pretending to comfort him, while he refused all comfort.

3. Meanwhile the Midianite merchants carried Joseph to Egypt, and sold him to POTIPHAR,[2] "an officer of Pharaoh, and captian of the guard."

We have now reached the point at which the history of the chosen family interweaves itself with the annals of the mighty kingdom of Egypt. (See Sec. IV, *Egypt.*) It appears that Joseph came into Egypt in the reign of Senusret III, an outstanding Middle Kingdom pharaoh.

The sculptures and paintings of the ancient Egyptian tombs bring vividly before us the daily life and duties of Joseph. The property of great men is shown to have been managed by scribes, who exercised a most methodical and minute supervision over all the operations of agriculture, gardening, the keeping of live stock and fishing. Every product was carefully registered to check the dishonesty of the laborers, who in Egypt have always been famous in this respect. Probably in no country was farming ever more systematic. Joseph's previous knowledge of tending flocks, and perhaps of husbandry, and his truthful character, exactly fitted him for the post of overseer.

4. Joseph was seventeen when he was sold into Egypt, and thirty "when he stood before Pharaoh" (Gen. 41:46). We are not told what portion of these thirteen years he spent in Potiphar's house. Probably not long, as it was his youthful beauty that tempted his master's wife (Gen. 39:6-7), whose conduct agrees with the well-known profligacy of the Egyptian women. Her desire for revenge, when Joseph withstood the temptation, is in accordance with the worst parts of our nature —

"Hell has no fury like a woman scorned."

It may have been from a suspicion of her guilt that Potiphar,

---

1. See Gen. 42:36, "Me have *ye* bereaved of my children."
2. The name of Potiphar is written in hieroglyphics PET-PA-RA or PET-P-RA, and signifies "belonging to RA" (the sun). It occurs again, with a slightly different orthography, Potipherah, as the name of Joseph's father-in-law, priest or prince of On. It may be remarked that as Ra was the chief divinity of On, or Heliopolis, it is an interesting undesigned coincidence that the latter should bear a name indicating devotion to Ra.

instead of bringing Joseph before a tribunal, put him in the state prison.

This experience affected Joseph greatly (Gen. 40:15). Besides the shock of being sold into a strange land as a slave, and being falsely accused by Potiphar's wife, his treatment was at first severe;[1] but the same blessing that had raised him in the house of Potiphar followed him in the prison, of which the keeper gave him the entire charge, "because Jehovah was with him, and that which he did Joseph made it to prosper" (Gen. 39:23).

Some conspiracy at the court of Pharaoh led to the imprisonment of two of the king's great officers, the chief of the cup-bearers and the chief of the cooks. (The terms *chief butler* and *chief baker* in our version are misleading as to their dignity.) They were committed to the charge of Joseph, whom they too discovered to be specially favored by God, for they asked him to interpret the dreams which forewarned them of their fate, and in three days, as Joseph predicted, the one was hanged, and the other restored to his office on Pharaoh's birthday (Gen. 40).

5. The restored cup-bearer's office about the king's person gave him ample opportunities of fulfilling Joseph's pathetic request to make mention of him to Pharaoh, and his colleague's fate might have warned him against ingratitude. "Yet did not the chief cupbearer remember Joseph, but forgat him," till after two years, when Pharaoh was disturbed by dreams which none of the scribes or wise men of Egypt could interpret (Gen. 41:8). Then the chief cupbearer remembered his fault and told Pharaoh of Joseph, who was brought out of prison and set before the king. After bearing witness to the true God, as in the former case, by ascribing all the power of interpretation to Him who had sent the dreams (Gen. 40:8; 41:16), he explained to Pharaoh their significance, which, to an Egyptian, was most striking. The dream had been twofold, to mark its certain and speedy fulfillment (v. 32). Seven years of an abundance extraordinary even for fruitful Egypt were to be followed by seven years of still more extraordinary dearth. In the first dream, the seven years of plenty were denoted by seven heifers, the sacred symbols of Isis, the goddess of production, which came up out of the river, the great fertilizer of Egypt, whose very soil is well called by Herodotus "the gift of the Nile." These were beautiful and fat, as they fed on the luxuriant marsh grass by the river's bank; but

---

1. Psalm 105:17,18: "whose feet they hurt with fetters: he was laid in iron."

after them came up seven others, so ill-looking and lean that
Pharaoh had never seen the like for badness, which devoured the
seven fat kine, and remained as lean as they were before.

The second dream was still plainer. There sprang up a stalk of
branching Egyptian wheat. That seen by Pharaoh had the
unusual number of seven ears, full and good, denoting the seven
years of plenty. Then there sprang up another stalk, also bearing
seven ears, thin and blasted with the east wind, and so mildewed
that they infected and consumed the seven good ears. The wise
men of Egypt must indeed have been fools not to understand
these symbols, which embraced both the animal and vegetable
wealth of the land!

Joseph went farther, and counselled Pharaoh to give some
discreet person authority over all the land, that he might store up
the surplus corn of the seven years of plenty against the seven
years of famine. Pharaoh saw that none could be so fit for this
office as Joseph himself, "in whom was the Spirit of God." He
made him his vicegerent over Egypt, and gave him his own
signet,[1] the indisputable mark of royal power. Clothed with fine
linen robes, wearing a collar of gold, and riding in the second
royal chariot, before which the people were bidden to fall
prostrate, Joseph was proclaimed with all the ceremonies which
we still see represented on the monuments. He received the
Coptic name of ZAPHNATH-PAANEAH *(a revealer of secrets);* and
married Asenath, the daughter of Potipherah, priest or prince of
On (Heliopolis), who bore him two sons during the seven years of
plenty. As a token of the oblivion of his former life, he named his
elder son MANASSEH *(forgetting);* and he called the younger
EPHRAIM *(double fruitfulness),* in grateful commomoration of his
blessings. When Joseph afterward became his father's heir, the
double share of the inheritance which fell to him was indicated by
each of his sons ranking with the sons of Jacob as the head of a
distinct tribe.

6. Joseph's administration of Egypt has been greatly
misunderstood. First, as to his conduct during the years of plenty.
The vague statement, made in the language of Oriental
hyperbole, that "he gathered up all the food of the seven years"
(v. 48), "as the sand of the sea, very much, until he left
numbering" (v. 49), comes after the exacter estimate given in his
advice to Pharaoh, which makes it clear that "he took up the *fifth*

---

1. The signet was a stone or gem incised with the king's name or emblem. With this official stampings could
be made on clay tablets.

part of the land of Egypt in the seven plenteous years" (v. 34). The ordinary royal impost appears to have been a land-tax of *one-tenth,* and this was just a *double tithe.*

The grain was stored up in each of the cities from the lands of which it was collected; and it was thus secured for orderly distribution in the years of famine. When that season arrived, its consumption was guarded by the same wise policy that had preserved it from being wasted in the years of plenty. The demand was not only from Egypt, but from the neighboring countries, Canaan, and probably parts of Syria, Arabia and Africa, to which the famine extended, and whose corn was soon exhausted. We may assume that the Egyptians also soon used up their private stores. Joseph then opened all the store-houses and sold unto the Egyptians; "and the famine waxed sore in the land of Egypt. And all countries came into Egypt to buy corn, because the famine was so sore in all lands" (Gen. 41:56-57).[1]

At the end of two years (see Gen. 45:6) all the money of the Egyptians and Canaanites had passed into Pharaoh's treasury (Gen. 47:14). At this crisis we do not see how Joseph can be acquitted of raising the despotic authority of his master on the broken fortunes of the people; but yet he made a moderate settlement of the power thus acquired. First the cattle and then the land of the Egyptians became the property of Pharaoh, and the people were removed from the country to the cities. They were still permitted, however, to cultivate their lands as tenants under the crown, paying a rent of one-fifth of the produce, and this became the permanent law of the tenure of land in Egypt: but the land of the priests was left in their own possession (Gen. 47:15-26).

7. The seven years' famine had the most important bearing on the chosen family of Israel. When all the corn in Canaan was exhausted, Jacob sent his sons to buy in Egypt; but he kept back Benjamin "lest mischief should befall him" (Gen. 42:4). Probably he would not trust Rachel's remaining child with his brethren. We need not recount that well-known narrative, the most beautiful and touching page of all history, of their two visits to Joseph and his final discovery of himself (Gen. 42-45). It seems hardly necessary to vindicate Joseph from the charge of harshness toward his brethren. We do not think that he went a step farther

---

1. Famines in Egypt caused by failure of the Nile to rise as usual each year have been experienced at various times, e.g. A.D. 1200. A famine of seven years duration occurred 1064-1071. This famine brought such misery that people ate corpses and animals that died of themselves.

than was required, in order to gain over them the power which he was ready to use for their good. We rather see in his conduct a faithful imitation of the divine discipline, by which man is restored to favor through suffering just enough to bring him to true repentance.

The short imprisonment of Simeon was but a taste of the sorrow to which he and his brothers had subjected their brother for many years. The getting of Benjamin into his power was needful, lest Jacob's fondness should frustrate all his plans. The roughness of his manner was surely not a thing to be complained of, where every step taken was one of kindness, while, in the final scene of recognition, hurried on by Joseph's tenderness of heart, there is not a word of upbraiding or reproach: "Now therefore be not grieved or angry with yourselves, that ye sold me hither. It was not you that sent me hither, but God" (Gen. 45:5,8). And at the very moment when Joseph kindly saw in his brethren only the unconscious instruments of God's providence, he was serving it almost as unconsciously by his plan for securing his father and brethren a safe and happy settlement in Egypt.

8. The removal of the chosen family to Egypt was an essential part of the great plan which God had traced out to their father Abraham. The promise had now been given two hundred years (Gen. 15), and they had neither possessions nor family alliances in the promised land. But they would soon have sought for both; and the character already manifested by Jacob's sons augured ill for their preserving either purity or piety amid the Canaanites. The chosen line was no longer to be severed from the rejected branches, as in the case of Ishmael and Esau; but the twelve sons of Jacob were to found the twelve tribes of Israel, even the sons of Zilpah and Bilhah being legitimated and reckoned as belonging to Leah and Rachel respectively. Their present relation to Canaan must be broken off, that it might be formed anew in due time. They must be placed among a people with whom they could not mix, but from whom they might learn the arts of civilization and industry; and there, under the discipline of affliction, the family must be consolidated into the nation.

9. So Joseph sent for his father and the whole family came from Beersheba into Egypt. God encouraged Jacob by a vision, commanding him to go down, and promising to bring him up again in the person of his descendants, who are henceforth called by the collective name of Israel (Gen. 47:11), and assuring him that Joseph should close his eyes (Gen. 46). So he went down, with

his sons and their wives and children, and all their cattle. The house of Israel now numbered 70 souls, without reckoning wives. The number is thus made up:

a. The children of Leah, 32, viz.:[1]
    1. Reuben and four sons 5
    2. Simeon and six sons[2] 7
    3. Levi and three sons 4
    4. Judah and five sons (of whom two were dead) and two grandsons 6
    5. Issachar and four sons 5
    6. Zebulun and three sons 4
       Dinah 1

b. The children of Zilpah, considered as Leah's, 16, viz.:
    7. Gad and seven sons 8
    8. Asher: four sons, one daughter, and two grandsons .. 8

c. The children of Rachel, 14, viz.:
    9. Joseph (see below).
    10. Benjamin and ten sons[3] 11

d. The children of Bilhah, considered as Rachel's, 7, viz.:
    11. Dan and one son 2
    12. Naphtali and four sons 5

Total of those "that came with Jacob into Egypt"   66
To these must be added Jacob, Joseph and two sons 4

Total of Israel's house 70

These are the numbers of the Hebrew text (Comp. Deut. 10:22), but the LXX completes the genealogy by adding the children of Manasseh and Ephraim, who of course ranked with those of the sons of Jacob, namely, Machir, the son of Manasseh; and Galeed (Gilead), the son of Machir (2); Sutalaam (Shutelah) and Taam (Tathath), the sons of Ephraim; and Edom, the son of Sutalaam (3); making five in all.[4] St. Stephen naturally quotes the LXX, the version commonly used, especially by the Hellenistic Jews, with whom his discussion began (Acts 7:14).

Thus, instead of any real difficulty, we have in this apparent difference an example of those undesigned coincidences amid variety, which are among the strongest internal evidences of the

---

1. Jacob himself is included in the 33 of v. 15, but he is excluded from the total of 66 in v. 26.
2. One of these is called the son of a Canaanitish woman; whence we may infer that all the rest were born from wives of the Hebrew race, and probably in nearly all cases of the stock of Abraham.
3. These are evidently added to complete the second generation, for Benjamin was only 23 years old, and the tone of the whole narrative is scarcely consistent with his yet having a family.
4. Gen. 46:20 LXX. Comp. I Chron. 7:14,20.

truth of Scripture. It is most interesting to compare these numbers with those to which the family of Israel had grown at the Exodus (Num. ch. 1).

10. On their arrival in Egypt, Joseph after a most affecting meeting with his father, presented five of his brethren to Pharaoh; and the king being informed that they were shepherds, a class held in abomination by the Egyptians, gave them for their separate abode the land of Goshen or Rameses, which was the best pasture-ground in all Egypt,[1] and intrusted to them his own flocks, while Joseph supplied them with bread during the remaining five years of famine. That they were tillers of the land, as well as shepherds, is clear from their being employed "in all manner of service in the field" (Exod. 1:14), and from the allusion of Moses to "Egypt, where thou sowedst thy seed and wateredst it" (Deut. 10:11).

Joseph next brought his father before Pharaoh, and the aged patriarch bestowed his blessing on the mighty king. In reply to Pharaoh's inquiry about his age, he said: "The days of my pilgrimage are 130 years: few and evil have the days of the years of my life been, and have not attained unto the days of the years of the life of my fathers in the days of their pilgrimage" (Gen. 47:9). Besides their testimony to the gradual decline of human life, and their affecting allusion to his trials, these words are a memorable example of how the patriarchs "confessed that they were strangers and pilgrims on the earth," and how "they desired a better country, that is, a heavenly," even the "city" which their God has "prepared for them" (Heb. 11:13-16).

11. The few remaining years of Jacob's life were spent in tranquillity and abundance. He lived seventeen years in Egypt, and beheld his descendants "multiply exceedingly" (Gen. 47:27). The chief record of this period is his prophetic blessing on his sons — one of the most important passages in the whole Bible.

First, as his end approached, he sent for Joseph, and made him swear that he would not bury him in Egypt, but carry him to the

---

1. The "land of Goshen," also called Goshen simply appears to have borne another name, "the land of Rameses" (Gen. 47:11), unless this be the name of a district of Goshen. It was between Joseph's residence at the time and the frontier of Palestine, and apparently the extreme province toward that frontier (Gen. 46:29). Gen. 46:33,34, shows that Goshen was scarcely regarded as a part of Egypt proper, and was not peopled by Egyptians — characteristics that would positively indicate a frontier province. The next mention of Goshen confirms the previous inference that its position was between Canaan and the Delta (Gen. 47:1,5,6,11). Goshen was a pastoral country, where some of Pharaoh's cattle were kept. The clearest indications of the exact position of Goshen are those afforded by the narrative of the Exodus. The Israelites set out from the town of Rameses in the land of Goshen, made two days' journey to "the edge of the wilderness," and in one day more reached the Red Sea. From these indications we infer that the land of Goshen must have in part been near the eastern side of the ancient Delta, Rameses lying within the valley now called the *Wadi-Tumilat*.

sepulchre of his fathers (Gen. 47:29-31). There is one point in this passage which must not be passed over. "Israel bowed himself upon the bed's head." An act of worship is certainly intended, doubtless a thanksgiving to God for the peaceful close of his troubled life, and for the assurance of being soon "gathered to his fathers."

Whether in this act Jacob bent his head reverently as he raised himself on his bed, or whether he supported himself on the head of his bedstead, as in the next chapter (v. 2), or on the top of that shepherd's staff, "which he had carried all his life" (Gen. 32:10), is in itself of little consequence. The latter meaning is the most natural, and is that given by the LXX, and followed by Paul (Heb. 11:21). However it has been strangely perverted. The Latin Bible (Vulgate) translates the passage, *worshipped the top of his staff;* and the text is cited as an authority for image worship!

12. Soon after this, Joseph heard that his father was sick; and he went to visit him with his sons, Manasseh and Ephraim (Gen. 48). The dying patriarch blessed Joseph and his sons, in the name of the "God, before whom his fathers Abraham and Isaac had walked, the God who had fed him all his life long, the Angel who had redeemed him from all evil." He claimed Ephraim and Manasseh for his own, placing them even before Reuben and Simeon, who by lust and violence had forfeited their birthright; and henceforth they were numbered among the heads of the tribes of Israel. Throughout the whole scene, he gave Ephraim the precedence over Manasseh; and, though unable to see, he crossed his hands, disregarding Joseph's opposition; so that in blessing them his right hand was on Ephraim's head, and his left on Manasseh's. Thus was added one more lesson of God's sovereign choice to the examples of Abel, Shem, Abram, Isaac and himself, who were all younger sons. He foretold for them a prosperity which would make them the envy of the other tribes of Israel; and he ended by giving Joseph an extra portion above his brethren, thus marking him as his heir, in respect of *property;* for the *royal power* was given to Judah, and the *priesthood* was afterward assigned to Levi. The *division* of these three great functions of the patriarchal government is already a mark of the transition from the *family* to the *nation.*

13. Having thus given Joseph his separate and special blessing for himself and his two sons, Jacob called all his sons to hear the last words of Israel their father (Gen. 49). He plainly declared that his words were of prophetic import, and that their

fulfillment would reach even *to the last days* (v. 1). Could we expound them fully, we should probably find that, in most, if not all the several blessings, there is a reference — first, to the personal character and fortunes of the twelve patriarchs; secondly, to the history and circumstances of the tribes descended from them; and, lastly, a typical allusion to the twelve tribes of the spiritual Israel (Rev. 7). We can trace the first two elements in all cases, and the last is conspicuous in the blessings on Judah and Joseph, the two heads of the whole family. But the details of the interpretation are confessedly most difficult.[1] The whole prophecy should be compared with "the blessing, wherewith Moses, the man of God, blessed the children of Israel before his death" (Deut. 33). Like the latter, Jacob's prophecy contains a *blessing* on each tribe, though in some cases it is almost disguised under the censure which his sons had incurred.

a. REUBEN, the eldest son, is acknowledged as his father's "strength and the beginning of his might," and as "excelling in dignity and power"; for such was his privilege by right of birth. He is always named first in the genealogies, and his numerous and powerful tribe took the lead in war. But he had forfeited his special birthright by a shameful act of wantonness, which is compared to water bursting its bounds (Gen. 49:4). And not only did Reuben yield the royal dignity to Judah, but, the possessions of the tribe lying in the most exposed position east of the Jordan, they were the first to become subject to a foreign power (I Chron. 5:26).

b. and c. SIMEON and LEVI are named together (Comp. Gen. 29:33-34), as akin in character, and together they are cut off from succeeding to the place forfeited by Reuben, for their cruelty to the Shechemites. The penalty of being "scattered in Israel," instead of having a share in the inheritance, reads like a curse; but it was turned into a blessing. The tribe of Levi, having redeemed its parent's fault by taking the Lord's side in the matter of the golden calf, was consecrated to the priesthood (Ex. 32:26-29), and, though they had no inheritance in Israel, they enjoyed a part of the inheritance of all the rest. Simeon early lost consequence among the tribes. His territory, which lay on the extreme southwest border, was never wrested from the Philistines. Many members of the tribe gained subsistence and honor as teachers, "scattered" among all the other tribes.

---

1. See DeWelt, *Sacred Hist. & Geog.* pp. 118-139.

d. JUDAH is announced, in a grand burst of prophetic fervor, as adding to his other dignities that of being the ancestor of the Messiah. In fact, the promise, which has been traced step by step is now centered in this tribe. The keynote of the whole blessing is in the meaning of Judah's name, PRAISE;[1] and it includes the following points:

1. Precedence among his brethren and victory over his enemies.

2. He is denoted by a fit symbol, which is varied to give it a complete force — the lion's whelp, exulting over the prey in youthful vigor, the lion crouching in his den, the lioness whom none may provoke but at their peril. It was doubtless from this prophecy that the tribe of Judah took a lion's whelp for its standard, with the motto, "Rise up, Jehovah, and let thine enemies be scattered."

3. Then follows a plain declaration of the *royalty* of Judah. From him was descended David, the son of Jesse, and in his house the sceptre of Judah remained, while the rebellious kingdom of the other tribes had many different dynasties, till the Babylonian Captivity. The civil rulers of the restored state after the Babylonian Captivity (now called *Jews, Judaei,* because belonging chiefly to this tribe) were at first of the house of David, as in the case of Zerubbabel (Ezra 3:2). Even though the peculiar religious character of the new commonwealth threw the chief power into the hands of the priests, and though Judas Maccabaeus and his line of princes were of the race of Levi, the nation which they governed was composed essentially of the tribe of Judah. And thus "the sceptre did not depart from Judah, nor a lawgiver from between his feet," till the usurpation of the Idumaean Herod gave a sign of "the coming of the SHILOH,"[2] which was verified by the birth of Jesus Christ, the Son of David and of Judah. (See p. 9.)

e. ZEBULUN'S lot is predicted in terms which exactly describe the position of the tribe between the Lake of Tiberias and the Mediterranean, bordering on the coasts of the Phoenicians, and sharing in their commerce.

---

1. We have here an example of the double significance of Scripture names, with reference, *primarily,* to the circumstances of the person's birth (Gen. 29:35), and *prophetically* to the destiny of his race.

2. *Shiloh* has been variously interpreted to mean *Restgiver* (Leupold, *Exposition of Gen.*), or *He whose it is.* Both of these explanations point to Christ Jesus, the former suggesting Matt. 11:28, and the latter the fact that the kingship and scepter belong to Christ (Ezek. 21:26-27; Luke 1:32).

f. ISSACHAR is described by "the image of the 'strong-boned he-ass' — the large animal used for burdens and fieldwork, not the lighter and swifter she-ass for riding — 'couching down between the two hedgerows,' chewing the cud of stolid ease and quiet — which is very applicable, not only to the tendencies and habits, but to the very size and air of a rural agrarian people, while the sequel of the verse is no less suggestive of the certain result of such tendencies when unrelieved by any higher aspirations — 'He saw that rest was good, and the land pleasant, and he bowed his back to bear and became a slave to tribute' — the tribute imposed on him by the various marauding tribes who were attracted to his territory by the richness of the crops." The vale of Esdraelon, which just corresponds to the territory of Issachar, was the most fertile land in Palestine.

g. DAN, like Judah, is described by the significance of his own name. His territories were at the two opposite extremities of the land, and it is doubtful whether the delineation of Dan in Jacob's blessing relates to the original settlement on the western outskirts of Judah, or to the northern outpost. "Dan," the judge, "shall judge his people"; he, the son of the concubine no less than the sons of Leah; he, the frontier tribe no less than those in the places of honor, shall be "as one of the tribes of Israel." "Dan shall be a serpent by the way, an adder in the path" — that is, of the invading enemy by the north or by the west, "that biteth the heels of the horse," the indigenous serpent biting the foreign horse unknown to Israelite warfare, "so that his rider shall fall backward." And his war-cry as from the frontier fortresses shall be, "For Thy salvation, O Lord I have waited!"[1]

h. GAD's fortune, too, is contained in his name, which is repeated with a play on the word: "*A plundering troop* shall *plunder* him, but he will plunder at their heels." As one of the tribes east of Jordan, Gad was among the first carried captive (I Chron. 5:26); and perhaps Jacob refers to this, promising that his enemies shall not triumph to the end — a promise which belongs also to the spiritual Israel.

i. ASHER (the *happy* or *blessed*) is promised the richest fruits of the earth. His land, some of the most fertile in the north of

---

1. According to Jewish tradition, Jacob's blessing on Dan is a prophetic allusion to Samson, the great 'Judge' of the tribe; and the ejaculation with which it closes was that actually uttered by Samson when brought into the temple at Gaza (Judges 16:28).

Palestine, yielded him "fat bread" and "royal dainties," and enabled him to "dip his foot in oil" (Deut. 33:24). But this wealth was purchased by inglorious ease and forbidden alliances with the heathen, whom he failed to drive out (Judges 1:31-32). No great action is recorded of this tribe, and it furnished no judge or hero to the nation. "One name alone shines out of the general obscurity — the aged widow, 'Anna, the daughter of Phanuel of the tribe of Asher,' who, in the infancy age of our Lord departed not from the Temple, but 'served God with fastings and prayers night and day' " (Luke 2:36-37).

j. NAPHTALI's blessing, also highly figurative, is obscured in our version by a mistranslation. It should be:

> "Naphtali is a towering terebinth;
> He hath a goodly crest."

The description, like Deborah's (Judges 5:18), of

> "Naphtali on the high places of the field,"

agrees with the position of the tribe among the highlands between Lebanon and the Upper Jordan, from its sources to the Sea of Galilee (Comp. Deut. 33:23; Josh. 20:7).

k. The blessing on JOSEPH forms the climax of the father's fondness and the prophet's fervor. Taking his name *(adding* or *increase)* as a sign both of his past abundance and his future enlargement, he compares him to a fruitful vine, or rather a branch of the vine of Israel, throwing its shoots over the wall of the cistern by which it is planted; and he promises his favorite son every form of blessing that man could desire or enjoy. As in all his history, so in this prophecy especially, Joseph is one of the most eminent types of Christ. The symbols of the vine, of which He is the root, and the members of His church the branches, and of the living water by which the living tree is nourished, are expounded by himself (John 15:1ff; 4:14; 7:38; 6:41-58; etc.).

l. BENJAMIN is described as a wolf, ravening for his prey, and successful in obtaining it — an image taken perhaps from the wild beasts, such as wolves, foxes, jackals and hyenas, which infest the defiles of the territory of Benjamin. Marked as is the contrast to the majestic strength of Judah the lion, the warlike character is common to both tribes, and they were as closely connected in their history as the lion and the jackal are believed to be in fact.

The concluding words (v. 28) show that this was a formal

appointment of Jacob's twelve sons to be the twelve heads of the chosen race, now becoming a nation, instead of its having one head as hitherto; and also that the blessings and prophecies of the dying patriarch had respect rather to the tribes than to their individual ancestors; and henceforth the tribes are continually spoken of as if they were persons.

14. Having added one more injunction to all his sons, to bury him in the Cave of Machpelah, Jacob "gathered up his feet into the bed, and yielded up his spirit, and was gathered unto his people" at the age 147 (Gen. 49:33; 47:28). After a burst of natural grief, Joseph gave orders for his embalment, and kept a mourning of forty days, according to the Egyptian custom (Gen. 50:1-3). He then went, by Pharaoh's permission, with all his brethren, and the elders both of Israel and Egypt, and a great military retinue, to carry the body of Jacob into Canaan. Avoiding the warlike Philistines, they made a circuit to Atad, near the Jordan, where they kept so great a mourning for seven days, that the astonished Canaanites called the place Abel Mizraim *(the mourning of Egypt)*. Proceeding thence to Hebron, Jacob's sons buried him in the Cave of Machpelah (Gen. 50:1-13).

15. On their return to Egypt, Joseph's brethren, fearing the effect of their father's removal, sought his forgiveness, and made submission to him. With tears of love, and disclaiming the right to judge them, which was God's alone, he returned the memorable answer — "Ye thought evil against me, but God meant it unto good." He promised still to nourish them and theirs: "And he comforted them, and spake kindly unto them" (Gen. 50:15-21).

16. Joseph survived his father for fifty-four years, still enjoying, as we may assume, his honors at the court under the same dynasty, though possibly under a succession of kings. He saw Ephraim's children of the third generation, and had Manasseh's grandchildren on his knees. At length he died at the age of 110. He was embalmed and placed in a sarcophagus, but not buried. For before his death he had predicted to his brethren[1] their return from Egypt to the promised land; and he had bound them by an oath to carry his remains with them. "By *faith* Joseph, when he died, made mention of the departing of the children of Israel; and gave commandment concerning his bones" (Gen. 50:22-26; Heb. 11:22).

Through all their afflictions, the children of Israel kept the

1. This word has no doubt the extended sense of the heads of his tribes, including any of Jacob's sons who were still alive; but Joseph would naturally be one of the last survivors of the twelve.

sacred deposit of Joseph's bones, and doubtless they often consoled themselves with his dying promise and the memory of his greatness. Amid the terrors of that "memorable night," when God led the people out of Egypt, Moses did not forget the trust (Ex. 13:19). When the people were settled in Canaan, they buried Joseph at Shechem, in the parcel of ground which Jacob bought from the Amorites, and which he gave as a special inheritance to Joseph (Josh. 24:32; Comp. Gen. 33:19; 48:22).

17. Of the other patriarchs we are only told that "Joseph died, and all his brethren, and all that generation" (Ex. 1:6). But Stephen adds this remarkable statement: "Jacob went down into Egypt and died, *he and our fathers,* and *were carried over into Sychem,* and laid in the sepulchre that *Abraham* bought for a sum of money of the sons of Emmor, the father of Sychem" (Acts 7:16).

Though all the Hellenistic Jews "were unable to resist the wisdom and spirit by which he spake" (Acts 6:10), modern Christian critics have discovered that Stephen confounded Abraham's purchase of Machpelah from the Hittites with Jacob's purchase near Shechem from the Amorites! But after we have corrected the obvious blunder of a copyist, by reading *Jacob* for *Abraham,* the question remains — Were Jacob and all his sons buried at Shechem, in the same sepulchre as Joseph's? Not necessarily. The passage may simply mean that Joseph's tomb at Shechem was regarded as the family sepulchre. Whether the bones of his brethren were placed in or beside the sarcophagus of Joseph, and whether the remains of Jacob were removed from Hebron to Shechem, are questions suggested, but we scarcely think determined, by the words of Stephen.

18. The interval between the death of Joseph and the beginning of the bondage in Egypt is dismissed with the brief but emphatic statement, that "the children of Israel were fruitful, and increased abundantly, and multiplied, and waxed exceedingly mighty; and the land was filled with them" (Ex. 1:7). The last words may imply that, while their main settlement was still at Goshen, members of the race were scattered over the country; and, in spite of the system of caste, they may have found employment as artificers and soldiers, as well as shepherds. If this were so, they were again restricted to the land of Goshen by the king who began to oppress them (Ex. 8:22; 10:23), and were thus collected for their departure. Besides the information contained in the genealogies, only one event is recorded during this period — the unsuccessful predatory expedition of Zabad, the sixth in

descent from Ephraim, against the Philistines (I Chron. 7:20-22). This repulse happening only a short time before the Exodus, will help to account for the people's fear of the Philistines (Ex. 13:17). As Stephen brings down the prosperity of the people till near the time of the Exodus, the bondage must have begun only a short time before the birth of Moses (Acts 7:17-18; Comp. Ps. 105:24-25).

19. *Chronology of the pilgrimage in Canaan and Egypt.* The times of events from Abraham to Joseph are clearly indicated in Scripture. (See chart *Chronology of Patriarchs,* p. 147.) A summary of these times is as follows:

a. *Abraham* (2166-1991 B.C.)
  1. Entered Canaan at 75 (Gen. 12:4).
  2. Isaac born, 100 (21:5).
  3. Death, 175 (25:7).
b. *Isaac* (2066-1886 B.C.)
  1. Married, 40 (25:20).
  2. Twins born, 60 (25:26).
  3. Death, 180 (35:28).
c. *Jacob* (2006-1859 B.C.)
  1. Before Pharaoh, 130 (47:9).
  2. At birth of Joseph, 91.

    Joseph was 30 (41:46), plus 7 (41:53), plus 2 (45:6) (total 39) when Jacob came before Pharaoh. Thus to obtain Jacob's age at the birth of Joseph, subtract 39 from 130. Note Gen. 37:3, "child of his old age."

    All of Jacob's children, except Benjamin, were born within the second seven-year period of his work for Laban (29:20,30; 30:25; 31:38). Thus Reuben, the oldest, was probably about six years older than Joseph, and was born when Jacob was about 85.
  3. Death, 147 (47:28).

The period of time from Jacob's entry into Egypt to the exodus is not as certainly indicated as the time from Abraham to Jacob. The whole period of the sojourn of the Israelites in Egypt is reckoned at 430 years in the account of their departure (Ex. 12:41). A similar period of bondage is also indicated by God's word to Abraham (Gen. 15:13), and by Stephen (Acts 7:6).

However, the words of Paul in Gal. 3:17 and the LXX rendering of Ex. 12:41 give the idea that the 430 years included the years the Israelites were in Egypt *and* the time from Abraham's entry into Canaan to Israel's migration into Egypt (a period of 215 years[1]), thus reducing the actual sojourn in Egypt to a like period of 215 years.

A summary of the dating obtained by these interpretations (when related to known dates) is as follows:

a. *Long chronology*

> 966 B.C.—4th year of Solomon's reign (I Kings 6:1).
> 480 yrs. (from Exodus to Solomon's fourth year).

> 1,446 B.C.— Date of exodus.
> 430 yrs. in Egypt.

> 1,876 B.C. — Jacob's entry into Egypt.
> 215 yrs. (from Abram's entry into Canaan to Jacob's entry into Egypt).

> 2,091 B.C.— Abram's entry into Canaan.

b. *Short chronology*

> 1,446 B.C.—The exodus.
> 215 yrs. in Egypt.

> 1,661 B.C.—Jacob enters Egypt.
> 215 yrs. (from Abram to Jacob).

> 1,876 B.C.—Abram's entry into Canaan.

In this book we have followed the longer chronology. Neither interpretation is free from difficulties.[2] Future archaeological discoveries may help clear up the problem; other obscurities have been cleared up in this manner.

The descent of Moses from Levi, through Kohath and Amram, seems to support the short chronology (Num. 3:17-19; 26:57-59; Ex. 6:16,18,20; I Chron. 6:1-3; 23:6, 12-13). Also the fact that Moses' mother is said to have been a sister of Kohath, the son of Levi (Ex. 6:20) supports the short chronology. However, Biblical genealogies very often have names omitted, as, for example, the genealogy of Christ in Matt. 1. A different Kohath may be referred to.

The fact that there are eleven known generations from Jacob to Joshua supports the longer chronology (I Chron. 7:29-27). It is further supported by the fact that at the time Israel was numbered at Sinai Moses' father Amram and his brothers had multiplied into clans (Num. 3:27). However, the plainest evidence of the long chronology remains the unambiguous

---

1. Calculated by adding the time of Abram's residence in Canaan before Isaac's birth (25 yrs), to the age of Isaac at Jacob's birth (6;), to Jacob's age when presented before Pharaoh (130).
2. See Zondervan *Pictorial Bible Dictionary* for details and bibliography, pp. 166-167, 170.

statement of Ex. 12:40-41. (The reading of the Hebrew text must be regarded as more authoritative than that of the LXX.)

Questions Over Section VII
Joseph and Jacob in Egypt

1. How old was Joseph when he reported evil of his brothers (Gen. 37:2)?
2. What special gift did Jacob give to Joseph (37:3)?
3. What were the two dreams of Joseph, and what did they mean (37:5-10)?
4. Where did Jacob send Joseph to find his brothers (37:13)?
5. Where had the brothers gone (37:17)?
6. Which brother kept the others from killing Joseph (37:21)?
7. Who suggested that Joseph be sold (37:26-27)?
8. To what people was Joseph sold (37:28)?
9. What was the price for Joseph (37:28)?
10. What was done with Joseph's coat (37:31-32)?
11. What did Jacob say when he saw the coat (37:33,35)?
12. To whom was Joseph sold in Egypt (37:36)?
13. What office did Joseph's Egyptian owner hold (39:1)?
14. How did Joseph get along in his master's house (39:2)?
15. How greatly did Joseph's master trust him (39:6)?
16. Who tempted Joseph (39:7)?
17. Joseph declared that his sin would be against whom (39:9)?
18. How did Joseph escape the woman (39:12)?
19. What lie did the woman tell (39:14)?
20. What did the master do with Joseph (39:20)?
21. What prisoners were kept in the place where Joseph was (39:20)?
22. How did Joseph get along in prison (39:21-23)?
23. What two officials of the king were placed in prison (40:1)?
24. What made these prisoners sad (40:8)?
25. What was the butler's dream (40:10-11)?
26. What interpretation did Joseph give of this dream (40:12-14)?
27. What request did Joseph make of the butler (40:14)?
28. What was the baker's dream (40:16-17)?
29. What interpretation did Joseph give of his dream (40:18-19)?
30. Who forgot Joseph (40:23)? For how long (41:1)?
31. What were Pharoah's two dreams (41:1-6)?

32. Who among the Egyptians could interpret the dreams (41:8,24)?
33. Who told Pharaoh of Joseph (41:9,12)?
34. What preparations did Joseph make before coming before Pharaoh (41:14)?
35. Whom did Joseph give credit to for interpreting dreams (41:16)?
36. What did Joseph say the dreams of Pharaoh meant (41:26-27)?
37. Why was Pharaoh's dream doubled (41:32)?
38. What advice did Joseph give Pharaoh (41:33-36)?
39. Why did Pharaoh select Joseph as grain collector (41:38-40)?
40. How high did Joseph rank in Egypt (41:40)?
41. Who was given to Joseph as a wife (41:45)?
42. Who was Joseph's father-in-law (41:45)?
43. What was Joseph's age when he stood before Pharaoh (41:46)?
44. How much grain did Joseph gather (41:49)?
45. What were the names of Joseph's two sons? Which was the older (41:51-52)?
46. What area did the famine cover (41:54,56)?
47. Why should Jacob's sons have gone into Egypt (42:1-2)?
48. Why did they look at one another instead of going to Egypt (42:1)?
49. Which son of Jacob did not go into Egypt (42:4)? Why not?
50. Whom did the brothers face in Egypt (42:6)?
51. How did their visit fulfill a dream (42:6; 37:9)?
52. What did Joseph accuse the brothers of (42:9)?
53. How long were the brothers kept in ward (jail) (42:17)?
54. Who were the brothers ordered to bring back to Egypt (42:19-20)?
55. Why did the brothers think they suffered this penalty (42:21)?
56. How had Joseph talked when he was sold (42:21)?
57. What made Joseph weep (42:22-24)?
58. Which brother was detained in Egypt (42:24)?
59. What did Joseph have placed in the brothers' sacks (42:25)?
60. How did the brothers react when they discovered the contents of their sacks (42:28,35)?
61. What did Jacob accuse the brothers of (42:36)?

62. What security did Reuben offer Jacob as proof he would care for Benjamin (42:37)?
63. Why did the brothers return to Egypt a second time (43:2)?
64. Who told Jacob that they had to take Benjamin to Egypt (43:3)?
65. Who promised to be surety for Benjamin (43:8-9)?
66. What did Jacob tell the brothers to take into Egypt (43:11-12)?
67. What hospitality did Joseph show to the brothers when they returned to Egypt (43:16)?
68. What did Joseph say when the brothers tried to return their money (43:23)?
69. What did the brothers offer to Joseph (43:25-26)?
70. Whom did Joseph ask the brothers about (43:27)?
71. How did Joseph react when he saw Benjamin (43:29-30)?
72. Why didn't Joseph sit at the table with his brothers (43:32)?
73. How were the brothers arranged at the table (43:33)?
74. Who got the most food? How much more (43:34)?
75. What was placed in the brothers' sacks and in Benjamin's sack (44:1-2)?
76. What did Joseph have the steward accuse the returning brothers of taking (44:4-5)?
77. What was the cup of Joseph (supposedly) used for (44:5)?
78. What did the brothers say could be done to them if they were guilty (44:9)?
79. How did the brothers react when the cup was found (44:12-13)?
80. How did Joseph say that Benjamin would be punished (44:17)?
81. Who interceded for Benjamin (44:18)?
82. What did the interceding brother offer to do to get Benjamin released (44:33)?
83. Why did he make this offer (44:31,34)?
84. Why did Joseph send everyone except his brothers out of the room (45:1)?
85. Whom did Joseph ask about first after revealing his identity (45:3)?
86. How did the brothers react when Joseph identified himself (45:3)?
87. Who did Joseph say had sent him into Egypt (45:5,8)?
88. How many years of the famine had passed by then (45:6)?
89. What instructions did Joseph send to his father (45:9)?

90. In what land was Jacob to dwell in Egypt (45:10)?
91. How were Joseph's feelings toward Benjamin revealed (45:14)?
92. How did Pharoah react to the coming of Joseph's brothers (45:16)?
93. What arrangements for transporting Jacob's family did Pharaoh make (45:17-19)?
94. What clothing was given to the brothers? What clothing and what else was given to Benjamin (45:22)?
95. How did Jacob react to the news about Joseph (45:26)?
96. Did Jacob agree to go into Egypt (45:28)?
97. At what city did God speak unto Jacob in a vision as he went to Egypt (46:1-2)?
98. What did God promise Jacob that he would do for him in Egypt (46:4)?
99. What does "Joseph shall put his hand upon thine eyes" mean?
100. How many souls (people) of the house of Jacob came into Egypt (46:27)?
101. Who was sent ahead of Jacob to direct the way into Goshen (46:28)?
102. Describe the meeting of Joseph and Jacob. Where did this meeting occur (46:29)?
103. What were the Israelites to tell Pharaoh was their occupation (46:32,34)?
104. How did the Egyptians feel about sheep herders (46:34)?
105. How many brothers of Joseph went in with him to see Pharaoh (47:2)?
106. In what land in Egypt did Pharaoh let them dwell (47:6)?
107. What job offer did Pharaoh make to the brothers (47:6)?
108. With what sort of speech did Jacob talk to Pharaoh (47:7,10)?
109. How old was Jacob then (47:9)?
110. What was another name for the area where Jacob's family lived (47:11)?
111. What three things did Joseph get from the people for Pharaoh (47:14,16,20,23)?
112. Who relocated the people of Egypt (47:21)?
113. What class of people retained their land (47:22)?
114. What part of the production of the land was collected for Pharaoh (47:24)?
115. How did the Israelites fare in Egypt (47:27)?

116. How long did Jacob live in Egypt (47:28)?
117. What promise did Jacob require Joseph to make to him (47:29-30)?
118. Who was brought to Jacob when he was sick (48:1)?
119. What event did Jacob recall before Joseph and his sons (48:3-4)?
120. What relationship did Jacob claim toward Joseph's sons (48:5)?
121. By what names was Joseph's inheritance to be called (48:6)?
122. What is another name for Bethlehem? What had happened to Jacob there (48:7)?
123. How did Jacob show affection for Joseph's sons (48:10)?
124. How did Jacob arrange his hands on Joseph's sons (48:14)?
125. How did Joseph react to Jacob's hand position on his sons? Why (48:17-18)?
126. Which of Joseph's sons was to become greater (48:19-20)?
127. How had Jacob acquired land from the Amorites (48:22)?
128. What did Jacob call his sons together to tell them (49:1-2)?
129. What honor and position did Jacob foretell for the tribe of Judah (49:10)?
130. Explain the term *Shiloh* in Gen. 40:10. What Messianic application is in it?
131. Where did Jacob command his sons to bury him (49:29-30)?
132. What five other persons besides Jacob were buried there (49:31)?
133. What class of Egyptians embalmed Jacob (50:2)?
134. How long did the embalming take (50:3)?
135. What request did Joseph make of Pharaoh after Jacob died (50:5)?
136. Who all went up into Canaan to bury Jacob (50:7-9)?
137. What did the Canaanites notice about the mourning for Jacob and what did they call it (50:10-11)?
138. What did the brothers of Joseph fear after Jacob was buried (50:15)?
139. How did Joseph react to their fears and message (50:17,21)?
140. How long did Joseph live (50:22)?
141. How many generations of his descendants did Joseph live to see (50:23)?
142. What did Joseph make the children of Israel swear to do when they left Egypt (50:24-25)?
143. Where was Joseph's body kept (50:26)?

CHRONOLOGY OF PATRIARCHS

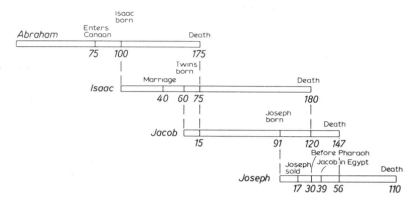

Period IV
Period of Bondage
(Exodus 1-12)

The period of bondage extends from Israel's going into Egypt unto their departure under the leadership of Moses 430 years later (1876-1446 B.C.). During this time Israel multiplied from a family into a great nation.

Section I
The Book of Exodus

1. The name EXODUS means a "going out" or a "going forth." The name is taken from the Greek Old Testament (Septuagint). The name applies more to the early part of the book than to the entire book.
2. Exodus continues the history at the point that Genesis left off. It starts with the bondage in Egypt and ends with the building of the tabernacle.
3. Moses was the author of Exodus, as he was of Genesis. See Mark 12:26. Moses was the author of the first five books of the Old Testament (called the Torah, or the Pentateuch).

4. There are two important breaks (or dividing lines) in the book of Exodus:
   (1) The Israelites in Egypt / The Israelites in the desert
   12:36 / 12:37
   (2) Patriarchal dispensation / Mosaic dispensation
   Exodus 19 / Exodus 20
   (During the patriarchal dispensation, God dealt with individuals and families of all nations. During the Mosaic dispensation God dealt almost exclusively with the nation of Israel to prepare them for the coming of the Messiah.)
5. Outline of Exodus (memorize)
   Part I—The Hebrews in Egypt; 1:1-12:36
      1. The Egyptian bondage; Ch. 1
      2. The preparation of Moses; Chs. 2-4
      3. The struggle with Pharaoh; Chs. 5-11
      4. The passover; 12:1-36
   Part II—The Hebrews from Egypt to Sinai; 12:37-ch. 18
      1. The exodus; 12:37-15:21
      2. The journey to Sinai; 15:22-ch. 17
      3. The visit of Jethro; Ch. 18
   Part III—The Hebrews at Sinai; Chs. 19-40
      1. The law given; Chs. 19-24
      2. The pattern of the tabernacle given; Chs. 25-31
      3. The idolatry of the people; Chs. 32-34
      4. The construction of the tabernacle; Chs. 35-40

Questions

1. What does the name *Exodus* mean?
2. Where does the history in Exodus begin and end?
3. Who was the author of Exodus?
4. Where are the two important breaks in Exodus, and between what do the breaks come?
5. Give from memory the outline of Exodus.

Section II
The Hebrews in Egypt (Ex. 1:1-12:36)

1. The people of Israel oppressed. 2. The birth and education of Moses. 3. His choice to suffer with his people. 4. His flight from Egypt and residence in Midian. 5. God appears to him in the burning bush —

The mission of Moses and Aaron to Israel and Pharaoh.
6. Moses returns to Egypt and meets Aaron — Their
reception by the people. 7. Their first appeal to
Pharaoh — Increase of the oppression — The renewal
of Jehovah's covenant. 8. The conflict with Pharaoh —
The Ten Plagues of Egypt. 9. Institution of the Passover.
10. The death of the first-born of Egypt, and the Exodus
of the Israelites. 11. Hebrew calendar — Weights and
measures.

1. *The people of Israel oppressed.* "Now *there arose up a new king over Egypt, which knew not Joseph*" (Ex. 1:8). So begins the story of the affliction of the Israelites in Egypt, and of that marvellous deliverance, which has given to the second book of the Bible its Greek title of Exodus. The date of this event may be placed about 1700 B.C., and it probably signifies a change of dynasty. This was the period when lower Egypt was taken over by Asiatic invaders called *Hyksos (rulers of foreign lands).*[1] There is considerable uncertainty about the history of Egypt in this period, but it would appear that Hyksos feared and oppressed the Israelites, who had been in favor with the Egyptians. The Hyksos had taken over the land by the use of horse-drawn chariotry. It seems unlikely that the millions of Egyptians would have regarded the Israelites with 600,000 men as more numerous and mighty than they. This would be likely, however, in the case of the Hyksos warrior invaders[2] (Ex. 1-9).

Even if it was the Hyksos kings who started the oppression, the mighty XVIII dynasty kings, who expelled the Hyksos, continued the oppression.

At all events, we see the new monarch dreading some war, in which the enemy might be aided by the people of Israel, who were "more numerous and mightier than his own subjects," and dreading also their escape out of the land (Ex. 1:8,9; Ps. 105:24). He therefore adopted the policy of reducing them to slavery (Ps. 105:25; Acts 7:19; Prov. 21:30), which was made more rigorous the more the people increased. Their labor consisted in field-work, and especially in making bricks and building the "treasure-cities" (probably for storing up corn) Pithom and

1. An alternate time for the beginning of the oppression could be the time of the beginning of the XVIII dynasty at the expulsion of the Hyksos from Egypt, about 1550 B.C.
2. See Gleason Archer, *A Survey of O.T. Introduction*, pp. 206-208, for further arguments that the oppression of Israel was started by the Hyksos and not the XVIII dynasty kings.

Raamses.[1] Still they multiplied and grew; and Pharaoh adopted a more cruel and atrocious course. He commanded the Hebrew midwives to kill the male children at their birth, but to preserve the females (Acts 7:19). The midwives, however, "feared God" and disobeyed the king; and they were rewarded by being made mothers of households in the families of Israel. Their names were Shiphrah and Puah. The king then commanded the Egyptians to drown the new-born sons of the Israelites in the river, but to save the daughters (Ex. 1:15-21).

2. *The birth and education of Moses.* Pharaoh's edict of infanticide led, by the providence of God, to the rearing up at his own court of the future deliverer of Israel. AMRAM, a descendant of Kohath, son of Levi, had espoused Jochebed, who was also of the tribe of Levi; and they had already two children, a daughter called MIRIAM (the same name as the *Mary* of the New Testament), and a son named AARON. Another son was born soon after the king's edict. With maternal fondness, increased by the boy's beauty, and in faith (as it seems) on a prophetic intimation of his destiny, his mother hid him for three months (Ex. 2:1-2; Comp. Heb. 11:23). When concealment was no longer possible, Jochebed prepared a covered basket of papyrus daubed with bitumen to make it water-tight, and placed it among the rushes on the banks of the Nile, or one of the canals, leaving Miriam to watch the result at a distance. To that very spot the daughter of Pharaoh came down to bathe. She saw the ark, and sent one of her maidens to fetch it. As she opened it, the babe wept, and touched with pity, she said, "This is one of the Hebrew's children." At this moment Miriam came forward, and having received the princess's permission to find a nurse, she went and fetched the child's mother. While she reared him as the son of Pharaoh's daughter, she doubtless taught him the knowledge of the true God and the history of the chosen race. In all other respects MOSES[2] was brought up as an Egyptian prince, and "he was educated in all the wisdom of the Egyptians" (Acts 7:22). St. Stephen adds that "he was mighty in words and in deed"; and whatever we may think of the traditions about this period of his life, it was certainly a part of his training for his great mission.

There are numerous reasons for believing that the daughter of

---

1. These two cities were in the land of Goshen. We read that Joseph settled his father and brethren "in the land of Rameses" (Gen. 47:11), which was a part of the land of Goshen. The name Rameses is derived from the Egyptian sun-god Ra, but came into greatest prominence during the XIX dynasty when several kings took the name Rameses.
2. In Egyptian *Moses* means "son of the water." In Hebrew, *"drawing out."*

Pharaoh who adopted Moses was none other than the famous queen Hatshepsut, who ruled Egypt about 1501-1479.

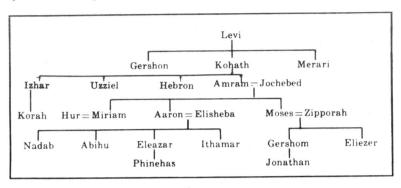

3. *Moses' choice to suffer with his people.* The narrative in Exodus passes over this period, to the crisis at which he decided to cast in his lot with his own people, when "by *faith* he refused to be called (renounced the rank of) the son of Pharaoh's daughter; choosing rather oppression with the people of God than the fleeting enjoyment of sin, deeming the reproach of Christ greater wealth than the treasures of Egypt, for he regarded the recompense" (Heb. 11:26) — a most striking passage, which not only implies *a deliberate choice,* but the hope of Messiah's coming and the expectation of rewards and punishments. So St. Stephen says that *it came into his heart* to visit his brethren the children of Israel, and that he supposed his brethren would have understood how that God by his hand would deliver them (Acts 7:23-25). These passages bring out the full meaning of his own simpler statement that "he went out unto his brethren, and looked on their burdens" (Ex. 2:11).

The time of this event was "when Moses was grown," or "when he was come to years" (Heb. 11:24), or, as St. Stephen states, "when he was full forty years old" (Acts 7:23). This date is confirmed by the whole narrative in the Pentateuch, which divides the life of Moses into three equal periods of 40 years each. We may say that for his first forty years he was an Egyptian; for the second forty an Arabian; and for the third forty the leader of Israel.

Moses then went forth to view the state of his brethren. The first sight he saw was one so common that our eyes can see it on the monuments of Egypt at this very day — an Egyptian overseer beating one of the slaves who worked under him. But the sight was new to Moses, and stung with indignation, after looking round to see that no one was near, he killed the Egyptian on the spot, and buried his body in the sand. His hope that this deed might prove a token of the coming deliverance was soon checked. On his next visit he found that the oppressed could oppress each other, and his interference was scornfully rejected by the wrong-doer, with a dangerous allusion to his having killed the Egyptian. The expression — "Who made thee a prince and a judge over us?" — seems to imply a willful rejection of his mission; at all events, it was a token of that spirit of which he had long after such terrible experience in the wilderness (Acts 7:35-41).

It seems to us very noteworthy that the year when Moses went out to visit his brethren (1486 B.C.) was very close to the time when Thutmose III, the mightiest King of all the Egyptians, took over power from Hatshepsut, who was both his step-mother and mother-in-law. Was Moses attempting to lead the Israelites to revolt and gain independence from Egypt as Hatshepsut's power was waning and Thutmose's was rising? The panic of Moses when his efforts to save his people failed suggests that his plans were bigger than delivering one Israelite from one Egyptian who was beating him. With his protectress Hatshepsut now losing power in Egypt, it was a time for Moses either to fight or flee. (See Acts 7:25.)

4. *Moses' flight from Egypt and residence in Midian.* The story reached the ears of Pharaoh, and the life of Moses was threatened. He fled into the desert which surrounds the head of the Red Sea, and which was inhabited by the people of Midian, who were descended from Abraham and Keturah.[1] As he sat down beside a well (or rather, *the* well, for it was one famous enough to be so distinguished), the seven daughters of JETHRO (elsewhere called REUEL and RAGUEL), the priest and probably prince of the Midianites, came to water their flocks, probably at a regular noontide gathering of the sheep. They were rudely repulsed by the shepherds, but Moses helped them and watered their flock. Their father welcomed the "Egyptian"; and Moses dwelt with him for forty years, like Jacob and Laban, feeding his flocks, and married his daughter Zipporah (Ex. 2:15-21, 3:1). She bore him a son whom he named Gershom *(a stranger here)* in memory of his sojourn in a strange land, but whose circumcision was neglected till enforced by a divine threat on his way back to

---

1. The land of Midian lay principally east of the Gulf of Akabah. However, the Midianites also dwelt in the peninsula of Sinai, and it was probably there where Moses took up his abode. See p. 355 for a special study of the Midianites.

Egypt (Ex. 2:22; 4:25). We read afterward of a second son, named Eliezer *(my God is a help)*, in memory of his father's deliverance from Pharaoh (Ex. 18:3,4; Acts 7:29).

5. *The burning bush – Mission of Moses to Israel and Pharaoh.* Moses had been forty years in Midian (Acts 7:30), musing amid the seclusion of his shepherd life over the past history of his people and his own destiny, when God's time arrived for the crowning revelation of all, and for the deliverance of his people. The return of Moses to Egypt during the lifetime of the king from whom he had fled would have been certain death. But that king died. The oppression of the Israelites under his successor seems to have been even more severe, "and they cried, and their cry came up to God by reason of their bondage. And God heard their groaning, and *God remembered his covenant* with Abraham, with Isaac, and with Jacob. And God looked upon the children of Israel, and God knew them" (Ex. 2:23-25).

The scene chosen for the revelation to Moses of his divine mission was the same amid which the Israelites, led out by him from Egypt, were to see God's presence again revealed, and to receive the law from His own voice. Unchanged in its awful solitary grandeur from that day to this, it is one of the most remarkable spots on the surface of the earth. The *Peninsula of Sinai* is the promontory enclosed between the two arms of the Red Sea, and culminating at its southern part in the terrific mass of granite rocks known by the general name of Sinai. This desert region bordered on the country of Jethro. It still furnishes a scanty pasturage, and its valleys were probably at that time better watered than now. As Moses led his flock to its inmost recesses (on its west side) he came to a mountain, which was even then called the "mount of God" from its sanctity among the Arabs, "even *Horeb.*" He saw one of the dwarf acacias *(seneh),* the characteristic vegetation of the desert, wrapt in a flame beneath which the dry branches would soon have crackled and consumed, had it been a natural fire; but "behold the bush burned with fire, and the bush was not consumed." It was the fit symbol of God's afflicted people in Egypt, and of His suffering church in every age.

As Moses turned aside to behold the marvel, the "angel Jehovah" (See Special Study, p. 354) called to him out of the bush, and after commanding him to remove his shoes, for the ground was holy, he announced himself as the God of his fathers, Abraham, Isaac and Jacob; declared that He had seen the affliction of his people in Egypt, and was come down to deliver them, and to lead them into the promised land; and called Moses to be his messenger to Pharaoh, and the leader of his people. Moses pleaded his unworthiness, but was assured of God's presence till his mission should be fulfilled by bringing the people to worship in that mountain. Then another difficulty arose. So corrupted were the people by the idolatry of Egypt, that they would not know what deity was meant by "the God of their fathers." They would ask, "What is his name?" Besides the common name expressive of their divinity, the gods of the heathen had proper names: Amon, Baal and the like; and that He might be distinguished from all these, God revealed to Moses the name by which the God of the Hebrews has ever since been known, JEHOVAH, the self-existent and eternally the same: — He that *is,* and *was,* and *ever will be what he is.* "I AM THAT I AM! — *What that is,* I have written on the consciousness of man" (Rom 1:19); I have revealed it by word and by act to your fathers; and I ever will be to my people what I was to them; for He repeats this character once more, and adds, "This is my name forever, and this is my memorial unto all generations" (Ex. 3:11-15).

God then unfolded his plan of deliverance. He bade Moses repeat to the elders of Israel the revelation he had now received. He assured him that they would believe, and bade him go with them and demand of Pharaoh, in the name of God, leave to go three days' journey into the wilderness to sacrifice to Jehovah. He warned him of Pharaoh's refusal,[1] and announced the signs and wonders He would work to make him yield, and ended by commanding the people to spoil the Egyptians of their jewels.

To these assurances God added *two signs,* to remove the doubts of Moses about his reception by the people. These were the signs of the hand made leprous and then cured, and the shepherd's staff which turned into a serpent and then resumed its former shape. To these signs, which were exhibited on the spot, was added a third, the power to turn the water of the Nile to blood.

But the more his mission is made clear to him, the more is Moses staggered by its greatness. He pleads his want of eloquence, which seems to have amounted to an impediment in his speech (Ex. 4:10), a sorry qualification for an ambassador to a hostile king. Notwithstanding the promise that He who made man's mouth and has the command of all the senses would be with

---

1. Ex. 3:19. This is the first reference to Pharaoh's stubbornness, and he himself was the stubborn one. In the subsequent experience God hardened Pharaoh's heart on several occasions. God is not to be blamed for punishing Pharaoh for doing only as God compelled him. God only punished Pharaoh by forcing him farther down the path that Pharaoh had himself first chosen.

him and teach him what he should say, he desires to devolve the whole mission on some other. Then did God in anger punish his reluctance, though in mercy he met his objections, by giving a share of the honor, which might have been his alone, to his brother Aaron, a man who could speak well. But yet the word was not to be Aaron's own. He was to be the mouth of Moses; and Moses was to be to him as God, the direct channel of the divine revelation. The rod of power became "Aaron's rod," though the power itself was put forth by the word of Moses. The two great functions conferred by the divine mission were divided: Moses became the *prophet,* and Aaron the *priest;* and the whole arrangement exhibits the great principle of *mediation* (Ex. 3:16-4:17).

6. *Moses returns to Egypt and meets Aaron — Their reception by the people.* Moses obtained his father-in-law's permission to return to his brethren in Egypt; and he received the signal of God for his departure, in the assurance that "the men were dead that sought his life" (Comp. Matt. 2:20). His mission to Pharaoh was summed up in the statement: that God claimed the liberty of Israel as his first-born son; and if Pharaoh refused to let him go, He would slay his first-born. To this last infliction all the plagues of Egypt were but preludes. After the scene at the inn, already referred to, in which his family, hitherto regarded as Arabian, received circumcision, the seal of the covenant (Gen. 17:9-14), Moses was met by Aaron, as God had foretold to him, on the very spot where he had received the commission which he rehearsed to his brother, with its attendant miracles, in the mount of God. On reaching Egypt they assembled the elders of Israel, "And Aaron spake all the words which Jehovah had spoken to Moses, and did the signs in the sight of all the people. And the people believed: and when they heard that Jehovah had visited the children of Israel, and that He had looked upon their affliction, then they bowed their heads and worshiped" (Ex. 4:18-31). We shall soon see that they were far from being finally weaned from the false religion of Egypt.

7. *First appeal to Pharaoh — Increase of oppression — Renewal of Jehovah's covenant.* Moses and Aaron next sought the presence of Pharaoh to demand leave in the name of Jehovah, the God of Israel, for His people to hold a feast to Him in the wilderness. It was to be a solemn festival, shared in by all the people, who, as a nomad race, would of course travel with their flocks and herds.

When they had once gone three days' journey into the wilderness, they would be at the disposal of their God and father, to lead them back or forward as He pleased; and he claimed of Pharaoh that they should be placed at his disposal (Ex. 4:22-23), without telling him of their farther destination, which had been long since revealed to Abraham, and lately made known to Moses (Ex. 5:1-3).

Pharaoh answered, "Who is Jehovah? . . . I know not Jehovah, and moreover I will not let Israel go." Pharaoh was soon to become well-acquainted with Jehovah, and to regret his refusal to let Israel go.

Refusing alike to acknowledge Jehovah as a god, and to let the people go, Pharaoh hounded back Moses and Aaron to their burdens. We may suppose that, though Moses' personal enemies at the court were dead, he was still sufficiently well known there for pleasure to be taken in his humiliation. Their repulse was followed by an increase of the people's oppression. The Egyptian taskmasters, whose office it was to regulate the amount of work, were bidden no longer to give them the chopped straw which was necessary to bind the friable earth into bricks. The people lost their time in searching the fields for stubble to supply its place. But still the full quota of bricks was exacted from them; and when they could no longer supply it, the Hebrew overseers, who were under the Egyptian taskmasters, were scourged and beaten. Their appeal to Pharaoh being rejected in the true spirit of unreasoning tyranny, they turned upon Moses and Aaron, whom they accused of making them odious to Pharaoh (Ex. 5:4-21).

In this strait Moses complained to God, that his mission had increased the people's misery, and yet they were not delivered: and God assured him that His time was at hand. With a plainer revelation of his great name, JEHOVAH renewed his ancient covenant, to bring them into the promised land (Ex. 6:1-8). Though the people were too heart-broken to accept the consolation, Jehovah gave Moses and Aaron (whose descent from Levi is now formally set forth) their final charge to Pharaoh; once more warning them of the king's resistance, which should only give occasion for more signal proofs of God's power, that the Egyptians might know Jehovah (Ex. 6:9; 7:5). Moses was now eighty years old, and Aaron eighty-three (7:7).

8. *The conflict with Pharaoh – The ten plagues of Egypt.* Then began that memorable contest, the type of all others between the

---

The Ten Plagues

1. Water to blood
2. Frogs
3. Lice
4. Flies
5. Murrain of cattle

6. Boils
7. Hail
8. Locusts
9. Darkness
10. Death of firstborn

---

power of God and the hardened heart of man, which was only stilled in the waters of the Red Sea.[1] Moses and Aaron resorted to the miracles provided for them by God. That of the leprous hand was omitted, having been only for the Israelites; but Aaron's rod was changed into a serpent. The miracle was imitated by the magicians of Egypt, headed by *Jannes* and *Jambres,* whose names are preserved by Paul (II Tim. 3:8). We say *imitated,* to express at once the conviction, that their apparent success was an imposture. Possibly their miracles were done by Satanic power (Matt. 24:24; II Thess. 2:9; Rev. 13:13). Or they may have been done by sheer human trickery. We may not be able to explain all their imitations (though very possible explanations have been suggested), but we have a perfectly satisfactory test of their imposture in the limit at which their power ceased. Their own exclamation, "This is the finger of God" (Ex. 8:19), involves the confession that they had been aided by no divine power, not even by their own supposed deities.

We do not read of any attempt on the part of Moses to expose their imposture. In the first miracle, he was content with the superior power shown by Aaron's serpent devouring theirs; and the rest he answered by still greater miracles, till he came to one which they could not imitate, and then their confession left no need for refutation.

The first miracle, that of the rod, was a display of God's power

---

1. It would almost seem as if it were the design of the sacred narrative to confine our attention to the moral and religious aspect of this great conflict of the King of Egypt with the King of kings, by its silence respecting those details which antiquarian curiosity has never since suceeded in solving. The sovereign's own name is not given although we suppose that he was Amenhotep II. We are not told whether he was a Theban or Memphite king; but this much is clear from the whole narrative — that the scene of the contest was in Lower Egypt, is inconsistent with the evident presence of the great mass of the Israelites, who were certainly still resident in Goshen (Ex. 7:22, 10:23). If we may take the passage in Psalm 78:43, literally — "His wonders in the field of Zoan" — the locality is expressly defined to the neighborhood of that great city of the Delta (the *Tanis* of the Greek writers), which was on the borders of Goshen, Zoan or Tanis. Zoan had been the Hyksos capital, and was a site of later building by Rameses II of the XIX dynasty. However, there is no reason to assert that the XVIII dynasty kings did not have a regional headquarters in the delta area, and did not conduct some business from there.

given to his prophet, for the conviction of Pharaoh and the Egyptians; but when their hearts were hardened against conviction, it became needful to teach them by suffering. The miracles that followed were *judgments,* on the king, the people and their gods, forming the TEN PLAGUES OF EGYPT (Ex. 7-12; Comp. Ps. 78, 105).

a. *The Plague of Blood.* — After a warning to Pharaoh, Aaron, at the word of Moses, waved his rod over the Nile, and the river was turned into blood, with all its canals and reservoirs, and every vessel of water drawn from them; the fish died and the river stank. The pride of the Egyptians in their river for its wholesome water is well known, and it was the source of all fertility. But besides this, it was honored as a god, and so were some species of its fish (as the *oxyrhynchus*); and to smite "the sacred salubrious Nile," was to smite Egypt at its heart. There was, however, mercy mingled with the judgment, for the Egyptians obtained water by digging wells. The miracle lasted for seven days; but as it was imitated by the magicians, it produced no impression on Pharaoh (Ex. 7:16-25).

b. *The Plague of Frog* — These creatures are always so numerous in Egypt as to be annoying; but at the appointed signal, they came up from their natural haunts, and swarmed in countless numbers, "even in the chambers of their kings" (Ps. 105:30), and defiled the very ovens and kneading-troughs. Here too it was an object of their reverence that was made their scourge, for the frog was one of the sacred animals. From this plague there was no escape; and though the magicians imitated it, Pharaoh was fain to seek relief through the prayer of Moses, and by promising to let the people go. "Glory over me," said Moses: he waived all personal honor that the contest might bring him, and allowed Pharaoh to fix the time for the removal of the plague. The king named the morrow; and then, by the prayer of Moses, the frogs died where they were, a far more striking confirmation of the miracle than if they had retired to their haunts. Pharaoh abused the respite, and even while his land stank with the carcasses of the frogs, he refused to keep his promise (Ex. 8:1-15).

c. *The Plague of Lice.* — From the waters and marshes, the power of God passed on to the dry land, which was smitten by the rod, and its very dust seemed turned into minute noxious insects, so thickly did they swarm on man and beast, or rather *"in"* them (Ex. 8:17). The scrupulous cleanliness of the Egyptians[1] would add intolerably to the bodily distress of this plague, by which also they again incurred religious defilement. As to the species of the vermin there seems no reason to disturb the authorized translation of the word.

In this case we read that "the magicians *did so* with their enchantments, *to bring forth lice,* but *they could not."* They struck the ground, as Aaron did, and repeated their own incantations, but it was without effect. They confessed the hand of God; but Pharaoh was still hardened (Ex. 8:16-19).

d. *The Plague of Flies or Beetles.* — After the river and the land, the air was smitten, being filled with winged insects, which swarmed in the houses and devoured the land, but Goshen was exempted from the plague. The word translated "swarms of flies" most probably denotes the great Egyptian beetle *(Scaraboeus sacer),* which is constantly represented in their sculptures. Besides the annoying and destructive habits of its tribe, it was an object of worship, and thus the Egyptians were again scourged by their own superstitions.

Pharaoh now gave permission for the Israelites to sacrifice to their God in the land; but Moses replied that the Egyptians would stone them if they sacrificed the creatures they worshiped (and almost *every* animal was sacred to some god of Egypt), a striking example, thus early, of the tendency to religious riots which has marked all the successive populations of Egypt. He repeated the demand to go three days' journey into the wilderness, there to place themselves at God's disposal. Pharaoh now yielded; but as soon as the plague was removed at the prayer of Moses, he "hardened his heart at this time also, neither would he let the people go" (Ex. 8:20-32).

Pharaoh's offer to let Israel go and sacrifice in the land was the first of four compromise proposals offered by Pharaoh to Moses. None of these compromises would have allowed the Israelites liberty to leave Egypt permanently, and all were rejected. For the sake of seeing all of them at once, we list the compromises here; they will be discussed individually later.

1. Go sacrifice; but stay in the land (Ex. 8:25).
2. Go, but do not go far (Ex. 8:28).
3. The men alone may go sacrifice (Ex. 10:11).
4. Everyone may go, but do not take your cattle (Ex. 10:24).

---

1. The priests used to shave their heads and bodies every third day, for fear of harboring lice when they entered the temples (Herodotus 2:37).

e. *Plague of the Murrain of Beasts.* — Still coming closer and closer to the Egyptians, God sent a disease upon the cattle, which were not only their property, but their deities. At the precise time of which Moses forewarned Pharaoh, all the cattle of the Egyptians were smitten with a murrain and died, but not one of the cattle of the Israelites suffered. Still the heart of Pharaoh was hardened, and he did not let the people go (Ex. 9:1-7).

Nearly all of the plagues were directed against particular Egyptian gods. Since the Apis bull was sacred to the Egyptian creator-god Ptah of Memphis, this plague of murrain of beasts particularly showed the superiority of Jehovah over the gods of Egypt.

f. *The Plague of Boils and Blains.* — From the cattle, the hand of God was extended to their own persons. Moses and Aaron were commanded to take ashes of the furnace, and to "sprinkle it toward the heaven in the sight of Pharaoh." It was to become "small dust" throughout Egypt, and "be a boil breaking forth (with) blains upon man, and upon beast." This accordingly came to pass. The plague seems to have been the black leprosy, a fearful kind of elephantiasis, which was long remembered as "the botch of Egypt" (Deut. 28:27,35; Comp. Job 2:7). This also was a terrible infliction on their religious purity, and its severity prevented the magicians from appearing in the presence of Moses. Still Pharaoh's heart was hardened, as Jehovah had said to Moses (Ex. 9:8-12).

g. *The Plague of Hail.* [1] — The first six plagues had been attended with much suffering and humiliation, and some loss; but they had not yet touched the lives of the Egyptians, or their means of subsistence. But now a solemn message was sent to Pharaoh and his people, that they should be smitten with pestilence and cut off from the earth. First of all, they were threatened with a storm of hail. "Behold to-morrow about this time, I will cause it to rain a very grievous hail, such as hath not been in Egypt since the foundation thereof even until now" (Ex. 9:18). Pharaoh was then told to collect his cattle and men into shelter, for that every thing should die upon which the hail descended. Some of the king's servants heeded the warning now given, and brought in their cattle from the field. On the rest there burst a terrific storm of hail, thunder and "fire running along

---

1. Hail and even rain are rare occurrences in Egypt. This intensified the supernatural appearance of this disaster to the Egyptians.

upon the ground," such as had never been seen in Egypt. Men and beast were killed, plants were destroyed and vines, figs and other trees broken to pieces (Ps. 105:33). Of the crops, the barley and flax which were fully formed were destroyed, but the wheat and rye (or spelt) were spared, for they were not yet grown up; mercy was still mingled with the judgment. This distinction, which could only have been made by one familiar with Egypt, marks the season of the events. Barley, one of the most important crops, alike in ancient and modern Egypt, comes to maturity in March, and flax at the same time, while wheat and spelt are ripe in April. Both harvests are a month or six weeks earlier than in Palestine.

Pharaoh, more moved than he had yet been, renewed his prayers and promises; and Moses, without concealing his knowledge of the result, consented to prove to him once more that "the earth is Jehovah's." The storm ceased at his prayer, and Pharaoh only hardened his heart the more (Ex. 9:13-34).

h. *The Plague of Locusts* (Ex. 10:1-20). — The herbage which the storm had spared was now given up to a terrible destroyer. After a fresh warning,

> *"The potent rod of Amram's son, in Egypt's evil day,*
> *Waved round her coasts, called up a pitchy cloud*
> *Of locusts, warping on the eastern wind,*
> *That o'er the realm of impious Pharaoh hung*
> *Like night, and darkened all the land of Nile."*

Approaching thus, the swarm alights upon fields green with the young blades of corn; its surface is blackened with their bodies, and in a few minutes it is left black, for the soil is as bare as if burnt with fire. Whatever leaves and fruit the hail had left on the trees were likewise devoured; and the houses swarmed with the hideous destroyers. No plague could have been more impressive in the East, where the ravages of locusts are so dreadful that they are chosen as the fit symbol of a destroying conqueror.[1] The very threat had urged Pharaoh's courtiers to remonstrance (Ex. 10:7), and he had offered to let the men only depart, but he had refused to yield more, and had driven Moses and Aaron from his presence. Now he recalled them in haste, and asked them to forgive his sin "only this once," and to

---

1. In the present day locusts suddenly appear in the cultivated land, coming from the desert in a column of great length. They fly rapidly across the country, darkening the air with their compact ranks, which are undisturbed by the constant attack of kites, crows and vultures, and making a strange whizzing sound like that of fire, or many distant wheels. Where they alight they devour every green thing, even stripping the trees of their leaves. (Comp. Joel 2:1-10).

entreat God to take away "this death only." A strong west wind removed the locusts as an east wind had brought them; but their removal left his heart harder than ever.

i.-j. *The Plague of Darkness* and the *Prediction* of the *Death of the First-born* (Ex. 10:21-29; 11). — The ninth plague was a fearful prelude to the last. For three days there was thick darkness over the sunny land of Egypt, "even darkness which might be felt"; while "all the children of Israel had light in their dwellings."[1] Unable to see each other, or to move about, the Egyptians had still this one last opportunity for repentance; but Pharaoh would only let the people go if they left their flocks and herds behind. With threats he forbade Moses to see his face again; and Moses sealed this rejection of the day of grace with the words: "Thou hast spoken well, I will see thy face again no more."

The fulfillment of this threat is obscured, in our version, by the division of chapters 10 and 11, and by the want of the pluperfect in 11:1: "The Lord *had said* unto Moses." The interview, which thus appears to end with the tenth chapter, is continued at 11:4. Moses ends by announcing the final judgment, which had been the one great penalty threatened from the beginning, for the midnight of this same day; and then "he went out from Pharaoh in a great anger" (Ex. 11:4-8; Comp. 4:21-23). The rest of the chapter 11 is a recapitulation of the result of the whole contest, nearly in the same words in which it had been described by God to Moses, when He gave him his mission (Comp. Ex. 11:1-3,9,10, with 3:19-22).

9. *Institution of the Passover.* The contest was now over. The doom of Pharaoh and of his people, who had oppressed the children of God, was now certain. Their own first-born sons would be slain by God. For the remainder of the third day of darkness, they sat awaiting the terrible stroke which was to fall on them at midnight. Meanwhile the Israelites, in the light of favored Goshen, were preparing for the night in the way prescribed by God. Now was instituted the great observance of the Mosaical dispensation, the FEAST OF THE PASSOVER.

The primary purpose of this festival was to commemorate Jehovah's "passing over" the houses of the Israelites when he "passed through" the land of Egypt to slay the first-born in every house (Ex. 12:11-12). But just as the history of Israel was typical

---

1. The sun-god *Ra* was the national god of Egypt. The plague of darkness was an assault on one of Egypt's principal deities.

of the whole pilgrimage of man, and as their rescue from Egypt answers to that crisis in the life of God's redeemed people, at which they are ransomed by the blood of the atonement from the penalty of sin, to which they also are subject, so we trace this wider and higher meaning in every feature of the institution.

The day, reckoned from sunset to sunset, in the night of which the first-born of Egypt were slain and the Israelites departed, was the fourteenth of the Jewish month *Nisan* or *Abib* (March to April), which began about the time of the vernal equinox, and which was now made the *first month* of the *ecclesiastical year*.[1] This was the great day of the feast, when the paschal supper was eaten. But the preparations had already been made by the command of God (Ex. 12:1-27). On the tenth day of the month, each household had chosen a yearling lamb (or kid, for either might be used) (Ex. 12:5), without blemish. This "Paschal Lamb" was set apart till the evening which began the fourteenth day, and was killed as a sacrifice (Ex. 12:27) at that moment in every family of Israel. But before it was eaten, its blood was sprinkled with a bunch of hyssop on the lintel and door-posts of the house: the divinely-appointed sign, that Jehovah might *pass over* that house, when He passed through the land to destroy the Egyptians (Ex. 12:7,12,13, 22-23). Thus guarded, and forbidden to go out of doors till the morning, the families of Israel ate the lamb, roasted and not boiled, with unleavened bread and bitter herbs. The bones were not suffered to be broken, but they must be consumed by fire in the morning, with any of the flesh that was left uneaten. The people were to eat in haste, and equipped for their coming journey. For seven days after the feast, from the fourteenth to the twenty-first, they were to eat only unleavened bread, and to have no leaven in their houses, under penalty of death. The fourteenth and twenty-first were to be kept with a holy convocation and Sabbatic rest. The Passover was to be kept to Jehovah throughout their generations, "a feast by an ordinance forever" (Ex. 12:14). No stranger might share the feast, unless he were first circumcised; but strangers were bound to observe the days of unleavened bread (Ex. 12:18-20, 43-49). To mark more solemnly the perpetual nature and vast importance of the feast, fathers were especially enjoined to instruct their children in its meaning through all future time (Ex. 12:25-27).

10. *Death of the Firstborn of Egypt – Exodus of the Israelites.* As the

---

1. The civil year began, like that of the Egyptians, about the autumnal equinox, with the month *Tishri.*

Passover was killed at sunset, we may suppose that the Israelites had finished the paschal supper, and were awaiting, in awful suspense, the next great event, when the midnight cry of anguish arose through all the land of Egypt (Ex. 12:29). At that moment Jehovah slew the first-born in every house, from the king to the captive; and by smiting also all the first-born of cattle, He "executed judgment on all the gods of Egypt" (Ex. 12:12).

The hardened heart of Pharaoh was broken by the stroke; and all his people joined with him to hurry the Israelites away. The Egyptians willingly gave them the jewels of silver and gold and the raiment, which they asked for by the command of Moses; and so "they spoiled the Egyptians."[1] They had not even time to prepare food, and only took the dough before it was leavened, in their kneading-troughs bound up in their clothes upon their shoulders, and baked unleavened cakes at their first halt (Ex. 12:34-35). But amid all this haste, some military order of march was preserved (Ex. 13:18), and Moses forgot not to carry away the bones of Joseph. The host numbered 600,000 men on foot, besides children (Ex. 12:37), from which the total of souls is estimated at not less than 2,500,000 (Comp. Num. 1:45; 11:21). But they were accompanied by "a mixed multitude," or great rabble, composed probably of Egyptians of the lowest caste, who proved a source of disorder.[2] Their march was guided by Jehovah himself, who, from its commencement to their entrance into Canaan, displayed His banner, the *Shekinah*, in their van: "Jehovah went before them by day in a pillar of a cloud, to lead them the way; and by night in a pillar of fire, to give them light; to go by day and night" (Ex. 13:21-22).

This Exodus, or departure of the Israelites from Egypt, closed the 430 years of their pilgrimage. Having learned the discipline of God's chosen family, and having been welded by the hammer of affliction into a nation, they were now called forth, under the prophet of Jehovah, alike from the bondage and the sensual pleasures of Egypt, to receive the laws of their new state amid the awful solitudes of Sinai. Egypt had been their home for many years, during which "the Israelites to all outward appearances became Egyptians. . . . The shepherds who wandered over the

---

1. The common objection to the morality of this proceeding is only founded on the word "borrow" (v. 22), which should be "ask." There was no promise or intention of repayment. The jewels were *given* for *favor* (v. 21), as well as fear; and they were slight recompense for all of which the Egyptians had robbed the Israelites during a century of bondage.

2. Num. 11:4. It would seem, from Deut. 29, that these people settled down into the condition of slaves to the Hebrews: "Thy stranger that is in thy camp, from the hewer of thy wood to the drawer of thy water."

pastures of Goshen were as truly Egyptian Bedouins as those who of old fed their flocks around the Pyramids, or who now, since the period of the Mohammedan conquest, have spread through the whole country. . . . Egypt is the background of the whole history of the Israelites, the prelude to Sinai and Palestine. . . . Even in the New Testament the connection is not wholly severed; and the Evangelist emphatically plants in the first page of the Gospel history the prophetical text, which might well stand as the inscription over the entrance to the Old Dispensation, OUT OF EGYPT HAVE I CALLED MY SON" (Matt. 2:15).

Hebrew Calendar

MONTH	OUR MONTH	FESTIVALS	SEASON
1. Abib or Nisan Ex. 23:15; Neh. 2:1	Mar./Apr.	14. Passover 15-21. Feast of Unleavened Bread	Latter rains. Jordan in flood. Barley ripe in lowlands.
2. Ziv or Iyar I Ki. 6:1, 37	Apr./May	14. Passover for those who could not keep regular one. Num. 9:10-11	Early figs. Barley harvest in hill country.
3. Sivan Esth. 8, 9	May/June	6. Feast of Weeks	Wheat harvest.
4. Tammuz	June/July		Dry season from late April to early Oct. First ripe grapes.
5. Ab	July/Aug.		Olives in the lowlands
6. Elul Neh. 6:15	Aug./Sept.		Grape gathering. Summer figs.
7. Ethanim or Tishri I Ki. 8:2	Sept./Oct.	1. Feast of Trumpets 10. Day of Atonement 15-22 Feast of Ingathering or Tabernacles	Pomegranates ripe. Former or early rains begin.
8. Bul or Marcheshvan I Ki. 6:38	Oct./Nov.		Olives gathered in northern Galilee. Planting time for barley and wheat.
9. Chisleu Zech. 7:1	Nov./Dec.	25. Feast of Dedication	
10. Tebeth Esth. 2:16	Dec./Jan.		
11. Shebat Zech. 1:7	Jan./Feb.		
12. Adar Esth. 3:7	Feb./Mar.	14-15. Feast of Purim	Oranges and lemons ripe in lowlands. Almond trees blossom.

11. Each month (new moon) began with the blowing of trumpets and offering of sacrifices (Numbers 28:11; 10:10; Psalm 81:3).

Three Periods of Moses' Life

1. First 40 years — In Egypt (as a prince)
2. Second 40 years — In Midian (as a shepherd)
3. Third 40 years — Leading Israel in the Wilderness

Hebrew Weights and Measures

Weights (Often used as monetary units)

Talent (Ex. 38:25; 60 minehs) . . . . .About 75 pounds
  (A talent of gold would be worth about $400,000,
      and a talent of silver about $2,000.)
Mineh (or maneh) (I Kings 10:17; 50 shekels) . . . . .20 oz.
Shekel (2 bekas) . . . . .4 oz.
Beka (Half-shekel; Ex. 38:26)
Gerah (1/20 shekel; Lev. 27:25; Num. 3:47; 18:16)

Liquid Measure

Log (Lev. 14:10) . . . . .Approx. pint
Kab (4 logs) . . . . .2 qts.
Hin (12 logs; Ex. 20:24) . . . . .1 gal.
Ephah or bath (Ezek. 45:10) . . . . .6 gal.
Homer or cor (Ezek. 45:14) . . . . .60 gal.
  (10 omers in an ephah.)

Dry Measure

Kab (II Kings 6:25) . . . . .2 pints plus
Omer (Ex. 16:16) . . . . .Approx. ½ gal.
Seah (I Kings 18:32) . . . . .Slightly less than a peck
Ephah (Ex. 16:36) . . . . .Approx. ³/⅔ bushel
  (10 omers in an ephah.)
Homer or cor . . . . .6¼ bushels
  (A cubit is approximately 1½ feet.)

Questions Over Section II
The Hebrews in Egypt

1. List the 12 sons of Jacob (Ex. 1:2-6).
2. How many descendants of Jacob came into Egypt (1:5)?
3. How greatly did the children of Israel multiply (1:7)?

4. Why did the new king oppress Israel (1:8-10)?
5. What two store-cities did Israel build (1:11)?
6. What type of slave work did Israel do (1:14)?
7. Name the two Egyptian midwives (1:15).
8. Why did not the midwives kill the Israelite babies (1:17)?
9. What commandment did the king make about the Hebrew babies (1:22)?
10. Of what tribe was Moses (2:1)?
11. How long was the baby Moses hid (2:2)?
12. Who raised Moses (2:8-9)?
13. Who adopted Moses (2:10)?
14. How much education did Moses receive (Acts 7:22)?
15. Which did Moses choose when he became a man — Egypt or Israel (Heb. 11:26)?
16. Why did Moses flee Egypt (Ex. 2:11-15)?
17. To what land did he flee (2:15)?
18. How many daughters did Reuel have (2:16)?
19. Who became Moses' wife (2:21)?
20. Who were Moses' sons (2:22; 18:3-4)?
21. How long did Moses live in Midian (Acts 7:30)?
22. Near what mountain did Moses see the burning bush (Ex. 3:1)?
23. Who spoke to Moses from the bush (3:2, 6)?
24. What was Moses sent to do (3:10)?
25. What four excuses did Moses give to God (3:11,13: 4:1,10)?
26. What did God say his name was (3:14; Cf. John 8:58)?
27. To whom was Moses to go first (3:16-17)?
28. What did God foreknow about Pharaoh's reaction to Israel's proposed departure (3:19)?
29. Explain, "Ye shall not go empty" (Ex. 3:21).
30. What three miracles was Moses empowered to perform (4:3,6,9)?
31. What made God angry with Moses (4:10-14)?
32. Who was to be the spokesman for Moses (4:14)?
33. What threat was to be made about Pharaoh's firstborn (4:22-23)?
34. Why did God try to slay Moses (perhaps by a deadly plague) (4:24-26)?
35. Where was Zipporah sent as Moses went into Egypt (4:26; 18:2)?
36. How did the Israelites accept Moses and Aaron (4:29-31)?

37. With what question did Pharaoh respond to Moses' request that he let Israel go (5:2)?
38. What did Moses ask permission for the Hebrews to do (5:3)?
39. Why did Pharaoh increase the work loads of the Israelites (5:5-9)?
40. Why did the Israelites become displeased with Moses (5:19-21)?
41. By what name had God been known to Abraham? What name was not made known to him (6:3)?
42. Name the generations from Levi to Moses (6:16-20).
43. Who was Moses' mother (6:20)?
44. What relation was Korah to Moses (6:16-21)?
45. Who were Aaron's four sons (6:23)?
46. Why did God harden Pharaoh's heart (7:3-5)?
47. Ages of Moses and Aaron when they led Israel out of Egypt (7:7)?
48. What miracle of Moses did Pharaoh's magicians (apparently) duplicate (7:10-11; Cf. II Tim. 3:8)?
49. List the ten plagues in order.
50. How many of the plagues did Pharaoh's magicians duplicate?
51. What four compromise offers did Pharaoh make to Moses during the plagues (8:25,28; 10:11,24)?
52. Why had God made Pharaoh to be king (9:14-16)?
53. What did Pharaoh's servants urge him to do (10:7)?
54. What did Pharaoh threaten Moses with after the ninth plague (10:28)?
55. How safe were the Israelites to be during the last plague (11:7)?
56. What feast marked the beginning of months, the start of the new year (Ex. 12:2,11)?
57. When was the Passover lamb selected? When slain and eaten (12:3,6)?
58. What was to be done with the blood of the lamb (12:7)?
59. What were the Israelites to be ready to do on the night of the Passover (12:11)?
60. On what condition would Jehovah pass over any house (12:13)?
61. What period (or feast) followed the Passover for a week (12:15-20)?
62. How often was the Passover to be observed (12:24-27)?
63. What happened at midnight in Egypt (12:29)?

64. What did the Israelites ask the Egyptians for when they departed (12:35-36)?
65. Name the months of the Hebrew calendar.
66. How much is a talent? What was its value in gold and in silver?

Period V
Period of Wandering

From the Exodus from Egypt, to Entry into Canaan (Ex. 12:37-Ch. 40; Leviticus, Numbers, Deuteronomy)

Section I
From Egypt to Sinai

1. The Sinaitic peninsula. 2. General view of the journey from Egypt to Canaan — Its three divisions: a. From Egypt to Sinai — b. From Sinai to the borders of Canaan — c. The wandering in the wilderness and final march to Canaan. 3. From Egypt to the Red Sea — Point of departure — Rameses — Succoth — Etham — Pihahiroth. 4. Crossing the Red Sea. 5. Wilderness of Shur — Thirst — Marah — Elim — Encampment by the Red Sea. 6. Wilderness of Sin — Hunger — The Manna — The Sabbath. 7. Dophka, Alush and Rephidim — The water from the rock. 8. The battle with Amalek — Jehovah-Nissi — Doom of Amalek. 9. Visit of Jethro — Appointment of assistant judges.

1. *The Sinaitic Peninsula*

a. The Sinaitic peninsula is a large triangular desert area, bordered on the north by the Mediterranean Sea, on the west by the Gulf of Suez and on the east by the Gulf of Akabah and the Arabah. It is of interest to Old Testament history because

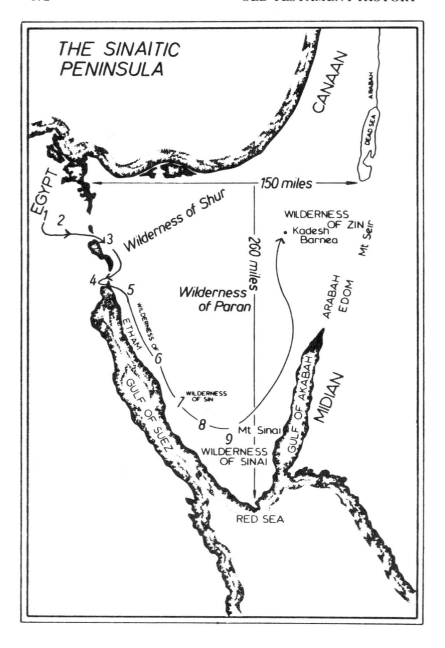

the children of Israel wandered there for forty years after leaving Egypt under the leadership of Moses.

b. Dimensions — 150 miles wide across the north; 260 miles deep from north to south.

c. Inhabitants — Israel's enemy, the *Amalekites,* wandered as nomads between Mt. Sinai and Canaan.

d. The wildernesses (or deserts) of the Sinaitic peninsula.

  1. *Wilderness of Shur* — A sandy desert in the northwest.
  2. *Wilderness of Etham* — A southward extension of the wilderness of Shur along the Red Sea (Numbers 33:8; Exodus 15:22).
  3. *Wilderness of Paran* — A large stony desert in the central area. Sterile tableland of limestone, 2000 to 3000 feet above sea level. Rolling plains with a gravel surface. Springs of impure water in a few places.
  4. *Wilderness of Sin* — A small plain northwest of Mt. Sinai, between Elim and Sinai (Exodus 16:1).
  5. *Wilderness of Sinai* — A rugged mountainous wasteland around Mt. Sinai. Mountains up to 8000 feet high.
  6. *Wilderness of Zin* — A desert in the northeast. It included the Arabah and the area around Kadesh Barnea (Numbers 34:3; 20:1; 33:36; Deuteronomy 32:51; Joshua 15:1).

e. Locations in and around the Sinaitic peninsula.

  1. *Land of Midian* — East of the Gulf of Akabah.
  2. *The Arabah* — A continuation of the deep depression of the Jordan valley south of the Dead Sea to the Gulf of Akabah. The Jordan valley north of the Dead Sea is also called Arabah.
  3. *Edom* — The mountainous area *(Mt. Seir)* east of the Arabah inhabited by the descendants of Esau.
  4. *Kadesh-Barnea* — Center of the Israelites' wilderness wanderings for many years.
  5. The locations marked by numbers on a line are part of the stations in Israel's journey from Egypt to Canaan. (See chart on p. 175).

Questions on the Sinaitic Peninsula

1. What is the general shape of the Sinaitic peninsula.
2. What borders the Sinaitic peninsula on the north, west and east.
3. What are the dimensions of the Sinaitic peninsula?
4. What people inhabited the Sinaitic peninsula?

5. On a blank map of the Sinaitic peninsula locate the wildernesses of Shur, Etham, Sin, Paran, Sinai and Zin.

6. On the blank map locate Midian, the Arabah, Edom and Kadesh-Barnea.

2. *General view of the journey from Egypt to Canaan – Its three divisions: a. From Egypt to Sinai – b. From Sinai to borders of Canaan c. The wilderness wanderings and final march to Canaan.* The whole journey of the Israelites, from Egypt into the land of promise, may be divided into three distinct portions:

a. *The march out of Egypt to Mount Sinai,* there to worship Jehovah, as he had said to Moses (Ex. 3:12). This occupied six weeks, making, with the fourteen days before the Passover, two months (Ex. 19:1); and they were encamped before Sinai, receiving the divine laws, for the remaining ten months of the first ecclesiastical year (Comp. Ex. 12:2). The tabernacle was set up on the first day of the first month (Abib) of the second year (about April 1, 1445 B.C.); and its dedication occupied that month (Ex. 40:17). On the first day of the second month, Moses began to number the people (Num 1:1), and their encampment was broken up on the twentieth day of the second month of the second year, about May 20, 1445 (Num. 10:11).

b. *The march from Sinai to the borders of Canaan,* whence they were turned back for their refusal to enter the land. This distance, commonly eleven days' journey (Deut. 1:2), was divided by three chief halts (Num. 33:16-18). The first stage occupied three days (Num. 10:33), followed by a halt of at least a month (Num. 10:20). The next halt was for a week at least (Num. 12:15). After the third journey, there was a period of forty days, during which the spies were searching the land (Num. 13:25); and they returned with ripe grapes and other fruits (Num. 13:24). All these indications bring us to the season of the Feast of Tabernacles, just six months after the Passover (Oct. 1445 B.C.).

c. *The wandering in the wilderness, and entrance into Canaan.* This is often vaguely spoken of as a period of forty years, but in the proper sense, the *wanderings* occupied thirty-seven and a half years. The people came again to Kadesh, whence they had been turned back, in the first month of the fortieth year (Num. 20:1). Advancing thence, they overthrew the kings Sihon and Og, and spoiled the Midianites; and reached the plains of Moab, on the east of Jordan, opposite to Jericho, by the end of

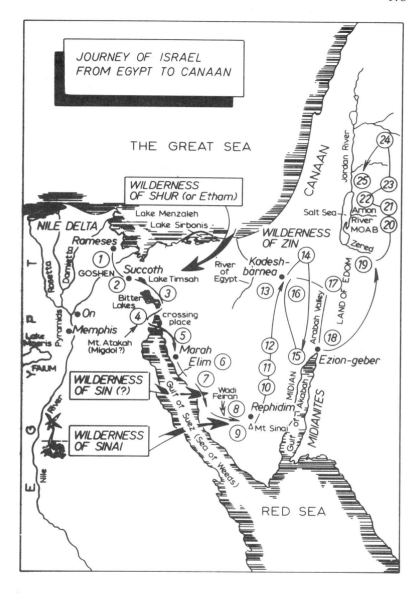

JOURNEY OF ISRAEL
FROM EGYPT TO CANAAN

THE GREAT SEA

WILDERNESS
OF SHUR (or Etham)

Lake Menzaleh
Lake Sirbonis

NILE DELTA

CANAAN

Jordan River

Salt Sea

WILDERNESS
OF ZIN

Rameses

GOSHEN

Succoth
Lake Timsah

River of
Egypt

Kadesh-
barnea

Amnon
River
MOAB

Zered

On

Memphis

Bitter
Lakes

crossing
place

Mt. Atakah
(Migdol?)

Marah
Elim

WILDERNESS
OF SIN (?)

Wadi
Feiran

Rephidim

WILDERNESS
OF SINAI

Mt Sinai

Ezion-geber

Araban Valley

LAND OF EDOM

MIDIAN

Gulf of Akabah

Gulf of Suez (Sea of Weeds)

MIDIANITES

RED SEA

Nile

FAIUM

Lake
Moeris

Pyramids

Rosetta

Damietta

Nile River

EGYPT

the tenth month, early in January, 1406 B.C. (Deut. 1:3). The
rest of the year was occupied by the final exhortations and
death of Moses (Book of Deut.). We are not told the exact date
of the passage of the Jordan; but the harvest-time identifies it
with the season of the Passover (Joshua 3:15); and thus the
cycle of forty years is completed, from the beginning of Abib,
to the same date of 1406.

Places and Events in Israel's Journey
From Egypt to Canaan (condensed list)

1. *Rameses*
   a. Starting point (Exodus 12:37).
2. *Succoth*
3. *Etham*
   a. Pillar of cloud and fire (Exodus 13:21-22).
4. *Camp facing Pihahiroth*
   a. Pursuit by Egyptians.
   b. Crossing Red Sea.
5. *Marah*
   a. Bitter water made sweet (Exodus 15:22-26).
6. *Elim*
   a. Twelve springs and 70 palm trees (Exodus 15:27).
7. *Wilderness of Sin*
   a. Quails and manna provided (Exodus 16:1-36).
8. *Rephidim*
   a. Water from the rock (Exodus 17:1-7).
   b. Attack by Amalek (Exodus 17:8-16).
   c. Jethro meets Moses (Exodus 18:1-12).
   d. Judges appointed (Exodus 18:13-27).
9. *Mt. Sinai*
   a. The law given. (By this means Israel became a nation, a
      theocracy.)
   b. Idolatry of the people (Exodus 32-34).
   c. Construction of the tabernacle (Exodus 35-40).
   d. Consecration of the priests (Leviticus 8-9).
   e. Death of Nadab and Abihu (Leviticus 10:1-7).
   f. A blasphemer stoned (Leviticus 24:10-23).
   g. The first census taken (Numbers 1).
   h. The Passover kept (Numbers 9).
10. *Taberah*
    a. Murmurers burnt (Numbers 11:1-3).

11. *Kibroth-hattaavah*
    a. Lust for flesh and food; quails given (Numbers 11:4-34).
    b. Seventy elders appointed.
    c. Eldad and Medad prophesy.
12. *Hazeroth*
    a. Miriam gets leprosy for criticizing (Numbers 11:35-12:15).
13. *Kadesh-barnea*
    a. Expedition of twelve spies (Numbers 13:1-14:38).
    b. Futile invasion of Canaan (Numbers 14:39-45).
    c. Korah's rebellion (Numbers 16).
    d. Budding of Aaron's rod (Numbers 17).
       "Ye abode many days at Kadesh" (Deuteronomy 1:46).
14. *Seventeen stations* (Numbers 33:18-34). No events are associated with these places. All are unknown except Moseroth, which is the same as Moserah in Deuteronomy 10:6. This was near Mt. Hor, where Aaron later died.
15. *Ezion-geber* (Numbers 35:35).
16. *Kadesh-barnea* (Numbers 33:36; 20:1-21). (This was the second sojourn around Kadesh, and was in the 39th or 40th year of wandering. See Numbers 33:37-38.)
    a. Death of Miriam (Numbers 20:1).
    b. Water from the rock (Numbers 20:2-13).
    c. Passage through Edom refused (Numbers 20:14-21).
17. *Mt. Hor* (Moserah)
    a. Death of Aaron (Numbers 20:22-29; Deut. 10:6).
    b. Attack by King of Arad (Numbers 21:1-3).
18. *Ezion-gerber* and *Elath*
    a. Fiery serpents sent (Numbers 21:4-9; Deuteronomy 2:8).
19. *Valley of Zered*
    a. Camps were set up in the valley itself and at nearby locations (Numbers 21:10-12).
20. *Arnon River* (Numbers 21:13-15). (Note that Israel went around the land of Moab. Judges 11:18)
21. *Beer*
    a. Water provided from a well (Numbers 21:16-19).
22. *Pisgah*
    a. View into promised land (Numbers 21:20).
23. *Jahaz*
    a. Defeat of Sihon, king of Amorites (Numbers 21:21-32).
24. *Edrei*
    a. Defeat of Og, king of Bashan (Numbers 21:33-35).

25. *Plains of Moab*
   a. Balaam's prophecies (Numbers 22-24).
   b. The sin of Peor (Numbers 25).
   c. The second census (Numbers 26).
   d. Midianites destroyed (Numbers 31).
   e. Messages of Deuteronomy.
   f. Death of Moses.

Complete List of the Stations in Israel's Journey to Canaan

(The places enumerated on the map of Israel's journey are a condensed list adapted from this complete list. Many of these places are not now identifiable geographically, nor do they have events associated with them. Hence our memory list is condensed and simplified.)

1. Rameses (Ex. 12:37; Num. 33:3). 2. Succoth (Ex. 12:37; Num. 33:5). 3. Etham (Ex. 13:20; Num. 33:6). 4. Pihahiroth (Ex. 14:2; Num. 33:7). 5. Red Sea. 6. Desert of Shur or of Etham (Ex. 15:22; Num. 33:8). 7. Marah (Ex. 15:23; Num. 33:8). 8. Elim (Ex. 15:27; Num. 33:9). 9. By Red Sea (Num. 33:10). 10. Desert of Sin (Ex. 16:1; Num. 33:11). 11. Dophkah (Num. 33:12). 12. Alush (Num. 33:13). 13. Rephidim (Ex. 17:1; Num. 33:14). 14. Sinai (Ex. 19:1; Num. 33:15). 15. Taberah (Num. 11:3; Deut. 9:22). 16. Kibroth-hattaavah (Num. 11:34; 33:16; Deut. 99:22). 17. Hazeroth (Num. 11:35; 33:17). 18. Mt. of the Amorites (Deut. 1:19). 19. Kadesh-barnea (Num. 13:26; Deut. 1:19. See King James Vers.). 20. Rithmah. 21. Rimmon-parez. 22. Libnah. 23. Rissah. 24. Kehelathah. 25. Mount Shapher. 26. Haradah. 27. Makheloth. 28. Tahath. 29. Tarah. 30. Mithcah. 31. Hashmonah. 32. Moseroth. 33. Benejaakan. 34. Hor-hagidgad. 35. Jotbathhah. 36. Ebronah (Places 20-36 listed in Num. 33:18-34). 37. Ezion-geber (Num. 33:35). 38. Kadesh-barnea (Num. 20:1; 33:36). 39. Beeroth Benejaakan (Wells of the sons of Jaakan (Deut. 10:6). 40. Moserah (Mt. Hor. Num. 20:22; 33:37; Deut. 10:6). 41. Gudgodah (Deut. 10:7). 42. Jotbath (Deut. 10:7). 43. Ezion-geber (Num. 21:4; Deut. 2:8). 44. Elath (Deut. 2:8). 45. Zalmonah (Num. 33:41). 46. Punon (Num. 33:42). 47. Oboth (Num. 21:10; 33:43). 48. Ije-abarim (Num. 21:11; 33:44). 49. Brook Zered (Num. 21:12; Deut. 2:13). 50. River Arnon (Num. 21:13; Deut. 2:24). 51. Dibon-gad (Num. 33:45). 52. Almon-diblathaim (Num. 33:46). 53. Beer (Num. 21:16). 54. Mattanah (Num. 21:18). 55. Nahaliel (Num. 21:19). 56. Bamoth (Num. 21:19). 57. Abarim, Nebo or Pisgah (Num. 21:20; 33:47). 58. Plain of Moab or Jordan (Num. 22:1; 33:48).

3. *From Egypt to Red Sea – Rameses – Succoth – Etham – Pihahiroth*
Had the object been to lead them by the shortest route out of
Egypt into Canaan, it might have been accomplished in a few
days' journey along the shore of the Mediterranean. But they
were not thus to evade the moral discipline of the wilderness.
Their first destination was fixed for "the mount of God";
furthermore they were quite unprepared to meet the armies of
the Philistines, and so "God led the people about through the way
of the wilderness of the Red Sea" (Ex. 14:2-3).

The exact route of Israel's departure is difficult to determine
accurately. It is evident that they were gathered together in
Goshen before their departure; and they are expressly said to
have started from RAAMSES (Ex. 12:37). If the city of Raamses is
meant, this is believed to be the same as Tanis, or Zoan; perhaps,
however, the district of Raamses (Gen. 47:11) is meant, and if so
the Israelites need not have been as far north as Tanis. From the
starting point the general direction was south and a little east.

As to further details, the name of the first stopping place,
SUCCOTH, affords no help, as it only means *booths*. The next place
ETHAM, which is associated with God's leading by the pillar of
cloud and fire (Ex. 13:20-22), seems to have been some place near
the north end of the Gulf of Suez. Here God directed Israel to
make a turn and encamp before PIHAHIROTH, an unknown place
west of the Gulf of Suez, between Migdol (a *tower*) and the Red Sea
(Ex. 14:1-2).

This incomprehensible movement led Pharaoh to exclaim,
"They are entangled in the wilderness, the sea hath shut them in."
And well might he say so, if their position was enclosed between
the sea on their east, the *Jebel Atakah,* which borders the north side
of the *Wady et-Tih,* on their south and west, and the wilderness in
their rear, with the pursuing army pressing on to cut off their
retreat. Add to this that the sea, where they encamped by it, must
have been narrow enough for the host to pass over in a single
night, and yet broad enough to receive the whole army of
Pharaoh; and lastly, that the opposite bank must not be rocky or
precipitous. These conditions seem to limit the area of the
crossing to neighborhood of Suez.

4. *Crossing the Red Sea.* [1] The great miracle itself, by which a way
was cloven for the people through the sea, was a proof to them, to
the Egyptians, and to all the neighboring nations, that the hand of

---

1. The name *Red Sea (Yam Suph)* should be rendered "Reed Sea" or "Marsh Sea." However, this does not
prove that the Israelites crossed at a very shallow marshy location where no miracle was required for crossing.
The name "Reed Sea" is applied to the entire sea, not just the tip of the Gulf of Suez. Furthermore, no reeds
grow in the Red Sea.

Jehovah was with them, leading them by His own way, and ready to deliver them in every strait through all their future course. In this light it is celebrated in that sublime hymn of triumph, which furnishes the earliest example of responsive choral music (Ex. 15). In this light it is looked back upon by the sacred writers in every age, as the great miracle which inaugurated their history as a nation.

The King of Egypt and his servants, with hearts hardened even against the lesson taught by the death of the first-born, repented of letting their slaves depart (Ex. 15:4,5). With six hundred chosen chariots, and all his military array, he pursued and overtook them at Pi-hahiroth. The frightened people began to raise the cry, with which they so often assailed Moses, "Better for us to serve the Egyptians than that we should die in the wilderness (Ex. 14:10-12). But the way was made clear by faith and obedience. "Fear ye not, stand still, and see the salvation of Jehovah . . . He shall fight for you, and ye shall hold your peace," was the answer of Moses to the people, while God's word to him was that which generally opens a way out of danger and distress: — "Speak unto the children of Israel, that *they go forward.*" At the signal of the uplifted rod of Moses, a strong east wind blew all that night, and divided the waters as a wall on the right hand and on the left, while the children of Israel went into the midst of the sea on dry land. The guiding pillar of fire (with the angel of Jehovah himself) moved from their van into the rear, casting its beams along their column, but creating behind them a darkness amid which the host of Pharaoh went after them into the bed of the sea. But, at the morning watch, Jehovah looked out of the pillar of fire and cloud, and troubled the Egyptians. Panic-stricken, they sought to flee; but their chariot-wheels were broken: the host of Israel had now reached the bank: the rod of Moses waved again over the gulf: "and the sea returned to his strength when the morning appeared; and the Egyptians fled against it"; but not one of them was left alive. "And the people feared Jehovah, and believed his servant Moses." The waters of the Red Sea were thenceforth a moral, as well as a physical gulf between them and Egypt. Its passage initiated a new dispensation: "they were all *baptized to Moses* in the cloud and in the sea" (I Cor. 10:2).

5. *Wilderness of Shur – Thirst – Marah – Elim – Encampment by the Red Sea.* Their route now lay southward down the east side of the *Gulf of Suez,* and at first along the shore. They marched for three days through the wilderness of SHUR or ETHAM, on the south-west

margin of the great desert of Paran where they found no water (Ex. 15:22; Num. 33:8). The tract is still proverbial for its storms of wind and sand. It is a part of the belt of gravel which surrounds the mountains of the peninsula, and is crossed by several *wadys,* whose sides are fringed with tamarisks, acacias and a few palm trees. Near one of these, the *Wady el'-Amarah,* is a spring called *Ain Awarah,* not only in the position of MARAH, but with the *bitter* taste which gave it the name. The people, tormented with thirst, murmured against Moses, who, at the command of God, cast a certain tree into the waters which made them sweet. This was the first great trial of their patience; and God, who had healed the waters, promised to deliver them from all the diseases of Egypt if they would obey Him, and confirmed the promise by the name of "Jehovah the Healer" (Ex. 15:26).

They must have been cheered at reaching the oasis of Elim, now called the *Wady Gharandel,* whose twelve wells and seventy palm-trees mark it as one of the *wadys* that break the desert. After passing the *Wady Taiyibeh,* the route descends through a defile on to a beautiful pebbly beach, where Dean Stanley places the ENCAMPMENT BY THE RED SEA, which is mentioned in *Numbers* (33:10) next to Elim, but is omitted in *Exodus.*

6. *Wilderness of Sin – Hunger – The Manna – The Sabbath.* Moving southward from this point, they entered the WILDERNESS OF SIN[1] (probably the plain of *Murkhah*), which leads up from the shore to the entrance to the mountains of Sinai (Ex. 16:1). Here occurred their second great trial since leaving Egypt. Their unleavened bread was exhausted; and they began to murmur that they had better have died by the fleshpots of Egypt than have been led out to be killed with hunger in the wilderness. But God was teaching them to look to him for their "daily bread," which He now rained down from heaven in the form of *manna,* and continued the supply till they reached Canaan.[2] The truth was most emphatically enforced by the impossibility of gathering more or less than the prescribed portion of the manna, or of keeping it over the day (Ex. 16:17; II Cor. 8:13-15). But the manna was designed to teach them a deeper lesson. They had not only distrusted God's providence as to their food, but were regarding that food itself as the chief thing they were to live for; and so "God

---

1. This must be carefully distinguished not only from the *wilderness of Sinai,* but also from the *wilderness of Zin,* which lies north of the *Gulf of Akabah.*
2. The natural products of the Arabian deserts and other Oriental regions which bear the name of manna, have not the qualities or use ascribed to the manna of Scripture. The manna of Scripture must be regarded as wholly miraculous, and not in any respect a product of nature.

humbled them and suffered them to hunger, and fed them with a food unknown to them, that He might make them know that *man doth not live by bread alone,* but by *every word that proceedeth out of the mouth of Jehovah* doth man live" (Deut. 8:3). And so the manna was a type of Christ, the Word of God, who came down from heaven as the bread of life, to give life to all who believe in Him (John 6:15-59).

The rules laid down for the gathering of the manna gave occasion for instruction about the *Sabbath* day (Ex. 16:22-30). Contrary to general opinion, the Sabbath was not made known to humanity at creation (Gen. 2:3), but on Mt. Sinai in the time of Moses (Neh. 9:13-14). The first mention of it to men is in connection with the giving of the manna, shortly before Israel arrived at Mt. Sinai. The way it is introduced in this connection confirms that Israel was entirely unfamiliar with its observance. The Sabbath day was part of the covenant of the ten commandments (Ex. 34:28), which has been replaced by a new and better covenant mediated by Christ (Heb. 8:6-13). The Sabbath was only a shadow of things to come, but the body that cast the shadow is Christ (Col. 2:16-17).

7. *Dophka, Alush, Rephidim – The water from the rock.* From the plain of Murkah the valleys lead up into the recesses of Sinai, resembling the beds of rivers but without water, and separated by defiles which sometimes become staircases of rock. Such were no doubt the stations of Dophkah and Alush (Num. 33:12-13) and such are the *Wadys Shellal* and *Mukatteb.* From the latter the route passes into the long and winding *Wady Feiran,* with its groves of tamarisks and palms, overhung by the granite rocks of *Mount Serbal,* perhaps the Horeb of Scripture. This valley answers in every respect to Rephidim (the *plains*) (Ex. 17:1).

Here the cry for water burst forth into an angry rebellion against Moses; and God vouchsafed a miracle for a permanent supply during their abode in the wilderness of Sinai. Moses was commanded to go before the people, with the elders of Israel, and to smite the rock in Horeb, and water flowed forth out of it. The place was called Massah *(temptation),* and Meribah *(chiding* or *strife),* in memory of the rebellion by which the people tempted Jehovah and doubted His presence among them (Ex. 17:2-7). The spring thus opened seems to have formed a brook, which the Israelites used during their whole sojourn near Sinai (Deut. 9:21; Comp. Ps. 78:15-16; 105:41). Hence the rock is said to have *"Followed* them" by St. Paul, who makes it a type of Christ, the source of the spiritual water of life (I Cor. 10:4; Comp. John 4:14; 7:35; Isa. 55:1; Ezek. 47:1; Zech. 14:8). Lastly, it should be remembered that the miracle was repeated at a much later period in another part of the peninsula (Num. 20:1-13).

8. *The battle with Amalek – Jehovah-nissi – Doom of Amalek.* It was in Rephidim that the new-formed nation fought their first great battle. As yet they have seemed alone in the desert; but now an enemy comes against them, their kinsman AMALEK, a nomad tribe descended from Eliphaz, the son of Esau. The range of the Amalekites seem to have been at this time over the south of Palestine and all Arabia Petraea; so that they commanded the routes leading out of Egypt into Asia. Whether they regarded the Israelites as intruders, or whether for the sake of plunder, they seem first to have assaulted the rear of the column and cut off the infirm and stragglers before the great encounter in Rephidim. The battle lasted till sunset. The chosen warriors of Israel fought under JOSHUA, whose name is now first mentioned, while Moses stood on a hill with the rod of God outstretched in his hand. He was attended by his brother Aaron and by Hur, the husband of Miriam, who held up his hands when he became weary, for only while the rod was stretched out did Israel prevail. We see in this incident a lesson of the power of prayer: but its exact meaning seems to have been a sign of God's presence with His hosts, held forth as a *standard* over the battlefield; and this was taught by the name given to the altar of thanksgiving then set up, JEHOVAH-NISSI, *Jehovah is my Banner.*

For this treacherous attack the tribe of Amalek were henceforth doomed to execration and ultimate extinction (Ex. 17:14-16; Num. 24:20; I Sam. 15:2-7). A very interesting point in the narrative is the command of God to Moses, to write the whole transaction in a book; one of the passages in which we learn from the sacred writers themselves their authorship of the books that bear their names (Ex. 17:14; Comp. Ex. 34:37).

9. *Visit of Jethro – Appointment of assistant judges.* The visit of Jethro, the father-in-law of Moses, took place probably during the encampment at Rephidim. The Israelites being now near Midian, Jethro brought to Moses his wife and children, whom he had sent back into Midian, probably after the scene related in Exod. 4:24-26. Moses received Jethro with high honor, and recounted to him all that Jehovah had done for the people. The priest of Midian joyfully acknowledged the God of Israel, and offered sacrifices to Jehovah; and henceforth there was the

closest friendship between Israel and the Kenites, his descendants (I Sam. 15:6). Seeing Moses overburdened with judging the people, he advised him to organize an administration of justice by a gradation of rulers over tens, fifties, hundreds and thousands, and to reserve himself for the harder cases to lay them before God, as mediator for the people (Ex. 18:13-26). It would seem that, on Jethro's return to his own land (Ex. 18:27), he left behind him his son Hobab, who became the guide of the people from Sinai to the border of Canaan (Num. 10:29-30).

Questions Over Section I
From Egypt to Sinai

1. List the first nine places on the map of Israel's journey from Egypt to Canaan, and give at least one event at each place where events are indicated.
2. Who left Egypt with Israel (Ex. 12:38)?
3. How long had Israel dwelt in Egypt (12:40)?
4. What regulation was given about the bones of the passover lamb (Ex. 12:46; Cf. John 19:36)?
5. What people and animals were claimed by the Lord (13:2)?
6. What was the feast of unleavened bread to remind the people of (13:7-10)?
7. What was to be done with firstborn animals (13:2-13,16; Num. 18:15-17)?
8. Why did not God lead Israel into Canaan by the short way of the land of the Philistines (13:17)?
9. Whose bones were carried out of Egypt by Moses (13:19)?
10. Where did the pillar of cloud begin to lead Israel (13:20-21)?
11. Before what place did the Israelites camp by the Red Sea (14:2)?
12. Why did Pharaoh think Israel was trapped (14:3)?
13. Why did Pharaoh desire to keep Israel in Egypt (14:5)?
14. How many Egyptian chariots struck out after Israel (14:7)?
15. How did Israel react when they saw the Egyptians coming (14:10)?
16. What was Israel told to do to see the salvation of Jehovah (14:13)?
17. What separated Israel from Egypt at night (14:19-20)?
18. What cleared a path across the sea (14:21)?
19. What hindered the Egyptians as they tried to follow Israel (14:25)?
20. What was the fate of the Egyptians (14:28)?

21. How did the Israelites feel toward God and toward Moses after they crossed the Sea (14:31)?
22. Who sang a song after the deliverance (15:1)?
23. Who sang and danced and played music (15:20)?
24. Into what wilderness did Israel enter after crossing the sea (Ex. 15:22; Num. 33:8)?
25. Name the place where Israel found bitter water (15:23)?
26. How was the water sweetened (15:25)?
27. What would guarantee the health of the Israelites (15:26)?
28. What was found at Elim (15:27)?
29. What did Israel lack in the Wilderness of Sin (16:1-3)?
30. How many days was food provided for Israel each week (16:4-5)?
31. When was twice as much food to be gathered (16:5)?
32. What meat was given to Israel (16:13)?
33. What does the name *manna* mean (16:15)?
34. How much manna was gathered each day for each person? What happened to those who gathered more or less (16:16-18)?
35. On what day was no manna found (16:23-27)?
36. Where was a pot of manna to be kept as a memorial (16:32-34; Heb. 9:4)?
37. Where did Israel come and find no water (17:1)?
38. How was the water provided for Israel (17:6)?
39. What do the names *Massah* and *Meribah* mean? To what were they applied (17:7)?
40. What tribe attacked Israel? Where (17:8)?
41. Who held up Moses' arms? Why (17:10-12)?
42. Who led Israel's army in battle (17:10)?
43. What was written in a book about the attacking tribe (17:14)?
44. What does the name *Jehovah-nissi* mean (17:15)?
45. Whom did Jethro bring to Moses (18:1-5)?
46. What did Jethro conclude after hearing the report of Moses' deeds (18:11)?
47. How long was Moses occupied in judging the people (18:13)?
48. What did Jethro counsel Moses (18:17-22)?
49. In what month after the departure from Egypt did Israel arrive at Sinai (19:1)?

Section II
Giving of the Law
(Exodus 19-24, 32-34)

1. The Wilderness of Sinai — Encampment before the mount — Israel's covenant with Jehovah — Preparations. 2. God's descent on Sinai — The Ten Commandments — Other precepts given to Moses — The Angel Jehovah their guide — The law given by angels. 3. The covenant recorded and ratified by blood — The elders behold God's glory — Moses in the mount. 4. The gloden calf — Intercession of Moses — Tables of the law broken — Punishment — Fidelity of Levi — Self-sacrifice of Moses — God shows Moses his glory — Moses' second abode in the mount — The tables renewed — Moses' face shines. 5. Divine origin of the law. 6. The law a Theocratic Constitution. 7. Classifications within the law: a. Laws criminal; b. Laws religious, moral and ceremonial; c. Laws constitutional and political; d. Laws civil. 8. Righteousness not by the law.

1. *The Wilderness of Sinai – Encampment before the mount – Israel's covenant with Jehovah – Preparations.* The next stage brought the Israelites to the WILDERNESS OF SINAI on the first day of the third month (Sivan, *June),* and here they encamped before the mount (Ex. 19:1-2). The site of their camp has been identified, to a high degree of probability, with the *Wady er-Rahah* (the *enclosed plain)* in front of the magnificent cliffs of *Ras Safsafeh.* Never in the history of the world was such a scene beheld as that plain now presented! A whole nation was assembled alone with God. His hand had been seen and his voice heard at every step of their history up to this great crisis. He had called their progenitor Abraham from his father's house, and made with him the covenant, which had now reached its first great fulfillment. He had guided the family by wondrous ways till He brought them down to Egypt, where they grew into a nation under the discipline of affliction. Thence He had brought them forth with a mighty hand and an outstretched arm, proving that He was the only God, and they the people of His choice. He had severed them from all the nations of the earth, and had divided the very sea, to let them pass into this secret shrine of nature, whose awful grandeur

prepared their minds for the coming revelation. Thus far they only knew the token which God had given to Moses, "When thou hast brought forth the people out of Egypt, ye shall serve God upon this mountain." They had reached the place, and they waited in awful adoration for what was to follow.

There was a season of preparation before the great appearance of God on Sinai to give the law. First, Moses went up to God, whose voice called to him out of the mountain, telling him to remind the people of the wonders already wrought for them, and promising that, if they would obey God and keep His *covenant,* "then shall ye be a peculiar treasure unto me about all people (for all the earth is mine), and ye shall be unto me a kingdom of priests, and an holy nation" (Ex. 19:5-6). These words mark the special character assigned to the Israelites, and still more to the spiritual Israel (I Pet. 2:5,9; Rev. 1:6; 5:10). Not that they were to be separated from all nations in proud exclusiveness for their own sake: this was the great mistake of their history (Deut. 7:7). But as "all the earth is Jehovah's," they were His in a special sense, to bring all nations back to Him; kings and priests for others' good, and a holy nation for a pattern to all the rest. True, they failed in this great mission; but only for a time: their history is not finished, for it is only the first step in that of the spiritual Israel, who are yet to reign as kings and priests to God, and to bring all nations to the obedience of Christ. Meanwhile the elders and people accepted the covenant, and said, "All that Jehovah hath spoken, we will do," and Moses returned with their words to Jehovah.

Moses was next warned of the coming appearance of God in a thick cloud, to speak to him before all the people, that they might believe him forever. He was commanded to purify the people against the third day, and to set bounds round the mount, forbidding man or beast to touch it, under penalty of death; and these preparations occupied the next day.

2. *God's descent on Sinai – The Ten Commandments – Other precepts given to Moses – The Angel Jehovah their guide – The law given by angels.* The same reverence that was then enjoined forbids the vain attempt to describe the scene, which is related in the simple but sublime words of Moses (Ex. 19:16-20; Deut. 5:1-5), and recounted in the noblest strains of poetry (Ps. 68:7-8), and whose terrors, which made even Moses himself to fear and quake (Ex. 19:16), are most beautifully contrasted with the milder glories of the spiritual Zion (Heb. 12:18-29). From amid the darkness, and

above the trumpet's sound, God's voice was heard calling Moses up into the mount, to bid him charge the people lest they should break the bounds to gaze on God, and to prepare the elders to come up with him and Aaron when God should call them. Moses returned to the people and repeated these injunctions.

Then followed the greatest event of the Old Covenant. The voice of God himself gave forth the law by which his people were to live; the TEN COMMANDMENTS, on which all other laws were to be founded, and which were themselves summed up under the Old Covenant as well as the New, in two great principles: — "Thou shalt love the Lord thy God with all thy heart and soul and mind and strength, and thy neighbor as thyself" (Ex. 20:1-17; Deut. 5:6-22).

The Ten Commandments were the only part of the law given by the voice of God to the assembled people: "He added no more," and they alone were afterward written on the two tables of stone (Deut. 5:22). The form of the revelation was more than they could bear; and they prayed Moses that he would speak to them in the place of God, lest they should die. God approved their words, and Moses was invested with the office of *Mediator,* the type of "the Prophet raised up like him," the "one Mediator between God and man, the man Christ Jesus" (Ex. 20:18-21). He drew near to the thick darkness where God was, while the people stood aloof; and he received a series of precepts, which stand apart from the laws afterward delivered, as a practical interpretation of the Ten Commandments (Ex. 20:22-26; 21; 22; 23).

These precepts were concluded by promises relating to the people's future course. Their destination was clearly stated (Ex. 23:23), their bounds assigned (Ex. 23:31), the conquest assured to them by a gradual exertion of the power of God (Ex. 23:28-29), the blessings of life promised if they served God, and a special warning given against idolatry (Ex. 23:24-26). Above all, the ANGEL JEHOVAH, who had already guided them out of Egypt (Ex. 13:21; 14:19,24), was still to be their guide to keep them in the way, and to bring them to the place appointed for them, and their captain to fight against their enemies (Ex. 23:20,22). But if provoked and disobeyed, He would be a terror to themselves, "for *my name is in Him*" (Comp. Num. 20:16). Thus the whole promise is crowned with Christ. For this ANGEL is identified with God's own presence. (See *The Angel of Jehovah,* p. 354). So ended the great day on which God came down to the earth to announce the law.

One circumstance remains to be noticed. St. Stephen upbraids the Jews for not keeping the law, though they had received it by the *disposition of angels* (Acts 7:53; Heb. 2:2). This appears evidently to be an allusion to those hosts of angels or "holy ones" whose presence at Sinai is more than once mentioned (Deut. 33:2; Ps. 68:17), and whom the Apostle contrasts with the innumerable company of angels on the spiritual Zion (Heb. 12:22). These angels seem to have been present, not only to swell Jehovah's state, but to declare the consent of the whole intelligent universe to that law, which is forever "holy, just, and good."

3. *The covenant recorded and ratified by blood – The elders behold God's glory – Moses in the mount.* The element of *terror*, which prevailed in the revelation given on Sinai, was the true type of the aspect of the law to the mind of sinful man. Pure and holy in itself, it became "death" when proposed as the condition of life; for its great purpose was to reveal to self-righteous man "the exceeding sinfulness of sin," that he might be led to receive the grace of God in Christ (Gal. 3:21-25; Rom. 7:7-25). Thus the clouds of Sinai did not exhibit, but concealed, the true glory of Jehovah: and He now presented a vision of that glory to Moses, with Aaron and his sons Nadab and Abihu, and seventy of the elders of Israel (Ex. 24:1-2). But first Moses wrote the precepts already given, and set up an altar and memorial pillars, one for each tribe, and sacrificed burnt-offerings and peace-offerings of oxen, and sprinkled with the blood the book of the covenant which he then read to the people, who renewed their promise of obedience, and were themselves also *sprinkled with the blood,* and so the "covenant of works" was ratified (Ex. 24:1-8; Heb. 9:18-20). The chosen parties now went up, and saw God enthroned in his glory, as he was afterward seen by Ezekiel and John, and yet they lived (Ex. 24:9-11). Moses was then called up alone into the mount, to receive the tables of stone and the law which God had written, while Aaron and Hur were left to govern the people. Followed only by his servant Joshua, Moses went up into the mount,[1] which a cloud covered for six days, crowned with the glory of God as a burning fire. On the seventh day Moses was called into the cloud, and there he abode without food forty days and forty nights.

---

1. Moses seems to have made seven ascents into Mt. Sinai: (1) Ex. 19:3 — God's call for Israel to become his covenant people; (2) 19:20 — A warning for the people; (3) 20:21 — Various laws given. Aaron went with Moses (Ex. 19:24); (4) 24:9 — Moses, with numerous others, goes up and sees God; (5) 24:13 — Moses and Joshua go up, and receive the first set of tablets during forty days; (6) 32:30-31 — Moses goes up to pray after Israel's sin; (7) 34:4 — Second stay of forty days. Second set of tablets given to Moses. Moses returns with shining face.

4. *The golden calf – Intercession of Moses – Tables of law broken – Punishment – Fidelity of Levi – Self-sacrifice of Moses – God shows Moses His glory – Moses' second abode in the mount – The Tables renewed – Moses' face shines.* During the forty days in the mount, God gave Moses the instructions about building a sanctuary, the tabernacle (Ex. 25-31). While God was instructing Moses in the ordinances of divine worship, the people had already relapsed into idolatry. We must remember that, as Egypt had been the scene of the people's childhood, their sojourn in the wilderness was their spiritual youth, the age of sensuous impressions and of unstable resolutions. The great works done for them were soon forgotten, while each present difficulty seemed unbearable. As the weeks passed by without the return of Moses, they began to think they had lost both their leader and their new-found God. They recalled the visible objects of worship to which they had been used in Egypt, and they asked Aaron to make them gods to go before them (Ex. 32:1). Weakly yielding to their demand (Ex. 32:22,23), and perhaps hoping that they would not make the costly sacrifice, Aaron asked for their golden ear-rings, from which he made a "molten calf," the symbol of the Egyptian Apis. This he exhibited to the people as the image of the God who had brought them out of Egypt, and he built an altar before the idol. But yet it was in the name of Jehovah that he proclaimed a festival for the morrow, which the people celebrated with a banquet, followed by songs and lascivious dances (Ex. 32:6,18,25; I Cor. 10:7). This was on the last of the forty days, and God sent Moses down from the mount, telling him of Israel's sin, and declaring his purpose to destroy them, and to make of him a new nation. With self-denying importunity, Moses pleaded for the people, by the honor of God in the eyes of the Egyptians, and by His covenant with Abraham, Isaac and Israel, "and Jehovah repented of the evil which he thought to do unto his people" (Ex. 32:7-14).

Moses now descended from the mount, carrying in his hands the two tables of stone, on which God's own finger had written the Ten Commandments (Ex. 31:18). His path lay through a ravine, which cut off his view of the camp, but he soon heard their cry of revelry, which his warlike attendant Joshua mistook for the noise of battle. As he reached the plain, the disgraceful scene burst upon him, and in righteous anger he dashed the tables out of his hands, and broke them in pieces at the foot of the mount; giving at once a terrible significance for all future time to the phrase, a *broken law,* and a sign of man's inability to keep the law given on Sinai. For both Moses and the people, though in different ways, were showing by their acts that the first use to which man puts God's law is to break it.

He next destroyed the calf by fire and pounding, strewed its dust upon the stream from which the people drank, and reproached Aaron, who could only offer feeble excuses. Then he executed a terrible example on the people. Standing in the gate of the camp, he cried, "Who is Jehovah's? to me!" and all his brethren of the tribe of Levi rallied round him, and went through the camp at his command, slaying about three thousand men, and not sparing their own kindred. This was the consecration of Levi to the service and priesthood of Jehovah. The blood shed by His righteous sentence expiated the violence done to the Shechemites, and turned into a blessing the curse that deed had brought on the father of their tribe (Gen. 34:30; 49:5-7), and their sacrifice of their own feelings and affections for the cause of God marked them as fit to offer continual sacrifices for His people (Deut. 33:9-10).

The self-sacrifice of Moses went far greater lengths. On the morrow, he reproved the people for their sin, but promised to intercede for them; and then he addressed to Jehovah these awful words: "Yet now, if thou wilt forgive their sin; — and if not, *blot me, I pray thee, out of thy book which thou hast written*" (Ex. 32:32). The one and only parallel is the cry of Paul: "I could wish that myself were accursed from Christ for my brethren" (Rom. 9:3). It seems incredible to suppose them willing to renounce their hope of eternal life; but we must not question the earnestness of their self-sacrificing petitions. The exact sense of the prayer must remain an unfathomable mystery: its *spirit* was the spirit of Him of whom Moses as mediator was the type, who sent through with the like self-sacrifice, and drank its cup to the dregs: "Christ hath redeemed us from the curse of the law, *being made a curse for us*" (Gal. 3:13).

But no mere man could drink of that cup, and God replied to Moses that the sinner himself should be blotted out of His book (Ex. 32:33), and He sent plagues upon the people (Ex. 32:35). Once more he promised to send His Angel before them, to be a mediator as well as leader (Ex. 32:34; 33:1-4). At this the people murmured, thinking that they were to lose God's own presence, and they put themselves into mourning. Moses removed the sacred tent, called the "*tabernacle* of the congregation,"[1] out of the camp which had been profaned, and all who sought Jehovah went out to it. When Moses himself went out, and entered the tabernacle, the pillar of cloud descended to its door, "and Jehovah spake unto Moses, face to face, as a man speaketh unto his friend," while all the people looked on from their tent doors and worshiped. When Moses returned into the camp, Joshua remained in the tabernacle.

Having obtained pardon for the people, Moses prayed for a special encouragement to himself: — "Shew me now thy way, that I may know thee." Receiving the assurance that God's presence should be with him, to give him rest, he renewed the prayer, "Shew me thy glory." The answer seems to intimate that God's glory is in His goodness and in His grace and mercy; but that, in our present state, we can only follow the track which His glory leaves in the works of grace He does: we can not bear to look face to face at His perfections in their essence. He vouchsafed to Moses the outward sign for which he asked, promising to place him in a cleft of the rock, and to hide him while the glory of Jehovah passed by, so that he could only see the train behind Him (Ex. 33:12-23).

Moses went up alone into the mount, which was secured against intrusion, carrying with him two tables of stone to replace those which he had broken, for God made repeated trials of the people's faith. Then Jehovah descended in a cloud, and proclaimed His name as the God of mercy, grace, long-suffering, goodness and truth, from generation to generation. At this proclamation of God's true glory, Moses came forth to intercede once more for his people; and God renewed His covenant to work wonders for them, and to bring them into the promised land, adding a new warning against their falling into the idolatry of Canaan (Ex. 33:1-17). This time also, Moses remained in the mount for forty days and forty nights, and received anew the precepts of the law, as well as the two tables he had carried up, inscribed with the Ten Commandments by God himself (Ex. 33:18-28; Deut. 9:18-25; 10:1-5).

When Moses came down from the mount, the light of God's glory shone so brightly from his face, that the people were afraid

---

1. This was, of course, not *the tabernacle* itself, which was not yet made, nor was it the tent of Moses, for Moses himself went to it out of the camp, and returned again. It would seem, therefore, that before the tabernacle, there was a sacred tent in the midst of the camp, at which perhaps the elders met and Moses judged the people, and where they assembled in the congregation. Afterward the tabernacle of Jehovah became the "tent of the congregation," for the sanctuary belonged to the people, and not only to the priests.

to look at him, till he had covered it with a veil. This he did so that they might not witness the passing away of the glory (II Cor. 3:12-18). Meanwhile he recited to them the commandments that God had given him (Ex. 34:29-35).

5. *Divine origin of the law.* A large portion of the books of *Exodus* and *Numbers* and nearly the whole of *Leviticus* and *Deuteronomy* are occupied with the LAWS, which Moses was the instrument of giving to the Jewish people. He keeps ever before our eyes the fact that the Law was the LAW OF JEHOVAH. Its outline was given from Sinai by the voice of God himself (Ex. 20:23). One whole section of it, containing the ordinances of divine worship, was communicated to Moses by a special revelation, in the secrecy of the mount (Ex. 25-31). And even in the case of those precepts, which were enacted as the occasion for each arose, we find Moses invariably referring the question to the express decision of Jehovah.

6. *The law a Theocratic Constitution.* The basis of the whole commonwealth of Israel, as well as of its law, is the THEOCRATIC CONSTITUTION. Jehovah was present with the people, abiding in his tabernacle in their midst, visible by the symbol of His presence, and speaking to them through Moses and the High-priest. The whole law was the direct utterance of His will; and the government was carried on with constant reference to His oracular decisions. Thus He was to Israel what the king was to other nations; and hence their desire to have another king is denounced as treason to Jehovah. But more than this: He was, so to speak, the proprietor of the people. They were His *possession,* for He had redeemed them from their slavery in Egypt, and had brought them out thence to settle them in a new land of His own choice; and they, on their part, had accepted his relation to Jehovah by a solemn covenant. His right over their *persons* was asserted in the redemption of the first-born, and in the emancipation of the Jewish slave in the year of release. His right over their *land* was the fundamental law of property among the Jews. The tithes were a constant acknowledgment of this right; and the return of alienated land, in the year of Jubilee, to the families who had at first received it by allotment from Jehovah, was the reassertion of His sole propriety.

On their part, the people were required to believe in this supreme and intimate relation of Jehovah to them. They accepted it at first by the "covenant in Horeb," and into it every Israelite was initiated by circumcision, the common seal of this covenant and of that with Abraham, of which this was the sequel. They were to observe it in practice by the worship of Jehovah as the only God, by abstaining from idolatry, and by obedience to the law as the expression of His will.

Of this relation of Jehovah to the people the whole law was the practical development; and from it each separate portion may be derived.

7. *Classifications within the law – a. Laws criminal – b. Laws religious, moral and ceremonial – c. Laws constitutional and political – d. Laws civil.* The sacred scriptures themselves do not analyze or separate the law into categories or types of laws, and we do so only at great risk of misrepresenting the law. It can be safely asserted that the basis of the whole law is laid in the TEN COMMANDMENTS, as we call them, though they are nowhere so entitled in the Mosaic books, but the "TEN WORDS" (Ex. 34:28; Deut. 4:13), the "COVENANT," or, very often, as the solemn attestation of the divine will, the TESTIMONY. The term "Commandments" had come into use in the time of Christ. Most, if not all, of the law is merely an exposition and application of the ten commandments. For convenience sake, however, we may summarize the laws into four classifications as follows.

a. *Laws criminal.* We place this first because the law was added to the promise God made to Abraham and his descendants *because of transgressions* (Gal. 3:18-19). Through the law comes the knowledge of what is sin, and what is its penalty (Rom. 3:20; 7:7-8). The Ten Commandments form the core of criminal law, as of all the law.

1. OFFENSES AGAINST GOD— *First Commandment.* — Acknowledgment of false gods (Ex. 22:20), as *e.g.,* Moloch (Lev. 20:1-5), and generally all *idolatry* Deut. 8; 9:2-5). Idolatrous cities to be utterly destroyed (Deut. 13:12-16). All witchcraft and false prophets forbidden (Ex. 22:18; Deut. 18:9-22).

Second Commandment. — No idols to be carved ("graven"), or cast of molten metal (Ex. 34:7).

Third Commandment. — Use of God's name for useless and trivial purposes (Ps. 139:20; Job 35:13), or false swearing (Ps. 26:4; Isa. 59:4), or in blasphemy (Lev. 24:15-16) forbidden.

Fourth Commandment. — Sabbath-breaking (Num. 15:32-36). Punishment, in all cases, death by stoning.

2. OFFENSES AGAINST MAN. — *Fifth Commandment.* —

Disobedience to, or cursing or smiting of, *parents* (Ex. 21:15,17; Lev. 20:9; Deut. 21:18-21), to be punished by death by stoning, publicly adjudged and inflicted; so also of disobedience to the priests (as judges) or Supreme Judge. — Comp. I Ki. 21:10-14 (Naboth); II Chr. 24:21 (Zechariah).

Sixth Commandment. — (1) *Murder,* to be punished by death without sanctuary or reprieve, or satisfaction (Ex. 21:12,14; Deut. 19:11-13). Death of a slave actually under the rod to be punished (Ex. 21:20,21). (2) *Death by Negligence* to be punished by death (Ex. 21; 28:30). (3) *Accidental Homicide,* the avenger of blood to be escaped by flight to the cities of refuge till the death of the high-priest (Num. 35:9-28; Deut. 4:41-43; 19:4-10). (4) *Uncertain Murder,* to be expiated by formal disavowal and sacrifice by the elders of the nearest city (Deut. 21:1-9). (5) *Assault* to be punished by *lex talionis,* or damages (Ex. 21:18,19, 22-25; Lev. 24:19,20).

Seventh Commandment. — (1) *Adultery* to be punished by death of both offenders; the rape of a married or betrothed woman, by death of the offender (Deut. 22:13-27). (2) *Rape or Seduction* of an unbetrothed virgin, to be compensated by marriage, with dowry (50 shekels), and without power of divorce; or, if she be refused, by payment of full dowry (Ex. 22:16,17; Deut. 22:28,29). (3) *Unlawful Marriages* (incestuous, etc.) to be punished, some by death, some by childlessness (Lev. 20).

Eighth Commandment. — (1) *Theft* to be punished by fourfold or double restitution; a noctural robber might be slain as an outlaw (Ex. 22:1-4). (2) *Trespass* and injury of things lent to be compensated (Ex. 22:5-15). (3) *Perversion of Justice* (by bribes, threats, etc.), and especially oppression of strangers, strictly forbidden (Ex. 23:9, etc.). (4) *Kidnapping* to be punished by death (Deut. 24:7).

Ninth Commandment. – *False Witness* to be punished by *lex talionis* (Ex. 23:1-3; Deut. 19:16-21). Slander of a wife's chastity by fine, and loss of power of divorce (Deut. 22:18,19).

Tenth Commandment. — The sin of coveting could not be brought under the scope of a definite criminal law. But the numerous acts of meanness, injustice, oppression and unkindness, which are its consequences, are repeatedly forbidden; and their punishment sprang from the curse which God would bring on the disobedient. Indeed the final and highest system of rewards and punishments is to be found in the "Blessing and the Curse" which Moses set before the people (Deut. 27-28).

b. *Laws religious, moral and ceremonial.* These laws concern the people's devotion to God, the holiness (separation) of his people, and the rituals in worshipping God. Since God's nature is absolute holiness, it is impossible to separate moral from ceremonial law. Laws that could be classified as religious, moral and ceremonial concern such matters as: (1) the tabernacle, its furniture and priesthood (Ex. 25:31, 35-40); (2) the laws of sacrifice and offerings (e.g. Lev. 1-7); (3) the holiness of His people in person and actions (e.g. Lev. 11-15, 18); (4) the sacred seasons and feasts (e.g. Lev. 16, 23:25).

c. *Laws constitutional and political.* The Political Constitution of the Jewish Commonwealth, as we have seen, is founded entirely upon a religious basis. In its form it is THEOCRATIC — a *monarchy,* with JEHOVAH for the only king, all magistrates and judges being His ministers: in its *substance* and *spirit,* it is a *commonwealth,* in the strict sense, its object being the highest welfare of the whole people, who enjoy equal rights as being all the children of God, and united by the bond of holiness. The formal constitution grew out of the wants of the people. When the people left Egypt, they could not be called a nation in the political sense, but a body of tribes united by the bonds of grace and religion, and especially by "the promise given to the fathers."

Each of these tribes had its own patriarchal government by the "princes" of the tribe, and the "heads" of the respective families, and we find their authority subsisting through the whole history of the nation. But no central government was as yet provided. God preserved it in his own hands, and committed its administration to Moses as His servant. The people were all collected in one encampment around the tabernacle of Jehovah, their ever present king. They were commanded by His voice, whether directly or through Moses, and their movements were guided by His visible signs. If any doubtful case arose of law or policy, there was His oracle to be consulted. If any opposition was made to the authority of His minister, Jehovah summoned the rebels to His presence at the door of the tabernacle, smote them with leprosy, consumed them with pestilence, devoured them with fire, or sent them down alive into the pit. Such was the simple constitution of this period; God governing by His will, while embodying that will in the law.

The law, however, made regulations for the kings who should rule over Israel in later times (Deut. 17:14-20). Also it gave the judicial responsibilities to the priests, Levites and judges (Deut. 17:8-13; Compare II Chron. 19:8-10).

d. *Laws civil; human duties and rights.* These laws involve such matters as: (1) Relation of fathers and sons (Ex. 21:15,17; Lev. 20:9); (2) Inheritances (Deut. 21:15-17; Num. 27:6-8); (3) Relation of Husband and wife (Num. 30:6-15); (4) Divorce (Deut. 24:1-4); (5) Relation of masters and slaves (Ex. 21:20,26,27); (6) Land ownership, and return of land at the Jubilee (Lev. 25:25-27); Debts and usury (Deut. 15:1-11; 23:19-20); (7) Taxes (Ex. 30:12-16); (8) Tithes (Lev. 27:30-33) — The tithes operated in cycles. The tithes of two years supported the Levites (Num. 18:20-24). The tithes of the third year were shared with the poor as well as the Levites (Deut. 14:28-29). After two cycles of this, the seventh year would come, in which there was no crop planted and hence no tithes of the field (Ex. 23:10-11). (9) Poor laws: gleanings (Lev. 19:9-10; Deut. 24:19-22).

8. *Righteousness not by the law* (Gal. 3:21). The law gave in detail God's requirements for a perfect man and a perfect society. If anyone had obeyed *all* that was written in the law, he would have been accepted by God on that basis, for "The man that doeth them (the commandments of the law) shall *live* in them" (Lev. 18:5; Gal. 3:12). However, because of the weakness of the flesh (Rom. 8:3), the law proved to be a yoke which neither our fathers nor we were able to bear (Acts 15:10). God foreknew that this situation would prevail, and hence the law was not given to provide man a way of being right with God, but to make men so aware of their sinful condition and shortcomings that they would seek justification by the favor (grace) of God through Jesus Christ. Those who are thus justified by faith will seek to fulfill the righteousness of the law by serving one another in love (Rom. 3:31; 13:10).

Questions over Section II
Giving of the Law

1. From what place did God call Moses in the wilderness of Sinai (Ex. 19:1-3)?

2. What was God's condition for Israel to become his own possession from among all peoples (19:5-6)?
3. What did Israel promise Moses and God that they would do (19:8)?
4. When God came unto Israel, within what did He come (19:9)?
5. How many days' notice of His coming did God give Israel (19:11)?
6. What was the danger in touching the mount (19:12-13; Cf. Heb. 12:18-22)?
7. Describe the scene as God descended on Mt. Sinai (19:16-18).
8. About how many times did Moses go up on Mt. Sinai?
9. Who all heard the words of the ten commandments (Ex. 20:22,18; Deut. 5:22-23)?
10. Write from memory Exodus 20:2-17.
11. How did Israel react when they heard God's voice (20:19-20)?
12. What material was Israel to use in making God an altar (20:24-25)?
13. How long could a Hebrew servant be held in slavery (21:2)?
14. What responsibility did a man with a mean ox have (21:28-29)?
15. What people were especially under God's protection and concern (22:22)?
16. How long could a man's garment be held as security for a loan (22:26)?
17. What law was given about following a mob (23:2)?
18. How often did the land lie fallow for a year (23:10-11)?
19. How many compulsory feasts were to be kept each year? Name them (23:14-16; 34:22-23; Deut. 16:16).
20. Who was sent before Israel to keep them (23:20-21)?
21. What did the people promise concerning the words of the covenant which God spoke (Ex. 24:3-5)?
22. By what means did Moses ratify the covenant between God and Israel (Ex. 24:8; Cf. Heb. 9:18-26)?
23. What group of people went up on Mt. Sinai with Moses on one trip (24:1,9)?
24. Describe the appearance of God to Moses and the others (24:10).
25. Who went up with Moses when he received the tables of the ten commandments (24:12-13)?

26. How long did Moses stay up on the mount on that trip (24:18)?

27. What did the people say when Moses delayed coming down (32:1)?

28. What was used to make an idol? Who built it (32:2-4)?

29. What did the people do before the idol (Ex. 32:6; I Cor. 10:7)?

30. What did God threaten to do to Israel, and do with Moses (32:10; Deut. 9:14,20)?

31. What saved Israel from God's wrath (32:11-14)?

32. What did Moses do with the tables of the ten commandments (32:19-20)?

33. What tall tale did Aaron tell Moses (32:24)?

34. What tribe stood by Moses against the idolatry (32:26)?

35. How many died because of the idolatry (32:28; Cf. Acts 2:41)?

36. With what words did Moses pray God to forgive Israel (32:32)?

37. Why did God not go with Israel, but rather sent an angel (33:1-3)?

38. What was the tent called where Moses sought Jehovah? Where did Moses pitch it (33:7)?

39. How did God speak unto Moses (33:11)?

40. What did Moses ask God to show him (33:13,18)?

41. Why did Moses not see God's face (33:20)?

42. Where did God hide Moses as His glory passed by (33:21-23)?

43. What was Moses to bring up upon the mountain during his final ascent (34:1-2)?

44. What did God promise and covenant to do before Israel and all people (34:10-11)?

45. What was Israel to do to the Canaanites (34:11-16)?

46. What words are called "the words of the covenant" (34:28)?

47. What was noticeable about Moses' appearance when he came down from the mount (34:29)?

You be the Judge (Exodus 21-23)

Case A — A Hebrew by the name of Dan bought a slave from one of his brothers. The slave served the alloted six years, but during that time he married, with the help and encouragement of his master, the niece of his master. They had three children. Now he wishes to leave, but the master says that the wife and children belong to him and that he must leave by himself. What is to be done?

Case B — While securing lumber for the building of the tabernacle, a workman felled a tree which fell on another workman and killed him. The man who was killed had a brother working in the crew and he swears that he has the right to avenge the blood of his brother. Has he? If so, what is to be done?

Case C — Here appear four brothers who all state that they caught their sister cursing their mother. What is to be done?

Case D — A man startled out of his sleep one night saw someone in his tent. He reached under his pillow and took hold of his sword. Almost before he knew it, he had run the intruder through and he lay dead on the tent floor. What is to be done?

Case E — A man comes to say that he has borrowed his neighbor's ox, and it had fallen sick while with him, and finally died. What shall be done?

Section III
The Tabernacle and Priesthood
(Ex. 25:1-31:11; 35:4-40:38; Lev. 8-10)

A. The Tabernacle.

    1. Importance of the tabernacle. 2. What was the tabernacle? 3. Information about the tabernacle. 4. Those camped about the tabernacle. 5. Names for the tabernacle. 6. Source of tabernacle materials. 7. Tabernacle workmen. 8. Tabernacle was One. 9. Maintenance of tabernacle. 10. How the tabernacle was sanctified. 11. Cloud of glory over the tabernacle. 12. Value of the tabernacle. 13. Layout and furniture of the tabernacle. — a. Layout — Court — Holy Place — Holy of Holies — Curtains and veils. b. Furniture — In the outer court: Altar of burnt offering, Brazen Laver — In the Holy Place: Altar of Incense, Table of Showbread, Golden Candlestick — In the Holy of Holies: Ark of the Covenant. 14. Typology of the tabernacle. 15. The tabernacle set up — The cloud of glory.

B. The Priesthood.

    1. Institution of the priesthood. 2. The High Priest —

a. His consecration — b. His peculiar garments —
c. His peculiar functions. 3. The Priests —
Consecration and dress — Regulations respecting
them — Their duties — Maintenance of them. The
Levites — Their duties in general — Division into
three families — Their support and settlement in the
Promised Land — Duties in later times.

A. The Tabernacle

1. *Importance of the tabernacle.* During Moses' first stay of forty days on Mt. Sinai (Ex. 24:18), God gave him instructions concerning the construction of a sanctuary for God, where God might dwell among them (Ex. 25:8). This sanctuary we call the tabernacle.

STANDARD PUBLISHING —Used by permission

This was an appeal to the senses of a people whose spiritual discernment was underdeveloped. God's presence among them was plainly indicated by the daily manna, the pillar of cloud and the miracles that occurred during their journeyings. But to a people brought up amidst the idolatry of Egypt, a centralized shrine was more readily comprehended than an omnipresent spiritual God.

The importance of this tabernacle can be seen in several ways:

a. The details of its construction are described *twice* in Exodus, and much information is found about it throughout the rest of the Bible.

b. The tabernacle is presented as a *type* of the Christian religion now operative (Heb. 9:8-9). (See "Typology of the Tabernacle," p. 215.)

c. God's insistence that it be made according to the precise pattern he had showed in the mount stresses the importance of each detail of it.

2. *What was the tabernacle?*

a. The tabernacle was that beautiful place of worship made by the children of Israel in the days of Moses. It was a sanctuary, a holy place set apart for God. God showed His presence at the tabernacle, and there received the worship of the people (Exodus 29:43-46).

b. It was a portable house of worship. When we go on camping trips, we carry with us a "house" that we can move about, a tent. Out in the desert the Israelites were constantly moving about. Therefore they had to have a house of worship that could easily be moved with them. The very word "tabernacle" means a "tent," and the word "tent" certainly suggests a portable dwelling. God gave instructions about how to transport the tabernacle in Numbers 4:5-15.

   1. Some pieces of furniture in the tabernacle had staves on each side, so men could carry them on their shoulders.
   2. The heavier parts of the tabernacle were carried by six wagons pulled by oxen (Numbers 7:1-7).

c. It was the meeting place of God and Israel. God dwelt among his people, Israel (Exodus 25:8). God particularly revealed His presence around the tabernacle, and especially in that part of it called the Most Holy Place (Exodus 25:22).

   The fact that God dwelt in the midst of Israel was the central fact of their life. To Israel God's presence meant plan, protection and provision. If God had not manifested His presence in the tabernacle, the tribes of Israel would have been scattered about helter-skelter, with no one to protect or provide for them.

   Today God dwells in the midst of his *church,* just as He dwelt among the Israelites (II Cor. 6:16). The presence and worship of God give order, protection and purpose to our lives. The worship of God should be as central to us as the tabernacle was central in the camp of Israel.

3. *Where is the information given about the tabernacle?*

a. The instructions about its building are given in Ex. 25-31.

b. The account of its construction and erection are in Ex. 35-40. Most of the information in this section is a repetition of that in Ex. 25-31.

c. The book of Hebrews, chs. 9-10, discusses the significance of the tabernacle at length.

d. Many other references throughout the Bible refer to it. The legislation in Leviticus and Numbers and Deuteronomy was primarily to be carried out in the tabernacle rituals.

4. *Who were camped around the tabernacle?*

a. The Israelites camped all around the tabernacle. Each tribe camped by itself in its designated place. Although each tribe camped separately, the three on each of the four sides of the tabernacle were grouped together into larger encampments, called the Camp of Dan, the Camp of Judah, the Camp of Reuben and the Camp of Ephraim. See Numbers 2:1-3:39. (See p. 207, fig. 2.)

b. Moses and the priestly families of Gershon, Merari and Kohath were camped around the tabernacle up close to it.

5. *What were the names which were given to the tabernacle?* God not only ordains things to exist, but He gives them their names as well. Let us use "Bible names for Bible things." Here are the names for the tabernacle:

a. "Tabernacle" (Exodus 26:1). This word is the translation of several Hebrew words (2 main ones). One *(ohel)* means "tent." The other *(mishkan)* means "dwelling place."

b. "Tent" (Exodus 26:36).

c. "Sanctuary" (Exodus 25:8). This word means " a place set apart."

d. "Tabernacle of the congregation" (Exodus 29:42,44; 30:36; etc.). This name is rendered "tent of meeting" in the Revised Version. The name "tabernacle of the congregation" is applied to that room in the tabernacle called "the holy place" (Exodus 27:21).

e. "House of the Lord" (Deut. 23:18). (The church is now the house of the Lord, and God dwells in it through the Holy Spirit [Eph. 1:22]).

f. "Temple of the Lord" (I Samuel 1:9). This name suggests the magnificence of the tabernacle, as if it were a palace or temple. The church is now the temple of God.

6. *How were materials obtained for the tabernacle?* Free-will offerings provided the materials. See Exodus 25:1-9; 35:4-29; 36:5-7. When the call was made for materials, the people responded liberally. No doubt the things that they gave had mostly been taken from the Egyptians on the night when they left Egypt (Exodus 12:35-36). The Israelites had earned all these things during years of slavery with no wages.

Even as the tabernacle was constructed of free gifts, so today the church is made by people who freely give themselves and their substance to the Lord. "Whosoever will may come" (Rev. 22:17; II Cor. 8:5, 2-3; 9:7).

7. *Who actually constructed the tabernacle?* It was constructed by men specially called and filled and guided by the Spirit of God to have wisdom and skill. God called them by name. Among these builders were Bezaleel and Aholiab (Ex. 36:1; Ex. 35:30-36:1).

These builders of the tabernacle correspond to the apostles of Christ in the church. Christ specifically called His apostles, and filled them with the Holy Spirit so that they could establish the church without error (Acts 1:8; John 16:13).

8. *How many tabernacles did all the parts of the tabernacle combine to form?* Just one. It was ONE tabernacle (Ex. 26:6). All its parts formed one harmonious whole.

Accordingly we find a unity pervading the whole church of Christ. There are many different members of it, but all produce one body (I Cor. 12:2).

9. *How was the tabernacle maintained?* It was maintained by an offering of "atonement money." Every person over twenty had to give a half-shekel (Ex. 30:11-16). This was an annual offering (Matt. 17:24). The fact that God provided through the tabernacle a means of atonement (or covering) for sins made the people indebted to God and to His tabernacle.

We who have a perfect atonement through Christ are just as obligated to support the work of the church as the Israelites were obligated to contribute for the service of the tabernacle (I Pet. 1:17-19; Rom. 15:27).

10. *By what act was the tabernacle "sanctified" or set apart for holy use?* It was set apart by anointing with holy oil. The tabernacle, all its pieces of furniture, and its priests were anointed with a holy oil, so that it was sanctified and became "most holy" (Ex. 30:22-23; 40:9-16).

Anointing oil, as used in the Old Testament, was symbolic of the Holy Spirit. See Luke 4:18; Psalm 133:2; Hebrews 1:9; Acts 10:38.

As every part of the tabernacle was anointed with the holy oil, so every feature of the Christian faith is anointed with the Holy Spirit. See Ephesians 1:22; I Corinthians 12:13; Acts 2:17. Our religion is therefore divine, holy, precious, anointed of God.

11. *What covered over, or lodged above, the tabernacle?* The cloud of God's glory covered over or lodged above the tabernacle

(Exodus 40:34-39; Numbers 9:15-23). This glory cloud is called the SHECHINAH.

God's presence has frequently been associated with a cloud, or a shining light, or smoke, or fire (Ex. 16:10; 24:16-17; Num. 20:6; Isa. 6:4; Luke 2:9). This creates a great sense of God's presence and majesty.

This cloud also guided and led the Israelites. When the cloud lifted up, this was a sign for the Israelites to pack up for moving on. When the cloud moved, they followed. When the cloud stopped, they camped.

The Scripture indicates that God intends to glorify His people today with a glory like that which crowned the tabernacle (Isaiah 60:2; 4:5).

12. *What was the value of the material in the tabernacle?* The value was tremendous. See Exodus 38:24-29. The exact value is impossible to determine, but a million and a half dollars has been suggested as a conservative figure. The worship of God is not a cheap, trifling and inconsequential thing.

13. *Layout and furniture of the tabernacle.*

a. The layout of the tabernacle.

   1. The *court of the tabernacle,* in which the tabernacle itself stood, was an oblong space, 100 cubits by 50 (i.e., 150 feet by 75), having its longer axis east and west, with its front to the *east.* It was surrounded by canvas screens 5 cubits in height, and supported by pillars of brass 5 cubits apart, to which the curtains were attached by hooks and fillets of silver.[1] This enclosure was broken only on the eastern side by the entrance, which was 20 cubits wide, and closed by curtains of fine twined linen, wrought with needle-work, and of the most gorgeous colors (Ex. 27:9-19; 38:9-20).

     In the outer or eastern half of the court was placed the altar of burnt-offering, and between it and the tabernacle itself, the laver at which the priests washed their hands and feet on entering the temple.

   2. The *tabernacle itself* was placed toward the western end of this enclosure. It was an oblong rectangular structure, 30 cubits in length by 10 in width (45 feet by 15), and 10 in height; the interior being divided into two chambers, the first or outer of 20 cubits in length, the inner of 10 cubits, and consequently an exact cube. The former was the *holy*

---

1. The *fillets* appear to have been thin rods or rails between the pillars of the court.

place, or *first tabernacle* (Heb. 9:2), containing the golden candlestick on one side, the table of shew-bread opposite, and between them in the center the altar of incense. The latter was the *most holy place,* or the *holy of holies,* containing the ark, surmounted by the cherubim, with the two tables inside.

The two sides, and the further or western end, were enclosed by boards of shittim-wood overlaid with gold, twenty on the north and south sides, six on the western side, with the corner-boards doubled. They stood upright, edge to edge, their lower ends being made with tenons, which dropped into sockets of silver, and the corner-boards being coupled at the top with rings. They were furnished with golden rings, through which passed bars of shittim-wood, overlaid with gold, five to each side, and the middle bar passing from end to end, so as to brace the whole together (Ex. 26:15-26; 36:20-70).

Four successive coverings of curtains looped together were placed over the open top, and fell down over the sides. The first, or inmost, was a splendid fabric of linen, embroidered with figures of cherubim, in blue, purple and scarlet, and looped together by golden fastenings. The next was a woolen covering of goats' hair; the third, or rams' skins dyed red; and the outermost, of badgers' skins[1] (Ex. 26:1-14; 36:8-19).

The question as to whether the curtains were laid flat across the top of the tabernacle, or were suspended across some ridge-pole running the length of the tabernacle has been disputed. To us it seems more likely that the coverings were laid flat across the top of the tabernacle, hanging vertically down the sides. This might appear to produce sagging on top. However, the pillars and fillets at the front entrance and at the entrance to the Holy of Holies would help to hold the coverings up without sagging. Also the considerable length of curtains hanging down each side would be heavy enough to prevent serious sagging. The picture presented to our minds by the word "tent" does not, when used in its oriental meaning, necessarily convey the idea of a sloping roof; biblical tents were long, low and more or less flat on top. Although the Scriptures give precise details about most of the tabernacle, not a hint of a

---

1. The "badger skins" were probably seal skins or porpoise skins, or (most probably) dugong (sea-cow) skins.

1. General view of the tabernacle and court.

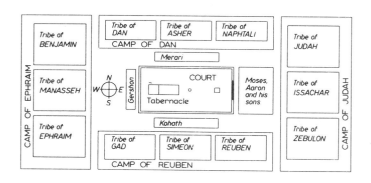

2. The encampments of Israel around the tabernacle.

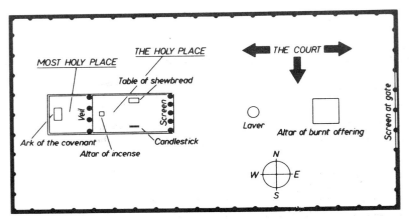

3. Floor plan of the tabernacle and court.

4. Altar of burnt-offering or brazen altar.

5. The laver and its base.

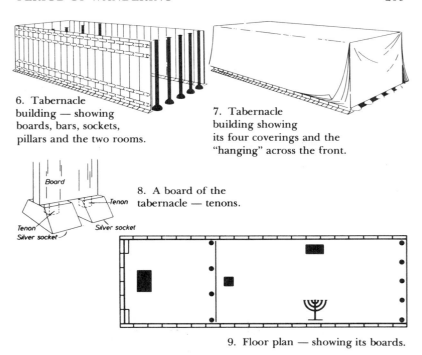

6. Tabernacle building — showing boards, bars, sockets, pillars and the two rooms.

7. Tabernacle building showing its four coverings and the "hanging" across the front.

8. A board of the tabernacle — tenons.

9. Floor plan — showing its boards.

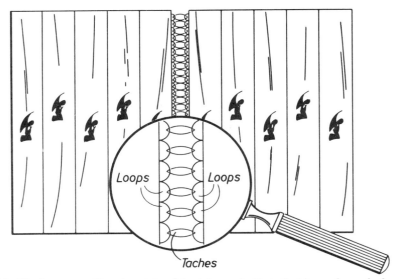

10. The innermost (linen) curtain of the tabernacle. Note that it was formed of two groups of five curtains decorated with cherubim, and joined by loops and taches (or clasps).

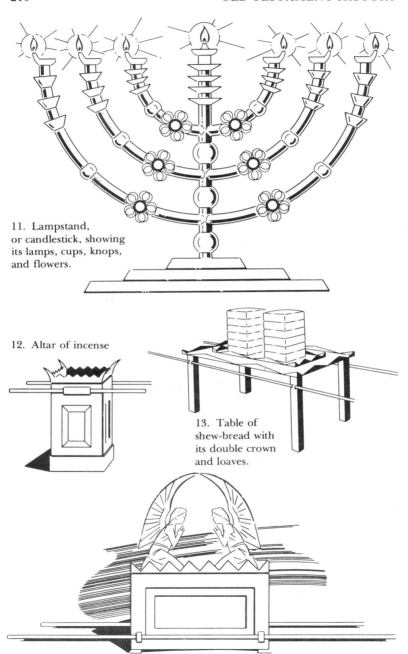

11. Lampstand,
or candlestick, showing
its lamps, cups, knops,
and flowers.

12. Altar of incense

13. Table of
shew-bread with
its double crown
and loaves.

14. The Ark of the Covenant and the mercy-seat with cherubim.

ridge-pole or a sloping roof is given. We read that the curtains hung down over the back of the tabernacle (Ex. 26:12). It is difficult to comprehend how the curtains could be suspended over a ridge-pole and yet hang down "over the backside of the tabernacle."

The front of the sanctuary was closed by a hanging of fine linen, embroidered in blue, purple and scarlet, and supported by golden hooks, on *five* pillars of shittim-wood overlaid with gold, and standing in brass sockets; and the covering of goats' hair was so made as to fall down over this when required. A more sumptuous curtain of the same kind, embroidered with cherubim, hung on *four* such pillars, with silver sockets, divided the Holy from the Most Holy Place. It was called the VEIL, as it hid from the eyes of all but the high-priest the inmost sanctuary, where Jehovah dwelt on his mercy-seat, between the cherubim above the ark. Hence, "to enter within the veil" is to have the closest access to God. It was only passed by the high-priest once a year, on the Day of Atonement, in token of the mediation of Christ, who with his own blood, hath entered for us within the veil which separates God's own abode from earth (Heb. 6:19). The veil was at last rent by the hand of God himself, at the same moment that the body of Christ was rent upon the cross, to indicate that the entrance into the holiest of all is now laid open to all believers "by the blood of Jesus, by a new and living way which He hath consecrated for us, through the veil, that is to say, His flesh" (Heb. 10:19-20). The *Holy Place* was entered daily by the priests only, to offer incense at the time of morning and evening prayer, and to renew the lights on the golden candlestick; and on the Sabbath, to remove the old shew-bread, and to place the new upon the table.

b. Furniture of the tabernacle.
  1. In the Outer Court.
      a. *The Altar of Burnt-offering* (Ex. 27:1-8; 38:1-7; Psalm 118:27) stood in the midst of the court, and formed the central point of the outer services, in which the people had a part. On it all sacrifices and oblations were presented, except the sin-offerings, which were burnt without the camp. It was a large hollow case or coffer, 5 cubits square by 3 in height, made of shittim-wood, overlaid with plates of brass, and with a grating of brass

halfway up the sides and under a ledge. At the four corners were projections called "horns," the "laying hold" of which was the sign of throwing one's self upon the mercy of God, and a means of fleeing to take sanctuary from man's vengeance. Like the ark, the altar of incense and the table of shew-bread, it was furnished with rings, through which were passed bars to carry it when the people were on the march. Its utensils of brass are enumerated in Ex. 38:3. The priests went up to it, not by steps, but by a slope of earth (Ex. 20:26).

Upon this altar fire was always burning (Lev. 6:13-19). Continual burnt-offerings occupied it. A lamb was offered every morning and evening (Ex. 29:38-42; Num. 28:3-8). This suggests to us that as the sacrifice was constantly upon the altar, so also the atoning death of Christ is always available to us for forgiveness of sins. Also as different types of offerings were made on the altar as need arose, so the death of Christ is adequate to meet every special need of our souls.

b. The *Brazen Laver* (Ex. 30:17-21; 38:8; 40:7,11; Lev. 8:10-11; Ex. 29:4), a vessel on a base, to hold water for the washings of the priests, stood between the altar of burnt-offering and the entrance to the Holy Place. It was made of the brass mirrors which were offered by the women. Its size and form are not mentioned: it is commonly represented as round; it need not have been very large, as the priests washed themselves *at* not *in* it.

The priests washed there when they were consecrated into office (Ex. 29:4; Lev. 8:6). The priests had to wash at the laver every time they went into the Holy Place, or burned offerings at the altar (Ex. 30:20-21). It was thus used for an *initial* and a *continual* washing.

2. In the Holy Place. The furniture of the court was connected with *sacrifice,* that of the sanctuary itself with the deeper mysteries of mediation and access to God. The *first sanctuary* contained three objects: the *altar of incense* in the center, so as to be directly in front of the ark of the covenant, the *table of shew-bread* on its right or north side, and the *golden candlestick* on the left or south side.

a. The *Altar of Incense* (Ex. 30:1-10, 34-38; 37:25-29; Lev. 10:1-2), a double cube of 1 cubit square by 2 high, with horns of shittim-wood, overlaid with gold, whence it is often called the *golden altar* (Ex. 39:38), to distinguish it from the altar of burnt-offering, which was called the *brazen altar* (Ex. 38:30). It had a cornice of gold, and two golden rings to receive the staves of shittim-wood overlaid with gold, for carrying it. Neither burnt-offering, nor meat-offering, nor drink-offering, was to be laid upon it; but the blood of the sin-offering of atonement was sprinkled upon its horns once a year. The incense burnt upon it was a sacred composition of spices of divine prescription. It was offered every morning and evening, at first by Aaron and his sons, and afterward by the priests officiating in weekly course, and by the high-priest on great occasions. The priest took some of the sacred fire off the altar of burnt-offering in his censer, and threw the incense upon it: then, entering the Holy Place, he emptied the censer upon the altar, prayed and performed the other duties of his office. Meanwhile the people prayed outside (Luke 1:10); and thus was typified the intercession of Christ in heaven, making his people's prayers on earth acceptable. It was highly criminal to offer "strange" incense or "strange" fire upon the altar, or for any one to usurp the function of the priests, or to make, or apply to any other use, the sacred incense. Nadab and Abihu were slain for the first of these offenses (Lev. 10:1-7); King Uzziah was smitten with leprosy for the second (II Chron. 26:16-21); and the punishment of death was appointed for the third.

b. The *Table of Shew-bread* (or *Presence-bread* (Ex. 25:23-30; 37:10-16; Lev. 24:5-9) was an oblong table, with legs, 2 cubits long, 1 broad, and 1½ high. It was of shittim-wood, covered with gold and finished, like the altar, with a golden rim and four rings and staves. It was furnished with dishes, spoons, covers and bowls of pure gold. It stood on the north or right side of the altar of incense. Upon this table were placed twelve cakes of fine flour, in two rows (or piles) of six each, with frankincense upon each row. This "*Shew*-bread," as it was called from being exposed before Jehovah, was placed fresh upon the table every Sabbath by the priests, who ate the old loaves in the Holy Place. Each loaf was made of two tenth parts of an ephah (about one-half peck) of flour. This much flour would have produced huge loaves.

c. The *Golden Candlestick* (Heb. *Menorah;* Ex. 25:31-40; 27:20-21; 37:17-24; Lev. 24:1-4; Num. 8:1-4), more properly called a *lampstand,* was placed on the left or south side of the altar of incense. It was made of pure beaten gold and weighed, with its instruments, a talent: its value has been estimated at $40,000, besides workmanship. Its form, as described in the Book of Exodus, agrees with the figure of the candlestick of the second temple, as represented, together with the table of shew-bread and other Jewish trophies, on the arch of Titus. It had an upright stem, from which branched out three pairs of arms, each pair forming a semicircle, and their tops coming to the same level as the top of the stem, so as to form with it supports for seven lamps. It was decorated by ornamental knobs and flowers along the branches and at their junction with the stem. There were oil-vessels and lamp-tongs, or snuffers, for trimming the seven lamps, and dishes for carrying away the snuff; an office performed by the priest when he went into the sanctuary every morning to offer incense. All these utensils were of pure gold. The lamps were lighted at the time of the evening oblation. They are directed to be kept burning perpetually; but from their being lighted in the evening, this seems to mean only during the night.

3. In the Holy of Holies.

a. The Ark of the Covenant. In the *Holy of Holies,* within the veil and shrouded in darkness, there was but one object, the most sacred of the whole. The *Ark of the Covenant,* or the *Testimony,* was a sacred chest, containing the two tables of stone,[1] inscribed with the Ten Commandments. It was two cubits and a half in length, by a cubit and a half both in width and height. It was of shittim-wood, overlaid with pure gold, and had a golden mitre round the top. Through two pairs of golden rings on its sides passed two staves of

---

1. It seems also to have contained the pot of manna and Aaron's rod that blossomed (Heb. 9:4). However, these objects generally appear to have been laid up "before" the testimony (Num. 17:10; Ex. 16:34), that is, probably, beside the ark. In the time of Solomon there was nothing in the ark except the stone tablets of the Ten Commandments (I Kings 8:9).

shittim-wood, overlaid with gold, which were drawn forward so as to press against the veil, and thus to remind the priests in the Holy Place of the presence of the unseen ark. The cover of the ark (called the *mercy-seat)* was a plate of pure gold, overshadowed by two cherubim, with their faces bent down and their wings meeting. This was the very *throne* of Jehovah, who was therefore said to "dwell between the cherubim."[1] It was also called the *mercy-seat* or *covering,* because Jehovah there revealed himself, especially on the great Day of Atonement, as "God pardoning iniquity, transgression and sin." Nor was it without the profoundest allusion to the coming dispensation of the Gospel, that God's throne of *mercy* covered and hid the tables of the *law.* The attitude of the cherubim was significant of the desire of angels to learn the Gospel mysteries that were hidden in the law (I Peter 1:12).

14. *Typology of the Tabernacle.* A *type* is some person, thing or event in the Old Testament age which foreshadowed some person, thing or event in the New Testament age. The *antitype* is that person, thing or event in the New Testament age which was foreshadowed by the Old Testament type. We are expressly told in Heb. 9:8-9 that the first tabernacle is a figure or type for the time present. The typology is given for many parts of the tabernacle.

a. The entire tabernacle — A type of the Christian religion (Heb. 9:8-9).
b. The Holy of Holies — A type of heaven (Heb. 9:24).
  1. The Ark of the Covenant — A type of God's throne (?)[2] (Ps. 99:1, RV marg.).
  2. The Mercy Seat — A type of Christ, our place of mercy (Rom. 3:25; I John 2:2; 4:10. "Propitiation" means "mercy seat.").
  3. The veil between the Holy and Most Holy Places — A type of Christ's flesh which was broken on the cross (Heb. 10:19-20; Luke 23:44-45).

---

1. Though the exact form of the cherubim is uncertain, they probably bore a general resemblance to the composite religious figures found upon the monuments of Egypt, Assyria, Babylonia and Persia. Compare the description in Ez. 1:5, seq., who speaks of them as living creatures with animal forms: that they are cherubim is clear from Ezek. 10:20. The symbolism of the visions of Ezekiel is more complex than that of the earlier Scriptures, and he certainly means that each composite creature-form had four faces so as to look for ways at once, was four-sided and four-winged, so as to move with instant rapidity in every direction without turning, whereas the Mosaic idea was probably single-faced, and with but one pair of wings.

2. Question marks (?) indicate that the antitypes given are not specifically stated in the Scripture. In such cases obvious inferences may usually be drawn from Scripture that will enable us to determine the antitypes.

   c. The Holy Place — A type of the church (?). (As the Holy of Holies was entered only from the Holy Place, so heaven is entered only from the church. As the Holy Place was for priests only, so the church is for priests (Christians) only.)

     1. Altar of Incense — A type of prayer (Rev. 5:8; 8:3-4; Ps. 141:2).

     2. Table of Shew-bread — A type of God's people in God's presence (?). (The twelve loaves obviously represented Israel. Shew-bread means presence-bread. Thus the shew-bread symbolized Israel's being in God's presence, and foreshadowed our fellowship in God's presence (I John 1:3). Some think the table of shew-bread represented the communion. This seems unlikely unless we are willing to construe the Lord's supper as a type of sacrifice [Lev. 24:9].)

     3. Lampstand — A type of the light of the Gospel (?) (Eph. 5:7-8). We walk in the light. God is light (I Jn. 1:5). Christ is the light (John 8:12). The scriptures are a light (Ps. 119:105; II Pet. 1:19). Churches are lights (Rev. 1:12,20). Christians are lights (Phil. 2:15).

   d. The Court — A type of the world, or God's outreach into the world (?). (As God placed in the court, within the reach of all Israelites, the means for forgiveness, so God has placed in the world the means for forgiveness to all who will draw near seeking God.)

     1. Altar of Burnt Offering — A type of Christ's death (Heb. 13:10; John 1:20).

     2. Laver — A type of baptism (Eph. 5:26; Titus 3:5). The word "washing" in Greek means "laver". Also a type of the daily cleansing available to Christians (I John 1:9).

   e. The Priesthood.

     1. Aaron, the high priest — A type of Christ our high priest (Heb. 4:14).

     2. Aaron's sons (lesser priests) — A type of Christians; all Christians are priests (Rev. 1:6; I Peter 2:9).

Garments of the High Priest (Exodus 28, 38)

   1. *Breast Plate* (Ex. 28:15-30). Four rows of three gems were set upon a beautiful cloth backing. Each gem was incised with the name of one of the twelve tribes. Golden chains and rings held the breastplate upon the ephod.

2. *Ephod* (Ex. 28:6-13). The ephod was an apron-like garment with straps over the shoulders. It may have had a back section joined to the front section at the shoulders. See Ex. 28:25.

3. *Robe of the Ephod* (Ex. 28:31-35). This was a blue garment worn underneath the ephod. Apparently it was like a sleeveless dress and had alternating golden bells, and purple, gold and scarlet pomegranates hanging about the bottom of the skirt.

4. *Coat* (Ex. 28:39). This seems to have been the white linen undergarment of the priest.

5. *The Band* (or girdle) (Ex. 28:8). This was a wide sash made of the same material as the ephod, and used to bind the ephod about the waist.

6. *Mitre* (or turban) (Ex. 28:36-38). This was the priest's headdress. Upon its front was attached a golden plate inscribed HOLY TO JEHOVAH.

Besides the dress garments of the high priest, Aaron and his sons had white linen coats, headtires, girdles and breeches to be worn in their routine work (Ex. 28:40-43).

---

15. *The tabernacle set up – The cloud of glory upon the tabernacle.* When all of the various parts of the tabernacle were prepared, Moses was commanded to set up the tabernacle and place in it the ark of the covenant, and to anoint Aaron and his sons to the priesthood. The solemn ceremony took place on the first day of the first month of the second year from the epoch of the exodus, March to April, 1445 B.C. Jehovah gave a visible token of His presence and approval by covering the tabernacle with the cloud and filling it with His glory, so that Moses could not enter into the tabernacle, and by sending down on the altar the sacred fire, with which alone the sacrifices were henceforth to be offered (Ex. 40; Num. 9:15-16). The scene thus simply and briefly related by Moses should be compared with the more elaborate description of the dedication of Solomon's temple, of which the tabernacle was the model (I Kings 8; II Chron. 6,7). A whole month was spent in arranging the service of the sanctuary, as it is set forth in the Book of Leviticus, before the people prepared for their onward journey.

B. The Priesthood

1. *Institution of the priesthood.* "Now when these things were thus ordered, the priests went always into the first Tabernacle,

accomplishing the service of God. But into the second went the high-priest alone once every year, not without blood, which he offered for himself and the errors of the people: the Holy Ghost thus signifying, that the way into the holiest of all was not yet laid open, while the first Tabernacle was yet standing" (Heb. 9:6-8). Such is the apostolic summary of the offices of the priesthood. The whole of the people were holy, and in a spiritual sense, they were a nation of priests; but from among them the tribe of Levi were chosen, as the reward of their devotion in the matter of the golden calf, to be the immediate attendants on Jehovah, that they might *"minister* in His *courts."* Out of that tribe again, the house of Amram was chosen to perform the functions of the priesthood, which devolved on Aaron, as the head of that house. He was appointed to the office of HIGH-PRIEST, at first simply THE PRIEST, as representing the whole order, the intercessor between Jehovah and the people; his sons became the *Priests,* who alone could offer sacrifices; and the rest of the tribe formed the class of *Levites,* who assisted in the services of the tabernacle. For this purpose the Levites are said to be "given" to Aaron and his sons; but afterward they were relieved of some of their enormous labor by a separate class of servants, such as the Gibeonites, who were made "hewers of wood and drawers of water"; and in the later history of the Jews such servants formed a distinct body, under the name of *Nethinim* (I Chron. 9:2; Ezra 2:43).

2. *The High-Priest – a. His consecration – b. His peculiar garments – c. His peculiar functions.* The HIGH-PRIEST — We find from the very first the following characteristic attributes of Aaron and the high-priests, his successors, as distinguished from the other priests:

a. In the consecration to the office Aaron alone was anointed (Lev. 8:12), whence one of the distinctive epithets of the high-priest was "the anointed priest" (Lev. 4:3,5,16). This appears also from Ex. 29:29,30. The anointing of the sons of Aaron, *i.e.,* the common priests, seems to have been confined to sprinkling their garments with the anointing oil (Ex. 29:21; 28:41). Both Aaron and his sons had blood placed on their right ears, thumbs and big toes, symbolizing the consecration of their ears, hands and feet (Lev. 8:23-24).

b. The high-priest had special garments, which passed to his successor at his death. This dress consisted of six parts: the *breastplate,* the *ephod* with its curious girdle, the *robe* of the ephod, the *mitre,* the *broidered coat* and the *girdle,* the materials being gold, blue, red, crimson and fine (white) linen (Ex. 28). To the above are added (Ex. 28:42) the *breeches* of linen; and some reckon the high-priest's mitre, or the plate separately from the bonnet; while others reckon the curious girdle of the ephod separately from the ephod. Of these six articles of attire, four — viz., the coat or tunic, the girdle, the breeches and the bonnet or turban, instead of the mitre, belonged to the common priests. The most remarkable and most important parts of the breastplate were the twelve precious stones, set in four rows, three in a row, thus corresponding to the twelve tribes, and divided in the same manner as their camps were; each stone having the name of one of the children of Isreal engraved upon it. Either these stones, or some unknown item(s) within the breastplate, constituted the *Urim* and *Thummim*. By means of the Urim and Thummim the priest was able to discern information, guidance and secrets from God. "Urim" and "Thummim" means "lights" and "perfections" (Ex. 28:15-30; Num. 27:21; Deut. 33:8,9; I Sam. 14:3, 18-19; Ezra 2:63; et al.).

c. Aaron had peculiar functions. To him alone it appertained, and he alone was permitted to enter the Holy of Holies, which he did once a year, on the great Day of Atonement, when he sprinkled the blood of the sin-offering on the mercy-seat, and burnt incense within the veil (Lev. 16). He is said by the Talmudists not to have worn his full pontifical robes on this occasion, but to have been clad entirely in white linen (Lev. 16:4,32).

The high-priest had a peculiar place in the law of the manslayer, and his taking sanctuary in the cities of refuge. The manslayer might not leave the city of refuge during the lifetime of the existing high-priest, who was anointed with the holy oil (Num. 35:25,28). It was also forbidden to the high-priest to follow a funeral or rend his clothes for the dead, according to the precedent in Lev. 10:6.

The usual age for entering upon the functions of the priesthood (II Chron. 31:17) is considered to have been twenty years. Again (Lev. 21), no one that had a blemish could officiate at the altar, and illegitimate birth was also a bar to the high-priesthood. The high-priest held his office for life; and it was the universal opinion of the Jews that the deposition of a high-priest, which in later times became so common, was unlawful.

The Epistle to the Hebrews sets forth the mystic meaning of his office, as a type of Christ, our great High-priest, who has passed into the heaven of heavens with his own blood, to appear in the presence of God for us; and this is typified in the minutest particulars of his dress, his functions and his privileges. In the Book of Revelation, the clothing of the son of man "with a garment down to the foot," and "with a golden girdle about the breasts," are distinctly the robe and the curious girdle of the ephod, characteristic of the high-priest.

3. *The Priests – Consecration and dress – Regulations respecting them – Their duties – Maintenance of them.* The PRIESTS — All the sons of Aaron formed the order of the priests. They stood between the high-priest on the one hand and the Levites on the other. The ceremony of their consecration is described in Ex. 29:8, Lev. 8. The dress which they wore during their ministrations consisted of linen drawers, with a close-fitting robe also of linen, white, but with a diamond or chessboard pattern on it (Ex. 29:8-9). Upon their heads they were to wear caps or bonnets in the form of a cup-shaped flower, also of fine linen. In all their acts of ministration they were to be barefooted.

Before they entered the tabernacle they were to wash their hands and their feet (Ex. 30:17-21). During the time of their ministrations they were to drink no wine or strong drink (Lev. 10:9). Except in the case of the nearest relationships (Lev. 21:1-5), they were to make no mourning for the dead. They were not to shave their heads. They were to go through their ministrations with the serenity of a reverential awe, not with the orgiastic wildness which led the priests of Baal in their despair to make cuttings in their flesh (Lev. 19:28; I Kings 18:28). They were forbidden to marry an unchaste woman, or one who had been divorced, or the widow of any but a priest (Lev. 21:7,14).

Their chief duties were to watch over the fire on the altar of burnt-offerings and to keep it burning evermore both by day and night (Lev. 6:12), to feed the golden lamp outside the veil with oil (Ex. 27:20-21), to offer the morning and evening sacrifices, each accompanied with a meal-offering and a drink-offering, at the door of the tabernacle (Ex. 29:38-44). They were also to teach the children of Israel the statutes of the Lord (Lev. 10:11). During the journeys in the wilderness it belonged to them to cover the ark and all the vessels of the sanctuary with a purple or scarlet cloth before the Levites might approach them (Num. 4:5-15). As the people started on each day's march they were to blow "an alarm" with long silver trumpets (Num. 10:1-8). Other instruments of music might be used by the more highly-trained Levites and the schools of the prophets, but the trumpets belonged only to the priests.

Functions such as these were clearly incompatible with the common activities of men. On these grounds therefore a distinct provision was made for them. This consisted — (1) of one-tenth of the tithes which the people paid to the Levites, *i.e.,* one per cent, of the whole produce of the country (Num. 18:26-28). (2) Of a special tithe every third year (Deut. 14:28; 26:12). (3) Of the redemption-money, paid at the fixed rate of five shekels a head, for the firstborn of man or beast (Num. 18:14-19). (4) Of the redemption-money paid in like manner of men or things specially dedicated to the Lord (Lev. 27). (5) Of spoil, captives, cattle and the like taken in war (Num. 31:25-47). (6) Of the shew-bread, the flesh of the burnt-offerings, peace-offerings, trespass-offerings (Num. 18:8-14; Lev. 6:26,29); and, in particular, the heave-shoulder and the wave-breast (Lev. 10:12-15). (7) Of an undefined amount of the first-fruits of corn, wine and oil (Ex. 23:19; Lev. 2:14). Of some of these, as "most holy," none but the priests were to partake (Lev. 6:20). It was lawful for their sons and daughters (Lev. 10:14), and even in some cases for their home-born slaves, to eat of sacrifices (Lev. 22:11). The stranger and the hired servant were in all cases excluded (Lev. 22:10). (8) On their settlement in Canaan the priestly families had thirteen cities assigned them, with "suburbs" or pasture-grounds for their flocks (Josh. 21:13-19). These provisions were obviously intended to secure the religion of Israel against the dangers of a caste of pauper-priests, needy and dependent, and unable to bear their witness to the true faith. They were, on the other hand, as far as possible removed from the condition of a wealthy order. The standard of a priest's income, even in the earliest days after the settlement in Canaan, was miserably low (Judges 17:10; II Chron. 31:10).

4. *The Levites – The duties in general – Division into three families – Their support and settlement in the Promised Land – Duties in later times.* The LEVITES were the assistants of the priests, and included all the males of the tribe of Levi who were not of the family of Aaron, and who were of the prescribed age, namely, from thirty to fifty (Num. 4:23,30,35). Their duties required a man's full strength; after the age of fifty they were relieved from all service, except that of superintendance (Num. 8:25-26). They had to assist the

priests, to carry the tabernacle and its vessels, to keep watch about the sanctuary, to prepare the supplies of corn, wine, oil and so forth, and to take charge of the sacred treasures and revenues.

The Levites were divided into three familes, which bore the names of the three sons of Levi: the GERSHONITES, the KOHATHITES and the MERARITES; and each had their appointed functions in the service of the tabernacle.

a. The KOHATHITES had the precedence, as the house of Amran belonged to this family. They were to bear all the vessels of the sanctuary, the Ark itself included (Num. 3:31; 4:15; Deut. 31:25), after the priests had covered them with the dark-blue cloth which was to hide them from all profane gaze.

b. The GERSHONITES had to carry the tent-hangings and curtains (Num. 4:22-26).

c. The MERARITES had the heavier burden of the boards, bars and pillars of the tabernacle. But the Gershonites and Merarites were allowed to use the oxen and the wagons which were offered by the congregation (Num. 7:1-9). The more sacred vessels of the Kohathites were to be borne by them on their own shoulders (Num. 7:9).

The whole tribe of Levi encamped close round the tabernacle: the priests in front on the east, the Kohathites on the south, the Gershonites on the west and the Merarites on the north.

The Levites had no territorial possessions. In place of them, they received from the other tribes the tithes of the produce of the land, from which they, in their turn, offered a tithe to the priests (Num. 18:21,24,26). On their settlement in the promised land, the most laborious parts of their duty were over, and they were relieved from others by the submission of the Gibeonites and the conquest of the Hivites, who became "hewers of wood and drawers of water" (Josh. 9:27). Hence their concentration about the tabernacle was no longer necessary, and it was more important for them to live among their brethren as teachers and religious guides. Forty-eight cities were assigned to the whole tribe, that is, on an average, four in the territory of each tribe; thirteen being given to the priests, and the rest to the Levites. Six of these cities, three on each side of Jordan, were *cities of refuge* for the manslayer; an institution which invested the Levites with the sacred character of protectors from danger. The suburbs of these cities gave pasture to their flocks.

After their settlement in their cities they took the place of the household priests (subject, of course, to the special rights of the

Aaronic priesthood), sharing in all festivals and rejoicings (Deut. 12:19; 14:26-27). They preserved, transcribed and interpreted the law (Deut. 17:9-12; 31:26), which they solemnly read every seventh year at the Feast of Tabernacles (Deut. 31:9-13). They pronounced the curses from Mount Ebal (Deut. 27:14).

At a still later time they became the learned class in the community, the chroniclers of the times in which they lived. One of the first to bear the title of "scribe" is a Levite (I Chron. 24:6), and this is mentioned as one of their special offices under Josiah (II Chron. 34:13). They are described as "officers and judges" under David (II Chron. 17:8; 30:22), and as such are employed "in all the business of Jehovah, and in the service of the king." Now that the heavier work of conveying the tabernacle and its equipments from place to place was no longer required of them, and that temple music had become the most prominent of their duties, they were to enter on their work at the earlier age of twenty (I Chron. 23:24-27).

Questions Over Section III
The Tabernacle and Priesthood

1. Where did God give Moses instructions about the tabernacle?
2. What was the tabernacle?
3. Why is the tabernacle important to us?
4. Where did God dwell in the time of the tabernacle?
5. Where within the tabernacle did God particularly reveal His presence?
6. Who were camped about the tabernacle?
7. What were some of the names for the tabernacle?
8. Who were the materials obtained for the tabernacle?
9. What men actually constructed the tabernacle?
10. What special guidance did the builders of the tabernacle have?
11. How many tabernacles did all the parts of the tabernacle combine to form?
12. What kind of money was collected for the service of the tabernacle?
13. By what means was the tabernacle sanctified for holy use? Of what is anointing oil a symbol?
14. What covered over (or hovered over) the tabernacle?
15. What is the estimated value of the materials in the tabernacle?
16. Draw a sketch of the tabernacle floor plan showing the court.

the Holy Place and the Holy of Holies, and the location of all items of furniture.

17. Give the dimensions of the court, including its entrance (Ex. 27:9-16).
18. What items or materials were used in making the court (Ex. 27:9-18).
19. What were the dimensions of the altar of burnt offering (Ex. 27:1)?
20. When was fire kept burning on the altar of burnt offering (Lev. 6:12-13)?
21. Of what material was the laver made (Ex. 30:17-21)?
22. Where was this material for the laver obtained (Ex. 38:8)?
23. When did the priests wash in the laver (Ex. 29:4; 30:20-21)?
24. What were the dimensions of the Holy Place? The Holy of Holies? The entire tabernacle building?
25. What were the walls of the tabernacle made of (Ex. 26:15-25)?
26. What held the boards together (Ex. 26:26-29)?
27. What materials were used in the four coverings of the tabernacle (Ex. 26:1-14)?
28. What separated the Holy Place from the Most Holy Place (Ex. 26:31-35)?
29. What does the name shew-bread mean (Ex. 25:30)?
30. How many loaves were placed on the table of shew-bread? How often were new loaves put out (Lev. 24:5-9)?
31. How often was the lampstand tended to (Lev. 24:1-4)?
32. How often was incense burned on the altar of incense (Ex. 30:1-10)?
33. Name the three items kept in or beside the ark of the covenant (Heb. 9:4)?
34. What was the lid or covering of the ark called (Ex. 25:17-22)? Describe this lid or covering.
35. Describe the ark of the covenant. Give its dimensions (Ex. 25:10-16).
36. Who only went into the Holy of Holies? How often? At what time (Heb. 9:7; Lev. 16; 23:27-28)?
37. Of what was the altar of burnt offering a type?
38. Of what was the laver a type?
39. Of what was the altar of incense a type?
40. Of what was the veil a type? What would the rending of the veil when Christ died represent (Matt. 27:51; Heb. 10:19-20; 9:7-8)?
41. Of what was the Holy of Holies a type (Heb. 9:11-12,24)?

The Priesthood

1. Who was Israel's first high priest (Lev. 8:12)?
2. List the distinctive garments of the high priest and describe them briefly.
3. What was *Urim* and *Thummim* (Ex. 28:30)?
4. What was the high priest's distinctive function on the Day of Atonement (Lev. 16)?
5. What was the high priest's distinctive function in the cities of refuge (Num. 35:25)?
6. List three duties of the priests (Lev. 6:12; Ex. 27:20-21; 29:38-44; Lev. 10:11).
7. How were the priests supported (Num. 18:26-28)?
8. Who were the assistants of the priests (Num. 3:6-9)?
9. Name the three families of the Levites (Num. 3:17-20).
10. How were the Levites supported (Num. 18:21)?
11. How many cities were given to the Levites (Num. 35:6-7)?

Section IV
The Book of Leviticus

1. Sacrifices — a. The burnt-offering — b. The meal-offering — c. The peace-offering — d. The sin-offering — e. Trespass-offering. 2. Holiness of the people — a. The principle of holiness — b. Circumcision — c. Dedication of first-born — d. Personal purity — e. Provisions for purification — f. Clean and unclean animals — g. Laws against disfigurement — h. Provisions for the poor — i. Humanity enforced. 3. Leprosy. 4. Sacred Seasons — a. Festivals connected with the Sabbath: (1) The Sabbath; (2) Feast of the New Moon; (3) Sabbatical Month and Feast of Trumpets; (4) The Sabbatical Year; (5) The Year of Jubilee — b. The three great historical festivals: (1) Passover; (2) Pentecost or Feast of Weeks; (3) Feast of Tabernacles — c. The Day of Atonement — d. Festivals after the captivity: (1) Feast of Purim; (2) Feast of Dedication.

A. Introduction

1. The name LEVITICUS is taken from the Greek and Latin names for this book. It is derived from LEVI, the priestly tribe.

The word Leviticus is actually an adjective, meaning the "Levitical" (book).

2. The book contains mostly ceremonial laws for priests and people. Some brief historical sections are included. Chapter 10 and 24:10-23 are historical sections.

3. Moses was the author of Leviticus. Compare Lev. 14:1-4 with Matthew 8:4. However, no other book of the Bible affirms its divine authorship as frequently as Leviticus does. No less than thirty-eight times it declares that Jehovah spoke the words.

4. The key idea and word in Leviticus is HOLINESS. The word "holy" is found about eighty times in the book. Leviticus 19:2 is a key verse. (Memorize this verse and Lev. 17:11.)

5. Leviticus was written while Israel was at Mt. Sinai and in the years of the wilderness wandering (Lev. 16:34). It was written after the tabernacle was built (Lev. 8:1-4).

6. Outline of Leviticus

I. The five sacrificial offerings (Chs. 1-7)

II. Consecration of priests (Chs. 8-10)

III. Clean and unclean things (Chs. 11-15)

IV. Day of Atonement (Ch. 16)

V. Prohibitions for people (Chs. 17-20) and for priests (Chs. 21-22)

VI. Feasts (Chs. 23-25)

VII. Blessings and curses (Ch. 26)

Vows and tithes (Ch. 27)

7. Leviticus tells (1) the means of approach to God (as through sacrificial offerings and the ministry of the priests), and (2) the means of maintaining fellowship with God (through the feasts, avoiding unclean things, etc.)

8. Leviticus is meaningful to us because Christ is the fulfillment of all the sacrifices, priesthood and ritual in Leviticus. An acquaintance with Leviticus will help us to comprehend the unsearchable riches of Christ, who is our priest, our sacrifice, our Passover, our altar, our atonement, our all!

Questions

1. Where do we get the name Leviticus and what does it mean?
2. What does Leviticus mostly contain?
3. Who was the author of Leviticus?
4. What is the key word and idea in Leviticus?

5. Write Leviticus 19:2 and 17:11 from memory.
6. Where and when was Leviticus written?
7. Memorize the outline of Leviticus.
8. Why is Leviticus meaningful to us?

B. Information Pertaining to Leviticus

1. *Sacrifices.* Leviticus 1-7 deals with five types of sacrifices or offerings to God. Sacrifices had been offered ever since the fall. We read of the whole burnt-offerings, such as those of Abel and Noah, the *thank-offering,* as that of Jethro, and the sacrifices by which *covenants* were ratified. To these the law of Moses added the *special sacrifices for sins and trespasses,* and for particular classes of persons *(as the priests),* the *meal-offerings,*[1] and the *drink-offerings.*

Most of the sacrifices were bloody; however some were unbloody, involving meal, grain, etc. In some of the sacrifices the victim was not entirely burnt, a portion of it was used as food, both by the priests, who were "to live of the altar," and also by the offeres themselves. All of these offerings are types or symbols of the offerings provided by God in Christ Jesus for our salvation. The fact that one offering was shared of the offerer as well as the altar and the priest shows us that the offerings of God are not only to satisfy the justice of God, but are for our *life* in God.

The sacrifices are divided into *burnt-offerings* with the accompanying *meal-offerings, peace-offerings, sin-offerings* for sins of ignorance, and *trespass-offerings* for various legal violations. The three former were of the nature of *gifts,* the two latter of *propitiatory* sacrifices; but even in the gift, as coming from a sinful man, there was present the idea of propitiation by the blood of the victim, and it was always preceded by a sin-offering.

At the risk of extreme oversimplification we will summarize the typology and significance of the sacrifices: a. *Burnt-offering* — The death of Christ for our sins; b. *Meal-offering* — Our gift of ourselves in accompaniment with Christ's gift of Himself for us; c. *Peace-offering* — Expressions of joy and peace in salvation; d. *Sin-offering* — Sacrifices for sins done ignorantly; e. *Trespass-offering* — For trespasses of ceremony, oaths, property.

a. The *Burnt-offering* or whole burnt-offering (Lev. ch. 1; 6:8-13), was so called because the victim was wholly consumed

---

1. The term *meal-offering* is consistently rendered *meat-offering* in the King James Bible. But the term *meat* is used as a general term for food, especially for grain and flour. We shall use the name *meal-offering* consistently as it more plainly indicates the nature of the offering.

by fire upon the altar of burnt-offering, and so, as it were, sent up to God on the wings of fire. This idea, which is expressed in the account of Noah's sacrifice, and which constantly recurs, both in the Scriptures and in profane authors, is implied in the Hebrew word which signifies to ascend. And every such sacrifice was a type of the perfect offering made by Christ on behalf of the race of man, of his human nature and will to do the will of the Father (Eph. 5:2).

Burnt-offerings were either made on behalf of the whole people, or by one or more individuals, who must bring them of their own free-will. Only four kinds of animals might be offered and they must be free from disease or blemish. To offer the unclean, maimed or diseased in sacrifice was an abomination to Jehovah.

1. Of the *herd,* a young bullock of not less than one nor more than three years, generally of the third year.
2. Of the *flock,* a lamb or kid, a male of the like age, but generally of the first year.
3. Of *birds,* turtle-doves or young pigeons, without distinction of sex. The victim was brought to the north side of the altar in the court of the tabernacle, where the offerer laid his hand upon its head, in token of its being a substitute for his own life, and slew it himself by cutting its throat, or if a bird, wringing off its head and pressing out the blood. In public sacrifices, these acts were done by the priest. The Levites assisted and in later times they slew all the victims. The blood, "which is the *life,*" was received in a basin, and sprinkled by the priest around the altar. The victim was then flayed and cut in pieces, the complete ruination of the sinner. The pieces were laid upon the wood on the altar and consumed, but the birds were not divided. Each day's sacrifices burnt on through the night, the sacred fire never being suffered to go out; and in the morning the ashes were carried by the priest into a clean place without the camp (Ex. 29:38-42; Lev. 1).

Burnt-offerings were made on the following occasions:

1. The *Daily Sacrifice* of a yearling lamb or kid was offered at the times of morning and evening prayer, the third and ninth hours from sunrise, before the priest went into the tabernacle to burn incense. This sacrifice especially typified the offering of Christ, who was pointed out by John the Baptist (about the third hour, it is supposed) as

"the Lamb of God, that taketh away the sin of the world," and who died upon the cross at the very time of the evening sacrifice.

2. The *Sabbath burnt-offering* was the daily sacrifice doubled (Num. 28:8-10).

3. The *burnt-offerings at the Festivals* of the *New Moon,* the *three great feasts,* the *Day of Atonement* and the *Feast of Trumpets,* generally two bullocks, a ram and seven lambs (Num. 28:11-29,39).

4. *Private burnt-offerings prescribed by the law:* at the consecration of priests, the purification of women, the removal of leprosy or other ceremonial uncleanness, the performance or the accidental breach of the vow of a Nazarite (Ex. 29:15; Lev. 12:6,8; 14:19; Num. 6).

5. *Free-will burnt-offerings* were made either in general acknowledgment of God's mercies (a *thank-offering)* or in performance of a vow. They were chiefly brought on occasions of great solemnity, as at the dedication of the tabernacle and of the temple (Num. 15:1-3:7).

b. The *Meal-offering* (Lev. 2:1-16; 6:14-23, 7:9-10) and the *Drink-offering* (Num. 15:1-4) always accompanied the burnt-offering. The name of the meal-offering *(Minchah)* signified in old Hebrew a *gift* in general, and especially one from an inferior to a superior. It is applied alike to the offerings of Cain and Abel, as a general name for a sacrifice (Gen. 4:3-5). The Hebrew word *corban* (meaning "an oblation," "a thing brought near"; Mark 7:11; Lev. 2:4,5,7,12,13) is often used to describe the meal-offering, and this strengthens the idea that the meal-offering was a *gift.*

In the law of Moses, it consisted of an offering of grains, usually in the form of flour, with oil and frankincense, the quantities varying for a lamb, a ram or a bullock. It was sometimes made with the oil into cakes or wafers, which must be free from leaven and honey. A special form of meal-offering was that of the first-fruits of corn in the ear, parched and bruised. All meal-offerings were to be seasoned with "the salt of the covenant," as a sign of incorruptness and of the savor of earnest piety (Lev. 2:13). A portion of the meal-offering and of the oil was burnt by the priest upon the altar of burnt-offering, with all the frankincense; and the rest belonged to the priests, who must eat it without leaven beside the altar, as "a thing most holy of the offerings of Jehovah made by fire" (Lev. 2:3). The meal-offerings of the priests themselves were to be wholly burnt. The drink-offerings of the daily and special sacrifices were poured out before Jehovah in the Holy Place (Num. 28:7); and it does not appear that the priests were ever permitted to partake of them. Indeed, to have done so would have been a breach of the prohibition of wine during their service (Deut. 32:38).

c. The *Peace-offering* (Lev. 3:1-17; 7:11-38; 9:18-21; 10:12-15) was not an atoning sacrifice to make peace with God, but a joyful celebration of *peace made* through the covenant. In this part of the ritual, more than in any other, we see Jehovah present in His *house,* inviting the worshiper to *feast with Him.* Peace-offerings were presented either as a *thanksgiving* or in fulfillment of a *vow,* or as a *free-will offering* of love and joy. They were of the flock or the herd, like the burnt-offerings, but they might be male or female. They were slain with the same ceremonies as the burnt-offering; but only a part was burnt upon the altar, namely, all the fat, the kidneys, the caul or midriff, and in the case of a lamb, the rump. The breast and the shoulder were the portion of the priests, who might eat them in any clean place with their sons and daughters. They were called the *wave-breast* and the *heave-shoulder,* from the motions made in offering them before Jehovah. The priest also took one of the unleavened cakes or leavened loaves, which were offered as a meal-offering with the peace-offering, having first heaved it before God. These motions seem to indicate the joy of a feast; and with joy the *worshiper* was to eat the rest of the flesh of the sacrifice and the bread of the meal-offering, under certain restrictions, to insure ceremonial purity.

Peace-offerings might be brought at anytime; but they were prescribed on the following occasions: at the consecration of priests, the dedication of the tabernacle, the purification of a leper and the expiration of a Nazirite's vow.

d. The *Sin-offering* was an expiatory sacrifice for sins of ignorance, committed either by a *priest,* unconsciously contracting sins from the people in his office; or by the *congregation,* incurring the displeasure of Jehovah for a reason not discovered; or by a *ruler,* ignorantly transgressing any of God's laws; or by one of the *people,* finding that he had unintentionally been guilty of any sin; and also as a purification from possible sin and uncleanness in general. For each of these cases special victims were to be offered with special ceremonies. The most important of these were, in the two former cases, the sprinkling of the blood seven times before the veil, and placing it on the horns of the altar and burning the flesh of the victim without the camp — a type of Christ's suffering without the gate for the people's sin. The flesh of the other sin-offerings belonged to the priests; in all cases the fat was burnt on the altar. Sin-offerings formed a part of all great solemnities, especially on the day of atonement. They were also offered at the purification of a leper or of a woman after child-birth. In the latter case, the offering was a lamb; or for the poor, a pair of turtle-doves or pigeons, one for the burnt-offering and other for the sin-offering (Luke 2:24).

e. *Trespass-offerings* (Lev. 5:1-19; 6:1-7; 7:1-8) for sins committed knowingly, as well as for acts of ceremonial uncleanness, are not very clearly distinguished from sin-offerings. The chief difference of form,[1] besides some points in the ceremonial, was that they were offered only for individuals. As to spirit and motive, the distinction seems to be that sins committed in rashness, as by an oath, or in ignorance of a law that ought to have been known, came under the head of *trespass:* "Though he wish it not, yet he is quilty, and shall bear in iniquity." The chief offenses which required trespass-offerings were: keeping back evidence, touching unclean things, swearing rash oaths, sins in holy things, violation of trust and some others. In every case of injury to property, the offering must be accompanied with *restitution* to the whole value, and one-fifth in addition.

2. *Holiness of the people – a. The principle of holiness – b. Circumcision – c. Dedication of first-born – d. Personal purity – e. Provisions for purification – f. Clean and unclean animals – g. Laws against disfigurement – h. Provisions for the poor – i. Humanity enforced.*

a. The holiness of the people, as the children of God, His "saints who had made a covenant with Him by sacrifice," was a principle as sacred as the consecration of the priests. They, like the children of the New Covenant, were "a chosen generation, a royal priesthood, *an holy nation,* a peculiar people," the purchased possession of Jehovah (I Pet. 2:9; Ex. 19:5-6); and for both there was the same simple law: "BE YE HOLY, FOR I AM

---

1. The poor might substitute flour, without oil or frankincense, for the two turtle-doves or pigeons of the sin-offering, so as to leave no excuse for neglecting the sacrifice.

HOLY." Holiness means *separation* or *withdrawal*. This principle, from which Paul so often deduces the spiritual law of the complete devotion of the whole nature to God's service, was enforced upon the Jews by ceremonies and restrictions reaching to every detail of their daily lives. It is the central subject of the Book of Leviticus, which gradually rises from the laws of sacrifice to the assertion and development of the holiness and purity of the people, in person, act, speech and property (Lev. 11-18). The following institutions were founded on this principle:

b. *Circumcision* is only enjoined in one passage of the law of Moses (Lev. 12:3). It had already been fully established, and Moses alludes to its spiritual sense, the circumcision of the heart, in language similar to that of Paul. The words of Christ, "Moses gave you circumcision, not because it is of Moses, but of the fathers" (John 7:22), refer to the full account of the institution in the Book of Genesis, which rendered its repetition in the later books unnecessary.

c. The *Dedication of the First-born* of men and beasts and the offering of the *First-fruits* of all produce (Ex. 13:2, 12-13; Deut. 26:1-11).

d. The *Preservation of Personal Purity*, especially by the strict laws against all unnatural marriages and lusts, and against fornication and prostitution. The law of Moses, like that of Christ, takes cognizance of sins against *a man's own self*, and that not so much in the light of self-interest, or even of self-respect, but from that principle of holiness to God which is so emphatically laid down by the Apostle Paul (Lev. 17-19).

e. *Provisions for Purification:* (1) As a religious ceremonial, observed both by priests and people in divine worship (Num. 19). (2) From personal uncleanness. (3) From leprosy, in persons, clothes or houses. The means of purification were washing, the sprinkling of blood, anointing with oil and the washing by the ashes of the *red heifer*. In some cases, as in leprosy, unclean persons were shut out from the camp (Num. 12:15).

f. The distinction between *clean* and *unclean animals* for food as well as sacrifice. Unclean animals were those strangled, which had died a natural death, or had been killed by beasts or birds of prey; whatever beast did not both part the hoof and chew the cud; and certain other smaller animals rated as "creeping things"; certain classes of birds mentioned in Lev. 11 and

Deut. 14, twenty or twenty-one in all; whatever in the waters had not both fins and scales; whatever winged insects had not, besides four legs, the two hind-legs for leaping; besides things offered in sacrifice to idols; and all blood, or whatever contained it; as also all fat, at any rate that disposed in masses among the intestines, and probably wherever discernible and separable among the flesh (Lev. 3:14-17). The eating of blood was prohibited even to "the stranger that sojourneth among you" (Lev. 17:10-14). The fat was claimed as a burnt-offering, and the blood enjoyed the highest sacrificial esteem. In the two combined the entire victim was by representation offered, and to transfer either to human use was to deal presumptuously with the most holy things. But besides this, the blood was esteemed as "the life" of the creature, and a mysterious sanctity beyond the sacrificial relation thereby attached to it. Hence we read, "Whatsoever soul it be that eateth any manner of blood, even that soul shall be cut off from his people." The offender in other dietary violations was merely "unclean until even" (Lev. 11:40). Sanitary reasons have been sought for these laws, and there may be something in this view, though their first signification was religious. The apostles and the primitive Church extended to Gentile converts the restriction about eating blood and things strangled (Acts 15:20,29).

g. The *Laws against Personal Disfigurement,* by shaving the head and cutting the flesh, especially as an act of mourning, have also reference to the customs of the heathen. The humane restriction on the number of stripes that might be inflicted was designed to prevent a man's degradation in the eyes of his brethren (Lev. 19:27-28; Deut. 25:3).

h. The *Provisions for the Poor.* The poor were regarded as brethren in the covenant of God. *Gleanings* in the field and vineyard were their legal right (Lev. 19:9-10); *slight trespass* was allowed, such as plucking corn (Deut. 27:24-25) while passing through a field, provided that it was eaten on the spot; *wages* were to be paid day by day (Deut. 24:15); *loans* might not be refused, nor usury taken from an Israelite (Ex. 22:25-27); *pledges* must not be insolently or ruinously exacted (Deut. 24:6, 10-13); no favor must be shown between rich and poor in dispensing justice (Lev. 19:15); and besides all this, there are the most urgent injunctions to kindness to the poor, the widow and the orphan, and the strongest denunciations of all oppression (Deut. 15:7-11).

i. The care taken to enforce *humanity* in general may be regarded as an extension of the same principle; for the truest motive to humanity is the constant sense of man's relation to his Heavenly Maker, Father and Master. For example, the state of *slavery* was mitigated by the law that death under chastisement was punishable, and that maiming at once gave liberty (Ex. 21:20, 26-27). *Fugitive slaves* from foreign nations were not to be given up (Deut. 23:15); and *stealing and selling a man* was punished with death (Ex. 21:16). The law even "cared for oxen" declaring, "Thou shalt not muzzle the ox when he treadeth out the corn" (Deut. 25:4). It went further and provided against that abominable law of our corrupt nature, which finds pleasure in wanton cruelty, adding such precepts as those which forbade the parent bird to be captured with its young (Deut. 22:6-7), or the kid to be boiled in its mother's milk. The latter custom is known to have been practiced by the heathen Canaanites at Ugarit as a milk charm (Ex. 23:19).

3. *Leprosy* (Lev. 13-14). The predominant and characteristic form of leprosy in Scripture is a white variety, covering either the entire body or a large tract of its surface; which has obtained the name of *lepra Mosaica*. Such were the cases of Moses, Miriam, Naaman and Gehazi (Ex. 4:6; Num. 12:10; II Kings 5:1,27; Comp. Levit. 8:13). The Egyptian bondage, with its studied degradations and privations, and especially the work of the kiln under an Egyptian sun, must have had a frightful tendency to generate this class of disorders; hence Manetho asserts that the Egyptians drove out the Israelites as infected with leprosy — a strange reflex, perhaps, of the Mosaic narrative of the "plagues" of Egypt, yet probably also containing a germ of truth. The principal morbid features mentioned in Leviticus are a rising or swelling, a scab or baldness, and a bright or white spot (8:2). But especially a white swelling in the skin, with a change of the hair of the part from the natural black to white or yellow (3,10,4,20,25,30), or an appearance of a taint going "deeper than the skin" or again "raw flesh" appearing in the swelling (10,14,15) were critical signs of pollution.

The foregoing remarks and other facts make it appear that the leprosy of the Bible is not the same disease as the disfiguring and fatal Hansen's disease called leprosy in modern times.

Biblical leprosy often produced white patches on the skin. Hansen's disease never produces whiteness.

Biblical leprosy is spoken of as being *cleansed*, but never as being *healed* (Matt. 10:8; 8:2-3; Lev. 14:2).

Biblical leprosy could be cleansed in a matter of days sometimes (Lev. 13:3-6). Hansen's disease requires months to heal, even with modern drugs.

Biblical leprosy seems to have been some skin ailment such as psoriasis or ringworm or leucoderma. The leprosy of houses and garments was some fungus infestation, mildew, mold or dry rot (Lev. 13:47-58; 14:37-53).

4. *Sacred Seasons* (Lev. 23,25). The SACRED SEASONS ordained in the law fall under three heads:

a. Those connected with the institution of the Sabbath — namely.
  1. The weekly Sabbath itself.
  2. The Feast of the New Moon.
  3. The Sabbatical Month and the Feast of Trumpets.
  4. The Sabbatical Year.
  5. The Year of Jubilee.
b. The Three Great Historical Festivals — namely,
  1. The Passover.
  2. The Feast of Pentecost.
  3. The Feast of Tabernacles.
c. The Day of Atonement. To these must be added d., the festivals established after the captivity — namely,
  1. The Feast of Purim or Lots.
  2. The Feast of Dedication.
a. FESTIVALS CONNECTED WITH THE SABBATH.
  1. The SABBATH is so named from a word signifying *rest*. No work was to be done on that day, the seventh day of the week, i.e. our Saturday (Lev. 2:1-3; 19:3; Ex. 31:17-19; 35:2-3; 20:8-11; Deut. 5:12-15). A great snare, too, has always been hidden in the word *work*, as if the commandment forbade occupation and imposed idleness. A consideration of the spirit of the law and of Christ's comments on it will show that it is *work for worldly gain* that was to be suspended. Christ taught that it was lawful to do good on the Sabbath, and the Jews themselves understood that it was permissible to do absolutely necessary work (Matt. 12:11-12).

The prohibitory part of the law is general; and the only special cases mentioned relate to the preparation of food. The manna was not given on the Sabbath, but a double supply was to be gathered on the day before, just as the rest of the *Sabbatic year* was compensated by the extraordinary fertility of the year before. No fire was to be kindled on the Sabbath, under the penalty of death (Ex. 35:2-3), which was inflicted on a man who went out to gather sticks on the Sabbath (Num. 15:35). Its observance is enjoined in the time of eating and harvest, when there was a special temptation to find an excuse for work (Ex. 24:21).

The Sabbath was a perpetual *sign* and *covenant,* and the holiness of the day is connected with the holiness of the people: "That ye may know that I am Jehovah that doth sanctify you" (Ex. 31:12-17). *Joy* was the key-note of their service.

The Sabbath is named as a day of special worship in the sanctuary (Lev. 19:30). It was proclaimed as a holy convocation (Lev. 23:3). The public religious services consisted in the doubling of the morning and evening sacrifice, and the renewal of the shew-bread in the Holy Place. In later times the worship of the sanctuary was enlivened by sacred music (Ps. 68:25-27). (For more concerning the Sabbath, see page 182.)

2. The completion of the month was observed by the FEAST OF THE NEW MOON. In every nation which uses a strictly lunar calendar, it is necessary to have a distinct public announcement of the beginning of each month, whether it be determined by an exact astronomical computation of the time of the moon's change, or by the first sight of her new crescent. This announcement was made to Israel by the sounding of the two sacred silver trumpets (Num. 10:10). The day was not kept as a Sabbath, but besides the daily sacrifice, a burnt-offering was made of two bullocks, a ram and seven lambs, with a meat and drink offering and a goat for a sin-offering (Num. 28:11-14).

3. The SABBATICAL MONTH and the FEAST OF TRUMPETS. — The month of Tishri, being the seventh of the ecclesiastical and the first of the civil year, had a kind of Sabbatic character (Lev. 23:24). The calendar was so arranged that the first day fell on a Sabbath (that, no doubt, next after the new moon), and this, the civil *New Year's Day,* was ushered in by the blowing of trumpets and was called the *Feast of Trumpets.* It was a holy convocation; and it had its special sacrifices, in addition to those of other new moons, namely for the burnt-offering, a young bullock, a ram and seven lambs, with a meat and drink offering and a young goat for

a sin-offering (Num. 29:1-6). This month was also marked by the great Day of Atonement on the tenth, and the Feast of Tabernacles, the greatest of the whole year, which lasted from the fifteenth to the twenty-second of the month.

4. The SABBATICAL YEAR. — As each seventh day and each seventh month were holy, so was each seventh year. It was based on the principle of Jehovah's property in the land, which was therefore to keep its Sabbath to Him; and it was to be a season of rest for all and of especial kindness to the poor. The land was not to be sown, nor the vineyards and olive-yards dressed; and neither the spontaneous fruits of the soil, nor the produce of the vine and olive, were to be gathered; but all was to be left for the poor, the slave, the stranger and the cattle (Ex. 23:10-11; Lev. 25:1-7). The law was accompanied by a promise of treble fertility in the sixth year, the fruit of which was to be eaten till the harvest sown in the eighth year was reaped (Lev. 25:20-22). But the people were not debarred from other sources of subsistence, nor was the year to be spent in idleness. They could fish and hunt, take care of their bees and flocks, repair their buildings and furniture and manufacture their clothing. Still, as an agricultural people, they would have much leisure; they would observe the Sabbatic spirit of the year by using its leisure for the instruction of their families in the law and for acts of devotion; and in accordance with this there was a solemn reading of the law to the people assembled at the Feast of Tabernacles (Deut. 31:10-13). The Sabbatic year is also called the "year or release," because in it creditors were bound to release poor debtors from their obligations; with a special injunction not to withhold a loan because the year of release was near (Deut. 15:1-11). The release of a Hebrew slave took place likewise, not only in the Sabbatic year, but in the seventh year of his captivity (Deut. 15:12-18).

5. The YEAR OF JUBILEE was every fiftieth year, coming therefore after a Sabbatic series of Sabbatic years. The notion that it was the forty-ninth and not the fiftieth year is an assumption from the improbability of the land being left untilled for two successive years; but it is opposed to the plain statement of the law, which directs seven Sabbaths of years to be counted, even forty-nine years, and then that the jubilee should be proclaimed by the sounding of the

trumpet (Lev. 25:8). Thus the Year of Jubilee completed
each half-century and formed a Pentecost of years.

Its beginning is fixed for the tenth of the seventh month
(Tishri), the great Day of Atonement. It was doubtless after
the sacrifices of that solemn day were ended that the
trumpet of jubilee pealed forth its joyful notes,
proclaiming "liberty to the captive, and the opening of the
prison door to them that were bound." The land was left
uncultivated as in the Sabbatic year. The possessions which
poverty had compelled their owners to alienate returned to
the families to whom they had been allotted in the first
division of the Holy Land. This applied to fields and houses
in the country, and to the houses of Levites in the walled
cities; but other houses in such cities, if not redeemed
within a year from their sale, remained the perpetual
property of the buyer. In all transfers of property, the
value was to be computed by the number of "years of fruits"
(that is, apparently, exclusive of Sabbatic years) till the next
Jubilee: so that what was sold was the possession of the land
for that term. A property might be redeemed at any
intervening period, either by its owner or by his nearest
kinsman (the Goel), at a price fixed on the same principle.
Land sanctified to Jehovah by the owner might be
redeemed at any time before the next Jubilee, by payment
of one-fifth in addition to the estimated value of the crops;
but if not redeemed before the Jubilee, it then became
devoted forever. Land sanctified by its owner after he had
sold it could not be redeemed, and land devoted by the
purchaser returned at the Jubilee to the owner (Lev.
27:19-24). The whole institution was based on the principle
that the land was God's, who granted to each family its own
portion (Lev. 25:23,38). It was a practical solution of the
most perplexing questions concerning the right of
property in the land, and a safeguard against its
accumulation in the hands of great proprietors.

All Hebrew slaves, whether to their brethren or to
resident foreigners, were set free in the Year of Jubilee.
This applied alike to those who had fallen into servitude
since the last Sabbatic year, and to those who had chosen to
remain in servitude by the ceremony of boring the ear (Lev.
25:39; Ex. 21:2-6). Provision was made for the redemption
of the slave meanwhile in a manner similar to that of the

redemption of the land. Thus, as in the restitution of the land, the principle was asserted that the people were Jehovah's only, His servants redeemed from Egypt and incapable therefore of becoming bondsmen to any one but Him (Lev. 25:42,45).

It has been asserted that debts were remitted in the Year of Jubilee, and some go so far as to maintain that the remission in the Sabbatic year was merely a suspension of their exaction. But the Mosaic law plainly states that debts were remitted in the Sabbatic year and says nothing of their remission at the Jubilee.

The Jubilee had a higher spiritual meaning, often alluded to by the prophets, and at length fulfilled by Christ when he recited the words of Isaiah proclaiming the *acceptable year of the Lord,* good tidings to the poor, healing to the broken-hearted, deliverance to the captive, sight to the blind and liberty to the oppressed; and added, "This day is his scripture fulfilled in your ears" (Luke 4:18-21). It also seems to point to the time of the new heaven and earth when all things shall be made new and forever free from sin (Rev. 21:1-5).

b. THE THREE GREAT HISTORICAL FESTIVALS. In these the whole people were united to seek the face of God and to celebrate His mercies. Thrice in the year, at these feasts, all males were required to appear before Jehovah, that is, at the tabernacle or the temple, not empty-handed, but to make an offering with a joyful heart (Ex. 2:14-17; Deut. 16:16). From the examples of Hannah and Mary (Luke 2:41; I Sam. 1:3-5), it appears that devout women went up to one of the annual festivals. There is no such requirement with reference to the Day of Atonement; but viewing it as a public reconciliation of the people with Jehovah, preparatory to their most joyful feast, it seems natural to suppose that most of those who went up to the Feast of Tabernacles would go early enough to be present on the Day of Atonement. These periodical assemblages of the people, including in later times even those who lived in foreign countries (Acts 2:5-11), were a powerful means of preserving the unity of the nation.

These festivals not only commemorated great events in the history of Israel, but they had each its significance in reference to God's gifts at the seasons of the year. The Passover marked the beginning of the harvest, the Pentecost its completion and the Feast of Tabernacles the vintage and the ingathering of all the fruits of the year.

1. The PASSOVER was the most solemn of the three festivals, as the memorial of the nation's birth and the type of Christ's death. The Passover was followed by the *Feast of Unleavened Bread,* which lasted for *seven days,* from the *evening* which closed the fourteenth to the end of the twenty-first of the first month of the sacred year, Abib or Nisan *(April).* The Paschal Lamb was eaten on the first evening and unleavened bread throughout the week, and the first and last days (the fifteenth and twenty-first) were holy convocations. We have already noticed its first institution in Egypt and its second celebration before Sinai. It was slain in each house and its blood was sprinkled on the door-posts; the supper was eaten by all members of the family, clean and unclean, standing and in haste, and without singing; and there were no days of holy convocation from the nature of the case, though their future observance was named in the original law (Ex. 12). But in the "Perpetual Passover," as arranged by the law and by later usage, the Paschal Lamb was selected any time up to the day of the supper (Mark 14:12-16); it was sacrificed at the altar of burnt-offering; its fat was burnt and its blood was sprinkled on the altar (Deut. 16:1-6); the supper was eaten only by men (Ex. 23:17; Deut. 16:16), and they must be ceremonially clean (Num. 9:6-14); they sat or reclined at the feast, which they ate without haste (Matt. 26:20), with various interesting ceremonies and with the accompaniment of the *Hallel* or singing of Psalms 113-118.

In the twelfth and thirteenth chapters of Exodus there are not only distinct references to the observance of the festival in future ages, but there are several injunctions which were evidently not intended for the first Passover, and which indeed could not possibly have been observed. In the later notices of the festival in the books of the law, there are particulars added which appear as modifications of the original institution (Lev. 23:10-14; Num. 28:16-25; Deut. 16:1-6).[1]

The Second or Little Passover. — When the Passover was celebrated the second year in the wilderness, certain men

---

1. For a description of the Passover ritual in N.T. times, see Edersheim, *Life & Times of Jesus the Messiah,* Vol. II, p. 490ff., or earlier editions of Smith's *O.T. History,* pp. 262-263.

were prevented from keeping it, owing to their being defiled by contact with a dead body. Being thus prevented from obeying the Divine command, they came anxiously to Moses to inquire what they should do. He was accordingly instructed to institute a second Passover, to be observed on the fourteenth of the following month for the benefit of any who had been hindered from keeping the regular one in Nisan (Num. 9:11; Cf. II Chron. 30:14-20). The Talmudists called this the Little Passover.

The Chagigah. — The daily sacrifices are enumerated in the Pentateuch only in Num. 28:19-23, but reference is made to them (Lev. 23:8). Besides these public offerings, there was another sort of sacrifice connected with the Passover, as well as with the other great festivals, called in the Talmud *Chagigah, i.e., "festivity".* It was a voluntary peace-offering made by private individuals. The victim might be taken either from the flock or the herd. It might be either male or female but it must be without blemish. The offerer laid his hand upon its head and slew it at the door of the sanctuary. The blood was sprinkled on the altar and the fat of the inside, with the kidneys, was burned by the priest. The breast was given to the priest as a wave-offering and the right shoulder as a heave-offering (Lev. 3:1-5; 7:29-34). What remained of the victim might be eaten by the offerer and his guests on the day on which it was slain and on the day following; but if any portion was left till the third day it was burned (Lev. 7:16-18). The eating of the Chagigah was an occasion of social festivity connected with the festivals and especially with the Passover. This seems to have been the "Passover" of John 18:28, which was on the day after the regular Passover supper.

2. The PENTECOST,[1] HARVEST FEAST or FEAST OF WEEKS, may be regarded as a supplement to the Passover. This feast was originally a feast commemorating harvest and was held 50 days after the first sheaf of grain was cut (Lev. 23:10-16). This would cause its date to vary accordingly as the harvest was early or late in any given year. However, long before New Testament times, the Jews began to regard this feast as a commemoration of the giving of the law on Mt. Sinai,

---

1. The name Pentecost means "fiftieth" and refers to the fiftieth day. This Greek name is not the translation of any corresponding word in the Pentateuch; but the later name of the feast, which naturally grew out of the calculation of its interval from the Passover.

which occurred approximately fifty days after the Passover in Egypt. Not only was its meaning changed (without divine authorization), but the date of the feast was made uniform from year to year by setting it 50 days after their Passover feast.

The First Sheaf of Harvest. — The offering of the Omer or sheaf is mentioned nowhere in the law except Lev. 23:10-14). It is there commanded that when the Israelites reached the land of promise, they should bring on "the morrow after the Sabbath" (i.e. Sunday), the first sheaf of the harvest to the priest, to be waved by him before the Lord. The sheaf was of barley, as being the grain which was first ripe (II Kings 4:42). From this event the time of the Feast of Weeks was to be reckoned.

The feast arrived fifty days later and was so counted that it fell on the morrow after the Sabbath (Lev. 23:15). It lasted *only for* one day but the modern Jews extend it over two. The people, having presented before God the first sheaf of the harvest, departed to their homes to gather it in and then returned to keep the harvest feast before Jehovah. From the sixteenth of Nisan (counting from the passover, as the Jews later did) seven weeks were reckoned inclusively, and the next or fiftieth day was the Day of Pentecost, which fell on the sixth of Sivan (about the end of *May).* The intervening period included the whole of the grain harvest, of which the wheat was the latest crop. Its commencement is also marked as from the time when "thou beginnest to put the sickle to the corn."

The Pentecost was the Jewish harvest home and the people were especially exhorted to rejoice before Jehovah with their families, their servants, the Levite within their gates, the stranger, the fatherless and the widow, in the place chosen by God for His name, as they brought a freewill-offering of their hand to Jehovah their God (Deut. 16:10-11). That offering, of course, included the *Chagigah;* but the great feature of the celebration was the presentation of the *two loaves* made from the first-fruits of the wheat-harvest, and *leavened,* that is, in the state fit for ordinary food. With the loaves two lambs were offered as a peace-offering and all were waved before Jehovah and given to the priests; the loaves, being leavened, could not be offered on the altar. The other sacrifices were: a burnt-offering of a young bullock, two rams and seven lambs, with a meat and drink offering, and a kid for a sin-offering (Lev. 23:18-19). Till the pentecostal loaves were offered, the produce of the harvest might not be eaten, nor could any other first-fruits be offered. The whole ceremony was the completion of that dedication of the harvest to God, as its giver, and to whom both the land and the people were holy, which was begun by the offering of the wave-sheaf at the Passover.

We have classified the Feast of Weeks as one of the three *historical* feasts because the Jews observed it as such in commemoration of the giving of the law at Mt. Sinai, though without divine warrant for so doing. Pentecost is of greatest interest to Christians because on that feast after Christ ascended, the Holy Spirit came and the church of Christ was brought into existence (Acts 2). The symbolism of the Feast of Harvest typifying the harvest of souls that began on Pentecost is very impressive, but is not specifically developed in the scripture.

3. The FEAST OF TABERNACLES or FEAST OF INGATHERING completed the cycle of the festivals of the year and was celebrated with great rejoicings. It was at once a thanksgiving for the harvest and a commemoration of the time when the Israelites dwelt in tents during their passage through the wilderness (Ex. 23:16; Lev. 23:43). It fell in the autumn when the whole of the chief fruits of the ground, the corn, the wine and the oil, were gathered in (Lev. 23:39; Deut. 16:13-15). Its duration was strictly only seven days but it was followed by a day of holy convocation, distinguished by sacrifices of its own, which was sometimes spoken of as an eighth day (Lev. 23:36). It lasted from the fifteenth till the twenty-second of the month of Tishri.

During the seven days the Israelites were commanded to dwell in booths or huts *(tabernacles)* formed of the boughs of trees, etc. The boughs were of the olive, pine, myrtle and other trees with thick foliage (Neh. 8:15-16). The command in Lev. 23:40 is said to have been so understood that the Israelites, from the first day of the feast to the seventh, carried in their hands "the fruit" (as in the margin of the A.V., not *branches,* as in the text) "of goodly trees, with branches of palm-trees, boughs of thick trees, and willows of the brook."

The burnt-offerings of the Feast of Tabernacles were by far more numerous than those of any other festival. There were offered on each day two rams, fourteen lambs and a kid for a sin-offering. But what was most peculiar was the arrangement of the sacrifices of bullocks, in all amounting to seventy. Thirteen were offered on the first day, twelve on the second, eleven on the third, and so on, reducing the number by one each day till the seventh when seven bullocks only were offered (Num. 29:12-38). When the Feast of Tabernacles fell on a Sabbatical year, portions of the law were read each day in public to men, women, children and strangers (Deut. 31:10-13).

c. THE DAY OF ATONEMENT. The Day of Atonement (Lev. 16; 23:26-32; Num. 19:1-11) is the one single fast or day of humiliation prescribed by the Mosaic law; whence it is called the *Fast* (Acts 27:9), and by the Talmudists, *the Day*. It was observed on the tenth day of Tishiri, the seventh sacred and first civil month, five days before the Feast of Tabernacles. Thus it was interposed between the Feast of Trumpets, which ushered in the Sabbatic month, and the most joyous festival of the year.

It was kept as a most solemn Sabbath, when all must abstain from work, and "afflict their souls" on pain of being "cut off from among the people." Its ceremonies signified the public humiliation of the people for all the sins of the past year, and the remission of those sins by the atonement which the high-priest made within the veil, whither he entered on this day only. All the sacrifices of the day were performed by the high priest himself. He first washed his body in the Holy Place and put on his white linen garments, not the robes of state. Coming out of the tabernacle, he first brought forward the sacrifices for himself and his family, which were provided at his own cost: a young bullock for a sin-offering and a ram for a burnt-offering. This part of the ceremony set forth the imperfection of the Levitical priesthood, even in its highest representative. Sanctified by God himself, washed with pure water and clad in spotless garments, the high-priest was the type of the true Intercessor and eternal Priest; but still, as himself a sinner, he was infinitely below the "high-priest needed by us, who is holy, harmless, undefiled, separate from sinners, who needeth not, *as those high priests*, to offer up sacrifice, *first for his own sins,* and then for the peoples" (Heb. 7:26-28).

The high-priest then led forward the victims for the people's sins, which were provided at the public cost. There were a ram for a burnt-offering and two young goats for a sin-offering. Presenting these two goats before Jehovah at the door of the tabernacle, he cast lots upon them, the one lot being inscribed FOR JEHOVAH, the other FOR AZAZEL (a word probably meaning *removal*). The matter was called the *Scape-goat.*

The victims being thus prepared, the high-priest proceeded to offer the young bullock as the sin-offering for himself and his family. Having slain it at the altar, he took some of its blood with a censer filled with live coals from the altar and a handful of incense; and entering into the *Most Holy Place,* he threw the incense on the coals, thus enveloping the ark in a fragrant cloud, and then sprinkled the blood seven times before the mercy-seat on the east side of the ark.

The goat "of Jehovah" was then slain as a sin-offering for the people, and the high-priest again went into the Most Holy Place and performed the same ceremonies with its blood. As he returned through the Holy Place, in which no one else was present, he purified it by sprinkling some of the blood of both victims on the altar of incense. This completed the purification of the sanctuary, the second stage of the atonement.

Then followed the remission of the people's sins by the striking ceremony of devoting the *Scape-goat,* the one on which the lot had fallen *"for Azazel."* The high-priest having laid his hands upon its head and confessed over it the sins of the people, the victim, loaded as it were with those sins, was led out, by a man chosen for the purpose, to the wilderness into "a land not inhabited" and there let loose. This idea of remission seems to be involved in the name to which the scape-goat was devoted, "for Azazel" signifying "for complete removal."

The great ceremony of the remission of sins being thus completed, the high-priest, after again washing his body in the Holy Place and resuming his robes of state, completed the offering of the slain victims. The two rams were burnt upon the altar with the fat of the two sin-offerings, but the flesh of the later was carried away and burnt without the camp. Those who performed this office, and the man who had led away the scape-goat, washed their bodies and their clothes before returning to the camp.

The significance of this type of the true atonement, not by the blood of bulls and goats, but by the precious blood of Christ himself, our high-priest, is set forth in the Epistle to the Hebrews (Heb. 9-10).

d. FESTIVALS AFTER THE CAPTIVITY

1. The FEAST OF PURIM or of LOTS was an annual festival instituted to commemorate the preservation of the Jews in Persia from the massacre with which they were threatened through the machinations of Haman (Esther 3:7; 9:24).

    The festival lasted two days and was regularly observed on the fourteenth and fifteenth of Adar.

2. The FEAST OF DEDICATION was the festival instituted to commemorate the purging of the temple and the rebuilding of the altar after Judas Maccabaeus had driven out the Syrians, 164 B.C. It is named only once in the Canonical Scriptures (John 10:22). Its institution is recorded in I Macc. 4:52-59. It commenced on the twenty-fifty of Chisleu, the anniversary of the pollution of the temple by Antiochus Epiphanes, 167 B.C. Like the great Mosaic feasts, it lasted eight days but it did not require attendance at Jerusalem. It was an occasion of much festivity. It is called *Hanukkah* or the Feast of Lights by modern Jews, and is practically the Jewish Christmas.

Questions Over Leviticus

Chapter 1 (also 6:8-13) — "The burnt offering"
1. What animals could be offered as burnt offerings (4 answers)?
2. Who killed the burnt offering?
3. What was done with the blood of the burnt offering?
4. What was done to the body of the burnt offering?
5. When were burnt offerings regularly made (Compare Ex. 29:38-42)?
6. What regulation was made about the fire on the altar of burnt offering?

Chapter 2 (also 6:14-23 and 7:9-10) — "The meal offering"
1. In what three forms could a meal offering be brought?
2. What three things were always added to the meal offering?
3. What was done with the meal offering?
4. What was done with the meal offerings of the priests?

5. What was excluded from the meal offering?

Chapter 3 (also 6:12 and 7:11-38) — "The peace offerings"

1. What part of the peace offering was burned?
2. Where was it burned?
3. What two parts of an animal were not to be eaten?
4. Name three purposes for which peace offerings might be made?
5. Who ate the flesh of peace offerings?

Lev. 4:1-5:13 (also 6:24-30) — "The sin offering"

1. What type of sins were sin offerings offered for?
2. From the scriptures give two types of sins requiring sin offerings?
3. What was done with the blood of the sin offering?
4. What classes of people are mentioned as possibly offering sin offerings and what was each required to bring?
5. What provision was made for poor people who had to bring sin offerings? See Luke 2:22-24.
6. What was done with the body of the sin offering?

Lev. 5:14-6:7 (also 7:1-8) — "The trespass offering"

1. What types of sins were trespass offerings offered for?
2. What was required in addition to the sacrifice when trespass offerings were made (2 things)?

Summary from Leviticus 1-7 (See 7:37-38)

1. List the 5 types of offerings described in Lev. 1-7.
2. Which offering was wholly burned?
3. Which offerings were partly eaten by priests?
4. Which offering was shared by priest and offerer?

Questions on Leviticus 8

1. What is the topic of chapter 8?
2. Who were set apart to be the priests?
3. Where was the blood placed upon the priests?
4. How many days did the consecration ritual last?

Questions on Leviticus 9

1. When Aaron entered into his office what four offerings did he offer?
2. How was Aaron's burnt offering on the altar consumed?

Questions on Leviticus 10

1. What is the topic of chapter 10?
2. Which of Aaron's sons died and why?
3. Why was Aaron not to mourn over the death of his sons?
4. What were the priests not to do when they entered the tent of meeting?

Questions on Leviticus 11
1. What is the topic of chapter 11?
2. What were the two qualifications of animals that could be eaten?
3. What word describes the type of life the people were to live?

Questions on Leviticus 12
1. What is the topic of chapter 12?
2. When was a baby circumcised?
3. How long after the birth of a male child was it until sacrifice was offered? A female child?
4. Why did Joseph and Mary offer turtle doves (See Luke 2:22-24)?

Questions on Leviticus 13
1. What is the topic of Lev. 13?
2. What did a leper in public have to cry out?
3. What did leprosy affect besides people?

Questions on Leviticus 14
1. What creatures were employed in the ceremony for cleansing lepers?
2. What could leprosy affect besides people and garments?

Questions on Leviticus 15
1. What is the general topic of chapter 15?

Questions on Leviticus 16
1. What is the topic of chapter 16?
2. On what month and day was the ritual described in chapter 16?
3. How often did Aaron enter the (Most) Holy Place?
4. What was done with the two goats?

Questions on Leviticus 17
1. Where were the people required to offer sacrifices?
2. What item was not to be eaten? Why?
3. Where is the life of the flesh?

Questions on Leviticus 18
1. Israel was not to do according to the doings of what two countries?
2. What was the penalty for moral violations?

Questions on Leviticus 19
1. What character were the children of Israel to have?
2. What was to be left at harvest time? Why?
3. How much time was to elapse before fruit from trees could be eaten?
4. What restriction was placed on cattle breeding?

5. How were the old people to be treated?

Questions on Leviticus 20

1. What were people not to give to Moloch?
2. What was the penalty for one who had a familiar spirit?

Questions on Leviticus 21

1. Could the priest weep for the dead? Could the high priest?
2. What disqualified a man for the priesthood?

Questions on Leviticus 22

1. Were the priests always as holy as the things in the tabernacle?
2. What made animals not acceptable for sacrifice?
3. How old did an animal have to be before it could be sacrificed?

Questions on Leviticus 23

1. What was the date of the Passover and the feast of unleavened bread?
2. What was done with the first sheaf of the harvest?
3. How many days from the bringing of the first sheaf to the next feast (the feast of weeks or Pentecost)?
4. What three feasts were in the seventh month?
5. Where were the people to live during the feast of tabernacles?

Questions on Leviticus 24

1. What was burned in the candlestick?
2. When was bread placed on the table of shew-bread?
3. What was done to the man who cursed God's name?

Questions on Leviticus 25

1. How would the land keep a Sabbath?
2. What was released on the Year of Jubilee? How often did this year occur?
3. What was the law about taking interest?

Questions over Leviticus 26

1. List three of the blessings for obedience.
2. List three of the punishments for disobedience?

Questions on Leviticus 27

1. What was to be given when a vow was accomplished (or fulfilled)? (Cf. Acts 21:23-24)
2. What had to be done with all things given or devoted to Jehovah?
3. What part of all produce was Jehovah's?

Israel, a Type of the Church (I Cor. 10:1-11)

ISRAEL	Bondage in Egypt Deliverer (Moses) Moses believed Egypt forsaken Passover	RED SEA	Freedom from Egypt Heavenly food provided Law of Moses Tabernacle worship Unfaithful perished Faithful entered	JORDAN	CANAAN

CHURCH	Bondage in sin Deliverer (Christ) Christ believed Sin forsaken Death of Christ	BAPTISM	Freedom from sin Heavenly food provided Law of Christ Church worship Unfaithful to perish Faithful enter	DEATH	HEAVEN

Section V
The Book of Numbers

1. Numbers gets its name from the fact that it records the two enumerations (or censuses) of Israel. We could also call it the "Book of Journeyings" because it gives an account of Israel's wilderness wanderings from Sinai to Moab. The Hebrew name for the book is *Bemidbar* meaning "in the wilderness."

2. Moses was the human author of the book. See Num. 1:1.

3. The history in Numbers takes up where Exodus leaves off. Numbers covers a time span of about 39 years. Compare Num. 1:1; 33:38 and Deut. 1:3. This would be 1445-1407 B.C.

4. "The spiritual lesson enforced throughout the book (of Numbers) is that God's people can move forward only so far as they trust His promises and lean upon His strength" (Gleason L., Archer, A. *Survey of O.T. Intro.* p. 246).

5. Numbers records seven murmurings of Israel against God

or Moses: (1) 11:1; (2) 11:4; (3) 14:2; (4) 16:1; (5) 16:41 and
17:12; (6) 20:2-3; (7) 21:5.

  6. Outline of the book. (Memorize the main headings and
scripture references.)

a. *Events at Sinai in preparation for departure* (1:1-10:10).
  1. Numbering and arrangement of the people (Chs. 1-2).
  2. Levites numbered and instructed (Chs. 3-4).
  3. The people protected from defilement (Ch. 5).
  4. Law of the Nazirite (Ch. 6).
  5. Gifts of the princes (Ch. 7).
  6. The Levites cleansed and installed into office (Ch. 8).
  7. First annual Passover (9:1-14).
  8. Following the pillar of cloud, the trumpet signals
     (9:15-10:10).

b. *From Sinai to Kadesh-Barnea* (10:11-ch. 14).
  1. Events during the trip (10:1-ch. 12).
  2. Unbelief and rejection at Kadesh (Chs. 13-14).

c. *From Kadesh to Moab* (Chs. 15-21).
  1. Laws about offerings; a Sabbath-breaker punished (Ch.
     15).
  2. Rebellion of Korah; Aaron's rod (Chs. 16-17).
  3. Laws for priests and Levites (Ch. 18).
  4. Water for purification (Ch. 19).
  5. Death of Miriam; second smiting of rock, etc. (Ch. 20).
  6. Brazen servant; arrival in Moab (20:1-20).
  7. First permanent conquests; defeat of Sihon and Og
     (21:22-36).

d. *Events in the Plains of Moab* (Chs. 22-36)
  1. Balaam's prophecies and the sin at Baal-Peor (Chs. 22-25).
  2. Second census (Ch. 26).
  3. Various laws (Chs. 27-30).
  4. Vengeance on Midian (Ch. 31).
  5. Transjordanian land allotted (Ch. 32).
  6. Summary of journeys of Israel (Ch. 33).
  7. Regulations for division of Canaan (Chs. 34-36).

Questions

1. Where does the book of Numbers get its name?
2. What is the Hebrew name of the book?
3. Where does the history in Numbers begin?
4. How long a time span does Numbers cover?
5. Give the main headings of the outline of Numbers and the
   Scripture references for each.

Section VI
From Sinai to Moab (Book of Numbers)

1. Numbering of the people — Order of the camp and march. 2. Numbering of the firstborn and of the Levites. 3. Other events at Sinai — Purification of the camp — Order of the Nazirites — Second Passover — Nadab and Abihu — The blasphemer stoned. 4. Departure from Sinai — Hobab their guide — Manner of the march. 5. The route from Sinai — Entrance intended by way of Hebron — The wilderness of Paran — Taberah. 6. Kibroth-hattaavah — Quails — Pestilence — Appointment of seventy elders — The gift of prophesying. 7. Hazeroth — Opposition of Miriam and Aaron — The meekness and fidelity of Moses. 8. Kadesh-barnea — Difficulties in tracing the journeys. 9. Spies sent out — Their return and report — Rebellion of the people — Fidelity of Caleb and Joshua. 10. Attempt to invade Canaan defeated. 11. Beginning of the thirty-eight years' wanderings — Their direction and object. 12. Some events of these years — a. A Sabbath-breaker stoned — b. Rebellion of Korah, Dathan and Abiram — c. The plague stopped by Aaron — d. The blossoming of Aaron's rod — Charge of the sanctuary given to the Levites. 13. Last encampment at Kadesh — Death of Miriam. 14. Water again given from the rock — The sin and sentence of Moses and Aaron. 15. Passage refused through Edom. 16. March from Kadesh to Mt. Hor — Death of Aaron. 17. March down the Arabah around Mt. Seir — The fiery serpents and the brazen serpent. 18. Arrival at Brook Zered — March through the desert of Moab — Territories of Moab and Ammon — Conquests of the Amorites in Moab and Basham. 19. Defeat and destruction of Sihon and Og. 20. Last encampment on the plains of Moab — Balak and Balaam — New census — Consecration of Joshua — Slaughter of the Midianites. 21. Settlement of Reuben, Gad and half of Manasseh east of Jordan.

1. *Numbering of the people – Order of the camp and march.* On the first day of the second month of the second year from the epoch of the exodus (May, 1445), Jehovah commanded Moses to number the people able to bear arms, from twenty years old and

upward. The census was to be taken by Aaron with a chosen assistant from each tribe, except that of Levi. The Levites were exempted from military service and numbered separately.

The other tribes were made up to twelve by the division of Joseph into Ephraim and Manasseh. The following is the result, in the order given in the book of *Numbers,* which takes its title from this census:

Reuben	46,500	(Joseph): Ephraim 40,500
Simeon	59,300	(Joseph): Manasseh 32,200
Gad	45,650	Benjamin 35,400
Judah	74,600	Dan 62,700
Issachar	54,400	Asher 41,500
Zebulun	57,400	Naphtali 53,400
Total of the military array		603,550

These may be taken as the exact figures corresponding to the round number of 600,000 as given at the exodus. From the identity of the total and the improbability of there being two numberings in one year, this seems to be the same as the census mentioned before, in connection with the half-shekel tax for the service of the sanctuary (Ex. 38:26).

The object of the census was military, in preparation for the march to Canaan. A captain was appointed for every tribe and the whole host was divided into four camps, which surrounded the tabernacle during a halt and went before and after it on the march, in the following order (based on Num. 2):

a. On the *East* and in the *front rank:* the camp of JUDAH, with Issachar and Zebulun, 186,400 men.

b. On the *South* and *second:* the camp of REUBEN, with Simeon and Gad, 151,450 men.

   The TABERNACLE and Levi.

c. On the *West* and *next to last:* the camp of EPHRAIM, with Manasseh and Benjamin, 108,100 men.

d. On the *North* and in the *rear:* the camp of DAN, with Asher and Naphtali, 157,600 men.

   Each tribe had its standard.

2. *Numbering of the firstborn and of the Levites.* Another object of the census was religious. The above numbers, besides excluding the tribe of Levi, included some who had no right there, as the *firstborn,* who were consecrated to Jehovah (Ex. 13:1,2, 11-16). Of both these classes, the Levites and the firstborn, the census included the males from one month old and upward, and there were found to be:[1]

---

1. The separate numbers in Num. 3. (Gershon, 7500; Kohath, 8600; Merari, 6200) give a total of 22,300. The received solution of the discrepancy is that 300 were the first-born of the Levites, who as such were already consecrated, and therefore could not take the place of others.

Of the firstborn 22,273
Of the tribe of Levi 22,000

Difference...273

The Levites were taken for the service of Jehovah in place of the firstborn, man for man; the remaining 273 were redeemed for five shekels each and the sum of 1365 shekels was given to Aaron and his sons. The cattle of the Levites were taken instead of the firstborn cattle (Num. 1-3,8).

The substitution of the Levites for the firstborn gave the Levites a sacrificial as well as a priestly holiness to Jehovah, an idea extended to all the redeemed, as "the church of the firstborn" (Heb. 12:23).

The Levites were again numbered, from thirty[1] to fifty years, for the service of the sanctuary; and to each of their three families their respective duties were assigned. (See chap. 15.) The numbers were:

Of the Kohathites 2750
Of the sons of Gershon...2630
Of the sons of Merari 3200

Total of priests and Levites 8580

3. *Other events at Sinai – Purification of the camp – Order of the Nazirites – Second Passover – Nadab and Abihu – The Blashemer stoned.* The description of this census in the book of *Numbers*, immediately after the setting up of the tabernacle, anticipates some events which occurred in the interval before the march was resumed — such as the purification of the camp by excluding the unclean (Num. 5:1-4), the institution of the order of *Nazirites* (Num. 6:1-21), and the offerings of the princes of Israel (the heads of the twelve tribes) at the dedication of the temple and of the altar (Num. 7). Here also we read the beautiful form prescribed for the blessing of Aaron and his sons upon the people in God's name:

> "Jehovah bless thee: and keep thee.
> Jehovah make His face to shine upon thee:
>   and be gracious unto thee.
> Jehovah lift up His countenance upon thee:
>   and give thee peace."
>   (Num. 6:24-26)

A special mention is made of the second celebration of the

---

1. The mention of twenty-five in Num. 8:24, as the age of entrance, must be understood either of a probationary period during which they were trained for their duties, or of the lighter work of keeping the gates of the tabernacle.

Passover in the wilderness of Sinai, with the addition of a new law permitting those who were defiled or travelling to keep it a month later (Num. 9:1-14). The Book of Numbers also mentions, incidentally, the death of Nadab and Abihu, the sons of Aaron, by fire from Jehovah for offering "strange fire" on the altar of incense, instead of the sacred fire sent down from God. It appears from the sequel that the sacrilege was committed in drunken recklessness. Aaron and his surviving sons were forbidden to defile the priesthood by the utterance of their natural grief, and commanded to remain within the tabernacle leaving the congregation to "bewail the burning which Jehovah had kindled." The law was laid down that the priests should drink no wine or strong drink when they went into the tabernacle, lest they should be incapacitated from distinguishing between the holy and the unholy, between the unclean and the clean. Even the survivors incurred the severe displeasure of Moses for not eating the sin-offering in the Holy Place (Lev. 10). Such were the terrors that beset the dignity of the priesthood, conferred by the law on "men compassed with infirmity" (Heb. 5:2; 7:28).

To this interval belongs also the death by stoning of a man who had blasphemed "the NAME." This blasphemer was the son of a Hebrew woman named Shelomith and of an Egyptian father; and here we have an example of the evils introduced by the "mixed multitude" who came with the people out of Egypt, as well as of the fact that such marriages were made before the exodus (Lev. 24).

4. *Departure from Sinai – Hobab their guide – Manner of the march.* At length the word of Jehovah came to them that they had dwelt long enough in this mountain, and commanding them to turn and journey onward (Deut. 1:6,7). The land of their destination was described with reference to the promises to Abraham, Isaac and Jacob (Deut. 1:8), but in more minute detail. They were directed to go, as the first aim of their journey, "to the *mount of the Amorites,*" that is, the highlands of Judah and Ephraim, which rise on the north of the desert of *et-Tih* and fill the central part of southern Palestine. To this is added the mention of "all the places nigh thereunto, in the *plain (Arabah),*" which seems here to mean the whole valley of the Jordan, and its lakes; "in the *hills,*" probably of Judah, and perhaps including Mount Gilead, east of the Jordan; "in the *vale (shephelah),*" that is, the lowlands situated in the land of the Philistines; "in the *south,*" the special portion of Judah; "by the *seaside,*" the great littoral region north of Carmel,

as far as Phoenicia; to *the land of the Canaanites*" or northern Palestine; "and unto *Lebanon;* "to the *great river, the river Euphrates*" (Cf. Gen. 15:18).

On the twentieth day of the second month of the second year (about May 20, 1445 B.C.), the cloud of Jehovah's presence was lifted up from the tabernacle, as the sign of departure, and the tabernacle itself was taken down (Num. 10:11-17). At the alarm blown by the two silver trumpets, which God had commanded to be made (Num. 10:1-10), each of the four camps set forward in its appointed order and the host followed the cloud into the wilderness of Paran (Num. 10:12). This divine guidance relieved Moses from all responsibility as to the direction of the journey (Num. 9:17-23). Moses invited Hobab, either his father-in-law or brother-in-law,[1] to go with them, in those memorable words so often quoted in a wider sense — "We are journeying unto the place of which Jehovah said, I will give it you: come with us, and we will do thee good: for Jehovah hath spoken good concerning Israel"; and Hobab consented to guide them through the desert (Num. 10:29-32). He appears as the experienced Bedouin sheikh, to whom Moses looked for the material safety of his cumbrous caravan in the new and difficult ground before them. The tracks and passes of that "great terrible wilderness" were all familiar to him, and his practiced sight would be to them "instead of eyes" in discerning the distant clumps of verdure which betokened the wells or springs for the daily encampment, and in giving timely warning of the approach of Amalekites or other spoilers of the desert. "The ark of the covenant of Jehovah went before them, to search out a resting-place for them. And the cloud of Jehovah was upon them by day, when they went out of the camp" (Num. 10:33-34). When the ark set forward, Moses cried, "Rise up, O Jehovah, and let thine enemies be scattered; and let them that hate thee flee before thee." And when it rested he said, "Return, O Jehovah, unto the ten thousand thousands of Israel" (Num. 10:35-36; Cf. Ps. 132:8). Thus they went three days' journey into the wilderness of Paran (Num. 10:12,33).

5. *The route from Sinai – Entrance intended by way of Hebron – The wilderness of Paran – Taberah.* In following the route of the

---

1. In favor of his being the brother-in-law of Moses there is the express statement that Hobab was "the son of Raguel" (Num. 10:29); Raguel or Reuel — the Hebrew word in both cases is the same — being identified with Jethro, not only in Exod. 2:18 (comp. 3:1, etc.), but also by Josephus, who constantly gives him that name; but the addition "the father-in-law of Moses," though in most of the ancient versions connected with Hobab, will in the original read either way, so that no argument can be founded on them.

Israelites, we must try to determine two or three chief positions.
The general direction is northward from Sinai "to the mount of
the Amorites," the highlands of southern Palestine. The two
extremes are the camp before Sinai on the south and the "city" of
KADESH, or Kadesh-barnea, on the north (Num. 13:26; 20:6;
32:8). The distance between these points was eleven days' journey
"by the way of Mount *Sier*" (Deut. 1:2). This is evidently
mentioned as the ordinary route, and it seems to be implied
(though this must not be assumed as certain) that it was followed
by the Israelites. If it were so, their course would lie nearly along
or parallel to the *Gulf of Akabah,* and up the wide plain of the
Arabah which runs northward from the head of the gulf, between
Mount Seir on the east and the desert of *et-Tih* (or *Paran)* on the
west. Their present journey must be carefully distinguished from
their final march into Palestine, at the end of the thirty-eight
years' wandering in the wilderness. On that occasion they
descended the *Arabah,* after being refused permission to pass
through Edom, rested at Elath *(Akabah)* at the head of the Gulf of
Akabah (Deut. 2:8); and whence, turning the southern point of
Mount Seir, they skirted its eastern side to the country of Moab,
east of the Jordan. But on their first march, there is no clear
evidence that they rested at the head of the *Gulf of Akabah* or
passed up the *Arabah;* and the probabilities are very nicely
balanced. Much of the difficulty arises from confounding the
directions in which they proposed to enter Palestine on the two
occasions. Their final entrance was made from the east by way of
the plains of Moab, but their first entrance was to have been from
the south by way of Hebron. This is clear from the command to
march to the mountain of the Amorites, from the description of
the circuit made by the spies, and especially from their visiting
Hebron and Eshcol (Num. 13:17-25). Whatever, therefore, the
route to Kadesh may have been, that station was a final
starting-point for Hebron; and thus we have some guide for the
latter part of the journey.

Between "the mount of the Amorites" and Mount Sinai lies the
great table-land now called the desert of *et-Tih* (the *wandering).*
There can be no doubt of its general correspondence to the
wilderness of Paran, in which the cloud rested when it was first
lifted up from the tabernacle (Num. 10:12). This arid tract of
limestone answers well to the description of Moses: "When we
departed from Horeb, we went through *all that great and terrible
wilderness,* which ye saw by the way of the mountain of the

Amorites; and we came to Kadesh-barnea" (Deut. 1:19). Its limits
are clearly marked out by the mountain ranges, which divide it on
the southwest from the desert of Shur, on the south from that of
Sinai and on the east from the *Arabah.* The range which divides it
on the south from the desert of Sinai is also called *et-Tih,* and this
the Israelites seem to have crossed in passing out of the wilderness
of Sinai to that of Paran. But it is not clear that they made this
passage in their first journey of three days (Num. 10:33). It took
them some time to get clear of the *wadys* about Sinai, and although
Paran is mentioned from the first as the region into which they
passed, the three important stations of TABERAH,
KIBROTH-HATAAVAH and HAZEROTH (Num. 11:3,34,35; 33:17)
can hardly be reckoned to Paran, as they are said to have
encamped in the wilderness of Paran after leaving Hazeroth
(Num. 12:16). Unfortunately these three names furnish little, if
any, clue to the route they took from Sinai. TABERAH (a *burning)*
records the awful judgment that befell the people, who now
began again to murmur against Jehovah. "Fire burnt among
them, and consumed those that were in the uttermost parts of the
camp" (Num. 11:2-3); doubtless, from the order of the
encampment, the mixed multitude who came with the people out
of Egypt.

6. *Kibroth-hattaavah – Quails – Pestilence – Appointment of seventy
elders – Their gift of prophesying.* The name of the next station,
KIBROTH-HATTAAVAH (the *graves of lust),* is of similar origin. On
this occasion too the rebellion began with "the mixed multitude"
(Num. 11:4). Their lust for better food spread to the Israelites,
who, remembering the fish and the vegetables of Egypt, loathed
the manna and asked for flesh. God sent them quails on which
they surfeited themselves for a whole month (Num. 11:20); and
while the flesh was yet between their teeth, they were smitten with
a great plague, which gave the place its name. The mention of the
sea in two passages of this narrative has been used as an argument
that the route thus far was along the valleys which run eastward
from Sinai to the Gulf of Akabah, but the sea is near to any part of
the peninsula and the flights of birds which have attracted the
attention of travellers are characteristic of the whole region.

A very important institution arose out of this rebellion. Moses
complained to Jehovah that the burden of the people was too
great for him to bear alone. He was directed to choose seventy of
the elders of Israel and to present them before the tabernacle,
where Jehovah came down in the cloud and gave them a share of

the Spirit that was on Moses, and they prophesied. Two of them who had not come out to the tabernacle, Eldad and Medad, prophesied in the camp, an intimation of the truth so often taught by the prophets, that even in the old dispensation the power of God's Spirit transcended the forms and places of his own appointment. But the devout zealot is slow to receive this truth; and so Joshua prayed Moses to forbid them, just as the disciples asked Christ to forbid those who wrought miracles, but did not follow in his train; and both received answers in the same spirit (Num. 11:24-29; Cf. Mark 9:38).

The appointment of the seventy elders has often been regarded as the germ of the *Sanhedrin*. They seem rather to have been a Senate, whose office was confined to assisting Moses in the government and ceased with the cessation of his leadership. No trace of the Sanhedrin is found till the return from the Babylonian captivity. It is more certain that the manner of their consecration prefigured the order of the *Prophets*.

7. *Hazeroth – Opposition of Miriam and Aaron – The meekness and fidelity of Moses.* For the next halting-place, HAZEROTH *(courts or villages)*, a site has been found at the *Wady Huderah* on the main route from Sinai to the shores of the Gulf of Akabah (Num. 11:35). Close to *Huderah* is a brook called *El-Ain (the* water), of itself a strong argument for this route, and inviting an encampment for a considerable time, such as the name seems to imply.

At Hazeroth Moses was troubled by a seditious opposition from Miriam and Aaron. They spake against him because of the *Cushite* woman whom he had married, probably his Midianite wife, Zipporah; and placed their authority on a level with his. On this occasion we have that celebrated description of the character of Moses: "Now the man Moses was very meek, above all the men that were on the face of the earth." We have also that testimony to his faithfulness as a servant set over the house of God, which the Apostle uses as a type of Christ's government over His own house, the Church. Jehovah called forth Aaron and Miriam, with Moses, to the tabernacle, and declared His pleasure to converse with Moses openly, mouth to mouth, and not, as to other prophets, in visions, dreams and dark speeches (parables); and reproved them for speaking against him. Miriam was smitten with leprosy; and though she was healed at the prayer of Moses, Aaron, as the high-priest, was obliged to shut her out from the camp for seven days, after which "the people removed from Hazeroth and pitched in the wilderness of Paran" (Num. 12:16; Cf. Num. 33:18).

8. *Kadesh-barnea – Difficulties in tracing the journeys.* The encampment in the wilderness of Paran involves us in difficulties in tracing Israel's journeys. We are not told at what point they passed into the wilderness of Paran, nor how many stops they made in it. We find them next at KADESH, whence the spies were sent out (Num. 13:26; Deut. 1:19). Kadesh is the oasis *Ain Qedeis* (or the nearby *Ain Qudeirat*) in the extreme south of the Negev of Palestine. In the list of stations in Numbers 33 Kadesh is not mentioned; and the name of Hazeroth is followed by several unknown places, of which it is even uncertain whether they belong to this journey or to the years of wandering in the wilderness. The latter seems the more probable alternative, since the mention of Mount Hor (Num. 33:37-41) clearly refers to the fortieth year, and at least the eight preceding stations (Num. 33:31-37) are closely connected with it (Comp. Deut. 10:6-7); while the halt at Kadesh (Num. 33:36-37) must be understood of a return to that place after the long wanderings (Comp. Num. 20:1). The escape from these difficulties is by the hypothesis that Kadesh served as a sort of headquarters during the thirty-eight years of wandering. The Israelites arrived at Kadesh forty days before the vintage or about the latter part of August; and they made there a longer halt than at any other place, except before Sinai.

9. *Spies sent out – Their return and report – Rebellion of the people – Fidelity of Caleb and Joshua.* At Kadesh, Jehovah declared to the people that they had reached the mountain of the Amorites into which they were to ascend, to possess the land He had given them (Deut. 1:20-21). But first the country was explored by twelve spies, who were heads of their respective tribes (Num. 13:1-16; Deut. 1:22-23). Their names are given at length, but only two of them are memorable: Caleb, the son of Jephunneh, of the tribe of Judah; and Oshea, the son of Nun, of the tribe of Ephraim, whom Moses had called *Joshua,* i.e., *Saviour.* They searched the land for forty days, ascending the Ghor and the valley of the Jordan as far as Rehob, on the way to Hamath on the Orontes in the extreme north. Thence they returned to Hebron and explored the region round that city in which their father Abraham had dwelt as a stranger, near the Amorite princes Aner, Mamre and Eshcol — the last of whom seems still to have given his name (*Eshcol* — a cluster of grapes) to the rich vineclad valley of which he was the

prince. From that valley the spies brought a cluster of grapes so large that it was borne between two men upon a staff, together with pomegranates and figs: for it was the season of the first ripe grapes (Num. 13:20-25; Deut. 1:24-25). These proofs confirmed their report that the land was all that Jehovah had promised, "It is a good land that Jehovah our God doth give us" (Deut. 1:25); "surely it floweth with milk and honey" (Num. 13:27; Ex. 3:8,17; 13:5).[1] Indeed we can but faintly judge the impression made upon them — after a year and a half of confinement to the desert — by the glowing description of travellers who have entered Palestine from the same side. But when they went on to tell of the people they had seen there, inhabiting great walled cities — the Amalekites in the south; the Hittites, Jebusites and Amorites in the mountains; and the Canaanites along the seashore and in the valley of the Jordan, and especially the giant sons of Anak, before whom they felt themselves as grasshoppers, their good report became an evil one. Caleb alone, supported afterward by Joshua, tried to calm the people, assuring them that they were able to conquer the land. The other spies not only exaggerated the strength of the enemy, but began to find fault with the land itself, as "a land that eateth up the inhabitants thereof" (Num. 13:32).[2] The people spent the night in bewailing their lost hopes (Num. 14:1).

In the morning they broke out into open rebellion and proposed to elect a captain and to return to Egypt. Neh. 9:17 indicates that a captain was actually chosen. In vain did Moses and Aaron fall down before the people; in vain did Caleb and Joshua reiterate their assurance of victory in the strength of Jehovah's promise and presence, and exhort the people, above all things, not to rebel against Him. All the congregation had already taken up stones to stone them when the glory of Jehovah shone forth from the tabernacle, and He spake to Moses, declaring that He would disinherit the people and make of him a nation. Once more, as before Sinai, the intercession of Moses prevailed; but in pardoning the nation, Jehovah swore by himself that "the whole earth should be filled with His glory," by the example he would make of the men who had rebelled against him, not one of whom,

---

1. This too often suggests only a vague idea of luxuriant plenty to readers who forget that, in the absence of the sugar-cane, *honey* is a necessity of life.
2. Num. 13:32 seems to mean that the enjoyment of the abundant produce of the land was marred by the constant danger from surrounding enemies, as attacks were invited by its fertility.

save Caleb,[1] should see the promised land. The execution of the sentence was to begin on the morrow by their turning into the wilderness by the way of the Red Sea. There they were to wander for forty years — a year for each day that the spies had searched the land — till all the men of twenty years old and upward had left their carcasses in the desert; and then at length their children, having shared their wanderings, should enter on their inheritance (Num. 14). As an earnest of the judgment, the ten faithless spies were slain by a plague (Num. 14:36-37).

10. *Attempt to invade Canaan defeated.* Now that it was too late the people changed their mind, and having lost the opportunity given them by God, they tried to seize it against His will. In the morning they marched up the mountainpass, in spite of the warning of Moses that it should not prosper; and the Amalekites and Canaanites, coming down upon them with the Amorites of the mountain, defeated them with great slaughter and chased them as far as Hormah,[2] and even to Mount Seir (Num. 14:40-45; Deut. 1:41-44). The entrance to the promised land on this side was now hopelessly barred, and their forlorn state is thus described by Moses — "And ye returned and wept before Jehovah; but Jehovah would not hearken to your voice nor give ear unto you" (Deut. 1:45-46).

11. *Beginning of the thirty-eight years' wanderings – Their direction and object.* The thirty-eight years (or rather exactly thirty-eight years and a half) occupied in the execution of God's judgment on "the generation that grieved him in the wilderness, and to whom he sware in his wrath, "They shall not enter into my rest," form almost a blank in the sacred history. Their close may be fixed at the period of the final march from Kadesh to Mount Hor, and thence down through the *Arabah* and up the eastern side of Mount Seir to the plains of Moab (Num. 20:1; 33:37; Deut. 2:23). But the intervening portions of the narrative are most difficult to assign to their proper place — whether to the first or final stay at Kadesh, or to the years between. The mystery which hangs over this period seems like an awful silence into which the rebels sink away.

---

1. Joshua is not mentioned here (Num. 14:24), probably because his destined leadership was already known to Moses, as his new name implies; but he is expressly named with Caleb in the repetition of the sentence to the people (Num. 14:30). Still, as Caleb was the first to withstand the rebellion, he receives the higher praise and reward (Num. 14:24; Deut. 1:36). Hebron itself was made his inheritance (Josh. 14:6-15).

2. The ancient name of Hormah was Zephath (Judg. 1:17). The name *Hormah* means a *devoted place*, i.e., one set apart for destruction. Hormah is perhaps *Tell es-Sheriah*, a place north of the road about midway between Gaza and Beersheba.

After the rout in Hormah, the people "abode in Kadesh many days" (Deut. 1:46). This phrase may possibly cover the whole period of the wandering and Kadesh may very well be taken for a general name of the wilderness (See Ps. 29:8). The direction in which the people started on their wanderings is defined, "*by the way of the Red Sea*" (Num. 14:25; Deut. 1:40), which seems clearly to mean down the *Arabah* to the head of the Gulf of Akabah. Now it seems that the passage in Deut. 2:1 must be referring to this same "turning into the wilderness by the way of the Red Sea," and not to the final march, the signal for which is recorded at v. 3;[1] and this is confirmed by the computation of the thirty-eight years of wandering from the time they left Kadesh-barnea (Num. 14:14). If this be so, we have a clue to the direction of the wandering in the words, "and we compassed Mount Seir many days"; words which point to the *Arabah*. With this agrees the notice of their last march back to Kadesh, being from Eziongeber at the head of the *Gulf of Akabah* (Num. 33:36).[2]

There is another light in which the question has hardly been yet regarded. We have often felt staggered at the idea of this vast multitude being led up and down the awful desolations of *Paran*, amid terrific sufferings to men, women, children and cattle, with no assignable purpose except to spend out the allotted years; and we would rather believe that God mitigated their punishment, than that He added any unnecessary suffering to the sentence of the gradual death of the grown-up generation. Nor do we read of any such sufferings as they must have endured had they plunged into the *Tih;* it is not till their return to Kadesh that we find them wanting water (Num. 20). Is it not more consistent with the spirit of the narrative, and with the ways of God, to suppose that their wanderings had at least an apparent object which determined their direction and extent? When they found that they could not scale the mountain passes of the Amorites, their southward journey might well have for its object to find some passage through Edom to the east by the route they at last followed; and it may have been with this hope that "they compassed Mount Seir for many days." Then, as in the end, they may have met with a refusal from the Edomites, and so have waited about their headquarters at Kadesh, trying sometimes one passage and

---

1. The direction *northward* is that which they would have taken if the Edomites had not refused them a passage (comp. Num. 14:4-7, with Num. 20:14-19); and the change of route is indicated at Num. 14:8.
2. The few preceeding stations to which we have any guide seem also to be near the Edomites.

sometimes another, but shut out on both sides;[1] and meanwhile leading a nomad life, chiefly among the pastures of the Arabah, till God's appointed time had come. This view is strongly confirmed by *Judges* 11:16-18, where it is said that, *on coming up out of Egypt,* Israel sent messengers both to the kings of Edom and of Moab, asking for a passage; and *after their refusal,* Israel *abode in Kadesh. Then* they went along through the wilderness and encompassed the land of Edom, etc. In the poetry of the Hebrews, Mount Seir and Edom are constantly connected with the wanderings (Judges 5:4; Deut. 33:2; Hab. 3:3).

Such a lot was hard enough, with all its necessary trials and with its hope constantly deferred; but it is consistent and intelligible. It may be left to imagination to fill up the picture of the doomed generation dropping off year by year and of the lesson impressed on their children by seeing their carcasses left in the wilderness. Nor must it be forgotten that this passage also of their history is emblematic of the whole pilgrimage of man, who must toil on to his rest through a path marked by the graves of his illusions and his sins.

12. *Some events of these years – a. A Sabbath-breaker stoned – b. Rebellion of Korah, Dathan and Abiram – c. The plague stopped by Aaron d. The blossoming of Aaron's rod – Charge of the sanctuary given to the Levites.* There are five chapters in the *Book of Numbers* (Num. 15-19) referring to this interval, but to what part of it we cannot say. Besides sundry religious laws, they record the following events:

a. The death by stoning of a man who was found gathering sticks on the Sabbath day (Num. 15:32-36). His offense was the doing *servile work;* its spirit was presumptuous disobedience to Jehovah and the penalty had already been declared (Deut. 5:15; Ex. 31:15; 35:2-3). The case was expressly referred by Moses to Jehovah and it is recorded as an example that the law of the Sabbath was not to be a dead letter.

b. The rebellion of Korah, Dathan and Abiram was an attempt to deprive the priesthood of its special sanctity, by a perversion of the truth declared by God himself that all the people were "an holy nation and a royal priesthood" (Num. 16:1-3; Cf. Ex. 19:6). It was led by Korah, a Levite, with 250 princes famous in the congregation, who claimed equality with the priests; and he was joined by Dathan and Abiram and others of the tribe of

---

1. Their encounter with Arad the Canaanite at Hormah seems to indicate another attempt to force a passage to the north-west (Num. 21:1,2; ver. 3 seems to be an anticipation of Judg. 11:30).

Reuben, whose claim probably rested on the primogeniture of their ancestor. At God's command, Korah and his company presented themselves with Moses and Aaron at the door of the tabernacle, each with his censer, favored as it would seem by the congregation (Num. 16:19). Then the voice of God called to Moses and Aaron to separate themselves from the congregation, that He might destroy them. For the third time the intercessor obtained the people's pardon: they were bidden to remove from the tents of Korah, Dathan and Abiram, and at the word of Moses, the earth opened and swallowed up the rebels with their families and all that belonged to them, while fire burst out from the tabernacle and consumed the 250 princes. Their brazen censers, as being sacred, were gathered by Aaron out of the fire to make plates for a covering of the altar of burnt-offering (Num. 16:1-40). The Apostle Jude uses those who "perished in the gainsaying of Korah" as a type of the "filthy dreamers" who, in the last days, shall "despies dominion and speak evil of dignities" (Jude 11).

c. The people now murmured at the fate of the men whose rebellion they had favored, and at the very moment when they gathered against Moses and Aaron before the tabernacle, Jehovah appeared in the cloud and sent a pestilence among them. Then followed one of the most striking examples of the intercession of Moses and the mediation of the high-priest. Seeing that "wrath was gone out from Jehovah," Moses bade Aaron to fill his censer with coals from the altar and with incense, as an atonement for the people, and to stand between the living and the dead; and so the plague was stayed (Num. 16:41-50). This is a most striking symbol of Christ's mediation to save those who are doomed to the death of sin.

d. After these things, a new sign was given of Jehovah's special favor to the house of Aaron. Twelve rods or sceptres were chosen for the several tribes and laid up in the tabernacle before the ark, the name of Aaron being inscribed on the rod of Levi. In the morning Moses went into the tabernacle and brought forth the rods, and returned them to the princes of the tribes when Aaron's rod was seen covered with buds and blossoms and fullgrown almonds. The rest were still dry sticks but his was a living and fruitful sceptre. It was a vivid emblem of "the rod of Jesse," the "Branch" springing up without the sustenance of nature, which in the prophets represents the spiritual and life-giving power of Messiah. By the command of God it was laid up in the ark, for a perpetual memorial against the like rebellions (Num. 17; Is. 11:1; 53:2; Zech. 6:12; Rev. 5:5). The people, now terrified into submission, cried that they only drew near the tabernacle to perish, and Jehovah repeated the law, committing the charge of the sanctuary to the Levites (Num. 17:12-13; 18).

13. *Last encampment at Kadesh – Death of Miriam.* In the first month of the fortieth year (Num. 33:38) from the epoch of the exodus (April, 1407), we find the Israelites again in the wilderness of Zin, at Kadesh, whither they seem to have marched up the *Arabah* from Ezion-geber, at the head of the *Gulf of Akabah* (Num. 20:1; 33:36). The doom under which most of the old generation had by this time perished, now reached the house of Amram. Miriam, the elder sister of Moses and Aaron, died and was buried here (Num. 20:1). We have seen her as a young girl watching the cradle of Moses and aiding in his deliverance. She is spoken of as sharing in the sacred mission of her brothers (Micah 6:4). When she leads off the song of triumph on the shore of the Red Sea, she is expressly called "Miriam, *the prophetess*"; and the ground on which she and Aaron rebelled against Moses implies their possession of the prophetic gift: "Hath Jehovah spoken by Moses? Hath He not also spoken by us" (Num. 12:1-2, 6-8)? The delay of the march till she was free from the defilement of her leprosy proves her high consideration (Num. 12:15). Lastly, she bore the name of the mother of our Lord. Tradition makes her the wife of Hur and grandmother of the artist Bezaleel; and it is said that the mourning for her, as for her brothers, lasted thirty days (Josephus, *Ant. III,* 3:2).

14. *Water again given from the rock – The sin and sentence of Moses and Aaron.* Here, too, Moses and Aaron committed the sin which brought them also under the sentence of death, without entering the promised land. The people murmured for water, as at Rephidim; and the repetition of the same scene by the new generation, even after the discipline of the thirty-eight years' wandering, is true to human nature — not theirs only, but ours, of which theirs was the type (Num. 20:2-6; Cf. Ex. 17:1). Jehovah interposed in the same manner as before: "He clave the rocks in the wilderness . . . and caused waters to run down like rivers" (Ps. 78:15,16,20; Neh. 9:15). But as the miracle had been wrought once already, He designed to show His power by a great wonder: Moses and Aaron were to stand before the rock (or cliff) in the

sight of the people; and Moses, holding the rod in his hand, was only to *speak* to the rock. But this time the trial was too strong, both for his patience and his humanity. Upbraiding the people as rebels, he asked, "Must *we* fetch you water out of this rock?" — and he *smote the rock* twice with the rod (Num. 20:7-11). The water gushed out in an abundant stream, which probably followed the march of the people down the Arabah. But at the same time the word of Jehovah came to Moses and Aaron that, because they had not believed and honored Him before the people, they should not bring them into the promised land. The place was called MERIBAH *(strife)*, or more fully, KADESH-MERIBAH (Num. 20:13; Deut. 32:51; Ezek. 47:19; 48:28).

15. *Passage refused through Edom* (Num. 20:14-21). After the experience with the waters of Meribah, Israel prepared to leave Kadesh and march northeastward via Edom. Before leaving Kadesh, Moses sent messengers on ahead of the people to the king of Edom, requesting passage through his land. This passage would have gone through the narrow canyon leading into Petra (Sela) and on eastward to the point where they could have gone north toward Moab. The messengers appealed to the brotherly relationship of Edom and Israel and to the natural sympathy of men for those who have been enslaved. Moses promised that Israel would stay strictly on the highway and molest nothing, and would pay for everything they might consume as they passed. To all this the Edomites gave a blunt refusal and barred the passage with an armed force. This refusal stands in sharp contrast to Edom's subsequent fearful deference to Israel after Israel went around Mt. Seir and came up along the east side of Edom (Deut. 2:1-8; Judges 11:17).

16. *March from Kadesh to Mt. Hor—Death of Aaron.* The only way now open was down the *Arabah,* and accordingly "they passed by from the children of Esau, which dwelt in Seir, *through the way of the Arabah*" (Deut. 2:8).[1] Their first march was to MOUNT HOR (i.e., *the* mountain), "in the edge of the land of Edom" (Num. 20:22-23; 33:37). Here we once more reach certain ground; for the whole course of the narrative confirms the tradition which identifies Hor with the majestic "mountain of the prophet Aaron" *(Jebel Nebi-Harun),* which stands on the eastern edge of the *Arabah,* above which it rises 4000 feet, having Petra at its eastern foot. "In this great valley," says Dean Stanley, "there is no more question of the course of the Israelites. It is, indeed, doubtful

---

1. The word *Arabah,* which means *desert,* is rendered *plain* in the King James version.

whether they passed up it on the way to Canaan; but no one can doubt that they passed down it, when the valleys of Edom were closed against them."

It is very probable that Hor, like Sinai, was already a sanctuary of the desert tribes. To this dignity and its natural grandeur was now added the solemnity of Aaron's death, which was appointed by Jehovah to take place here. This event was not only the decease of so great a personage as the colleague and elder brother of Moses, but it involved the demise of the first high-priest and the investiture of his successor. In the sight of all the congregation, Moses led up Aaron and his son Eleazar to Mount Hor, and stripped Aaron of his garments and put them upon Eleazar; and Aaron died in the top of the mount. Travellers have found a position on the summit well suited for the public ceremony, but we need not suppose that Aaron actually died in the sight of the people. He was buried either on the mountain or at its foot and the people mourned for him thirty days (Num. 20:23-29; 33:38; Deut. 10:6; 32:50).

Aaron died on the first day of the fifth month, forty years after the exodus *(Ab–* July and August, 1407 B.C.), at the age of 123. As the first-born of the house of Amram, the priesthood *of that house* would be a part of his birthright. His natural eloquence fitted him to be the organ of Moses in his mission to Egypt; and he not only spoke for him, but wrought the miracles at his bidding. Throughout the scenes in the desert, he is associated with Moses in leading the people; but Moses stands above him as mediator with God, and as favored with His direct and open revelations. Even when Aaron is made high-priest, he receives his authority from Moses. When left alone to govern the people, he at once yielded to their willfulness, believing probably that it was a wise concession to give them a visible symbol of God's presence; and so he became the minister of idolatry and debauchery. His feeble excuse on this occasion betrays that unstable character, which could not go alone without his brother; but as is usual with such characters, he made a rash attempt to assert his independence under the influence of Miriam. On all other occasions we find him sharing the cares of Moses and joining even in his errors, as in the sin which shut them both out from the promised land. It has been well observed that the very defects of Aaron's character, and especially his sin and repentance in the matter of the golden calf, fitted him the more for the office of a high-priest — "Who can have compassion on the ignorant and the erring, for that he himself also is compassed with infirmity" (Heb. 5:2; 7:28). And he could also sympathize with deep suffering, such as he felt when his sons Nadab and Abihu were slain for their sacrilege — "and Aaron held his peace" (Lev. 10:3). All these points are placed by the Apostle in striking contrast to His priesthood, whose perfect and sinless human nature makes Him have sympathy without infirmity (Heb. 5-8).

Aaron's wife was named Elishaba (Ex. 6:23). Of his four sons, two survived him — Eleazar and Ithamar. The family of the former held the high-priesthood till the time of Eli, who belonged to the house of Ithamar. The descendants of Eli retained it down to the reign of Solomon, who deposed Abiathar and gave the office to Zadok, of the family of Eleazar (I Sam. 2:30-36; I Kings 2:27). The traditional tomb of Aaron, on one of the two summits of Mount Hor, is marked by a Mohammedan chapel, the dome of which forms a white spot on the dark red sandstone.

17. *March down the Arabah around Mt. Seir – The fiery serpents and the brazen serpent.* The march of the Israelites was now down the *Arabah,* out of which they turned by way of Ezion-gerber and Elath into the wilderness of Moab. *Ezion-geber* lay about a mile from *Elath,* on the shore at the north end of the *Gulf of Akabah,* and was a great port for the commerce with the Indian Ocean, which took that route in the days of Solomon and Jehoshaphat. It was afterward eclipsed by ELATH near the modern port of EILAT. The *Gulf of Akabah* yielded its importance as a highway of commerce to the *Gulf of Suez,* in consequence of the building of Alexandria; but the beauties of its red shores and clear blue waters filled with red coralline sea-weed are still the same.[1] To this place "the Israelites came on their return from Kadesh and through a gap in the eastern hills they finally turned north to Moab. It was a new Red Sea for them, and they little knew the glory which it would acquire when it became the channel of all the wealth of Solomon."

They now finally passed out of the neighborhood of the Red Sea into the elevated region which lies to the east of the series of valleys that extend from the head of the Gulf of Akabah to the sources of the Jordan. Here they found, not the Canaanites whom they were to subdue, but tribes kindred to themselves, whom they were forbidden to molest: the descendants of Esau and of Lot. First they skirted the eastern side of Mount Seir, the

---

1. These are the features of the whole sea, which caused it to be called the Red Sea, and by the Hebrews the Sea of Weeds.

home of the Edomites, who would seem to have yielded them, in this direction, the friendly passage which they could hardly have resisted on the open desert (Deut. 2:29). The route lay along the margin of the great *desert of Nejd*, "and the soul of the people was much discouraged because of the way" (Num. 21:4). God punished their murmurs by sending among them serpents, whose fiery bite was fatal. On their prayer of repentance a remedy was found. Moses was commanded to make a serpent of brass, whose polished surface shone like fire, and set it up on the banner-pole in the midst of the people; and whoever was bitten by a serpent had but to look up at it and live (Num. 21:4-9). In recounting the perils of the wilderness, Moses speaks of the "fiery serpents and scorpions" (Deut. 8:15); and these reptiles still abound in the region about the Gulf of Akabah. But a far deeper interest belongs to this incident of the pilgrimage of Israel: "As Moses lifted up the serpent in the wilderness, even so must the Son of man be lifted up; that whosoever believeth in him should not perish, but have eternal life" (John 3:14-15).

Preserved as a relic, the Brazen Serpent, called by the name of Nehushtan, became an object of idolatrous veneration, probably in connection with the snake worship that was adopted in the reign of Ahaz, with all the other idolatries of the neighboring nations; and the zeal of Hezekiah destroyed it with the other idols of his father (II Kings 18:4).

18. *Arrival at Brook Zered – March through the desert of Moab – Territories of Moab and Ammon – Conquests of the Amorites in Moab and Bashan.* We may assume that the brazen serpent was set up either at ZALMONAH or PUNON (Num. 33:41-42), which are equally unknown with the next station, OBOTH (Num. 21:10-11; 33:43-44). Then follows IJE-ABARIM (the *ruins of Abarim),* in the wilderness on the east border of Moab (Num. 21:11; 33:44), a name suggesting the foothills of the "mountains of ABARIM," which are mentioned four stages farther on (Num. 33:47), and which are a limestone range, running north and south through Moab along the east side of the Dead Sea and the lower Jordan, opposite the region about Jericho. Their highest point was NEBO, the "head" of the PISGAH or "height", from which Moses viewed the promised land (Num. 27:12; Deut. 32:49). They entered these highlands after crossing the valley and brook at *Zered* at the southeast corner of the Dead Sea, which Moses marks as the terminus of the thirty-eight years' wandering (Deut. 2:14).

From the Wady of Zered on the south to the broad canyon of

the River Arnon[1] on the north, lay the territory of Moab, also called *Ar*, along the southern half of the eastern shore of the Dead Sea; and a southern branch of the Arnon bounded their country on the east. Sometime before the exodus, the warlike Amorites had driven the Moabites out of the region between the Arnon and the Jabbok, so that these rivers were now the southern and northern boundaries of the kingdom of SIHON, the warlike king of the Amorites, whose capital was Heshbon (Num. 21:26-30). *North* of the Jabbok, the great upland territory of BASHAN, extending to Mount Hermon, formed the kingdom of the giant OG, who is also called an Amorite (Deut. 3:8). Such was the state of the country east of Jordan, which formed no part of the land marked out for the first settlement of the Israelites, but events drew them on to its conquest.

Having been forbidden to molest Moab or Ammon, they asked for a peaceable passage through the former, which would seem from some statements to have been granted and from others to have been refused (Deut. 2:28-29; 23:4; Judges 11:17). But the last of these passages may refer, as we have seen, to an earlier period, and the second only speaks of the withholding of actual assistance in supplies. Probably, as in the case of Edom, a direct passage was refused, but the people were left unmolested in passing over the upper courses of the Zered and the Arnon, and round the eastern slope of the intervening hills by the margin of the desert. Such a course would bring them "to the mountains of Abarim, before Nebo," on "the top of Pisgah," facing the JESHIMON or wilderness (Num. 33:47; 21:20); and their march from the Arnon to this position is expressly said to have been from the wilderness (Num. 21:18) and on the *border* of Moab (Num. 21:15).

Another indication that the people passed through the desert and not through the fertile lands of Moab is furnished by the very interesting notice of the station of BEER, so called from the well which was opened before all the people at the command of Jehovah (Num. 21:16).

19. *Defeat and destruction of Sihon and Og.* From their encampment in the wilderness of Kedemoth (the position of which is unknown), the Israelites sent a message to Sihon asking for a passage through his territory to the fords of Jordan opposite

---

1. The River Arnon formed the boundary between Moab and the Amorites, on the north of Moab (Num. 21:13,14,24,36; Judg. 11:22), and afterward between Moab and Israel (Reuben), Deut. 2:24,36; 3:8,12,16; 4:48; Josh. 12:1,2; 13:9,16; Judg. 11:13,26). It is now called *Wady el-Mojeb*, and flows through a deep canyon into the Dead Sea.

to Jericho, where they designed to enter the promised land and promising to asbtain from every disorder (Num. 21:21-22; Deut. 2:16-30). The Amorite king not only refused the request, but marched out with all his forces against Israel into the wilderness. A decisive battle at JAHAZ gave to Israel his whole territory. Sihon was slain, with his sons and all his people, even to the women and children, and Israel dwelt in their cities from Aroer on the Arnon to the Jabbok (Num. 21:23-30; Deut. 2:30-36; Judges 11:19-22). To the east of the southern branch of this river lay the territory of Ammon, too strong to be attacked even had it been permitted (Num. 21:24; Deut. 2:37). They followed up their victory by taking JAAZER, a stronghold of the Amorites in Mount Gilead, and then they crossed the Jabbok into the district of Bashan. Here they encountered the giant King Og, who ruled over sixty fenced cities in the district of *Argob*.[1] He was defeated at Edrei and slain with his sons and his people, as had been done to Sihon. Among the spoil was the iron bedstead of Og, 9 cubits long and 4 cubits broad (13½ feet by 6), which was preserved in Rabbath-ammon as a memorial of his vast stature, for he was the last of the giant race of the Rephaim who had dwelt of old in Ashteroth-karnaim, the capital of Og (see *Canaanites and Rephaim*, p. 90).

These first great victories of the new generation of Israel gave them the whole region east of Jordan as far as the desert, from the Arnon on the south to Mount Hermon or Sirion on the north, the region soon after allotted to the tribes of Reuben, Gad and half the tribe of Manasseh. But still more, they were an earnest of the conquest of the promised land; and they are ever after commemorated among the most signal mercies of Jehovah by the responsive anthems of the temple-service, giving thanks to Jehovah (Ps. 135:10-12; 136:17-22).

20. *Last encampment on the plains of Moab – Balak and Balaam – New census – Consecration of Joshua – Slaughter of the Midianites.* At length the Israelites made their last encampment on the east side of the Jordan in "the desert plains of Moab." Their tents were pitched among the long groves of acacias *(shittim)* which cover the topmost of the three terraces that form the basin of the Jordan, from ABEL-SHITTIM (the *meadow of acacias)* on the north, to *Beth-jeshimoth* (the *house of the wastes)* on the south. As in the

---

1. The limits of Bashan are very strictly defined. It extended from the "border of Gilead" on the south to Mount Hermon on the north (Deut. 3:3,10,14; Josh. 12:5; I Chron. 5:23), and from the Arabah or Jordan valley on the west to Salchah and the border of the Geshurites, and the Maacathites on the east (Josh. 12:3-5; Deut. 3:10). Argob, which means the *stony*, with its sixty strongly-fortified cities, formed a principal portion of Bashan (Deut. 2:4,5).

tropical climate of the valley, they enjoyed the shelter of the cool groves and the abundant springs; they could see on the opposite terrace the green meadows of Jericho, their first intended conquest. But there still remained work for them on the left bank. The hills of Abarim, which rose close behind them, were presently occupied by a watchful and wily enemy.

The conquest of the Amorites had roused the Moabites from their doubtful neutrality. Their king, Balak, the son of Zippor (the king who had been defeated by Sihon), seeing that Israel was too strong for him in the field, made a confederacy with the sheikhs of Midian, several of whom appear to have led their Bedouin life within the territories of Moab, owning a certain allegiance to the king (Num. 21:4; 31:8; Josh. 13:21). The united forces encamped on the heights of Abarim while Balak sought mightier help from another quarter.

There was living at Pethor in Mesopotamia, a prophet named BALAAM, the son of Beor, one of those who still retained the knowledge of the true God by whom he was favored with prophetic visions. He seems, however, to have practiced the more questionable arts of divination and to have made gain of his supernatural knowledge. His fame was spread far and wide among the tribes of the desert. "I know that he whom thou blessest is blessed, and he whom thou cursest is cursed" (Num. 22:6), is the belief on which Balak grounded his invitation to Balaam to come and curse Israel, after which he hoped he might prevail against them and drive them out of the land. The message was carried by the elders, both of Moab and of Midian, with the rewards for his divinations in their hand. The temptation was too great for the prophet's integrity, and he "forsook the right way and went astray" into that which the Apostle Peter calls "the way of Balaam, the son of Bosor, who loved the wages of unrighteousness" (II Pet. 2:15; Jude 11). Both as a prophet and from the fame which had spread over all the surrounding countries, he must have known that Israel were the people of his God, and that he had nothing to do with the messengers of Balak. He hesitated and was lost, but not without repeated warnings. Instead of dismissing the messengers, he invited them to remain for the night while he consulted God. He received the plain answer: "Thou shall not go with them; thou shall not curse the people, for they are blessed"; and in the morning he sent them away (Num. 22:1-14).

Balak again sent more numerous and more honorable envoys,

with a more pressing message and promises of great honors and rewards. Balaam declared his inability, for all the wealth of Balak —*not* to entertain the proposal for a moment, but — to go beyond the word of the Lord his God, to whom he again referred the case. And this time God visited him with the severest punishment, which He reserves for the willful sinner: "He "gave him his own desire" (Ps. 78:29); but while delivering him to the destruction he courted, He made him the instrument of blessing Israel in strains among the sublimest of sacred poetry. Balaam was commanded to go with the men, but as he himself had already said, to utter only the words that God should put in his mouth; and in all that follows, we see how vainly he strove to break through the prescribed limit and to earn the wages of his apostasy (Num. 22:15-21).

He received one last warning in a miracle that befell him on the road. The beast that bore him swerved twice from the way, and saved him from the uplifted sword of the Angel-Jehovah, who had come out to withstand him; and the third time, where the pass was too narrow to escape, she fell down beneath him, and on his smiting her again, "the dumb ass speaking with man's voice, forbad the madness of the prophet" (II Pet. 2:16). His eyes were now opened and he beheld the angel, who refused the offer which he now made to turn back, and repeated the injunction to go with the men but to speak only what He should say to him.[1]

Balak went to meet Balaam at a city on the Arnon (perhaps Aroer), and brought him to the city of *Kirjath-huzoth,* where the king held a great feast in the prophet's honor. On the morrow, Balak and Balaam began their unhallowed ceremonies (Num. 22:41-23:26). Thrice they ascended those eminences, which were consecrated to the worship of the heathen deities (Deut. 12:2), as places whence the prophet might see and curse the people, and thrice did "Jehovah their God turn the curse into a blessing, because Jehovah loved them." Lest Balaam's courage should fail him at the sight of the vast encampment surrounding the tabernacle, with its sign of Jehovah's presence in the cloud, Balak took him first to a hill sacred to Baal, whence he could see the utmost part of the people. Here Balaam bade Balak prepare seven altars, on each of which he offered a bullock and a ram, and then retired to another hill to consult Jehovah. From His mouth the prophet received the word; and he returned to confound Balak and his princes by asking, "How shall I curse whom God

---

1. Num. 22:22-35. Here is one of the many identifications of the *Angel-Jehovah* with God himself.

hath not cursed? or how shall I defy whom Jehovah hath not defied?" — at the same time prophesying Israel's separation from all nations and their countless numbers, and concluding by the oft-quoted ejaculation, "Let me die the death of the righteous, and let my last end be like this!"

The experiment was repeated from another eminence, "the field of Zophim, on the top of Pisgah," a more elevated point of observation, but still not commanding the great body of the camp. Here the same ceremonies were repeated with the same result; and God's message by the prophet declared His own eternal truth; His forgiving love to His people; His perpetual presence among them, making them proof against enchantment; and their future career of lion-like prowess against their enemies. Balak vented his disappointment in the cry, "Neither curse them at all, nor bless them at all"; but he would not give up without a last trial (Num. 23:14-26).

This third time he brought Balaam up to the very sanctuary of the national deity Peor, the same topmost summit — Nebo, the *head* of Pisgah — from which Moses soon after viewed the promised land. The sevenfold sacrifice was repeated, but Balaam laid aside his arts of divination, for he saw that it pleased Jehovah to bless Israel. His view embraced the whole camp of Israel, spread out among the acacia groves by the river at his feet; it ranged over their promised possessions in the hills of Judah, Ephraim and Gilead; and as "he saw Israel abiding in their tents according to their tribes, the Spirit of God came upon him, and he took up his parable," the prophecy of the man whose eyes were at length opened. In the goodly array of their tents he saw the omen of the destruction of the nations around; and ended, "Blessed is he that blesseth thee; and cursed is he that curseth thee" (Num. 23:27-24:9). Heedless of the rage of Balak or of his cruel sarcasm, "*I* thought to promote thee to great honor; but lo, *Jehovah* hath kept thee back from honor," Balaam declared that, before returning to his home, he must complete his prophecy of what the people should do to the heathen in the last days (Num. 24:10-14). For the fourth time he opened his mouth and proclaimed his distant vision of the "Star of Jacob," the "Sceptre of Israel," who should smite Moab — a prophecy in part fulfilled by the victories of David (II Sam. 8:2); but as the titles plainly show, pointing forward to the kingdom of Messiah over the outcast branches of the chosen family. Then as his eye ranged over the distant mountains of Seir, the home of Edom, and the table-land of the desert, over which the children of Amalek wandered, and the home of the Kenites full in his sight, among the rocks of Engedi on the farther shores of the Dead Sea, he predicted their destruction; till the vision carried him back to the banks of his native Euphrates, and he saw the conquests of Asshur overturned by ships coming from the coasts of Chittim, the unknown lands beyond the Western Sea, and he exclaimed, "Alas! who shall live when God doeth this!" And he rose up, and returned to the place assigned for his abode (Num. 24:15-25).

Can we read the sublime prophecies of Balaam without wishing that his desire for his latter end might have been fulfilled? Doubtless *it might have been,* had he renounced the vain hope of gain and honor and returned to repent of his sin and thank the God who had turned it into a blessing. But he remained among the Moabites and Midianites, clinging doubtless to the chance of reward; and provoked his fate by a new and more effectual plot against Israel. By his advice the people were tempted to share in the lascivious rites of Peor, and to commit whoredom with the daughters of Moab (Num. 25:1-3; 31:16). The wrath of Jehovah was shown in a plague which broke out in the camp and destroyed 24,000 men. Moses doomed all the offenders to death and Phinehas, the son of Eleazar, the high-priest, set an example of zeal by transfixing with a javelin a man of Israel in the arms of a woman of Moab, whom he had brought into his tent in the face of the congregation as they wept before Jehovah. The plague was stayed and the covenant of Jehovah was renewed with the house of Eleazar, assuring him a perpetual priesthood (Num. 25:4-15).

For these plots against Israel, as well as for their former inhospitality, the Moabites were excluded from the congregation to the tenth generation,[1] and the Midianites were doomed to destruction (Num. 25:16-18). The execution of this sentence was the last act of the government of Moses. All the men of Midian were slain, with the princes who had been allied with Balak, and Balaam died in the general slaughter. Their cities were burnt and their spoil taken, and the women, who had been saved alive, were slain by the command of Moses, the female children only being spared. At the same time a law was made for the equitable division of the spoil between those who went forth to battle and those who remained in the camp (Num. 31).

Before this war another census had been taken, by which the

---

1. Deut. 31:3-6; this is interpreted by Nehemiah (13:1) to mean *forever.* The inclusion of the Amorites in the sentence is another proof of the close connection between the two peoples. The Edomites might enter the congregation in the third generation.

number was found to be about the same as before Sinai, 38½ years before (the exact decrease was 1820) (Num. 26); and JOSHUA was consecrated by the high-priest Eleazar to be the successor of Moses (Num. 27:15-23).

21. *Settlement of Reuben, Gad and half of Manasseh east of Jordan.* After the slaughter of the Midianites, the tribes of Reuben and Gad came to Moses and Eleazar and the elders, with the request that they might have for their possession the conquered land on the east of Jordan, the upland pastures of which made it desirable for their numerous cattle. Moses at first rebuked them sharply, as if they were repeating the sin of their fathers at Kadesh-barnea; but on their promise that they would only leave their families and their cattle in their new abodes, while they themselves would march armed in the van of their brethren till the whole land should be subdued, he yielded to their request and bound them solemnly to their engagement (Num. 32; Deut. 3:12-20).

The tribe of Reuben was settled in the south of the region beyond Jordan, from the Arnon to the southern slopes of Mount Gilead. That mountain was given to Gad, whose northern border just touched the sea of Chinnereth (lake of Gennesareth). The northeast part of Gilead and the land of Bashan, as far as Mount Hermon, were at the same time allotted to half the tribe of Manasseh, who came under the same engagement as their brethren. In the final account of the settlement of the country we read how faithfully the two tribes and a half fulfilled their promise (Josh. 4:12-13; 22:4). Still they can hardly be acquitted of a certain selfish grasping at present advantage; and their fault brought its own punishment, for their position exposed them to attack and they were the first of the Israelites who were carried into captivity (II Kings 15:29).

Questions Over Numbers

Numbers, Chapter 1
1. What is the topic of chapter one?
2. What people were counted in the numbering?
3. Make a list of the tribes, their populations and the total number.
4. Which tribe was not numbered and why not?

Numbers, Chapter 2
1. What is the topic of chapter two?
2. List the order (or positions) of the various camps as Israel moved about.

3. As the tribes marched, where was the tabernacle carried in relation to the camps?

Numbers, Chapter 3

1. What is the topic of chapter three?
2. Whom did God take instead of the firstborn of Israel?
3. Name the three families of the Levites.
4. What was the total number of the Levites?
5. Were there more Levites or firstborn Israelites? How many more?
6. What was done to adjust the difference between the number of Levites and the number of the firstborn?

Numbers, Chapter 4

1. Give the chapter topic for chapter four.
2. How was the ark of the covenant packed up for moving?

Numbers, Chapter 5

1. What was used to determine if a wife had committed adultery?

Numbers, Chapter 6

1. What is the topic of most of chapter six?
2. What things was a Nazirite not to do (Compare Judges 13:4-5,7,24)?

Numbers, Chapter 7

1. What was given to help in transporting the tabernacle?
2. Did the princes of the various tribes offer different gifts for the tabernacle?

Numbers, Chapter 8

1. What is the topic of 8:5-26?

Numbers, Chapter 9

1. What feast was kept early in the second year after Israel left Egypt?
2. What rule was given about those who could not keep the Passover because they were unclean?
3. What guided the Israelites and determined their moving about?

Numbers, Chapter 10

1. What was used for calling the congregation of Israel together?
2. How long after leaving Egypt was it when Israel left Sinai?
3. How long were the Israelites at Mt. Sinai altogether (see Ex. 19:1)?
4. Into what wilderness did Israel come after leaving Sinai?
5. Whom did Moses ask to accompany Israel from Mt. Sinai?

   6. Did he desire to accompany Moses and Israel?

Numbers, Chapter 11

   1. What happened when the people murmured?
   2. What was the place called where they murmured?
   3. What did the mixed multitude lust after?
   4. How did God react to their lustful weeping?
   5. How did Moses react to it?
   6. Whom did God appoint to help Moses bear the burden of the people?
   7. How long did God promise that Israel would eat flesh?
   8. What did the men who were appointed to help Moses do when the Spirit rested on them?
   9. What two men prophesied in the camp?
  10. How did Joshua react to their prophesying?
  11. What type of meat was given to the people?
  12. With what did Jehovah smite the people?
  13. What was the place called where God gave them meat and what did its name mean?

Numbers, Chapter 12

   1. What did Miriam and Aaron speak against Moses about?
   2. How is Moses described in this chapter?
   3. How did Jehovah feel about their speaking against Moses?
   4. How was Miriam punished?
   5. How long did Miriam's sin delay Israel's progress?

Numbers, Chapter 13

   1. What did Jehovah command Moses to do?
   2. Who were the spies from the tribes of Judah and Ephraim?
   3. How much of the land did the men look over?
   4. What was obtained at Eshcol?
   5. How long did the men take on their trip?
   6. How did the spies describe the land and its inhabitants?
   7. Which spy said that Israel could possess the land?
   8. How did the men say they looked to the inhabitants of the land?

Numbers, Chapter 14

   1. How did the people react to the words of the ten unbelieving spies?
   2. Whom did the Israelites say would be a prey and perish?
   3. Did the Israelites appoint a captain to lead them back to Egypt (Cf. Neh. 9:17)?
   4. What did God threaten to do to Israel?

5. What prevented God from killing Israel?
6. What judgment and punishment did God pronounce upon Israel?
7. What happened to the ten spies?
8. What was the result of Israel's attempted invasion of Canaan?

Numbers, Chapter 15

1. What two offerings were to be made along with burnt or peace offerings?
2. If a person sinned unknowingly what types of offerings did he have to bring?
3. What was to be done to those who sinned "with the high hand"?
4. What was the punishment upon the man who gathered sticks on the Sabbath?
5. What were the Israelites to place on the borders of their garments?

Numbers, Chapter 16

1. What is the chapter topic of Numbers 16?
2. Who rebelled against Moses (3 names)? How many men joined the rebels?
3. What did Moses tell the rebels to do to determine whom Jehovah had chosen to be priests?
4. Was the congregation of Israel favorable to Moses or to the rebels (16:19)?
5. What was the fate of the rebel leaders? Of their followers?
6. What was done with the censers of the rebels?
7. How did the congregation react to the deaths of the rebels?
8. How many in the congregation died as a result of this?

Numbers, Chapter 17

1. What did God use to demonstrate which man was his chosen priest?
2. Where was the rod to be kept? Why?
3. What was Israel's reaction to the budding of Aaron's rod?

Numbers, Chapter 18

1. What was the penalty upon unauthorized people who did the work of priests?
2. What was to be given to Aaron and his sons to provide for their needs?
3. What was to be done with firstborn animals?
4. What was the redemption price of firstborn sons?
5. Why did the priests receive no inheritance of land?

6. What was to be given to the Levites as their inheritance?
7. What were the Levites to take out of their tithes? To whom was this given?

Numbers, Chapter 19

1. What were the ashes of a red heifer to be used for (Compare Heb. 9:13)?
2. How long was a man unclean after touching a dead body?

Numbers, Chapter 20

1. Where did Miriam die?
2. What did God tell Moses to do unto the rock? What did Moses do?
3. What was Moses' punishment?
4. What unkind thing did Edom do to Israel?
5. Where did Aaron die?
6. Who became Aaron's successor as high priest?

Numbers, Chapter 21

1. What Canaanite king attacked Israel?
2. What was the result of this attack?
3. How did the Israelites feel as they went around the land of Edom?
4. What was the brass serpent used for? What did Jesus compare this incident to (John 3:14-15)?
5. What was the border between Moab and the Amorites?
6. What did Moses and Israel do at Beer?
7. Who was Sihon?
8. What was the extent of Sihon's kingdom (Compare Joshua 12:2-3)?
9. What did Israel request of Sihon?
10. Where did Sihon fight against Israel?
11. Between what two rivers did Israel occupy the land of Sihon?
12. What was the capital city of Sihon's kingdom?
13. What land had Sihon previously captured?
14. Who was Chemosh (Compare I Kings 11:33)?
15. To what city did Moses send spies?
16. Who was Og?
17. What was the extent of Og's kingdom (Compare Joshua 12:4-5)?
18. How big was Og's bedstead (Deut. 3:11)?
19. Where did Israel fight Og?
20. What encouragement did Israel receive for the battle against Og?
21. What was the outcome of the battle of Og?

Numbers, Chapter 22
1. Who was Balak?
2. What was worrying Balak?
3. Who was Balaam?
4. What did Balak want Balaam to do?
5. What did God tell Balaam not to do?
6. How did Balak try to persuade Balaam?
7. What blocked Balaam's path as he rode to Balak?
8. What unusual thing did Balaam's ass do (Compare II Peter 2:15-16 and Jude 11)?
9. Did Balaam really want to please God or to please Balak?

Numbers, Chapter 23
1. What did Balaam do in the hope that God might change his mind?
2. In Balaam's first prophecy did he curse or bless Israel?
3. What was done in preparation for the second attempt to curse Israel?
4. Did God change his mind about Israel, according to Balaam's second prophecy?
5. What did Balak say after Balaam's second prophecy?
6. Did Balak think that God was the same everywhere? Give a reason for your answer.

Numbers, Chapter 24
1. What had Balaam used enchantments for?
2. What is the main point in Balaam's third prophecy?
3. What (apparently) good statement did Balaam give to Balak after the third prophecy?
4. In Balaam's fourth prophecy what did he say would rise out of Jacob and Israel?
5. Relate this prophecy (24:17) to Matthew 2:2.
6. What nations did Balaam predict in his fourth prophecy that God would destroy?

Numbers, Chapter 25
1. What sin did Israel fall into?
2. Whose counsel had brought about this sin by Israel (See Numbers 31:16)?
3. What priest slew a couple? How? Why?
4. How many Israelites died as a result of this sin (Compare I Cor. 10:8)?
5. What did God tell the Israelites to do to Midian?

Numbers, Chapter 26
1. What is the topic of chapter 26?

  2. Prepare parallel lists of the populations of the tribes in the two censuses (Numbers 1 and 26).

  3. How many men survived the 40 years' wilderness wanderings?

Numbers, Chapter 27

  1. What did the daughters of Zelophehad want?

  2. Was their request granted?

  3. What dramatic demand did God make to Moses?

  4. What did Moses ask God to do before he (Moses) died?

  5. Who was appointed as leader to succeed Moses?

Numbers, Chapter 28

  1. On what occasions were the Israelites to offer additional sacrifices besides the daily continual burnt offerings?

Numbers, Chapter 29

  1. What three feasts were to be observed in the seventh month (Compare Lev. 23:23-36)?

  2. On what days of the month were these feasts to be observed?

Numbers, Chapter 30

  1. How seriously were vows to be taken (Compare Ecclesiastes 5:4-6)?

  2. Who had power to break a vow made by a woman? A wife? A widow?

Numbers, Chapter 31

  1. With whom did Israel go to war?

  2. What prophet was slain in the war?

  3. How did the war come out?

  4. How were the prisoners of war divided?

  5. What part of the prisoners were given to Jehovah from the men of war? From the congregation of Israel?

Numbers, Chapter 32

  1. What land did the children of Reuben and Gad request?

  2. How did Moses react to their request?

  3. What did the tribes of Reuben and Gad promise to do if they could have the requested land?

  4. What other tribe received land in the same area as Gad and Reuben?

  5. Who dispossessed the Amorites in Gilead?

Numbers, Chapter 33

  1. What is the general topic of chapter thirty-three?

  2. What caused Moses to write a record of the journeys of Israel?

3. What were the Egyptians doing while the Israelites left Egypt?
4. In what year of Israel's wanderings did Aaron die?
5. What did God command Israel to do to the inhabitants of Canaan?
6. What would the Canaanites be to the Israelites if the Israelites failed to drive them out?

Numbers, Chapter 34

1. What was the south border of the promised land (Compare Gen. 15:18)?
2. What was the north border of the promised land?
3. What part of the land was allotted to Gad, Reuben and half of Manasseh?

Numbers, Chapter 35

1. How many cities were to be given to the Levites altogether?
2. What six special cities were included in this number?
3. How much territory surrounding these cities was to be given to the Levites?
4. What were the cities of refuge used for?
5. Where were the cities of refuge to be located?
6. What was the penalty for murderers?
7. Who decided if a man had a right to safety in a city of refuge?
8. How long did a manslayer have to stay in a city of refuge?
9. How could a manslayer lose his security in a city of refuge?
10. How many witnesses were required to convict a killer?

Numbers, Chapter 36

1. What problem worried the descendants of Manasseh?
2. What restriction about marriage was placed on women who inherited property?

Section VII
Book of Deuteronomy

1. Introduction to the book. 2. Final addresses of Moses: the Book of Deuteronomy — a. His first discourse: Review and introduction — b. His second discourse: Repetition of the law — c. His third discourse: The blessing and the curse — d. The law rewritten — The "Song of Moses" — e. The "Blessing of Moses." 3. Moses' view of the Promised Land — His

death and burial. 4. The character of Moses — Moses a type of Christ.

1. *Introduction to Deuteronomy*

a. The name DEUTERONOMY means "Second Law" (or "The Law repeated"). It is called by this name because in Deuteronomy Moses repeated much of the law that had been given nearly forty years before at Mt. Sinai. Note that the Ten Commandments are given in Deuteronomy 5 as well as in Exodus 20.

This repetition of the law was necessary because a new generation had grown up in the wilderness who had not heard the law at Mt. Sinai. Also all the Israelites who had once heard it assuredly needed to hear it again.

b. Author, date and place of writing.

   1. *Author.* Moses was the author of all the book except probably the last chapter, which tells of his death (Deut. 1:1; 4:44; 31:1). The last chapter was probably written by Joshua after Moses' death. See Josh. 8:32 and 24:26.

   2. *Date:* 1407 B.C. Deuteronomy was delivered in the fortieth year, the eleventh month, after the exodus, and it took approximately one month. It was a thirty-day revival. This was about two months before Israel crossed over into the promised land (Deut. 1:3; Josh. 4:19).

      (Note — Joshua 4:19 tells us that Israel crossed into Canaan in the 41st year, the first month, tenth day. This was seventy days after Moses began to deliver Deuteronomy. Between Deuteronomy and the crossing into Canaan lay: (1) Moses' death; (2) a thirty-day period of weeping for Moses (Deut. 34:8); (3) the sending of spies into Jericho, an event that occupied several days (Joshua 2:22). These events took about forty days, leaving about thirty days for the delivering of the messages in Deuteronomy.)

   3. *Place.* Deuteronomy was delivered in the "plains of Moab by Jordan at Jericho" (Num. 36:13). This place is otherwise described as "beyond (east of) the Jordan in the wilderness, in the Arabah" (Deut. 1:1).

c. *Character of the book.*

   1. The book consists of three extended addresses by Moses (chapters 1-30), followed by certain closing words and events (chapters 31-34).

2. Deuteronomy contains (mainly in chapters 12-26) laws of social, civil and political nature such as Israel would need when they entered the promised land, but which would have been superfluous in the desert.

3. The book mostly has the style of a sermon or a fatherly exhortation. It contains the closing messages of Moses to his people.

d. *Outline of Deuteronomy*
1. Three addresses by Moses *(Chapters 1-30).*
   a. Historical review of God's dealings with Israel (1:1-4:40). Transjordanian cities of refuge set apart (4:41-43).
   b. Laws and exhortations (4:44-ch. 26).
      (1) Chs. 5-11: an extended exposition of the Ten Commandments.
      (2) Chs. 12-26: a code of special statutes to be observed in Canaan.
   c. Blessings of obedience and curses of disobedience (Chs. 27-30).
2. Closing words and events (Chs. 31-34).
   a. Final charges (Ch. 31).
      (1) Charge concerning conquering the land (31:1-8).
      (2) Charge to read the law every seven years (31:9-13).
      (3) Charge to Joshua (31:14-23).
      (4) Charge to keep the law by the ark (31:24-29).
   b. The song of Moses (Ch. 32).
   c. The blessing of Moses (Ch. 33).
   d. Death of Moses (Ch. 34).

e. *New Testament uses of Deuteronomy.*
1. Jesus quoted Deuteronomy three times during his temptations (Matthew 4:4-10; Deut. 6:16; 8:3).
2. The apostle Paul often quoted and used passages from Deuteronomy to prove the teachings of the Gospel. See Romans 10:8.
3. Peter quoted Deuteronomy 18:15 in his sermon on Solomon's porch (Acts 3:22-23).

f. *We suggest that you memorize the following passages from Deuteronomy:* 4:2; 6:4-5; 8:3; 10:12; 11:26-28; 18:15; 24:29; 31:6; 33:27.

Questions Over the Introduction to Deuteronomy

1. What does the name Deuteronomy mean? Why is it called that?

2. Who was the author of Deuteronomy? Its date? Place of writing?

3. In what two places are the Ten Commandments given?

4. Memorize the outline of Deuteronomy.

5. When did Jesus make a conspicuous use of passages from Deuteronomy?

2. *Final Addresses of Moses – The Book of Deuteronomy.* The work of Moses was now finished: he had already received the command of God to ascend Mount Abarim and view the land into which he must not enter, and his successor had been solemnly ordained. But before his departure he assembled all the people, rehearsed to them the dealings of Jehovah and their own conduct since they had departed from Egypt; repeated the law, with certain modifications and additions, and enforced it with the most solemn exhortations, warnings and prophecies of their future history. This address (or rather series of addresses) is contained in the Book of DEUTERONOMY *(the repetition of the law).* It was delivered in the plains of Moab, in the eleventh month of the fortieth year from the epoch of the exodus (Adar — February, 1407 B.C.). It consists of *three discourses,* followed by the *Song of Moses,* the *Blessing of Moses* and the *story of his death.*

a. In the *First Discourse* (Deut. 1:1-4:40), Moses strives briefly, but very earnestly, to warn the people against the sins for which their fathers failed to enter the promised land, and to impress upon them the one simple lesson of *obedience;* that they might in their turn be ready to enter into the land. With this special object, he recapitulates the chief events of the last forty years in the wilderness, and especially those events which had the most immediate bearing on the entry of the people into the promised land.

b. The *Second Discourse* (Deut. 5-26. 4:44-49 introduces the discourse) enters more fully into the actual precepts of the law: in fact, it may be viewed as the body of the whole address, the former being an introduction. It contains a recapitulation, with some modifications and additions, of the law already given on Mount Sinai. Yet it is not bare recapitulation or naked enactment, but every word shows the heart of the lawgiver full at once of zeal for God and of the most fervent desire for the welfare of his nation. It is the Father no less than the Legislator who speaks. And while obedience and life are throughout bound up together, it is the obedience of a loving heart, not a service of formal constraint, which is the burden of his exhortations.

c. The *Third Discourse* (Deut. 27-30) relates almost entirely to the solemn *sanctions* of the law: the *blessing* and the *curse*. Moses now speaks in conjunction with the elders of the people (Deut. 27:1), and with the priests and Levites (Deut. 27:9), whose office it would be to carry out the ceremony, which was prescribed in anticipation of the people's settlement in Palestine (Deut. 27:8).

The place selected was that sacred spot in the centre of the land, where Abraham and Jacob had first pitched their tents under the oaks of Moreh, and where the first altar to God had been erected. Here the green valley of Shechem is bounded by two long rocky hills on the north and south, the former being the MOUNT EBAL, the latter the MOUNT GERIZIM.

As soon as they should have crossed over Jordan, the people were commanded to set up, on the summit of *Ebal,* great stones covered with plaster and inscribed with the law of God. They were also to build an altar; and this seems to have been distinct from the stones, though the point is somewhat doubtful. Then (to use the historical form of expression, as the scene is described more fully here than on its actual performance under Joshua), the twelve tribes were divided between the two hills. On Gerizim stood Simeon, Levi, Judah, Issachar, Joseph and Benjamin, to *bless* the people: on Ebal, Reuben, Gad, Asher, Zebulun, Dan and Naphtali, to utter the *curses,* which are then fully recited (Deut. 27).

Moses then proceeds to amplify the blessing and the curse, but chiefly the latter, as the warning was more needed. That sad prophetic anticipation of the course actually followed by the Israelites, which runs through the whole book, becomes now especially prominent; and he denounces, with terrible explicitness, the curses of disease and pestilence, death and famine, failure in every work, subjection to their own servants, invasion by a mighty nation, with all the horrors of defeat and siege, ending in the forlorn lot of the captive in a foreign land, oppressed by his tyrants and uncertain of his very life. "In the morning thou shalt say, Would God it were even! and at even thou shalt say, Would God it were morning!" and, to crown all, they would be led back at last to their bondage in Egypt (Deut. 28).

d. Having finished these discourses, Moses encouraged the people and Joshua, their new leader, to go over Jordan and take possession of the land (Deut. 31:1-8). He then wrote "this law" and delivered it to the Levites, to be kept in the ark of the covenant as a perpetual witness against the people; and he commanded them to read it to all Israel when assembled at the Feast of Tabernacles every seventh year, in the solemnity of the Sabbatic year (Deut. 31:9-13, 24-30).[1]

e. By the command of Jehovah, who appeared in the cloud to Moses and Joshua when they presented themselves at the door of the tabernacle, Moses added to the book of the law a *song*, which the children of Israel were enjoined to learn, as a witness for Jehovah against them (Deut. 31:13-23). This "Song of Moses" recounts the blessings of God, the ROCK — His perfect work, His righteous ways, and the corrupt response by His foolish people, though He was their father, who bought and created and established them. It contrasts His mercies with their sins; declares their punishment and the judgment of their oppressors, as alike displaying the glory and vengeance of Him beside whom there is no god; and it concludes by prophesying the time when the Gentiles should rejoice with His people, and all should join to celebrate His marvellous works and judgments in "the song of Moses, the servant of God, and the song of the Lamb" (Deut. 32:1-47; Rev. 15:3).

3. *Moses' View of the Promised Land – His death and burial.* Moses now received the final summons for his departure (Deut. 32:48-52). But first he uttered, not now as the legislator and teacher of his people, but as the prophet wrapt in the visions of the future, his blessing on the twelve tribes (Deut. 33). This *blessing of Moses* closely resembles, in its structure and contents, the dying blessing of Jacob on his sons, but with very interesting differences. Besides the new and fervent description of Levi's priesthood (Deut. 33:8-11), it is remarkable for the absence of those darker shades, which were cast over Jacob's language by the faults of his sons. It speaks only of the favors that God would shower on the tribes;[2] and it describes most richly the happiness of the whole people who are mentioned, here and in the preceding song, but the symbolical name of JESHURUN, which is only used again by Isaiah.[3]

---

1. This is the most striking of the passages in which the books of Scripture contain in themselves the record of their composition.
2. It is curious that *Simeon* is not named.
3. Jeshurun is a poetic and idealized name for Israel (which name it resembles) meaning *the righteous one* (Deut. 32:15; 33:5,26; Isa. 44:2).

"And Moses went up from the plains of Moab unto the mountain of Nebo, the summit of Pisgah, that is over against Jericho. And Jehovah showed him all the land of Gilead unto Dan, and all Naphtali, and the land of Ephraim, and Manasseh, and all the land of Judah, even unto the utmost sea, and the south, and the plain of the valley of Jericho the city of palm-trees, unto Zoar" (Deut. 34:1-3). Thus minutely does the supplement to the Book of Deuteronomy describe the scene which lay open before Moses, when he was alone with God upon the sacred mountain of the Moabites — embracing the four great masses of the inheritance on the east, the north, the centre and the south, with the plain that lay at his feet. After receiving the last assurance that this was the land promised to Abraham and his seed, *"Moses the servant of Jehovah died there in the land of Moab, according to the word of Jehovah"* (Deut. 34:5). *God himself buried him "in a ravine before Bethpeor," in front of the very sanctuary of "the abomination of the Moabites."* An allusion in Jude 9 reveals that Michael, the archangel, engaged in dispute with the devil about the body of Moses, and that Michael did not presume to speak to the prince of evil spirits in a railing manner (comp. Zech. 3:2). We know nothing further about this matter.

No man knows the place of Moses' burial. That of him which it was really left for posterity to seek, besides the record of his deeds, was his living likeness in the prophet whom God promised to raise up of his brethren, as He had raised up him, even Christ.

The children of Israel mourned for Moses in the plains of Moab thirty days; and they rendered obedience to Joshua, the son of Nun, on whom Moses had laid his hands and who was full of the spirit of wisdom (Deut. 33:8,9).

4. *The Character of Moses – Moses a Type of Christ.* In portraying the character of Moses, we avail ourselves of the graphic description of Dean Stanley from Smith's *Dict. of Bible,* art. Moses:

It has sometimes been attempted to reduce this great character into a mere passive instrument of the Divine Will, as though he had himself borne no conscious part in the actions in which he figures or the messages which he delivers. This, however, is as incompatible with the general tenor of the scriptural account as it is with the common language in which he has been described by the Church in all ages. The frequent addresses of the Divinity to him no more contravene his personal activity and intelligence than in the case of Elijah, Isaiah or Paul. In the New Testament the Mosaic legislation is especially ascribed to him: — *"Moses* gave you circumcision" (John 7:22). *"Moses,* because of the hardness of your hearts, suffered you" (Matt. 19:8). "Did not *Moses* give you the law" (John 7:19)? *"Moses* accuseth you" (John 5:45). St. Paul speaks of him as the founder of the Jewish religion: "They were all baptized *unto Moses*" (I Cor. 10:2). He is constantly called "a Prophet." In the poetical language of the Old Testament, and in the popular language both of Jews and Christians, he is known as "the Lawgiver" (Num. 21:18; Deut. 33:21). He must be considered, like all the saints and heroes of the Bible, as a man of marvelous gifts, raised up by Divine Providence for a special purpose, but as led into a closer communion with the invisible world than was vouchsafed to any other in the Old Testament.

There are two main characters in which he appears: as a leader and as a prophet.

a. Of his natural gifts as a *leader,* we have but few means of judging. The two main difficulties which he encountered were the reluctance of the people to submit to his guidance and the impracticable nature of the country which they had to traverse. The patience with which he bore their murmurs has been described — at the Red Sea, at the apostasy of the golden calf, at the rebellion of Korah, at the complaints of Aaron and Miriam. On approaching Palestine, the office of the leader becomes blended with that of the general or the conqueror. By Moses the spies were sent to explore the country. Against his advice took place the first disastrous battle at Hormah. To his guidance is ascribed the circuitous route by which the nation approached Palestine from the east, and to his generalship the two successful campaigns in which SIHON and OG were defeated. The narrative is told so shortly, that we are in danger of forgetting that at this last stage of his life Moses must have been as much a conqueror and victorious soldier as Joshua.

b. His character as a *prophet* is, from the nature of the case, more distinctly brought out. He is the first as he is the greatest example of a prophet in the Old Testament. The name is indeed applied to Abraham before (Gen. 20:7), but so casually as not to enforce our attention. But in the case of Moses, it is given with peculiar emphasis. In a certain sense, he appears as the centre of a prophetic circle, now for the first time named. His brother and sister were both endowed with prophetic gifts. Aaron's fluent speech enabled him to act the part of prophet for Moses in the first instance, and Miriam is expressly called "the Prophetess." The seventy elders, and

Eldad and Medad also, all "prophesied" (Num. 11:25-27). But
Moses (at least after the exodus) rose high above all these. The
others are spoken as of more or less inferior. Their
communications were made to them in dreams and figures
(Deut. 13:1-4; Num. 12:6). But "Moses was not so." With him
the divine revelations were made, "mouth to mouth, even
openly, and not in dark speeches, and the form of JEHOVAH
shall he behold" (Num. 12:8).

The prophetic office of Moses, however, can only be fully
considered in connection with his whole character and
appearance. "By a prophet Jehovah brought Israel out of
Egypt, and by a prophet was he preserved" (Hosea 12:13). He
was, in a sense peculiar to himself, the founder and
representative of his people. And in accordance with this
complete identification of himself with his nation, is the only
strong personal trait which we are able to gather from his
history. "The man Moses was very meek, above all the men
that were upon the face of the earth" (Num. 12:3). The word
"meek" is hardly an adequate reading of the Hebrew term,
which should be rather "much enduring"; and, in fact, his
onslaught of the Egyptian and his sudden dashing the tables
on the ground, indicate rather the reverse of what we should
call "meekness". It represents what we should now designate
by the word "disinterested". All that is told of him indicates a
withdrawal of himself, a preference of the cause of his nation
to his own interests, which makes him the most complete
example of Jewish patriotism. He joins his countrymen in
their degrading servitude (Ex. 2:11; 5:4). He forgets himself
to avenge their wrong (Ex. 2:14). He desires that his brother
may take the lead instead of himself (Ex. 4:13). He wishes that
not he only, but all the nation, were gifted alike: — "Enviest
thou for my sake" (Num. 11:29)? When the offer is made that
the people should be destroyed and that he should be made "a
great nation" (Ex. 32:10), he prays that they may be forgiven
— "if not, blot me, I pray Thee, out of Thy book which Thou
hast written" (Ex. 32:32). His sons were not raised to honor.
The leadership of the people passed, after his death, to
another tribe. In the books which bear his name, Abraham,
and not himself, appears as the real father of the nation. In
spite of his great pre-eminence, they are never "the children of
Moses."

In the New Testament Moses is spoken of as a likeness or

type of Christ. This comparison was clearly foretold in Deut. 18:15,18 — "The Lord thy God will raise up unto thee a prophet from the midst of thee, from thy brethren, *like unto me;* unto him ye shall harken . . . I will raise them up a prophet from among their brethren, *like unto thee,* and will put my words in his mouth; and he shall speak unto them all that I shall command him. And it shall come to pass, that whosoever will not hearken unto my words which he shall speak in my name, I will require it of him." This passage is also quoted by Peter and by Stephen (Acts 3:22-23; 7:37), and it is probably in allusion to it that at the transfiguration, in the presence of Moses and Elijah, the words were uttered, "Hear ye him." There are several points of similarity between Moses and Christ:

1. Christ, like Moses, was a prophet (Matt. 13:47).
2. Christ, like Moses, was a lawgiver (John 14:15).
3. Christ, like Moses, was saved as a babe.
4. Christ, like Moses, came as a peacemaker (Matt. 19:42; Ex. 2:13).
5. Christ, like Moses, was commissioned by God (John 5:30).
6. Christ, like Moses, came working miracles.
7. Christ, like Moses, came proclaiming deliverance (Luke 4:18).
8. Christ, like Moses, was rejected by many (Acts 7:23-39, 51-52).
9. Christ, like Moses, put His brethren (the church!) before His own interests. As Moses was the entire representative of his people, feeling for them more than for himself, absorbed in their interests, hopes and fears, so with reverence be it said, was Christ.

Questions Over Deuteronomy

Deuteronomy 1
1. In what year and month did Moses speak the words of Deuteronomy?
2. Why had Moses appointed wise men from the tribes to be heads over the people?
3. What sort of a place was the wilderness which Israel passed through after leaving Horeb?
4. How did the Lord feel toward Moses when the Israelites did not have faith to conquer the Promised Land?

5. How did the invasion of Canaan work out when Israel decided they would try to enter?
6. How long did Israel abide at Kadesh?

Deuteronomy 2

1. With what three peoples was Israel not to contend (2:4-5,9,19)?
2. How many years did it take Israel to get from Kadesh-barnea to the brook Zered (2:7,14)?
3. Who was Sihon?
4. How did Sihon respond to Israel's messengers of peace?

Deuteronomy 3

1. Who was Og? What did Israel do to him?
2. How big was Og's bed?
3. What tribe received the land of Bashan?
4. What command was given to the men of the Israelite tribes which inherited land east of the Jordan?
5. What request of Moses did God deny (3:25-26)?

Deuteronomy 4

1. What was Israel neither to add to nor diminish from?
2. What words comprised God's covenant which he commanded to Israel (4:13)?
3. What lesson was Israel to learn from the fact that they saw no form of God on the day God spoke the law to them in Horeb?
4. What would be Israel's punishment if they made graven images in the land (4:26)?
5. Name the three cities of refuge east of (or beyond) Jordan.

Deuteronomy 5

1. What did God make with the Israelites at Horeb (5:2)?
2. What notable words are repeated in Deuteronomy 5?
3. What was the Sabbath day to cause Israel to remember besides the seventh day of creation?
4. How did the Israelites react when they heard the voice of the Lord at Sinai (5:23-25)?

Deuteronomy 6

1. What wonderful truth about God is given in this chapter (6:4)? (This verse is called the *Shema,* from the opening word in Hebrew, meaning "Hear".)
2. How important is the command in 6:5? (See Matthew 22:37-38.)
3. Where was the law to be placed (6:8-9)? (For further study, look up "Phylactery" in a Bible dictionary. Matt. 23:5)

4. How can men *tempt* the Lord (6:16; Ex. 17:2,7)?

Deuteronomy 7

1. How many nations of Canaanites were in the Promised land?
2. What was Israel to do (and *not* do) with these nations (7:2-5)?
3. Did God promise to cast out these nations suddenly?

Deuteronomy 8

1. Why did God give them manna (other than to keep them alive)?
2. What agricultural products and minerals were in the Promised Land?
3. What was Israel likely to forget when they enjoyed abundance (8:11-14)?

Deuteronomy 9

1. What was the reason for which God determined to drive out the Canaanites?
2. How long had Israel been rebellious against the Lord (9:24)?
3. What had made God angry with Israel?
4. How did God feel toward Aaron when he made the golden calf?

Deuteronomy 10

1. Who wrote on the second set of tables of ten commandments?
2. What did God require of Israel (10:12)?
3. Why were the Israelites to love sojourners?

Deuteronomy 11

1. What did Moses declare that the Israelites had seen (11:7)?
2. How was the land of Egypt and the land of Canaan watered?
3. What two things did Moses set before Israel?
4. Where were the blessings to be read (or set) and where were the curses to be read?

Deuteronomy 12

1. What was to be done to Canaanite places of worship?
2. Where were the Israelites to offer their burnt offerings?
3. Were the Israelites ever allowed to eat unclean beasts?

Deuteronomy 13

1. Were the people to believe prophets because they worked miracles?
2. What was to be done to relatives who tried to get the people to worship other gods?
3. What was to be done to cities that served other gods?

Deuteronomy 14

1. Of whom were the Israelites called children?

2. What was taken out of the yearly increase of crop and livestock?
3. What was the tithe of the third year to be used for (14:28-29)?

Deuteronomy 15

1. What was to be released every seven years?
2. How were Israelites to treat the poor of their people?
3. What could Israelites do unto other nations that they could not do unto their own people?
4. What was to be given to a Hebrew bondservant when he was released?

Deuteronomy 16

1. All three of the compulsory feasts were to be observed in a certain place. Where was it?
2. At what hour of the day was the Passover to be eaten?
3. How was the date of the feast of weeks determined?
4. What does the command "They shall not appear before the Lord empty" mean?
5. What is the effect of a bribe upon a wise man?

Deuteronomy 17

1. What rendered an animal unfit for sacrifice?
2. How was a person who transgressed God's covenant to be slain?
3. Who gave the judgment concerning hard cases of disagreement?
4. Who was to select the king over the Israelites?
5. What three things was a king not to multiply to himself?
6. What was the king to read every day?

Deuteronomy 18

1. How did the Levites get their living?
2. What is a necromancer?
3. What individual did God promise to raise up?
4. How would the people know when God had not spoken to a prophet?

Deuteronomy 19

1. How many cities west of Jordan were to be set apart as cities of refuge?
2. What was the purpose of the cities of refuge?
3. How many additional cities might have been designated as cities of refuge (19:9)?
4. What law was given about landmarks?
5. What punishment was to be given to false witnesses?

Deuteronomy 20
1. How could Israel confidently face greater armies than they had?
2. What four classes of men were excused from military duty?
3. What offer was to be made to every city the Israelites attacked?
4. How were the Israelites to treat differently the Canaanite cities from distant cities under siege?
5. What restriction was imposed about cutting down trees during a siege?

Deuteronomy 21
1. Who was held responsible for an unknown man who was slain?
2. What could be done to a stubborn and rebellious son?
3. How long were those who were hanged to remain on a tree?

Deuteronomy 22
1. What was a man to do when he found his neighbor's lost ox?
2. What restriction was imposed about types of clothing that could be worn?

Deuteronomy 23
1. What peoples could not enter the assembly of Jehovah for several generations?
2. What interest could be charged on money lent to an Israelite?
3. What was the law about eating grapes from a man's vineyard?

Deuteronomy 24
1. What was to be given to a woman by her husband if he hated her (Cf. Matt. 19:7-9)?
2. What freedom did a new bridegroom have?
3. What was the law about taking a garment as security for a loan?

Deuteronomy 25
1. How many stripes could be given to a criminal?
2. What privilege did an ox treading grain have?
3. What was to be done for a childless widow by her husband's brother? (This is called "Levirate" marriage.)
4. What was to be done to the tribe of Amalek? Why?

Deuteronomy 26
1. What was to be done with part of all the firstfruits of the ground?

Deuteronomy 27
1. Where was the law to be written after Israel crossed Jordan?
2. Upon what mountain were curses to be pronounced? Blessings?

Deuteronomy 28
1. What was to happen to Israel if they hearkened and obeyed the Lord's commandments?

2. What was to happen if Israel did not hearken and obey God's commandments?
3. What would other nations do to Israel if Israel was disobedient to God (28:49-52; II Kings 17:7-18)?
4. What would cause cannabalism (28:53; Cf. II Kings 6:28-29)?
5. To what nation would God bring Israel back if they were disobedient (28:68)? (Compare Josephus, *Wars* VI, ix, 2)

Deuteronomy 29

1. What does Moses in this chapter remind the Israelites that they had seen (29:2)?
2. How did Israel have shoes during the forty years' wanderings?
3. What did Moses want Israel to enter into that day, as they were all camped on the plains of Moab (29:10-13)?

Deuteronomy 30

1. What would happen when Israel returned unto God while in captivity (30:1-4)?
2. Where did God say that his word and commandments were (30:11-14; Cf. Rom. 10:6-8)?
3. What two things did Moses set before the people?

Deuteronomy 31

1. How old was Moses when he spoke the words in Deuteronomy?
2. How often was the law to be read orally? At what time of the year?
3. What did God foretell that the Israelites would do (31:16)?
4. Why was Moses to teach Israel a song?
5. What charge was given to Joshua?
6. Where were the Levites to keep the copy of the law?

Deuteronomy 32

1. Is the song of Moses mainly a song of warning or of joy or of praise?
2. What does the name *Jeshurun* mean (32:15)?
3. Where was Moses told to go to die?

Deuteronomy 33

1. To whom did Moses address the various parts of his blessing? (For further study, make a comparison of this chapter with Genesis 49. See also pp. 134-138 of this book.)
2. What was the dwelling place of Israel and what was underneath Israel (33:27)?

Deuteronomy 34

1. Where did Moses die?
2. What did God show Moses before he died?
3. How old was Moses when he died?

4. How long did Israel lament for Moses?
5. How did Moses compare to other prophets?

Period VI
Period of Conquest
Book of Joshua

Section I
The Book of Joshua

1. Name of the book. 2. Beginning and ending points.
3. Date — Author. 4. Pertains to Period of Conquest.
5. Reveals that God's saints are irresistible. 6. Outline.
7. Verses to memorize.

1. This book gets its name from its principal character, Joshua.

2. The book begins with events after the death of Moses
(Joshua 1:1). It tells of the invasion and conquest of Canaan, the
division of the land and ends with the death of Joshua.

3. Date of the book: 1406-1400 B.C. Author: The book was
mostly written by Joshua himself. Note the first person references
in 5:1,6. The last chapter, telling of Joshua's death, was probably
composed by Phinehas, the grandson of Aaron, or Samuel the
prophet (Joshua 24:33).

4. The book of Joshua gives the information about that period
of sacred history called the PERIOD OF CONQUEST of Canaan.

(Note: The conquest of Canaan lasted about seven years. Caleb
was forty years old when he served as a spy in Canaan (Joshua
14:7; Number 13:1-6). The wilderness wanderings that followed
lasted about thirty-eight years. Caleb was eighty-five years old

when the conquest was completed (Joshua 14:10). Thus $85 - (40 + 38) = 7$.)

5. The book reveals that God's saints are irresistible when they rely on God's power and faithfully set forth to do God's commandments.

6. Outline of the book. (Memorize this.)

a. Invasion and Conquest of Canaan (Chapters 1-12).
   1. Preparations for invasion (Chs. 1-2).
   2. Crossing the Jordan (Chs. 3-4).
   3. Conquest in three campaigns (Chs. 5-12).
      a. Central campaign (5:1-10:15).
      b. Southern campaign (10:15-43).
      c. Northern campaign (11:1-15).
      d. Summary (11:16-ch. 12).

b. The Land Divided (Chapters 13-22).
   1. Inheritance of the two and one-half tribes (Ch. 13).
   2. Inheritance of the nine and one-half tribes (Chs. 14-19).
   3. Cities of refuge (Ch. 20).
   4. Levitical cities (Ch. 21).
   5. Return of the two and one-half tribes (Ch. 22).

c. Joshua's Farewell Addresses, Death and Burial (Chapters 23-24).

   7. Memorize Joshua 23:14 and 24:15.

Questions on Section I — Book of Joshua

1. Where does the book of Joshua get its name?
2. Where does the book of Joshua begin?
3. What does the book of Joshua tell of?
4. Date and author of the book.
5. What period of sacred history does Joshua tell of?
6. How long did this period last?
7. Write from memory the outline of the book.
8. Write from memory Joshua 23:14 and 24:15.

Section II
Invasion and Conquest of Canaan
(Joshua 1-12)

1. Joshua the leader of Israel. 2. Two spies sent to Jericho and saved by Rahab. 3. Passage of the Jordan. 4. Circumcision and passover at Gilgal — Cessation of

1. MOSES, the lawgiver, was succeeded by JOSHUA, the military chief, on whom devolved the work of leading the people into their inheritance and giving them "rest" (Heb. 4:8). He was the son of Nun of the tribe of Ephraim (I Chron. 7:27). His name at first was Hoshea *(help,* or *Saviour),* which Moses changed by prefixing the name of Jehovah to JOSHUA,[1] that is, *God is the Saviour;* and this name, so descriptive of his work, was a type of the higher work of Jesus, in "saving his people from their sins" (Matt. 1:21). He was probably above eighty years of age, having been above forty at the beginning of the wandering in the wilderness.[2] He had grown up to mature age in the state of Egyptian bondage; he had shared the experience and trials of the wilderness, as the chosen servant of Moses; he had proved his military capacity at Rephidim and in the conquest of the land east of Jordan; and his steadfast obedience at Kadesh, when he stood alone with Caleb, "faithful among the faithless"; and he lived for about twenty-five years more to finish his allotted work. These three periods of his life thus embrace the whole history of the moulding of the nation from its state of hopeless bondage, when Moses fled to Midian, till God "brought them in and planted them in the mountain of his inheritance" (Ex. 15:17). His character was in accordance with his career: a devout warrior, blameless and fearless, who has been taught by serving as a youth how to command as a man; who earns by manly vigor a quiet honored old age; who combines strength with gentleness, ever looking up for and obeying the Divine impulse with the simplicity of a child, while he wields great power and directs it calmly, and without swerving, to the accomplishment of a high unselfish purpose. He is one of the very few worthies of the Old Testament on whose character there is no stain, though his history is recorded with unusual fullness. We have already

---

1. The fuller form is *Jehoshua;* another form is *Jeshua;* and in Greek the name is *Jesus,* as in Acts 7:45; Heb. 4:8.

2. The Jewish tradition made him eighty-five: Joseph. *Ant.* v. 1,29, which agrees with his age at his death (Josh. 24:29).

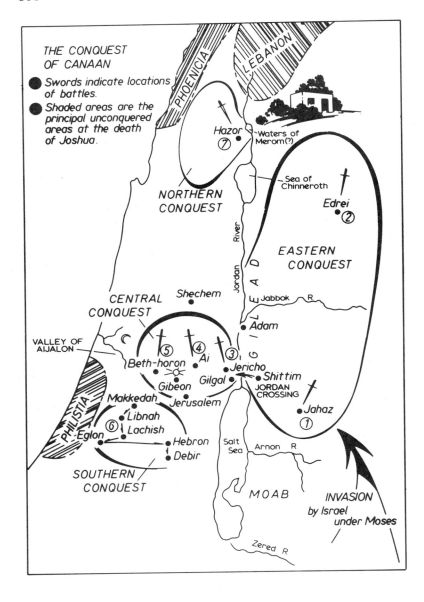

noticed his appointment and consecration as the successor of Moses.

2. As soon as the mourning for Moses was ended, God appeared to Joshua and commanded him to lead the people over Jordan, with a renewed description of their land as assurance of victory, an exhortation to courage and to obedience maintained by meditation on the book of the law and a promise of God's presence (Josh. 1:1-10). Joshua prepared the host against the third day and summoned the two tribes and a half to perform their promise of marching in for war. He had already sent two spies to Jericho, which was to be the first object of attack. This great city stood in a spacious plain, about six miles west of Jordan and opposite to the camp of Israel, in the midst of a grove of noble palm-trees, whence it was called "Jericho, the city of palms" (Deut. 34:3). It had a "king" like all the great cities of Canaan. The description of its spoil proves the wealth it derived from its position on the high road of the commerce that passed from the East over the Jordan to Philistia and Egypt; and the "goodly Babylonish garment" in particular attests its use of the products of the Chaldaean capital. It appeared to possess advantages for a capital far exceeding those of Jerusalem, to which it might have become a formidable rival, but for the curse laid upon it by Joshua. It was strongly fortified and well guarded, the gates being shut at night. The houses on the walls indicate the size of the walls themselves.

The two spies were received into one of these houses by a harlot named RAHAB, in whose mind the terror that had fallen on the Canaanites, when they heard all that God had done for Israel, had produced belief in Jehovah, as the God of heaven and of earth, and in his purpose to give them the land. In this faith she hid the spies, misdirected the officers of the king, who came in search of them, and sent them out of the city in fruitless pursuit; and then let down the spies from a window of her house over the city wall, after they had sworn to save her family in the destruction of the city. A scarlet thread, in the window from which she had let them down, was the sign by which the house was to be known. The spies fled to the mountain for three days, to avoid the pursuers who had gone out in search of them, and then returned to Joshua with the report that Jehovah had delivered the land into their hands; for all the inhabitants were fainting with fear because of them (Josh. 2; Comp. Ex. 15:14-15).

3. The next morning Joshua broke up the camp at Shittim,

and moved down to the edge of the Jordan which at this season, the harvest *(April)* (Josh. 3:15), overflowed its banks, in consequence of the melting snow about its sources in the Anti-Lebanons. On the third day, the officers instructed the people in the order of their march, and Joshua bade them sanctify themselves in preparation for the wonder that God should do on the morrow. In the morning, the priests that bore the ark advanced in front of the host to the water's edge; and their feet were no sooner dipped in the water, than the river was divided, the waters that came down from above being heaped up as a heap,[1] and the lower portion flowing down toward the Dead Sea, and leaving the channel bare (Josh. 3:16).[2] The priests advanced into the midst of the river's bed with the ark, and there stood firm till all the people had passed over. Meanwhile twelve chosen men, one from each tribe, took twelve stones from the spot where the priests stood firm, and brought them out of the river, leaving in their place twelve other stones from the dry land. When all this was done, Joshua commanded the priests to come up out of Jordan; and the moment that their feet were lifted over the margin of the water into the dry land, the waters of the river returned and overflowed the banks as before.

The host encamped that night at Gilgal in the plains of Jericho,[3] and there Joshua set up the twelve stones that had been brought out of the river's bed for a perpetual memorial of the division of the waters before the ark of Jehovah, to let his people pass into their land, just as the Red Sea had been divided to let them pass out of Egypt (Josh. 3,4).

4. The passage of the Jordan was completed on the tenth day of the first month (Nisan = April, B.C. 1406) (Josh. 4:19). This was the day appointed for the selection of the Paschal Lamb, and on the evening of the fourteenth the people kept the Passover for the first time on the sacred soil of their inheritance, exactly forty years after their fathers had first kept it before leaving Egypt (Josh. 5:10). But first, God commanded Joshua to circumcise the people; for the circumcised generation who had left Egypt had died in the wilderness, and none of the present generation had been circumcised (Josh. 5:2-9). It seems strange that this essential seal of the covenant should have been neglected under the

---

1. The waters were held back at Adam near Zarethan, about 25 miles upstream from the place of crossing.
2. Comparing this passage with Ex. 14:22, we see how exactly the two descriptions suit the two cases of the river and the sea.
3. Gilgal was at the eastern side, Jericho at the western side of the plain. Gilgal was about five miles from the Jordan.

leadership of Moses himself; but his attention may have been too closely occupied with the public affairs of the people to inquire into a matter which rested with the heads of families. Be this as it may, the omission led to a great national observance, which may be regarded as a renewal of the covenant with Abraham in the very land the promise of which had been sealed with the same sign. Perhaps this is implied in the terms of the command to Joshua to "circumcise the people *again.*" In memory of the "rolling away of their reproach," the place was called *Gilgal,* i.e., *rolling.*

Here, on the morrow after the Passover, the new generation tasted bread for the first time. They ate unleavened bread and parched corn of the old crop of the land, and at the same time the manna ceased. From that day forward they began to eat the fruits of the year (Josh. 5:12).

We must not fail to notice the picture of their security and their command of the open country implied in these proceedings. They were not only unmolested during their circumcison and the Passover, but they were supplied with old and new corn, whether by the help or by the flight of the country people, while the cities were "closely shut up for fear of them (Josh. 6:1); and the news of their passage of the Jordan had so terrified the kings of the Amorites and the Canaanites, from the Jordan to the sea, "that their heart melted, neither was there any spirit in them any more, because of the children of Israel (Josh. 5:1).

5. As Joshua was by Jericho, he received a divine revelation to teach him that the work was God's. Looking up toward the city, he saw a warrior opposite to him with a drawn sword in his hand, who in reply to Joshua's challenge, announced that he had come forth as the "Captain (or prince) of the host of Jehovah." This title, so often afterward applied to the Son of God, revealed him to Joshua, who fell down before him to worship and to receive the commands of his supreme general. After bidding him to put off his shoe, for the place was holy (Josh. 5:13,15), Jehovah promised him the conquest of Jericho and prescribed the manner of its capture. The host were to compass the city for seven days: the first six days once, the chosen warriors marching in front of the ark, before which seven priests bore seven trumpets of ram's horns; the rest of the people following, and all preserving silence, while the trumpets alone sounded a continued defiance. On the seventh day the circuit was repeated seven times; and at the seventh, the trumpets pealed forth one long loud blast; and each

loud blast; and each man rushed in straight from the place where he had stood, as Joshua had commanded (Josh. 6). Before its capture, the city, with all its inhabitants, was "accursed" or "devoted," as the first-fruits of the spoil of Canaan — a thing "most holy to Jehovah"; and the law prescribed that all living beings so devoted should be put to death without redemption, and all the property destroyed or dedicated to God (Lev. 27:28-29; Josh. 6:17). Only the household of Rahab were excepted from the curse; and the two spies were sent to bring her and her kindred safe out beyond the camp. Then the men and women, young and old, and the oxen, sheep and asses were put to the edge of the sword: the city was burnt with fire, and its buildings razed to the ground; the silver and gold, and vessels of brass and iron, were placed in the sacred treasury; and Joshua imprecated a solemn curse on the man who should rebuild Jericho (Josh. 6:21-27). The curse was literally fulfilled in the fate of Hiel, the Bethelite, who rebuilt Jericho in the reign of Ahab (about 870 B.C.): his first-born son, Abiram, died as he was laying the foundation, and his youngest son, Segub, while he was setting up the gates (I Kings 16:34).

No less striking was the blessing which followed Rahab for her conduct, which is recorded as the greatest example of *faith* and of the *works* which spring from faith in the old heathen world (Heb. 11:31; James 2:25). Besides being a heathen, she was a harlot, for there is no ground for the interpretation of the word as meaning an inn-keeper; though there is much to prove that she was not utterly depraved. But her mind and heart received in simple faith the proofs of Jehovah's power and purposes; she served his people with courage, ingenuity and devotion; and so she "entered into the kingdom of God" (Matt. 21:31). She was rewarded by a most distinguished place among the families of Israel. She married Salmon (perhaps one of the spies), and became the mother of Boaz, the great-grandfather of David (Matt. 1:5). Hers is thus one of the four female names, all of them foreigners, recorded in the genealogy of Christ;[1] and it is one of the profoundest moral, as well as spiritual, lessons of His Gospel, that He did not disdain such an ancestry.

The fall of Jericho itself is placed by the Apostle among the great triumphs of *faith* (Heb. 11:30). It was an example of the power of simple obedience to plans of action prescribed by God, and an earnest of the conquests to be achieved by the same

---

1. The four are Tamar, a Canaanite, the concubine of Judah; Rahab; Ruth, the Moabite; and Bathsheba, the Hittite.

principle. And this is true also of the destruction of the city. Not only as the first which the Israelites took, but as perhaps the most conspicuous city of Canaan for the advantages of its position, its commerce, wealth and luxury, and unquestionably also for the abominable vices that had now "filled up the iniquity of the Canaanites," its doom was the pattern of that denounced on the cities of the land.

6. There was, however, one man among the Israelites, whose lust of spoil made him unfaithful (Josh. 7). His act brought a curse upon all Israel, so that they failed in their next enterprise, the attack on Ai. This was the place east of Bethel, between which and Bethel Abraham had pitched his tent (Gen. 12:8); it lay among the hills, probably at the head of one of the valleys leading up from the valley of the Jordan. The spies whom Joshua had sent reported it an easy conquest; and only about 3000 men were detached to take it. They were repulsed and chased to Shebarim, with the loss of thirty-six men. The hearts of the people melted and Joshua, with all the elders, fell down before the ark as mourners and uttered earnest expostulations to Jehovah. The Lord replied that Israel had sinned in taking of the accursed thing and concealing it among their goods. Joshua was commanded to sanctify the people against the morrow, and then to cast lots for the offender, who was to be slain and burned with all belonging to him. This decision by lot involved no chance, but in the whole history of the Jews it was one of the most regular methods of revealing the will of God, especially in reference to some individual. "The lot is cast into the lap, but the whole disposal thereof is Jehovah's" (Prov. 16:33). Accordingly, the lot fell first on the tribe of Judah, then on the family of Zerah, then on the house of Zabdi, whose members were brought individually before Jehovah, and Achan the son of Carmi was taken. Exhorted by Joshua to give glory to God, Achan confessed that he had taken from the spoil of Jericho a goodly Babylonish garment, and 200 shekels of silver, and a wedge of gold of fifty shekels' weight, and had hid them in the earth in his tent, where they were found by men sent by Joshua. The offender was stoned and afterward burned, with his children, his cattle and his tent, and a great heap of stones was raised over them to mark the place, which received the name of Achor *(trouble)*. [1] The fact that his family was also slain suggests that they had known about and consented to his sin. His case is also a striking example of the effect of sin, as involving the

---

1. The meaning common to the words *Achan* and *Achor* is alluded to by Joshua: "Why hast thou *troubled* us? The Lord shall *trouble* thee this day" (Josh. 7:25).

destruction of the guiltless: "That man perished not alone in his iniquity" (Josh. 22:20).

Encouraged anew by God, Joshua formed a plan for taking Ai by an ambush, which met with complete success. The city was destroyed with all its inhabitants, the cattle only being reserved as the spoil of Jehovah. The King of Ai was hanged on a tree and buried under a great heap of stones, the only memorial of the city (Josh. 8:1-29). It seems to be implied that Bethel was taken at the same time (Josh. 5:17; 12:16).

The victory at Ai secured the passes from the valley of the Jordan and gave the Israelites access to open country in the center of Palestine. Joshua now marched to a place near Shechem, where he held the solemn ceremony of the Blessing and the Curse on Mounts Gerizim and Ebal, as prescribed by Moses (Deut. 27:12-13). On his return, a force was doubtless left at Ai to secure the passes, but the main body of the army remained encamped at Gilgal in the valley of the Jordan (Josh. 9:6).

The above events form the first stage in the conquest of Canaan.

7. A great league was now formed by all the kings west of Jordan in the hills, the valleys and the sea-coasts, as far north as Lebanon against the Israelites (Josh. 9:1-2). The people of Gibeon alone sought for peace by a curious strategem. Gibeon (now *El-Jib*) "a royal city, greater than Ai" (Josh. 10:2), was the chief of the four cities of the Hivites,[1] lying immediately opposite the pass of Ai, and at the head of the pass of Beth-horon. It would therefore have been the next object of the attack of the Israelites. Assuming the appearance of wayworn travellers, with old shoes and sacks, rent and patched wineskins, and dry and mouldy bread, an embassy of the Gibeonites went to Joshua, and declared that they had come from a very far country, where they had heard the name of Jehovah and the fame of His mighty deeds, to seek for a league with His people. Their bread had been hot, they said, and their garments and wine and skins new when they started.

The trick deceived Joshua and the princes of the congregation, who neglected to consult the Lord (Josh. 10:14). They made peace with the Gibeonites and swore to them by Jehovah to save their lives. Three days afterward they learned the truth and reached their cities by a three days' march. The oath was held sacred, in spite of the murmurs of the congregation; but to punish their deceit, Joshua put the Gibeonites under a curse, by

1. The others were Chephirah, Beeroth and Kirjath-jearim (Josh. 10:17).

which they became devoted to Jehovah in irredeemable bondage, and they were employed as "hewers of wood and drawers of water for the house of God" forever.[1] The treaty evidently included all the four cities, of which Gibeon was the chief. The transaction affords a memorable example of a principle more than once insisted on in the law, and expressed by the Psalmist, that God requires that all oaths be honored, even when the oaths are foolish (Ps. 15:4).

8. Alarmed by the defection of Gibeon, Adoni-zedek, king of Jerusalem, made a league with the kings of Hebron, Jarmuth, Lachish and Eglon, and laid siege to the city. The Gibeonites sent for help to Joshua, who marched by night from the camp at Gilgal, took the confederated Amorites by surprise and utterly routed them near Beth-horon.[2] "The battle of Beth-horon or Gibeon," remarks Dean Stanley, "is one of the most important in the history of the world." Beth-horon was the name of two villages, an "upper" and a "nether" or lower (Josh. 16:3,5; I Chron. 7:24), on the steep road from Gibeon to Azekah and the Philistine plain (Josh. 10:10,11; I Macc. 3:24), which is still the great road of communication from the interior of the country to the sea-coast.

From Gibeon to the Upper Beth-horon is a distance of about four miles of broken ascent and descent. The ascent, however, predominates, and this therefore appears to be the "going up" to Beth-horon which formed the first stage of Joshua's pursuit. With the upper village the descent commences; the road is rough and difficult, even for the mountain-paths of Palestine, now over sheets of smooth rock flat as the flag-stones of a London pavement, now over the upturned edges of the limestone strata, and now among the loose rectangular stones so characteristic of the whole of this district. After about three miles of this descent, a slight rise leads to the lower village standing on the last outpost of the Benjamite hills.

This rough descent from the Upper to the Lower Beth-horon is the "going down to Beth-horon," which formed the second stage of Joshua's pursuit. As they fled down this steep pass, the Canaanites were overtaken by a miraculous hail-storm, which slew more than had fallen in the battle. It was then that Joshua, after a prayer to Jehovah, who had promised him this great victory, "said in the sight of Israel:

---

1. They formed the class of servants called Nethinim (Neh. 7:73).
2. The exact place is the steep road between the two villages of the name, the Upper and Lower Beth-horon. The two Beth-horons are approximately two miles apart. Upper Beth-horon is 2,022 ft. in elevation, and lower (or nether) 1,210 ft.

'Sun, stand thou still upon Gibeon;
And thou, Moon, in the valley of Aijalon.' "

It was doubtless early in the day when Joshua uttered this
prayer. Behind the army of Israel lay Gibeon four miles to the
east. At that hour it appeared that the sun was standing over
Gibeon. Apparently the moon was in its waning phrase and
appeared in the west over the valley of Aijalon, seven miles
beyond Beth-horon. When Joshua prayed, the sun and moon
stood still in their apparent positions and hasted not to go down
about a whole day (Josh. 10:13) until the people had avenged
themselves of their enemies. Is not this writing in the *Book of
Jasher?*"[1] The miraculous stoppage of the "greater and the lesser
light" in their full course enabled Joshua to continue his pursuit
to Makkadah, a place in the Shephelah or maritime plain where
the five kings hid themselves in a cave. Joshua stayed not even
then, but bidding the people roll great stones to the mouth of the
cave, and set a guard over it, he pressed the rear of the fugitives
and "made an end of slaying them with a very great slaughter till
they were consumed, that the rest which remained of them
entered into fenced cities. And all the people returned to the
camp to Joshua at Maakadah in peace; none moved his tongue
against any of the children of Israel" (Josh. 10:20-21; Comp. Ex.
11:7).

The five kings were now brought forth from the cave and
Joshua bade all the captains place their feet upon their necks, in
token of what Jehovah would do to all their enemies. Then he
slew them and hanged them on five trees till the evening (Josh.
10:22-27). Their bodies were cast into the cave and its mouth was
closed with great stones, just as that most memorable sun at
length went down and closed the day, "like which there was none
before it or after it, that Jehovah hearkened unto the voice of a
man; for Jehovah fought for Israel" (Josh. 10:14).

This great battle was followed by the conquest of the seven
kings of Makkadah, Libnah, Lachish, Gezer, Eglon, Hebron and
Debir, whose cities, chief and dependent, were utterly destroyed,
with all their inhabitants and all creatures that breathed, as
Jehovah had commanded (Josh. 10:28-39). In this one campaign
(Josh. 10:42) Joshua subdued the southern half of Palestine, both
highlands and lowlands, from Kadesh-barnea to Gaza, the

---

1. The Book of Jasher (the *Righteous*) is mentioned elsewhere only in II Sam. 1:18. It seems to have been a
book of Hebrew hero stories written in verse.

eastern and western limits of the southern frontier; and he led back the people to the camp at Gilgal.[1]

9. Our attention is now called to the north, the country about the "Sea of Chinneroth" (the Lake of Galilee), the Upper Jordan and the bases of Mount Lebanon (Josh. 11). Jabin,[2] king of Hazor, the chief city of northern Palestine, formed a league against Israel with all the kings of the north as far as Mount Hermon, and with all the nations that were still unsubdued. Their army was "as the sand on the sea-shore for multitude," and they had many chariots and horses.[3] Joshua routed them by the waters of Merom, and chased them as far as "Great Sidon" and the valley of Mizpeh (probably the great valley of Coele-Syria). In obedience to God's prohibition of calvary, Joshua cut the hoof-sinews of the horses and burnt the chariots, which he might have been tempted to keep as the choicest prizes of victory (Josh. 11:9). Joshua next "turned back," perhaps on some new provocation, and took Hazor, putting its king and all the inhabitants to the sword, and likewise with the other cities of the confederates; but the cities themselves were left standing except Hazor,[4] which he burnt, as being "the head of all those kingdoms." As the result of this *third campaign,* Israel was master of the whole land from Mount Halak (the *smooth mountain*) at the ascent to Mount Seir on the south, to Baal-gad, under Mount Hermon on the north. But a much longer time was required for the subjugation of the numerous kings, who held each his own fortified city, and "Joshua made war a long time with all those kings" (Josh. 11:18). It was five years at least, and probably six, before the land rested from war. Even then the old inhabitants held out in many separate parts, for the further trial of Israel's faith and courage as Moses had foretold.

The results of the whole conquest, besides the previous victories over Sihon and Og, are summed up in the subjugation of thirty-one kings of cities of the west of the Jordan, belonging to the seven nations, which had been mentioned in the first promise to Abraham: the Amorites, Canaanites, Girgashites, Hittites, Hivites, Jebusites and Perizzites (Josh. 12). Special notice is taken of the extermination of the giant Anakim, who had struck such terror into the spies, and who were only left in the Philistine cities

---

1. It may be inferred from Joshua 11:13,14, that this destruction extended only as far as the entire desolation of the cities, and that they were not burnt.
2. Jabin seems to have been a hereditary title (Judges 4).
3. Josephus gives them 300,000 foot soldiers, 10,000 horses and 20,000 chariots.
4. The phrase, "cities that stood still in their strength," is correctly rendered, "cities that stood on their mounds." These mounds are the familiar built-up hills or *tells* in the near East.

of Gaza, Gath and Ashdod, though they had before occupied the whole of the central highlands, with Hebron and other cities (Josh. 11:21-22).

Questions Over Section II
Invasion and Conquest of Canaan

1. When did God speak to Joshua (1:1)?
2. How much of Canaan was to be given to Israel (1:3)?
3. Who was able to stand and resist Joshua (1:5)?
4. What was Joshua to do with the book of the law (1:8)?
5. How many days' notice of the crossing of Jordan did Joshua give the people (1:11)?
6. What command of Moses to the tribes of Gad, Reuben and half-Manasseh did Joshua remind them of (1:13-15)?
7. From what place did Joshua send spies? How many spies? To what city (2:1)?
8. Into whose house did the spies come (2:1)?
9. Who came looking for the spies (2:2)?
10. Where were they hidden (2:6)?
11. Where did the men pursue after the spies (2:7)?
12. What feeling did the people in Canaan have about the invading Hebrews (2:9-11)?
13. What promise did the woman ask of the spies (2:12-13)?
14. How did the spies escape (2:15)?
15. What sign or token was the woman to hang in her window? When (2:18)?
16. Who was Rahab to gather in her home (2:18)?
17. What was the woman not to talk about (2:20)?
18. Who led the procession across Jordan (3:3,14)?
19. How much space was to be left between the ark and the people (3:4)?
20. Where did the priests stand during the crossing of Jordan (3:8,17)?
21. What was the crossing of Jordan to reassure the people about (3:10-11)?
22. What was the condition of Jordan when Israel crossed it (3:15)?
23. Where did the Jordan waters stop and rise up (3:16)?
24. What were twelve men appointed to do after the Jordan was crossed (4:1-3)?
25. Where were the stones to be set (4:3,20)?
26. What purpose were the stones from Jordan to serve (4:7)?

27. Where was a second group of stones set up? By whom (4:9)?
28. How did the crossing of Jordan cause Israel to feel toward Joshua (4:14)?
29. What was the place of the first encampment after crossing Jordan (4:19)?
30. How did the crossing of Jordan affect the Canaanites (5:1)?
31. Where were the people circumcised (5:9)?
32. Why was the mass circumcision necessary (5:5)?
33. What does the name Gilgal mean, and why was that name given to the place (5:9)?
34. What feast was kept in Gilgal (5:10)?
35. When did the manna cease (5:12)?
36. Who appeared to Joshua when he was by Jericho (5:13-14)?
37. What did Jehovah's prince tell Joshua to do (5:15)?
38. How many times did Israel march around Jericho (6:3-4)?
39. What was the daily schedule of the marches around Jericho (6:3-4)?
40. Describe the order of the various groups as they marched around Jericho (6:4, 6-7,9,13).
41. What sound was heard during the marching (6:9,13)?
42. When did the people shout (6:16)?
43. What does *devoted* mean (6:17)?
44. What was to be done with the goods of Jericho (6:17-19)?
45. What was done to Jericho itself (6:21,24)?
46. Who brought Rahab and her family out (6:22-23)?
47. Where did Rahab dwell after that (6:25)?
48. What curse did Joshua pronounce about Jericho (6:26)?
49. Who committed a trespass at Jericho? What was the trespass (7:1)?·
50. What did Joshua's spies report about Ai (7:2-3)?
51. How many Israelites died in the assault on Ai (7:4-5)?
52. How did the defeat at Ai affect Israel's courage (7:5)?
53. What did Joshua do after this defeat (7:6-7)?
54. Why did God say that Israel had been defeated (7:11-12)?
55. How was the sinner pointed out (7:13-14)?
56. What did Joshua tell Achan to say (7:19)?
57. What things had Achan stolen (7:21)?
58. What penalty was inflicted on Achan (7:24-25)?
59. What was the place of Achan's death called? What does the name mean (7:26)?
60. How was the spoil of Ai differently handled than that of Jericho (8:2)?

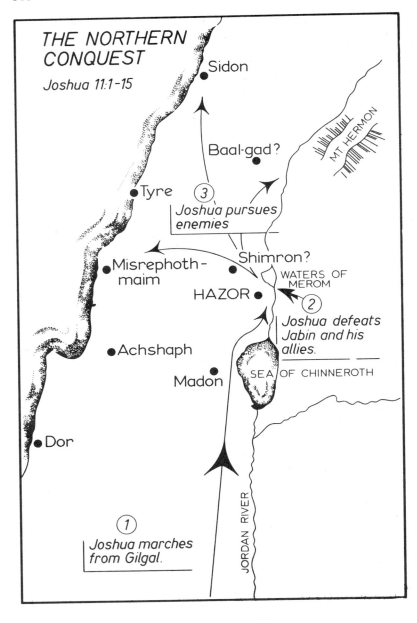

THE NORTHERN
CONQUEST
Joshua 11:1–15

Sidon

Baal-gad?

MT HERMON

Tyre

③
*Joshua pursues
enemies*

Misrephoth-
maim

Shimron?

WATERS OF
MEROM

HAZOR

②
*Joshua defeats
Jabin and his
allies.*

Achshaph

Madon

SEA OF CHINNEROTH

Dor

①
*Joshua marches
from Gilgal.*

JORDAN RIVER

61. How was Joshua directed to capture Ai (8:3-7)?
62. What city had joined with Ai (8:17)?
63. What signal did Joshua give to his hiding men (8:18)?
64. How many people of Ai were slain (8:25)?
65. What was done to the city (8:28)?
66. What was done to the king of Ai (8:29)?
67. Tell four things done at Mt. Ebal (8:30-32,34).
68. What did the kings in Canaan gather to do (9:1-2)?
69. What city craftily made a covenant with Joshua (9:3-6)?
70. How did they deceive and convince Israel (9:4-5, 11-13)?
71. What did Israel neglect to do before making the covenant of peace (9:14)?
72. When was the deception discovered (9:16)?
73. What four cities were in the group that deceived Israel (9:17)?
74. How did the congregation respond when the deception became known (9:18)?
75. Why was the covenant of peace not broken (9:20)?
76. What were the Gibeonites made to be (9:23)?
77. For how long did Joshua sentence the Gibeonites to be bondsmen (9:23)?
78. Who was king of Jerusalem (10:1)?
79. How great a city was Gibeon (10:2)?
80. How many kings allied against Gibeon (10:3)?
81. What did the Gibeonites do when attacked (10:6)?
82. Where did Joshua come upon the armies attacking Gibeon (10:10)?
83. To what place did he chase them (10:10)?
84. How did the Lord help in the battle (10:11)?
85. Over what places did the sun and moon stand still (10:12)?
86. Where did the kings hide (10:16)?
87. What significance was there in putting feet on the kings' necks (10:24-25)?
88. How were the kings slain (10:26)?
89. What five cities were taken after Makkedah fell (10:29-39)?
90. How much of the South did Joshua take? What places were the limits of this part of the conquest (10:40-41)?
91. Who was Jabin (11:1)?
92. How many people gathered to fight Israel (11:2-4)?
93. Where did they gather (11:5)?
94. What was Joshua to do with their chariots and horses (11:6)?

95. How far did Joshua pursue these northern enemies (11:8-9)?
96. What city in the north was taken and burned (11:10-11)?
97. Was Joshua's conquest brief or lengthy (11:18)?
98. Why did the Canaanites not make peace with Joshua (11:19-20)?
99. Where did the Anakim live (11:21-22)?
100. How fully did Joshua conquer the land (11:23)?
101. What two kings beyond (east of) the Jordan did Israel defeat (12:1-5)?
102. How many kings in all did Israel smite (12:24)?

Section III
The Twelve Tribes in Canaan
(Joshua 13-24)

1. Considerable land unconquered. 2. Division of the land east of Jordan — Reuben, Gad, Manasseh. 3. West of Jordan — Judah, Ephraim, Manasseh. 4. The Tabernacle set up at Shiloh — Possessions of Benjamin, Simeon, Zebulun, Issachar, Asher, Naphtali and Dan — Lot of Joshua. 5. Cities of Refuge and of the Levites. 6. Altar of the two-and-a-half tribes — The schism healed. 7. Last exhortations of Joshua. 8. The covenant renewed at Shechem — Deaths of Joshua and Eleazar — Burial of Joseph's bones — Bright period of national fidelity.

1. The defeat of the thirty-one kings did not involve, in every case, the capture of their cities. Jerusalem, for example, was not taken till after the death of Joshua (Judges 1:8), and its citadel remained in the hands of the Jebusites till the time of David. Many other cities held out for a long time.

But besides such isolated posts, there were whole tracts of country — "very much land" — yet to be subdued within the limits which God had originally named, and which He now once more promised (Josh. 13:1). These were, speaking generally: (1) the plains along the Mediterranean, (2) the coast of Phoenicia and (3) the ranges of Lebanon. On the southwest, there was the whole country and five cities of the Philistines, who were destined to be such formidable enemies to Israel, from Sihor on the frontier of

THE TWELVE TRIBES

Joshua. 13 - 24

☆ Cities of Refuge

Sidon

MT HERMON

Tyre

PHOENICIA

Kadesh

Laish or Leshem
(Dan)

☆

BASHAN

ASHER

ZEBULUN

NAPHTALI

MANASSEH

Sea of Chinnereth

☆ Golan

ISSACHAR

Megiddo

R.

☆ Ramoth-gilead

THE GREAT SEA

MANASSEH

JORDAN R

GAD

GILEAD

Shechem

☆

EPHRAIM • Shiloh

G

Timnath-serah

Jazer

DAN

BENJAMIN

Jericho
Gilgal

AMMON

Jerusalem

☆ Bezer

JUDAH

REUBEN

Debir

☆
Hebron

Salt
Sea

Aroer

SIMEON

ARNON R.

• Beersheba

MOAB

• Kadesh-barnea

Egypt to Ekron (Josh. 13:2-4). Next were the Canaanites of the west coast, as far as Aphek, which seems to have been near Sidon, the Sidonians "and all Lebanon" which is, however, so described as to include only the southern slopes or foot-hills (Josh. 13:5-6). These conquests were not reserved for Joshua, who was now "old and stricken in years," but he was commanded to include them in the division of the land.

2. Joshua was now commanded to divide the land by lot among the nine tribes and a half, the two and a half having already received their allotment from Moses on the east of Jordan (Josh. 13:8-13; 18:7), and the Levites receiving no inheritance among their brethren, "for Jehovah, God of Israel, was their inheritance" (Josh. 13:14,33). Their withdrawal from the number of the tribes was compensated by the division of Joseph into the two tribes of Ephraim and Manasseh (Josh. 14:3-5). In describing the allotment generally, we follow the order of the Book of Joshua.

First, the territories of the two and a half tribes on the east of Jordan.

a. REUBEN lay first on the south from the Arnon, over the kingdom of Sihon, the northern boundary being a little above the latitude of Jericho (Josh. 13:15-23).

b. GAD came next to the north, possessing Mount Gilead and half of Ammon. On the side of Jordan, their northern border just touched the Sea of Chinneroth, and was drawn thence toward the southeast. The Jabbok divided their territory into two nearly equal parts (Josh. 13:24-28).

c. The *half-tribe of* MANASSEH had all the kingdom of Og, king of Bashan, including half of Mount Gilead, which was the special inheritance of Machir, the son of Manasseh, and reaching to the base of Mount Hermon on the north (Josh. 13:29-33). In all three cases, the eastern frontier toward the desert was necessarily indefinite. These allotments are expressly mentioned as having been made by Moses.

3. The division of the land among the nine and a half tribes west of Jordan was made by Eleazar, the high-priest, and Joshua, with "the heads of the fathers of the tribes," by a solemn lot cast before Jehovah (Josh. 14:1-2; 18:6,10). It took place on two different occasions. First, while the people were still encamped at Gilgal and perhaps before the conquest of the north was finished, the tribes of Judah and Joseph received, as their respective

allotments, the greater part of the south and the center of the land.

a. JUDAH seems to have had the first share in consequence of Caleb's laying claim to Hebron, the special inheritance promised by Moses as a reward of his fidelity. His claim was admitted and Joshua added his blessing. Caleb, who at the age of eighty-five, was still as strong for war as when he was forty, drove out the Anakim from Hebron and then attacked Debir, which was taken by his nephew Othiniel, whose valor was rewarded with the hand of Caleb's daughter, Achsah. Her demand of a special inheritance from her father, who gave her the upper and the nether springs, is an interesting picture of patriarchal life (Josh. 14:6-15; 15:13-19). The general inheritance of Judah began at the wilderness of Zin, on the border of Edom, while their southern border stretched across the wilderness to "the river of Egypt." The Dead Sea formed their east coast, and the northern border was drawn from the mouth of Jordan westward, past the south side of the hill of Jerusalem (which lay therefore outside the boundary)[1] to Kirjath-jearim, in Mount Ephraim, whence the western border skirted the land of the Philistines, and touched the Mediterranean (Josh. 15:1-12, 21-63).

b. The tribe of JOSEPH had the center of the land across from Jordan to the Mediterranean. EPHRAIM lay north of Judah but between them were the districts afterward allotted to Benjamin and Dan. The southern border was drawn from the Jordan along the north side of the plain of Jericho to Bethel, whence it took a bend southward to Beth-horon and thence up again to the sea near Joppa. The northern border passed west from the Jordan opposite the mouth of the Jabbok past Michmethah to the mouth of the river Kanah (which flows into the Mediterranean Sea just north of Joppa). Besides the sacred valley of Shechem, it included some of the finest parts of Palestine, the mountains of Ephraim and the great and fertile maritime plain of Sharon, proverbial for its roses (Josh. 16).

MANASSEH, in addition to the land of Bashan and Gilead east of the Jordan, which had been allotted to Machir and his son Gilead, had a lot on the west of Jordan north of Ephraim (Josh.

---

1. This was not because it belonged to another lot, but because it was not yet conquered. See Josh. 15:63. In the second division it was allotted to Benjamin, but it was secured to Judah by David's conquest.

17). The extent of the territories of this tribe is accounted for, first by the reward due to the valor of Machir, and next by the right established by the daughters of Zelophehad to a share of the inheritance (Comp. Num. 26:33; 27:1; 36:2). The northern frontier is very difficult to determine, some very important towns of Manasseh being expressly named as within the lots of Asher and Issachar (Josh. 17:11). Further we find the children of Joseph complaining to Joshua that they had only one lot, namely, Mount Ephraim, instead of the two given them by Jacob, and that they could not drive out the Canaanites from Beth-shean and the valley of Jezreel, because of their chariots of iron, and Joshua assigns to them "the wooded mountain," which can hardly be any other than Carmel (Josh. 17:14-18).

4. During the long time that the encampment at Gilgal remained the headquarters of the Israelites, they seem to have preserved the military system organized in the desert, with the tabernacle in the center of the camp. But at length they removed to SHILOH, south of Shechem, in the territory of Ephraim, and there they set up the tabernacle, where it remained till the time of Samuel (Josh. 18:1; Judges 18:31; I Sam. 4:3). There were still seven tribes that had not received their inheritance and Joshua reproved them for their slackness in taking possession of the land. We are not told on what principles the portions already allotted had been divided, except that on the east of Jordan the boundaries were assigned by Moses. Now, however, three men were apointed from each tribe to make a survey of the rest of the land, and to divide it into seven portions, which with their several cities, they described in a book. The survey being finished, Joshua cast lots for the seven portions before the tabernacle in Shiloh (Josh. 18:1-10). The result was as follows, the tribes being named in the order in which their lots came out:

a. BENJAMIN had the eastern part of the territory that lay between Judah and Ephraim, embracing the plain of Jericho and the northern highlands of the later Judaea, a region admirably suited to the wild and martial character of the tribe (Josh. 18:11-28). Jerusalem was in Benjamin, by its south border.

b. SIMEON had an inheritance taken out of the portion already allotted to Judah, for whom it was found to be too large, namely, the southwestern part of the maritime plain, with the land bordering on the desert as far eastward as Beer-sheba. Their western coast lay along the Mediterranean to the north of Ashkelon (Josh. 19:1-9). Simeon was truly scattered in Israel (Gen. 49:7).

c. ZEBULON received the mountain range which forms the northern border of the great plain of Jezreel or Esdraelon, between the eastern slopes of Carmel on the west, and the southwest shore of the Sea of Chinneroth and the course of the Jordan, to about opposite the mouth of the Yarmuk river on the east (Josh. 19:10-16). The rich mountain passes which led down to the valley of Jezreel seem to be referred to in the blessing of Moses, "Rejoice, O Zebulon, in thy goings out" (Deut. 33:18).

d. ISSACHAR'S inheritance corresponded almost exactly to the great valley of Jezreel, otherwise called the plain of Esdraelon, which opened to the Jordan on the east (Josh. 19:22), and was enclosed on the south by the hills of Gilboa, and on the north by the highlands of Issachar, among which Mount Tabor was conspicuous on the frontier (Josh. 19:17-23). The territory seems to have been taken out of that of Manasseh, as Simeon's was out of Judah. The effect of its richness and seclusion on the character and history of the tribe has been noticed in connection with Jacob's blessing.

e. ASHER has the rich maritime plain extending from Mount Carmel to "great Sidon" and "the strong city Tyre": the territory of the former was included in their inheritance, though they failed to possess it. In their case too, both Jacob and Moses had given a prophetic intimation of the influence of the tribe's position (Josh. 19:24-31).

f. NAPHTALI, the most powerful of the northern tribes, obtained the highlands which form the southern prolongation of the range of Lebanon, bounded on the east by the Upper Jordan, the "waters of Merom," and the Sea of Chinneroth; and looking down on the west upon the maritime plain of Asher, just as Zebulon looked down from the southern part of the same highlands into the valley of Esdraelon (Josh. 19:32-39).

g. DAN had at first a very small territory northwest of Judah, from Japho (Joppa) to the border of Simeon, almost entirely occupied by the Philistines. For this reason, and because they found their lot too small for them, they made an expedition against Leshem or Laish, in the extreme north of the land, at the sources of the Jordan. They took the city and destroyed the inhabitants and gave it the name of Dan. It became one of the two landmarks in the phrase which was used to describe the whole extent of the land from north to south, "from Dan even to Beersheba." In the Book of *Judges*, we have a fuller account of the expedition at the time when Dan conquered Laish (Judges 18).

Lastly, Joshua himself received, as his personal inheritance, the place he asked for, namely, Timnath-serah, in Mount Ephraim, and he built the city of that name (Compare Judges 2:9).

It must be remembered that the allotments were made not only to the tribes as a whole, but to the families of each tribe, as in expressly stated in each case: "This is the inheritance of the tribes *by their families.*" Thus we shall expect to find the possessions of each tribe proportional to the number of its families, as determined by the census taken in the plains of Moab (Num. 26). This is generally the case, but there still remain inequalities which can only be accounted for by the relative importance assigned to the tribes, on principles already indicated in the dying prophecy of Jacob. The great preponderance of Judah and Joseph relates to their respective pre-eminence as the prince and heir of the whole family.

5. Each of the twelve tribes having received the lot of its inheritance, provision was next made for the habitation of the Levites and the cities of refuge. Six cities of refuge were appointed by the people themselves (Josh. 20): three on the west of Jordan, namely, *Kedesh*, in Galilee, in the highlands of Naphtali; *Shechem*, in Mount Ephraim, and *Hebron*, in the mountains of Judah; and three on the east of Jordan, namely, for Reuben, *Bezer*, in the wilderness; for Gad, *Ramoth*, in Gilead; for the half-tribe of Manasseh, *Golan*, in Bashan.

The Levites having claimed the right given to them by Moses, received forty-eight cities and their suburbs, which were given up by the several tribes in porportion to the cities they possessed (Josh. 21; Comp. Num. 35:1-8).

Thus did Jehovah give Israel the land which He had sworn to their father, and they dwelt in it. They had obtained their promised rest in this world, though a better rest remained, and still remains (Heb. 4:8-9). Their enemies were delivered into their hand and all open resistance ceased. "There failed not aught of any good thing which Jehovah had spoken to the house of Israel: all came to pass" (Josh. 21:43-45). The failures afterward brought to light were in the people themselves.

6. Their peace was, however, soon threatened by the danger of a religious schism. The two tribes and a half, having kept their

promise to their brethren, were dismissed by Joshua with a blessing and with an earnest exhortation to cleave to Jehovah their God and keep his commandments (Josh. 22:1-6). Abundantly enriched with their share of the spoil of Canaan, they crossed the Jordan into the land of Gilead. Close to the ford, "the passage of the children of Israel," they built a great altar (doubtless a huge erection of earth and stones), of the same form as the altar of burnt-offering. Hastily inferring their intention to establish a separate place of sacrifice, in violation of God's command, the other tribes prepared for war. But first they sent Phinehas, the son of the high-priest Eleazar, with ten princes of the respective tribes, to remonstrate with their brethren and to remind them of the consequences of former public sins. The two tribes and a half replied that they had not acted in the spirit of rebellion against Jehovah. They had feared lest a time should come when their more favored brethren might forget their common interest in Jehovah, the God of Israel; and therefore they had erected the altar, not to burn sacrifices upon it, but as a perpetual memorial of their part in the altar of which it was the likeness. Thus interpreted, their act was accepted by the envoys and afterward by all the people as a new proof that Jehovah was among Israel; and the children of Reuben and Gad called the altar ED (a *witness*):[1] "for," said they, "it shall be a witness between us that Jehovah is God" (Josh. 22). We hear nothing further of this erection: its meaning may have been forgotten in later times.

7. The closing records of the history of Joshua show us a solemn pause and crisis in the career of Israel. They had now attained that first success which is always a trial of human power and endurance, and which, in their case, was the test of their faithfulness to Jehovah. In Joshua they had a leader equal to the crisis. He lived long after God had given them rest from their enemies; and he was now "going the way of all the earth" (Josh. 23:1,14). His last care was to set clearly before the people their true position and to bind them to Jehovah by another solemn covenant. The last two chapters of Joshua seem to refer to two distinct transactions.

First, he sent for all the heads of the tribes, the judges and the officers, and gave them an exhortation, which may be summed up in the words, "Be ye therefore *very courageous* to keep and to do all that is written in the book of the law of Moses." He knew the

---

1. The name *Ed* is the Hebrew word meaning *witness*. It is supplied into the English Bible because no name is actually given to the altar in the Hebrew text.

danger of their resting satisfied with what was done or of their thinking it hopeless to do more; and he knew that, if once they ceased before the heathen remnant was destroyed out of the land, they would be corrupted by their idolatries and vices. He well remembered all the experience of the desert and all the warnings of Moses. He reminds them of all that God had done to the Canaanites for their sakes; and promises that the land divided to them should be wholly theirs, and the heathen be driven out before them. On their part they had thus far been faithful; let them still thus cleave to Jehovah their God! Let them not mix with the people that remained; nor name their gods, nor swear by them, nor worship them! If once they began this course, and if they intermarried with them, God would cease to drive out those nations, which would become to them as snares and scourges and thorns, till they themselves should perish from the land. In the prospect of his own death, he testifies that not one good thing had failed of all that God had spoken; and that God would be as faithful to His word in bringing upon them all the evils that He had spoken. The distinctly prophetic character of this last warning deserves special notice; for he does not say *if*, but "*when* ye have transgressed the covenant of Jehovah your God, and served other gods, ye shall perish from off the good land which he hath given you."

8. This exhortation was followed up by a great public transaction between Joshua and all Israel. He gathered them together at Shechem, the sacred home of Abraham and Jacob. From out of the mass he called forth the elders, the heads of families, the judges and the officers, who "presented themselves before God"; that is, not before the tabernacle, which was then at Shiloh, but at the place which Abraham and Jacob had sanctified by their altars to God (Josh. 24:1; Comp. Gen. 12:6,7; 33:20). Joshua addressed them in the same strain as before; but going back to the call of Abraham, he reminded them of the time when their fathers "on the other side of the flood" (the Euphrates) had served other gods. Briefly mentioning the history of Abraham, Isaac, Esau and Jacob, till the descent into Egypt, he recounts the mission of Moses and Aaron, the passage of the Red Sea and the sojourn in the wilderness, the conquest of the Amorite kings (Josh. 24:12; Comp. Ex. 23:28; Deut. 7:20), and the turning of Balaam's intended curse into a blessing; the passage of the Jordan, the capture of Jericho and the deliverance of the nations of Canaan into their hands, "but not with thy sword, nor with thy

Dow" (Josh. 24:12; Comp. Ps. 44:3,6); and he reminds them that all they possessed was the gift of God, and the fruit of others' labors: "I have given you a land for which ye did not labor, and cities which ye built not, and ye dwell in them; of the vineyards and olive-yards which ye planted not, do ye eat" (Josh. 24:13). From all this he deduces the exhortation to fear Jehovah, and serve Him in sincerity and in truth, and to put away the gods which their fathers had served beyond the flood and in Egypt. This is not a demand to purge themselves from actual idolatry, into which they had not yet fallen, but to renounce forever the examples which might seduce them to it. He ends with an appeal, unequaled in simple force except by that of Elijah to Israel; if they found fault with the service of Jehovah, let them at once choose whom they would serve, whether the idols of their fathers, or the gods of the Amorites; but his own choice was made: "As for me and my house, we will serve Jehovah" (Josh. 24:15).

The appeal was irresistible: the people swore by God, not to forsake Him who had done all these wonders for them. Thus did Joshua make a covenant with the people and set them a statute and an ordinance in Shechem. It was, for that generation and their posterity, the counterpart of the covenant which Moses had made on the part of God with their fathers in Mount Horeb. Joshua added the record of this great transaction to the book of the law of God, and set up a monument of it in the form of a great stone under an oak by the sanctuary of Jehovah, perhaps the very oak beneath whose shadow Abraham and Jacob had pitched their tents.

The people were dismissed to their homes and Joshua soon after died at the age of 110, and was buried in the border of his own inheritance at Timnath-serah (Josh. 24:29-30). His decease was soon followed by that of Eleazar, the high-priest, the son of Aaron: he was also buried in Mount Ephraim, in a hill belonging (as a burying-place) to his son and successor, Phinehas (Josh. 24:33). The bones of Joseph, which the Israelites had brought up out of Egypt, were duly interred at Shechem, in the plot of ground which Jacob had bought of Hamor (Josh. 24:32). This bright period of Jewish history is crowned by the record that "Israel served Jehovah all the days of Joshua, and all the days of the elders that outlived Joshua, and which had known all the works of Jehovah that He had done for Israel" (Josh. 24:31). The lessons of the wilderness had not been lost upon them. Not in vain had they seen their fathers drop and die till they were all consumed for their rebellion. We search the sacred history in vain, from the exodus to the captivity, for another generation that was so wholly faithful to Jehovah.

Questions Over Section III
The Twelve Tribes in Canaan

1. What three principal areas were not conquered by Joshua (Joshua 13:2-5)?
2. How many tribes received inheritance in the land west of Jordan (13:7)?
3. Which tribes received land east of Jordan (13:8,32)?
4. Which tribe received no inheritance of land (13:14)?
5. Where, in general terms, was the land of Reuben (13:15-23)?
6. Where was the land of Gad (13:24-27)?
7. Where was the eastern half-tribe of Manasseh (13:29-31)?
8. How were the inheritances for each tribe determined (14:2; 18:8-10)?
9. How old was Caleb when the land was divided (14:10)?
10. What had Moses promised Caleb (14:9)?
11. What city was given to Caleb? What was its former name (14:13,15)?
12. Whom did Caleb drive out of this city (15:14)?
13. Who took Debir? What was his reward for taking it (15:15-17)?
14. What did Caleb's daughter request (15:19)?
15. Where was the territory of Judah (15:1-8)?
16. What city was just north of Judah's land (15:8)?
17. What people occupied Jerusalem? Were they driven out (15:63)?
18. Where was the land of Ephraim (16:5ff.)?
19. From what city did the Ephraimites not drive the Canaanites (16:10)?
20. Where, in general terms, was the land of Manasseh west of Jordan (17:1ff.)?
21. What man of Manasseh had daughters that inherited his land (17:3-6)?
22. What cities did Manasseh have in Asher and Issachar (17:11)?
23. Who dwelt in these cities (17:12)?
24. What tribes complained that their territory was too small (17:14,17)?

25. What reply did Joshua give to the complaint of these tribes (17:15,18)?
26. Where was the tabernacle set up (18:1)?
27. How many tribes were slow to possess their land (18:2-3)?
28. Where was the land of Benjamin (18:11ff.)?
29. What was the chief city of Benjamin (18:28)?
30. Where was the inheritance of the tribe of Simeon (19:1)?
31. Where was the land of Zebulun (19:10ff.)?
32. Where was the land of Issachar (19:17ff.)?
33. Where was the land of Asher (19:24ff.)?
34. What foreign area was near Asher (19:28-29)?
35. Where was the tribe of Naphtali (19:32ff.)?
36. Where was the tribe of Dan (19:40ff.)?
37. What other area was conquered by Dan (19:47)?
38. What city was given to Joshua? In what tribe was it (19:49-50)?
39. At what place was the land divided (19:51)?
40. What were the cities of refuge used for (20:1-6)?
41. Give names of the six cities of refuge. Tell what tribe each city was in (20:7-8).
42. What was given to the Levites (21:2)?
43. How many cities altogether did the Levites get (21:41)?
44. How fully had the promises of God been fulfilled (21:45)?
45. What tribes had kept a promise (22:2-3)?
46. What were these tribes to take heed to as they returned home (22:5)?
47. What did the tribes take back home with them (22:8)?
48. What did these tribes build? Where (22:10-11)?
49. What did the other tribes assemble to do to these returning tribes? Why (22:12,16)?
50. Who was sent to question the returning tribes (22:13-14)?
51. Why had the returning tribes built the altar (22:24-28)?
52. What was the altar called (22:34)?
53. What was Joshua's physical condition after the land was divided (23:1)?
54. Who was present at Joshua's address in Joshua 23 (23:2)?
55. What did Joshua charge Israel to do (23:6)?
56. What was Israel to do to the people remaining in Canaan (23:7-10)?
57. What would the remaining Canaanites be unto the Israelites if they did not drive them out (23:13)?

58. What was to happen when Israel transgressed the covenant of God (23:16)?
59. Where was Joshua's final address delivered (24:1)?
60. To whom was this address spoken (24:1,16)?
61. What evil thing had Terah done (24:2)?
62. What history did Joshua review in his farewell address (24:2-13)?
63. What choice did Joshua call on the people to make (24:14-15)?
64. What choice had Joshua made (24:15)?
65. What promise did the people make to Joshua (24:18)?
66. Why did Joshua say the people could not serve God (24:19-20)?
67. What did Joshua command the people to put away (24:23)?
68. What did Joshua write (24:26)?
69. Why did Joshua set up a great stone (24:26-27)?
70. How long did Joshua live (24:29)?
71. Where was Joshua buried (24:30)?
72. How long did Israel serve Jehovah (24:31)?
73. Where were Joseph's bones buried (24:32)?
74. What priest died after Joshua's lifetime (24:33)?

Period VII
Period of Judges
From the death of Joshua to King Saul's accession (Judges, Ruth, I Samuel 1-7)

Section I
Introduction to Judges and Ruth

1. The books of Judges and Ruth, along with I Sam. 1-7, tell of that period of Bible history we call the *Period of Judges.*

2. The *book* of Judges begins with the history after the death of Joshua and ends (chronologically speaking) with the death of Samson. This history covers slightly more than 300 years. The events in the last few chapters (17-21) of Judges occurred long before most of the events recorded previously in the book.

3. The book of Judges appears to have been written by some *prophet,* for it condemns the wrongdoings of leaders in the true spirit of a prophet. It was written before David's capture of Jerusalem (Judges 1:21; 1003 B.C.), and apparently after Israel had a king (after 1050). *Samuel,* the prophet of that time, was probably the author.

4. The book of Judges tells of repeated cycles of history in Israel. The diagram on p. 332 illustrates these cycles.

5. The history in the book of Judges is dark, sordid, repetitious and TRUE. The verse that most sharply characterizes the entire book of Judges is Judges 21:25: "In those days there was no king of Israel; every man did that which was right in his own eyes." (Memorize this verse.)

6. The book of Ruth gives the lovely story of one family in the time of the judges. The love and goodness described in Ruth make a welcome contrast to the ugliness of much of Judges. The book gives a marvelous picture of family affection and devotion.

331

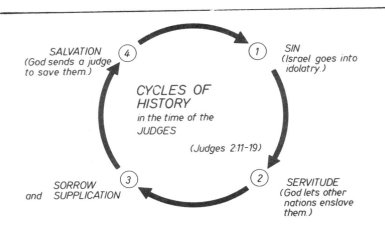

SALVATION
(God sends a judge
to save them.)   ④   ①   SIN
                                                              (Israel goes into
                                                              idolatry.)

                    CYCLES OF
                    HISTORY
                    in the time of the
                    JUDGES

                            (Judges 2:11-19)

SORROW   ③   ②   SERVITUDE
and   SUPPLICATION   (God lets other
                                                              nations enslave
                                                              them.)

The book shows God's marvelous grace in accepting Gentiles into
the chosen nation of Israel. Ruth, the Moabite foreigner, became
the great-grandmother of King David. Another value of the book
is that it traces the chosen line of Abraham's descendants down
from Judah's son Perez through David the king (Ruth 4:18-22).
The book was probably composed in the time of King David. Its
author is unknown. Memorize Ruth 1:16-17.

   7. Outline of Judges. (Memorize this outline.)
I. Events and conquests after Joshua's death (1:1-2:5).
II. History of the judges (2:6-ch. 16).
       A. Cycles of history in the time of the judges (2:6-3:6).
       B. The 7 oppressions and 13 judges (3:7-ch. 16).
1. Oppression of Mesopotamia (1) Othniel (3:8-11)
2. Oppression of Moab   (2) Ehud (3:12-30)
3. Attack of Philistia   (3) Shamgar (3:31)
4. Oppression of Canaan   (4) Deborah (Chs. 4-5)
5. Oppression of Midian   (5) Gideon (Chs. 6-8)
                                (6) Abimelech (Ch. 9)
                                (7) Tola (10:2)
                                (8) Jair (10:1-5)
6. Oppression of Ammon   (9) Jephthah (10:6-12:7)
                                (10) Ibzan
                                (11) Elon
                                (12) Abdon (12:8-15)
7. Oppression of Philistia   (13) Samson (Chs. 13-16)
III. Events showing conditions in the time of the judges (Chs.
17-21, Book of Ruth).

A. Idolatry of Micah (Ch. 17)
B. Migration of the Danites (Ch. 18)
C. Crime and civil war involving Benjamin (Chs. 19-21)
D. The story of Ruth (Ruth 1-4)

8. *Chronology of the Judges.* The chronology of the judges is difficult. Several facts and problems must be faced as the chronology is considered.

a. 480 years elapsed between King Solomon's fourth year (966 B.C.) and the exodus from Egypt (1446 B.C.). The judges fit into this period (I Kings 6:1). Paul the apostle refers to this period in a rather indefinite manner as being 450 years (Acts 13:19-21).

b. Several other events must also be fitted into this 480 year period. Among these are 4 years of Solomon's reign, 40 years of David's reign (I Kings 2:11), 40 years of Saul's reign (Acts 13:21), approximately 20 years of Samuel's judgeship (I Sam. 7:1; 14:18), the life of Joshua and the faithful elders after the conquest (Josh. 24:31), 7 years of conquest, 40 years of wilderness wanderings (Num. 33:38). These items total more than 150 years.

c. The book of Judges gives the number of years occupied by the various oppressions of Israel and the periods of peace that followed the oppressions: 8 years servitude to Mesopotamia (3:8); 40 years peace under Othniel (3:11); 18 of servitude to Moab (3:14); 80 of peace after Ehud delivered them (3:30); 20 of Canaanite oppression (4:3); 40 of peace under Deborah (5:31); 7 of Midianite oppression (6:1); 40 of peace under Gideon (8:23); 3 under Abimelech (9:23); 23 under Tola (10:2); 22 under Jair (10:3); 18 of Ammonite oppression (10:8); 6 under Jephthah (12:7); 7 under Ibzan (12:9); 10 under Elon (12:11); 8 under Abdon (12:14); 40 under Philistine oppression (13:1); 20 under Samson (15:20; 16:31). Total, 410 years.

It will be immediately apparent that this period of 410 years when added to the 150 years or more of other known events is much more than the 480 years of I Kings 6:1.

d. Another chronological note is the statement of Jephthah in Judges 11:26, where it is indicated that about 300 years elapsed from the time Israel first dwelt in Hesbon until the Ammonites took it over shortly before Jephthah's judgeship. Israel came into Hesbon in the fortieth year of their wanderings (1406 B.C.; Num. 21:25; 20:23-24; 33:38). Thus Jephthah must have been judge after 1106 B.C.

e. The frequent occurrence of the number 40 in the list of judges suggests that the numbers may be rounded off (3:11; 5:31; 8:23; 13:1).

f. The explanation of the chronological difficulty in Judges seems to be that several of the judges were contemporary, or at least had overlapping judgeships. Judges 10:7 suggests that the Ammonite oppression associated with Jephthah east of Jordan was near the same time as the Philistine oppression associated with Samson along the Mediterranean coast. It is likely that the judges Shamgar, Tola, Jair, Ibzan, Elon and Abdon, about whom very little is said, were limited in their activities to their own tribal areas and overlapped one another and the periods before and after them.

It appears that the judges Othniel to Abimelech were successive in rule, but the judges Tola through Samson overlapped one another considerably.

g. The chronology of the judges works out very well when we take into account the foregoing considerations. Furthermore there appears a noteworthy correlation between the history in Judges and the history of Egypt and other nations around Israel. Generally the periods when Israel was living in peace were the periods when the Egyptians or the Hittites were strong and holding in submission the small nations that frequently oppressed Israel. The times when Israel was enslaved by surrounding nations were the times when Egypt was very weak and unable to send military forces into Palestine and nearby areas to crush the restless and rampaging small nations.[1]

We are not suggesting that this is a necessary explanation for the history related in Judges. But we see no reason for arguing that God did not use the power of Egypt as a tool to suppress Israel's enemies during those times when Israel sought Him faithfully.

h. The events in the last chapters of Judges, 17-21, occurred long before most of the events recorded previously in the book, perhaps back in the time of Othniel. This is indicated by the fact that Judges 18:30 mentions Moses' grandson Jonathan as living when the events occurred. Since Moses' son was born long before the exodus, perhaps around 1470 B.C., it is not likely that his grandson lived after 1300. See Exodus 2:22.

---

1. M.F. Unger. *Arch. & O.T.* ch. xvi.

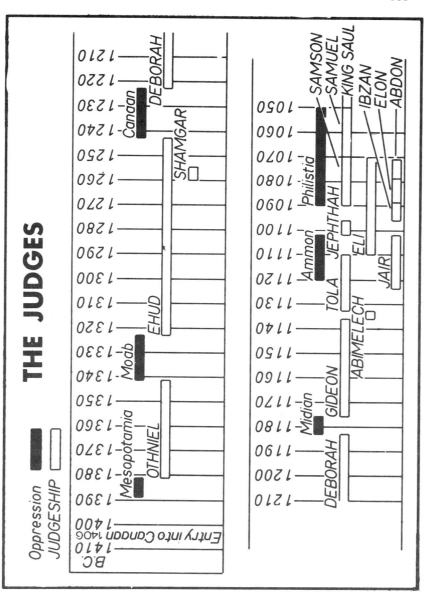

THE JUDGES

Furthermore, Hosea 10:9 speaks of the sin at Gibeah, described in Judges 19 as the *beginning* of Israel's sins in the land.

i. Dates of the judges and related events. (This chronology must be calculated backward from the known date of King Saul's accession, since we do not know the date of Joshua's death. However, we here give the events in the order of their occurrence.)

1. Wilderness wanderings of Israel — 1446-1406.
2. Conquest of Canaan — 1406-1399. (7 yrs. The Hittites who had controlled Palestine had been so weakened by attacks of Thutmose III and the Egyptians in the 15th century that they could offer no interference with Israel's conquest.)
3. Peace following Joshua's death — 1399-1389 (?).
4. Mesopotamian oppression — 1389-1381. (8 yrs. Judges 3:8. This was a period of weakness in Egypt under Amenhotep III, 1412-1376. After 1380 Egypt lost all dominance in Palestine to the Hittites.)
5. Peace under Othniel — 1381-1341. (40 yrs. Judges 3:11. Under Suppiluliuma, king of the Hittites, 1385-1345, peace and order was brought to all Syria and Palestine. Egypt was weak under Amenhotep IV, 1376-1362, and Tutankhamon, 1360-1350.)
6. Moabite oppression under Eglon — 1341-1323. (18 yrs. Judges 3:14. Egypt again began to challenge Hittite supremacy, leaving Moab free to oppress Israel.)
7. Peace under Ehud — 1323-1243. (80 yrs. Judges 3:30. Under Seti I of Egypt, 1320-1300, Palestine and Syria again came mostly under Egyptian control. The strong Rameses III, 1197-1165, a strong king in Egypt, ruled and defeated restless nations in Syria and Palestine.)
8. Canaanite oppression — 1243-1223 (20 yrs Judges 4:3).
9. Peace under Deborah — 1223-1183 (40 yrs. Judges 5:31. Rameses III, 1197-1165, a strong king in Egypt, ruled during much of this time. This was also the time of the invasion of the Sea Peoples from the Mediterranean islands into the land of the Hittites and the Palestine coast. These peoples probably included most of the Philistines.)
10. Midianite oppression — 1183-1176 (7 yrs. Judges 6:1. Weak kings in Egypt from 1165 to 1085 permitted Bedouin invaders like the Midianites to maraude freely.)

11. Peace under Gideon — 1176-1136 (40 yrs. Judges 8:28. The prolonged weakness of Egypt may have contributed to Israel's desire to have a king of its own. See Judges 8:22.)

12. Abimelech — 1136-1133 (3 yrs. Judges 9:22).

13. Tola and Jair — 1133-1110. (Tola 23 yrs., and Jair 22. Judges 10:1-5. Because of the necessity of squeezing the events from Jephthah [after 1106] to Samuel into about 35 years, we assume the judgeships of Tola and Jair overlapped one another and also overlapped the Ammonite oppression preceding Jephthah. Jair, who definitely came *after* Tola (10:3), doubtless extended further into the Ammonite oppression than did Tola.)

14. Ammonite oppression — 1120-1102 (18 yrs. Judges 10:8).

15. Jephthah — 1102-1096 (6 yrs. Judges 12:7).

16. Ibzan, Elon, Abdon — 1096-1071 (25 yrs. Judges 12:8-15). These judges overlap the Philistine oppression associated with Samson.

17. Samson — 1090-1070 (20 yrs. Judges 16:31). Samson is expressly said to have judged Israel 20 years *in the days of the Philistines* (Judges 15:20). The Philistines oppression lasted 40 years (Judges 13:1). It would appear that the first twenty years of the Philistine oppression are the 20 years of Samson's judgeship.

The Philistine oppression of Israel did not cease, as far as we know, until Samuel's victory at Eben-ezer (I Sam. 7), shortly before the accession of Saul. Samuel's judgeship lasted about 20 years (compare I Sam. 7:2; 13:1; 14:18), and this period doubtless constituted the remaining 20 years of the Philistine oppression.

18. Eli — 1110-1070. Probably contemporary with Samson.

19. Samuel — 1070-1050.

Questions Over Section I
Introduction to Judges and Ruth

1. What period of Bible history do the books of Judges and Ruth tell of?
2. With what events does Judges begin and end?
3. How many years of history are covered in Judges?
4. Who was the probable author of Judges?

5. Give the four (or five) words that describe the cycles of history in Judges.
6. Write from memory Judges 21:25.
7. What relation was Ruth to David?
8. What genealogical information is given in Ruth?
9. How does Ruth contrast with the history in Judges?
10. Write from memory Ruth 1:16-17.
11. Write the outline of Judges from memory.
12. How many years elapsed from the exodus to Solomon's fourth year?
13. What difficulty is encountered in the chronology of Judges?
14. What is the possible explanation for this difficulty?
15. Where do the events in Judges 17-21 fit into the chronology?
16. How does the chronology in Judges coincide with the history of Egypt and the Hittites?
17. What two judges judged during the 40 years of Philistine oppression?

Section II
The Earlier Judges
Othniel to Deborah (Judges 1-5)

1. The period of the judges — The books of Judges and Ruth. 2. General character of the period. 3. Efforts to drive out the heathen nations. 4. The fifteen judges — Servitude to Cushanrishathaim — Othniel, the first judge. 5. Oppression by Eglon, King of Moab — Ehud, the second judge. 6. Shamgar, the third judge. 7. Tyranny of Jabin and Sisera — Deborah and Barak jointly as fourth judge — The Song of Deborah. 8. Moral difficulties of the narratives.

1. The period of Jewish history from the death of Joshua to the choice of Saul as king was one of great disorganization, and the records of it involve certain difficulties. Our sole authority, besides a few incidental allusions, is the *Book of Judges,* to which *Ruth* forms a supplement. See p. 333 for a discussion of the chronology of the book.

2. The history of the whole period is summed up in a passage which connects the Book of *Judges* with that of *Joshua* (Judges 2:6-19). After the death of Joshua, the people remained faithful to Jehovah so long as the generation lasted which had seen all His mighty works (Judges 2:7). "And there arose another generation

after them which knew not Jehovah, nor yet the works which he had done for Israel" (Judges 2:10). They fell into the worship of "Baalim," the idols of the country, and especially of Baal and Ashtaroth;[1] and they were given over into the hands of the enemies whose gods they served. Their career of conquest was checked and heathen conquerors oppressed them, but though punished, they were not forsaken by God. As often as they were oppressed, He raised up "Judges,"[2] who delivered them from their oppressors (Judges 2:16). But as often as they were delivered, they disobeyed their judges and declined into idolatry; and "when the judge was dead they returned, and corrupted themselves more than their fathers" (Judges 2:19). For this unfaithfulness on their part to the covenant, God kept back the full accomplishment of His promise to drive out the nations before them, who were left at Joshua's death; indeed, it was in foresight of their sin that He had not entirely delivered those nations into the hand of Joshua (Judges 2:20-23; 3:1-4). We sum up the cycles of history in Judges as periods of (1) sin, (2) servitude, (3) sorrow and supplication, and (4) salvation through a judge.

Such is the summary which is filled up in the first sixteen chapters of *Judges:* the rest of the book (chs. 17-21) is occupied with two or three striking examples of the idolatry and anarchy thus generally described.

3. The history of the Judges is prefaced by some account of the efforts of the several tribes to drive out the heathen nations after the death of Joshua. In these efforts JUDAH took the lead, by the direction of God's oracle, and in association with SIMEON. These two tribes gained a great victory over the Canaanites and Perizzites in Bezek,[3] and took prisoner Adoni-bezek (the *Lord of Bezek),* one of those tyrants who have become famous for some special cruelty to their captives. He had cut off the thumbs and great toes of seventy kings, and amused himself with their attempts to pick up the food that fell from his table; and now, himself thus mutilated, he confessed that God had requited him

---

1. *Baal* was the Phoenician and Canaanite god of rain and storm and fertility. The name *Baal* means simply "Lord" or "Master". The name Baal was applied to the gods of many localities, e.g. Baal-Gad, Baal-Peor, Baal-Zebub, etc.

Ashtoreth (plural, Ashtaroth) was one of the Canaanite goddesses of love, sex and war. She is often associated with, or confounded with similar goddesses — Anath, Astarte and Asherah. These were frequently associated with Baal as wife, sister or lover. Their worship included acts of prostitution.

2. The Hebrew word *Shophet* is the same as that for an ordinary *judge.* However, the judges under consideration were first of all military leaders and deliverers. When they delivered Israel from enemies, then they administered justice to the people and their authority supplied the want of a regular government.

3. This Bezek, in the lot of Judah, seems to have been distinct from the Bezek named in I Sam. 11:8, which was more central.

justly (Judges 1:4-7). He died at Jerusalem, the lower city of which the men of Judah succeeded in taking.[1] This example of the wanton cruelty of the chiefs of Canaan throws a light on the state of the country before its conquest.

Next we have the account of the exploits of Caleb and Othniel, already anticipated in *Joshua* (Judges 1:9-15); and of the settlement of the Kenites, the children of Jethro, the father-in-law of Moses, in the wilderness of Judah, to the south of Arad. Here they dwelt as a free Arab tribe among the people of the desert, but in close alliance with Israel (Judges 1:16; Comp. 4:11; I Sam. 15:6; 27:10; 30:29). Judah then aided Simeon in recovering his lot. They took Zephath (which they called Hormah), and fulfilled by its utter destruction the vow long since made by Israel (Judges 1:17, Comp. Num 21:3; I Chron. 4:30). They also took Gaza, Askelon and Ekron from the Philistines, but the strength of those people in war-chariots prevented their expulsion and enabled them soon to regain these cities. The tribe of BENJAMIN failed to drive out the Jebusites from Jebus, the citadel of Jerusalem, which belonged to their lot (Judges 1:21). The men of EPHRAIM took Bethel by the treachery of an inhabitant, whom they caught outside the gate of the city. It was now finally called by the name of Bethel, which was first given to it by Jacob, and had been commonly applied to it by the Jews. Its old name of *Luz* was given to a city which its betrayer went and built among the Hittites (Judges 1:22-26). Ephraim failed, however, to drive out the Canaanites from Gezer; and MANASSEH only reduced those of the valley of Esdraelon to tribute after some time. Several cities of the northern highlands proved too strong for ZEBULUN and NAPHTALI, but some of them were made tributaries, as Beth-shemesh and Beth-anath. ASHER did not even attempt to take Accho, Sidon and the other cities of the Phoenician seacoast and the Lebanon, but they dwelt among the people of the land. Lastly, the men of DAN were forced back by the Amorites from the valleys of their lot into the mountains; and even there the Amorites retained some strongholds, which were ultimately reduced to tribute by the power of Ephraim. This was no doubt the chief motive of the northern expedition of the Danites, which has been already mentioned, and to which we shall have to recur. The Amorites also kept possession of the *"Pass of*

---

1. Judg. 1:5-8. That it was only the lower city which was taken is expressly stated by Josephus (*Ant.* v. 2. 23); and we also learn from the biblical narrative that the upper city remained in the hands of the Jebusites till the time of David. Comp. Josh. 15:63; Judges 1:21.

Scorpions" (Akrabbim), from "Selah" (the *cliff*, Petra?) upward, south of the Dead Sea (Judges 1:27-36).

These fitful efforts were reproved by an angel (or messenger) of the Lord who went forth from Gilgal to some solemn assembly of the people in that neighborhood; and told them that, as they had failed to keep God's covenant, He would not drive out the people before them. They kept a great act of public humiliation, with sacrifices to Jehovah; and from their cries of repentance the place received the name of *Bochim* (the *weepers*) (Judges 2:1-5).

4. After this introduction we have the general summary of the vicissitudes of idolatry and repentance, servitude and deliverance, which we have already noticed (Judges 2:6-3:7). It ends with the enumeration of the heathen nations who were still left, "to prove Israel by them": a trial in which they failed, intermarrying with them, worshiping their gods, doing evil in the sight of Jehovah, forgetting their own God and serving Baal and the Ashtaroth (Judges 3:4-7; Comp. Deut. 7:3-4).

These statements are illustrated by the dark records of idolatry, vice and cruelty which occupy the closing chapters of the book. These are expressly presented as examples of the disorder in those days when "there was no King in Israel, but every man did that which was right in his own eyes" (Judges 17:6; 18:1; 19:1; 21:25).

5. Having given this introductory summary, the Scriptures then turn to the history of the judges themselves. They were fifteen in number, Deborah, the prophetess, being reckoned with her male associate, Barak: (1) Othniel; (2) Ehud; (3) Shamgar; (4) Deborah and Barak; (5) Gideon; (6) Abimelech; (7) Tola; (8) Jair; (9) Jephthah; (10) Ibzan; (11) Elon; (12) Abdon; (13) Samson; (14) Eli; (15) Samuel. The mission of most of the judges was preceded by a period of oppression under a foreign conqueror.

The first of these conquerors was Chushan-rishathaim, king of Aram-naharaim *(Aram of the two rivers, i.e.,* Mesopotamia), the home of the family of Abraham (Judges 3:8). Concerning Cushan-rishathaim we know only the facts related in the Scripture. Since the Hittites had occupied the land of Mesopotamia around Haran at this time, we suspect that he was a Hittite conqueror. After the people had served him eight years, 1389-1381 B.C., God raised up Othneil, Caleb's nephew, whose valor has already been mentioned, to be their deliverer and the *first judge*. Of him it is recorded what is not said of all the judges,

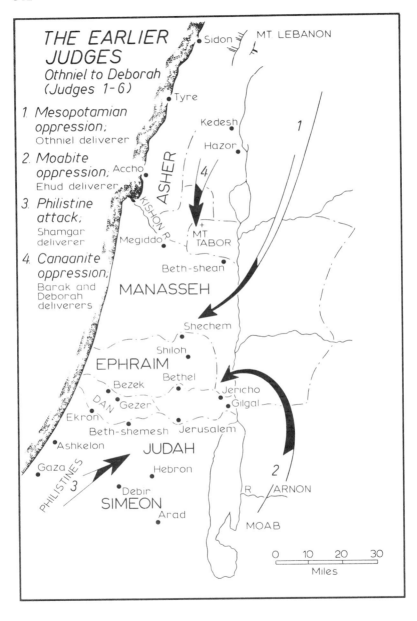

THE EARLIER
JUGES
*Othniel to Deborah
(Judges 1-6)*

1. *Mesopotamian
   oppression;*
   Othniel deliverer

2. *Moabite
   oppression;*
   Ehud deliverer

3. *Philistine
   attack;*
   Shamgar
   deliverer

4. *Canaanite
   oppression;*
   Barak and
   Deborah
   deliverers

MT. LEBANON

Sidon

Tyre

Kedesh

Hazor

Accho

ASHER

KISHON R.

Megiddo

MT. TABOR

Beth-shean

MANASSEH

Shechem

Shiloh

EPHRAIM

Bezek   Bethel

DAN   Gezer

Ekron   Jericho

Beth-shemesh   Gilgal

Ashkelon   Jerusalem

JUDAH

Gaza

PHILISTINES

Debir

SIMEON

Hebron

Arad

R. ARNON

MOAB

0   10   20   30
Miles

that "the spirit of Jehovah was upon him." The land had rest under his government for forty years (1381-1341 B.C.).

6. The next enemy who prevailed against Israel was *Eglon,* king of Moab, who formed a great league with the Ammonites and Amalekites. He crossed the Jordan, defeated the Israelites and took possession of "the city of palm-trees," that is, Jericho (Deut. 34:3; Judges 1:16). His power endured for eighteen years (Judges 3:12-14; 1341-1323 B.C.) till a deliverer was raised up in EHUD, the son of Gera, who is reckoned the *second judge.* He was one of those left-handed, or ambidextrous Benjamites, already alluded to, and his skill with the left hand was fatal to the King of Moab. As a Benjamite, he was naturally deputed to carry a present to Eglon at Jericho, which lay within the territory of that tribe. He prepared a double-edged dagger, a cubit long, and girded it on his right thigh under his garment. Having offered the present, he went away as far as "the graven images"[1] at Gilgal, where he dismissed his attendants and returned to the king, whom he found in the retirement of his summer parlor. On Ehud's telling him that he had a secret message to him from God, Eglon dismissed his attendants and rose to receive it without fear, when Ehud plunged his dagger into the body of the king, whose obesity was such that the weapon was buried to the handle and Ehud could not draw it out again. Ehud locked the doors of the summer parlor and went out through the porch. It was long before the attendants ventured to break in upon the king's privacy, and meanwhile Ehud escaped beyond the graven images at Gilgal to Seirath, in Mount Ephraim. The children of Israel rallied at the sound of his trumpet in those highland fastnesses, and he led them down into the plain. First seizing the fords of the Jordan, he fell upon the Moabites, who were completely defeated, with the loss of 10,000 of their best warriors. And so the land had rest for eighty years (1323-1243 B.C.). It is to be observed that Ehud is not called a judge throughout the narrative, but only a deliverer; still the way in which his death is mentioned at the beginning of the next chapter seems to imply that he held the regular power of a judge to the end of his life.

7. The place of *third judge* is commonly assigned to SHAMGAR, the son of Anath,[2] who delivered Israel from the tyranny of the *Philistines,* and displayed his strength by killing 600 of them with an ox-goad (Judges 3:31). But there seems no reason for

---

1. This is the meaning of the word rendered "quarries" (Judg. 3:19,26); it may refer to the twelve stones taken out of the bed of the Jordan and set up there (Josh. 4:20).
2. The fact that Shamgar's father was named *Anath,* the name of an immoral Canaanite goddess, suggests that idolatry had infected his grandparents.

reckoning this as a deliverance of the whole land from a positive subjection. The Philistines were a constant "thorn in the side" to Israel on the south-west frontier, in addition to all the other enemies they had to encounter; but it was not till the time of Eli and Samson and Samuel that they became the chief oppressors of the people. Shamgar is not called a judge; and his exploits seem to have been of the same nature as those of Samson, irregular acts of personal prowess, having but little lasting effect on the condition of the people at large. His time and acts may, therefore, be safely included in the preceding period of eighty years. Accordingly the next captivity is said to have begun "after the death of Ehud" (Judges 4:1).

8. After the death of Ehud, the people were again sold, for their sins, into the hand of the Canaanite *Jabin, king of Hazor;* who, like his ancestor of the same name, was the head of a great confederacy in Northern Palestine (Judges 4; Comp. Josh. 11). He had 900 war-chariots of iron, and his host was commanded by a mighty captain, named Sisera, who dwelt in Harosheth of the Gentiles, a city in the north, deriving its epithet probably from its mixed population (like Galilee in later times), over whom Sisera ruled as a chieftain. The site of Hazor is about four miles southwest of the "waters of Merom," in the territory of Naphtali, in which also Hazor was situated. Here then we have not, as in the two former cases, an invasion from without, but the rebellion of a state already once subdued, a sad sign of the decay of Israel. For twenty years Jabin "mightily oppressed" the land, but both his power and the life of his captain Sisera were given as a spoil to the hands of women.

At this time Israel was judged by a prophetess named DEBORAH,[1] the wife of Lapidoth, who is reckoned with Barak as the *fourth judge.*[2] Her abode was under a palm-tree which bore her name, a well-known solitary landmark, between Ramah and Bethel; and thither the people came to her for judgment. She sent an inspired message to Barak, the son of Abinoam, of Kedesh, in Naphtali, bidding him assemble 10,000 men of Naphtali and Zebulun at Mount Tabor; for Jehovah would draw Sisera and his host to meet him at the river Kishon, and would deliver them into his hand. Barak consented, only on the condition that Deborah would go with him to the battle, though she warned him that he would reap no honor, for Jehovah would sell Sisera into the

---

1. Her name means *bee* — a very ancient symbol both of royal power and of inspired poetry.
2. It seems more proper to consider her as the prophetess, inspiring and directing Barak, the judge. See Heb. 11:32.

hands of a woman. The forces of Zebulun, Naphtali and Issachar were gathered together at Kadesh, with some help from the central tribes, Ephraim, Manasseh and Benjamin, as well as from the half-tribe of Manasseh beyond Jordan. Those of the east and south took no part in the contest; Sisera advanced from Harosheth to the great plain of Esdraelon or Jezreel, which is drained by the river Kishon. He took up his position in the south-west corner of the plain near "Taanach by the waters of Megiddo" (Judges 5:19), where were numerous rivulets flowing into the Kishon. Barak marched down from his camp on Mount Tabor with his 10,000 men. "It was at this critical moment that (as we learn directly from Josephus and indirectly from the song of Deborah) a tremendous storm of sleet and hail gathered from the east, and burst over the plain, driving full in the face of the advancing Canaanites. 'The stars in their courses fought against Sisera.' The rain descended, the four rivulets of Megiddo were swelled into powerful streams, the torrent of the Kishon rose into a flood, the plain became a morass. The chariots and the horses, which should have gained the day for the Canaanites, turned against them. They became entangled in the swamp; the torrent of Kishon — the torrent famous through former ages — swept them away in its furious eddies; and in that wild confusion 'the strength' of the Canaanites 'was trodden down,' and the 'horse-hoofs stamped and struggled by the means of the plungings and plungings of the mighty chiefs' in the quaking morass and the rising streams. Far and wide the vast army fled far through the eastern branch of the plain by Endor. There, between Tabor and the Little Hermon, a carnage took place long remembered, in which the corpses lay "fattening the ground." Psalm 83:10 speaks of Sisera's and Jabin's bodies, "Which perished at Endor, and became as dung for the earth."

Sisera escaped by dismounting from his chariot, and fled on foot to the tent of Heber the Kenite. This Arab sheikh had separated from the encampment of his brethren, the children of Hobab, the brother-in-law of Moses, and removed northward to "the oaks of the wanderers" *(Zaanaim)*, near Kedesh, preserving, it should seem, friendly relations both with the Jews and the Canaanites. At all events, it is distinctly stated that there was peace between Jabin and Heber; and Sisera fled to the tent of Jael the wife of Heber. Jael met him at the tent door, and pressed him to come in. He accepted the invitation, and she flung a mantle (or rug) over him as he lay wearily on the floor. When thirst prevented sleep, and he asked for water, she brought him buttermilk in her choicest vessel, thus ratifying the sacred bond of Eastern hospitality. But anxiety still prevented Sisera from composing himself to rest until he had exacted a promise from his protectress that she would faithfully preserve the secret of his concealment, till at last, with a feeling of perfect security, the weary and unfortunate general resigned himself to the deep sleep of misery and fatigue. Then it was that Jael took in her left hand one of the great wooden pins (in the Authorized Version "nail") which fastened down the cords of the tent, and in her right hand the mallet (in the Authorized Version "a hammer") used to drive it into the ground, and creeping up to her sleeping and confiding guest, with one terrible blow dashed it through Sisera's temples deep into the earth. With one spasm of fruitless agony, with one contortion of sudden pain, "at her feet he bowed, he fell; where he bowed, there he fell down dead" (Judges 5:27). She then waited to meet the pursuing Barak, and led him into her tent that she might in his presence claim the glory of the deed.

The narrative closes with the *Song of Deborah and Barak* (Judges 5), one of the most picturesque remains of Hebrew poetry, and deserves to rank with the song of Moses and Miriam. After praising God for the avenging of Israel, and for the willingness with which the people offered themselves, it goes back to the glories displayed by Jehovah amid the hills of Seir and the mountains of Sinai. It describes the desolation of the land in the time just past, when the highways were empty, and travellers passed through byways; when the villages were deserted, and not a spear or shield was to be found among 40,000 in Israel till Deborah arose, a mother in Israel. The princes, who had willingly offered themselves, are called on to bless Jehovah, with the judges riding on their white asses,[1] and the people who could not draw water at the wells unmolested by the archers of the enemy, and could not go up in security to the gates of Jehovah. The high notes of victory are then pealed forth:

> "Awake! Awake, Deborah!
> Awake! awake, utter a song!
> Arise, Barak!
> And lead thy captivity captive,
> Thou son of Abinoam!"

The tribes are celebrated that joined in the battle, Ephraim, Benjamin, Machir the son of Manasseh, Zebulun, and the

---

1. The horse was never used by the Hebrews for peaceful purposes.

princes of Issachar; and reproaches are cast upon the secession of Reuben, who stayed among the sheepfolds, to hear the bleating of his sheep; on the men of Gilead, who abode beyond Jordan; on Dan, who kept to his ships; and on Asher, who continued on the sea-shore, by the banks of his creeks." The chief praise is given to Zebulun and Naphtali:

"A people that jeoparded their lives
Unto the death in the high places of the field."

Then the battle is described, in which

"They fought from heaven—
The stars in their courses fought against Sisera,"

till the ancient river Kishon swept away the slain, and their horsehoofs were broken by their prancings. Meroz is devoted with a double curse.[1]

"Because they came not to the help of Jehovah—
To the help of Jehovah against the mighty";

and Jael is pronounced "blessed above women" for the slaughter of Sisera, which is described in the most poetic language. But the gem of the whole piece is the concluding description of Sisera's mother opening her lattice to look for his return, and wondering why the wheels of his chariots tarry; while her ladies remove her fears and confirm her hopes of victory and spoil.

"So let all thy enemies perish, O Jehovah!
But let them that love Him be
As the sun when he goeth forth in his might."

The land had rest forty years (Judges 5:31; 1223-1183 B.C.).

We may at this point conveniently divide the history of the judges and consider a question that demands notice. Many persons have pointed to the treachery of Ehud and Jael as impossible to be mentioned without indignant reprobation. It is not quite clear whether the same view would be taken of similar actions when perpetrated by the patriot deliverers of other countries, whose names are not free from the blots of treachery and assassination. Nor is it easy to draw the line of moral demarcation between the deeds which are permitted against an enemy in open war, however slight may be the cause involved, and those which are forbidden even when the salvation of our country is at stake. For example, Jael herself is requested by Sisera to tell a lie to save his life.

---

1. Meroz was evidently near the Kishon, perhaps at *Merasas*, four miles northwest of *Beisan*, on the southern slope of the hills called the Little Hermon, and commanding the chief pass from the valley of Jezreel to that of Jordan. The offense of the people may have consisted in their neglecting to stop this pass. The fact that the city is not mentioned again makes it probable that it was destroyed in consequence of its curse by Deborah.

But even if the conduct objected to be morally indefensible, it does not follow that the discredit of it belongs to the God of Israel or to the Bible, as claiming to be His word. Here, again, comes in the principle on which we have had to insist in the history of the patriarchs, that the Bible does not adopt the morality of all the acts that it records, not even of those done by the servants of God. We must look through the record to the influences under which the actors lived, and not expect chivalrous honor from a fierce Benjamite, or scrupulous fidelity from a Bedouin woman. Had such qualities been ascribed to them, the record would have been assailed on the ground of its untruthfulness to nature.

But it is said these acts are more than simply recorded. Ehud is immortalized as a deliverer and ruler in Israel; Jael receives the magnificent eulogy of the inspired prophetess. But the employment of the former for the work for which he was fitted does not imply approval of all his acts; and the latter is honored for her services to Israel, without any judgment being passed on the means by which they were rendered.

Questions Over Section II
The Earlier Judges

1. What tribe was sent up first to fight the Canaanites after Joshua died (1:1-2)?
2. What was done to Adonibezek? Why (1:6-7)?
3. Who took Jerusalem (1:8)?
4. Did they keep Jerusalem (1:21)?
5. Who was Achsah (1:12)?
6. Who took Debir, and what was his reward (1:12-13)?
7. Where did the Kenites go from and go to (1:16)?
8. Why could not Judah drive out the inhabitants of the valleys (1:19)?
9. What people occupied Jerusalem (1:21)?
10. Who took Bethel (1:22)?
11. Who built a new city called Luz? Where did he build it (1:26)?
12. What six tribes did not drive out the inhabitants in their territories (1:21-34)?
13. What message did the angel of the Lord give to Israel (2:1-3)?
14. What does the name *Bochim* mean? What happened there (2:4-5)?
15. Who were Baal and the Ashtaroth (2:13)?
16. What happened to Israel in Canaan when they went into idolatry (2:14)?

17. What were the people who saved Israel called (2:18)?
18. Why did not God drive out all the nations before Israel (2:20-22)?
19. What were the three principal areas not conquered by Israel (3:3)?
20. What forbidden marriages occurred (3:6)?
21. Who was Cushan-rishathaim (3:8)?
22. Whom was Othniel related to (3:9)?
23. Who was king of Moab (3:12)?
24. What city did the Moabites and their allies take over (3:13)?
25. Who was left-handed (3:15)?
26. What is said of Eglon's size (3:17)?
27. Where was Eglon slain? By whom (3:20-21)?
28. Where did Israel block off the Moabites from escaping (3:28)?
29. What people did Shamgar fight? With what weapon? How many did he slay (3:31)?
30. Who was the king of the Canaanites (4:2)?
31. Who was captain of the army of the Canaanites (4:2)?
32. How many chariots did the Canaanites have (4:3)?
33. Where did Deborah dwell (4:5)?
34. Whom did Deborah call to save Israel (4:6)?
35. To what place was he called (4:6)?
36. Why did a woman get the honor a man was to receive (4:8-9)?
37. Where had Heber the Kenite moved to (4:11)?
38. By what river did Israel confront the Canaanites (4:13)?
39. To what place did Sisera flee (4:17)?
40. Who met Sisera (4:18)?
41. How did Sisera die (4:21)?
42. How were the dangerous conditions in Israel during the time of the judges shown by the travellers (5:6)?
43. Which tribes did Deborah praise? Which did she condemn (5:14-18)?
44. What had helped the Israelites defeat Sisera (5:20-21)?
45. In her song what did Deborah picture the mother of Sisera as worrying about (5:28)?

Section III
Later Judges, Gideon to Samson (Judges 6-16)

1. Oppression of the Midianites. 2. Call of Gideon, the fifth judge — The Angel Jehovah — Gideon overthrows the Altar of Baal — Surnamed Jerubbaal. 3. Gideon musters Israel — The signs of the fleece. 4. Choice of 300 men — The trumpets, lamps and pitchers — Slaughter of Midian in Jezreel — Pursuit beyond the Jordan — Fate of Succoth and Penuel. Special studies — The Angel of Jehovah; the Midianites. 5. Gideon refuses the crown — Makes an ephod. 6. Abimelech murders Gideon's sons and becomes king at Shechem — The parable or fable of Jotham. 7. Revolt against Abimelech — Destruction of Shechem — His death — Erroneously ranked as the sixth judge. 8. Tola and Jair, the seventh judges — Overlapping judgeships. 9. Oppression of the Philistines and Ammonites — Rise of Jephthah, the ninth judge — Embassy to Ammon — Jephthah's vow — The Ammonites subdued — The fate of Jephthah's daughter — Massacre of Ephraim — Shibboleth and Sibboleth — Death of Jephthah. 10. Ibzan, Elon and Abdon, the tenth, eleventh and twelfth judges — Philistine battles in Judah. 11. Chronology of Samson, the thirteenth judge — Contemporary with Eli, the fourteenth judge. 12. The situation in Southern Palestine. 13. Birth of Samson, the Nazirite. 14. His first exploits and establishment as judge. 15. The gates of Gaza — Delilah — Captivity and death of Samson.

1. The peace purchased by the victory of Deborah and Barak was again misused by Israel, and the next scene of their history opens upon a more shameless idolatry, and a more complete subjection to their enemies. The worship of Baal was publicly practiced, and the people were ready to display zeal for the false god (Judges 6:25-32). They were now delivered over to their old enemies of the desert, the Midianites and the Amalekites, who came up every year in entire hordes, "as locusts for multitude," with their cattle and their tents, covering the whole breadth of the land as far as Gaza and devouring its produce, so that the

Israelites had no food left, nor sheep, nor ox, nor ass. The only refuge of the people was in dens, caves and fortresses in the mountains. Egypt at this time had a series of weak kings who could not keep the Palestinian tribes in subjection, and this allowed Bedouin invaders like the Midianites to maraude freely. This oppression lasted seven years. Once more the people cried to Jehovah, who sent a prophet to reprove them for the evil they had done since their deliverance from Egypt (Judges 6:1-10). But the reproof was the prelude to effectual aid.

2. As in the former oppressions, there were still stout hearts in Israel ready to come forth at the call of Jehovah. Such a man was GIDEON, the son of Joash, of the distinguished family of the Abi-ezrites (Josh. 17:2), at Ophrah, in the tribe of Manasseh. He was grown up and had sons, and had obtained the character of "a mighty man of valor" (Judges 6:12; 8:20). Gideon was threshing in his father's wine-press to hide it from the Midianites, when he saw the "angel of Jehovah" sitting under an oak which formed a landmark, who saluted him with the words "Jehovah is with thee, thou mighty man of valor." "If Jehovah be with us," pleaded Gideon, "why is all this befallen us, and where are all His wonders that our fathers told us?" The reply was a command to go in his might and save Israel from the Midianites, for he was sent by God. Gideon pleaded the poor estate of his family, and his own lowly position in his father's house; but the reply was a renewed promise of God's presence, and an assurance that he should smite the Midianites. These words, spoken by the angel in his own name, could have left little doubt in Gideon's mind concerning the identity of his visitant. He prayed him to give a sign of his favor by accepting, not any ordinary refreshment, but an offering of unleavened cakes, with a kid, and the broth in which it was boiled for a drink-offering. These things the angel commanded him to lay upon a rock in the very form of a sacrifice prescribed by the law, and at the touch of the angel's staff they were consumed by fire which burst out of the rock, and the angel vanished from his sight. When Gideon knew that he had spoken with the ANGEL JEHOVAH he feared that he should die, because he had seen Jehovah face to face; and on receiving the divine assurance of peace, he built an altar on the spot where the sacrifice had been offered, and called it JEHOVAH SHALOM, *Jehovah* [*is our*] *peace*. It was still to be seen at Ophrah when the Book of Judges was written (Judges 6:11-24).

The altar thus directly sanctified by God himself became, of

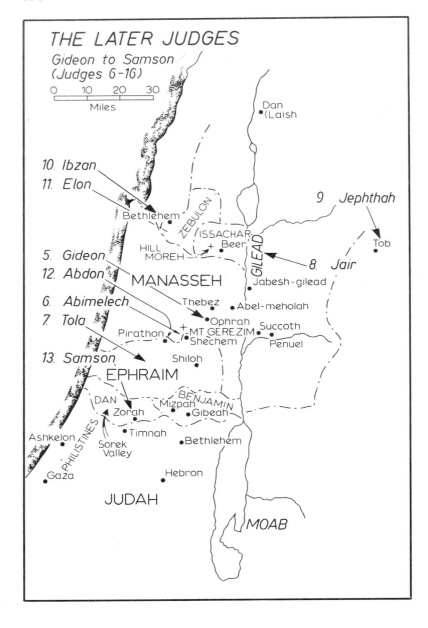

course, a lawful place of sacrifice, and Gideon was invested for the time with a sort of priesthood, apparently in contrast with his father's position as priest of Baal, for the altar of Baal in Ophrah belonged to Joash. By a dream or vision in the following night, Gideon was commanded to take his father's "second bullock of seven years old" (probably one devoted to Baal), and having overthrown the altar of Baal, and cut up the *Asherah*,[1] or wooden image of the goddess Ashtoreth, to use its fragments for burning the bullock as a sacrifice upon the altar of Jehovah. Aided by ten of his servants, he performed this deed by night for fear of his father's household and the men of the city. In the morning all was discovered, and the men of the city came to Joash demanding the life of Gideon. But Joash replied by the argument so conclusive against idols, and so often since repeated both in word and deed, "Let Baal plead his own cause." The citizens seemed to have shared the conviction which led Joash to take his son's part; and Gideon's new name of JERUBBAAL, that is, *Let Baal contend,* at once commemorated the triumph of the day, and became a watchword to deride the impotence of the false god (Judges 6:25-32).

3. Whether in consequence of this deed, or in the ordinary course of their annual invasion, the Midianites and Amalekites, with all the nomad nations east of Palestine, mustered their forces and pitched in the valley of Jezreel (Judges 6:35).[2] Then "the spirit of Jehovah clothed Gideon," and his trumpet called round him the house of the Abi-ezrites. By means of messengers, he gathered Manasseh and the northern tribes who had followed Barak; but now even Asher came with Zebulun and Naphtali; and he encamped on Mount Gilboa, overlooking the myriad tents that whitened the plains of Esdraelon. Before the conflict, Gideon prayed for a sign that God would save Israel by his hand. He spread a fleece of wool on his threshing-floor, and asked that it might be wet with dew while the earth around was dry, and in the morning he wrung a bowlful of water from the fleece.

At Gideon's renewed prayer, put up in the same spirit in which Abraham pleaded for Sodom, the sign was repeated in a form which puts the miracle beyond all cavil. Heavy dews are common enough in the highlands of Palestine, and water has been wrung out of clothes that have been exposed throughout the night; but when the fleece remained dry, while the earth around was wet

---

1. This is the word wrongly rendered *grove* in our version. The plural of *Asherah* is *Asherim*, a word that usually refers to the many images of Asherah.
2. Their force amounted to 120,000 warriors, for this number seems to be *inclusive* of the remnant of 15,000 (Judg. 8:10).

with dew, there could be no doubt that the required sign had been vouchsafed by God.

So remarkable a test must surely have been more than merely arbitrary; but its significance is not very evident. "His own character," says Dean Stanley, "is well indicated in the sign of the fleece — cool in the heat of all around, dry when all around were damped with fear. Throughout we see three great qualities, decision, caution and magnanimity."

Special Study

The Angel of Jehovah

There are frequent references in the Old Testament to the angel of the Lord which suggest that the angel of the Lord in those cases is none other than the Lord Jehovah himself.

1. Genesis 16:10 — The *angel* tells Hagar, "I will greatly multiply thy seed." Hagar called the name of the one who spoke unto her, "Thou art a *God* that seeth" (16:13).
2. Genesis 22:11-18 — In this passage it is the *angel* of Jehovah that calls Abraham, but when the angel speaks he says, "I know now that thou fearest *God,* seeing thou hast not withheld thy son, thine only son from *me*" (22:12).
3. Genesis 31:11-13 — The *angel* of God spoke to Jacob and said, "I am the *God* of Bethel."
4. Genesis 32:24-30 — Jacob after wrestling with the man (angel) said, "I have seen *God* face to face."
5. Genesis 48:15-16 — Jacob speaks of the angel who redeemed him as identical with God.
6. Exodus 3:2 — An angel appears to Moses at the burning bush, but the speaking is attributed to God.
7. Exodus 13:21 — Jehovah went before Israel as they left Egypt in the pillar of cloud and fire. However, Exodus 14:19 and Numbers 20:16 indicate that it was an angel that went before them.
8. Edodus 23:30-21 — The angel that was sent before Israel had power to forgive transgressions (Mark 2:7), and God's name was in him.
9. Judges 2:1-5 — The *angel* of Jehovah appeared, but the angel said, "I said, *I* will never break my covenant with you." "*I* will not drive out the inhabitants of the land before you." Only God would speak thus.

10. Judges 6:11-16 — The angel of Jehovah is specifically called "Jehovah."

The Scripture also records numerous appearances of God during the Old Testament age with no reference to the angel.
1. To Abraham (Gen. 18:1).
2. To Jacob (Gen. 28:13; 32:24).
3. To the elders of Israel (Exodus 24:10).
4. To Isaiah (Isaiah 6:1. Compare John 12:37-41).
5. To Ezekiel (Ezek. 1:1).

This is especially interesting because the Scriptures repeatedly declare that no man has seen or can see God (Exodus 33:20; John 1:18; 6:46; Col. 1:15; I Tim. 6:16; I John 4:12).

How are these facts to be explained? It would seem that the appearances of Jehovah and the angel (or messenger) of Jehovah who has the characteristics of Jehovah were appearances of that one who was called the Word (John 1:1), and who later came into the world in the person of Jesus Christ. This appears to be likely for several reasons:
1. God has always revealed himself through Christ, the Word (John 1:18): "No man hath seen God at any time; the only begotten Son, who is in the bosom of the Father, he hath declared him."
2. Even before he was born of Mary, Christ was *"in the world,* and the world was made through him, and the world knew him not" (John 1:10).
3. The God whom Isaiah saw (Isaiah 6:1ff) is specifically identified in John 12:37-41 as Christ Jesus.
4. If it was Christ Jesus the Word who appeared as God during the Old Testament age, then it can both be true that men saw God in the Old Testament times, and that no man hath seen the Father at any time.
5. Christ the Word was both God himself and with God (John 1:1). Jesus said, "He that hath seen me hath seen the Father" (John 14:9).

Special Study

The Midianites

1. The Midianites were descendants of Abraham and Keturah (Gen. 25:1-2, 6).
2. They seem to have been a nomadic people, residing in Siniatic peninsula and the area east of the Gulf of Akabah in

the time of Moses. They were later found northward in Moab and still northward in Gilead, east of the Jordan.

3. Moses stayed with the priest of Midian and married his daughter (Ex. 2:15-21).

4. Midian allied with Moab against Israel late in the period of Israel's wilderness wanderings (Num. 22:4). They led in seducing Israel into sin at Baal-peor (Num. 25:3-6, 14-15). This caused them to be condemned by God (Num. 25:16-18). In the ensuing battle the Midianites were almost annihilated (Num. 31:1-9). The Midianites must have been wealthy and numerous, because 675,000 sheep were taken from them as spoil of battle along with many other things (Num. 31:32-35).

5. Twice in the Scriptures the Midianites are associated with or called Ishmaelites (Gen. 37:25,36; Judges 8:22,24). Both of these races descended from Abraham, but the Ishmaelites came from Hagar and Ishmael. The association of the two races together may be due to (1) the fact that they lived in the same general areas, intermarried and actually mixed; or to (2) the fact that the people referred to were Ishmaelites by race but dwelt in the territory of Midian.

6. The Midianites swarmed over the land of Israel in the days of the judges, allowing the Israelites to plow and sow, but they (the Midianites) did the reaping (Judges 6:1-6).

7. The Midianites have long since disappeared from the earth.

---

4. On the morning of the decisive day Gideon was encamped by the "well of trembling" (*Harod,* probably *Ain Jalud),* as the spring was called from what ensued, at the head of 32,000 men (Judges 7). But these forces were not destined to gain another such victory as that over Sisera in the same plain. The repetition of Deborah's eulogy on the men of the north would have made them vaunt themselves against Jehovah, saying, "Mine own hand hath saved me," when in truth they were wanting in the first requisite of courage. Accordingly, when Gideon proclaimed at God's command, "Whosoever is fearful and afraid, let him return and depart early from Mount Gilead," 22,000 slunk away (Deut. 20:8). We feel sure that Asher went, to a man; and by a curious coincidence, those who remained were the same number as the 10,000 chosen warriors of Zebulun and Naphtali that had followed Barak. Still Jehovah said that the people were too many, and they were brought to another test by their manner of drinking at the "well of trembling." All those who knelt down to

drink were rejected, and those who lifted the water in their hands and lapped it like a dog were set apart for the service. They proved to be only 300, and thus Gideon was left with the same number that remained with Leonidas at Thermopylae. They took their provisions and trumpets and waited for the night.

At nightfall God commanded Gideon to go down with his servant Phurah to the host of Midian, where he overheard a man relate a dream to his comrade, from which he learned that God had already stricken the Midianites with terror at "the Sword of Gideon, the son of Joash," and he returned to tell the Israelites that Jehovah had delivered Midian into their hand. The cake of barley bread, seen in the Midianite's dream (Judges 7:13-14), tumbled into their camp and smote the tent, doubtless the king's tent. The Midianite perhaps associated the barley cake with Israel under Gideon, because the barley suggested the poverty of Israel under Midianite oppression. Because of its somewhat bitter taste the Israelites used barley to make bread only in times of distress, famine or poverty.

Gideon formed a plan admirably adapted to cause in the demoralized host one of those panics to which the undisciplined armies of the East have always been liable. Dividing his 300 men into three bands, he furnished each man with a trumpet and a torch shrouded by a pitcher, thus forming a dark lantern, and bade them all, at the signal of his trumpet, to sound their trumpets too, and to shout his battle-cry, "The sword of Jehovah and of Gideon," at the same time breaking the pitchers that covered their lights. Just as the middle watch was set, they took their posts on three sides of the host of Midian. The sudden shouts and flashing lights bewildered the Midianites; and as Gideon's handful of men stood firm with the torches in their left hands and the trumpets in their right, they "ran and cried and fled." No attack was needed. Their own swords were turned against each other as they fled down the pass leading to the Jordan to the "house of the acacia" *(Bethshittah)* and the "meadow of the dance" *(Abel-meholah).*

While Naphtali, Asher and Manasseh gathered themselves in pursuit of the Midianites, Gideon sent word to the men of Ephraim to seize the "waters" as far as Beth-barah and Jordan.[1] There a second battle ended in the capture of the chieftains Oreb

---

1. Beth-barah *(House of the Ford)* seems to have been the chief passage of the Jordan between Central Palestine and the East; probably the same by which Abraham and Jacob entered the land, and at which Jephthah slew the Ephraimites. The "waters" seized were perhaps the wadys leading down from the highlands of Ephraim to this ford.

and Zeeb (the *Raven* and the *Wolf*, names doubtless answering to their standards). They were slain at spots which thenceforth bore their names, and their heads were sent to Gideon (Judges 7:25).

That leader had already passed the Jordan in pursuit of Midian, after pacifying, by one of those proverbial phrases which in the East serve for conclusive arguments, the complaints of the men of Ephraim because he had not called them to the battle (Judges 8:1-3). The two great sheikhs of Midian, Zebah and Zalmunna, had escaped into the eastern side of Jordan with 15,000 men, all that were left of their hosts. Faint, but still pressing the pursuit, Gideon and his chosen 300 arrived at Succoth, whose princes refused them supplies for fear of the Midianites. The like scene was repeated at Penuel, the city whose name commemorated Jacob's wrestling with Jehovah; and Gideon left both places with threats of signal vengeance. He found the Midianites encamped in careless security at Karkor, somewhere in the southern part of the desert highlands east of the Jordan, frequented by the pastoral tribes "that dwelt in tents." Passing up out of the Jordan Valley by one of the lateral wadys east of Nobah and Jogbehah, he fell upon them unawares and gained a third great victory. Zebah and Zalmunna were taken prisoners, and led back in triumph before sunrise to be shown to the men of Succoth and Penuel, who now suffered the penalty of their cowardice in the form which Gideon had promised. At Succoth he "taught" the princes who had refused him succor "with thorns and briers of the wilderness," and at Penuel he broke down the great tower which was its strength and pride, and slew the men of the city (Judges 8:13-17). Dr. Kitto adds that the idea of a punishment which must appear so strange to us is not unnaturally suggested in the East, where men are continually lacerating their half-clothed bodies with thorns in passing through thickets.

Gideon dealt next with Zebah and Zalmunna. Bringing them to a sort of trial, he asked what kind of men they were whom they had slain at Mount Tabor. "Such as thou art; each one like the children of a king," was the reply by which they sealed their fate while seeking to flatter their conqueror. "They were my brethren, the sons of my mother," exclaimed Gideon; and he called on Jether, his first-born son, to rise up and slay them. The youth hesitated, and the kings prayed Gideon to slay them with his own manly hand. Having killed them, he took off the ornaments shaped like the moon, which hung upon their camels' necks (Judges 8:18-21), for a use which will presently appear.

This deliverance was the greatest, and the three victories the most signal that Israel had known since the time of Joshua, and they are often referred to in the later records of the nation, and celebrated in their hymns of praise (I Sam. 12:11; Ps. 83:11; Isa. 9:4, 10:6; Heb. 11:32).

5. The people's gratitude to their deliverer displayed itself in a form which shows how fast they were approaching the revolution which Moses had foreseen and provided for, even while he warned them against it. They offered Gideon the rank of a HEREDITARY KING: "Rule thou over us; both thou, and thy son, and thy son's son also" (Judges 8:22). The answer shows that Gideon himself remembered with reverance the great principle of the theocracy: "I will not rule over you, neither shall my son rule over you: *Jehovah shall rule over you.*" He was content with the position of a judge, and in the succession of the judges, he is reckoned as the *fifth* and greatest, being excelled by Samuel in holiness of character, but by none in dignity and prowess. His princely appearance has been already mentioned (Judges 8:18), and he dwelt in his own house in all the dignity of a numerous harem. He had a family of seventy sons, besides Abimelech, the son of his concubine at Shechem. This departure from domestic simplicity brought its retribution in the next generation. The only other blot on the character of Gideon was his mistaken, though doubtless well-intentioned, innovation on divine worship. Presuming, probably, on his having been permitted to build an altar and to offer sacrifice, he made a jeweled ephod, adorned with 1700 shekels of gold, which the people gave him from their share of the spoils of Midian, besides the ornaments he had taken from off the kings and their camels. The Israelites came from all quarters to consult the ephod, and Gideon and his house were thus enticed into a system of idolatrous worship (Judges 18:24-27).

The rule of Gideon or Jerubbaal lasted forty years (1176-1136), during which time the Midianites never lifted their heads again. The complete tranquility of the period from the defeat of the Midianites to the death of Gideon is expressed in the statement that Jehovah had delivered the people "out of the hands of *all their enemies on every side,*" which seems quite to exclude the notion of wars going on at the same time in other parts of Israel. He died in a good old age and was buried at his native city of Ophrah. After his death the children of Israel returned to the worship of Baalim and installed Baal-berith *(Lord of the Covenant)* as their national god. They forgot alike Jehovah, who had delivered them, and Gideon, whose sword had been God's instrument. Their ingratitude to the house of their late ruler was shown by the events that happened soon after his death (Judges 8:28-35).

6. The royal power which Gideon had refused was coveted after his death by ABIMELECH, the son of his concubine at Shechem, who really succeeded in establishing a kingdom at that place, though only for three years (Judges 9). But from the limited extent of his rule, and from the absence of a general consent of the people, it is incorrect to reckon Abimelech, as the first King of Israel. It seems indeed not improbable that the usurpation of Abimelech was effected by the support of the old Amorite population of Shechem. The point cannot be decided clearly, as we have no further information about the "house of Millo," who were his chief adherents. Having formed a conspiracy with his mother's family, who seem to have been of great weight in Shechem, he harangued the men of that city on the absurdity of committing the supreme power to the seventy sons of Gideon, and the advantage of entrusting it to a single hand, and he reminded them that he was one of themselves. Meanwhile his mother's brethren intrigued privately among the Shechemites, who were at last gained over. They gave Abimelech money out of the sacred treasury of Baalberith, with which he hired "vain and light persons," the refuse of society, to form a band of attendants (Judges 9:1-4). Abimelech led them to his father's house at Ophrah, and there he slew Gideon's seventy sons on one stone, except Jotham, the youngest, who had hidden himself (Judges 9:5). All was now prepared for the crowning measure of universal suffrage. The men of Shechem, headed by the house of Millo, assembled and made Abimelech king at the very oak where Joshua had set up the pillar that commemorated Israel's solemn engagement to Jehovah (Judges 9:6). The election, however, did not pass unchallenged. Jotham, the surviving son of Gideon, had the courage to show himself upon Mount Gerizim and call the men of Shechem to listen to that parable, or rather *fable*,[1] the most ancient upon record, which has become celebrated under his name. It is a most interesting

---

1. The fable differs from the parable by its use of physical impossibilities, as the conversations of trees, beasts, etc.

example of parabolic wisdom, but there is hardly a hint of its having the authority of inspiration.

The trees once went forth to anoint a king over them, and their choice fell first upon the best and the most useful. They asked the olive-tree to reign over them. But the olive-tree said, "Should I leave my fatness, wherewith by me they honor God and man, and go up and down for other trees?" They next applied to the fig-tree; but the fig-tree said, "Should I forsake my sweetness, and my good fruit, and go up and down for other trees?" Then they asked the vine; but the vine said, "Should I leave my wine, which cheereth God and man, and go up and down for other trees?" Thus rebuffed, they turned to the worthless and thorny bramble (or thorn), and said to it, "Come thou, and reign over us." Instead of refusing, like the rest, the bramble gave them fair warning of the consequences of his election in words both of irony and terror: "If in truth ye anoint me king over you, come and put your trust in my shadow; and if not, let fire come out of the bramble, and devour the cedars of Lebanon."

The general meaning of the fable is obvious. The trees that have any virtue in them prefer cultivation and fruitfulness to the thankless office of "going up and down," bearing all the cares of government for the rest; but the thorn, which has nothing to give, and is itself fit for nothing but the fire, accepts the dignity, in return for which it ironically offers the protection of its shadow, and more seriously threatens that the fire to which it is destined will consume the nobler trees. So the men who are endowed with beneficient qualities will hesitate to leave their work to rule the populace, while he who accepts the tyrant's throne will first deceive, and then destroy those who put their trust in him.

Such, added Jotham, should be the reward of the Shechemites. If they had dealt well with the house of Jerubbaal, who had saved them, in killing his sons and choosing the son of his maid-servant to rule over them, then let them rejoice in their king! But if not, let fire come out from Abimelech and devour the men of Shechem and the house of Millo, and let them, in their turn, devour him! Having said these things, Jotham fled to Beer, and we hear of him no more.

7. His curse was not long in being fulfilled. After three years God sent an evil spirit between Abimelech and the Shechemites. The Shechemites revolted from Abimelech, and plotted against his life. Bands of men lay in wait for him in the passes on the neighboring hills, and robbed all travellers while Abimelech was

absent from the city. The insurgents found a leader in Gaal, the son of Ebed, who in the excitement of a vintage feast in the temple of Baal, while the people mingled curses on Abimelech with their sons and merriment, openly declared that it would be better to serve the old princes of the city, the family of Hamor, the father of Shechem, and declared that he would dethrone Abimelech. But Abimelech had still a strong party in the city; and Zebul, the governor, sent privately to inform him of the words of Gaal, and of the preparations to defend the city. Abimelech surrounded Shechem by night, and defeated Gaal and the Shechemites with great loss when they came out to meet him. What follows is obscure. While Abimelech remains at Arumah, Zebul expels Gaal and his party, but the city is still hostile to Abimelech. It would seem as if the old Amorite population had now got the upper hand, and had resolved to hold it to the last. But Abimelech took the city by a stratagem, and utterly destroyed it, slaying all the inhabitants, except about a thousand men and women, who had taken refuge in a tower sacred to Baalberith. Abimelech led his army to Mount Zalmon, and ordering his men to follow his example, he cut down a bough, and each of the men having done the same, they piled up the wood against the tower and burnt it, and all who were within.

The cruel deed was soon avenged. Abimelech had besieged Thebez,[1] where also there was a tower to which the people fled when the city was taken. Abimelech had approached the wall to apply fire as at Shechem, when a woman threw down a piece of a millstone upon his head and broke his skull (Judges 9:53). In the agony of death, he had just time to call upon his armor-bearer to dispatch him with his sword, that it might not be said of him "a woman slew him." Thus God rendered both to Abimelech and the Shechemites their wickedness in slaying the sons of Jerubbaal. "The bramble Abimelech, the only one in the line of the judges who attained to greatness without any public services," had devoured the men who elevated him, and had been devoured by them.

He is commonly reckoned as the *sixth judge,* but it may be questioned whether his lawless usurpation, extending but little beyond Shechem, justifies the title: and not a word is said of his being raised by Jehovah, or of the spirit of God coming upon him. Of his relations to Israel in general we are told nothing, for no

---

1. Thebez was situated 13 Roman miles from Shechem, on the road to Scythopolis. There it still is, its name – *Tubas* – hardly changed.

conclusion can be fairly drawn from the isolated mention of his reigning "over Israel" (Judges 9:22). But the conclusion of his story seems to imply a combined action against the tyrant: "And when the men of Israel saw that Abimelech was dead, they departed every man into his place" (Judges 9:55).

8. Among the six judges who succeeded Abimelech, Jephthah's is the only conspicuous name. Of the two who preceded him, the first was TOLA, the son of Puah, the son of Dodo, of the tribe of Issachar, who dwelt at Shamir, in Mount Ephraim, and judged Israel twenty-three years. He was the *seventh judge;* and though he is said to have arisen to *defend* (or *deliver*) Israel, there is no mention of any enemy who oppressed them in his time. His judgeship may therefore be regarded as a continuance of the period of quiet obtained by the victories of Gideon (Judges 10:1-2).

This is true also of the *eighth judge,* JAIR, a man of Gilead, on the east of Jordan, who is not even called a deliverer. The peaceful character of this twenty-two years' rule is further indicated by the dignified state in which he maintained his family of thirty sons, who rode on white asses, and had dominion over thirty cities of Mount Gilead, which retained the name of the "villages of Jair" *(Havoth-jair)* (Judges 10:3,5; 5:10; 12:4; Num. 32:41; Deut. 3:14).

Because of the necessity of squeezing the judges from Jephthah to Samson into a period of about 35 years to account for known chronological data, we assume that the times of Tola and Jair overlap and both are included in the approximate time of 1133-1110 B.C. Jair, who definitely came after Tola (10:3), doubtless extended some years after 1110. Both of these judges seemingly judged during part of the Ammonite oppression preceding Jephthah's deliverance (see Chronology of the Judges, p. 337).

9. The whole pattern of this period of the history of Israel leaves no doubt that so long an interval of rest would involve a more serious backsliding than any of those before it. Accordingly we find them serving all the gods of all the nations around them, "Baalim and Ashtaroth, and the gods of Syria, of Sidon, of Moab, of Ammon, and of the Philistines," except Jehovah. Him they forsook and served not (Judges 10:6). This time the punishment was as signal as the crime. Two nations at once attacked Israel on the west and on the east — the Philistines and the children of Ammon. Of the former we shall soon hear again. The oppression of the latter lasted for eighteen years (Judges 10:8; 1120-1102

B.C.), especially in the land of Gilead, on the east of Jordan. But they also passed the Jordan and fought against the tribes of Judah, Benjamin and Ephraim, so that Israel was sore distressed (Judges 10:7-9).

Nor was their cry of penitence at once successful. They were told (probably by the mouth of a prophet) to cry to the gods whom they had chosen. Once more they humbled themselves before Jehovah, confessing their sin and praying Him to deliver them only this once; and they proved their repentance by putting away the false gods from among them and serving Jehovah; "And His soul was grieved for the misery of Israel," is the powerful figure of the sacred record. The two nations gathered their forces for a decisive contest: the sons of Ammon in Gilead and the Israelites in Mizpeh. A captain alone was wanting, and the people and princes of Gilead offered to make the man who would lead them against the Ammonites the head over all the inhabitants of Gilead (Judges 10:10-18).

Now there was in Gilead a man who had given proofs of the highest valor in a predatory war against the neighboring tribes. This was JEPHTHAH, the son of Gilead[1] by a concubine of the lowest class. On his father's death, he had been thrust out by his legitimate brethren, and fleeing to the land of Tob, apparently on the border of the Ammonites, he became the leader of a band of "vain persons," such as afterward restored to David at Adullam, and who obtained their living as freebooters, preying on the Ammonites — a mode of life not disgraceful in the East then, any more than now. When war broke out with the Ammonites, the elders of Gilead sent to Jephthah and prevailed on him, with some difficulty, to become their leader. He exacted from them an oath, in confirmation of the promise that their deliverer should be head over all Gilead; and when he joined the army at Mizpeh, the oath was ratified before Jehovah at that sacred place (Judges 11:1-11).[2]

Jephthah first sent messengers to the King of Ammon to demand by what right he made war on Israel, and the discussion that followed is an important passage for the history of the war under Moses on the east of Jordan. The Ammonite averred that Israel had at that time taken away his land along the Jordan between the Arnon and the Jabbok, and demanded its restoration. Jephthah replied that Israel had taken nothing either

---

1. As this was the name of Machir's son, Manasseh's grandson, we may fairly suppose that Jephthah's father was his descendant, and the prince of the half-tribe.
2. These present important evidences of Jephthah's adherence to the worship of Jehovah.

from Moab or from Ammon. They had driven out Sihon, king of the Amorites, and possessed his land from the Arnon to the Jabbok, and from Jordan to the wilderness. Since Jehovah had dispossessed the Amorites before Israel, was Ammon to take the land? No! Let them take what Chemosh, their god, would give them, and we will hold all that Jehovah our God shall give us. Israel had dwelt for 300 years in the territories of Hesbon, Aroer and all the cities north of the Arnon: why had not Ammon recovered them within that time? In fine, said Jephthah, we have not wronged you, but you wrong us in making war: let "Jehovah the Judge" be judge between us!

The appeal was in vain. Then the spirit of Jehovah came to Jephthah, and he went through Gilead and Manasseh, and mustered their forces at Mizpeh, whence he marched against Ammon. As he set forth, he made that rash vow which has ever since been associated with his name, devoting to Jehovah, as a burnt-offering, whosoever should come forth out of his door to meet him, if he returned in peace a victor over the Beni-ammi. His expedition was crowned with complete success: Jehovah delivered Ammon into his hands: he defeated them with great slaughter; and he took from them twenty cities, from Aroer on the Arnon to Minnith and the "plain of the vineyards" (*Abel-keramim*), and entirely subjected them to Israel from that time to the reign of Saul (Judges 11:32-33; Comp. I Sam. 11).

Jephthah returned a victor to his house at Mizpeh, to receive the promised supremacy over Gilead, and alas! To pay his rash vow to Jehovah. For as he approached his house, his own daughter came out to meet him with timbrels and with dances, like another Miriam; and to make the blow more terrible, she was his only child. Our natural horror at the consequences of such a meeting is mitigated by the sublime scene of resignation that passed between the rash father and the submissive daughter. "Alas! my daughter! thou has brought me very low," cried Jephthah, as he rent his clothes; "and thou art one of them that trouble me: for I have opened my mouth unto Jehovah, and I can not go back." "My father!" she replied, "if thou hast opened thy mouth unto Jehovah, do to me according to the word which hath proceeded out of thy mouth." To crown such a victory as God had given to Israel, she grudged not her own sacrifice. She only prayed for a respite of two months, that she might wander over the mountains of Gilead with the companions whom she had fondly led out to swell the chorus of her father's victory, bewailing that which, to a Hebrew woman, was the worst part of her doom, the loss of the hope of offspring, and so of the possible honor of being the mother of the Messiah. At the end of the two months she returned to her father, "who *did with her according to his vow which he had vowed,*" words which can leave no possible doubt of her fate.[1] The custom was established in Israel that the daughters of Israel went out every year for four days to lament the daughter of Jephthah the Gileadite (Judges 11:34-40).

Some persons, mindful of the enrollment of Jephthah among the heroes of faith in the Epistle to the Hebrews (Heb. 11:32), as well as of the expression "the Spirit of the Lord came upon him" (Judges 11:29), have therefore scrupled to believe that he could be guilty of such a sin as the murder of his child. But the deed is recorded without approval, and it becomes a moral difficulty only to those who persist in the false principle, already more than once referred to, of identifying the record of actions in Scripture with their approval. It should be recollected that Jephthah was a rude Gileadite, whose spirit had become hardened by his previous life as a freebooter.

The victory over the Ammonites was followed, like Gideon's over the Midianites, by fierce jealousy on the part of the men of Ephraim because they had not been called to share the enterprise, and the rough warrior had not the same skill to turn aside their wrath. They threatened to burn Jephthah's house over his head, and taunted the men of Gilead with being outcasts of the tribe of Joseph, apparently in allusion to their predatory habits. The Ephraimites were utterly defeated in Gilead, and the men of Gilead, seizing the fords of Jordan, put the fugitives to that curious test which shows that differences of dialect already existed among the tribes, and which has passed into a proverb for minor differences in the Church. Every one who demanded a passage westward was asked, "Are you an Ephraimite?" If he said "No," he was required to pronounce the *Shibboleth,* and on his betraying himself by saying *Sibboleth,* he was put to death, "for he could not frame to pronounce it right" (Judges 12:1-6). The whole loss of Ephraim in this campaign was 42,000 men. It seems to have been characteristic of that tribe to hold back from great enterprises, and yet arrogating to themselves a sort of supremacy as the representatives of Joseph, to be bitterly jealous of their brethren's success (Ps. 78:9; Isa. 11:13; Hosea 7:8).

---

1. It has been said that the succeeding clause, "and she knew no man," suggests an escape from such a conclusion in a sentence of perpetual virginity; but it seems almost certain that this circumstance is added to set forth in a stronger light the rashness of Jephthah and the heroism of his daughter.

Jephthah lived only six years to judge Israel (Judges 12:7; 1102-1096 B.C.), and was buried in Mount Gilead.

10. A bare mention will suffice of the *tenth, eleventh* and *twelfth judges.* These judges clearly came *after* Jephthah, but seem to have overlapped the time of the Philistine oppression and Samson (Judges 12:7-8).

IBZAN, of Bethlehem, in Zebulun, judged Israel for seven years, and was buried in Bethlehem[1] (1096-1089 B.C.). Like Jair, he used his position for the aggrandizement of his family, which consisted of thirty sons and thirty daughters. He married his daughters abroad, and took wives for his sons from abroad, that is, among the surrounding nations.

He was succeeded by another Zebulonite, ELON, who judged Israel ten years, and was buried at Aijalon in Zebulun (Judges 12:11-12; 1089-1079 B.C.), which seems to have been named after him.

ABDON, the son of Hillel, the Pirathonite, judged Israel for eight years (1079-1071 B.C.). He also had a family of forty sons and thirty nephews, who rode on seventy white asses' colts. He is perhaps identical with Bedan, who is enumerated by Samuel among the judges (Judges 12:13-14; I Sam. 12:11).

There is one feature in the history of this period which should not be overlooked: the remarkable silence of the Scripture narrative respecting the tribe of Judah, and those whose lot fell within its territory in the wider sense, namely, Simeon and Dan. While the scene changes between the highlands of Zebulun and Naphtali, the valley of Jezreel, the mountains of Ephraim and those of Gilead, and while we have a succession of judges belonging to the northern, central and eastern tribes, Judah is only once mentioned as suffering from the incursions of the Ammonites in the time of Jephthah. Only two explanations of this silence appear possible: that Judah, retaining its distinction as the princely tribe, loyal to Jehovah, enjoyed a comparative exemption both from the sins and the sufferings of the other tribes, or that it was occupied by its own conflicts with the Philistines. Both of these circumstances seem to have been true. There was a state of war, more or less constant, with the Philistines, and Samson's conflict with them seems to have been contemporary with Ibzan, Elon and Abdon, if indeed not also with Jephthah. However, the warfare with the Philistines was sustained chiefly by the tribes of Simeon and Dan, within whose

1. This was not the famous Bethlehem of Judah, but another Bethlehem in Zebulun, about seven miles NW of Nazareth (Josh. 19:15,10).

lots they lay, while Judah formed a compact government under its own princes, in loyal union with the high-priest at Shiloh. The truth of this view will be seen in the subsequent history.

11. We have now reached a point at which the history becomes most interesting and the chronology most difficult. We read that the children of Israel did evil again in the sight of Jehovah; and he delivered them into the hand of the Philistines *forty years* (Judges 13:1).[1] Then we have the story of the birth and exploits of SAMSON, the thirteenth judge, who is expressly said to have judged Israel twenty years, *in the days of the Philistines* (Judges 15:20). The fair inference from these words is, that the forty years' oppression of the Philistines is to be reckoned from the beginning of Samson's exploits against them, and that the story of his birth is retrospective. The history in the Book of Judges ends with the death of Samson (Judges 16:31), but the interposition of the supplemental chapters and of the Book of Ruth breaks the connection of the story with its continuation in the Book of Samuel. There we find Israel under the government of ELI, who resided at Shiloh by the tabernacle of Jehovah, and who was at once the high-priest and the fourteenth judge, an office which he is said to have held for forty years, dying at the age of ninety-eight, at the time of the capture of the ark by the Philistines (I Sam. 4:15-18). Meanwhile Samuel had been born and dedicated to Jehovah, who made to him, while yet a youth, that signal revelation which established his character as a prophet of Jehovah (I Sam. 3). This revelation may be regarded also as Samuel's designation to his future office as the fifteenth judge of Israel, and hence we may explain the statement that "Samuel judged Israel *all the days of his life*" (I Sam. 7:15).

From these facts it would follow that the forty years' domination of the Philistines was about equally divided at the death of Eli, whose last twenty years would thus be contemporary with the twenty years of Samson's judgeship (I Sam. 4:18; Judges 16:31).

There is nothing surprising in this result. The exploits of Samson were so entirely a personal character, as episodes in the constant war between the Philistines and the tribe of Dan, that his position is not at all inconsistent with the judgeship of Eli over Israel in general. It is also quite natural that the Philistines should have seized the occasion of Samson's death to make that great

---

1. This follows the death of Abdon, but it is not expressly said to have occurred *after his death*, as in some other cases, e.g., Judg. 4:1.

attack on Israel which led to the capture of the ark, and the death of Eli and his sons; for the loss of 3000 men by the fall of the Temple of Dagon, though a terrible blow for the moment, would soon stimulate them to seek revenge.

12. We return to the narrative, which could scarcely have been made intelligible without a discussion of the connection of its several threads. We have seen that the fierce conflicts in which the northern tribes and those east of Jordan were engaged with the heathen, under Barak, Gideon and Jephthah, only partly involved the tribe of Ephraim, and scarcely touched the southern tribes of Judah, Dan and Simeon. The part of the country which may be roughly marked off by a line drawn south of the valley of Shechem had a history of its own, upon which we have little light till the period we have now reached. In this region, though unquestionably not free from idolatry, the authority of the high-priest at Shiloh seems to have been generally respected. That office was now held by ELI, a man of venerable age,[1] of the house of Ithamar, Aaron's younger son (I Kings 2:27; Comp. I Chron. 24:3). We are not told when the high-priesthood was transferred from the house of Eleazar to that of Ithamar; but we find that the arrangement had the divine sanction, and was only reversed as a judgment on the house of Eli.[2] Himself a man of the most sincere piety, he was guilty of sinful weakness in the indulgence he showed to the vices of his sons, whose profligacy disgraced the priesthood and ruined the people (I Sam. 2:12-17). To the office of high-priest, Eli added that of judge, having entered on his office about or soon after the birth of Samson. The postponement of Eli's history till after that of Samson is the natural result of his intimate connection with Samuel, whose life begins the book that bears his name.

While Eli was high-priest, it pleased God to raise up two champions for Israel whose characters form a contrast far more remarkable than any of Plutarch's parallels. Alike in the divine announcement of their birth, in being devoted at Nazirites[3] from the womb, and in being early clothed with the spirit of Jehovah, Samson and Samuel exhibit the two extremes of physical energy and moral power, with all the inherent weaknesses of the former, and the majestic strength of the latter. In Samson we see the utmost that human might can do, even as the instrument of the

---

1. According to the above computation, he was seventy-eight, and had ruled already for twenty years.
2. I Sam. 2:30. These words agree very well with the notion that Eli was the first of the new line.
3. On the laws respecting the Nazirites, see Num. 6:1-21.

divine will; in Samuel we behold the omnipotence of prayer. The great faults of the former seem almost inseparable from his physical temperament: the faultlessness of the latter is the fruit of a nature early disciplined into willing subjection to the laws of God.

13. SAMSON, the *thirteenth judge,* belonged to that part of the tribe of Dan which had not migrated from its original allotment on the borders of the Philistines between Judah and Ephraim. His father was Manoah, a man of Zorah, on the confines of Judah. Manoah's wife had long been barren, when she was favored with the visit of the ANGEL-JEHOVAH, announcing the birth of a son,[1] who was to be devoted by the vow of "a Nazirite from the womb," and who should begin to deliver Israel from the Philistines. She herself was to abstain from wine and strong drink, and from all unclean food; and the child was to practice the same abstinence, and no razor was to come upon his head. The woman having called her husband, the angel revealed his divine character by a sign similar to that vouchsafed to Gideon; and while Manoah dreaded death, because they had seen God, his wife drew that juster inference of God's favor which has often since consoled His people: "If Jehovah were pleased to kill us, he would not have received a burnt-offering and a meat-offering at our hands, neither would He have showed us all these things." The child thus promised was born, and named Samson, and he grew up blessed by Jehovah (Judges 13).

The promise that Samson should begin to deliver Israel from the Philistines implies that their power was already severely felt by the tribe of Dan. From the very first the Philistines had kept them out of their possessions on the maritime plain and driven them into the hills; and we may be sure that there was a constant state of war, in which the Israelites had certainly not the better. We have seen that the power of the Philistines was severely felt at the same time that the Ammonites oppressed those east of the Jordan. By the time that Samson reached manhood their power was established, and their forty years' oppression had begun; "At that time the Philistines had dominion over Israel" (Judges 14:4). The princely tribe of Judah had sunk into submission, as we see from their readiness to deliver up Samson, and from their plain avowal on that occasion, "Knowest thou not that the Philistines are rulers over us?" (Judges 15:11). The hardy warriors of Dan lived as soldiers in the field, in the permanent camp which they had

---

1. The appearance of the angel to Manoah was the last "open vision" till the voice which called Samuel (I Sam. 3:1).

formed at Mahaneh-Dan *(the camp of Dan)*, near Kirjathjearim, in the central highlands, between Zorah and Eshtaol. Here "the spirit of Jehovah began to move Samson at times" (Judges 13:25; 18:12).

14. This divine inspiration, which is often mentioned in his history, and which he shared with Othniel, Gideon and Jephthah, assumed in him the unique form of vast personal strength, animated by undaunted bravery. It was inseparably connected with the observance of his vow as a Nazirite: "his strength was in his hair." Conscious of this power, he began to seek a quarrel with the Philistines; and with this view he asked the hand of a Philistine woman whom he had seen at Timnath. One day, as he passed by the vineyards of the city on a visit to his intended bride a young lion rushed out upon him: the spirit of Jehovah came on Samson, and without a weapon, he tore the lion as he would have torn a kid, but he told no one of the exploit. As he passed that way again, he saw a swarm of bees in the carcass of the lion; and he ate of the honey, but still he told no one.[1] He availed himself of this circumstance, and of the custom of proposing riddles at marriage-feasts, to lay a snare for the Philistines. Thirty young men had been assigned to him as companions or groomsmen, and to them he proposed a riddle, to be solved within the seven days of the marriage-feast, for a stake of thirty tunics and thirty changes of raiment. This was the riddle:

> "Out of the eater came forth food,
> And out of the strong came forth sweetness."

On the seventh day they asked Samson's wife to entice her husband to tell the riddle, threatening to burn her and her father's house if she refused. With that fatal subjection to a woman's wiles and tears which at last destroyed him, Samson told the riddle to his wife, and she told it to the men of the city, so that before sunset on the seventh day they came to Samson and said,

> "What is sweeter than honey?
> And what is stronger than a lion?"

"If ye had not ploughed with my heifer," rejoined Samson, "ye had not found out my riddle." The spirit of Jehovah came again upon him; and going down to Askelon, he slew thirty men of the city, and gave their spoil to their fellow-countrymen of Timnath. He then returned to his own house (Judges 14).

His wife was given to one of the groomsmen, and on Samson's

---

1. The eating of honey was a breach of the Nazirite's vow, which shows Samson for the first time trifling with temptation. Josephus, by making him give the honey to his wife, evades this point.

visiting her soon after, her father refused to let him see her. Samson revenged himself by taking 300 foxes (or rather jackals) and tying them together two by two by the tails, with a firebrand between every pair of tails, and so he let them loose into the standing grain of the Philistines, which was ready for harvest. The Philistines took vengeance by burning Samson's wife and her father; but he fell upon them in return, and smote them "hip and thigh with a great slaughter," after which he took refuge on the top of the rock of Etam, in the territory of Judah.

The Philistines gathered an army and marched against the men of Judah, who hastened to make their peace by giving up Samson. Three thousand of them went up to the rock of Etam to bind him, and he submitted on their promise not to fall upon him themselves. Bound with two new cords, he was brought down to the camp of the Philistines, who received him with a shout of triumph; but the spirit of Jehovah came upon him, he broke the cords like burnt flax, and finding a jawbone of an ass at hand, he slew with it a thousand of the Philistines. The place was henceforth called Ramath-lehi *(the height of the jawbone)*. The supernatural character of the exploit was confirmed by the miraculous bursting out of a spring of water to revive the champion as he was ready to die of thirst. He called the spring *Enhakkore*, that is, *the well of him that cried*. This achievement raised Samson to the position of a judge, which he held for twenty years (Judges 15).

15. After a time he began to fall into the temptations which addressed themselves to his strong animal nature, but he broke through every snare in which he was caught so long as he kept his Nazirite's vow. While he was visiting a harlot in Gaza, the Philistines shut the gates of the city, intending to kill him in the morning; but at midnight he went out and tore away the gates, with the posts and bar, and carried them to the top of a hill looking toward Hebron (a distance of over 30 miles).

Next he formed his fatal connection with Delilah, a woman who lived in the valley of Sorek. She was bribed by the lords of the Philistines to entice Samson to tell her the secret of his strength; and though not at once betraying it, he played with the temptation. Thrice he suffered himself to be bound with green withes, with new ropes, and by weaving the seven locks of his hair to the beam of a loom; and each time, when Delilah gave the signal, "The Philistines are upon thee, Samson," he burst the withes and ropes, and tore away the beam, with its pin. Instead of resenting Delilah's evident treachery, he seems to have enjoyed the certainty of triumph over each new snare, till he was betrayed into the presumption that perhaps his strength might survive the loss of his Nazarite's locks. Wearied out with her importunity, he at last "told her all his heart," and while he was asleep, she had him shaven of his seven locks of hair. For the last time he was awakened by her cry, "The Philistines are upon thee Samson," and thought he had only to go out and shake himself, as at the other times, for "he wist not that Jehovah was departed from him." They put out his eyes, and led him down to Gaza, bound in brazen fetters, and made him grind in the prison. The silence of the Scripture on this period of his life is supplied, as far as is possible by sanctified human genius, in Milton's *Samson Agonistes*. God had not deserted his champion, though he had so severely rebuked his confidenece in his own strength, and punished the violation of his vows. It is very instructive that the last triumph, the price of which was his own life, was not granted to his cries of penitence until he was again restored to the state of a Nazirite. As his hair grew, his strength returned; but his infatuated foes only saw in this the means of their diversion. The lords and chief people of the Philistines held a great festival in the Temple of Dagon to celebrate their victory over Samson. They brought forth the blind champion to make sport for them. At his request they placed him between the two chief pillars which supported the roof that surrounded the court, which, as well as the court itself, was crowded with spectators to the number of 3000. Samson asked the lad who guided him to let him feel the pillars, to lean upon them. Then with a fervent prayer that God would strengthen him only this once to be avenged on the Philistines, he bore with all his might upon the two pillars: they yielded, and the house fell upon the lords and all the people. "So the dead which he slew at his death were more than they which he slew in his life." His kinsmen took up his body, and buried him in his father's burying place between Zorah and Eshtaol (Judges 16). His name is enrolled among the worthies of the Jewish Church who "*through faith* obtained a good report, stopped the mouths of lions, out of weakness were made strong, turned to flight the armies of the aliens" (Heb. 11:2,32,33,34).

Questions Over Section III — The Later Judges

1. What people enslaved Israel after the peace under Deborah (6:1)?

2. How severe was this oppression (6:2-3)?
3. Why did a prophet say that Israel was oppressed (6:10)?
4. Where was Gideon threshing wheat? Why there (6:11)?
5. What was Gideon told to do for Israel (6:14)?
6. What did the angel do with Gideon's offering (6:21)?
7. What did Gideon do with his father's altar to Baal (6:25)?
8. What does the name *Jerubbaal* mean? Why was Gideon called that (6:30-32)?
9. How did Gideon use a fleece to test God's being with him (6:36-40)?
10. How many men came to Gideon? How many fearful ones went home (7:3)?
11. How were the men who were to go with Gideon selected? How many were selected (7:4-6)?
12. What dream did Gideon overhear a Midianite telling of (7:13-14)?
13. How many groups did Gideon divide his men into (7:16)?
14. What three things did he give to each man (7:16)?
15. What did Gideon's men shout (7:20)?
16. How were the Midianites routed (7:22)?
17. Who were the princes of Midian? Who slew them (7:24-25)?
18. What did the Ephraimites complain of (8:1)?
19. What two cities would not assist Gideon when he pursued the Midianite kings (8:5,8)?
20. Name the two Midianite kings (8:12).
21. What was done with the cities that refused to help Gideon (8:16-17)?
22. What had the Midianite kings done that made Gideon slay them (8:18-19)?
23. Who was Gideon's firstborn son (8:20)?
24. What did Israel request Gideon to become (8:22)?
25. Who should have been Israel's real king (8:23)?
26. What did Gideon make of the earnings from the spoil (8:21-27)?
27. What result followed the making of the ephod (8:27)?
28. How many sons did Gideon have (8:30)?
29. Who was Gideon's son by the concubine in Shechem (8:31)?
30. What god did the Israelites serve after the death of Gideon (8:33)?
31. How did Abimelech win favor at Shechem (9:1-3)?
32. What relatives did Abimelech slay (9:5)?
33. Who escaped Abimelech's massacre (9:5)?

34. What fable did the one who escaped tell (9:8-15)?
35. Who was symbolized by the bramble bush?
36. Who led the revolt against Abimelech in Shechem (9:26-28, 39)?
37. Who was Zebul? Whose side was he on (9:30-31)?
38. Who won in the fight between Abimelech and the men of Shechem (9:40)?
39. How did Abimelech defeat those in the tower of Shechem (9:48-49)?
40. Where did Abimelech die (9:50)?
41. What two things caused Abimelech to die (9:53-54)?
42. Of what tribe was Tola (10:1)?
43. Which judge had thirty sons that rode on ass colts (10:3-4)?
44. What sarcastic command did God give when the Israelites cried to him in distress (10:13-14)?
45. What did Israel need to fight against Ammon (10:18)?
46. Why had Jephthah been driven out from his family (11:1-2)?
47. What followers had Jephthah collected (11:3)?
48. What bargain did Jephthah make with the Gileadites (11:9)?
49. What first contact did Jephthah have with the king of Ammon (11:12)?
50. How long had Israel dwelt in Heshbon (11:26)?
51. What vow did Jephthah make (11:30-31)?
52. Who met Jephthah first when he returned home (11:34)?
53. How long did the daughter bewail her virginity (11:38)?
54. Why was Ephraim angry with Jephthah (12:1)?
55. Who won the fight, Ephraim or the Gileadites (12:4)?
56. What was the password? How did the Ephraimites say it (12:5-6)?
57. What chapters in Judges tell of Samson?
58. Who was Samson's father (13:2)?
59. Where did he live (13:2)?
60. Who foretold Samson's birth (13:3)?
61. What prohibitions were imposed on Samson, and on his mother before his birth (13:4-5, 14)?
62. Why did the messenger return and repeat the prophecy about Samson's birth (13:8-9)?
63. Where did Samson see a woman he wanted (14:1-2)?
64. How did it happen that Samson became involved with the Philistine woman (14:4)?
65. What did Samson kill with his hands (14:5-6)?
66. Where had bees swarmed and settled (14:8)?

67. What was Samson's bet and his riddle (14:12-14)?
68. How was the answer to his riddle discovered (14:15-16)?
69. How did Samson pay off his bet (14:19)?
70. What made Samson burn the Philistines' fields (15:1-2,6)?
71. What did Samson use to spread the flames (15:4)?
72. Where did Samson dwell after slaughtering Philistines (15:8)?
73. Who delivered Samson to the Philistines (15:11-13)?
74. What did Samson use to slay Philistines? How many did he slay with it (15:15)?
75. Where did Samson get water after the slaughter (15:18-19)?
76. Where did Samson go in to a harlot (16:1)?
77. With what on his shoulders did Samson leave this town (16:3)?
78. Where did Delilah live (16:4)?
79. What three lies did Samson tell Delilah about the source of his strength (16:7,11,13)?
80. Where was Samson when his hair was shaved (16:19)?
81. How did the Philistines abuse Samson (16:21)?
82. To what Philistine god was a great sacrifice made (16:23)?
83. Why was Samson brought to the Philistine temple (16:25)?
84. Where did Samson ask to stand in the temple (16:26)?
85. How many Philistines were on the temple roof (16:27)?
86. How did Samson die (16:30)?
87. How long did Samson judge Israel (16:31)?

Section IV
Conditions in Times of Judges
(Judges 17-21; Book of Ruth)

1. Judges 17-21 early in period of judges. 2. Scenes of idolatry and wickedness — The story of Micah and the Danites. 3. Extermination of the Benjamites. 4. The reverse of the picture — Story of Ruth and Boaz.

1. We have previously indicated that the events related in Judges 17-21 occurred early in the period of judges. This is indicated by: (1) the reference to Moses' grandson Jonathan (Judges 18:30); (2) Hosea's reference to the sin at Bigeah as Israel's first sin in the land (Hosea 10:9); (3) the fact that the tribe of Benjamin had time to replenish its number from 600 men (Judges 20:47) to many thousands by David's seventh year

(I Chron. 12:29); (4) Phinehas' being the priest (Judges 20:28; Num. 28:7).

2. *The story of Micah and the Danites* (Judges 17-18). A man of Mount Ephraim, named Micah, had stolen from his mother 1100 shekels of silver. She cursed the unknown thief and devoted the silver to Jehovah to make a graven and a molten image, a sign of that first step in idolatry, when forbidden symbols were intruded into the worship of the true God. Micah confessed the theft and restored the silver to his mother, who dedicated 200 shekels of it to the fulfillment of her vow. The two images were set up in the house of Micah, who made also an *ephod* (the garment of a priest)[1] and *teraphim* (minor household gods), and consecrated one of his sons as priest; thus making a complete patriarchal establishment for the worship of Jehovah, but with the addition of idolatrous symbols.[2] He soon obtained for his priest a young Levite who had removed from Bethlehem-judah, and who was no less a person than the grandson of Moses (see below). Micah hired him for ten shekels a year, besides garments and food; and though the law forbade a Levite to intrude into the priests' office, Micah felt sure that Jehovah would bless him, now he had a Levite for his priest.

About this time the Danites sent out five spies, to prepare for their great expedition against Laish. In passing the house of Micah, the spies recognized the voice of the Levite, who received them, inquired of Jehovah respecting the issue of their journey, and gave them a favorable response.[3] The spies having accomplished their mission, 600 men of war started from the Danite cities of Zorah and Eshtaol, and after a halt at Kirjath-jearim in Judah, they entered Mount Ephraim; and as they passed by the house of Micah, they stole his carved image, ephod and teraphim, and enticed his priest to go with them. Having taken the city of Laish by surprise, and called it by the new name of DAN, they set up there the graven image and established a sanctuary for themselves, and probably for others of the northern tribes, all the time that the tabernacle remained at Shiloh. The family of the Levite, whose name was Jonathan, the son of Gershom, the son of Moses,[4] continued to be priests to the tribe of Dan down to the Captivity (Judges 18:30,31). The

---

1. This was, no doubt, an imitation of the sacred ephod of the high-priest, with the "breastplate of judgment" and the Urim and Thummim, the use of which for divination is referred to in Judg. 18:5,6. Gideon made a smiliar ephod (Judg. 8:27).

2. The phrase "Michah had a house of idols" (17:5) may refer either to his own house or to a separate chapel for the idol figures.

3. It cannot be supposed that this reponse was anything but the invention of the hireling. The Levite is supposed to have been recognized from being — as the grandson of Moses — a well-known person.

4. The Masoretic text, followed by the King James version, has changed the name of Moses to *Manasseh;* inventing an absurd genealogy to cover the disgrace of a grandson of Moses!

circumstance of the priest's being the grandson of Moses helps to fix the time of the transaction to the earlier part of the period of the judges.[1] The whole narrative affords a lively picture of the frightful state of anarchy into which the nation had fallen; while it presents us, in the case of Micah, with a specimen of the family life of the Israelites in the country districts.

3. *The extermination of the Benjamites.* A certain Levite of Mount Ephraim had taken a concubine from Bethleham-judah. Having proved unfaithful to him, she returned to her father's house at Bethlehem and remained there four months. At length the Levite went to propose a reconciliation and to fetch her home. He was gladly welcomed by his father-in-law and we are presented with another interesting picture of Hebrew social life. After three days' feasting together and another two days' prolongation of the visit at the pressing instance of the host, the Levite at length resisted his entreaties to remain another night, and departed toward the evening of the fifth day. He travelled with his concubine, his servant and two saddled asses; and as night came on, they found themselves over against Jebus.[2] Refusing the proposal of his servant to ask hospitality from the natives, the man entered Gibeah[3] at sunset, to meet with worse treatment than he could have feared from the most licentious heathen. It would seem that the tribes had already begun to regard each other with the mutual jealousy of foreigners. Proverbial as is the hospitality of those countries and races, the little party sat down in the street or open square of the city, without being offered a lodging (which was all they needed, for they had food and provender with them) by any of the Benjamites. At length an old fellow-countryman from Mount Ephraim, who lived in the city, as he was returning from his work in the field, found the wayfarers in the street, and learning who they were, took them home and showed them all the duties of hospitality. Now the men of the city were "men of Belial," and had fallen into the worst vices which had brought down fire from heaven on the ancient cities of the land. When night came on, they beset the old man's house, and what followed may be best alluded to in the words in which Milton describes the power of Belial over his votaries.

---

1. The mention of *Mahaneh-dan* (Judg. 18:12) proves that it was at least earlier than the birth of Samson when the place already had that name (Judg. 13:25), but it seems to have had the name earlier still.
2. The citadel of Jerusalem, still held by the Jebusites.
3. The celebrated town, called more fully *Gibeah of Benjamin*, stood, as its name implies, on a height near the road from Jerusalem to Shechem. It corresponds with the height called *Tell el-Ful*, four miles north of Jerusalem, and to the right of the high-road.

> "In courts and palaces he also reigns
> And in luxurious cities, where the noise
> Of riot ascends above their loftiest towers,
> And injury, and outrage: and when night
> Darkens the streets, then wander forth the sons
> Of Belial, flown with insolence and wine.
> Witness the streets of Sodom, and *that night*
> *In Gibeah,* when the hospitable door
> Exposed a matron, to avoid worse rape."
> *(Paradise Lost,* book i. vs. 497-505)

In the morning, the Levite carried home his now-dead concubine; and having cut her body into twelve pieces, he sent them to the twelve tribes of Israel, who cried with one voice that no such deed had been done or seen since the children of Israel came up out of Egypt. With a unanimity which recalls the spirit shown in resenting the supposed defection of the two and a half tribes, the whole congregation of Israel, from Dan to Beersheba, gathered together at Mizpeh, were all the men of war, to the number of 400,000, presented themselves before Jehovah. Having called upon the Levite to recount the wrong, they bound themselves by a solemn vow of vengeance; resolved not to separate till it was fulfilled; and chose by lot one man in every ten to find provisions for the host. First, however, they sent messages through all the tribe of Benjamin, to demand the surrender of the culprits; but the Benjamites espoused the cause of the men of Gibeath with that fierceness and obstinacy which appear so often in their history, justifying the prophecy of Jacob, "Benjamin shall ravin as a wolf." They drew to a head at Gibeah, to the number of 26,000 fighting-men, besides those of the city, who numbered 700. It is particularly recorded that there were 700 left-handed men, who could sling stones to a hair-breadth (Comp. Judges 3:15; I Chron. 12:2).

The other tribes assembled at the sanctuary of Bethel, where the ark then was, Phinehas, Aaron's grandson, being high-priest (Judges 20:18,23,26-28); and in reply to their inquiry of the oracle of God, Judah was directed to lead the attack on Benjamin. Then followed a struggle almost unexampled in the history of civil wars. The army of Israel having been arrayed against Gibeah, the Benjamites sallied out and defeated them, slaying 22,000 men. They rallied their forces in the same place, and spent the next day in weeping before God; while the tone of their inquiry, "Shall I go up again to battle against the children of

Benjamin my *brother?*" seems to show some misgiving. But the
oracle bade them renew the attack, and for the second time they
were defeated with the loss of 18,000 men. Again the whole
congregation assembled at Shiloh to keep a solemn fast, with
burnt-offerings and peace-offerings, and again they consulted
the oracle through Phinehas the high-priest. They were bidden to
fight again and assured of victory on the morrow. They arranged
a stratagem, like that by which Joshua took Ai. An ambush was set
near Gibeah, while the main army were drawn up as before. This
time their flight was feigned. The Benjamites pursued them,
slaying about thirty men, till they were drawn from the city, over
which was now seen to rise the column of smoke, which first
apprised them of the stratagem, and was the signal of its success.
The Israelites turned upon their pursuers, who were stricken
with a panic and fled toward the wilderness. They were met by the
other body, who had sacked Gibeah, and 18,000 of them were left
dead upon the field. 500 fell on the highways and 2000 more were
slain, apparently in a last rally at Gidom.[1] The 600 men, who were
all now left of the 25,700 warriors of the tribe, fled to the rock of
Rimmon in the wilderness, and remained there four months,
while the Israelites burnt their cities and put the inhabitants and
the cattle to the sword.

At length their anger began to turn to pity and they assembled
again at the sanctuary to mourn before God, because a tribe was
cut off from Israel. Its total extinction seemed inevitable, for
when they made the league at Mizpeh, they had bound
themselves by a curse not to give their daughters in marriage to
the Benjamites. But a remedy was found in another curse which
they had imprecated on any of the tribes who neglected to come
up to the battle. On numbering the people, it was found that the
men of Jabesh-gilead were absent. That city was devoted to
destruction: 12,000 men were sent against it, with orders to
destroy all the men and women, except virgins; and these,
amounting to 400, were given for wives to the remnant of the
Benjamites. The remaining 200 were provided for by the
Benjamites seizing the maidens of Shiloh, who came out of the
city to dance at one of the great annual feasts; the elders of Israel
suggested the scheme, and made peace with the fathers of the
maidens. The children of Israel then departed to their homes.
The Benjamites returned to their inheritance and repaired their
cities. They regained something of their old martial fame and

---

1. These are round numbers; in v. 35 the total of the slain is 25,100.

gave Israel its second judge, Ehud, and its first king, Saul, the son of Kish; but they never recovered from this terrific blow. After hesitating between the two powerful tribes whose territories they parted, and ranging themselves at first on the side of Ephraim, they at last subsided, like the Simeonites, into a position entirely subordinate to Judah, and their territory was absorbed in Judea. Down to the latest period of Jewish history their crime was remembered as marking the time from which Israel began to sin, and the righteous indignation of the other tribes was commemorated as "the battle in Gibeah *against the children of iniquity*" (Hosea 10:9).

4. We must guard, however, against the impression that such scenes as these describe the whole, or even the chief part, of the history of Israel under the Judges. In the book itself, the intervals during which "the land had rest" make up a large aggregate of years, though we are apt to overlook them from the brevity of each notice. These hints are in some degree filled up to a finished picture, in the exquisite scenes of rural tranquility set before us in the Book of *Ruth*. The events there related are merely said to have happened "in the time of the Judges," but from the genealogies we gather that they fell in the generation after the troubles above related (Ruth 4:18-22).

A man named Elimelech, an Ephrathite of Bethlehem-judah, had been driven by a famine into the country of Moab, with his wife Naomi, and their two sons, Mahlon and Chilion. The sons married women of Moab, named Orpah and Ruth; and the family resided in that country for about ten years. The father died and both his sons, and Naomi rose up to return to her own land. She gave leave to her daughters-in-law to go back to their families but both declared they would return with her. On her urging the point, for their own sakes, Orpah bade her an affectionate farewell and went back "to her people and her gods," but Ruth cast in her lot wholly with Naomi (Ruth 1:15-18). They reached Bethlehem at the beginning of barley harvest and Ruth sought subsistence as a gleaner. What followed turns entirely upon the provisions of the Mosaic law for the "Levirate" marriage of a widow and the redemption of her husband's inheritance by the "Goel", or nearest whose grandfather, Nahshon, was prince of the tribe of Judah (I Chron. 2:10), was a very near kinsman (though not the nearest) to Naomi's deceased husband Elimelech, and consequently to Ruth, as the widow of his son. It chanced that Ruth went to glean in this man's field; and the mind, distressed with the fatal story of other inhabitants of the same city, finds exquisite relief in the picture of Boaz visiting the gleaners, not like a grudging farmer, but in the spirit of kindness prescribed by Moses; blessing them, and blessed by them in the name of Jehovah. Ruth attracted his attention; and when he learned who she was, he bade her glean only in his field, and enjoined the reapers to show her kindness. In reply to her thanks, he praised her devotion to her mother-in-law, and her coming to place her trust under the wings of Jehovah, God of Israel. Thus passed the whole harvest, Ruth following the reapers, who were instructed by Boaz to throw handfuls of grain in her way, and sharing their daily meal (Ruth 2). Meanwhile Naomi, full of gratitude to God, who had thus guided her to her husband's nearest kinsman, instructed Ruth to claim her rights under the Levirate law (Ruth 3).[1] Boaz blessed her in the name of Jehovah; praised her virtue and her fidelity to him whom the law had made her rightful husband; exercised the most scrupulous modesty toward her; and promised to do the part of a kinsman by her.

In the morning he kept his word (Ruth 4). We have a truly partriarchal picture of this wealthy and powerful man of Bethlehem sitting, like Job, in the gate of the city; and as all the inhabitants came forth, calling first the "Goel", or nearest kinsman of Elimelech, to sit beside him, and then asking ten of the elders to take their seats, to witness and ratify the transaction. In their presence, he informed the "Goel" that Naomi had a field to sell, which must be redeemed either by him or by Boaz himself; and the Goel consented to redeem it, thus admitting the claim of kindred. But when Boaz went on to say that, if the Goel took the field, he must take also Ruth, the Moabitess, the wife of the dead, "to raise up the name of the dead upon his inheritance," the kinsman found an excuse, and transferred the right of redemption to Boaz. The ceremony prescribed by the law was then performed (Deut. 25:7,9). The sandal of the kinsman was taken off in the presence of the elders and the people; and Boaz called them to witness that he had bought of Naomi all that had belonged to Elimelech, and to his sons Chilion and Mahlon, and that he had purchased Ruth, the Moabitess, the wife of Mahlon, to be his wife, to raise up the name of the dead upon his inheritance. The elders ratified the deed, invoking upon Ruth the blessing of Rachel and Leah, who had built the house of

---

1. We may safely assume that Naomi knew enough of the one still nearer kinsman to be aware that the appeal to him would be fruitless.

Israel, and that the house of Boaz might be made like that of his ancestor Pharez, the son of Judah. The blessing was fulfilled more highly than they thought. Ruth bore to Boaz a son, named Obed, the father of Jesse, the father of David; and so Christ, "the son of David," derived his lineage from a Moabitish woman, who had shown a faith rarely found in Israel, and whose husband was the son of the harlot Rahab (Ruth 4:17-22; I Chron. 2:10-12; Matt. 1:5; Luke 3:32).

Questions Over Section IV — Conditions in Times of Judges

1. What indications are there that Judges 17-21 tells of events early in the period of judges?
2. In what tribe did Micah live (17:1)?
3. How much money had been stolen? Who took it (17:2)?
4. What was done with the money (17:3-5)?
5. Where had the young Levite who visited Micah come from (17:7)?
6. What was the Levite's name? Who was his famous ancestor (18:30)?
7. What did the Levite become unto Micah (17:12)?
8. What did the tribe of Dan desire? Why (18:1)?
9. Where did the Danites stop overnight as they were out looking for land (18:2-3)?
10. What place did the Danites find that appealed to them (18:7)?
11. Whom did the Danites take with them to their new home (18:18-19)?
12. How did the one who was taken feel about being taken (18:20)?
13. What did the Danites call their new city (18:29)?
14. What did the Levite of Ephraim take unto himself (19:1)?
15. Why did he go to Bethlehem (19:2-3)?
16. In what city did he try to find lodging when he returned from Bethlehem (19:12-13)?
17. Who died as a result of abuse in this city (19:27)?
18. What was done with the body (19:29)?
19. Who assembled for war? Against what city and tribe (20:1,14)?
20. What unusual fighting force was among the Benjamites (20:16)?
21. How many days were required to defeat the Benjamites (20:24-28)?

22. How many Benjamites survived the war (20:47)?
23. What grieved the Israelites concerning the tribe of Benjamin (21:1-3)?
24. From what city were wives stolen for the Benjamites (21:10-12)?
25. From what city were the Benjamites to catch additional women for wives (21:19-21)?
26. What final descriptive verse describes conditions in the days of the judges (21:25)?

Questions on the Book of Ruth

1. During what period did the story of Ruth occur (Ruth 1:1)?
2. Who was Naomi's husband? Her two sons (1:2)?
3. Where did they live (1:1)?
4. Where did they all go to sojourn? Why (1:1-2)?
5. Who were the wives of Naomi's sons (1:4)?
6. Who died in the land where they sojourned (1:3,5)?
7. What did Naomi urge her widowed daughters-in-law to do (1:8)?
8. Which daughter-in-law stayed with Naomi (1:14)?
9. What did Ruth mean when she said, "God do *so* to me and more also . . ." (1:17)?
10. What do the names *Naomi* and *Mara* mean (1:20)?
11. Why did Naomi request that she be called Mara (1:21)?
12. At what season did Naomi return (1:22)?
13. Who was Naomi's husband's kinsman (2:1)?
14. What work did Ruth do (2:2)?
15. What kindnesses did Boaz show to Ruth (2:8-9, 14-16)?
16. How much grain did Ruth collect the first day (2:17)?
17. How did Naomi react to Ruth's experiences while gathering grain the first day (2:20-22)?
18. What did Naomi mean by saying, "Shall I not seek rest for thee"?
19. Where did Naomi send Ruth? Why (3:2-4)?
20. Where was Boaz the night when Ruth came to him (3:6-7)?
21. Explain, "Spread thy skirt over thy handmaid, for thou art a near kinsman" (3:9).
22. What does the Hebrew word *goel* mean (3:9)?
23. What did Boaz promise to do for Ruth? When (3:13)?
24. What hindered Boaz from marrying Ruth at once (3:12)?
25. What did Boaz give Ruth to carry home (3:15)?

26. Where did Boaz meet the other near kinsman? Who joined them (4:1-2)?
27. Did the near kinsman consent to buy the land of Elimelech (4:3-4)?
28. Why did he not buy it (4:5-6)?
29. What action showed that the land was legally purchased (4:7-8)?
30. What was the significance of the wish, "The Lord make the woman . . . like Rachel and like Leah" (4:11)?
31. What was the name of Ruth's son? Who gave him the name (4:17)?
32. Who became the nurse of Ruth's son (4:16)?
33. What relation was Ruth to king David (4:17)?
34. What significance does the genealogy in Ruth 4:18-22 have in the fulfillment of God's promise to Abraham (Gen. 22:18; Matt. 1:1-6)?

Section V
Introduction to I & II Samuel

1. Endings of Samuel, Kings and Chronicles (memorize these):
   a. I Samuel ends with the *death of Saul.*
   b. II Samuel ends near the *death of David.*
   c. I Kings ends near the *death of King Ahab.*
   d. II Kings ends with the Babylonian captivity.
   e. I Chronicles ends with the *death of David.*
   f. II Chronicles ends with the decree of Cyrus.
2. I Samuel begins with the birth of Samuel, and ends with the death of King Saul.
3. II Samuel tells of the reign of King David.
4. The books get their name from Samuel the prophet, who is the principal character in the first book, and who anointed the other two principal characters, Saul and David.
5. Author — the author is uncertain. He doubtless used various records and histories as source materials (I Sam. 10:25; I Chron. 29:29; II Sam. 1:18). (Certainly the Spirit of God brought things to the author's mind, and helped him to use any source materials without error.) The books were written *no later than the time of Solomon,* because the author was an eyewitness of the events in the latter part of David's reign (see II Sam. 17:17-20; 18:19). *Ahimaaz,* son of the priest Zadok

(II Sam. 15:36), has been proposed as the author. This is probably as good a guess as any.

6. I and II Samuel were originally one book but were divided into two books when the O.T. was translated into Greek. The two books were called I and II Kings, while our books of Kings, which deal with a later historical period, were called III and IV Kings (or Kingdoms). The Catholic Bible still uses the names I, II, III and IV Kings. However, other modern Bibles, including the Hebrew, list the books as we are familiar with them, I and II Samuel and I and II Kings.

7. Outline of the books of Samuel (memorize the three main headings):

Part I —Samuel's judgeship (I Sam. 1-7)
1. Samuel's birth and boyhood (I Sam. 1:1-2:10).
2. Eli's rejection and Samuel's call (I Sam. 2:11-3:21).
3. The ark among the Philistines (4:1-7:1).
4. Deliverance from Philistia by Samuel (7:2-17).

Part II — Saul's reign (I Sam. 8-31).
1. Rise of Saul (Chs. 8-14).
2. Decline of Saul and rise of David (Chs. 15-31).

Part III — David's reign (II Samuel)
1. David's lamentation over Saul (Ch. 1).
2. Reign and increasing strength at Hebron (Chs. 2-4).
3. Establishment of national and religious unity (Chs. 5-6).
4. God's covenant with David (Ch. 7).
5. David's conquests (Chs. 8-10).
6. David's sin and repentance (Chs. 11-12).
7. Amnon and Absalom's crimes (Chs. 13-14).
8. Absalom's rebellion (Chs. 15-18).
9. David's restoration to power (Chs. 19-20).
10. Famine and revenge of the Gibeonites (II Sam. 21:1-14).
11. Later wars with Philistines (21:15-22).
12. David's song and last words (22:1-23:7).
13. David's mighty men (23:8-29).
14. David's census and its punishment (Ch. 24).

8. Chronology of the period
a. Samuel born — about 1100 B.C.
b. Ark captured — 1070 B.C.
c. Saul crowned — 1050 B.C.
d. Saul's death and David's accession — 1010 B.C. (Note that David was king in 1000 B.C.)
e. David's death — 970 B.C.

9. A summary of the life of David (memorize these points).
   1. Boyhood and anointing.
   2. Advancement and Saul's jealousy (Goliath, Jonathan, Michal).
   3. David's outlaw life.
   4. Saul's downfall.
   5. The rival kingdoms and David's triumph (Ishbosheth, Abner).
   6. David's wars (Jerusalem, Syrians, etc.).
   7. David's spiritual triumphs (Ark, God's covenant, Mephibosheth).
   8. David's family troubles (Bathsheba, Amnon, Absalom).
   9. National calamities (famine, pestilence, Absalom's rebellion).
   10. David's final arrangements and closing days (temple preparations, Solomon crowned).
10. Memorize I Samuel 15:22; 16:7b; II Sam. 7:12-13.

Questions

1. With what events do the books of Samuel, Kings and Chronicles end?
2. Where does I Samuel begin and end?
3. What does II Samuel tell about?
4. Where do the books of Samuel get their name?
5. What is the latest time when I and II Samuel could have been written? Who has been suggested as author?
6. What are the three main sections (Parts I, II and III) of the books of Samuel and what are their Scripture limitations?
7. Who was king of Israel in 1000 B.C.?
8. Give the ten-point summary of the life of David.
9. Write from memory I Sam. 15:22; I Sam. 16:7b; and II Sam. 7:12-13.

Section VI
Eli and Samuel (I Samuel 1-7)

1. Samuel, the fifteenth judge — His prayers — Time of his entrance into office — Parentage and birth. 2. Eli, the priest — His ancestry — Wickedness of Eli's sons, Hophni and Phinehas — A prophet sent to Eli — The call of Samuel — His establishment as a prophet.

3. The first battles of Eben-ezer — Death of Eli and his sons — Capture of the ark — "Ichabod". 4. The ark among the Philistines — Its return to Beth-shemesh and Kiriathjearim. 5. Third battle and victory of Eben-ezer — End of Philistine oppression — Judgeship of Samuel and his sons.

1. The loss of Samson was more than supplied by the other leader of whom we have spoken, SAMUEL,[1] the *fifteenth* and last of the *judges;* the *first* in that regular succession of *prophets,*[2] which never ceased till after the return from the Babylonian Captivity; and the founder of the monarchy. His name is expressive of the leading feature of his whole history, *the power of prayer.* Himself the child of prayer, he gained all his triumphs by prayer; he is placed at the head of those "who called upon Jehovah, and He answered them"; and he is placed on a level with Moses as an intercessor (I Sam. 7:8,9; 12:18-19,23; 15:11; Ps. 99:6; Jer. 15:1). Nor should we overlook in him one striking character of sincere prayer — the patient waiting to hear, and the readiness to obey the voice of God: "Speak, Lord, for thy servant heareth."

The time of his actual entrance on his office is not expressly named. We suppose that there was a time interval between God's first revelation to him and the death of Eli. It would appear that the interval was long enough to give time for Samuel to grow up and to establish his character as a prophet throughout all Israel (I Sam. 3:19-21; 4:1) and if he was able to fulfill the part of a prophet, surely he could discharge the duties of a judge. We see no difficulty, therefore, in supposing that he at once succeeded Eli, and that he was then in his full manhood, about thirty years old, the period of entrance on public duties. The great victory, which his prayers obtained at Eben-ezer, when "the Philistines were subdued, and came no more into the coast of Israel . . . all the days of Samuel" (I Sam. 7:13, 5:3), seems clearly to mark the end of the forty years' servitude to them; and it seems equally clear that this victory was gained twenty years after the capture of the ark (I Sam. 7:1-2).[3] This victory may be regarded as the

---

1. Properly Shemuel, i.e., *asked of God* (I Sam 1:20); though other etymologies have been given, as *heard of God* and *name of God.*

2. Acts 3:24: "All the prophets, from Samuel and them that follow after." There had been great prophets before, as Moses, Miriam and Deborah, and others who are mentioned without their names; but the continuous series began with Samuel.

3. The seven months of its abode among the Philistines may be included in the twenty years; at all events, they do not affect the computation in round numbers. Some writers have most strangely confused this twenty years, during which the Israelites mourned for the ark before making an effort to shake off the yoke of the Philistines, with the whole space of its abode at Kirjath-jearim, whence it was only removed by David after he had reigned ten years, thus making its abode there about seventy years (II Sam. 6:1; I Chron. 13:4,6).

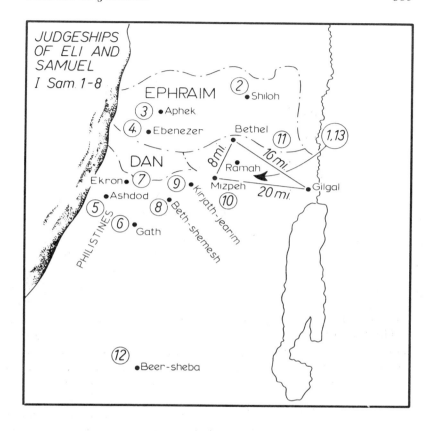

JUDGESHIPS OF ELI AND SAMUEL
I Sam. 1-8

Judgeships of Samuel and Eli
I Samuel 1-8

1. Ramah
   Birth of Samuel 1:1-20
2. Shiloh
   Dedication of Samuel 1:21-2:11
3. & 4. Aphek and Ebenezer
   Defeat of Israel by
   Philistines 4:1-22
5. Ashdod
   Fall of Dagon 5:1-7
6. Gath
   Ark there 5:8-9
7. Ekron
   Ark there 5:10-12

8. Beth-shemesh
   Ark sent to Israel 6:1-20
9. Kiriath-jearim
   Ark remains 20 years 6:21-7:2
10. Mizpah
    Samuel defeats Philistines 7:3-14
11. Bethel-Gilgal-Mizpah
    Samuel's circuit 7:15-17
12. Beersheba
    Samuel's sons judges 8:1-3
13. Ramah
    Israel requests a King 8:4-22

culminating point of Samuel's administration, and there seems no difficulty in supposing him to have been at least fifty years old at this time.

The Scripture narrative assigns no exact period to the judgeship of Samuel, from the battle of Eben-ezer to the election of Saul. We have a general description of his circuits as a judge (I Sam. 7:15-17); and then follows the misgovernment of his sons in his old age, which led the people to desire a king. We may fairly suppose that the complete establishment of his power would soon lead to that association of his sons in the administration which caused such disastrous results; and he was already getting old, if the above computations be correct. So many events fit into the period of about 1100-1050 B.C. that it is unlikely that more than two years elapsed between Samuel's victory at Eben-ezer and King Saul's accession.

Samuel's descent is uncertain. His father is called an Ephrathite, that is, one from Bethlehem-Judah (Gen. 35:19), or according to another reading, an Ephraimite; but it seems certain, from the evidence of the genealogies, that he was a descendant of Korah the Levite, of the family of the Kohathites (I Chron. 6:22-38). The two statements are easily reconciled by assuming that his family were settled in Mount Ephraim. The place of their abode was *Ramathaim-zophim* (the *double heights of the beacon* or *watch),* elsewhere called *Ramah.* Ramah is almost certainly to be located near modern Er-Ram, about five miles north of Jerusalem, two miles north of Gibeah (Comp. Judges 19:10-14). Traditionally Ramah has been considered to be the lofty hill of Neby Samwil (the prophet Samuel) four miles NW of Jerusalem. But this location seems improbable. Ramah was Samuel's usual residence to the end of his life (I Sam. 19:18).

His father, Elkanah, had two wives, an instance of polygamy rare in a private family, and entailing the usual consequences of bitterness and jealousy (I Sam. 1:6). The one wife, Peninnah, had borne several children, but the other, Hannah, was barren. With a pious regularity which deserves especial notice in those times of disorder, the whole family went up yearly to worship and sacrifice to Jehovah at Shiloh, where Eli ministered as high-priest, assisted by his sons, Hophni and Phinehas, as priests. As they feasted on their freewill-offering, according to the law (Deut. 12:17-18; 16:11), Elkanah gave Peninnah and her children their due portions, but to Hannah he gave a double portion. This proof of his affection brought on her the jealous provocations of her rival;

so that she wept and could not eat, and her husband tried in vain to console her, asking, "Am not I better to thee than ten sons"? In her bitterness of soul, she went and stood before the entrance of the tabernacle, where Eli sat in his usual place by one of the pillars (I Sam. 1:10, 4:18), and with many tears she prayed for a son, whom she devoted to Jehovah as a Nazirite. She prayed silently in her heart but her lips moved, and Eli, thinking that she was drunk after the feast, reproved her severely; but on her assurance that she was a woman of sorrowful spirit, and poured forth her soul before Jehovah, he gave her his blessing, praying that God would grant her petition. She departed with joy and returned to Ramah, and in due time she bore a son and called him Samuel. She waited to go up again to Shiloh till the child was weaned, when she presented him before Jehovah, to abide there forever. Her husband, who cordially entered into her pious designs (I Sam. 1:23), provided a freewill-offering of three bullocks, an ephah of flour, and a skin of wine;[1] and Hannah presented her son to Eli for the services of Jehovah, telling him of the fulfillment of the prayer he had witnessed. She uttered a hymn of praise, which served long after as a model for the song of Mary (the *Magnificat*) (I Sam. 2:1-10; Luke 1:46-55). Elkanah returned with his family to Ramah, leaving behind Samuel, who abode in the tabernacle and ministered before Jehovah, clad in a linen ephod, like those worn by priests. At their annual visit, Hannah brought Samuel a little coat or mantle, a miniature of the official priestly robe.[2] Eli blessed Elkanah and Hannah, who bore three sons and two daughters (I Sam. 2:18-21; I Chron. 6:26-27).

2. We have briefly considered ELI, the priest in the discussion of Samson, who was contemporary with Eli (see Sec. III, sub. 12). Eli was a descendant of Aaron through his son Ithamar. The priestly families are diagrammed on a chart on p. 392.

Samuel's growth in favor with God and man formed a striking contrast to the shameful profanation of the tabernacle by the sons of Eli, who were "sons of Belial." Instead of contenting themselves with the parts of the sacrifices allotted to them by the law, they invented strange and disorderly methods for obtaining what they pleased; and they practiced licentiousness at the very doors of the tabernacle (I Sam. 2:12-16,22). Their aged father reproved them in vain (I Sam. 2:22-25), and he was too indulgent

---

1. I Sam. 1:24. This offering is proof of his wealth.
2. This robe was the same that Samuel wore in mature years (I Sam. 11:27), and by which he was identified by Saul when raised by the witch of Endor (I Sam. 28:14).

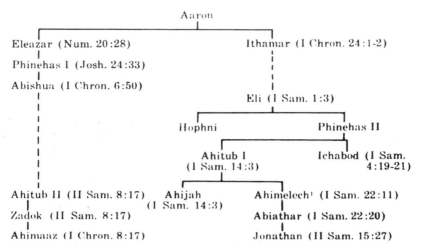

1. Since Christ referred to Ahimelech as "Abiathar" (Mark 2:26), we suppose that Ahimelech was also known by the name Abiathar, which was his son's name.

to use his authority as high-priest: "His sons made themselves vile, and he restrained them not" (I Sam. 3:13). Therefore a prophet was sent to announce the destruction of the house of Eli, as a sign of which both his sons should be slain in one day; a faithful priest should be raised up in his place; and those who remained of Eli's house should come crouching to him with the prayer to be put into one of the priest's offices to earn a morsel of bread (I Sam. 2:27-36). The judgment was fulfilled when Solomon deposed Abiathar, the last high-priest of the house of Ithamar, and restored the priesthood to the house of Eleazar in the person of Zadok (I Kings 2:27).

Another warning was sent to Eli by the mouth of the youthful Samuel. "The word of God was precious in those days; there was no open vision" (I Sam. 3:1); and this made the revelation to Samuel a more decided proof of his call to the office of a prophet. Eli's sight was now failing through old age, and he had laid himself down to sleep in a chamber attached to the tabernacle. Samuel had also lain down in the Holy Place itself, and the sacred lamp lighted at the time of the evening sacrifice was near expiring, when Jehovah called Samuel by name and he answered, "Here am I." He knew not as yet that "still, small voice," and he ran to Eli, thinking that he had called him. This was repeated thrice, but the third time Eli knew that Jehovah had spoken to the child, and he bade him reply to the next call by saying, "Speak,

Lord, for thy servant heareth." Then the word of God came to Samuel, confirming in more terrible terms the sentence already uttered on the house of Eli, and declaring that the iniquity of his house should not be purged with sacrifice forever. In the morning Samuel opened the doors of the tabernacle as usual; and being solemnly adjured by Eli, he told him all that Jehovah had said; and the old man exclaimed, like Job, "It is Jehovah! let Him do what seemeth him good!" (I Sam. 3:1-19). From that day Samuel was a prophet of Jehovah. His fame grew with his growth and none of his words failed. Whatever difficulty we have felt before as to the extent of the influence of the judges disappears entirely now: *"All Israel from Dan even to Beersheba,* knew that Samuel was established to be a prophet of Jehovah," and the words uttered by him at Shiloh came to pass throughout all Israel (I Sam. 3:19-4:1).

3. Encouraged, it would seem, by this reappearance of the prophetic gift, and at the same time, by the blow inflicted on the Philistines in Samson's dying effort, the Israelites went out to battle against their oppressors. The Israelites encamped at the place which afterward became so memorable by the name of Eben-ezer,[1] and the Philistines at Aphek, a place in the Plain of Sharon, about 25 miles west of Shiloh. In the first of the three great battles which signalized this neighborhood, the Israelites were defeated with the loss of 4000 men. The elders of Israel[2] then formed the rash project of fetching the ark of the covenant into the camp, that *it* might save them from their enemies. Thus all their memory of God's mighty deeds of old was summed up in a superstitious hope from the mere symbol of His presence, which they profaned even while they trusted to its help. The ark was brought from Shiloh by Hophni and Phinehas, the sons of Eli, fit ministers of such a sacrilegious act. The shout with which the ark was welcomed appalled the Philistines, who thought the gods of the Hebrews had come into the camp, those mighty gods "that smote the Egyptians with all the plagues in the wilderness."[3] But instead of panic fear, they assumed the courage of despair, while the God they so much feared was only present in the Hebrew camp to punish the presumption of the rulers and the wickedness of the priests. Israel was smitten with a panic rout;

---

1. I Sam. 4:1, 5:1, 7:12. It was between Mizpeh (the *watch-tower*) — one of the eminences a few miles north of Jerusalem — and Shen (the *tooth* or *crag*), the site of which is unknown.
2. I Sam. 4:3. This is an interesting proof that the patriarchal form of government was still in existence. Eli, though judge, seems to have been now a mere cipher and Samuel kept aloof from the whole proceeding. Eli's disapproval of the profanation of the ark is clear from I Sam. 4:13.
3. I Sam. 4:8. Such was the vivid but vague recollection handed down by tradition.

30,000 men were slain and among them Hophni and Phinehas, and the ark of God was taken. The news was carried to Shiloh by a Benjamite, who escaped from the battle, and arrived with his clothes torn and earth upon his head, in sign of the deepest mourning. As Eli sat by the side of the road at the gates of the tabernacle, waiting for tidings and trembling for the ark of God, he heard the cry of grief and terror raised by the whole city. The messenger was brought to Eli, who listened to the fate of the army and his own sons; but when he heard that the ark of God was taken, he fell back from his seat and broke his neck and died, for he was an old man and heavy. He was ninety-eight years old, and had judged Israel forty years. But the troubles of the day were not yet ended. The wife of Phinehas, on hearing the news, was seized with premature labor, and died in giving birth to a son, whom she named with her last breath ICHABOD *(there is no glory)*, for she said, "The glory is departed from Israel," because the ark of God was taken. That one phrase is the best description of the fearful issue of the battle of Eben-ezer (I Sam. 4).

4. The captured ark was carried by the Philistines to Ashdod (the later Azotus), to be laid up as a trophy in the temple of their deity Dagon, a grain god worshipped in Phoenicia and Canaan. But Jehovah, in punishing His people, was still jealous of His own glory. The comfort of His presence was withdrawn from Israel, but its terror, so often felt by them, was transferred to their foes. First, their god was laid prostrate:

"When the captive ark
Maimed his brute image, head and hands lopped off,
In his own temple, on the grunsel edge,
Where he fell flat, and shamed his worshipers."
        (Milton, *Paradise Lost,* Book 1, vss. 462-466)

The memory of his humiliation was perpetuated at Ashdod by the custom of the priests not to tread on the threshold of his temple. Next the men of Ashdod were smitten, many with death, and others by tumors, probably plague boils of bubonic plague.[1] Further we read that their land was ravaged by swarms of mice which doubtless spread the plague. They refused to keep the ark any longer, and by the decision of the lords of the Philistines, it was carried first to Gath and then to Ekron, only to inflict the like plagues and slaughter on those cities (Judges 5).

For seven months the ark was thus carried about through the cities of the Philistines, and at length they resolved to send it back.

1. See Zondervan *Pictorial Bible Dict.,* art. "Diseases," p. 219.

Under the advice of their priests and diviners, whom it is most interesting to find remonstrating with them for hardening their hearts as the Egyptians and Pharoah had done, they sent with it five golden images of mice and five such of the tumors, as a trespass-offering. They made a new cart on which they placed the ark, with a coffer containing the jewels of gold; and to prove the hand of God in its return, they harnessed to the cart two milk cows that had never borne the yoke, and took home their calves. The cows went straight up the road leading from Ekron to Bethshemesh *(House of the Sun,* now *Ain-Shems),* [1] lowing after their calves, but never turning aside; the five lords of the Philistines following after to see the result. As the cart reached the field of Joshua, the Bethshemite, the men of Beth-shemesh paused from their harvest-work, rejoicing at the sight; the Levites took down the ark and coffer, cut up the cart, and used the wood in sacrificing the cows as a burnt-offering. Overcome, however, by curiosity, the men of Beth-shemesh looked into the ark, and Jehovah smote 50,070 of them with death. In their terror they sent to the men of Kirjath-jearim to fetch away the ark, and in that city it remained till David removed it to Jerusalem. Its abode was in the house of Abinadab, a Levite, on the summit of the hill; and his son Eleazar was consecrated as the keeper of the ark (I Sam. 6; 7:1; II Sam. 6; I Chron. 13).

5. For twenty years the people mourned for the absence of the ark from Shiloh, and beneath the oppression of the Philistines, till Samuel summoned them to repentance and exertion. He bade them to put away Baalim and Ashtaroth, and all false gods, and prepare their hearts to serve Jehovah, and he would deliver them from the hand of the Philistines. He gathered all Israel at Mizpeh, that he might pray for them to Jehovah. There they held a solemn fast-day, confessing their sins, and pouring out libations of water and renewing the covenant. After this Samuel judged the people their repentance being thus connected with the redress of wrongs (I Sam. 7:3-6; Comp. Matt. 3:8; Luke 3:8). This assembly was the signal for a new muster of the Philistines, and the frightened Israelites entreated Samuel not to cease to cry to God on their behalf. He was in the very act of offering a burnt-offering and uttering his cries of prayer, when the Philistines drew near in battle array. Then God answered the prayers of Samuel by a violent storm of thunder, which discomfited the Philistines, and

---

1. This "suburb city" of the priests stood on the north-west slopes of the mountains of Judah, on a low plateau at the junction of two fine plains, about two miles from the edge of the great Philistine plain, and seven from Ekron (Josh. 21:16; I Chron. 6:59).

Israel pursued them with great slaughter to Bethcar (the *house of lambs*). This spot, at which the pursuit ceased, seems to have been the place where Samuel set up a stone as a memorial of the victory, between Mizpeh and Shen, and called it EBENEZER (the *stone of help*), saying, "Hitherto hath Jehovah helped us!" (I Sam. 7:7-12).

This third battle of Eben-ezer put an end to the forty years' oppression of the Philistines, who "were subdued, and came no more into the coast of Israel, and the hand of Jehovah was against the Philistines all the days of Samuel." The prophet was now, if not before, constituted the judge of Israel, the last who held that office before the monarchy; for though he is said to have made his sons Joel and Abijah judges, they must be regarded simply as his deputies, like the sons of Jair and of Abdon (Judges 10:4; 12:14; I Sam. 8:1-2; Comp. I Chron. 6:28). Their seat of judgment was at Beersheba, while Samuel himself dwelt at Ramah and made a circuit of the neighboring cities, judging the people of Bethel, Gilgal and Mizpeh, all four places being in the highlands of Benjamin. We have incidental pictures of this part of Samuel's life in the early history of Saul and David. We see the prophet receiving those who desired to inquire of Jehovah, and who came to him with a customary present, presiding at the sacrifices of his own city, and entertaining a select number of the most distinguished elders at the ensuing banquet, or going to hold a special sacrifice, at as Bethlehem, where the awe inspired by his presence bears witness to the authority of the judge. At this time too, we first hear of those *"Companies* (or as our version gives, *Schools) of the Prophets,"* where the young men on whom the Spirit of God had descended were trained, under Samuel's eye, in the art of sacred song, and doubtless in the knowledge of the Scriptures, in which David improved his powers as the great psalmist and of which we learn more under Elijah and Elisha (I Sam. 9,16). (See pp. 454-456.)

We cannot ascertain the exact span of time between the third battle of Ezenezer and the accession of Saul. It would appear, however, that the time was not more than two years. The period of Samuel's judgeship before Saul's accession was brought to an end by the misconduct of Samuel's sons in his old age.

Questions on Section VI — Eli and Samuel

1. Who was Elkanah (I Sam. 1:1, 19-20)?
2. Who were his wives (1:2)?

3. Where did he worship each year (1:3)?
4. Who was the priest? The priest's sons (1:3)?
5. From which son of Aaron was the priest descended?
6. What grieved Hannah (1:5-6)?
7. What request and promise did Hannah make to the Lord (1:11)?
8. Why did the priest think Hannah was drunk (1:13-14)?
9. Who was Hannah's son (1:20)?
10. Where did Hannah take her son? When (1:24)?
11. How did Hannah feel when she gave her child to the Lord (2:1)?
12. What song in the N.T. resembles Hannah's song (Luke 1:46ff)?
13. What work did Samuel do at the house of God (2:11)?
14. What sort of men were Eli's sons (2:12)?
15. What did Hannah bring to Samuel each year (2:19)?
16. What other children did Hannah have (2:21)?
17. Why would not Eli's sons hearken to their father (2:25)?
18. What did the prophet foretell about Eli's house (2:31,34)?
19. Explain the clause, "The word of the Lord was precious in those days" (3:1).
20. When did the Lord call to Samuel (3:2-4)?
21. How many times did the Lord call Samuel (3:8,10)?
22. What message did the Lord tell Samuel (3:12-14)?
23. What office did Samuel hold? Who knew this (3:20)?
24. Where did Israel encamp against the Philistines and where did the Philistines encamp (4:1)?
25. What did the Israelites propose to do after their defeat (4:3)?
26. How did the Philistines react to the presence of the ark (4:7-8)?
27. Tell three results of the second battle at Ebenezer (4:10-11).
28. How old was Eli at his death (4:15)?
29. What was his physical condition (4:15,18)?
30. How did Eli react to the news of the battle (4:18)?
31. What happened to Phinehas' wife (4:19-20)?
32. Who was called Ichabod? What does the name mean (4:21-22)?
33. Where was the ark taken first (5:1)?
34. Who was Dagon (5:2)?
35. What happened to Dagon (5:3-4)?
36. What happened to the people of Ashdod (5:6)?
37. Where was the ark sent next (5:8)?

38. Where was the third place the ark was sent (5:10)?
39. Where did the Philistines decide to send the ark? Why (5:11-12)?
40. How long was the ark in the land of the Philistines (6:1)?
41. What was sent back to Israel with the ark (6:3-4)?
42. By what means was the ark sent back (6:7-9)?
43. How did this show that the Lord had smitten the Philistines (6:9,12)?
44. Where in Israel did the ark return to (6:12)?
45. During what season of the year did the ark return (6:13)?
46. Why did the Lord smite the men of Bethshemesh? How many were smitten (6:19)?
47. Where was the ark then sent (6:21)?
48. How long was the ark at Kiriath-jearim (7:2)?
49. What did Samuel command the Israelites to do (7:3)?
50. Where did Samuel gather all Israel (7:5)?
51. Who attacked as Israel was assembled (7:7)?
52. What caused God to help the Israelites when they were attacked (7:9)?
53. How did God stop the attack (7:10)?
54. What does the name Ebenezer mean? To what was the name given? Why (7:12)?
55. How much deliverance did Samuel give Israel from the Philistines (7:13-14)?
56. What three cities formed Samuel's judicial circuit (7:16)?
57. Where was Samuel's home (7:17)?

Period VIII
The United Kingdom
The Reigns of Saul, David and Solomon (I Samuel 8-I Kings 11; I Chron. 10-II Chron. 9)

Section I
The Rise of King Saul (I Samuel 8-14)

1. End of the Theocracy: the people desire a king.
2. Saul: his character and family. 3. His visit to Samuel, designation, anointing and the signs of God's favor.
4. His election as king by lot, acceptance by the people and inauguration in the kingdom by Samuel. 5. His rescue of Jabesh-gilead from Nahash the Ammonite — Second inauguration of the kingdom at Gilgal and retirement of Samuel. 6. Saul's second year — The "War of Michmash" with the Philistines — The first case of Saul's disobedience and the first sentence of rejection — Jonathan surprises the camp of the Philistines — Their rout and Saul's foolish vow — Jonathan saved by the people — Other enemies subdued — Saul's kingdom fully established — His family, guards, officers and regal state.

1. The Philistine yoke was broken and the attacks of enemies on the other frontiers had ceased. Peace was restored to Israel

under Samuel, the wisest and holiest ruler they had had since Joshua, and it might have seemed that the theocracy was safely re-established.[1] And yet it is not surprising that the people should have thought less of their present security than of their past dangers, and that the season of tranquility was used as an opportunity for obtaining what they deemed a stronger and more permanent government. The offer of the crown to Gideon proves that this desire had long been growing, from envy of the splendor and power of the surrounding monarchies, and from a bitter sense of the disorders of those times when "there was no king in Israel, and every man did what was right in his own eyes." And just as we often see the effect of some inveterate evil reach its climax at the very moment when the cause itself seems to have been subdued, so the settlement of the government by Samuel failed to avert the revolution for which the misconduct of his sons gave the immediate occasion. The elders of Israel came to him at his house at Ramah, and pleading his own great age and the evils growing up again, their sense of which would be the keener for the remembrance of Hophni and Phinehas, they plainly made the request, "Make us a KING, to judge us, *like all the nations*" (I Sam. 8:5).

Their idea of a king may be summed up in the three points of: a *leader* always ready at their head in war, a *judge* provided without interruption by the law of hereditary descent,[2] and a *court* invested with dignity and magnificence. Their reference to the prophet proves that they wished to have the divine sanction to their desire.

It was a trying moment for Samuel, as a man, a father and a prophet of Jehovah: "The thing was evil in the eyes of Samuel." At his age and with his spirit, we cannot suppose him to have been much concerned at the loss of his own power. The slight to his government was excused by the misconduct of his sons; and keenly as we see that he felt the implied rebellion against Jehovah, the case was beyond the reach of mere reproof, and the people would not have been contented with the simple reply of Gideon, "Jehovah shall rule over you." Samuel applied himself to the resource that never failed him; he *prayed* unto Jehovah (I Sam. 8:6). His indignation was at once justified and chastened by the assurance, "They have not rejected *thee*, but they have rejected ME from reigning over them."

---

1. The passage in I Sam. 9:16, however, indicates a state of things in which the Philistines were always threatening to recover the ascendancy.
2. In ancient times and Eastern countries this notion was inseparable from royalty. That it was so understood by the Jews, is clear from the offer of the crown to Gideon (Judg. 8:22).

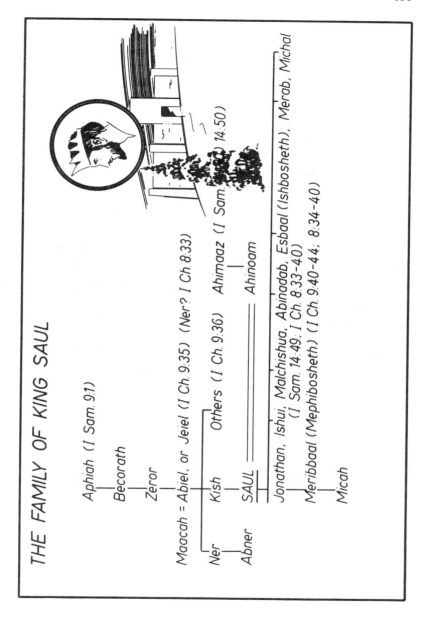

THE FAMILY OF KING SAUL

Aphiah (1 Sam. 9:1)

Becorath

Zeror

Maacah = Abiel, or Jeiel (1 Ch. 9:35) (Ner? 1 Ch. 8:33)

Ner   Kish   Others (1 Ch. 9:36)   Ahimaaz (1 Sam. 14:50)

Abner   SAUL ══════ Ahinoam

Jonathan, Ishui, Malchishua, Abinadab, Esbaal (Ishbosheth), Merab, Michal
(1 Sam. 14:49; 1 Ch. 8:33-40)

Meribbaal (Mephibosheth) (1 Ch. 9:40-44; 8:34-40)

Micah

These words are the key to the whole history of the Hebrew monarchy, but they must not be viewed as entirely words of anger. God pitied the infirmities of His people, even while He punished their self-will by granting their desire. So Samuel is instructed to grant them their request, but not till he had first solemnly warned them of its immediate results, in the oppression which their king would exercise till they should cry out to Jehovah against the master of their own choice (I Sam. 8:7-18). The prophet's description of a self-willed king should be compared with the law laid down by Moses in anticipation of the kingdom (Deut. 17:16-20). The expostulation had no effect and after once more laying before Jehovah their reply, "We *will* have a king over us," and again receiving the command to make them a king, Samuel sent them back to their cities, to await the man selected for them in the providence of God. We must not suppose that that man would be a ferocious tryant, at once beginning to inflict the retribution of their folly. Like their own idea of a monarchy, he covered, under a fair exterior, great possibilities of good and the seeds of still greater evil.

2. SAUL, a name rendered memorable in the annuals of the tribe of Benjamin and of the world, by the king and the apostle Paul, its first and last owners named in Scripture, was the son of Kish, a wealthy and powerful Benjamite, though of a family not conspicuous in the tribe, whose descendants can be traced to the time of Ezra (I Sam. 9:1,21; I Chron. 9:39-44). Saul is described as "a choice young man, and a goodly: there was not among the children of Israel a goodlier person than he;[1] from his shoulders and upward, he was taller than any of the people."[2] To this physical excellence, characteristic of his tribe, he added no small share of its ungovernable temper, which opposition and disappointment aggravated to madness, the common fate of despots. He was the creature of impulse; often kindly, as in his love for David and Jonathan, often noble, as in his patriotic zeal for God, but always wanting the control of steady principle.

His birthplace is uncertain. Zelah was the place of his father's sepulchre (II Sam. 21:14), but his royal residence was at Gibeah, thence called "Gibeah of Saul"; and this town seems to have been the abode of at least a part of the family. His age at the time of his election is not stated; but we can hardly suppose so great a dignity, involving the chief command in war and the judgeship, to have

---

1. Comp. II Sam. 1:19, where he is called "the gazelle of Israel."
2. I Sam. 9:2; comp. II Sam. 1:23, where he and Jonathan are described as "swifter than eagles and stronger than lions."

been conferred to a man under forty; and this agrees with what we know of the ages of his sons. Jonathan, his eldest son, appears as a warrior the year after Saul's accession, and Ish-bosheth, his younger son, was forty years old at his father's death (II Sam. 2:8).

According to the apostle Paul, Saul reigned forty years (Acts 13:21). His reign extended from 1050 to 1010 B.C.

3. Saul was led to Samuel to be anointed to his future office by what, to the eyes of men, might have seemed an accident (I Sam. 9:1-4). His father Kish, having lost his asses, sent Saul with a servant in search of them. They passed through Mount Ephraim and by Shalisha and Shalim, till they came on the third day to the neighborhood of Samuel's abode, here called the land of Zuph.[1] Saul now proposed to return, lest his father's care for the asses should pass into anxiety for him and the servant — a mark of his affectionate disposition. The servant, however, told him that in the city which they were approaching there dwelt a man of God who was held in the highest honor, and all whose words came to pass; perhaps he might direct them where to find the asses. Saul's difficulty about the gift which it was usual to offer when consulting a *seer* (for such was the name of a *prophet* in those days) was removed by the servant, who had with him the fourth part of a shekel of silver. As they ascended the hill on which the city stood, they learned from the maidens who had come out to draw water that the seer had just returned from one of his judicial circuits, and was expected to bless the sacrifice and festival which the people were holding on that day in the high place above the city; and just as they entered the city, they met Samuel coming forth for that purpose. Samuel was prepared for the interview. God had forewarned him the day before that he would send to him on the morrow a Benjamite, whom he should anoint to be captain over Israel, to deliver them out of the hand of the Philistines; and now as Saul approached, the word of Jehovah came to Samuel: "Behold the man whom I spake to thee of! this same shall reign over my people." Samuel made himself known to Saul and having told him that his father's asses were found, he astonished him by the salutation, "On whom is all the desire of Israel? Is it not on thee, and on all thy father's house?" Waiting as the people were for their destined king, Saul could not but suppose what Samuel meant; and he pleaded that his family was the least in Benjamin, itself the smallest tribe in Israel. Postponing

---

1. Some connect this name with the appellation of Samuel's city, *Ramathaim-Zophim*. It perhaps indicates that the whole region was a range of beacon-heights.

further explanation, Samuel led Saul and his servant into the banqueting-chamber on the high place, and seated them above all the thirty guests who were assembled, persons whose limited number proves their consequence in the city. Samuel then ordered the cook to place before Saul the portion which he had told him to reserve for an expected guest, namely, a boiled *shoulder,* at once the choicest part of the sacrifice, and the emblem of the weight of government which he was to sustain.[1] After the banquet they went down from the high place to the city, and Samuel lodged Saul on the top of his house, a favorite sleeping-place in the East.

At daybreak the prophet aroused his guest and led him out of the city; and then the servant having been sent on before them, Samuel bade Saul stand still to hear the word of Jehovah. Thereupon producing a vial of oil, he poured it on his head, adding the kiss of homage, and telling him that Jehovah had anointed him to be captain over His inheritance. The prophet named three incidents which would happen to Saul on his return, as signs that Jehovah was with him; the first, an assurance of the safety of his father's cattle, as the prophet had said; the second, a present which was to be an earnest of the future offerings of the people; the third, the descent of the spirit of Jehovah upon him, causing him to prophesy, and turning him into another man. The promised change began at the moment that Saul turned to leave Samuel: he felt that God had given him another heart, and the appointed signs were fulfilled in their order. The only remaining care of his past life was relieved by two men who met him by Rachel's sepulchre at Zelzah, and told him that the asses were found and that his father was anxious about him. At the oak of Tabor he met three men, who presented to him two loaves of bread out of the offerings which they were carrying up to God at Bethel. And in fine, when he reached "the hill of God" (probably Gibeah), which was occupied by a garrison of the Philistines, a company of prophets came down from the high place with the instruments of music which they were taught to use in the service of God; and as they began to prophesy, the spirit of God fell upon Saul and he prophesied among them. This sign of his inspiration was the more decisive, as he seems to have been a man unlikely to exhibit religious fervor. Those who had known him before expressed their amazement by the question, which passed into a proverb, "Is Saul also among the prophets?" and there were some

1. Comp. Lev. 7:32; Ezek. 24:; Is. 9:6.

The Beginning of Saul's Reign
I Samuel 9:1-12:25

1. Gibeah
—Saul sent to seek asses;
9:1-3

2. Ephraim, and lands of
Shalishah and Shaalim;
—seeking asses; 9:4

3. Land of Zuph
—Meeting with Samuel,
and anointing of Saul;
9:5-8

4. Between Zuph and Gibeah
—Saul meets three groups
of men, fulfilling Samuel's
prophecies; 10:9-13.

5. Gibeah
—Saul is questioned by his
uncle; 10:14-16

6. Mizpah
—Saul publicly proclaimed
king; 10:17-27

7. Jabesh-Gilead
—Attack by Nahash the
Ammonite; 11:1-5

8. Gibeah
—Saul gathers army;
11:6-10

9. Jabesh-Gilead
—Saul defeats Ammon;
11:11-13

10. Gilgal
—Samuel's address to
Israel; 11:14-12:25

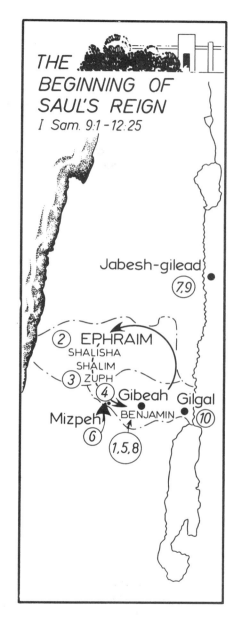

THE BEGINNING OF SAUL'S REIGN
I Sam. 9:1-12:25

who went so far as to question the source of such inspiration by suggesting, "But who is their father?"[1] Saul then went up to the high place, apparently the hill of Gibeah, to the residence of his uncle (or his grandfather), Ner, in reply to whose curious inquiries he told what Samuel had said about the asses, but said nothing about the matter of the kingdom. After this private designation to his office, he returned to his home (I Sam. 9; 10:1-16).

4. The time soon came for his public manifestation to Israel. Samuel convened the people at Mizpeh; and after once more reproving them for rejecting God and resolving to have a king, he called on them to present themselves before God by their tribes and their thousands. Then whether by lot or by the Urim and Thummim, or by any other mode of expressing the choice of God, the tribe of Benjamin was taken.[2] The tribe was brought by its families and the family of Matri was taken; and lastly, out of that family, the choice fell on SAUL, the son of Kish, but he was nowhere to be found. Again they consulted the oracle, which revealed his hiding-place; and he was found concealed among the baggage of the camp — so little eager was he to thrust himself into the office to which he knew his call. He was brought into the midst of the congregation and there he towered above all the people from his shoulders upward. His impressive appearance won universal favor; and when Samuel presented him as the king whom Jehovah had chosen, the like of whom was not to be found among all the people, they shouted with one voice *"God save the king."*[3] From this whole scene it is clear that what is said of the choice of God is not to be understood as an absolute preference for Saul as being the man best fitted for the king of Israel, but as the selection of one possessing the endowments which would recommend him to the people as the king that they desired. He is commended to the people for the goodliness of his outward form; and in the very same matter of the choice of a king, the same prophet was afterward instructed by God to "look not on his countenance or *the height of his stature:* . . . for man looketh on the outward appearance, but Jehovah looketh on the heart" (I Sam. 16:7). Throughout the whole transaction, God was giving the people their own desire and the history of Saul is the working out of the experiment.

---

1. Comp. Matt. 12:24-27.
2. It is most important to distinguish this choice from an election by the people.
3. Literally, "Let the king live!" but the case is one of those in which the popular pnrase has passed beyond the power of alteration.

In another sense, however, he was the king of Jehovah's choice. The whole circumstances of his selection and his anointing by the prophet, invested him with authority which bound the people to be subject to him as an ordinance of God. But he was also himself subject to a law. That law had been given through Moses, in anticipation of this day (Deut. 17:14ff), and now Samuel wrote it in a book and laid it up before Jehovah in the sanctuary, after he had rehearsed it to the people, whom he then dismissed to their homes. Saul retired at the same time to his home at Gibeah with no other retinue than a band of volunteers whose hearts God had touched. Some murmurs of contempt were heard against him at Gibeah, where his prophetic gifts had already been derided; but he held his peace, waiting for an opportunity to prove himself worthy of the crown by his services to his people (I Sam. 10:17-27).

5. That opportunity soon arrived. During the later years of Samuel the enemies of Israel had gained strength and this was one chief reason of the desire for a king (Comp. I Sam. 12:12). We have seen the Philistines in possession of the citadel that had subdued. Nahash the Ammonite marched against Jabesh-gilead, and would only listen to the offer of a capitulation on the cruel and shameful terms of putting out the right eyes of all the people and laying it as a disgrace on Israel. The men of Jabesh obtained a delay of seven days and sent messengers to all parts of Israel praying for someone to come and save them. Observe that the request for help was not addressed to Saul. Obviously he was not yet known or recognized as king in outlying areas such as Jabesh-gilead.

Saul was returning with his cattle from the field when he heard the cry of the people at the tidings. Then as we read of the other champions of Israel, the Spirit of Jehovah came upon him and he summoned Israel to the field by a token as powerful as the "fiery cross" of the Gailic chiefs. Cutting a yoke of oxen into small pieces, he sent them throughout all Israel, declaring that so it shall be done to the oxen of him who came not out after Saul and Samuel.[1] When the forces were numbered in Bezek, there were 300,000 warriors of Israel and 30,000 of Judah. On the sixth day of the truce, the men of Jabesh received Saul's promise of help before tomorrow's noon, and they sent word to Saul that they would place themselves in his hands. In the morning watch, Saul,

---

[1]. This association of Samuel with himself should be particularly observed; as should also the separate enumeration of Judah, which seems to indicate that there was already a lack of unity between the other tribes and Judah.

with his army in three divisions, fell upon the unsuspecting Ammonites and slaughtered them till the heat of the day put an end to the pursuit. His triumph was adorned by an act of regal clemency. The people called on Samuel to put to death the men who had despised the new-made king, but Saul declared that not a man should be put to death on that day in which Jehovah had saved Israel (I Sam. 11:12-13).

Having thus given proof of his merit, Saul was again solemnly inaugurated into his kingdom. For this purpose Samuel called the assembled hosts to follow him to Gilgal and there they held a high festival with sacrifices to Jehovah. But their joy was not unmingled. The time was come for Samuel to lay down his judicial office and the hoary prophet, protesting his own integrity in the sight of those before whom he had walked from his childhood to that day, and whose voice now bore witness to his words, reasons with them of all that God had done for them from the time that Jacob went down to Egypt till that hour. He recalls their deliverance from Egypt, from Sisera, from the Philistines, and from the King of Moab; their idolatries and their repentances, and the missions of Jerubbaal and Bedan,[1] and Jephthah and Samuel; and yet, he adds, when Nahash came against them, they must needs have a king, though Jehovah their God was their king. Now then they had their king, set over them by Jehovah, and it rested with them whether his kingdom should be established. If they would fear Jehovah and serve Him and keep His law, both king and people should continue to be His; but if they were rebellious, His hand would be against them, as it had been against their fathers. Then pointing to the sky, which had been brilliant with the unchanging clearness of an eastern June (for it was the season of the wheat-harvest), he prayed to God, who sent the portent of a thunder-storm to confirm his words. Such a storm in Palestine at that season of year is almost unheard-of. The terrified people confessed their latest sin and besought Samuel to pray for them that they might not die. He comforted them with the promise of the future, warning them not to let the sense of past guilt lead them into further sin and protested that he would never cease to pray for them and to teach them the good and right way.

With these words of comfort, Samuel closed his public life as the sole judge of Israel. But his office did not entirely cease, for as

---

1. *Bedan* appears to be a form of the name Barak. It is possible that Bedan was a judge whose name is not preserved in the book of Judges. Possibly also it may be a variant form of Abdon.

we have seen, "he judged Israel all the days of his life." In his subsequent relations to Saul, there is clearly more than the sort of authority which the later prophets never ceased to exercise as special messengers of Jehovah to reprove the sins of the king and direct him on great occasions. Samuel's is a power constantly present to check the waywardness of Saul and at last announcing God's rejection of Saul and designating his successor.

6. The preceding events occupied the first year of Saul's reign (I Sam. 13:1). In the second, he set to work systematically to deliver Israel from their enemies. He gathered a chosen band of 3000 men, two-thirds being with him in the camp at Michmash and the hills of Bethel,[1] and the other 1000 at Gibeah, with his son JONATHAN, whose name now first appears in the history. Jonathan's successful attack on the Philistine garrison in the hill of Geba opposite Michmash was the signal for Saul's summoning the Israelites to the war. His trumpet sounded throughout all the land, and his camp was fixed at Gilgal, the scene of his inauguration and the old camp of Joshua. The Philistines answered the challenge with an immense army, comprising 30,000 chariots and 6000 horsemen, besides infantry without number and encamped at Michmash, on the highlands which Saul had abandoned. The Israelites fled to woods and caves and the fastnesses of the rocks, while even the warriors trembled as they followed Saul. The king waited impatiently at Gilgal for the seven days within which Samuel had promised to come and offer sacrifice, while his forces were rapidly dispersing (Comp. I Sam. 10:8). On the seventh day he ventured to begin the sacrifices himself, and he had just ended the burnt-offering when Samuel arrived and asked him what he had done. Saul pleaded the danger of the Philistines coming down the pass to attack him at Gilgal, but Samuel declared that he had acted with sinful folly and uttered the first intimation thus early in his reign of what he had already threatened in case of disobedience (Comp. I Sam. 12:25), that his kingdom should not be lasting, for Jehovah had already sought out "a man after his own heart, to be captain over his people." After this threat, which seems to have been uttered privately to Saul, Samuel went away to Gibeah and Saul followed with his little band of only 600 men and encamped on the south side of the ravine, on the north of which lay the Philistines. He was

---

1. Michmash is a village about seven miles north of Jerusalem, on the northern edge of a ravine which forms the chief pass between the highlands of Benjamin and the valley of the Jordan about Jericho and Gilgal. Bethel is about four miles west of Michmash, and the intervening hills seem to form the "Mount Bethel" of the text. On the south side of the ravine was Geba, with its Philistine garrison, the furthest post which they held toward the east. Geba and Gibeah were very near each other and it is difficult to distinguish them clearly.

joined at Gibeah by the high-priest Ahijah, the son of Ahitub, son of Phinehas, son of Eli, and it would seem that the ark was brought up for the time from its house at Kirjath-jearim (I Sam. 13:1-16; 14:2,3,18). Meanwhile the Philistines overran the country from their headquarters at Michmash, whence three bands of spoilers issued forth. No smith was suffered to work in Israel, but the people went to the camps of the Philistines to sharpen their tools; Saul and Jonathan alone had swords and spears (I Sam. 13:17-23).

An unhoped-for deliverance was effected by God's blessing on the courage of Jonathan. Familiar as he must have become during the encampment at Michmash with the ravine at its foot, he planned a surprise of the Philistine camp without the knowledge of his father or the high-priest, but trusting in Jehovah, with whom said he, "there is no restraint to save by many or by few" (I Sam. 14:6). With one faithful comrade, his armor-bearer, who fully shared his spirit, he climbed up the opposite side of the ravine between two sharp crags, named Bozez and Seneh. They had resolved to show themselves to the Philistines, and to draw an omen from the words with which they might be received; and accordingly when the Philistines, who took them for two Hebrews wandering out of their hiding-places, said to them, "Come up, and we will show you something," Jonathan concluded that Jehovah had delivered them into the hands of Israel. Climbing with hands and feet up the face of the precipice, which was supposed to make the camp impregnable, Jonathan fell upon the enemy, his armor-bearer slaying after him. They killed at this first onset about twenty men and the rest were seized by a panic which was increased by an earthquake, so that they went on striking down each other. The Hebrews who frequented the camp of the Philistines now turned against them and others came out of the caves with which those rocks abound to join in the slaughter. The scene was witnessed with amazement by the watchmen in Saul's camp at Gibeah; and on counting the people, it was discovered that Jonathan and his armor-bearer had left the camp. Saul bade the high-priest to bring the ark that he might consult Jehovah, but as the noise in the Philistine camp increased, he rushed to the pursuit, driving the foe down the pass of Bethaven as far as Aijalon, the very ground over which Joshua had pursued the Canaanites in his most memorable victory. The pursuit was, however, hindered by the exhaustion of the people, consequent on Saul's rash vow devoting to a curse the man who

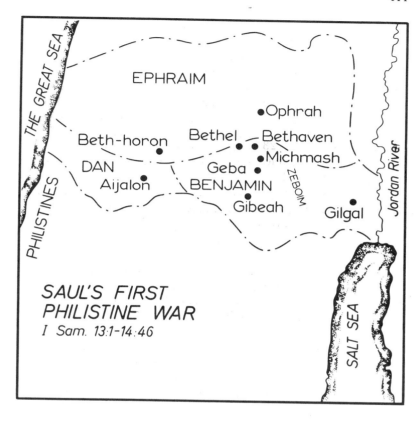

SAUL'S FIRST
PHILISTINE WAR
I Sam. 13:1-14:46

Saul's First Philistine War
I Sam. 13:1-14:36

1. Saul gathers 2000 men at Michmash, and Jonathan 1000 at Gibeah (13:1-2).
2. Jonathan smites Geba (13:3).
3. Saul goes to Gilgal and makes a foolish sacrifice (13:4-14).
4. Saul goes to Geba with 600 (13:15-16).
5. Philistines camp at Michmash and send out raiders toward Beth-horon, Ophrah and Valley of Zeboim (13:17-23).
6. Jonathan and armorbearer climb the pass between Geba and Michmash and smite Philistines (13:24-14:15).
7. Saul's troops join in and smite Philistines from Michmash to Aijalon (14:16-23:31).
8. Jonathan is saved from Saul's curse about eating (14:24-30, 32-46).

should taste food till sunset. They were passing through one of those woods where the wild bees build their combs in the branches in such numbers that the honey drops from the trees, and no man dared even to carry his hand to his mouth for fear of Saul's oath, when Jonathan, who had now rejoined the army, dipped the end of his staff in a honey-comb and put it to his mouth. His sense of new life caused him to inveigh bitterly against his fathers' vow, of which he was now informed for the first time. When evening came, the famished people flew upon the spoil and began to eat the cattle with the blood. Saul reproved their sin and building an altar, the first that he built to Jehovah, he bade the people bring each his ox or sheep and slay it there. He then prepared to continue the pursuit by night; but the high-priest reminded him that all this time they had not asked counsel of God. Saul now inquired if he should pursue the Philistines, but the oracle was silent. He set himself to find the hidden sin, swearing by the life of Jehovah that the man should die, were it Jonathan his own son. As no one answered, he cast lots, with prayer to God, between the people on one side and himself and Jonathan on the other, and Saul and Jonathan were taken. A second lot fell on Jonathan and Saul would have kept his oath, but the people interposed to save their champion's life. So Saul returned from the pursuit of the Philistines.[1]

The "War of Michmash," as the above campaign is called, was followed by a series of victories over all the other enemies of Israel: Moab, Ammon, Edom, the kings of Zobah, the Philistines again, and the Amalekites, of whom more will presently be said. This is the brightest period of the life of Saul, who now assumed his fully royal state: he "took the kingdom" (I Sam. 14:48-49). His own family made a goodly show. Besides Jonathan, his court was graced by two sons, Ishui and Melchishua, and two daughters, Merab and Michal, the children of his wife Ahinoam, daughter of his father's sister Ahimaaz.[2] His standing army of 3000 men was commanded by his cousin, ABNER, the son of Ner, one of the noblest men and greatest warriors in the history of Israel;[3] and he had a body-guard of Benjamites, chosen for their beauty and stature, as runners and messengers, of whom David afterward became the chief.[4] These two commanders sat at the king's table (I Sam. 20:25) with Jonathan, whose seat was opposite his

1. I Sam. 14:1-46. There are many points of likeness between Jephthah's vow and Saul's.
2. He had other children by his second wife Rizpah, who was also his cousin.
3. I Sam. 13:2, 14:50, 24:2; Comp. I Chr. 12:29.
4. I Sam. 16:15,17; 22:7,14,7; 26:22; Joseph. *Ant.* 6:6, 6; 7:14.

father's. In recruiting these guards, the king acted in the arbitrary manner which Samuel had predicted; "when he saw any strong man or any valiant man, he took him to himself" (I Sam. 14:52; Comp. 8:11). The herds of cattle which formed the chief part of the royal wealth, and the servants who had the charge of them, were under a chief officer, who had constant access to the king's presence. Saul gave this office to an Edomite, named Doeg, who became infamous as the slayer of the priests (I Sam. 21:7; 22:9-19). Even the high-priest, as we have seen, attended the commands of the king, both in the camp and court, with the sacred ephod, as a means of consulting the divine will; and Saul assumed the power of giving him orders at all times through his messengers.[1] The theocracy had sunk far from that state in which the people used to stand before the tabernacle to receive the sole behests of Jehovah their king through the prophet and the priest!

Whether sitting at table with these officers, whose attendance was especially required on the new moon and other festive days, or whether he appeared in public, surrounded by his body-guard, the king was distinguished by a tall spear, suited to his stature, which was placed beside his chair when he rested, and by his pillow when he slept and which he wielded with terrible effect in battle, where the mightiest weapons of Israel were the spear of Saul and the bow of Jonathan.[2] He wore over his armor a royal diadem and a golden armlet (II Sam. 1:10). He loved to hear the acclamations of the people, and the song with which the women greeted him as they came out of the cities of Israel to welcome his return from battle and to receive robes of scarlet and ornaments of gold from the spoil (I Sam. 18:6; II Sam. 1:24).

Questions on Section I — The Rise of Saul

I Samuel 8

1. Whom did Samuel make judges over Israel? Give their names.
2. What special request did the people of Israel make to Samuel? Why did they ask for this?
3. How did Samuel react to their request?
4. Whom did God say that the people had rejected?
5. Did God tell Samuel to grant the people's request?
6. What warning was to be given to the people?
7. Did the people change their request after the warning?

---

1. I Sam. 21:2. The practice may be inferred from David's pretense of such a commission.
2. I Sam. 18:10; 19:9; 22:33; 26:11; II Sam. 1:6.

I Samuel 9
1. Who was Kish?
2. How tall was Saul?
3. On what mission was Saul sent by his father?
4. Why did Saul want to return home after being unsuccessful in his search?
5. What was a *seer*? Who was the serr?
6. Why did Saul and his servant desire to go to the seer?
7. Who told Saul where he could find the seer?
8. What information had the Lord revealed to the seer?
9. From what enemy was the new king (prince) to save Israel?
10. Where did Saul sit while eating with the seer and what was given to him to eat?
11. Where did Saul and the seer commune (or converse) after coming down from the high place?
12. Why did Samuel ask Saul to stand still?

I Samuel 10
1. What was done to Saul when he was anointed?
2. What three groups of men was Saul to meet after leaving Samuel?
3. Where was Saul to tarry till Samuel came?
4. What proverbial saying arose after Saul prophesied?
5. What did Saul tell his uncle Ner and what did he not tell him?
6. Where did Samuel gather the people together?
7. From what tribe was Saul?
8. How was the new king selected and pointed out before the people?
9. Who said that Saul was hidden among the baggage?
10. How did the people react to the new king?
11. Was everyone satisfied with the new king?

I Samuel 11
1. Who was Nahash?
2. What city did Nahash attack and what was his condition for the people's surrender?
3. Where did the city send messengers seeking help?
4. What came upon Saul when he heard of the city's plight?
5. Describe Saul's draft call to all Israel.
6. How did Saul divide his troops when he attacked?
7. What words of kindness did Saul utter after the battle?
8. Where did Samuel call the people together?
9. For what purpose did he call the people together?

I Samuel 12
  1. To whom did Samuel speak?
  2. Was Samuel then young or old?
  3. Why did Samuel challenge the people to accuse him of wrongdoing?
  4. According to Samuel's speech had Israel always remembered God?
  5. Which judges does Samuel mention? Who is Bedan?
  6. What would happen to Israel and its king if they feared and served the Lord? What would happen if they didn't?
  7. What miraculous occurrence did Samuel cause to happen?
  8. What did Samuel say he would continue to do for Israel?
  9. What would be their punishment if Israel continued doing wickedly?

I Samuel 13
True or False? Correct all false statements.
  1. Saul chose an army of men when he had reigned two years.
  2. 2000 men were with Saul in Gibeah.
  3. Jonathan smote the Philistine garrison at Geba.
  4. The people gathered together after Saul in Gibeah.
  5. The Philistines encamped in Michmash after Saul left.
  6. The people of Israel stood up bravely against the Philistines.
  7. Saul waited seven days in Gilgal for Samuel.
  8. Saul had the priest to offer a burnt offering and peace offerings.
  9. Saul went out to meet Samuel and salute him.
 10. Samuel said that Saul had done foolishly and now his kingdom would not continue.
 11. Saul had 600 men with him in Gilgal.
 12. Saul and Jonathan came and abode in Geba.
 13. Philistine spoilers came out of Michmash in five companies.
 14. Israel had many iron workers to make weapons.
 15. The Philistines sharpened the Israelites' tools.

I Samuel 14
  1. Who was Jonathan?
  2. Where did Jonathan and his armor-bearer go?
  3. What priest was with Saul?
  4. Where were the rocky crags between which Jonathan and his armor-bearer passed?
  5. What did Jonathan call the Philistines?
  6. What gave Jonathan courage to attack the Philistines?

7. What did Jonathan say would be a signal for them to attack the Philistines?
8. How did Jonathan get up to the Philistines?
9. How many Philistines did they kill?
10. What caused a great trembling?
11. Who from a distance saw the Philistine multitude melting away?
12. Where was the ark of God? What did Saul want with the ark?
13. What did the fearful Israelites who had been hiding do when they saw Israel was winning?
14. What curse did Saul pronounce to the people?
15. Who violated the curse? How?
16. Why did the people fly (or pounce) on the spoil and eat meat with the blood?
17. Why could not Saul get an answer when he sought counsel from God about pursuing the Philistines?
18. What was Saul about to do with Jonathan?
19. Who rescued Jonathan?
20. What five foreign enemies did Saul fight?
21. Who were Merab, Michal, Abner, Ner and Kish?

King Saul's Philistine Wars
Saul's Philistine wars brought him no glory.

1. First war (at Michmash) — Jonathan was the hero.
2. Second war (at the vale of Elah) — David was the hero.
3. Third war (at Mt. Gilboa) — Saul killed himself.

Section II
Decline of Saul and Rise of David
(I Samuel 15-II Samuel 1)

1. Second period of Saul's reign — His mission against Amalek, disobedience and final rejection — Samuel's last parting with Saul and mourning for him. 2. Samuel sent to Bethlehem to anoint David the son of Jesse as the first true King of Israel — His lineage, character and early life — Sources of information. 3. The war of

1. During the period of Saul's rise the outward appearance of his reign was impressive and vigorous. But beneath it all was the remembrance of the doom pronounced by Samuel at Gilgal, and rendered irrevocable by Saul's conduct during the second stage of his career. (He seems like one impelled by the intoxication of power to brave the very fear that haunted him, and an act of open disobedience to God determined his fate.)

Amid his career of victory over the surrounding heathen, which tended to the twofold object of giving Israel the promised bounds of their possession and of punishing those nations for their past sins, Saul received a special commission to execute the vengeance long since denounced on Amalek for their treacherous attack on Israel in the wilderness of Sinai.[1] The command was given by the mouth of Samuel, and enforced by an appeal to Saul's allegiance to Jehovah's word by the prophet who had anointed him. He was commanded to destroy Amalek utterly, man and woman, infant and suckling, ox and sheep, camel and ass. He mustered the forces of Israel, 200,000 infantry, besides 10,000 of Judah, at Telaim, on the edge of the southern desert, near the border of Edom. Having first warned the old allies of Moses, the Kenites, to depart from among the

---

1. I Sam. 15:1-3. Compare Ex. 17:8; Num. 24:20; Deut. 25:17-19.

Amalekites,[1] he fell upon the tents of the tribe, and pursued them with great slaughter from Havilah to Shur, on the frontier of Egypt.[2] Agag, their king of sheikh, was taken prisoner; but all the rest of the people were put to death, clearly showing that Saul was not moved to disobedience by any feelings of humanity. There can be no doubt that Agag was spared to add splendor to Saul's triumphant return, as a king making war for himself rather than as the servant of Jehovah. The spoil was dealt with in like manner; and here the people shared the sin, sparing all the best of the cattle and all that was valuable, and destroying all that was vile and refuse. It was doubtless true in part, as Saul afterward declared, that he would have offered some of the cattle in sacrifice to God; but the chief motive in sparing them was clearly to enrich his followers with the spoil. Instead of pursuing the campaign and finishing the destruction of the fugitives, he returned by way of Carmel[3] to the old camp of Gilgal.

Meanwhile Samuel had been commanded to meet him at the place for the second time. The word of Jehovah had declared to the prophet that mysterious change in the divine purpose which is so often expressed by one striking word: "It *repenteth* me, that I have set up Saul to be king." The old man's affection for Saul overflowed in tears and cries of prayer all the night, but in the morning he rose up to fulfill his hard commission. No interview recorded in history has a deeper moral significance. Elated with his victory, and resolved to brave out the voice of conscience, Saul meets Samuel with affected pleasure and anticipates inquiry by claiming the praise of a duty well discharged: "Blessed be thou of Jehovah! I have performed the commandment of Jehovah!" "What meaneth, then," rejoined Samuel, "this bleating of sheep, and this lowing of oxen?" Descending one more step in prevarication and trying to evade the responsibility of the act, Saul replied that the people had reserved these for sacrifice, while they had destroyed the rest; but Samuel cuts short his excuses by bidding him hear the word of Jehovah. Before pronouncing the fatal sentence, he reminds him of his low estate before God exalted him, and asks why he had disobeyed the command of God. Saul repeats the same excuse, with another attempt to throw the responsibility on the people, and a word thrown in to propitiate the prophet, "to sacrifice unto Jehovah, *thy God,* in Gilgal." Then Samuel proclaims that eternal principle of *moral*

---

1. Comp. Num. 24:21; Judg. 1:16; 4:11.
2. I Sam. 15:4-7.
3. A place in the extreme south of Judah, which, of course, must not be confounded with Mount Carmel in the north.

duty in condemnation of every attempt to propitiate God, and yet to retain our sin and have our own way: "Hath Jehovah as great delight in burnt-offerings and sacrifices, as in obeying the voice of Jehovah! BEHOLD, TO OBEY IS BETTER THAN SACRIFICE, and to hearken than the fat of rams. For rebellion is as the sin of witchcraft,[1] and stubbornness is an iniquity and idolatry. *Because thou hast rejected the word of Jehovah, He hath also rejected thee from being king.*" Overwhelmed with remorse, Saul confesses his fault though still pleading that he had done it for fear of the people, and prayed Samuel to pardon his sin, and to turn back and join him in worshiping Jehovah. Samuel refused and reiterated the sentence. As he turned to depart, Saul caught at his prophet's mantle, but only to receive a new sign of his fate. The mantle was rent, and Samuel said that even so had Jehovah rent the kingdom of Israel from Saul, and given it to a neighbor of his, who was better than himself. He confirmed the sentence by a solemn observation: "THE STRENGTH OF ISRAEL will not lie nor repent, for He is not a man that he should repent!" It is beyond the power of human judgment to decide what might have been the result, even at this last moment, if Saul had betaken himself to public humiliation and importunate prayer; but his only prayer was to be saved from public humiliation. He entreated Samuel to honor him before the people by turning again to join in the sacrifices. Samuel consented but he used the opportunity to inflict the sentence of death on Agag. He sent for the King of Amalek, who approached with every mark of outward deference, believing that "the bitterness of death was past." The pity we are tempted to feel for him is silenced by Samuel's declaration of the justice of his doom: "As thy sword hath made women childless, so shall thy mother be childless among women." And Samuel hewed Agag in pieces before the Lord in Gilgal.

This was Samuel's last interview with Saul, for whom he still retained that affection which is a strong tribute to the better features of Saul's character. While Saul went to his royal residence at Gibeah, Samuel returned to his house at Ramah, where he mourned for Saul with a prolonged bitterness which at last incurred the reproof of God, who had new work for him to perform in the designation of Saul's successor. Meanwhile Jehovah's repentance at having made Saul king is emphatically repeated (I Sam. 15; 16:1).

---

1. A sin against which Saul was most zealous (I Sam. 28:3).

> **Saul's Punishments**
>
> 1. For offering sacrifice — His kingdom would not
>   continue, that is, his family or dynasty would not
>   continue to rule Israel.
> 2. For not destroying the Amalekites completely —
>   Saul was personally rejected by God as king.
> 3. For seeking the witch — Killed (I Ch. 10:13).

2. Samuel was recalled from the indulgence of his grief by a command to fill a horn with the consecrated oil and to go to Bethlehem, where God had chosen a king among the sons of JESSE, the grandson of Boaz and Ruth (I Sam. 16).

To remove his fear of Saul's anger, the prophet is directed to take with him a heifer and to invite Jesse to a sacrifice. His arrival caused much alarm, but he assured the elders that he came in peace and bade them and the house of Jesse to sanctify themselves for the sacrifice. There the family of Jesse made a goodly show. To his distinction as the chief man of the city, he added that of an age remarkable in those degenerate days, and he was surrounded by all his eight sons, except the youngest, who seems to have been of small consideration in the family and accordingly was sent abroad to tend the sheep. Struck with the noble figure of the eldest son, Eliab, the very counterpart of Saul, Samuel said to himself, "Surely the anointed of Jehovah is before me": but he was warned not to judge a second time by so false a standard. Jehovah said to him, "Look not on his countenance, or on the *height of his stature,* because I have refused him; for it is not as man seeth; for man looketh on the outward appearance, but *Jehovah looketh on the heart.*" In like manner the prophet rejected Abinadab, the second, Shammah, the third, and all the rest of the seven. Samuel asked Jesse, "Are all thy children here?" No, there still remained the youngest, who was with the sheep. "Send and fetch him" said the prophet, "for we will not sit down till he come." Soon there entered a fair youth, with reddish or auburn hair and keen bright eyes,[1] his beautiful countenance flushed with his healthy occupation, and his whole aspect pleasant to behold. Then Jehovah said to Samuel, "Up and anoint him: for this is he!" In the presence of his brethren Samuel poured the horn of sacred oil upon his head, and then returned to his house

---

1. I Sam. 16:12 in the Hebrew.

at Ramah, having performed his last public act. From that day forth the Spirit of Jehovah came on DAVID *("the beloved"),* for such was the name of Jesse's youngest son, the new "root" of the princely tribe of Judah, the first true King of Israel, and the greatest, since Abraham, of the progenitors of the CHRIST, who is often called "the son of David."

This is all that we are distinctly told of David's early life in Scripture, the simple records of which must not be contaminated with the oriental legends, nor even illustrated, without the greatest caution, from the Jewish traditions which are recorded by Josephus. It may be well here to notice the true authorities for the life of David.

a. Each of the three prophets with whom David lived in the closest intimacy, Samuel, Gad and Nathan, wrote a memoir of that part of his life which came respectively under their notice (I Chron. 29:29). We may be quite sure that Samuel, from the time of his mission to Bethlehem, would watch David's career with the deepest interest, and that he would record all that he could learn of him and his ancestry in the history of his own times, which we cannot doubt to have been the occupation of his last years at Ramah, "the *Book of the Prophet Samuel."* The close relation maintained between David and the prophet is shown by the former taking refuge with the latter when he fled from the court of Saul. Gad joined him in his wanderings and lived at his court, and Nathan was the faithful mentor of his later years. Though these books have not come down to us in their original form, we cannot doubt that we have their substance and generally their actual contents in the *First and Second Books of Samuel,* with I Kings 1,2.

b. Another contemporary authority was the *"Chronicles (or State Papers) of King David,"* a record which David undertook with his characteristic love of truth and order (I Chron. 27:24). That the substance of this work is preserved in the *"First Book of Chronicles"* is clear from its very form. Beginning from Adam, with the genealogies, which the Jews justly regarded as the basis of all history, and in them giving the most minute account of the tribe of Judah and the line of David,[1] it dismisses Saul with the genealogy of his family, and only breaks out into the form of a consecutive narrative with the battle in which he died, and from which the reign of David

---

1. Of course the continuation of his and the other genealogies belongs to the ultimate form of the book, which was probably compiled by Ezra about 450 B.C.

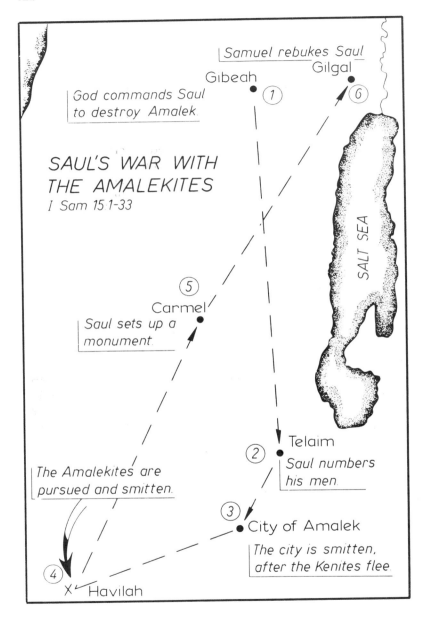

Samuel rebukes Saul

Gibeah   Gilgal

God commands Saul
to destroy Amalek.

① ⑥

SAUL'S WAR WITH
THE AMALEKITES
I Sam 15:1-33

SALT SEA

⑤
Carmel
Saul sets up a
monument.

The Amalekites are
pursued and smitten.

Telaim
② Saul numbers
   his men.

③
City of Amalek

The city is smitten,
after the Kenites flee.

④
X Havilah

began (I Chron. 10). The rest of the book is occupied entirely with the history of David.

c. Of still deeper interest for the true knowledge of David as a man and as the servant of Jehovah are his PSALMS, which serve as a mirror for his very nature. There are many critical difficulties in deciding which of the Psalms are David's and on what occasions they were written, what weight should be given to the titles and what to internal evidence; but there remains an ample store of his own undoubted utterances, of the deepest interest not only for his own life but in which his is the very pattern of the experience of humanity, and himself the type of the "Son of Man," the true head of the human race. The "threefold cord" of personal experience, sympathetic utterance on behalf of humanity in general, and Messianic prophecy must not be loosed in the vain attempt to discriminate each strand. In some sense all that David says of himself belongs to every servant of Jehovah and to the chief servant and son, who was the antitype of all the rest.

From these sources of information we can gather that David was a beautiful, though not a commanding person, strong and agile, and endowed with the exquisite organization of the poet and the musician. As the youngest in a large family, he was subject to the scorn of his elder brothers and his occupation as a shepherd was that which is usually allotted in the East to servants, women and dependents, as we see in the cases of Rachel and Zipporah, Jacob and Moses. But these apparent disadvantages became the very life-springs of his manly and devout character. It is, of course, impossible to draw the line of distinction between his life before and after his designation by Samuel, but we may well believe that those elements of character were already forming which began to shine forth when the Spirit of Jehovah came upon him. The lonely watches which he kept by night, amid the pastures for which Bethlehem was famed, opened his mind to revelations only surpassed by those made to later shepherds in the same fields at the advent of his Son and Lord. If he did not, like them, actually hear the heavenly host praising God and saying, "Glory to God in the highest! Peace on earth, good-will to man!" he was taught by the inward voice of God's Spirit to utter the same strains to the music of his harp; and his Psalms show how he used the imagery spread out before his eyes by day and night.[1] At this time he must have first acquired the art which gave him

1. See Psalms 7, 8, 19, 22, 23, 29, 42, 43, 147 and many others.

one of his chief claims to mention in after times, "the sweet singer of Israel" (II Sam. 23:1). But the character thus formed was not that of a religious recluse, unfitted for the active work of life. The personal prowess which he proved by his celebrated combat with a lion and a bear in defense of his father's flocks (I Sam. 17:34-35), appears to have been also exercised in conflicts with Bedouin robbers or Philistine marauders; for on his first introduction to Saul, he is already known as "a mighty valiant man and a man of war." At the same time he had already a reputation for the prudence which distinguished him in after life, and which was doubtless the fruit of the self-reliance demanded by his position in his father's house. It seems probable that he found congenial companions in his nephews — Abishai, Joab and Asahel — the sons of Zeruiah; and Amasa, the son of Abigail, who were probably about his own age and who afterward became his most famous champions in war, though the cause of many a trouble, from their want of sympathy with the gentler side of his character.

3. To complete his qualifications for his future dignity, David was introduced to the court of Saul, and after being displayed to the nation as a rival of the king even in warlike fame, his character was braced by a long persecution.

Meanwhile the mind of Saul was oppressed by forebodings of a war and by the foresight of the fate denounced by Samuel. "The spirit of Jehovah," which had descended upon him when he was anointed, now "departed from him, and an evil spirit from Jehovah terrified him" (I Sam. 16:14). His servants, who began to experience the terrible caprices of a despot's incipient madness, advised him to try the charms of music, always powerful against melancholy, and believed in the East to possess a magical influence over wild and venomous beasts as well as savage men. Saul consented and sent to Bethlehem for David, who was recommended to him. Jesse sent his son with a present to the king; and that harp, which has since cured many a disturbed spirit, refreshed the soul of Saul and dispelled his evil fancies (I Sam. 16:20-23).

Certain difficulties rise in our minds as we read I Sam. 16-17. Why did Saul not know David when he slew Goliath (I Sam. 17:55-58), when David had played the harp before Saul and so impressed Saul that he loved him (I Sam. 16:21-23)?

The explanation for this may lie in the fact that David's playing for Saul actually was done *after* the victory over Goliath and not before. There are other instances in the books of Samuel where events are related out of strict chronological order for various purposes. There was an evident reason for placing the account of the departure of the Spirit of God from Saul immediately after the notice of the Spirit's descent on David (I Sam. 16:13-14). The most vivid demonstration of the departure of God's Spirit from Saul lay in the dark depressed moods he had. Reference to these naturally led to a mention of David's playing for Saul, even though the account of David's playing actually followed the victory over Goliath recorded in the subsequent chapter (Comp. I Sam. 18:10-11). This interpretation is further strengthened by the fact that I Sam. 17:39 indicates that David had not tested Saul's armor. Thus it would seem that I Sam. 17 precedes portions of I Sam. 16.

Another explanation of the matter may be simply that David returned home after playing for Saul, and was absent from Saul for some months or even a year or more, before going out to the battle with Goliath (I Sam. 18:2). During that time David could have matured considerably and changed in appearance. This, combined with the fact that Saul had seen David in times of mental depression when his memory was faulty, can easily account for his not recognizing David when he came to oppose Goliath. A comparison of I Sam. 16:22 and 18:2 lends support to this view.

We are told that "there was sore war against the Philistines all the days of Saul" (I Sam. 14:52), and the whole system of God's dealings with Israel justifies our supposing that Saul's crowning act of disobedience was followed by a fresh assault of these enemies. The Philistines gathered their armies at Ephes-dammim (the *Boundary of Blood)*, between Scochoh and Azekah, on the border between their own great plain and the highlands of Judah.[1] Saul and the men of Israel were gathered to oppose them (I Sam. 17:2), and among those who followed him were the three eldest sons of Jesse — Eliab, Abinadab and Shammah (I Sam. 17:17). Not on one occasion only, but habitually, as we judge from the nature of the case, Jesse sent David to inquire of his brothers' welfare and to supply their wants (I Sam. 17:17). With his natural courage animated by the knowledge of his high destiny, we may be assured that David would not neglect the opportunity

---

1. I Sam. 7:1. Ephes-dammim lay on the mountain forming the south side of the valley of Elah *(Valley of the Terebinth)*, which is probably that now called *Wady es-Sumt. (Valley of the Acacia)*. It lies about fourteen miles south-west of Jerusalem, on the road to Gaza, and is intersected by a torrent whose bed is full of round pebbles, like those which David picked out of the brook. Ephes-dammim is elsewhere called Pas-dammim (I Chron. 11:13).

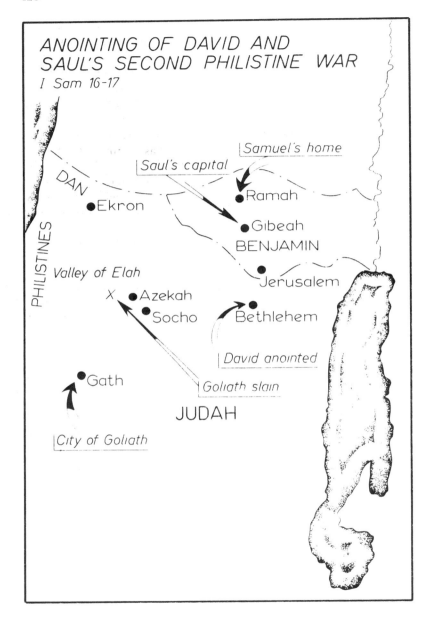

ANOINTING OF DAVID AND
SAUL'S SECOND PHILISTINE WAR
I Sam 16-17

Samuel's home

Saul's capital

DAN

●Ekron   ●Ramah

PHILISTINES   ●Gibeah
                           BENJAMIN

Valley of Elah   ●Jerusalem

X ●Azekah
   ●Socho   ●Bethlehem

                   David anointed

●Gath   Goliath slain

                   JUDAH

City of Goliath

afforded, by his visits to the camp to begin irregular essays in the art of war. The taunt of his brother Eliab that he had come down, in "the pride and naughtiness of his heart, to see the battle" (I Sam. 17:28), seems to breathe jealousy rather than contempt. The supposition that he had engaged in successful shirmishes with the Philistines as a visitor to the camp and that he had relieved the tedium of the watches by his playing, will account for his being known to Saul's servants as "a mighty valiant man, and a man of war, and prudent in affairs," as well as "cunning in playing on the harp" (I Sam. 16:18).

The camps of Philistia and Israel were pitched upon two heights, separated by the valley of Elah, across which the hosts confronted one another in battle array morning after morning. A strange cause delayed their conflict. Every morning a champion of Gath, named GOLIATH,[1] came forth out of the camp of the Philistines, and stalked down into the valley to offer single combat. His height was six cubits and a span; he was armed in full panoply of brass (a rare thing in those days, and especially among the Israelites),[2] and a coat of mail weighing 5000 shekels. His spear-head of iron, a metal then much rarer than brass, weighing 600 shekels and its shaft was like a weaver's beam. Before him marched an armor-bearer, carrying his shield. With a voice answering to his form, he demanded of "the *servants* of Saul" to find a warrior to meet him, a free-born Philistine, and proposed that the nation whose champion was defeated should serve the other. His appearance struck dismay into Saul and all his people; they stood motionless throughout the day, and at length the defiance having been repeated in the evening, both armies retired to their camps (I Sam. 17:4-11).

This scene had been repeated for forty days, when David returned to the camp, on a visit to his brethren. He reached the circle of baggage outside the camp at the moment when both armies were drawn up, and the battle-cry was already raised. The temptation was irresistible. He left the bread and parched corn and cheeses, which he had brought as presents for his brothers

---

1. It has been conjected that he was one of the giant race of the Rephaim, some of whom dwelt in the southern part of Canaan, and were called Anakim (Deut. 2:10-11). His height is stated as six cubits and a span (about nine and one-half feet). There is some confusion about his name; as Elhanan is said to have slain a Goliath of Gath whose description is like that of the text (II Sam. 21:19); but the parallel passage in I Chron. 22:5 gives "Lahmi, the brother of Goliath the Gittite." From these two passages we may infer that a certain giant of Gath, whose name, Rapha, seems to connect him with the Rephaim, had five sons, Goliath, Ishbibenob, Saph, Lahmi and a fifth who is not named by distinguished as having six fingers and toes on each hand and foot.
2. Comp. 1 Sam. 13:19-22. Even when Saul gives David his own armor we read of a brazen helmet and a coat of mail, but not of the greaves and target of brass (comp. I Sam. 17:5,6, with I Sam. 17:38).

and their captain, with the guard of the baggage, and ran into the ranks where his brethren stood. As he spoke to them, the champion of Gath approached and uttered his defiance and all who stood near fled before him. The Spirit which rested upon David moved him with indignation at such a reproach on Israel. "Who," he asked, "is this Philistine, that he should defy the armies of the living God?" The by-standers told him that Saul would give his daughter to the man who should kill the Philistine, and enrich him greatly and make his house free in Israel. Heedless of the taunts of Eliab, who rebuked his presumption with the authority of an elder brother, David repeated his inquiries till his words came to the ears of Saul. When brought before the king he bade Israel dismiss their fear, for he would go and fight with the Philistine. Not with proud contempt, but with generous anxiety, Saul reminded him that he was but a youth, and the Philistine a warrior from his youth. But David had a shepherd's exploits against wild beasts, not to boast of, but to plead in support of his faith, that "Jehovah, who had delivered him out of the paw of the lion, and out of the paw of the bear, would deliver him out of the hand of the Philistine." "Go! and Jehovah be with thee!" said Saul, his own early trust in God revived by the contagion of example. He armed David for the combat in his own armor, and girded him with his own sword; but David, after the first few steps, cast them off as an untried encumbrance and betook himself to those shepherd's weapons, for their skill in which we have already seen that his countrymen were famous. The only arms of David were his shepherd's staff and sling, with five pebbles which he took from the water-course and placed in his pouch. The Philistine's scorn for the ruddy youth swelled into rage at the mode of his attack: "Am I a dog," he asked, "that thou comest to me with staves?" He seems to have overlooked the sling, "and he cursed him by his gods." David answered his threats with the calm and certainty of victory which befitted a champion who avowed that the battle was Jehovah's. Both advanced, David with the swiftness of foot for which he was famous; but before his foe came close, he took a stone from his bag and slung it into the forehead of the Philistine, who fell to the ground upon his face. David rushed in and stood upon him, and drawing the Philistine's own sword from its sheath, cut off his head. At this sight the Philistine army fled, pursued by Israel with great slaughter as far as Gath, and even to the gates of Ekron, whence the victors returned to spoil their camp. David's own tropies were the head, the armor and the sword of the fallen champion. The first he exposed at Jerusalem, the second he put in his own tent and the last he laid up in the tabernacle at Nob, till he took it for his own weapon in his time of need (I Sam. 17:20-54).

As David had gone forth to the encounter, Saul had asked Abner whose son the young man was, but Abner could not tell him. Saul repeated the inquiry to David himself when Abner ushered the youth into his presence, with the head of the Philistine in his hand; and on learning his father's name, Saul sent to ask Jesse to let David remain in his presence and he made him his armor-bearer. Saul gave him the sunshine of royal favor, the warm love of his impulsive nature, while his son Jonathan conceived for David an affection which at once ripened into one of those friendships that have become proverbial in history — the perfect union of the "friend that sticketh closer than a brother." They made a covenant, which was faithfully observed even when Saul became David's enemy, and according to the custom in such cases, Jonathan clothed David with his own garments, to his sword and bow and girdle.

In this new position, David confirmed the character for prudence which had at first been given him. Employed by the king in various important matters, he is repeatedly said to have "behaved himself wisely in all his ways," "more wisely than all the servants of Saul," and the reason is given, "Jehovah was with him."[2] He needed all his prudence, for Saul's love began soon to turn to jealousy. It is a very interesting question, whether any tidings of Samuel's visit to Bethlehem had reached the court. It is alike difficult to understand the keeping of such a secret, and the conduct of Saul and Jonathan to David if it had transpired. But something may be ascribed, on the one hand, to the jealousy between Judah and Benjamin,[1] which would lead the elders of Bethlehem to keep a secret so vital to their tribe; or something, on the other supposition, to the fatalism of Saul and the romantic generosity of Jonathan, combined with his faith in the providence of Jehovah. On the whole, we can hardly think that David was yet viewed as Saul's anointed successor, though Jonathan afterward recognizes him in that character, and Saul openly denounces him as a rival.[3] The first occasion for this jealousy was given by the

---

1. I Sam. 18:5,14,15,30. The margin of our version gives "he *prospered*"; and we may well understand it of that perfect union of prudence and success which marks the very prosperous man.
2. Besides other proofs of this, Judah had been the leader in the massacre of Benjamin (Judg. 22:18).
3. I Sam. 20:15,31. Still later he acknowledges David as his destined successor (I Sam. 24:20, 26:25).

songs of the Hebrew women, who came out of every city to greet the victors on their return from the war with the Philistines; and as they trooped forth "singing and dancing, with tabrets, with joy, and instruments of music," they added to their wonted acclamation,

"Saul hath slain his thousands,"

the response of the whole chorus,

"And David his Ten Thousands."

From that hour Saul viewed David with the evil eye and his fits of melancholy became charged with impulses of murder. On the very next day he twice cast his spear at David as he sat at the royal table and David only escaped by fleeing from Saul's presence. The king's saner hours were haunted by a jealous fear, which increased with David's prosperity (I Sam. 18:12,15). He removed him from his office about his person and made him captain over a thousand, but the only result was that David became better known and more beloved by all the people (I Sam. 18, 13-14, 16). Saul then began to plot more systematically against his life. He offered to perform the promise held out to the conqueror of Goliath by giving him his daughter Merab, urging him to win the prize by new enterprises, in which he hoped he might fall by the hand of the Philistines. However, when the time for the marriage arrived, Merab was given to another. Meanwhile Saul's second daughter, Michal, had become enamored of David; and Saul, with the low cunning of a diseased mind, saw another opportunity for his destruction. He employed his servants to demand of David a dowry which could only be procured by the slaughter of a hundred Philistines; but David went down with his own troop and slew two hundred, and laid their bloody spoils at Saul's feet, thus at once disappointing the hope of his destruction and leaving him no excuse for breaking his word (I Sam. 18:17-27). He became the king's son-in-law, and as Saul would naturally keep up appearances, this was probably the occasion of his elevation to the command of the body-guard, a post only second to that of Abner.[1] David's wife proved, like Jonathan, his faithful friend; for which Saul only hated him the more and "became his enemy continually." He no longer concealed his thoughts but ordered Jonathan and his courtiers to kill David. Jonathan, however, tried the effect of an earnest remonstrance with his father, contriving that David should overhear the conversation, so as to be assured

---

1. I Sam. 17:5. Here the connection of thought in the writer's mind may have been preferred to the exact chronological order.

of Saul's real feelings and the result was the restoration of David to Saul's favor (I Sam. 18:28, 19:7).

4. This reconciliation lasted only for a short time. David's exploits in a new war with the Philistines again provoked the fury of Saul, who nearly pinned him to the wall with his spear for the second time. David fled to his house, round which Saul set a watch during the night, intending to kill him in the morning.[1] Michal saved her husband's life by letting him down out of a window. She placed an image[2] in his bed and told Saul's messengers that he was sick. Saul's persistent demand to have him brought to him exposed the deception, which Michal boldly justified. Meanwhile David went to Samuel at Ramah, and dwelt with him at Naioth (the pastures), near the city, among the "schools of the prophets."

When the messengers sent by Saul to take him saw the company of the prophets prophesying, the Spirit of God fell upon them also and they prophesied. This was repeated thrice and at last Saul went himself. No sooner had he reached the well of Sechu, at the foot of the hill of Ramah, than the Spirit of God came upon him and he prophesied all the way as he went to Naioth. There he stripped off his outer clothes and fell down before Samuel, prophesying all that day and night. Well might this melancholy exhibition of reluctant homage, so different from his first willing reception of the divine spirit, cause the repetition of the surprise then uttered in scornful incredulity, but now grounded in sad experience, which gave new force to the proverb, "Is Saul also among the prophets?" (I Sam. 19).

Saul seems to have returned from Ramah, professing to be reconciled to David, whom he expected to resume his place at court (I Sam. 20:25-29), but David only left his refuge at Ramah to appeal to Jonathan against his father's persecution (I Sam. 20:1-14). He obtained his friend's consent to a decisive experiment on Saul's intentions and they arranged a meeting, at which David was to learn his fate. At the same time they renewed their covenant, with the remarkable addition of the oath which Jonathan required of David, evidently in anticipation of his succeeding to the crown: "Thou shalt not cut off thy kindness from my house forever; no! not when Jehovah hath cut off the enemies of David every one from the face of the earth"; and David solemnly ratified this covenant for his descendants as well as himself, and afterward observed it faithfully (II Sam. 9; 21:7).

---

1. Psalm 59 is referred to this occasion, on the authority of the title.
2. In Hebrew *teraphim*, a proof that Michal had brought into the house of David that domestic idolatry which has often come under our notice.

The next day was the feast of the new moon and instead of appearing at the king's table, David hid himself in the place agreed upon with Jonathan, a great heap of stones, called Ezel, in a field near the residence of Saul. Saul sat down to the banquet with Abner and Jonathan, and said nothing of David's absence, but found an excuse for him in his own mind on the ground of ceremonial uncleanness. On the second day, however, his suspicions were thoroughly roused and he demanded of Jonathan the cause of David's absence. Jonathan's reply that he had given David leave to attend a family feast at Bethlehem (where, in fact, David may have spent these two days), brought down his father's rage upon his own head. With the deepest insult upon his birth, Saul taunted him with his friendship for David, told him that his kingdom would never be established during David's life, and ordered him to fetch him, that he might be slain. When Jonathan remonstrated, Saul hurled his spear at him as he had done twice before at David, and Jonathan left the room in fierce anger. The next morning he went out to the field where David was hiding and his manner of directing his attendant to gather up the arrows he shot gave David the signal to fly for his life. But first he came out from his hiding-place and the friends renewed their covenant before parting and with embraces and tears, in which David was the more vehement, they parted only to meet again for one brief interview (I Sam. 20; Comp. 23:16-18). It was reserved for David to give the last proof of his affection for Jonathan by his lamentation over his untimely fate and the protection which he gave to his son Mephibosheth. Meanwhile he found himself a solitary exile, soon to be hunted "like a partridge on the mountains."

The conqueror of Goliath now sought shelter from the Philistines, but first he betook himself to Nob, where the tabernacle then stood. The high-priest, Ahimelech,[1] was alarmed at his coming alone, but David pretended an urgent commission from Saul and saying that he had appointed his servants to meet him at a certain place, he asked five loaves of bread for himself and these imaginary attendants. The high-priest had none but the old shew-bread, which had just been removed and replaced by the hot loaves, for it was the beginning of the Sabbath; and he gave this to David, on his assurance that he and his attendants

---

1. Called Ahijah in I Sam. 14:3, and Abiathar in Mark 2:26. In the latter passage we have an interesting example of that truth to the spirit, rather than the letter, which marks the sacred writings. "Those who were with David" are spoken of as if his pretended appointment with his followers to meet him had been real.

were undefiled. This act was in direct violation of the law, but our Lord refers to it as justified by necessity, in illustration of the great principle, "I will have mercy and not sacrifice," which overrides the mere letter of the positive law.[1] David's next care was to arm himself. With the ambiguous explanation that he had had no time to take his weapons because *the king's business required haste,* he asked for a sword or spear; and the high-priest gave him the sword of Goliath, which had been laid up behind the ephod. We cannot think that David's excuses imposed upon the high-priest, but rather that Ahimelech's readiness to aid him was a sign of his attachment to David's cause, founded, perhaps on some knowledge of his divine designation. If any such feeling influenced him, however, he kept it to himself, and did not consult the oracle on David's behalf, as Saul afterward charged him with doing, on the report of Doeg, his chief herdsman, who happened to witness the transaction (I Sam. 21:1-7; 22:14-15).

From Nob David fled to Achish, king of Gath, but the Philistine chieftains showed so quick a memory of his slaughter of Goliath[2] that he only saved his life by feigning the madness of a slavering idiot and Achish dismissed him with contempt. He found a refuge for himself in the largest of the caves in the limestone rocks which 'border the *Shefelah,* or great maritime plain near Adullam, a city of Judah, not far from Bethlehem.[3] Here he became established as an independent outlaw. Besides his brethren, who fled to him from their neighboring native city, he was joined by all those classes who are ever ready for revolt — debtors, malcontents and persons in distress, such as those who had gathered round Jephthah in his outlawry.[4] His father and mother he placed in safety with the King of Moab, a people with whom the family were connected through Ruth. We must not think of David in the Cave of Adullam as a rebel against Saul, but rather as an independent chieftan, making war from his own stronghold against the Philistines. Among this band of 400 men, some performed deeds of valor which gave them a permanent precedence among his warriors. Two such trios were especially distinguished, and among the second three was Abishai, the son

---

1. Matt. 12:3; Mark 2:25; Luke 6:3,4. Often as David is mentioned in the N.T. as the ancestor of Christ, this is the only allusion to the incidents of his life.

2. The sword of Goliath may have been the means of his discovery. The title of Psalm 56 states that he was made prisoner by the Philistines of Gath.

3. I Sam. 22:1,2; II Sam. 23:13; I Chr. 11:15; Gen. 38:1,12,20; Josh. 12:15, 15:35; II Chron. 11:7; Neh. 11:30; II Macc. 12:38. It was probably the cave now called *Khureitun,* the only very large cavern in Palestine (Robinson, vol. 2, pp. 23, 51-53).

4. That some of these were Canaanites appears from the mention of Ahimelech the Hittite, I Sam. 26:6.

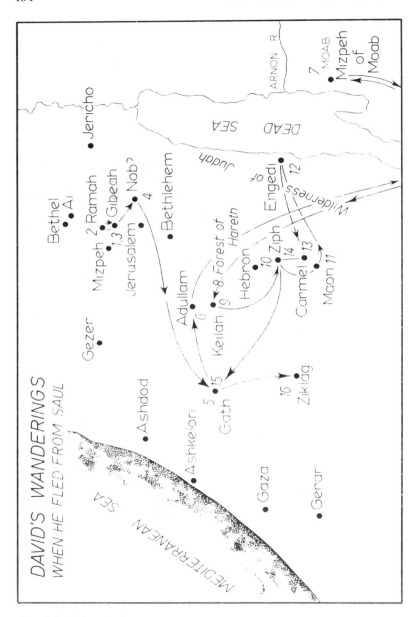

David's Wanderings
When He Fled From Saul

(The places listed are shown on the map.)

1. *Gibeah* (I Sam. 19:1-17)
   a. Jonathan intercedes for David (19:1-7)
   b. Saul tries to spear David (19:8-10)
   c. Michal helps David escape (19:11-17)
2. *Ramah* (I Sam. 19:18-24, Ps. 59 [?])
   a. David visits Samuel (19:18-19)
   b. Saul and his messengers prophesy (19:20-24)
3. *Gibeah* (I Sam. 20)
   a. David absent from feast of new moon (20:1-34)
   b. Jonathan warns David with arrows (20:35-42)
4. *Nob*[1] (I Sam. 21:1-9)
   a. Ahimelech gives David food and weapons (21:1-6, 8-9)
   b. Doeg the Edomite witnesses Ahimelech's act (21:7)
5. *Gath* (I Sam. 21:10-15, Ps. 34, 56)
   a. David feigns madness
6. *Adullam* (I Sam. 22:1-2; Ps. 142, perhaps I Chron. 12:16-18)
   a. David gathers 400 followers
7. *Mizpeh of Moab* (I Sam. 22:3-5)
   a. David leaves his parents here for safety
8. *Forest of Hareth* (I Sam. 22:5-23; Ps. 52)
   a. Saul slays priests at Nob (22:5-19)
   b. Abiathar comes to David (22:20-23)
9. *Keilah* (I Sam. 23:1-12)
   a. David saves Keilah from Philistines (23:1-6)
   b. Saul pursues David (23:7-12)
10. *Ziph* (I Sam. 23:13-23)
    a. David escapes to the wilderness (23:13-14)
    b. Jonathan's last visit with David (23:15-18)
    c. Ziphites reveal David's hiding place to Saul (23:19-23)
11. *Maon* (I Sam. 23:24-28)
    a. David narrowly escapes Saul
12. *Engedi* (I Sam. 23:29-24:22)
    a. David spares Saul
13. *Carmel* (I Sam. 25:1-44)
    a. Samuel's death (25:1)
    b. Nabal refuses food for David's men (25:2-13)
    c. Abigail's intercession (25:14-35)
    d. Death of Nabal (25:36-38)
    e. David marries Abigail (25:39-44)
14. *Ziph* (I Sam. 26:1-25)
    a. Ziphites reveal David's hiding-place again (26:1-3)
    b. David spares Saul (26:4-25)
15. *Gath* (I Sam. 27:1-4)
    a. David dwells with Achish
16. *Ziklag* (I Sam. 27:3-12; I Chron. 12:1-6)
    a. David receives Ziklag from Achish (27:5-7)
    b. David raids southern tribes (27:8-12)

1. The location of Nob is uncertain. It is thought to be near the Mt. of Olives near Jerusalem.

of David's sister Zeruiah, whose two other sons, Joab and Asahel, probably joined David at this time, though not yet mentioned by name. Another band joined him here of men of Judah and Benjamin, under Amasa, the son of his other sister Abigail and eleven men of Gad crossed the Jordan to his camp (I Chron. 12:8, 16-18). With them perhaps came the prophet GAD, who is now first mentioned (I Sam. 21:10-22:5).

By his direction, David left his concealment at Adullam for the forest of Hareth among the hills of Judah (I Sam. 22:5); and Saul no sooner heard of his appearance, than he set out in person to hunt him down. The king had begun to distrust his own immediate followers. As he stood with them under a grove at Ramah he taunted the men of his own tribe as having no feeling for him, and as conspiring with his own son on behalf of David, from whom *they* could not expect the benefits which would doubtless be reserved for Judah.[1] None responded to the appeal but his Edomite officer, Doeg. He recounted what he had witnessed at Nob, artfully suppressing the tale by which David had deceived Ahimelech and adding that the high-priest had asked counsel of the oracle for David. Ahimelech, summoned to Saul's presence, denied the latter charge and protested his ignorance of any treason on the part of David, whom he had treated as the king's son-in-law, honored in his court and entrusted with his confidence. Saul's fury regarded this plea as little as Ahimelech's sacred character and he called on his guards to slay him with all the priests of Nob. When none obeyed, he repeated the order to Doeg and this son of Esau put to death eighty-five priests on that one day. Nor was this all. The city of Nob was given up to massacre, and men, women, children and sucklings, oxen, asses and sheep were all put to the sword. Only one of the sons of Ahimelech, named Abiathar, escaped and fled to David, who now saw with remorse the effect of the deceit he had practiced on the high-priest in Doeg's presence and promised Abiathar his protection. We cannot fail to see in this massacre the working of the curse on the house of Eli (I Sam. 22:9-23).

David had now in his camp not only a prophet but the successor to the high-priesthood, and he placed his movements under the guidance of the oracle of Jehovah. With this divine sanction, he overbore the fears of his followers and fell upon the Philistines, who had plundered the threshing-floors of Keilah, and were

---

1. I Sam. 22:6-8; the appeal to the jealousy of the two tribes is clearly implied.

besieging the city. Having utterly defeated the Philistines and gained great booty from them in cattle, David established himself in Keilah. Here Saul imagined he had caught him, as in a trap; and David, learning from God by means of the sacred ephod that the men of Keilah would give him up, left the city with his little band, now amounting to 600 men, who were obliged to disperse themselves for safety (I Sam. 23:1-15). David moved from one lurking-place to another in the wilderness of Ziph, while Saul was in constant search of him. It was at this juncture that the last interview took place between David and Jonathan, who found his friend in a certain wood, "and strengthened his hand in God," assuring him that he should be king over Israel and expressing the vain hope that he himself would be next to him. When they had again renewed their covenant, Jonathan retired to his house instead of rejoining his father. The Ziphites betrayed David's movements to Saul, who left Gibeah in quest of him, preceded by the Ziphites, tracking his very footsteps like beaters after game. Thus hunted like a partridge over the hills of Judah, David fled to the wilderness of Maon, beyond Jeshimon, in the extreme south. Here Saul followed him so close that David fled from his rock of refuge to one side of a mountain, while the king was hunting for him on its other side; whence the place obtained the name of Sela-hammahlekoth *(the rock of divisions)*. At length Saul was called away by the news of an invasion of the Philistines, and David betook himself to the dreary fastnesses of the wilderness of Engedi, on the margin of the Dead Sea.[1] Saul, having repelled the invaders, returned with 3000 men, chosen out of all Israel, to the pursuit of David and his little band, who were now hunted from rock to rock like the wild goats of that desert. It happened that Saul went alone into a cave where David and his men were hidden in the lateral caverns. Urged to use so favorable an opportunity, David contented himself with creeping behind the king and cutting off the skirt of his robe. But his heart smote him even for this insult to the anointed of Jehovah. Following Saul out of the cave, he cried after him, "My lord the king," and bowing down before him, he showed him his skirt as a proof that he had spared his life and made a most pathetic appeal to the king's forbearance and protestation of his own innocence. The old impulsive

---

1. Engedi, "the fountain of the kid," was originally named Hazazontamar, "the pruning of the palm," on account of the palm-groves which surrounded it (II Chr. 20:2; Eccl. s. 24:14). It is about the middle of the western shore of the lake, and at an elevation of some 400 feet abov ɪe plain is the fountain of *Ain Jidy*, from which the place gets its name. Traces of the old city exist upon the plain and lower declivity of the mountain, on the south bank of the brook.

affection of Saul burst the barriers of jealous hatred. David had called him "Father," and with tears he responds, "Is this thy voice, my son David?" He confesses his injustice and David's magnanimity, acknowledges the divine decree which had given the kingdom of Israel into the hand of David, and takes an oath of him not to cut off his name and house in Israel. Saul returned home but David remained in his fastnesses (I Sam. 24).

About this time Samuel died and all Israel joined to mourn for him with a bitterness doubtless enhanced by the fulfillment of his warnings concerning their chosen king. They buried him at his house at Ramah and David, probably feeling that the last restraint on Saul was now removed, retired southward to the fastnesses of the wilderness of Paran. Here occurred a very interesting episode in his adventures. There lived at Maon a descendant of Caleb, named Nabal, possessed of great wealth. His flocks of 3000 sheep and 1000 goats fed on the pastures of Carmel. His wife Abigail was intelligent and beautiful, but the man himself was a mean, miserable churl. As his own wife said, he was Nabal (a *fool*, implying wickedness) by nature and by name. Amid the festivities of his sheep-shearing, David sent ten young men with a friendly greeting to ask Nabal for a present. The request was founded on the security of his flocks while David's band had been near them and it seems probable that Nabal had not only enjoyed immunity from any injury by the outlaws, but had even been protected by them from the Bedouin marauders. Such appears to have been David's mode of occupying his followers and obtaining subsistence in return for their services. But Nabal spurned the request and denied the claim with contempt. "Who is David?" he asked, "And who is the son of Jesse? There be many servants nowadays that break away every man from his master!" David received the message and prepared to avenge the insult, vowing the death of every man of Nabal's house. He took 400 men with him and left 200 to guard the baggage — the first example of a proportion which afterward became a rule (I Sam. 30:24). Meanwhile the prudent Abigail, being informed by a servant of her husband's behavior, hastened to provide, without his knowledge an abundant present of bread, parched corn, sheep ready dressed, skins of wine, clusters of raisins and cakes of figs. Sending forward her servants with the asses thus loaded, she went to meet David just as he emerged from the passes of the hills. Not content with entreating his forbearance, she acknowledged him as the champion who fought the battles of Jehovah, and as the future leader of Israel. Deploring the persecution he suffered from Saul, she used those powerful and oft-quoted figures: "The soul of my lord shall be *bound in the bundle of life* with Jehovah thy God: and the souls of thine enemies, *them shall He sling out, as out of the middle of a sling.*" Her beauty and sense made a deep impression upon David. For the present, he sent her home in safety, accepting her gift and thanking her for keeping him from shedding blood. Nabal had meanwhile feasted like a king till he was drunk so his wife kept her news till the morning. The shock was too great for his cowardice and avarice: "his heart died within him, and he became as a stone"; and in ten days he died. Abigail found a new husband in David, whose wife Michal had been given by Saul to another, and about the same time David also married Ahinoam of Jezreel (I Sam. 25).

Meanwhile Saul had forgotten the promises made under his transient impulse of kindness and repentance. David's old enemies, the Ziphites, came to tell the king that he was again in the stronghold of Hachilah, east of Jeshimon, and Saul again led his chosen army of 3000 men, under Abner in pursuit of him. Once more Saul fell into the power of David and was magnanimously spared. Informed by his spies of the position of Saul's camp, David went down with his nephew Abishai by night and found Saul asleep by the side of Abner in the midst of his body-guard, with his wellknown spear stuck into the ground at his head. Abishai proposed to smite Saul to the earth with that spear which had twice been hurled at David, but David left his fate in the hands of God and refused to stretch forth his hand against Jehovah's anointed. They took the spear and the cruse of water that was by his side and left the camp, where all were still sunk in a sleep sent by God. Retiring a safe distance to the top of a hill, David shouted to the people and to Abner, whom he taunted for the little care with which so valiant a man had watched over the king's life! Saul knew the voice and the scene of remonstrance, confession and forgiveness was again repeated but with some striking variations. Saul begged David to return to him, promising not to harm him and confessing that "he had played the fool";[1] and when David would only trust his life to God and not to him, he parted from him with the words of prophetic blessing: "Blessed be thou, my son David, thou shalt both do great things and also shalt still prevail" (I Sam. 26).

This was their last interview for David, despairing of safety

---

1. 1. Here, as in other passages, the present sense of the English word fool quite fails to express the degraded wickedness implied by the Hebrew.

while within reach of Saul, resolved finally to seek shelter among the Philistines. Their power was now such that Saul could scarcely make head against them, much less pursue David into their country, and, in fact. he abandoned the attempt (I Sam. 27:1-4). David went, as before, to Achish king of Gath, no longer as a solitary fugitive but with his whole household, and his band of 600 men. This force, and still more perhaps, the knowledge that he had finally broken with Saul, secured him respect, though the Philistine chieftains withheld from him their confidence. Achish assigned, for his residence and maintenance, the frontier city of Ziklag, which consequently belonged ever after to the kings of Judah. We have here the only note of time in the history of David's wanderings. The whole time he spent in the country of the Philistines, that is, to his departure for Hebron after the death of Saul (II Sam. 2:1), was a year and four months. This stay in the land of the Philistines suggests a reflection on the evils that sprang from his want of faith and patience for so short a period. His presence in Judah would have given an opportunity which Saul could hardly have refused for calling him forth as the champion of Israel. At all events, he would have been at hand to retrieve the disaster and would doubtless have been hailed as king by the united voice of Israel. As it was, however, his nation suffered a terrible defeat, which instead of doing his best to avert, he narrowly escaped taking a share in inflicting; his recognition as king of Israel was postponed for seven years and a half, at the cost of a civil war and the permanent alienation of Judah from the rest of Israel, and meanwhile he was involved in a course of pitiable deceit. He could not enjoy the protection of Achish without rendering him service against his country. So he sallied forth from Ziklag but instead of attacking Israel, he fell upon the tribes of the southern desert of Shur, toward the confines of Egypt, the Geshurites, the Gezrites and the Amalekites, and exhibited their spoil to Achish as having been won in the south of Judah, and from the allied tribes of the Jerahmeelites and the Kenites. To guard against detection, he put to the sword every man and woman of each settlement that he attacked. Achish himself was thoroughly imposed upon and put such unlimited confidence in David that he summoned him to join in a grand attack which the Philistines were preparing against Israel, and David sank so low as to boast of the courage he would display (I Sam. 27; 28:1-2). The distrust of the other lords of the Philistines saved him from this dilemma.

5. We must now look back to Saul. Since the death of Samuel and the flight of David, darkness had gathered about his declining path like clouds around the setting sun. The prophetic inspiration which had once marked him as the servant of Jehovah found vent, as we have seen at Ramah, in ravings scarcely to be distinguished from those of his madness. His religious zeal, always rash, as in the vow which so nearly cost the life of Jonathan, was now shown in deeds of sanguinary violence. If the slaughter of the witches and necromancers be defended by the strict letter of the Mosaic law, which however Saul himself had long permitted to slumber, the massacre of the Gibeonites was the violation of a covenant which formed one of the sacred traditions of the nation, and was afterward visited as such on "the blood-stained house of Saul" (II Sam. 21:1-9).[1] This deed may have been a sequel to Saul's inexpiable crime, the massacre of the priests at Nob. The day of retribution now came.

The hosts of the Philistines had assembled at the great battlefield of Palestine, the valley of Jezreel. They occupied the southern slopes of the "Little Hermon," by Shunem, while Saul and the Israelites were encamped on the opposite hills of Gilboa. A panic fear seized Saul at the sight of the army of the Philistines. Fain would he have inquired of Jehovah, but the high-priest was a fugitive from his murderous wrath; he had alienated the prophets and their chief was in the camp of David, and God gave him no answer, "neither by dreams, nor by Urim, nor by prophets." In his extremity, he resorted to the very imposters who had been the victims of his zeal. Among those who had escaped him was a woman who lived at Endor,[2] on the other side of the Little Hermon. Her supernatural pretensions are described by the epithet "a woman of *Ob*" (the skin or bladder), which the LXX, explains as a ventriloquist. Saul went to her abode by night and in disguise, with only two attendants and desired her to bring up from the dead the person whom he should name. Fearing a snare and having perhaps already some suspicions as to the identity of her visitors, the woman only consented on Saul's taking an oath that she should not be punished. She then inquired whom she should bring up, and Saul asked for Samuel. Then the

---

1. I Sam. 28:4,9; comp. Ex. 22:18; Lev. 19:31, 20:27; Deut. 17:10,11. It seems clear that this was a late act of Saul's reign.
2. The name still lingers attached to a considerable but now deserted village to the north of the Little Hermon (*Jebel Duhy*). The rock of the mountain, on the slope of which *Endur* stands, is hollowed into caves, one of which may well have been the scene of the incantation of the witch. The distance from the slopes of Gilboa to Endor is seven or eight miles, over difficult ground.

woman saw (or professed to see) the form of Samuel rising from the earth and, uttering a loud cry, she charged Saul with having deceived her, for she now knew him to be the king. He calmed her fears and demanded what she had seen. "I saw," she answered, "a god-like form rising up out of the earth." In reply to Saul's inquiries, she further described the apparition as that of "an old man covered with a mantle," perhaps the prophetic robe always worn by Samuel. By these tokens Saul recognized Samuel and bowed his face to the ground, while Samuel asked, "Why hast thou disquieted me, to bring me up?" Saul poured forth his sore distress, attacked as he was by the Philistines and abandoned by Jehovah. Samuel replied that it was in vain to resort to him, for this was but the fulfillment of his prophetic word; that Jehovah had torn he kingdom out of his hand, and given it to David, because he had disobeyed him in sparing the Amalekites. He foretold his defeat by the Philistines and added that on the morrow Saul and his sons should be with him among the dead. At this sentence, Saul fell prostrate his whole length upon the earth and fainted away with fear and exhaustion, for he had fasted all the day and night. Having at the urgent pressure of the woman and his attendants, partaken of a meal, the best that she could prepare for him, Saul returned to the camp the same night (I Sam. 28).

Such is the plain narrative of Scripture, which certainly conveys the impression that there was a real apparition in the form of Samuel and that the words heard by Saul were uttered by the spectre. It must be admitted, however, that the case before us has some peculiar features which suggest. not that the woman was other than an imposter, but that her juggleries were overruled by God in a way as surprising to herself as to the other witnesses of the scene. Her shriek of terror at Samuel's appearance, if it proves the reality of the apparition, equally disproves her claims to have raised him, for she evidently expected no such result. Different readers will of course form different opinions, whether the words introduced by the simple phrase, "And Samuel said to Saul," were heard by the witnesses of the scene or were repeated to them by Saul as the expression of an overburdened heart, but we incline to the opinion that in this unique case the spirit of Samuel actually returned to the land of the living to communicate with Saul in his reprobate and desperate state.

Such a night was a dismal preparation for the ensuing day, which sealed the fate of Saul. But while the two armies still hang, like thunder-clouds, on the opposing heights, let us see what is passing in the rear of the Philistines. There is David and his band, with the forces of Gath under Achish, no doubt hoping that his position would secure him from taking any decisive part in the battle. But he was soon relieved from his false position. The princes of the Philistines no sooner saw him than they asked, "What do these Hebrews here?" In vain did Achish plead his perfect confidence in David: the other lords called to mind again the old songs of the ten thousand slain by David, and declaring that he would side against them in the battle to reconcile himself with Saul, they insisted on his dismissal. After a show of great reluctance and renewed expressions of confidence from Achish, David and his men departed with the morning light.

Having thus escaped the great danger of having to fight against Israel, he found that another disaster had been occasioned by his march with the Philistines. The Amalekites had seized the opportunity to take vengeance for David's forays, and when he and his men arrived at Ziklag the third day after leaving the Philistine camp they found the city burnt and their wives and children carried away as captives, including the two wives of David himself. They wept over the ruin and began to threaten David's life, "but David encouraged himself in Jehovah his God." He summoned Abiathar with the oracular ephod and received the direction of Jehovah to pursue, with the promise of success. By means of a straggler, an Egyptian slave of one of the Amalekites, whom they found half dead with fatigue and hunger, they fell upon the enemy, who were feasting in all the disorder of security, and slaughtered them for a whole night and day, only 400 of the whole tribe escaping. Besides recovering their wives and children and all their property without any loss, they obtained a great booty in cattle from the enemy. A question now arose about the division of the spoil. It had happened that one-third of David's 600 men were too weary, after their long march, to keep up with the rest and they had been left behind at the brook Besor with the baggage. As they exchanged congratulations with David on his return, the worser part of David's followers, "all the men of Belial," proposed that they should have no share in the spoil. David sternly forbade this injustice and laid down what thenceforth became a law in Israel, that those who stayed with the baggage should have an equal share, man for man, with those who went to the fight. From his own share of the spoil he sent presents to the elders of Judah, to

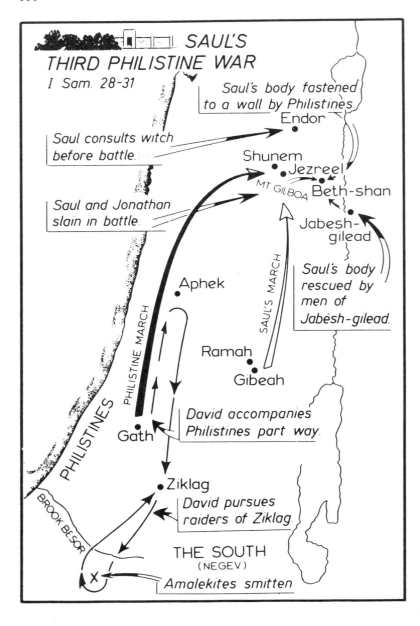

SAUL'S
THIRD PHILISTINE WAR
I Sam. 28-31

Saul's body fastened
to a wall by Philistines
Endor

Saul consults witch
before battle.

Shunem
Jezreel
MT GILBOA
Beth-shan

Saul and Jonathan
slain in battle.

Jabesh-
gilead

Saul's body
rescued by
men of
Jabesh-gilead.

Aphek

PHILISTINE MARCH

SAUL'S MARCH

Ramah
Gibeah

David accompanies
Philistines part way.

Gath

PHILISTINES

Ziklag

David pursues
raiders of Ziklag.

BROOK BESOR

THE SOUTH
(NEGEV)
Amalekites smitten

Bethel, Hebron and other cities that he had frequented with his bands, and to the friendly Arabs of the desert, the Jerahmeelites and the Kenites (I Sam. 29). These gifts certainly served a diplomatic purpose for David. He could not have been unmindful of the fact that he would soon become king over the cities which were receiving his gifts.

6. On the third day after this victory, David received news of the terrible overthrow of Saul and his army in Mount Gilboa on the day of his departure. The Philistines had occupied the valley of Jezreel (I Sam. 29:11), and the Israelites were driven before them up the slopes and over the crest of Mount Gilboa with immense loss (I Sam. 31:7). The hottest pursuit was made after Saul and the band who kept round him. His three sons, Jonathan, Abinadab and Melchishua, were slain, and he himself was mortally wounded by the Philistine archer. Disabled from flight, he begged his armor-bearer to draw his sword and slay him, that his last moment might not be insulted by the uncircumcised foes of God. On his refusal, Saul fell upon his own sword and died and his faithful attendant, who had feared to raise his hand against God's anointed, did not hesitate to share his fate. On the next day the Philistines found the bodies of Saul and his three sons among the dead, and messengers were instantly dispatched through all the cities of Philistia to command rejoicings in the idol temples. They carried Saul's remains from city to city and at last deposited the trophy in the temple of Ashtaroth. His head was struck from his body and placed in the temple of Dagon, probably at Ashdod, while the headless trunk was exposed, with those of his sons, on the wall of the Canaanitish city of Bethshan. In this extremity of shame and ruin, there was one city whose heroic people remembered that Saul had saved them from a fate as shameful. While the Israelites west of Jordan were abandoning their cities to be possessed by the Philistines, the men of Jabesh-gilead made a night march across the river and took down the bodies of Saul and his sons, which they carried to Jabesh and burnt.[1] They buried the bones under a tamarisk-tree, and observed a fast for seven days (I Sam. 31; I Chron. 10). The ashes were removed long

---

1. Bethshan, elsewhere called Bethshean (Josh. 17:11; I Chron. 7:9), one of the towns from which the Canaanites were not driven out (Judg. 1:27), still bears the name of *Beisan*. It lies in the Ghor, or Jordan Valley, about twelve miles south of the Sea of Galilee, and four miles west of the Jordan, on the brow of the descent, by which the great plain of Esdraelon (Jezreel) drops down to the level of the Ghor. A few miles to the southwest are the mountains of Gilboa, and close beside the town runs the water of the *Ain-Jalud*, the fountain of which is by Jezreel, and is in all probability the spring by which the Israelites encamped before the battle in which Saul was killed (I Sam. 29:1). Jabesh-Gilead is about twenty miles from Bethshan, an all night's journey east and south, across the Jordan.

afterward by David to the sepulchre of Kish at Zelah (II Sam. 21:14).

The sad tidings were brought to David at Ziklag by an Amalekite, who arrived with his clothes rent and earth upon his head, and said that he had escaped out of the camp of Israel and had been an eye-witness of Saul's death (II Sam. 1). He told the tale of the hot pursuit and then added (whether as an invention to please David, or whether he had really come up to the place where Saul had fallen upon his sword, while he was still alive) that the king, despairing of escape, had begged to be dispatched by his hand, and that he had dealt the last fatal blow. He produced the crown and armlet which Saul used to wear in battle and gave them to David. The news was received with an unfeigned grief and consternation worthy of the reverence and affection which David had never lost for Saul, and of his deep love for Jonathan. He rent his clothes and, with all his band, mourned and wept and fasted till the evening. Then he sent for the Amalekite and asking how he had dared to put forth his hand to slay the anointed of Jehovah, he caused him to be put to death as guilty by his own confession. Finally, he took his harp and poured forth a lamentation over Saul and Jonathan, which is the finest as well as the most ancient of all dirges. Under the title of "THE BOW," the favorite weapon of Jonathan, it was recorded in "The Book of Jasher," and taught as a standing lesson to the children of Judah. Its spirit is alike worthy of the poet and of the objects of his eulogy. A less generous heart and one less devoted to duty might have been content with the tribute of affection to his friend Jonathan and have left the memory of his unjust master to perish in silence. But David was not so insensible to Saul's better qualities, to his old affection and to the claim of the King of Israel to be celebrated in death by the same harp that had soothed his tortured mind while he lived. And so the poem has verified to every succeeding age its own most beautiful and touching words:

"Saul and Jonathan were lovely and pleasant in their lives,
And *in their death they were not divided.*"

Together they are celebrated as "swifter than eagles, and stronger than lions"; and equal prowess is ascribed to the bow of Jonathan and to the sword of Saul. The mourner depicts the joy of the Philistines over "the mighty who were fallen" in strains which have ever since been proverbial:

"Tell it not in Gath,
Publish it not in the streets of Askelon;

Lest the daughters of the Philistines rejoice,
Lest the daughters of the uncircumcised triumph."
Nature is called to sympathize with the sorrow of Israel by
devoting the scene of the disaster to a curse:
"Ye mountains of Gilboa, let there be no dew,
Neither rain upon you, nor fields of offerings:
For there the shield of the mighty is vilely cast away,
The shield of Saul,[1] as though he had not been anointed with oil."
Each of the fallen receives his special tribute. Saul is likened to:
"The *gazelle* of Israel, slain upon the high places";
and the daughters of Israel, who once celebrated the slayer of his
thousands, are called to weep for him:
"Who clothed them in scarlet, with other delights;
Who put ornaments of gold on their apparel."
But the grand outburst of love and grief is reserved for Jonathan:
"O Jonathan, thou wast slain in thy high places.
I am distressed for thee, my brother Jonathan:
Very pleasant hast thou been unto me:
Thy love to me was wonderful,
Passing the love of women."

This noble utterance of grief, in which David is the mouthpiece
of Israel, forms a fit conclusion to the second period of his own
life, as well as to the fatal experiment undertaken by the Israelites
and Saul, of establishing a kingdom on the principles of self-will,
and after the model of the nations around, in place of the royalty
of Jehovah.

To this period we owe several of those Psalms which, while
attesting the constancy of David's piety, have been ever since the
manual for the afflicted and the oppressed. The simple songs of
the shepherd "had prepared the way for his future strains, when
the anointing oil of Samuel came upon him, and he began to
drink in special measure, from that day forward, of the Spirit of
Jehovah." It was then that, victorious at home over the mysterious
melancholy of Saul, and in the field over the vaunting champion
of the Philistine hosts, he sang how from even babes and sucklings
God had ordained strength because of His enemies (Psalm 8). His
next Psalms are of a different character: his persecutions at the
hands of Saul had commenced. Psalm 58 was probably written

---

1. This is a figure for the utter destruction of Saul's power, as in Psalm 76:3; not a mere literal statement that
Saul left his shield on the field of battle. It is superfluous to multiply examples of the *shield* as the emblem of
martial power, under which the people dwell in safety — a figure used in the highest sense in Ps. 84:11,
"Jehovah God is a sun and shield"; and in Ps. 115:9, "He is their help and their shield." There is an interesting
variant reading: "The shield of Saul, the weapons of the anointed with oil."

after Jonathan's disclosure of the murderous designs of the court, Psalm 59 when his house was being watched by Saul's emissaries. The inhospitality of the court of Achish at Gath gave rise to Psalm 56; Psalm 34 was David's thanksgiving for deliverance from that court, not unmingled with shame for the unworthy stratagem to which he had there temporarily had recourse. The associations connected with the Cave of Adullam are embodied in Psalm 57; the feelings excited by the tidings of Doeg's servility in Psalm 52. The escape from Keilah, in consequence of a divine warning, suggested Psalm 31. Psalm 54 was written when the Ziphites officiously informed Saul of David's movements. Psalms 34 and 36 recall the colloquy at Engedi. Nabal of Carmel was probably the original of the 'fool' of Psalm 53, though in this case the closing verse of that psalm must have been added when it was further altered by David himself into Psalm 14. The most thoroughly idealized picture suggested by a retrospect of all the dangers of his outlaw-life is that presented to us by David in Psalm 22. But in Psalm 23, which forms a side-piece to it, and the imagery of which is drawn from his earlier shepherd days, David acknowledges that his past career had had its brighter as well as its darker side; nor had the goodness and mercy which were to follow him all the days of his life been ever really absent from him. Two more psalms, at least, must be referred to the period before David ascended the throne, Psalms 38 and 39, which naturally associate themselves with the distressing scene at Ziklag after the inroad of the Amalekites. Other Psalms referred by their traditional titles to this period are, Psalm 63, "When he was in the wilderness of Judah," and Psalm 142, "A prayer when he was in the cave."

Questions on Section II
Decline of Saul and Rise of David

I Samuel 15
1. What people was Saul told to destroy? Why?
2. Where were Saul's people numbered for war?
3. What people were told to depart from the battle area?
4. How fully did Saul destroy the enemy?
5. Who was king of the condemned people?
6. Where did Saul set up a monument?
7. Where did Samuel rebuke Saul for his sin?
8. Whom did Saul blame for his sin?

9. What is better than sacrifice? How did this truth apply to Saul?
10. What was Saul's penalty for this disobedience?
11. What was torn by Saul?
12. What name did Samuel use to describe God?
13. To what places did Samuel and Saul go after the execution of King Agag?

I Samuel 16

1. What was Samuel to do with his horn?
2. To what place was Samuel sent? To what man? Why?
3. How did the elders of the city react to Samuel's visit?
4. How many sons did Jesse have (Comp. I Sam. 17:12)?
5. Give the names of Jesse's three oldest sons.
6. How did Jesse's older son impress Samuel?
7. How does God look upon people differently than men do?
8. Describe David's physical appearance.
9. What came upon David after he was anointed?
10. What troubled King Saul?
11. How did Saul's servants seek to cheer him? Who was called to do the job?
12. How did Saul respond to David and to his playing?

I Samuel 17

1. Memorize the fact that I Sam. 17 contains the story of David and Goliath.
2. What people gathered to oppose Saul and the men of Israel?
3. Where were they gathered? In what vale did they encamp?
4. Who was the champion of the Philistines and where did he come from?
5. What was the champion's height?
6. What did Goliath offer if an Israelite defeated him?
7. Which of Jesse's sons were in Saul's army?
8. For how many days did the Philistine challenge Israel?
9. Why did David go to the battle area?
10. What rewards were promised to the one who defeated Goliath?
11. What were David's words concerning Goliath?
12. How did Eliab feel when he heard what David said to the men?
13. Why did Saul tell David that he could not go against Goliath?
14. What animals had David killed while shepherding his sheep?
15. Why wouldn't David wear Saul's armor?

16. What were Goliath's first words to David? How did David reply?
17. Whose sword did David use to slay Goliath?
18. How far did Israel pursue the Philistines?
19. What did David do with Goliath's head and his armor?
20. What did Saul ask Abner about David?

I Samuel 18

1. Who became David's friend? How close was the friendship?
2. What would Saul not allow David to do any more?
3. What items did David's friend give him?
4. What was the estimate of David among the people and Saul's servants?
5. What was the song of the women?
6. How did Saul react to the song?
7. Where did the evil spirit upon Saul come from?
8. How did Saul attempt to harm David?
9. Into what position did Saul set David?
10. Who was Saul's older daughter?
11. Why did Saul give his daughter Michal to David?
12. How many Philistines did David slay to provide a dowry to obtain Michal? Was this the number requested?
13. How did Michal feel toward David?

I Samuel 19

Why did these things happen?

1. That David was abiding in a secret place and hid himself?
2. That Saul swore and said concerning David, "As Jehovah liveth, he shall not be put to death"?
3. That Saul smote the spear into the wall?
4. That David escaped by night?
5. That Michal let David down through a window in a basket?
6. That a teraphim was put in David's bed?
7. That Michal lied to her father?
8. That David came to Samuel at Ramah?
9. That Saul's messengers failed in their mission?
10. That Saul stripped off his clothes and prophesied?

I Samuel 20

1. Whom did David come to see after leaving Ramah?
2. How far from death did David feel that he was?
3. What promise did Jonathan cause David to swear to him that he would do?

What part do these items have in the story?

4. New moon.

5. Yearly sacrifice at Bethlehem.
6. The stone Ezel.
7. Three arrows.
8. David's empty seat.
9. The second day.
10. Saul's anger at Jonathan.
11. A little lad.
12. Kissing one another.

I Samuel 21

True or false?
1. Then David came to Ahimelech, to Nob the priest.
2. The priest came to meet David trembling because of the soldiers with David.
3. David lied to Ahimelech.
4. David said that he had some young men with him but he had appointed them to another place.
5. David asked for five loaves of bread.
6. David said that his young men were (ceremonially) holy.
7. Doeg was an Ammonite.
8. Doeg was Saul's chief herdsman.
9. David said that the king's business required haste.
10. The sword of Goliath was wrapped in an ephod.
11. Nahash was king of Gath.
12. The song of the women of Gath refreshed David's heart.
13. David was sore afraid of Achish, the king of Gath.
14. David acted like a mad man before the king.

I Samuel 22

What events are associated with the following?
1. Adullam.
2. About four hundred men.
3. Mizpeh of Moab.
4. Gad.
5. The forest of Hareth.
6. Ahitub.
7. Doeg the Edomite.
8. Fourscore and five persons.
9. Abiathar.
10. Ahimelech.

I Samuel 23

Multiple choice:
1. The Philistines were robbing the threshing-floors of (1) Keilah; (2) Ziph; (3) Maon.

2. Abiathar, son of Ahimelech, came to David with (1) a sword; (2) an ephod; (3) a vessel.
3. From Keilah David went next to (1) the wilderness of Ziph; (2) Maon; (3) Engedi.
4. David then had about (1) 400; (2) 200; (3) 600 men.
5. Jonathan visited David in (1) the wilderness of Ziph; (2) Keilah; (3) Gibeah.
6. Saul wanted the Ziphites to (1) capture David and bring him to him; (2) locate David's hiding-places; (3) take news to David.
7. Saul pursued David in (1) the wilderness of Maon; (2) Engedi; (3) the land of the Philistines.
8. Saul (1) never got near David; (2) was on the other side of a mountain from David; (3) found David in the strongholds.
9. Saul returned from pursuing David because (1) he couldn't catch him; (2) he had a change of heart; (3) a Philistine raid was reported to him.

I Samuel 24
True or False?
1. Saul sought David on the rocks of the wild goats.
2. David said when he discovered Saul in the cave, "Behold, the day of which Jehovah said . . . I will deliver thine enemy into thy hand."
3. David's men were about to rise up against Saul and David prevented them.
4. David's heart troubled him (smote him) after he had cut off Saul's skirt.
5. David stood right up and spoke to Saul man to man.
6. David said that Saul had been hearkening to the words of men in his hatred for David.
7. David said that he would not hurt Saul because he loved his son Jonathan.
8. David called upon Jehovah to avenge him of Saul.
9. David called Saul a dead dog or a flea.
10. Saul wept. David's good overcame Saul's evil.
11. Saul actually asked God's reward in David's life.
12. Saul would not admit to David that David would ever be king.
13. Saul asked the same thing that his son did, namely that David would not cut off his posterity.
14. Saul went home and David went with him.

I Samuel 25
1. Where was Samuel buried?

2. Where did Nabal live? How wealthy was he?
3. Who was Nabal's wife?
4. What did David request of Nabal? How did Nabal respond?
5. What did David determine to do to Nabal?
6. Who prevented David's violence? How?
7. What does the name Nabal mean?
8. How did Nabal die?
9. What happened to Abigail after Nabal's death?

I Samuel 26

1. How many men came with Saul to pursue David?
2. Where did the events of this chapter take place?
3. Who accompanied David as he came to Saul at night?
4. What did David's companion desire to do to Saul?
5. What did David take from Saul?
6. Whom did David taunt?
7. To what two creatures did David compare himself?
8. How did Saul react when he realized how David had spared him?

I Samuel 27

True or False?

1. David said that even if he went to the land of the Philistines that Saul would pursue him there.
2. David had six hundred men with him when he went to Gath.
3. Nahash was the king of Gath.
4. David had two wives with him in Gath.
5. Saul never found out where David was staying.
6. David stayed in the country of the Philistines for sixteen months.
7. The city of Gath was given to David.
8. David smote the Amalekites and the Geshurites.
9. David brought back the kings of these nations alive.
10. David lied to Achish about the persons against whom he fought.
11. Achish was suspicious of David.

I Samuel 28

1. Between what two peoples did fighting arise again?
2. To what position did Achish appoint David?
3. What people had Saul put out of the land?
4. What sort of person did Saul seek to inquire of? Why?
5. Where did the woman (witch) live?
6. Whom did Saul seek to call back from the dead?
7. How did the woman react when she saw Samuel?

8. What was Samuel's message to Saul?
9. Describe Saul's physical condition after he heard Samuel.
10. What did the woman feed Saul?

I Samuel 29

1. Where did the Philistines gather and where did Israel encamp?
2. Who objected to David's presence among the Philistines?
3. Did David go with the Philistines to battle?

I Samuel 30

1. What did David find upon returning to Ziklag?
2. What two people special to David had been taken captive?
3. What reaction of the people greatly distressed David?
4. Who told David to pursue the attackers?
5. What brook did they cross? How many were left there? Why?
6. Who was found in the field?
7. What were the attackers doing when David overtook them?
8. How complete was the rescue?
9. What spoil was given to those who stayed by the baggage?
10. Where did David send spoil from this battle?

I Samuel 31

1. Where was Israel defeated in battle?
2. What princes were slain in the battle?
3. How did Saul die?
4. What was done with Saul's body by the Philistines?
5. Who rescued Saul's body? Why do you suppose they did this good deed?

II Samuel 1

1. How long after the death of Saul was it before David heard the news?
2. Who reported the news to David?
3. What did the Amalekite tell David about Saul's death? Was it true?
4. What possessions of Saul were brought to David?
5. What happened to the Amalekite?
6. What was the name of David's song of lamentation?
7. In what book was this song written?

Special Study

The Schools of the Prophets

The priesthood was originally the instrument by which the

members of the Jewish theocracy were taught and governed in things spiritual. But during the time of the judges the priesthood sank into a state of degeneracy, and the people were no longer affected by the acted lessons of the ceremonial service. They required less enigmatic warnings and exhortations. Under these circumstances a new moral power was evoked — the Prophetic Order. Samuel was the instrument used at once for effecting a reform in the sacerdotal order (I Chr. 9:22), and for giving to the prophets a position of importance which they had never before held. So important was the work wrought by him that he is classed in Holy Scripture with Moses (Jer. 15:1; Ps. 99:6; Acts 3:24), Samuel being the great religious reformer and organizer of the prophetical order, as Moses was the great legislator and founder of the priestly rule.

Samuel took measures to make his work of restoration permanent as well as effective for the moment. For this purpose he instituted companies or colleges of prophets. One we find in his lifetime at Ramah (I Sam. 19:19,20); others afterward at Bethel (II K. 2:3), Jericho (II K. 2:5), Gilgal (2 K. 4:38) and elsewhere (I K. 6:1). Their constitution and object were similar to those of theological colleges. Into them were gathered promising students and here they were trained for the office which they were afterward destined to fulfill. So successful were these institutions, that from the time of Samuel to the closing of the Canon of the Old Testament, there seems never to have been wanting a due supply of men to keep up the line of official prophets. The apocryphal books of the Maccabees (I. 4:46; 9:27; 14:41) and of Ecclesiasticus (36:15) represent them as extinct. The colleges appear to have consisted of students differing in number. Sometimes they were very numerous (I K. 18:4; 22:6; II K. 2:16). One elderly or leading prophet presided over them (I Sam. 19:20), called their father (I Sam. 10:12) or master (II K. 2:3), who was apparently admitted to his office by the ceremony of anointing (I K. 19:16; Is. 61:1; Ps. 105:15). They were called his sons. Their chief subject of study was, no doubt, the law and its interpretation; oral, as distinct from symbolical, teaching being henceforward tacitly transferred from the priestly to the prophetical order. Subsidiary subjects of instruction were music and sacred poetry, both of which had been connected with prophecy from the time of Moses (Ex. 15:20) and the judges (Judg. 4:4, v. 1). The prophets that meet Saul "came down from the high place with a psaltery and a tabret, and a pipe and a harp before them" (I Sam. 10:5). Elijah calls a minstrel to evoke the prophetic gift in himself (II K. 3:15). David "separates to the service of the sons of Asaph and of Heman and of Jeduthun, who should *prophesy* with harps and with psalteries and with cymbals. . . . All these were under the hands of their father for song in the house of the Lord with cymbals, psalteries and harps for the service of the house of God" (I Chr. 25:1-6). Hymns or sacred songs are found in the Books of Jonah (2:2), Isaiah (12:1; 26:1), Habakkuk (3:2). And it was probably the duty of the prophetical students to compose verses to be sung in the Temple (see Lowth, *Sacred Poetry of the Hebrews,* Lect. 18). Having been themselves trained and taught, the prophets, whether still residing within their college or having left its precincts, had the task of teaching others. From the question addressed to the Shunammite by her husband, "Wherefore wilt thou go to him today? It is neither new moon nor Sabbath" (II K. 4:23), it appears that weekly and monthly religious meetings were held as an ordinary practice by the prophets. Thus we find that "Elisha sat in his house," engaged in his official occupation (cf. Ezek. 8:1; 14:1; 22:1), "and the elders sat with him" (II K. 6:32), when the King of Israel sent to slay him. It was at these meetings probably that many of the warnings and exhortations on morality and spiritual religion were addressed by the prophets to their countrymen. The prophet's dress was a hairy garment, girt with a leathern girdle (Is. 22:2; Zech. 13:4; Matt. 3:4). He was married or unmarried, as he chose, but his manner of life and diet were stern and austere (II K. 4:10,38; I K. 19:6; Matt. 3:4).

Questions

1. What institution was originally designed to teach the Jews in things spiritual?
2. What made the prophets a necessary institution?
3. What man reformed the priesthood and organized the prophetic order?

Special Study

The Topography of Jerusalem

A. The hills of Jerusalem
    1. *Mt. Ophel*
        a. This was the southeast hill, the location of David's city.
        b. It was a long narrow hill, shaped something like a

gigantic human footprint, about 1250 feet long and 400 feet wide. Its walled-in area was not larger than about eight acres.

c. David called this hill *Zion* (Psalm 48:12; 76:1-2).

2. *Mt. Moriah*
   a. This was the hill north of Mt. Ophel. It was not actually in the city in David's time.
   b. It was the location of Solomon's temple and also later temples (II Chron. 3:1).
   c. A depression between Ophel and Moriah was filled in by David and later kings.

3. *Mt. of Olives* (II Sam. 15:30)
   a. This lies to the east of Jerusalem.

4. Zion (modern)
   a. This is the southwest hill, a hill larger in area than Ophel. It has been wrongly called Zion during the Christian era.
   b. It was not a part of David's city.

5. *Bezetha*
   a. A hill northwest of Moriah. While it was included within the walls of Jerusalem in later times, it is not mentioned in the Bible, nor was it part of David's city. "As the mountains are round about Jerusalem, so the Lord is round about his people" (Psalm 125:2).

B. The valleys of Jerusalem
   1. *Hinnom*
      a. This valley lies around the west and south of Jerusalem.
      b. It is also called Gehenna and Tophet (II Kings 23:10; Jer. 7:31).
      c. Steep cliffs rim this valley, particularly on the south of Jerusalem.

   2. *Kidron,* or Jehoshaphat (Joel 3:2; II Sam. 15:23)
      a. This is the valley east of Jerusalem, between the Mt. of Olives and Moriah and Ophel.
      b. It joins the Hinnom valley at the southeast corner of Jerusalem. The name *Kidron* is retained on southeast of the junction of the valleys. The Kidron extends on to the Dead Sea.
      c. Water runs in the Kidron during the rainy season.

   3. *Tyropoeon valley*
      a. This valley separated Mt. Ophel and the modern hill of Zion.

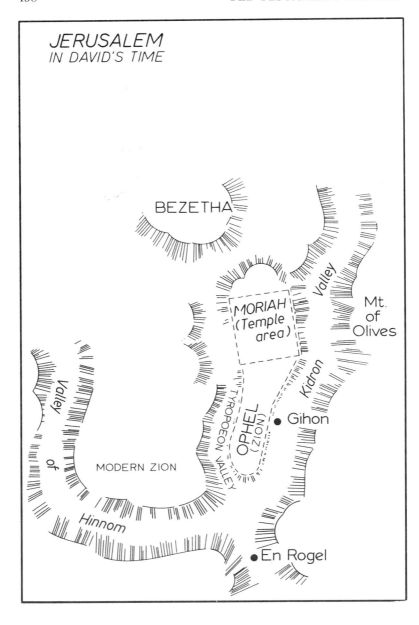

JERUSALEM
IN DAVID'S TIME

BEZETHA

MORIAH
(Temple
area)

Valley

Mt.
of
Olives

Kidron

TYROPOEON VALLEY

OPHEL (ZION)

Gihon

Valley

of

MODERN ZION

Hinnom

En Rogel

      b. It is not mentioned in the Scripture. It is partly filled with debris and dirt in modern times, except at the south end.

C. The springs of Jerusalem
   1. *Gihon* (I Kings 1:33,39,45; II Chron. 32:30)
      a. This was located in the Kidron valley, east of Ophel. It is now called the Virgin's fountain.
      b. Tunnels from this fountain westward to the city were dug in ancient times by the Jebusites and by King Hezekiah.
   2. *En Rogel* (Joshua 15:1; II Sam. 17:17)
      a. This spring (which is now a well, called Job's well) was also in the Kidron valley and was located south of the junction of the Kidron and Hinnom valleys.

Questions

1. Where was Mt. Ophel?
2. Where was Mt. Moriah?
3. Where is the Mt. of Olives?
4. Which hill was called Zion in David's time?
5. Where is the Kidron valley?
6. Where is the Hinnom valley?
7. Where is the Tyropoeon valley?
8. What and where was Gihon?
9. What and where was En Rogel?

Outline of the Reign of David[1]

1. Men who came to David at Ziklag (I Chron. 12:1-7).
2. Gadites join David[2] (I Chron. 12:8-15).
3. David dismissed from Philistine army (I Sam. 29, I Chron. 12:19-22).
4. David defeats Amalekites who destroyed Ziklag (I Sam. 30).
5. Saul visits witch at Endor (I Sam. 28:3-5).
6. Battle of Mt Gilboa (I Sam. 31; I Chron. 10).

---

1. This harmony of the data given in the books of Samuel, I Kings and I Chronicles concerning David is designed to serve students as a reading guide for the reign of David. It is impossible to produce a harmony of the life of David that cannot be questioned in some particulars. In our outline we have generally followed the order of events in the books of Samuel and Kings. Parallel and supplementary material from I Chronicles has been inserted wherever it appeared to fit best. Students should frequently consult *A Harmony of the Books of Samuel, Kings and Chronicles* by Wm. D. Crockett (Grand Rapids: Baker, 1961). Although our outline does not follow Crockett in many places, his arrangement of the scripture text is valuable.

2. Placing the account of the Gadites here instead of later during David's reign has the double advantage of following the order given in Chronicles and of avoiding the difficulty of explaining why the Gadites should have separated themselves unto David during his reign when many Gadites came to him at the start of his reign (I Chron. 12:37).

7. Mephibosheth injured (II Sam. 4:4).
8. David learns of Saul's death (II Sam. 1).
9. David anointed king over Judah (II Sam. 2:1-4a).
10. David's message to Jabesh-gilead (II Sam. 2:4b-7).
11. Ishbosheth made king over Israel (II Sam. 2:8-11).
12. Battle at Gibeon and pursuit of Israel (II Sam. 2:12-32).
13. Long civil war (II Sam. 3:1).
14. David's family in Hebron (II Sam. 3:2-5, I Chron. 3:1-4a).
15. Abner defects to David and is slain (II Sam. 3:6-39).
16. Ishbosheth slain (II Sam. 4:1-3, 5-12).
17. David made king over Israel (II Sam. 5:1-5, I Chron. 11:1-3, 12:23-40).
18. David captures Jerusalem (II Sam. 5:6-10, I Chron. 11:4-9).
19. Alliance with Hiram of Tyre (II Sam. 5:11-12, I Chron. 14:1-2).
20. David's family in Jerusalem (I Sam. 5:13-16, I Chron. 3:5-9, 14:3-7).
21. David's defensive wars against Philistines:
    (a) Victory at Baal-Perazim (II Sam. 5:17-21, I Chron. 14:8-12).
    (b) Second victory (II Sam. 5:22-25, I Chron. 14:13-17).
    (c) Water from Bethlehem (II Sam. 23:13-17, I Chron. 11:15-19).[1]
22. Removal of the ark from Kirjath-jearim (II Sam. 6:1-11, I Chron. 13:1-14).
23. Ark brought to Jerusalem (II Sam. 6:12-19, I Chron. 15:1-16:3).
24. David's psalm of praise (I Chron. 16:4-36).
25. Ministers appointed for the ark (I Chron. 16:37-43).
26. Michal scorns David (II Sam. 6:20-23).
27. David's desire to build a temple and God's reply (II Sam. 7, I Chron. 17).
28. Levites numbered and organized for service (I Chron. 23:3-32, 24:20-31).[2]
29. Twenty-four courses of priests appointed (I Chron. 24:20-31).
30. Twenty-four groups of singers (I Chron. 25:1-31).

---

1. The reference to the valley of Rephaim in II Sam. 23:13 seems to connect this incident with the Philistine battles of II Sam. 5:22ff.
2. The reference to Hushai and Ahithophel in I Chron. 27:33 indicates that the lists of priests and officials in I Chron. 23-28 pertain to the period in David's reign before Absalom's rebellion. See II Sam. 15:12. It is difficult to determine precisely when these appointments were made. Prof. Smith places them before the Ammonite-Syrian war. However, the difficulty of inserting them into the accounts of the wars described in II Sam. 8-12 has led us to insert the data about the civil and sacred appointments (I Chron. 23-28) here just before those wars.

31. Courses of doorkeepers (I Chron. 25:1-31).
32. Treasurers and officers over outward business (I Chron. 26:20-32).
33. Twelve captains of the army (I Chron. 27:1-15).
34. Chiefs of the tribes (I Chron. 27:16-24).
35. Overseers of the king's treasures (I Chron. 16:25-30).
36. The officers of state (I Chron. 27:32-34).
37. David's offensive wars against Philistines (II Sam. 8:1, I Chron. 18:1).
38. Moab smitten (II Sam. 8:2, I Chron. 18:2).
39. David's messengers humiliated by Ammon (II Sam. 10:1-5).[1]
40. **Battle of Medeba** (II Sam. 10:6-14, I Chron. 19:6-15).
41. Syrians defeated at Helam (II Sam. 10:15-19, I Chron. 19:16-19).
42. Syrian territories occupied (II Sam. 8:3-8, I Chron. 18:3-8).
43. Edom subjugated (II Sam. 8:13-14, I Chron. 18:12-13, I Kings 11:15-18).
44. Rabbah beseiged (II Sam. 11:1, I Chron. 20:1a).
45. Sin with Bathsheba and death of Uriah (II Sam. 11:2-27).
46. David's repentance (II Sam. 12:1-25, Psalm 51).
47. Capture of Rabbah (II Sam. 12:26-31, I Chron. 20:1b-3).
48. Spoils of war dedicated (II Sam. 8:11-12, I Chron. 18:11).
49. Officers of David's kingdom at this time (II Sam. 8:15-18, I Chron. 18:14-17).
50. David's mighty men (II Sam. 23:8-12, 18-39, I Chron. 11:10-14, 20-47).[2]
51. David's kindness to Mephibosheth[3] (II Sam. 9).
52. Amnon and Tamar (II Sam. 13:23-33).
53. Flight of Absalom (II Sam. 13:34-39).
54. Absalom recalled (II Sam. 14:1-33).
55. Absalom's rebellion (II Sam. 15:1-12).
56. David's flight (II Sam. 15:13-16:14).
57. Absalom counselled by Ahithophel and Hushai (II Sam. 16:15-17:14,23).
58. Priests' sons discovered and pursued (II Sam. 17:15-21).
59. David crosses Jordan (II Sam. 17:22, 24-29).

---

1. To us it seems necessary to interpret the Syrian wars of II Sam. 8:3-8 as a summary and sequel to the same war described in detail in II Sam. 10. It is difficult to see how the Syrians assisting the Ammonites (II Sam. 10:6) could have done this after David had occupied the Syrian territory, as described in II Sam. 8:3-6. This view is further confirmed by the reference to **Hadadezer** (or Hadarezer) in both II Sam. 8:5 and 10:16.

2. It seems natural to list David's mighty men here, following the list of his officers. Obviously, however, the mighty men had functioned as a body before this time.

3. Mephibosheth was but five years old at David's accession. He now has a son (**II Sam 9:12**). Therefore the account in II Sam. 9 could hardly have occurred until this later time in David's reign and the record in II Sam. 9 must be of proper chronological position.

60. Battle with Absalom (II Sam. 18:1-18).
61. News of Absalom's death brought to David (II Sam. 18:19-32).
62. David's grief over Absalom (II Sam. 18:33-19:8).
63. David restored as king (II Sam. 19:9-40).
64. Jealousy between Israel and Judah (II Sam. 19:41-43).
65. Rebellion of Sheba (II Sam. 20:1-23).
66. David's officers late in his reign (II Sam. 20:23-26, I Chron. 18:14-17).
67. The Gibeonites avenged on Saul (II Sam. 21:1-9).
68. Rizpah's devotion (II Sam. 21:10-11).
69. Saul and Jonathan buried (II Sam. 21:12-14).

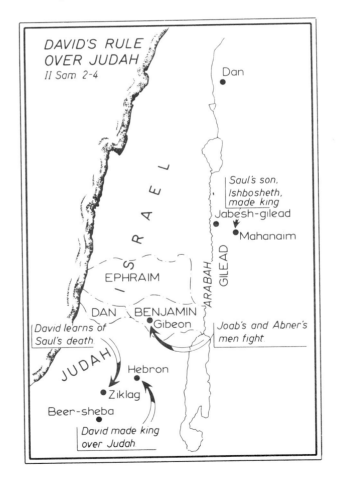

70. Four Philistine battles (II Sam. 21:15-22, I Chron. 20:4-8).[1]
71. David's song of deliverance (II Sam. 22:1-51).[2]
72. David numbers Israel (II Sam. 24:1-9, I Chron. 21:1-6).
73. The choice of punishments (II Sam. 24:10-14, I Chron. 21:7-13).
74. The pestilence (II Sam. 24:15-17, I Chron. 21:14-17).
75. Araunah's threshing-floor purchased (II Sam. 24:18-25, I Chron. 21:18-22:1).
76. David prepares material for temple (I Chron. 22:1-5).
77. David's charges to Solomon (I Chron. 22:6-16).
78. David's charge to the princes (I Chron. 22:17-19).
79. Solomon appointed king (I Chron. 23:1).
80. National convention called by David (I Chron. 28:1).
81. David's address concerning the temple and Solomon (I Chron. 28:2-29:22a).
82. David's last song (II Sam. 23:1-7).
83. David and Abishag (I Kings 1:1-4).
84. Usurpation of Adonijah (I Kings 1:5-27).
85. Solomon anointed king (I Kings 1:28-53, I Chron. 29:22b-25).
86. Final charges to Solomon (I Kings 2:1-9).
87. Death of David (I Kings 2:10-11, I Chron. 29:26-30).

Section III
David's Reign in Triumph
(From Kingship at Hebron to Conquest of Ammon, II Samuel 2-12)

1. David king of Judah at Hebron — Ish-bosheth proclaimed king of Israel by Abner — Civil War — Deaths of Asahel, Abner and Ish-bosheth. 2. David king of all Israel — His army at Hebron — He takes Jerusalem — Alliance with Hiram, King of Tyre — Forms a harem — Victories over the Philistines. 3. Removal of the ark from Kirjath-jearim — Death of Uzzah — Second removal from the house of Obed-edom to Zion — Psalms on this occasion — Divine service arranged — The building of God's house postponed by Divine

---

1. Crockett places these four Philistine battles after David's offensive wars against the Philistines (II Sam. 8:1; Sec. 37). I Chron. 20 places them after the subjugation of Ammon. We have chosen to leave the account in the position given in II Sam. 21.
2. This song is plainly out of chronological position in II Sam. It logically follows II Sam. 8:14. However, in its existing position it serves as a valuable concluding illustration of the character of David.

command — Messianic Psalms. 4. David's victories over the Philistines, Moabites, Syrians and Edomites — Israel reaches its fullest limits. 5. Character and Constitution of the kingdom — a. The royal family — b. Military organization — c. Civil administration — d. The religious institutions — David's prophetic character — Psalmody — Levites — Double high-priesthood — Courses of the priests — Order of prophets. 6. David's kindness to Mephibosheth — Touching story of Rizpah. 7. War with the Ammonites and Syrians — Victories of Joab and David — Siege of Rabbah — David and Bathsheba — Murder of Uriah — Mission of Nathan — David's repentance — Death of David's child — Birth of Solomon — Final conquest of Ammon.

1. The battle of Gilboa left Israel in a state as forlorn as that which ensued upon the defeat of Aphek, except that the ark was not lost and David was ready to be her deliverer. The country west of Jordan was overrun by the Philistines, who occupied the cities from which their inhabitants had fled (I Sam. 31:7). The surviving members of the house of Saul took refuge on the east of Jordan while David, at the command of God, removed with his band and all his family from Ziklag to Hebron, the ancient sacred city of the tribe of Judah. Here the men of Judah came to him and anointed him king over their tribe (II Sam. 1:1-7,11). Thence he sent a message to the men of Jabesh-gilead to thank them for the honor paid to Saul's remains and to announce his accession to the throne. He was now thirty years old and he reigned in Hebron 7½ years (B.C. 1010-1003). The next event recorded is Abner's proclamation of Ish-bosheth,[1] the eldest surviving son of Saul, as king over Gilead, the Ashurites, the valley of Jezreel, Ephraim and Benjamin, and nominally over all Israel: his residence was at Mahanaim, east of Jordan. It is added that Ish-bosheth was forty years old when he began to reign over Israel and that he reigned two years. Now as we cannot suppose an interval of five years from his death to David's full recognition, and as the Philistines were in full possession of all Israel west of Jordan except where David's power extended, it would seem that Abner was occupied for five years or more in recovering the territory of the other tribes from them, after which the two years of Ish-bosheth begin

---

1. II Sam. 1:8-10, he is called Eshbaal in I Chron. 8:33, 9:39. *Eshbaal* means *Man of Baal.* Possibly this was changed in common speaking to *Ishbosheth, Man of Shame,* because the people did not approve the use of the name *Baal.* Thus also *Meribbaal to Mephibosheth* (I Chron. 8:34; II Sam. 4:4).

to be reckoned so as to end just before David's full recognition as king of all Israel (B.C. 1003). Abner, not Ish-bosheth, was the real power.

When Abner had established Ish-bosheth's power west of the Jordan, he endeavored to conquer Judah and a civil war ensued, which was only ended by his own death and that of Ish-bosheth. The war was commenced by Abner's advancing to Gibeon, where he was met by the forces of Judah under JOAB, the son of David's sister Zeruiah, who now takes a foremost place in the history. The Pool of Gibeon,[1] on the opposite sides of which the armies encamped, was made memorable by the deadly combat of twelve Benjamites against twelve men of Judah, in which each man seized his adversary by the head with one hand and with the other thrust his sword through his side, so that all of them fell down dead together. The scene of this mutual slaughter received the name of Helkath-hazzurim (*the field of sharp knives*).[2] In the battle which ensued, the men of Israel were routed. Abner himself was closely pursued by Asahel, one of the three sons of Zeruiah, who were as swift-footed as the wild roe. Unable to escape and unwilling to kill Asahel, Abner twice entreated him to go after someone else, that he might have spoils to carry back with him, but as Asahel persisted, Abner thrust him through with a back stroke of his spear and he fell dead, to the dismay and grief of all who came up to the spot. His brothers, Joab and Abishai, pressed on the pursuit as far as the hill of Ammah, east of Giah in the wilderness of Gibeon. There at sunset the Benjamites rallied round Abner and after a parley between him and Joab, the latter sounded the trumpet of recall and both parties retired during the night — Abner to Mahanaim and Joab to Hebron. The former had lost 360 men, the latter only nineteen besides Asahel, whom they buried in his father's sepulchre at Bethlehem (II Sam. 2:17-32).

The war went on long without any decisive action but with a constantly increasing advantage to the side of David; "David waxed stronger and stronger, and the house of Saul waxed weaker and weaker" (II Sam. 3:1). At length Abner, on an insult received from Ish-bosheth, who was a mere puppet in his hands, made overtures to David, who required as a preliminary the restoration of his wife Michal. David made the demand of

---

1. Comp. Jer. 41:12. The great pool of Gibeon was discovered and excavated 1956-63 by James Pritchard. It was dug in solid rock and was 37 feet in diameter and 35 feet deep. See Pritchard, *Gibeon, Where the Sun Stood Still.*

2. II Sam. 2:12-16. The left-handedness of the Benjaminites may have contributed to the result.

Ish-bosheth, who took Michal from her second husband, Paltiel, and sent her to Hebron. Abner now entreated with the elders of Israel and especially with the tribe of Benjamin, reminding them of David's designation by Jehovah and of his services against the Philistines. So favorable was the response that he resolved to go in person to Hebron, with a guard of only twenty men, to represent to David the feelings of Israel and Benjamin. Having been welcomed and feasted by David, he promised to gather all Israel to his standard and went away in peace. But both his journey and his scheme were doomed to a sad miscarriage (II Sam. 3:6-21).

Joab, who stood to Abner in the relation of the avenger of blood on account of the death of Asahel, only returned to Hebron from an expedition against the Bedouins of the desert after Abner had departed. He accused the king of dismissing an enemy who had come only as a spy, and without David's knowledge he sent messengers after Abner, who brought him back to Hebron under the pretense of further conference. Drawing Abner aside under the gateway of the city for private converse, Joab smote him under the fifth rib, so that he died. In this treacherous revenge for blood shed most unwillingly, Joab was aided and abetted by his brother Abishai (II Sam. 3:22-27, 30).

Calling Jehovah to witness that he and his kingdom were guiltless for all future time of Abner's blood, David imprecated a terrible curse on Joab and his house. He then called his followers to bury Abner at Hebron with the honors due to a prince and chieftain. Joab was obliged to join in the universal mourning "and King David himself followed the bier." David's conduct formed the climax of his favor with the people, who well knew his innocence: "as whatsoever the king did pleased all the people." But he bitterly felt his impotence to restrain his too powerful relations and vented his indignation in the words which have become proverbial: "These men, the sons of Zeruiah, be too hard for me." He added threats that the doer of evil should be rewarded according to his wickedness but it was not till Joab had again mortally provoked him by killing Absalom, that he deposed him from his office of captain of the guard and gave it to Amasa, whose treacherous murder filled up the measure of Joab's crimes. Even then David left his punishment as a legacy to Solomon, by whom he was put to death (II Sam. 3:31-39, 19; I K. 2:5-6, 33-34).

Ish-bosheth, left helpless by the loss of Abner, fell a victim to the conspiracy of two of his captains, who slew him on his bed,

Mephibosheth, Jonathan's son, was lame. Being a child of five years old when the tidings were brought of the death of Saul and Jonathan, he was carried off by his nurse, who let him fall in the hurry of the flight and so lamed him for life. His royalty was as powerless as his person, but yet he was the least unfortunate of Saul's house, because of the favor which David showed him for his father's sake and in fulfillment of their covenant. We shall hear much of him afterward, but meanwhile it is not clear from the narrative whether he was ever proclaimed king or brought out from his place of refuge, which according to Josephus, was in the house of Machir ben-Ammiel, a prince of Gad or Manasseh at Lo-debar near Mahanaim.[1]

The murderers of Ish-bosheth carried his head to David at Hebron, only to meet the fate of the messenger of Saul's death. They were put to death, their hands and feet cut off and their bodies hanged over the Pool of Hebron, while the head of Ish-bosheth was buried in the sepulchre of Abner (I Sam. 4).

2. The minds of all the people were now united in favor of David. The elders came to him at Hebron, recognizing him as their brother, recalling his leadership of Israel in the time of Saul and acknowledging that God had appointed him "to feed His people Israel." So they anointed him as king of Israel at Hebron and he made with them a covenant, and the event was celebrated by a three days' feast (II Sam. 5:1-3; I Chron. 11:1-3; 12:39). David was now at the head of a powerful army, composed of the best warriors of all the tribes, who came ready armed to him at Hebron. Judah sent 6800, Simeon 7100, Levi 4600, besides 3700 priests, under Johoiada, with whom came the young Zadok, already famous for his valor and destined to bring back the high-priesthood into the house of Eleasar. Even Benjamin, which had hitherto stood fast by the family of Saul, contributed 3000 men, Ephraim, 20,800 and the half-tribe of Manasseh, 18,000. Two hundred captians led the whole tribe of Issachar, whose decision gained for them the praise that "they had understanding of the times to know what Israel ought to do." The 50,000 of Zebulun were all "expert in war, well armed, firm in their ranks, and of no double heart"; Naphtali furnished 37,000 such warriors, under 1000 captains, Dan, 28,600; and Asher, 40,000. The tribes of Reuben, Gad and half-Manasseh sent 120,000 well-armed warriors across the Jordan. The sum is 337,600 men,

1. I Sam. 4:4; I Chron. 8:34, 9:40; Josephus *Ant.* vii. 5, 5.

besides the whole tribe of Issachar (I Chron. 12:23-40).

Having this powerful army, David resolved to remove the seat of government from the remote Hebron nearer to the centre of the country, and his choice at once fell upon Jerusalem, the strong city of the Jebusites, situated on a rocky height 2600 feet above the level of the sea. But another reason also probably recommended Jerusalem to David as the capital of his kingdom. It was impossible for him to desert the great tribe to which he belonged and over which he had been reigning for some years. Now Jerusalem was the natural escape out of this difficulty, since the boundary between Judah and Benjamin ran at the foot of the hill on which the city stands. The city itself was actually in Benjamin but the territory of Judah lay just south across the narrow ravine of Hinnom.

David no doubt approached the city from the south. The city was at that time limited to an area on Ophel, the eastern hill between the ravines around Jersualem. A portion of the wall of the Jebusite city and one of its gates have been excavated in modern times. The wall was exceedingly strong, being twenty-seven feet in width and well-built. Therefore the Jebusites taunted the attacking Israelites, saying, "Except you take away the blind and the lame, you shall not come in." But they little understood the temper of the king or his men and even less Jehovah their God.

David's anger was roused and he at once proclaimed to his host that the first man who entered the city would be chief and captain (I Chron. 11:4-6). Joab the son of Zeruiah went up first. Entry was made into the city by its watercourse.[1] This was an underground tunnel going westward sixty-seven feet from the spring Gihon in the Kidron valley. At this point a forty foot vertical shaft extended down from the surface inside the walls to intersect the tunnel below. Thus water was available to the city even during seige.

Once entry was gained the intrepid Israelites quickly took the city. Thus David took the stronghold of Zion. This is the first time that that memorable name appears in the history. The fortress, which now became the capital of the kingdom, received the name of "the city of David" and David fortified its whole circuit round

---

1. Recent discoveries indicate the word translated "watercourse" may mean "hook." If so, it probably refers to scaling hooks by which David's men scaled the walls of Jerusalem, rather than their coming in by the underground watercourse.

about from Millo,[1] while Joab repaired the rest of the city (II Sam.
5:6-9; I Chron. 11:4-8). In this capital, the power of the king was
now thoroughly established: "David went on, and grew great; for
the Lord of hosts was with him" (II Sam. 5:10; I Chron. 11:9). His
power was acknowledged by Hiram king of Tyre, who sought for
the alliance which he henceforth steadily maintained with David
and Solomon, and who now sent cedar-timber from Lebanon,
with masons and carpenters, to build David a palace. But there
was already "a worm in the bud," which afterward blighted all
David's happiness. Disregarding the express command of Moses
(Deut. 17:17), he formed a numerous harem. Already, while at
Hebron, he had added to his first wife (1) Michael, restored to
him by Ish-bosheth, and to (2) Ahinoam, and (3) Abigail, the two
wives of his wanderings, four others, namely (4) Maacah, the
daughter of Talmai, king of Geshur, (5) Haggith, (6) Abital and
(7) Eglah; and each of them, except Michael who was childless,
had borne him one son at Hebron, namely (1; Amnon,
(2) Chiliab, (3) Absalom, (4) Adonijah, (5) Shephatiah and
(6) Ithream, and one daughter, Tamar, who was full sister to
Absalom by Maacah (II Sam. 3:2-5; I Chron. 3:1-4). At Jerusalem
he took more wives, whose names and number are not stated, and
who bore him ten more sons. Besides these, he had ten
concubines, whose children are not named. This list does not
include BATHSHEBA, whose story will be related soon. She
bore David five sons, of whom the youngest, SOLOMON, was his
successor (II Sam. 5:13-16; I Chron. 3). In all this David stopped
short of that fatal step contemplated in the warning of Moses, and
taken by Solomon, of multiplying to himself wives from heathen
nations, so as to turn away his heart from God (Deut. 17:17); but
the miseries he suffered in his family give the best answer to the
folly which quotes Scripture in sanction of polygamy. He reigned
at Jerusalem for thirty-three years, besides the seven years and a
half in Hebron, making his whole reign in round numbers forty
years. He was thirty years old at his first accession and seventy at
his death (I Sam. 5:4-5; I Chron. 3:4; 26:31; 29:27). It is
emphatically stated that "David perceived that Jehovah had
established him king over Israel, and that he had exalted his
kingdom *for his people Israel's sake*" (II Sam. 5:12).

A twofold work had been given him to perform: to establish the
worship of Jehovah in the place which he had chosen above all

---

1. Millo was probably a filled-in area behind stone terraces along the steep east side of Mt. Zion (Ophel).

others for his abode, and to extend the kingdom of Israel to the bounds promised to their fathers. With the former object first in his thoughts, he had proposed to the tribes who gathered at Hebron that the ark should be brought up from Kirjath-jearim but the project was delayed by war. The Philistines resolved not to give up without an effort their long domination over Israel, gathered their hosts in the valley of Rephaim, or the valley of the Giants. This is the fertile valley southwest of Jerusalem, about three miles from Bethlehem. At the command of God, David fell upon them with a fury as resistless as the outburst of water through a broken dike, whence the scene of slaughter was called Baal-perazim *(the place of breakings forth)*. The Philistines were not only routed but disgraced by the burning of their idols, which were left on the field of battle. A second victory was gained in the same valley by a stratagem prescribed by God, whose presence was indicated to the army of Israel by a rustling in the tops of the mulberry-trees, and the Philistines were smitten from Gibeon to Gezer. "And the fame of David went out into all lands; and Jehovah brought the fear of him upon all nations" (II Sam. 5:18-25; I Chron. 14:8-17; Comp. Isa. 28:21). Henceforth David is found acting on the offensive against the Philistines and meanwhile their defeat and the friendship of King Hiram secured peace along the whole maritime coast.

To this period belongs the touching story of the water of the well of Bethlehem. David expressed a longing for the water of which he used to drink as a boy and the three chief heroes cut their way through the army of the Philistines, which lay encamped in the valley of Rephaim, to the gate of Bethlehem and brought the water to David. But with self-denial like that of Alexander in the desert of Gedrosia, David poured the water on the ground, exclaiming, "Shall I drink the blood of these men, that have put their lives in jeopardy?" (II Sam. 23:13-19; I Chron. 11:15-21).

3. David had now the long desired opportunity for the removal of the ark. He had "sworn to Jehovah, and vowed to the mighty God of Jacob. Surely I will not come into the tabernacle of my house, nor go up into my bed; I will not give sleep to mine eyes, nor slumber to mine eyelids, until I find out a place for Jehovah, an habitation for the mighty God of Jacob" (Psalm 132:1-5). Since its restoration by the Philistines, the symbol of Jehovah's presence had had its stated abode at Kirjath-jearim, here called Baalah, under the care of Abinadab and his family (I

Sam. 6:21; 7:1). Thither David went with 30,000 men chosen from all the tribes and transported the ark with music and singing from Abinadab's house in Bigeah (the citadel of Kirjath-jearim) on a new cart, driven by Uzzah and Ahio, the two sons of Abinadab. But its progress to Jerusalem suffered a melancholy interruption. As the procession reached the threshing-floor of Nachon (or Chidon), the oxen shook the cart and Uzzah laid his hand upon the ark to steady it, forgetting that Jehovah needed not his aid. The profanation was named the place Perez-uzzah (the *breaking-forth on Uzzah*). But Uzzah's fate was not merely the penalty of his own rashness. The improper mode of transporting the ark, which ought to have been borne on the shoulders of the Levites, was the primary cause of his unholy deed and David distinctly recognized it as a punishment on the people in general, "because we sought Him not after the due order" (I Chron. 15:13; Num. 4:5,15, 17-20).

The terror of this proof of Jehovah's jealousy stayed further progress for the time, and the ark was carried aside to the house of Obed-edom, the Gittite. There it remained three months and during that time Jehovah blessed Obed-edom and all his house (I Sam. 6:1-11; I Chron. 13).

Meanwhile David prepared for its final transport to Jerusalem with a care suitable to the awful lesson he had received. Instead of removing the old tabernacle which was doubtless much impaired by age, he set up a new tent for it in the city of David. In the first procession, the king and his warriors had perhaps held too prominent a place, to the injury of the religious solemnity which was now duly preserved. David entrusted the duty of carrying it to those whom Jehovah had appointed. He assembled the three families of the house of Levi with the sons of Aaron and the high-priests of both the branches, Zadok, of the house of Eleazar, and Abiathar, of the house of Ithamar, and bade them sanctify themselves to bring up the ark of God; and so they carried it on their shoulders after the manner prescribed by Moses. They were escorted by David and his chosen warriors with the elders of Israel and the procession started with every sign of joy. The first movement was watched with deep anxiety lest there should still be some fault to provoke God's anger; but when the Levites had taken six steps in safety, it was seen that God helped them and the procession halted while David sacrificed seven bullocks and seven rams. He then took his place before the ark, clothed only with the linen ephod of the priestly order without his royal robes and danced with all his might, playing upon the harp as he led the way up to the hill of Zion amid the songs of the Levites, the joyful shouts of all the people and the noise of cornets and trumpets and cymbals and psalteries and harps. Having placed it in the tabernacle he had prepared and having offered burnt-offerings and peace-offerings, he blessed the people in the name of Jehovah and dealt to each of the multitude, women as well as men, a loaf of bread, a large piece of meat and a flagon of wine, doubtless from the offerings. He then returned to bless his household but his reception cast a shade even over this most joyful day of all his reign. His enthusiastic dance before the ark had been observed with scorn by his wife Michal from a window of the new palace; she met him on his return with insulting reproaches, to which he made an indignant answer and she remained barren to the day of her death (II Sam. 6; I Chron. 15-16).

In both these ceremonials a prominent feature was singing the praises of Jehovah to the music of various instruments. On the first removal of the ark we are told that "David and all Israel played before God with all their might, and with singing, and with harps, psalteries, timbrels, cymbals, and trumpets." On the second occasion David made a complete arrangement of the musical service, placing it under the direction of the priests, Zadok and Abiathar, and appointing the Levites for its performance, with ASAPH[1] at their head. The First Book of Chronicles describes the order of this "service of song," and preserves the Psalm of thanksgiving which David first delivered into the hand of Asaph and his brethren.[2] The comparison of this with several in the Book of Psalms shows that it is either an outline which was afterward expanded into separate poems or an epitome of the Psalms used on the occasion. For there are many Psalms to be referred to the removal of the ark to Jerusalem, both on the grounds of tradition and of their own internal evidence. At the head of these is the 132nd, in which David in his own name describes the removal of the ark from the first desire of his heart to its final accomplishment, records God's eternal covenant with him and his house, and celebrates Jehovah's choice of Zion for his abode. The 68th is equally suitable for the first removal of the ark,

---

1. Psalm 50 and 73 to 83 are attributed to Asaph. He was in aftertimes celebrated as a seer as well as a musical composer, and was put on a part with David (II Chron. 29:30; Neh. 12:46). His office appears to have remained hereditary in his family, unless he was the founder of a school of poets and musical composers, who were called after him "the sons of Asaph" (I Chron. 25:1; II Chron. 20:14; Ezra 2:41).

2. I Chron. 16. Compare Psalm 105:1-22; 96; 196:47-48.

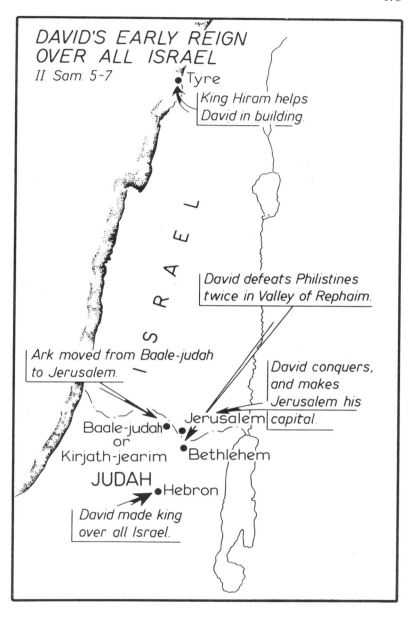

DAVID'S EARLY REIGN
OVER ALL ISRAEL
II Sam. 5-7

Tyre

King Hiram helps
David in building.

ISRAEL

David defeats Philistines
twice in Valley of Rephaim.

Ark moved from Baale-judah
to Jerusalem.

David conquers,
and makes
Jerusalem his
capital.

Jerusalem

Baale-judah
or
Kirjath-jearim

Bethlehem

JUDAH

Hebron

David made king
over all Israel.

for the solemn pause in which David offered sacrifice when the Levites had lifted it at its second removal or for its entrance into the city of David; it begins with words appointed by Moses to be sung when the ark was lifted, "Let God arise, let his enemies be scattered," and it advances from the record of victory after victory to the final establishment of God's house at Jerusalem and the prediction of the worship He should receive from all nations of the earth. The 24th marks the entrance of the ark into the citadel of Zion by its grand refrain,

> "Lift up your heads, O yet gates;
> And be ye lift up, ye everlasting doors;
> And the King of glory shall come in:"

words which clearly set forth the idea which runs through all these psalms, of victory as well as praise. They celebrate not only the inauguration of the place of religious worship but the installation of Jehovah, the glorious King, who has at length completed the victory over the heathen enemies of his people in the citadel from which he shall still go forth to conquer all the world. He is marked as the God of battles by the new name which heralds his entrance:

> *"Who is this King of glory?*
> Jehovah strong and mighty,
> Jehovah mighty in battle."
> *"Who is this King of glory?*
> The Lord of Hosts,
> He is the King of glory."

The 96th, 105th, 106th, as we have seen, are probably the full form, adapted to the Temple service of the Psalm which David delivered to Asaph and his brethren at the close of this great ceremony. Of others less certainly belonging to this occasion, the 15th describes the character of a true citizen of Zion and forms a sort of proclamation against impiety in the new city; the 101st is in a similar vein with more especial reference to David's conduct of his own house; the 29th (in the LXX) and the 30th have titles referring them to this time.

All other arrangements were made by David with equal care for the whole order of divine worship, according to the law of Moses. Asaph and his brethren were appointed to minister in the daily service before the ark. The office of chief doorkeeper was committed to Obed-edom in whose house the ark had rested. Zadok and the priests were charged with the daily and other sacrifices at the Tabernacle which remained at Gibeon (I Chron. 16:37-43).

David's zeal for the house of God was still only fulfilled in part. His new city was blessed with the symbol of Jehovah's presence but that sacred object had itself no worthy abode, The palace built for the king by Hiram's workmen was now finished and no war summoned him from its halls; but as he sat in it he was troubled by the thought which has so often since lighted up the "Lamp of Sacrifice"; "See now, I dwell in a house of cedars, but the ark of the covenant of Jehovah dwelleth within curtains." He uttered his feelings to the prophet Nathan, who now first appears as David's chief counselor; and as if there could be but one response to so pious a desire, without waiting to consult God, Nathan replied, "Do all that is in thy heart, for God is with thee" (II Sam. 7:1-3; I Chron. 17:1-2). But that same night the word of God came to Nathan, bidding him tell David that he was not to build a house for God to dwell in. He is reminded that Jehovah had been content to dwell in a tent ever since the Exodus and that He had not spoken a word to any of the tribes or the judges about building him a house of cedar. In these words, which sound like a gentle rebuke for a tendency to materialism in God's worship, we see the same principle which Solomon recognizes in the very act of dedicating his temple: "Behold! the heaven and heaven of heavens can not contain Thee; how much less this house that I have built!" (I Kings 8:27; II Chron. 2:6; Comp. Isa. 66:1; Acts 7:49; 17:24). But the design was only postponed, not forbidden. Just as God condescended to the wish of the people for a king and then made the stability of David's throne the new basis of the commonwealth, so he chose a habitation for himself in the city of David as a sign that the period of pilgrimage was ended and that his home was with the king and people of His choice. So Nathan was commissioned to tell David that Jehovah, who had been with him hitherto, would first establish *his* house and would raise up one of his sons, whose kingdom should be established forever and who should build the house of God in the place chosen by Himself (II Sam. 7:4-17; I Chron. 17:3-15). This prediction, referring first to Solomon, is expressed in terms that could only be fulfilled in the Messiah; and it is clear that David understood it so from the wonderful prayer which he poured out before God in thanksgiving for the honor put upon him (II Sam. 7:18-29; I Chron. 17:16-27). Similar feelings are uttered in several of the

"Messianic Psalms," which have therefore been regarded as written on the occasion of Nathan's prophecy, such as the 2nd, 45th, 22nd, 16th, 118th and 110th, in all of which the promises of God to David and his house are celebrated in that wonderfully expressive language which reveals Him who was at once David's Son and Lord (Matt. 22:44; Mark 12:36; Luke 20:42).

A KEY PASSAGE
God's Promise to King David — II Sam. 7:12-13

	SOLOMON	JESUS MESSIAH
"I will set up thy seed after thee."	Fulfilled. I Kings 2:12	Fulfilled. Matthew 1:1
"He shall build a house for my name."	Fulfilled. I Kings 7:51	Fulfilled. Eph. 2:21-22 I Pet. 2:5
"I will establish the throne of his kingdom for ever."	Did not fulfill. I Kings 11:43	Fulfilled. Luke 1:32-33 Rev. 1:9, Isaiah 9:7

4. His own throne and the service of God's sanctuary being thus established, David advanced to the final subjugation of the enemies of Israel.

a. We have already mentioned the two last invasions of the PHILISTINES: they were now, in their turn, invaded and subdued by David, who took the proud frontier city of Gath, called Metheg-Ammah or "The bridle of the mother-city" (II Sam. 8:1). Except one or two minor combats, we hear of no further trouble from the Philistines during David's reign. This conquest secured to Israel its promised boundary on the southwest, the "river of Egypt."

b. Turning to the eastern frontier, David exacted from MOAB a signal vengeance for all her enmity against Israel down from the time of Balak. Two-thirds of the people were put to death and the other third reduced to tribute (II Sam. 8:2; I Chron. 18:2). David's personal relations to this nation, whose blood he shared, had been so friendly that we have seen him committing his father and mother to the care of the King of Moab. A Jewish tradition says that they were foully murdered. There is not a word of this in the Scripture narrative but we may be quite sure that David's vengeance was provoked by some treacherous insult, as in the later case of Ammon. Thus was Balaam's prophecy fulfilled: "Out of Jacob shall come he that shall have dominion, and shall destroy him that remaineth of Ar" (the metropolis of Moab). To this war belong the exploits of Benaiah, the son of Jehoiada (II Sam. 23:20; I Chron. 11:22).

c. The eastern frontier being now secured, for Nahash the Ammonite was his friend, David advanced to the conquest of the promised boundary on the northeast, "the great river Euphrates" (II Sam. 8:3; I Chron. 18:3; Comp. Gen. 15:18). Two SYRIAN kingdoms lay between him and his purpose. That of ZOBAH, which has been mentioned more than once before, was then governed by Hadadezer, the son of Rehob, whom David defeated, taking from him his force of 1000 chariots, 700 horses and 20,000 infantry. The chariot-horses were hamstrung, according to the command of Moses, but David could not resist the temptation of reserving 100 chariots as an ornament for his royal state (II Sam. 8:3-4; I Chron. 18:3-4). The Syrians of Damascus, coming to the help of Hadadezer, were defeated with the loss of 22,000 men and that fairest and oldest of the cities of the world was made tributary to David and garrisoned by his troops. "Thus did Jehovah preserve David withersoever he went" (II Sam. 8:5-6; I Chron. 18:5-7).

These victories led to an alliance with Toi, king of HAMATH (a kingdom including both the city of Hamath and the valley of the Orontes), who sent his son Joram to congratulate David on the defeat of Hadadezer, his own enemy. This, together with the old friendship of Hiram king of Tyre, secured the northern frontier, and David returned to Jerusalem laden with the golden shields of Hadadezer's body-guard, the brass taken from his cities and the vessels of gold and silver and brass which Joram had brought as presents. All these, together with the spoils of Moab and the Philistines, the plunder formerly taken from Amalek, and that gained afterward from Edom and the sons of Ammon, he dedicated for the service of the future Temple (II Sam. 8:7-12; I Chron. 18:7-11).

d. The long conflict of EDOM with his brother Israel was now brought to its first decision by a great victory gained by Abishai, the son of Zeruiah, in "the valley of Salt" (on the south of the Dead Sea), in which the Edomites lost 18,000 men (II Sam. 8:13-14; I Chron. 18:12-13).[1] David was probably in Syria at the time of this battle, which was followed up by a great army under Joab, who in six months almost exterminated the male population. David then visited the conquered land and placed garrisons in all the cities. The young king Hadad, however, escaped to Egypt and became afterward a formidable enemy to Solomon (I Kings 11:14-22).

These victories which David celebrates in the 60th and possibly the 110th Psalms, carried the southern frontier of Israel to the eastern head of the Red Sea; and from that point to the frontier of Egypt, the Arab tribes had felt enough of his power as an exile not to molest him in the hour of his triumph. The bounds of the promised land were now fully occupied, though not even now so completely as if Israel had been faithful from the first. For besides the scattered remnants of the old inhabitants, several of whom (as Ittai the Gittite, Uriah the Hittite, and others) were conspicuous among the king's great men; besides that the Philistines and others who had been devoted to extermination were only reduced to tribute; there was one fair province unsubdued, the whole coast of Phoenicia, the great cities of which still flourished under their native kings, the chief of whom was David's firm ally.

These extended limits were only preserved during the reigns of David and of Solomon, a period of about sixty years. For that time, however, the state formed no longer a petty monarchy, barely holding its own among the surrounding nations, as under Saul; but it was truly one of the great Oriental monarchies; too truly, indeed, for the magnificence of Solomon sapped its strength and prepared its speedy dissolution. Meanwhile David's position is thus described by the prophet Nathan: "Thus saith Jehovah of hosts, I took thee from the sheepcote, from following the sheep, to be ruler over my people, over Israel: and I was with thee whithersoever thou wentest, and have cut off all thine enemies out of thy sight, and have made thee a great name, like unto the name of the great men that are in the earth" (II Sam. 7:9). Thus "David

---

1. Compare II Sam. 8:13 and I Chron. 19:12. The two very similar names, Edom and Aram (Syria), in the two accounts have led some to suppose that the reading in Samuel is in error. However, *both* Edom and *Syria* were actually conquered and the spoils of both dedicated by David.

reigned over all Israel and executed judgment and justice among all his people" (II Sam. 8:15; I Chron. 18:14).

5. The constitution which David established for his kingdom was preserved in its main forms to the end of the monarchy.

a. *The Royal Family*. We have already spoken of David's goodly progeny which well entitled him to the epithet of "patriarch" (Acts 2:29). The princes were under the charge of Jehiel, probably the Levite of that name (I Chron. 27:32; 15:21; II Chron. 20:14); but when Solomon was born, he was committed to the care of the prophet Nathan (II Sam. 12:25). The warm love of David for his sons (II Sam. 13:31,33,36; 14:33; 18:5,33; 19:4; I Kings 1:6) was shown in an indulgence that was the proximate cause of the family calamities which were visited on him as a judgment for his one great sin. But those dark clouds had not yet gathered and he had nothing to mar his pleasure in his children, two of whom, at least, Absalom and Adonijah, inherited his beauty.

b. The *Military Organization* was based on that of Saul.

1. "The *Host*" was composed, from the first formation of the nation in the desert, of all males capable of bearing arms, who were summoned to war by the judges or princes of tribes when the necessity arose. Saul formed a chosen band of 3000 as a standing army, the nucleus of the whole force, under ABNER as commander-in-chief. The same post was held under David by JOAB, who won it by the capture of the citadel of Jerusalem. He led out the host to war when the king did not take the field in person (II Sam. 12:26; I Kings 11:15). The standing organization was improved under David by the division of the whole host into twelve bodies of 24,000 each (288,000 in all), whose turn of service came every month, and each of which had a commander chosen from David's band of mighty men of valor (I Chron. 27:1-15). In accordance with the institution prescribed by Moses, the force was entirely of infantry; the 100 chariots reserved by David from the Syrians seem to have been only for purposes of state. The weapons constantly alluded to in the history and the Psalms are spears and shields, swords and bows. The use of body armor is mentioned in the story of Goliath.

2. The *Body-guard* was recruited to so great an extent from foreigners (and chiefly Philistines, a practice dating probably from David's exile) that the force bore a foreign

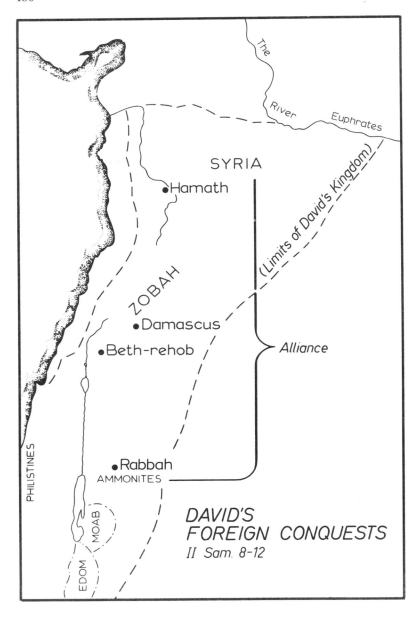

DAVID'S
FOREIGN CONQUESTS
II Sam. 8-12

name, like the *Scottish* archers and the *Swiss* guards of the French kings and the Pope. At least it seems most probable that "Cherethites and Pelethites" are proper names, the former of a Philistine tribe (I Sam. 30:14) and the latter a form of the word Philistines.[1] They are mentioned in close connection with the "Gittites," a body of 600 men who came to David from Gath under Ittai, but these seem only to have joined him on the special occasion of his flight from Absalom. The commander of the Cherethites and Pelethites was Benaiah, the son of Jehoiada, the priest of the line of Eleazar.

3. The *Heroes* or *Mighty Men,* were a peculiar and favored body, composed originally of the 600 warriors who joined David in his exile and afterward maintained at the same number. They were formed into three great divisions of 200 each and thirty bands of twenty each, with their respective leaders. The captains of twenties formed "the thirty" and the commanders of two hundreds "the three," above whom was "the captain of the mighty men." This post was held by Abishai, the son of Zeruiah, but though first in rank he was inferior in prowess to "the three," who were Jashobeam (or Adino) the **Hachmonite**; Eleazar, son of Dodo the Ahohite, who was with David at **Ephes-dammim**; and Shammah, son of Agee the Hararite. We have also a list of "the thirty," some of whose names occur also in other passages. It opens with the name of Asahel, the brother of Joab, who was slain by Abner, and closes with that of Uriah the Hittite, who fell by the treachery of David himself (II Sam. 23:8-39; I Chron. 11:10-14, 20-47).[2]

c. The *Civil Administration* was conducted under the eyes of the king himself, assisted by a council of which the chief members were Jonathan, the king's nephew,[3] son of his brother Shimeah, who seems to have been his chief secretary; Ahithophel of Gilo, afterward so famous as Absalom's adviser; his rival Hushai the Archite, the king's "friend" or "companion"; Benaiah, the son of Jehoiada; and Zadok and

---

1. The words are otherwise interpreted "executioners" and "couriers", functions certainly performed by the body-guard. See II Kings 11:4; I Kings 14:27.

2. The comparison of the two lists affords an interesting example of the minor variations of the sacred text. The excess above the number of thirty is naturally accounted for by the new appointments required to fill up vacancies.

3. I Chron. 27:32, it seems that "nephew" is the truer meaning of the word translated uncle, and that this is the same Jonathan as in II Sam. 21:21; I Chron. 20:7.

Abiathar, the high-priests; together with Joab and probably Benaiah, whose military rank gave them, like Abner and David under Saul, a high place at the court. Then there were the great officers of state, Sheva or Seraiah, the "scribe" or public secretary; Jehoshaphat, the "recorder" or historian; Adoram and Ira the Jairite, who was "a chief ruler about David" with functions probably judicial, and the same rank was held by David's sons (II Sam. 8:16-18; 20:23-26; I Chron. 18:14-27; 27:32-34). The royal possessions in the fields, cities, villages and castles, comprising farms, vineyards, olive and other trees, stores of wine and oil, herds of oxen and camels, and flocks of sheep, besides treasure, were entrusted to officers for each branch, all under a chief treasurer, Azmaveth, the son of Adiel (I Chron. 27:25-31). But a place was still found for the patriarchal government of the tribes, whose princes are enumerated (I Chron. 27:16-32), the prince of Judah being, not David himself, but his brother Elihu (doubtless the same as Eliab) (I Sam. 16:16) by the right of primogeniture.

d. The *Religious Institutions* were in part mixed up with the constitution of the monarchy itself. Like Saul and some of the judges, we see David offering sacrifices — an apparent usurpation of the priestly office, to be explained perhaps by the patriarchal priesthood which was vested in the chief of a family and therefore by a natural analogy in the chief of the state;[1] and he even gives the priestly benediction (II Sam. 6:6). But his peculiar character as the religious head of the state is seen in his inspiration as a prophet and psalmist. *"Being a prophet,"* as St. Peter explicitly declared (Acts 2:30), he foretold in plainer and more glowing language than any that had yet been used, those great events of which the whole ceremonial of the Jewish Church and even his own kingdom were but types, "the sufferings of Christ, and the glory that should follow." As a prophet too, he taught the people those principles of religious and moral truth of which the Psalms are full and which in the Proverbs were to a great extent learnt by Solomon from him. As "the sweet Psalmist of Israel," who said of himself "The Spirit of Jehovah spoke by men, and His word was in my tongue," it was his peculiar honor, not only for the Jewish Church, but for the Church Universal to the end of time to direct that part of God's worship which is the best

---

1. Even Samuel, though a Levite, was not a priest.

utterance of the heart, the tuneful notes of praise, inseparably blended with prayer and with the utterance of divine truth. His pre-eminence in this respect is unaffected by the doubts about the authorship of many of the Psalms. A great truth is expressed by the common title which names the whole Book "The Psalms of David," for he founded psalmody as an institution, taught it to Asaph and his other immediate successors and gave the model which all later psalmists followed.

While he thus furnished the matter of psalmody, he regulated its manner by arranging for the first time a full choral service. To this office David, in conjunction with the chiefs of the Levites, set apart three families, one from each of the three houses of the tribe, the Gershonites, Kohathites and Merarites. They were *prophets* as well as singers, "to prophesy with harps, with psalteries, and with cymbals" (I Chron. 15:16-22; 25:1-2; Comp. 23:6); and they handed down their art from generation to generation by a systematic course of instruction, "the teacher as well as the scholar" (I Chron. 15:3-8; II Chron. 23:13). These families were those of ASAPH, the son of Berechiah the Gershonite, the chief singer and also distinguished as a seer (II Chron. 29:30); of HEMAN the Kohathite, son of Joel and grandson of the prophet Samuel, and himself "the king's seer in the words of God" (I Chron. 15:5); and of JEDUTHUN (or Ethan), a Merarite, who is also called "the king's seer" (II Chron. 30:15). The names of each of these leaders are found in the titles of particular Psalms and the tripartite division was observed till the Captivity (II Chron. 29, 30), and probably restored after the return (Neh. 11:17; I Chron. 9:16). At first they were divided between the ark at Jerusalem and the tabernacle at Gibeon, the family of Asaph being assigned to the former and those of Heman and Jeduthun to the latter (I Chron. 16:37-42; 25:8-31). The three families numbered 288 principal singers, divided by lot into twenty-four courses of twelve each, but the total of the Levites engaged in praising Jehovah "with the instruments which David made" was 4000 (I Chron. 23:5). The rest of the Levites, amounting to 34,000 were arranged into the three families of Gershon, Kohath and Merari. Six thousand bore the dignity of officers and judges; 400 were set apart to the humbler office of door-keepers (I Chron. 23:4-5; Comp. Ps. 84:10); and the general service of the sanctuary, "the work of the house of

Jehovah," was committed to the remaining 24,000 (I Chron. 23:4). They were relieved of the hardest part of that work, carrying the tabernacle and its vessels, now that God had given rest to his people to dwell at Jerusalem forever (I Chron. 23:25,26); and as the offices which remained, though numerous, were comparatively light, David assigned them to the Levites above *twenty* years, though the census was still taken according to the ancient standard of *thirty* and upward (I Chron. 23:3,23,27). Their offices were to wait on the priests for the service of the house of Jehovah, purifying the holy place and the holy things, preparing the shew-bread and the meal-offerings, praising God at the morning and evening service, and assisting in offering the burnt sacrifices on the Sabbaths and the stated feasts (I Chron. 23:24-32).

For the higher duties allotted by the law of Moses to the priesthood, the sons of Aaron were arranged according to the two houses of Eleazar and Ithamar, his two elder sons, Nadab and Abihu, having died childless for their disobedience (Lev. 10; Num. 26:60-61). We have seen that Eleazar succeeded his father as high-priest but it is clear that the head of the house of Ithamar was in some sense co-heir to the office. In the person and family of Eli this state of things was reversed: the high-priesthood was vested in the house of Ithamar while that of Eleazar did not abdicate its claims. So under David we find both Zadok and Abiathar recognized as priests, the former being named first by the right of primogeniture while the latter actually held the office of high-priest. This double priesthood was in fact connected with a twofold service, Zadok ministering at the old tabernacle in Gibeon and Abiathar before the ark at Jerusalem. By the census taken toward the close of David's reign, it appeared that the families of the house of Eleazar were twice as many as those of the house of Ithamar, there being sixteen of the former and eight of the latter.[1] The twenty-four chiefs of these families were made the heads of twenty-four "courses," who were arranged in order by lot for the performance of the services of the sanctuary and named ever afterward from their present chiefs.[2] The courses were as follows:

---

1. The disparity may have been caused in part by the slaughter of the priests with Hophni and Phinehas, and in part by Saul's massacre of Ahimelech's family (I Sam. 22:16-19).

2. Even when, after the Captivity, the courses were found to be reduced to 4, these were again divided into 24, which were called by the ancient names (I Chron. 24).

1. Jehoiarib	9. Jeshuah	17. Hezir
2. Jedaiah	10. Shecaniah	18. Aphses
3. Harim	11. Eliashib	19. Pethahiah
4. Scorim	12. Jakim	20. Jehezekel
5. Malchijah	13. Huppoh	21. Jachin
6. Mijamin	14. Jeshebeah	22. Gamul
7. Hakkoz	15. Bilgah	23. Delaiah
8. Abijah	16. Immer	24. Mahaziah

To the eighth course (that of Abijah or Abia) belonged Zacharias, the father of John the Baptist (Luke 1:5-10,23). The term for which each course was on duty is not expressly stated but from the analogy of the service of the porters (I Chron. 9:25; II Kings 11:5) and from the testimony of the Jewish writers, it seems to have been weekly, beginning on the Sabbath, the services of the week being arranged among the members of the course by lot.[1] The twenty-four courses of singers were associated respectively with those of the priests (I Chron. 25).

These arrangements formed the model of the Temple service under Solomon, except that the separate worship of Gibeon was discontinued and the house of Ithamar was finally excluded from the high-priesthood by the deposition of Abiathar (I Kings 2:26-27).

Lastly, a special association was maintained by David with Jehovah through the *prophets;* first, SAMUEL, who anointed him and afterward protected him at Ramah; next GAD, who joined him in his exile; and lastly, NATHAN, the counselor of his throne and faithful reprover of his grievous sins.

6. Thus established in his kingdom, David had no further fear of rivalry from the house of Saul and he was anxious to find an opportunity of performing his covenant with Jonathan. He learned from Ziba, who had been one of Saul's courtiers, that Mephibosheth, the lame son of Jonathan, was living in the house of Machir at Lodebar; and having sent for him, he restored to him all the land of Saul and his family. Committing the charge of this property to Ziba, David retained Mephibosheth at Jerusalem and gave him a place at the royal table like his own sons (II Sam. 9). We do not know how long afterward but probably earlier than it stands in the order of the narrative, the king protected

---

1. Still the numbers raise the suspicion that the first arrangement may have been *monthly:* two courses being engaged each month, one at Gibeon and one at Jerusalem.

Mephibosheth from a great danger. The land was visited with a famine for three years, the cause of which was declared by the oracle of Jehovah to be "for Saul and for his bloody house, because he slew the Gibeonites" (II Sam. 21). This massacre, in shameful violation of the oath of Joshua and the elders of Israel, was one of those acts of passionate zeal in which Saul tried to drown the remorse of his later years. In reply to David's offer of satisfaction, the Gibeonites demanded the lives of seven of Saul's sons, and the king gave up to them the two sons of Saul by his concubine Rizpah and the five sons that Merab had borne to Adriel, to whom she was married when Saul took her from David. These seven were hanged by the Gibeonites on the hill of Gibeah, Saul's own city. They hung there from the beginning of barley harvest till the rains set in though the law provided that, in such cases, the bodies should be buried by sunset (Deut. 21:22-23). But Rizpah took her station upon the rock with only a covering of sackcloth to keep the bodies from the birds of prey by day and from the wild beasts by night till the rain began to fall. Touched with her devotion, David caused their remains to be taken down and interred in the sepulchre of Kish at Zelah, together with the bones of Saul and Jonathan, which he transported from Jabesh-gilead (Comp. I Sam. 31:10-13). Mephibosheth, the son of Jonathan, whom David had refused to give up to the Gibeonites (II Sam. 21:7), was now the sole survivor of the house of Saul, with his infant son Micah through whom the family was continued to the latest period of the nation's history. We hear of him again before the end of David's reign.

It has been observed that this famine was the first of those three great adversities of David's reign which are described in the alternative proposed by the prophet Nathan: a three years' famine, a three months' flight or a three days' pestilence; when David, having had bitter experience of the first two, chose the third as a dispensation direct from God (II Sam. 24:13; I Chron. 21:12).

7. This first period of David's reign is marked by another great success in war and in connection therewith by the fall which embittered the rest of his life and which, as the prophet declared at the time, has ever since "given great occasion to the enemies of Jehovah to blaspheme" (II Sam. 12:14). NAHASH, king of the children of Ammon who had been David's ally and some suppose his relation, died, leaving the throne to his son Hanun (II Sam. 10; I Chron. 19). David sent an embassy of condolence and

friendship to the new king but Hanun, persuaded by his counselors that the ambassadors only came as spies, sent them back with shameful personal insults. In anticipation of David's vengeance, the Ammonite obtained help from the Syrians of Beth-rehob, Zobah, Maacah and Ish-tob, who joined him with 33,000 men.[1] On the other side, Joab took the field with all the host of Israel. A decisive battle was fought before Medeba (I Chron. 19:7). While the Israelites had followed the Ammonites up to the gates, the Syrian allies had enclosed them in the rear. Joab took front against the Syrians with all the chosen warriors of Israel, leaving the rest under Abishai to make head against the Ammonites. The Syrians were routed and the Ammonites then fled and shut themselves up in their city, while Joab returned to Jerusalem. The defeated Syrians formed a grand confederacy under Hadarezer with their brethren beyond the Euphrates, but David crossed the Jordan with the whole force of Israel and defeated them in a pitched battle at Helam, where they lost 7000 charioteers, 40,000 infantry and their captain, Shophach. The Syrians became tributary to David and abandoned the cause of Ammon (II Sam. 10:15-19).

The next year at the return of the campaigning season, Joab again took the field and ravaged the lands of the Beni-ammi and shut them up in Rabbah, their chief city and a strongly fortified place.[2] David remained at Jerusalem and if this inaction arose from a growing inclination to a luxurious enjoyment of his royal state, his self-indulgence led him into a terrible temptation and wrought his fall. In the restlessness which follows a day of such indolence, he rose one evening from his bed to enjoy a walk upon the roof of his lofty palace of cedar, which overlooked the woman's court of a neighboring house; and there he saw a fair woman in her bath and became at once enamored. On inquiry, he found that she was BATHSHEBA (or Bathshua), the daughter of Eliam and the wife of one of his "thirty mighty men," Uriah the Hittite, who was then fighting the king's battles under Joab. Such a discovery might have checked the passion even of a heathen despot but David fell; and when the consequence of his crime exposed himself to discovery and Bathsheba to a shameful death, the king, after a vain attempt to conceal his guilt, which only

---

1. According to *Chronicles*, there were nearly as many chariots, 32,000, besides those of Maacah. It seems probable that the numbers in *Samuel* ought also to be referred to the chariots.

2. II Sam. 11:1, I Chron. 20:1. Rabbah, now called *Amman*, lies on a river about 22 miles from the Jordan, and on the road from Heshbon to Bosra. It consisted of an upper and a lower city, the latter being called by Joab "the city of waters" (II Sam. 12:37). The upper city rose abruptly on the north side of the lower town and was a place of very great strength.

showed more of the noble nature of the man he had outraged
(II Sam. 11:6-13), added treacherous murder to his adultery. He
made Uriah the bearer of his own death-warrant to Joab, who
exposed the brave man to a sally from the best warriors of the
Ammonites and he fell in ignorance of his sovereign's guilt and
his wife's involvement. The artifice was kept up by a message
from Joab to the king, excusing the apparent rashness of his
attack by the significant conclusion, "Thy servant, Uriah the
Hittite, is dead also," and the messenger was sent back to comfort
Joab with a cold-blooded allusion to the fortune of war. After the
customary mourning for her husband, Bathsheba, who seems
throughout to have consented to the sin, was taken to the house of
David and became his wife and soon afterward bore him a son
(II Sam. 11).

Thus far man's share in this drama of lust and blood, but now
another voice is heard: "THE THING THAT DAVID HAD DONE
DISPLEASED JEHOVAH" (II Sam. 12:27). He sent the prophet
Nathan to the king with that well-known parable of the rich man,
who spared his own abundant flocks and herds and seized for his
guest the one ewe-lamb of the poor man, his darling and his
children's pet (II Sam. 12:1-4). Our surprise that David's
conscience was not at once awakened may yield to the
consideration that his heart was not yet hardened in guilt, so that
his natural sense of justice broke forth in the indignant sentence,
"As Jehovah liveth, the man that hath done this thing is a son of
death"; and he was going on to describe the restitution he would
exact, when the lips of Nathan uttered those words, which have
from that day been echoed by every sinner's awakened
conscience, "THOU ART THE MAN!" Then the prophet pronounced
the sentence of the King of kings on him who had just been
sentencing the unknown culprit. Reproaching David with his
ingratitude for all that Jehovah had done and would yet have
done for him, he announced the appropriate punishment: that as
his sword had broken up the house of Uriah, the sword should
never depart from his own house; and that as he had outraged the
sanctities of domestic life, his own should be likewise outraged but
with the difference which God always makes between the secret
sin and the public punishment: "For thou didst it secretly, but I
will do this thing before all Israel and before the sun." Then
follow the few simple words of repentance and forgiveness: "And
David said unto Nathan, I have sinned against Jehovah. And
Nathan said unto David, Jehovah also hath put away thy sin; thou

shalt not die." But the path of repentance, however plain, is a "strait and narrow way," and how David "agonized" to enter into it, we may read in the fifty-first Psalm. In the bitterness of his anguish as well as in the fullness of his pardon, David once more appears as the type of the sinning, suffering, repenting and forgiven man, who has ever since found in that one psalm the perfect utterance of his deepest feelings.

But even the "godly sorrow, which worketh repentance unto life," does not avert the temporal consequences of sin, whether in the form of its natural fruits or of special judgments. And so Nathan not only does not recall the woes denounced on David's house, which were in part the natural consequence of his polygamy, and of that weak parental indulgence which has been the besetting sin of many a great man, but he goes on to declare a special punishment for that consequence of David's sin which we still see in action: "Because by this deed thou hast given great occasion to the enemies of Jehovah to blaspheme, the child also that is born unto thee shall surely die." And now David was called to prove the sincerity of his repentance by his submission to the punishment which began to work. No sooner had Nathan gone home, than God struck the newborn child with a mortal sickness; and David prayed and fasted and lay all night on the ground, refusing all comfort from his attendants. On the seventh day David learnt the child's death from the whisperings of the courtiers, who feared to crush him with the news. To their great surprise he put off all signs of mourning, went to worship in the house of God and then sat down to eat, explaining to his attendants that while there remained any hope of the child's life, he fasted and wept in the forlorn hope that God might yet grant him its life; but now mourning could not bring it back from the dead and he added those memorable words which we cannot but understand as expressing the higher hopes, with which they have so often been echoed by bereaved Christian parents: *"I shall go to him;* but he shall not return to me." The 32nd Psalm expresses David's return to hope and peace. And "God, who comforteth them that are cast down," ordained that his relation to Bathsheba should be the source not only of comfort to David himself but of glory to his kingdom and of blessing to all generations of mankind, by the birth of a son whom he named SOLOMON, in memory of the *peace* which was established at the same time and whom, at the command of Nathan, he also named JEDIDIAH (beloved of Jehovah), in token of the special favor which God showed him from his birth (II Sam. 12:24-25). He became the successor of David and the progenitor of the Messiah, of whose kingdom as "the prince of Peace" his peaceful reign was a conspicuous type.

The peace, which the name of Solomon commemorates, had been established by the final conquest of the Ammonites. Joab, having reduced Rabbah to the last extremities by taking the lower city with its waters, reserved the honor of the victory for David, who marched out at the head of all Israel and took the city. He placed on his own head the sacred crown called the "crown of Milcolm (or Moloch)," weighing a talent of gold and set with precious stones, and added the spoil of the city to the treasures prepared for the house of God (II Sam. 12:26,30; I Chron. 20:1-2). The crown is said to have been worn by David ever afterward but this could only have been on rare ceremonies and then for a few moments from its enormous weight, 114 pounds. The long resistance of the city and the insult which had provoked the war were punished by a cruel massacre in which all the cities of the Beni-ammi were involved. "David brought out the people, and put them under (or cut them with) saws, and harrows of iron, and axes, and made them pass through the brick-kiln" (II Sam. 12:31; I Chron. 20:3), the fire, perhaps, through which their children passed "to their grim idol."

The triumphant return of David and his army to Jerusalem concludes the first period of his reign, the glory of which is overshadowed by that great sin, the punishment of which was to render its second part so disastrous.

Questions on Section III
David's Reign in Triumph

1. Whom did David consult before going up to one of the cities of Judah (II Sam. 2:1)?
2. What was the name of David's wife from Jezreel (2:2)?
3. Who was the wife of Nabal who became David's wife (2:2)?
4. To what city of Judah did David first go to be anointed king (2:3)?
5. To the men of what city did David send thanks for their treatment of Saul's body (2:4)?
6. For how long did David reign from this city in which he was first anointed king (2:11)?
7. Whom did Abner, general of Saul's army, seek to make king (2:8)?

8. At what city was he anointed king (2:8)?
9. At what town did the first encounter take place between the two forces (2:12)?
10. Who pursued Abner and was finally killed by him (2:18)?
11. What does Scripture say concerning the duration of the civil strife (3:1)?
12. Of what did Saul's son accuse Abner (3:7)?
13. What was the reaction of Saul's son toward Abner when Abner announced his defection to David (3:11)?
14. What did David demand before accepting the peace agreement with the son of Saul (3:14)?
15. Who became infuriated because of David's conversation with Abner (3:24)?
16. Who killed Abner (3:30)?
17. Why were they interested in vengeance (2:22)?
18. Who killed Saul's son who had been made king by Abner (4:6)?
19. What did David command his young men to do to them (4:12)?
20. Were there many or few Israelites who came to make David king over all Israel (I Chron. 12:23,37)?
21. What two reasons did the tribes of Israel give for wanting to take part in the anointing of David king over all Israel (5:1,2)?
22. How old was David at the commencement of his reign (5:4)?
23. For how long was he king (5:4)?
24. What people lived in Jerusalem before David took it (5:6)?
25. Through what was entry made into Jerusalem (5:8)?
26. Which of David's men smote Jerusalem first (I Chron. 11:6)?
27. What is another name for Jerusalem given it at this time (5:9)?
28. What king made an alliance with David by sending him timbers and other materials with which to build his palace at Jerusalem (5:11)?
29. Of what city was he king (5:11)?
30. Where did the Philistines gather twice to fight David (5:18,22)?
31. In what town was the ark when David first decided to bring it to Jerusalem (6:1; I Chron. 13:6)?
32. At whose house had it been kept (6:3)?
33. Who were the two sons who accompanied the ark on its first journey (6:3)?
34. Which son was killed because he had touched the ark (6:7)?

35. To whose house was the ark then taken (6:11)?
36. For how long was the ark left before its final removal to Jerusalem (6:11)?
37. Whom did David call upon to bring up the ark at the second attempt (I Chron. 15:2,13)?
38. Who criticized David because of his actions when the ark was finally brought into Jerusalem (6:20)?
39. Why did David believe he ought to build a temple for the Lord (7:2)?
40. To whom did David make this proposal (7:2)?
41. Why was David forbidden to build the temple (I Chron. 22:8; II Sam. 7:6-7)?
42. What promises did God give David concerning his seed (7:12-13)?
43. What nations or peoples did David subjugate after becoming king over Israel? (List five. II Sam. 8)
44. Who was king of Hamath (8:9)?
45. Who was over David's army (host) (8:16)?
46. Who were the priests (8:17)?
47. What people served as David's body-guard? Who was their leader (8:18)?
48. What three men were appointed by David over the music and praise around the ark (I Chron. 15:19; 25:1)?
49. How many courses or divisions did David divide the priests into (I Chron. 24:1, 18-19)?
50. Who was the son of Jonathan befriended by David (9:3,6)?
51. How did David befriend Jonathan's son (9:3)?
52. Who was Ziba (9:2)?
53. Who was Machir (9:4)?
54. Why did the Gibeonites seek revenge on Saul's descendants (II Sam. 21:1-6)?
55. Who was Rizpah (II Sam. 21:7-11)?
56. Who was Hanun and how did he anger David (10:1,4)?
57. What people did the Ammonites hire to help them fight (10:6)?
58. Where were the forces of David fighting at the time he saw Bathsheba from the roof of the royal palace (11:1)?
59. Who was Bathsheba's husband (11:3)?
60. Where was her husband (11:5ff)? What was he doing?
61. How did David seek to cover his sin? (Give full account of the steps taken.)

62. What does the Scripture record concerning the attitude of the Lord toward the sin of David? (Be very specific. 11:27)

63. What prophet came to David to accuse him (12:1)?

64. What are the correct words for the following blanks: There were _____ men in a certain city, one of whom was _____ and the other _____. The _____ man had flocks and herds in great numbers, but the _____ man had nothing at all except one little _____ which he had bought and nurtured, so that it grew up with him, along with his children. It ate its part of his little food, drank out of his cup and lay down in his arms; . . . Then a _____ came to the _____ man who, unwilling to take an animal out of his own flock or herd for the use of his guest, took the _____ man's _____ to prepare for his visitor (12:1-4).

65. What was David's decree concerning the man who had wronged his neighbor (12:6)?

66. What were the prophet's words to David upon hearing David's decree? (Be specific. 12:7)

67. Did David confess his sin (12:13)?

68. Which Psalm expresses David's repentance?

69. Did God forgive David his sin (12:13,14)?

70. What was David's immediate punishmnet for his sin (12:14)?

71. What was the name of the son born to David by Bathsheba at Jerusalem (12:24)?

72. What was the name given him by the Lord through Nathan (12:24,25)?

Section IV
David's Reign in Tragedies
(II Samuel 13:1-I Kings 2:11)

1. Second period of David's reign — Family troubles — Amnon, Tamar and Absalom — Rebellion of Absalom — He is crowned at Hebron. 2. David's flight from Jerusalem — The priests and ark sent back — Ahithophel and Hushai — Ziba and Shimei — Absalom at Jerusalem — David at Mahanaim — Disappointment and death of Ahithophel — Absalom pursues David. 3. Battle in the wood of Ephraim — Death and burial of

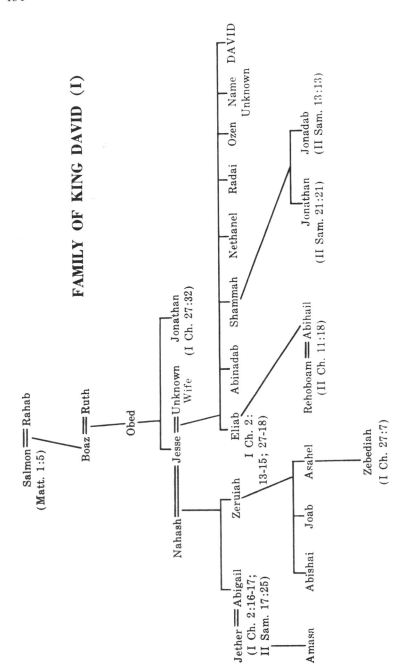

FAMILY OF KING DAVID (I)

FAMILY OF KING DAVID (II)

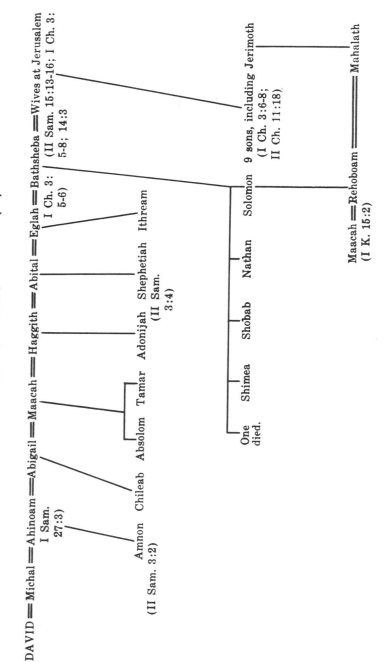

1. **Before his marriage with Bathsheba, David had sixteen sons**
who lived as princes among the people, each in his own house.
Only three of them are of any note in history: the eldest, AMNON,
son of Ahinoam of Jezreel; the third, ABSALOM, son of Maacah of
Geshur; and the fourth, ADONIJAH, son of Haggith. For the
precedence due to Amnon as the first-born he was likely to have a
formidable rival in Absalom, whose mother was a king's daughter
and who was himself unequaled for beauty among the people.
But we do not hear of any jealousy or dissension among the king's
sons till the following occasion led to fatal results. Absalom had a
sister named Tamar, who shared his beauty and of whom Amnon
became so violently enamored that he fell sick (II Sam. 13:1).
Marriage with a half-sister was forbidden by the Mosaic law (Lev.
18:9,11), though Tamar in pleading with Amnon suggested that
David might have consented to that alternative to avoid the crime
which Amnon effected by a base stratagem (II Sam. 13:1-14).
Amnon incurred the anger of David, who probably spared his life
because he was his first-born.   Absalom hated Amnon and
waited in silence an opportunity for revenge. When two years had
thus passed, Absalom invited the king with all his sons and
Amnon, in particular, to a sheep-shearing feast at Baalhazor on
the border of Ephraim. David seems to have had suspicions even
after such an interval of time but in the end he consented to his
sons' going, though he himself remained at home. Amid the
mirth of the feast, Absalom's servants, having received their
orders beforehand, slew Amnon when he was merry with wine.
The king's sons fled preceded by the rumor that they were all
slain, but they soon arrived weeping for Amnon, when the king

and all his servants joined them in their mourning. Absalom fled to his grandfather, Talmai, king of Geshur, a district northeast of the Sea of Galilee and remained there three years, while David, now comforted concerning the fate of Amnon, grieved for the loss of his living son.

To end this state of things, Joab employed a "wise woman" of Tekoa (afterward the birthplace of the prophet Amos), who appeared before the king in mourning with a fictitious tale similar to the case of his own family (II Sam. 14). One of her two sons, she said, had slain the other in a quarrel and all the family demanded the death of the killer, which would leave her childless and cut off her husband's name. The king promised her protection but the woman continued to plead until the king had promised a third time and sworn with an oath that her son would not be touched. Then she applied her parable to him and reproved him because he did not "fetch home again his banished." She enforced her request by the oft-quoted proverb, "We must needs die and are as water split on the ground, which can not be gathered up again" (II Sam. 14:14). She asserted that both David and Absalom would die. David should therefore act now to restore the boy while both were living. By doing this David would be like God, who does not take away life but devises means that he who is banished may be no more an outcast from him. This beautiful verse finds its utmost fulfillment in Christ, whom God sent into the world that sinners, banished from God by divine justice, might be no more outcasts from God.

The scarcely concealed reference to Absalom's recall was not lost on David. He sensed that someone (Joab) had put her up to this. The resemblance between the case of the woman's only surviving son and Absalom was not perfect: Absalom was not David's only son; neither was Absalom actually threatened with death by vengeful relatives. To refer to Absalom's case from the case of the woman's son was transparently contrived.

Learning from the woman by whom she had been prompted, David sent for Joab and bade him bring back Absalom, whom however the king refused to see. Absalom dwelt for two years in his house at Jerusalem with his three sons[1] and his beautiful daughter, Tamar, gaining favor with the people by his handsome person. There can be no doubt that he was already meditating, perhaps not the dethronement of his father but his own association in the kingdom as his heir. At length, impatient of his

---

1. They seem all to have died before Absalom (II Sam. 18:18).

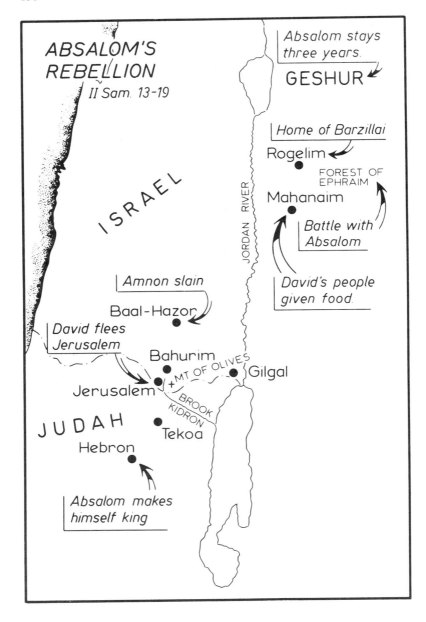

exclusion from the court, he sent for Joab who was too cautious to go to him, upon which Absalom compelled him to come by setting fire to one of his fields of standing grain. Joab interceded with the king who received his son and gave him the kiss of peace. We may suppose that the interview put an end to Absalom's hopes of sharing his father's throne, for he now began to prepare for rebellion (II Sam. 15).[1] He surrounded himself with a body of fifty foot-runners, besides chariots and horsemen, and taking his station beside the city gate, he met the suitors who came to the king with expressions of his regret that their causes were neglected and with the wish that he were judge over the land to give them redress, while every reverence made to him was returned with an embrace. "So Absalom stole the hearts of the men of Israel." This may partly be accounted for by the common love of change and impatience at long-continued prosperity, but besides this, Absalom's unchecked proceedings prove that David was not living as of old in sight of the people — a certain cause of loss of popularity: the affair of Bathsheba, though only known in part and his treatment of Absalom, may have bred discontent; and it has been conjectured from the choice of Hebron as the headquarters of the rebellion, that the men of Judah were offended at finding themselves merged with the other tribes. Absalom's chief captain and chief counselor, Amasa and Ahithophel, were of that tribe and there are symptoms of discord between Judah and the other tribes at the time of the king's return (II Sam. 14:41).

When the plot was ripe, Absalom obtained leave from the king to go to Hebron, the ancient sanctuary of his tribe, to pay a vow which he had made at Geshur in case he should return to Jerusalem (II Sam. 15:7).[2] He took with him 200 men not yet aware of his design and sent around secret messengers to all the tribes warning the adherents, whom we have seen him gaining at Jerusalem, that the trumpet would give the signal of his having been proclaimed king at Hebron. But perhaps his most prudent step was his sending for Ahithophel, David's most able counselor, . from his own city of Giloh.[3]

---

1. We may probably infer from the silence of Scripture that David's second son, Chileab, was dead.
2. The correct reading of 15:7 is probably, "After *four years*," as in Syriac, Josephus and some editions of LXX.
3. Some have supposed that Ahithophel was Bathsheba's grandfather and that David's treatment of her explains Ahithophel's defection. This is based on II Sam. 23:34 and 11:3. These verses give the name Eliam as that of Ahithophel's son and also Bathsheba's father. However, the verse parallel to II Sam. 23:34, I Chron. 11:36, gives "Ahijah the Pelonite" instead of "Ahithophel the Gilonite." David's age at the time he took Bathsheba (certainly past fifty) casts doubt on the likelihood of Bathsheba's having a grandfather as active as Ahithophel subsequently was. Probably Eliam the father of Bathsheba was a different man from Eliam the son of Ahithophel.

2. The first news of the conspiracy reached David as tidings of its success. He at once resolved to flee from Jerusalem, lest the city should be stormed and his servants consented. His departure from Jerusalem is related with a minuteness to which we have no parallel in the Scripture history of any single day, except that of which this was the type, when the son of David, betrayed by "his own familiar friend" and rejected by his own people, went out by the same path "bearing his reproach." It was early in the morning when the king, leaving his palace in the care of his ten concubines, went forth by the eastern gate with all his household and a crowd of people, for there were still many who showed him the deepest attachment. Among his faithful guard of Cherethites and Pelethites and his chosen heroes, the 600 who had followed him ever since his residence at Gath, was Ittai the Gittite. David released him and his countrymen from their allegiance but Ittai vowed that he would follow the king in life or death and David bade him lead the way. They passed over the brook Kidron (the Cedron of the New Testament) by the way that led over the Mount of Olives to Jericho and the wilderness, while "all the country wept with a loud voice." As David halted in the valley to let the people pass on, he was joined by Zadok and Abiathar, with all the Levites, bringing with them the ark of God. With self-renouncing reverence, David refused to have the ark removed, for his sake, from the sanctuary where he had fixed its abode and exposed to share his perils. If Jehovah willed to show him favor, he would bring him back to see both the ark and His habitation; if not — "Behold here am I! let Him do to me as seemeth good to Him!" He reminded the priests that they could do him effectual service in the city by employing their two sons, who were both swift runners, to bring him tidings and so he sent them back with the ark. The weeping troop then ascended the Mount of Olives in the garb of the deepest mourning, the king himself walking barefoot; and just as the grief reached its height at the last view of the towers of Jerusalem, word was brought to David that Ahithophel was among the conspirators. He had scarcely uttered the prayer that God would turn the wise counsel of Ahithophel into foolishness when the means of its fulfilment was presented. At the summit of the mount, he was met by his other counselor and chosen "friend," Hushai the Archite,[1] in the garb of mourning. David bade him to return into the city and offer his services to Absalom, in order to defeat the counsel of

---

1. The Archites were a clan of Benjaminites who lived near the border of the tribe of Ephraim.

Ahithophel and to place himself in communication with Zadok and Abiathar, whose sons would bring his messages to the king. Hushai returned to Jerusalem just as Absalom was entering the city and was received by him with taunts for his desertion of his "friend," which must have confirmed him in his purpose, though he answered them with professions of fidelity to his new master as the chosen of Jehovah and of Israel (II Sam. 15:37; 16:16-19).

Meanwhile, just at the height of noon, David passed over the brow of the hill into the territory of Benjamin, where he found himself among the friends of Saul. One of these, Ziba, the servant of Mephibosheth, met David with two asses laden with refreshments and, by a falsehood about his master's treason, obtained a gift of all his property. The other member of the house of Saul, Shimei, the son of Gera, a native of Bahurim, came out from the village as David passed by and pelted him and his retinue with stones, cursing him as the bloody murderer of Saul's house. Abishai would have avenged the insult but the king, with an outburst of impatience at the overbearing sons of Zeruiah, let him curse on, as the messenger of the curse of God — a submission which seems to express the voice of David's conscience for the murder of Uriah. And what was there, he asked, so strange in the curses of a Benjamite when his own son sought his life? Uttering a hope that Jehovah would requite him good for this cursing, he suffered the man to continue his insults down the hill-side. At the close of the day he reached the Jordan and rested at its fords, the place he had appointed with the priests (II Sam. 16:14; Comp. 15:28; 17:22; 10:18). Here they were roused at midnight by Ahimaaz, the son of Zadok, and Jonathan, the son of Abiathar, who had narrowly escaped with their lives, bringing a warning to cross the river the same night (II Sam. 17:15-22).

For the day had been a busy one at Jerusalem. Absalom had no sooner entered the city than, by the advice of Ahithophel — who acted on the favorite maxim of conspirators to commit their party by some unpardonable crime — he perpetrated the outrage which had been foretold by the prophet Nathan (II Sam. 16:20-22).[1] Ahithophel's next advice proved the sagacity for which he was unrivaled (II Sam. 16:23). He proposed to pursue David with 12,000 chosen men and to fall upon him when weary and dispirited; his followers would be sure to fly; the king's life only should be sacrificed; and the rest would return and dwell in peace (II Sam. 17:1-3). Absalom and the elders of Israel did not

---

1. In the East the harem of a king passes to his successor.

shrink from the atrocity of the scheme but it was thought better first to consult Hushai. With consummate art, he inspired Absalom with the fear that David had chosen some hiding-place where he and his men of war would be found chafing like a bear robbed of her whelps, and the first pursuers would certainly be smitten with an overthrow which would cause a panic through all the land. Let Absalom rather gather the whole multitude of Israel from Dan to Beersheba and take the field in person, with the certainty of falling upon David as the dew covers all the ground, or if he had taken refuge in a city, the force of Israel would drag it bodily with ropes into the river. The result was that which is usual with councils of war. The more daring plan and the first thoughts, which are generally best, were abandoned for the "safer" course: "For Jehovah had appointed to defeat the good counsel of Ahithophel, to the intent that Jehovah might bring evil upon Absalom" (II Sam. 17:14).

Before, however, this decision was fully taken Hushai advised the priests to send David warning of the plan of Ahithophel. On receiving it, as we have seen, David crossed the Jordan[1] with all his people before the morning and took up his abode at Mahanaim, the very place which had been the capital of his rival, Ish-bosheth, while he himself reigned at Hebron. Here he was visited by Shobi, the son of Nahash, whom David had no doubt set up as a vassal king of Ammon, in place of his brother Hanun, and by Machir, the former protector of Mephibosheth, and by Barzillai the Gileadite of Rogelim, whose touching farewell is recorded later. These faithful friends brought him all the supplies needful for the rest and refreshment of his exhausted followers (II Sam. 17:15-29).

Meanwhile Hushai was without a rival at the court of Absalom. Ahithophel was so mortified at the rejection of his advice and so convinced of the consequent ruin of Absalom's party, that he took his departure to his native city and having set his house in order, he hanged himself and was buried in the sepulchre of his fathers. His name has passed into a byword for the truth that "God taketh the wise in his own craftiness," and his unscrupulous treason forbids all sympathy with his fate. We may apply to him what was said of one of our own party leaders: "His great crimes were enhanced by his immense talents, of which God gave him the use, and the devil the application." Absalom assumed the royal state

1. The 3rd Psalm was probably composed in the morning after crossing the Jordan. Ps. 143 by its title in the LXX, "When his son was pursuing him," belongs to this time. Also, by long popular belief, Psalm 42 has been supposed to have been composed in the trans-Jordanic exile of David, and the complaints of Psalm 60, 69 and 109 to be leveled against Ahithophel.

and was solemnly anointed as king (II Sam. 19:10). Joab's office of captain of the host was conferred by him upon Amasa, the son of Ithra by Abigail, the daughter of Nahash, stepdaughter to Jesse and sister to Zeruiah; he was half-cousin to David and own cousin to Joab and Abishai (II Sam. 17:25). Absalom then crossed the Jordan in pursuit of David and pitched his camp in Mount Gilead (II Sam. 17:26).

3. David prepared to receive the attack with his usual skill (II Sam. 18). He divided his forces into three bodies under Joab, Abishai and Ittai, and yielding to the people's entreaties, he himself remained to hold out the city in case of a defeat. Confident, however, in his tried veterans and still more in the help of God, he was chiefly solicitous for the safety of his rebellious son. "Deal gently for my sake with the young man, even with Absalom," was his charge to the captains in the hearing of all the people, as he sat in the gate to see them march out to the battle. The armies met in "the forest of Ephraim"[1] in Mount Gilead, where the entangled ground was most unfavorable to the untrained hosts of Absalom. They were overthrown with a slaughter of 20,000 men, more of whom perished in the defiles of the forest than in the battle itself, if that might be called a battle, which consisted in a number of partial combats spread over the face of the country. Amid this scattered fight, Absalom was separated from his men and as he fled from a party of the enemy, the mule on which he rode carried him beneath the low branches of a spreading terebinth and left him hanging by the luxuriant hair which formed his pride.[2] The first soldier who came up spared his life because of the king's command and went to tell Joab. The unscrupulous chief hurried to the spot and thrust three javelins into Absalom's heart, while his ten armor-bearers joined in dispatching him. Having sounded the trumpet of recall, Joab took down the body and cast it into a pit, over which the people raised a great heap of stones as a mark of execration,[3] a burial which the historian contrasts with the splendid monument which Absalom had prepared for himself in Shaveh or the "King's Dale" (II Sam. 18:1-18).[4]

David waited at Mahanaim with an impatience which his

---

1. No very satisfactory explanation has been given of the use of this name on the east of Jordan. Perhaps Ephraim's pursuit of Midian into this area, and its subsequent fight with Gilead in the time of Jephthah, gave the name of Ephraim to the forest (Judges 7:24; 12:4).

2. Comp. II Sam. 14:26. Two things are to be noted as contributing to Absalom's fate: the ostentation of going into battle on the mule, which marked his rank as prince, instead of on foot like David and all the great warriors, and the vanity of wearing his hair in a style only becoming to a Nazarite.

3. As in the case of Achan (Josh. 7:26).

4. The so-called "Tomb of Absalom," just outside Jerusalem in the Valley of Kidron was probably built in Herodian times.

knowledge of Joab must have rendered doubly painful. Joab's manner of sending the message has been explained from a desire, which even he felt to spare the feelings of Ahimaaz, the young friend and messenger of the king. Bidding him wait till the morrow, Joab sent a Cushite follower of his own, unknown to the court with no other orders than to tell what he had seen. The blunt soldier, conscious of having done the king good service even by his disobedience, makes no attempt to break the news. But Ahimaaz was more considerate. Having prevailed on Joab to let him run after the Cushite, he outstripped him by his better knowledge of the ground (II Sam. 18:23).[1] David was sitting in the gateway of Mahanaim, when the watchman on the tower above announced first one and then a second runner. He presently recognized Ahimaaz by his style of running and David felt sure that his favorite messenger must bring good tidings. And so at first it seemed, for he offered his breathless congratulations on the king's deliverance from his enemies. But the eager question, "Is the young man Absalom safe?" was evaded by the mention of some strange confusion that prevailed when the runner left. Before the king had time to ascertain his meaning, the Cushite entered with his news of the victory. The inquiry about Absalom was repeated and called forth the answer, "The enemies of my lord the king and all that rise against thee to do thee hurt, be as that young man!" Then burst the floodgates of a father's heart. No scene in all history appeals to deeper feelings and none is related in such simple and pathetic words as this: "And the king was much moved and went up to the chamber over the gate, and wept: and as he went, thus he said, O my son Absalom! my son, my son Absalom! would God I had died for thee, O Absalom, my son, my son!" (II Sam. 18:33).

The king's grief turned the victory into mourning and the people stole back into the city like the remnants of a defeated army. David shut himself up, repeating the same mournful cry (II Sam. 19:1-4). The hand that had struck the blow roused him from his grief. Joab went into his presence and upbraided him with lamenting for his enemies instead of encouraging his friends, who would soon be driven away by his neglect. Most had already dispersed to their tents but they returned on hearing that David had resumed his post at the gate of Mahanaim. Confusion prevailed throughout the tribes. They remembered that it was

---

1. This disputed passage seems to mean that, while the Cushite followed a direct line over the hills, Ahimaaz took a more circuitous but easier course along the valley of the Jordan.

David who had delivered them from the Philistines and now that Absalom their anointed king was dead, they asked each other, "Why speak ye not a word of bringing the king back?" (II Sam. 19:5-10). At this crisis David sent for the priests, Zadok and Abiathar. Through them he appealed to the tribe of Judah, as his brethren, while he promised to make Amasa captain of the host in the place of Joab. The tribe, thus gained over as one man, invited him to cross the Jordan and met him at the ancient camp of Gilgal. David's triumphant return is related as fully as his sad departure. With the men of Judah came a thousand Benjamites under Shimei, who was eager to make his peace with his insulted king, and Ziba with his fifteen sons and twenty servants crossed the river to anticipate his master's claim for restitution. The ferry-boat, which carried over the king and his household, had scarcely touched the shore when Shimei fell down before him to confess his guilt and entreat pardon,[1] which was granted with another impatient rebuke of Abishai's remonstrances. The clemency, which David deemed becoming to the hour of victory, was sound policy toward Benjamin. He swore to preserve Shimei's life but he kept a close watch on a man who had proved so dangerous, and warned Solomon against him on his death-bed; and Shimei justified David's distrust and provoked his own fate by a new act of disobedience (I Kings 2:8-9, 36-46).[2]

David was next met by Mephibosheth, whose supposed ingratitude was only noticed by a gentle rebuke (II Sam. 19:25).[3] Mephibosheth, however, had a different tale to tell from that of Ziba, whom he accused of having compelled him to remain at Jerusalem while he went to slander him to the king. But he submitted all to David's disposal since his life had been spared, when all Saul's family were but dead men, and now he had come to meet the king in the deep mourning which he had worn since his departure. Ziba seems not to have denied the truth of Mephibosheth's statement but David, weary of the case and unwilling to leave any one discontented on that joyful day, divided the property between Ziba and Mephibosheth, who thus received half when he thought he had lost the whole (II Sam. 19:24-30).

---

1. In Shimei's confession he refers to the tribes other than Judah as the "house of Joseph" (19:20). This is the first such reference; many occur after this. This foreshadowed future division from Judah, with Ephraim being the center of opposition. Previously Mahanaim or Benjamin had been the ruling center in Israel. No longer was this to be so. Ephraim (Joseph) was thereafter dominant.

2. That David's injunction is only to be understood as a warning condition on Shimei's own conduct is proved by the course actually taken by Solomon.

3. To understand this verse we must read *"from Jerusalem."*

The most affecting incident of the day was the farewell of Barzillai, the wealthy Gileadite, who had supplied David's wants while he was at Mahanaim. He accompanied David over the Jordan and the king invited him to Jerusalem that he might return his hospitality. "How long have I to live?" asked Barzillai, who had reached his eightieth year, "that I should go up with the king to Jerusalem?" Contenting himself with escorting David a little beyond the Jordan, he left his son Chimham to receive the favors which he himself was too old to enjoy, and one of David's last acts was to commend the family to the generosity of Solomon (II Sam. 19:31-40).

4. The joy of the king's return was disturbed by the angry jealousy of the rest of Israel against Judah for beginning the movement without them (II Sam. 19:41-43). The fierce tone of Judah seems to have provoked the old animosity of Benjamin and Sheba, the son of Bichri, a Benjamite, proclaiming that the tribes had no interest in the house of Jesse, blew the trumpet of revolt and raised the cry, "Every man to his tents, O Israel!" The king, who had now returned to Jerusalem, ordered his new captian, Amasa, to muster the forces of Judah in three days, that the rebellion might be crushed while it was confined to Benjamin. Amasa's slowness compelled David to have recourse again to the sons of Zeruiah, and Abishai led forth the body-guard of Cherethites and Pelethites and the heroes, accompanied by Joab. Gibeon once more became the scene of battle. They found Amasa there before them with the main army and, under the show of an embrace, Joab dealt his favored rival one fatal blow and then pressed on the pursuit after Sheba with his brother Abishai. One of Joab's followers stood over Amasa as he lay wallowing in his blood on the highway, bidding all the friends of Joab and of David to go forward; but when he saw their hesitation, he carried the corpse aside into a field and covered it with a mantle and so the pursuit went on (II Sam. 20:1-13). Sheba fled northward, raising the tribes of Israel on his way, to Abel-beth-maachah near the sources of the Jordan, "a city and metropolis in Israel" (II Sam. 20:14-22).[1] The forces of Sheba seem to have melted away before Joab's hot pursuit and he was besieged in Abel. This city was proverbial for the oracular wisdom of its inhabitants, and "a wise woman" now saved it by first learning Joab's demands in a parley

---

1. Abel is also called Abel-maim *(the meadow of waters)*. Its site was probably in the marshy ground round the "Waters of Merom." Comp. I Kings 15:20; II Kings 15:29; II Chron. 16:4.

and then inducing the people to comply with them by throwing the head of Sheba over the wall.[1]

The suppression of this rebellion closes a second period of David's reign. Its remaining part was only disturbed by a war with the Philistines at Gezer, the date of which is unknown and in which several of David's heroes signaled their individual strength and prowess (II Sam. 21:15-22; I Chron. 20:4-8).

To this epoch ought probably to be referred the remarkable Psalm which is recorded in the *Second Book of Samuel* as "a song spoken by David to Jehovah in the day that Jehovah delivered him out of the hand of all his enemies and out of the hand of Saul" (II Sam. 22).[2] It stands in the *Book of Psalms* as the eighteenth, with the description of David in the title as "the servant of Jehovah," words no doubt intended to ascribe to Him all David's glories. Needless difficulty has been felt about the mention of Saul in the title, which even recent events might have suggested as Sheba's rebellion was the dying effort of Saul's party, but what is more natural than that, in thanking God for deliverance from all his enemies, David should lay the greatest emphasis on the earliest and the most dangerous of them all?[3]

5. David's life, in the very character of its separate parts, is typical of that whole course of experience which is seen in the men who best represent humanity: a youth of promise, a manhood of conflict, trouble and temptation, not free from falls and a serene old age. The work which was properly his own was now done and a third and closing period of his reign was occupied in preparing for the culminating glories of the *earthly* kingdom of Israel under his successor. But the parallel would scarcely have been true had the evening of his life been perfectly unclouded. As has been remarked before, the three periods of his reign were stamped each with a great external calamity, the lesson of which God made plainer by the *numerical* parallel: *three years of famine* to avenge the cruelties of Saul; *three months of flight* before rebellious Absalom; and now *three days of pestilence,* a form of judgment analogous to the offense that called it down.

"Satan stood up against Israel and provoked David to number

---

1. The whole history of Absalom's rebellion and the events that followed, down to the death of Sheba, is omitted in *Chronicles.*

2. Perhaps it may be placed after the pestilence, but the absence of any allusion to that deliverance and the specific reference to success in war, both in the title and the Psalm itself, best accord with the place here given to it. The title must be regarded as an integral part of the Psalm.

3. This view is confirmed by the allusions in II Sam. 22:5-7, 17-10; Psalm 18:4-6, 16-19 and especially the words "my *strong enemy,*" v. 17 of the Psalm.

the people."[1] That this was no ordinary census is clear, not only from the punishment that followed it, but from the remonstrances of Joab to whom the business was entrusted (II Sam. 24:3; I Chron. 21:3) and to whom it was so "abominable" that he omitted the tribes of Levi and Benjamin altogether.[2] By David's own desire, all under twenty were omitted "because Jehovah had said that he would increase Israel like to the stars of the heavens."[3] And that some distrust of this truth was at the root of David's sin is implied in the terms of Joab's remonstrance. The transaction seems to have sprung from a self-confident desire to consolidate the forces of the kingdom, to exult in their greatness and to hold them in the readiness of a full military organization for new enterprises. Nor is it unreasonable to suppose that some specific conquest was meditated beyond the limits of the promised land. And so God sent a punishment, which showed how easily He who had promised that Israel should be increased like the stars of heaven and the sand by the sea-shore (Gen. 15:5) and who could have added unto the people, how many soever they might be, a hundred-fold (II Sam. 24:3), could cut down their numbers at a stroke.[4]

Early in the morning after the work was finished, the prophet Gad was sent to David, whose conscience had already prepared him for the visit, to offer the choice of three modes of decimating the people: a three years' famine, a three months' flight before his enemies or a three days' pestilence. The king, who had experienced the two former calamities, now chose the latter with pious resignation, saying, "Let us fall now into the hand of Jehovah; for His mercies are great, and let me not fall into the hand of man." The pestilence raged for the appointed time and 70,000 of the people died from Dan to Beersheba (II Sam. 24:10-15; I Chron. 21:9-13). Its cessation was a turning-point in the history of the nation. The breaking out of the plague in Jerusalem itself was accompanied by the awful appearance of an angel hovering in the air just outside of the wall and stretching out a drawn sword toward the city. At this sight, David cried to Jehovah, praying that He would let the punishment fall on him

---

1. I Chron. 21:1. We learn from the parallel passage, II Sam. 24:1, that Satan was the allowed agent of Jehovah's anger, excited doubtless by the spirit which was the act displayed.

2. The numbers in II Sam. 24:9 differ from those in I Chron. 21:6 and 27:24, but there is no reason to suspect corruption in either text. Joab did the work unwillingly and imperfectly. Hence the final figures can only be rough estimates.

3. I Chron. 27:23. The result of the census was not recorded in the Chronicles of the kings of Judah. From II Sam. 24:9, we learn that it gave 800,000 valiant warriors for Israel and 500,000 for Judah. It occupied Joab 9 months and 20 days.

4. To take a census without collecting atonement money to ransom every man's soul was to invite a plague (Exodus 30:12).

and his house, "but these sheep, what have they done?" His intercession was accepted. The prophet Gad came to him again, bidding him to erect an altar to Jehovah on the spot over which the angel had been seen. That spot was occupied by *the threshing-floor of* ARAUNAH or ORNAN, one of the old Jebusites of the city. He was evidently a man of the highest consideration and from certain expressions it has even been supposed that he had been the king of Jebus before its capture by David (II Sam 24:23).[1] Araunah was engaged with his four sons in threshing corn by means of sledges drawn by oxen when the vision of the angel caused them to hide themselves for fear, but on seeing the king approach with his courtiers, Araunah came forth and bowed down before him, offering as soon as he learned his wish to give him the threshing-floor as a free gift and the oxen and the implements for a burnt-offering. But David refused to offer Jehovah that which had cost him nothing and paid to Araunah the royal price of 600 shekels of gold for the ground and 50 shekels of silver for the oxen. There he built an altar to Jehovah and offered burnt-offerings and peace-offerings, and the plague ceased (II Sam. 24:18-25; I Chron. 21:18-30).

This altar first distinctly marked the hill as the sacred spot which Jehovah had long promised to choose for his abode. The ark had indeed been placed for some time in the city of David, but the stated sacrifices had still been offered on the original brazen altar before the tabernacle of Gibeon (II Chron. 1:13), and even after the removal of the ark, God had spoken to David of His choice of a place to build His house as yet to be made (II Sam. 7:10,13). That choice was now revealed by the descent of fire from heaven on David's sacrifice, as upon the altar of burnt-offering in the wilderness (I Chron. 21:26); and David recognized the sign and said, "This is the HOUSE OF JEHOVAH GOD, and this is the altar of the burnt-offering for Israel" (I Chron. 22:1). The place received the name of MORIAH *(vision)* from the appearance of God to David as the first destroying angel, and then by the sign of fire (II Chron. 3:1).

David at once commenced his preparations for the edifice. We have seen him long ago devoting to this use the spoils of his victories, which now amounted to 100,000 talents of gold and 1,000,000 talents of silver;[2] and now he collected all the skilled

---

1. "All these things did Araunah, *a king,* give unto the king."
2. There has been much discussion concerning the enormous and seemingly incredible amount of the gold and silver; though, considering the way in which treasures have always been amassed in the East, it is hard to assign the limits of credibility.

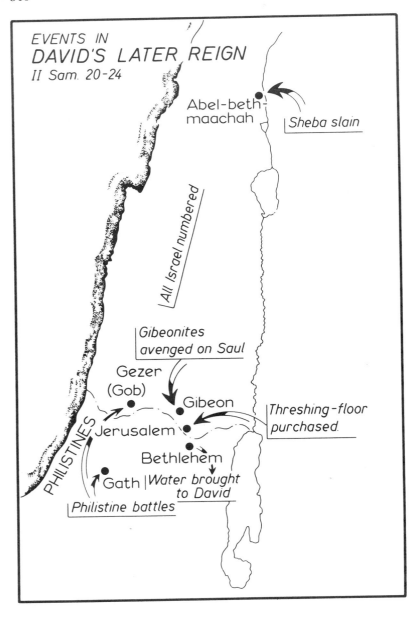

EVENTS IN
DAVID'S LATER REIGN
II Sam. 20-24

Abel-beth-
maachah

| Sheba slain

All Israel numbered

| Gibeonites
avenged on Saul

Gezer
(Gob)   Gibeon

PHILISTINES | Threshing-floor
Jerusalem   purchased

Bethlehem

Gath | Water brought
to David

| Philistine battles

foreign workmen that could be found in the land to hew stones and to do all other work: he prepared iron and brass without weight and procured the cedar-wood of Lebanon from the Sidonians and Tyrians. But the work itself was destined to another hand. To his son SOLOMON, now designated as his successor, he gave the charge to build a house for Jehovah, God of Israel. He told his son how God had denied him this desire of his heart because he had been a man of war and had shed much blood upon the earth; and how He had promised its fulfillment by a son, who was to be named Solomon *(peaceful)*, because under him Israel should have peace and whose throne should be established over Israel forever. He also charged the princes of Israel to help Solomon and to set their heart and soul to seek Jehovah (I Chron. 22; 28:2-8).[1]

6. The designation of Solomon gave the deathblow to the hopes of ADONIJAH, the son of Haggith, David's fourth and eldest surviving son, a man of great personal beauty whom his father had always treated with indulgence (I Kings 1:6). Taking advantage of David's increasing feebleness (I Kings 1:1-4), he resolved to make himself king. Like Absalom, he prepared a guard of chariots and horses and fifty foot-runners, and he gained over Joab and Abiathar. Zadok, however, with Benaiah, the captain of the body-guard, and David's heroes and the prophet Nathan, remained faithful to the king. When Adonijah thought his project ripe, he invited his adherents with all the king's sons (except Solomon), who seem to have shared his jealousy, to a great banquet at the rock of Zoheleth near Enrogel, where amid the mirth of the festival the cry was raised, "Long live King Adonijah."

The prophet Nathan informed Bathsheba of these proceedings and arranged with her a plan to secure the interests of her son. Bathsheba went into David's chamber followed soon after by Nathan, to tell him that Adonijah reigned in spite of his promise to Solomon. The aged king had lost nothing of his prudence and decision. At his command, Zadok the priest and Nathan the prophet, supported by Benaiah with the body-guard of Cherethites and Pelethites, proclaimed Solomon king amid the rejoicings of the people and anointed him with the sacred oil, which Zadok took out of the tabernacle. The guests of Adonijah

---

1. The comparison of these passages with II Sam. 7 suggests that David's renewed desire to build the Temple had called forth fuller intimations of God's will both in respect to himself and to Solomon. In another passage, Solomon himself assigns the *constant occupation* of David in war as the reason of the delay (I K. v. 3).

dispersed at the news which was brought by Jonathan, the son of
Abiathar, and Adonijah himself fled for sanctuary to the horns of
the altar; but on Solomon's assurance that his life should be
spared if he proved worthy of his clemency, he retired to his own
house (I Kings 1). David gathered all the people to an assembly in
which he gave a solemn charge to them and their new king, to
whom also he delivered patterns for the house of God and the
materials he had collected for the building. These were greatly
increased by the freewill-offerings of the princes and the people.
After David had offered thanksgiving and prayer for Solomon,
all the people feasted together and Solomon was inaugurated into
his kingdom for the second time, while Zadok was publicly
anointed as high-priest. The new king was established in
prosperity and in favor with the people before his father's death.
"And Jehovah magnified Solomon exceedingly in the sight of all
Israel, and bestowed upon him such royal majesty as had not been
on any king before him in Israel." A constant memorial of this
solemnity is preserved in that most magnificent of the Psalms of
David, the seventy-second, in which the blessings predicted for
the reign of Solomon form a transparent veil for the transcendent
glories prophesied for Christ's kingdom, and which is marked as
the crowning contribution of its author to the service of the
sanctuary by its concluding words, "The prayers of David, the son
of Jesse, are ended!"

7. Amid these happy omens for his house, David approached
the end of his life. His last act was to send for Solomon and renew
the charge to him to keep the statutes of Jehovah, as written in the
law of Moses, that so he might prosper in all his deeds" (I Kings
2:1-4). He added directions in reference to the men with whom
the young king might not know how to deal. JOAB was named as a
just object of vengeance for his two treacherous murders of
Abner and Amasa, which are described in very striking language
(I Kings 2:5-6). BARZILLAI and his house are commended to
Solomon's favor. The denunciation of SHIMEI has been already
noticed. We may here anticipate the first acts of Solomon's reign
and see how he dealt with these and his other enemies. No sooner
was David dead than Adonijah had the audacity to solicit,
through the intercession of Bathsheba, the hand of Abishag the
Shunammite, who had been the companion of David's old age,
though not exactly his concubine. In the latter case, marriage with
her would have been only permitted to the king's successor, and
in this light Solomon seems to have viewed the request. Indeed we

can only understand what followed on the supposition that this
was a first insidious step in a new conspiracy of Adonijah with
Abiathar and Joab, as Solomon's answer clearly implies (I Kings
2:13-25). Adonijah was put to death by the hand of Benaiah, but
Abiathar, in consideration of his office and his old
companionship with David, was only banished to his home at
Anathoth and deposed from the high-priesthood, which thus
passed from the house of Ithamar according to God's sentence
against Eli (I Kings 2:26-27; Comp. I Sam. 2:31-35). Upon this
Joab fled for sanctuary to the horns of the altar and there,
refusing to come forth, he was slain by the hand of Benaiah. His
death is regarded as a satisfaction for the blood of Abner and
Amasa, the guilt of which was thus removed from the house of
David, but his fate was sealed by his accession to Adonijah's
conspiracy. He was buried in his own house in the wilderness and
Benaiah succeeded to his command (I Kings 2:28-35). Shimei was
ordered by Solomon to dwell in Jerusalem, with the express
warning that his departure from the city, on whatever pretext,
would seal his fate. Three years afterward he went to Gath in
pursuit of two of his servants who had fled to Achish, and on his
return Solomon caused him to be put to death (I Kings 2:36-46).

To return to David: the short Psalm entitled "The last words of
David" seems, from its closing sentences, to have been uttered in
connection with his final words to Solomon (II Sam. 23:1-7). Its
opening sums up the chief features of his life: "David, the man
raised up on high, the anointed of the God of Jacob, and the sweet
Psalmist of Israel." After a reign of forty years, seven in Hebron
and thirty-three at Jerusalem, "he died in a good old age, full of
days, riches, and honor, and Solomon his son reigned in his
stead." He was buried "in the city of David." After the return
from the Captivity, "the sepulchres of David" were still pointed
out between Siloah and "the house of the mighty men" or "the
guard-house" (Neh. 3:16). His tomb, which became the general
sepulchre of the kings of Judah, was known in the latest times of
the Jewish people. "His sepulchre is with us unto this day," says
Peter at Pentecost (Acts 2:29).[1] His acts were recorded in the
Book of Samuel the seer, and of Nathan the prophet and of Gad
the seer, "with all his reign and his might, and the times that went
over him, and over Israel, and over all the kingdoms of the

---

1. The edifice shown as such from the Crusaders to the present day is on the southern hill of modern
Jerusalem, mistakenly called Mount Zion, under the so-called "Coenaculum." But this tomb was *outside* the
walls, and therefore cannot be identified with the tomb of David, which was emphatically *within* the walls.

countries." The substance of these records is preserved in the Books of Samuel and the beginning of the First Book of Kings (I Kings 2:10-11; I Chron. 29:26-30).

8. The character of David[1] has been so naturally brought out in the incidents of his life that it need not be here described in detail. In the complexity of its elements, passion, tenderness, generosity, fierceness — the soldier, the shepherd, the poet, the statesman, the priest, the prophet, the king — the romantic friend, the chivalrous leader, the devoted father — there is no character of the Old Testament at all to be compared to it. Jacob comes nearest in the variety of elements included within it. But David's character stands at a higher point of the sacred history and represents the Jewish people just at the moment of their transition from the lofty virtues of the older system to the fuller civilization and cultivation of the later. In this manner he becomes naturally, if one may so say, the likeness or portrait of the last and grandest development of the nation and of the monarchy in the person and the period of the Messiah. In a sense, more than figurative, he is the type and prophecy of Jesus Christ. Christ is not called the son of Jacob or of Moses, but he was truly "the son of David."

To his own people his was the name most dearly cherished after their first ancestor Abraham. "The city of David," "the house of David," "the oath sworn unto David" (the pledge of the continuance of his dynasty), are expressions which pervade the whole of the Old Testament and all the figurative language of the New, and they serve to mark the lasting significance of his appearance in history.[2]

His Psalms (whether those actually written by himself be many or few) have been the source of consolation and instruction beyond any other part of the Hebrew Scriptures. In them appear qualities of mind and religious perceptions not before expressed in the sacred writings, but eminently characteristic of David — the love of nature, the sense of sin and the tender, ardent trust in and communion with God. No other part of the Old Testament comes so near to the spirit of the New. The Psalms are the only expression of devotion which have been equally used through the whole Christian Church — Abyssinian, Greek, Latin, Puritan, Anglican.

The difficulties which attend on his character are valuable as

---

1. The following character of David is taken from Dean Stanley's art, David, in Smith's *Dict. of the Bible.*
2. It may be remarked that the name David never appears as given to any one else in the Jewish history.

proofs of the impartiality of Scripture in recording them, and as indications of the union of natural power and weakness which his character included. The Rabbis in former times and critics (like Bayle) in later times, have seized on its dark features and exaggerated them to the utmost. And it has been often asked, both by the scoffers and the serious, how the man after God's[1] own heart could have murdered Uriah and seduced Bathsheba, and tortured the Ammonites to death? An extract from one who is not a too indulgent critic of sacred characters expresses at once the common sense and the religious lesson of the whole matter. "Who is called 'the man after God's own heart?' David, the Hebrew king, had fallen into sins enough — blackest crimes — there was no want of sin. And therefore the unbelievers sneer, and ask 'Is this your man according to God's heart?' "

The sneer, I must say, seems to me but a shallow one. What are faults; what are the outward details of a life, if the inner secret of it, the remorse, temptations, the often baffled, never-ended struggle of it be forgotten? . . . David's life and history, as written for us in those Psalms of his, I consider to be the truest emblem ever given us of a man's moral progress and warfare here below. All earnest souls will ever discern in it the faithful struggle of an earnest human soul toward what is good and best. Struggle often baffled — sore baffled — driven as into entire wreck, yet a struggle never ended, ever with tears, repentance, true unconquerable purpose begun anew.

Questions on Section IV
David's Reign in Tragedies
(II Samuel 13:1-I Kings 2:11)

1. What was the name of Absalom's sister (13:1)?
2. What son of David fell in love with her (13:2)?
3. What friend helped him devise a plot against her (13:3)?
4. What plot was conceived to entrap the young woman (13:5ff)?
5. What was the attitude of the young man toward the young woman after the sinful act had taken place (13:15)?
6. How many years passed before Absalom took vengeance on his half-brother (13:23)?
7. What was the occasion when vengeance was taken?

---

1. This expression has been perhaps too much made of. It occurs only once in the Scriptures (I Sam. 13:14, quoted again in Acts 13:22), where it merely indicates a man whom God will approve, in distinction from Saul who was rejected. A much stronger and more peculiar commendation of David is that contained in I K. 15:3-5 and implied in Ps. 89:20-28.

8. To whom did Absalom escape after he took vengeance (13:37)?
9. What relationship was he to Absalom (3:3)?
10. How long did Absalom remain away from his father, the king (13:38)?
11. Who realized that David's heart went out toward Absalom (14:1)?
12. To what place did he send for a woman who would come to convince David to send for Absalom (14:2)?
13. For how long after his return to Jerusalem did Absalom wait before being allowed to see David (14:28)?
14. What did Absalom do to convince Joab that he wanted him to consult with David for him (14:30)?
15. How many men did Absalom obtain to run before him and his chariot as he went from place to place (15:1)?
16. By what method did Abaslom seek to steal the hearts of the people (15:2-6)?
17. How did Absalom deceive the king in order to get his permission to leave Jerusalem (15:7ff)?
18. How many men from Jerusalem accompanied Absalom on his mission to place agitators throughout all the tribes of Israel (15:11)?
19. What counsellor of David defected to Absalom (15:12)?
20. What was David's action upon hearing that Absalom was making himself king over Israel (15:14)?
21. What foreigner (a Gittite) would not forsake David (15:19-21)?
22. Did David give permission to the priests to bring the ark out of Jerusalem (15:25)?
23. What did David pray when he learned of his counsellor's going over to Absalom (15:31)?
24. Who were the sons of Zadok and Abiathar? What were they appointed to do for David (15:36)?
25. Who was Ziba and what message did he bring to David as he fled (16:1-3)?
26. Who was Shimei and what did he do to David (16:5)?
27. Why did David spare Shimei when Abishai desired to kill him (16:9-12)?
28. What counsel was given to Absalom about David's concubines? Who gave this counsel (16:20-21)?
29. How did each of the two counsellors advise Absalom to attack David (17:1-13)?

30. Whose counsel was followed (17:14)?
31. Who saw the sons of the priests and told Absalom (17:18)?
32. How did the sons of the priests escape death (17:18-19)?
33. Why did David and his people go across Jordan (17:21-22)?
34. How did Ahithophel die (17:23)?
35. Whom did Absalom set over his army (17:25)?
36. What three men brought food and beds to David and his people (17:27)?
37. Into how many groups did David divide his army? Who was appointed leader of each group (18:1-2)?
38. What command about Absalom did David speak before all the people (18:5)?
39. Where was the battle with Absalom fought (18:6)?
40. What killed more people than the sword (18:8)?
41. How did Absalom die? Who slew him (18:9-14)?
42. Who was sent to tell David of Absalom's death (18:21)?
43. Who also wanted to run and tell David the news (18:19)?
44. How did David react to Absalom's death (18:33)?
45. Who scolded David for his grief about Absalom (19:5)?
46. Why was it necessary for David to go forth and speak to his servants after Absalom's death (19:7-8)?
47. What tribe was summoned to bring King David back to his house in Jerusalem (19:11,14)?
48. Did David spare Shimei when he met him (19:16,23)?
49. How had Mephibosheth felt during David's absence (19:24)?
50. Who was given the land that had belonged to Saul (19:29)?
51. What aged man would not return with David to Jerusalem (19:32-34)?
52. Who was Chimham (19:37)?
53. What disagreement arose between Judah and the other tribes of Israel (19:41-43)?
54. Who was Sheba and what did he do (20:1-2)?
55. What did David do with his defiled concubines (20:3)?
56. Who was sent to gather an army to pursue Sheba (20:4)?
57. Who was sent later to pursue Sheba (20:6)?
58. Who slew Amasa? Where (20:8-10)?
59. Where did Sheba die? How (20:15,22)?
60. Why were there three years of famine in the land (21:1)?
61. Why were seven sons of Saul slain (21:3-6)?
62. Who was Rizpah (21:8)?

63. How long did Rizpah guard the bodies of her sons (21:9-10)?
64. Where were Saul's bones buried (21:14)?
65. Who saved David's life during a battle with a giant (21:16-17)?
66. What relative of Goliath was slain (I Chron. 20:5)?
67. How many fingers were on the hands of the giant from Gath (II Sam. 21:20)?
68. How many mighty men did David have (23:23-24)?
69. Who moved David to number Israel (24:1; I Chron. 21:1)?
70. Who objected to the numbering (24:3)?
71. About how many men were numbered (24:9)?
72. What three punishments did God offer David a choice of (24:13)?
73. How many people died as a result of David's numbering (24:15)?
74. Where did the angel stop slaying (24:16)?
75. Where was the angel seen (24:16; I Chron. 21:16)?
76. Where was David commanded to build an altar (II Sam. 24:18)?
77. What was built in later years on the site where David built the altar (I Chron. 22:1)?
78. What did Araunah offer David (24:22)?
79. Why would David not accept Araunah's gift (24:24)?
80. What happened to the burnt-offering on David's altar (I Chron. 21:26)?
81. Where was the altar of burnt-offering in David's time (I Chron. 21:29)?
82. What people were gathered together to work on temple preparations (I Chron. 22:2)?
83. What materials did David collect for the temple (I Chron. 22:3-4, 14)?
84. What charge did David give to Solomon (I Chron. 22:6)?
85. Whom did David appoint to be the next king (I Chron. 23:1)?
86. What did David organize the Levites to do (I Chron. 23:4-5, 28-32; 26:1,20,29)?
87. At what age did David cause the Levites to enter their work (I Chron. 23:24)?.
88. How did this differ from the age indicated in the law (Num. 4:1-3)?

89. How many courses (or groups) were the priest divided into (I Chron. 24:10; Luke 1:5)?

90. Which priestly course is mentioned in the New Testament (I Chron. 24:10; Luke 1:5)?

91. Whose sons (three names) were leaders in the temple music (I Chron. 25:1)?

92. Who was the young virgin brought to David in his old age (I Kings 1:3)?

93. Which son of David exalted himself and said, "I will be king," in David's old age (I Kings 1:5)?

94. What two leaders followed this would-be king (I Kings 1:7)?

95. Who told Bathsheba of the plot (I Kings 1:11)?

96. Who first told David of the plot (I Kings 1:15)?

97. Who then came and told David of the plot (I Kings 1:22)?

98. Who was summoned to anoint Solomon and announced that he was king (I Kings 1:33-34)? Where was the announcement made?

99. How did the people react to Solomon's being made king (I Kings 1:40)?

100. How did the would-be king and his followers react to the news of Solomon's having been made king (I Kings 1:49-50)?

101. Did Solomon kill the one who had tried to become king (I Kings 1:52-53)?

102. What dying charge did David give Solomon (I Kings 2:1-3)?

103. What instructions did David give to Solomon concerning Joab (I Kings 2:5-6)? Concerning Barzillai (2:7)? Concerning Shimei (2:8-9)?

104. Where was David buried (2:10)?

Section V
Introduction to the Books of Kings and Chronicles

A. Kings

1. I Kings begins with the account of David's old age and ends shortly after the death of King Ahab.

2. II Kings begins with Ahab's son Ahaziah and ends with the Babylonian captivity of Judah. Thus II Kings brings us almost down to the end of O.T. history.

3. There is a notable historical break between chapters eleven and twelve (11/12) of I Kings. This is the break between the United Kingdom period and the Divided Kingdom period. See the Outline of Old Testament History.

4. Outline of I and II Kings. (Memorize)

Part I — Reign of Solomon (I Kings 1-11).

Part II — Synchronous reigns of the kings of Judah and Israel (I Kings 12-II Kings 17).

Part III — Kings of Judah to the Babylonian captivity (II Kings 18-25).

5. Solomon's reign is dated 970-931 B.C. For the chronology of the Divided Kingdom, see Chronology of the Divided Kingdom in this book, pp. 570-575.

6. *Jeremiah* is thought to have been the final author and compiler of Kings. However, Kings had numerous earlier authors who drew upon the official records of Judah and Israel (See I Kings 11:41; 14:19,29), the writings of various prophets and their own knowledge of events.

The writers of Kings appear to have been *prophets*. Note the schools of prophets called "son of the prophets" in II Kings 2:15; 6:1; etc. These prophets knew the secrets of royal hearts and councils. They did not fear to condemn the sins of kings. They stressed the work of various prophets.

7. Since the writers and compilers of Kings were prophets, we are not surprised to find the great emphasis given to the prophets Elijah and Elisha. The records of their deeds occupy most of I Kings 17-21 and II Kings 1-8.

Questions

1. With what events does I Kings begin and end?
2. With what events does II Kings begin and end?
3. Where is the notable break in I Kings and what does it come between?
4. Write from memory the outline of I and II Kings.
5. Who is thought to have been the final author and compiler of the material in Kings?
6. What group of men were the writers of the information in Kings?
7. Which two great prophets have much told about them in I and II Kings?

B. Chronicles

1. There is much material in I and II Chronicles that is parallel to that in the books of Samuel and Kings. However, there are also important differences.

a. Kings tells about both the northern and southern kingdoms. Chronicles tells only about the Kingdom of Judah, and mentions the northern kingdom only when its history directly involved Judah.

b. Kings has a *prophetic* emphasis. Chronicles has a *priestly* emphasis, telling of the worship and temple activities of such men as David, Jehoshaphat, Hezekiah, etc. Chronicles shows the priestly interest in genealogies. (The genealogies are important, since the Messiah was to come from the family of Abraham and David.)

c. Chronicles covers a longer time span than do the books of Samuel and Kings.

d. Chronicles presents the *optimistic* and brighter side of Judah's history, omitting such dark events as David's taking Bathsheba or Absalom's rebellion.

2. *Chronicles begins with Adam* and carries the history down to the decree of Cyrus permitting the Jews to return from Babylonian captivity. The genealogies in the book even go further forward in history than that, telling of several generations of people who lived after the Babylonian captivity. See I Ch. 3:19-24. Thus Chronicles brings us down to about 420 B.C. to the time of the writing of the last O.T. book.

3. *Ezra*, the scribe and priest who came back from Babylonian captivity, is thought to be the author and compiler of chronicles. The last paragraph of II Chronicles is continued at the start of Ezra's book and is incomplete in Chronicles. Ezra doubtless used the old temple records as sources of the genealogies in Chronicles.

4. Outline of Chronicles. (Memorize.)

Part I — Genealogies from Adam to the return from Babylon (I Ch. 1-9).

Part II — History of King David (I Ch. 10-29).

Part III — History of King Solomon (II Ch. 1-9).

Part IV — History of the Kings of Judah (II Ch. 10-36).

5. A helpful book: Crockett, Wm. D. *A Harmony of the Books of Samuel, Kings and Chronicles* (Grand Rapids, Mich.: Baker Book

House, 1961). This book gives all the Scripture in Samuel, Kings and Chronicles in chronological order and puts related material in different books in parallel columns.

    6. Memorize II Chron. 7:14.

Questions

1. What difference is there between the information given about the kingdoms in Kings and in Chronicles?
2. What type of an emphasis does Chronicles give to its history?
3. Where does the material in Chronicles begin and where does it end?
4. Who is thought to be the author of Chronicles?
5. Write from memory the outline of Chronicles.
6. Write II Chron. 7:14 from memory.

Section IV
The Reign of Solomon
(I Kings 2:12-11:43; II Chron. 1-9)

1. Character of Solomon's reign. 2. His marriage with Pharaoh's daughter — Alliance with Hiram — The high places retained — God appears to him at Gibeon — His choice of wisdom — The judgment of Solomon. 3. Solomon's court and revenues — His personal qualities — His knowledge, writings and conversation — The Proverbs. 4. Building of the temple — Arrangements with King Hiram — Materials for the house — Hiram the architect. 5. Description of the edifice. 6. Dedication of the Temple — The prayer of Solomon. 7. Completion of Solomon's buildings — God's second appearance to him. 8. His works in the provinces — Conquest of Hamath — Building of Tadmor — Solomon's commercial enterprises — Voyages to Tharshish and Ophir — His works in gold, ivory, etc. 9. Visits of foreign kings — The queen of Sheba. 10. Solomon's declension — His tyrannical government and idolatries. 11. Troubles from Hadad, Rezon and Jeroboam — Prophecy of Ahijah. 12. Last days of Solomon — Book of Ecclesiastes — Death and burial of Solomon — Records of his reign.

    1. *Solomon reigned over Israel 970-931 B.C.* The epoch of

Solomon's reign marks the climax of the Hebrew monarchy and, according to the usual law of human greatness, the beginning of its decline. Starting from the vantage-ground on which the kingdom had been placed by the conquests of David, through the favor of Jehovah, he preserved its ascendancy by a wisdom which has become proverbial, and prepared its downfall by his luxury and arrogance. Having achieved the greatest work done by any ruler of Israel since Moses, the building of the house of God upon Mount Moriah and the settlement of His worship, he left to after times the name of

> "That uxorious kings, whose heart, though large,
> Beguiled by fair idolatresses, fell
> To idols foul."

The author and compiler of the richest maxims of wisdom in the literature of the world, he so used up the resources of intellectual as well as sensual pleasure as to end with the confession, "Vanity of vanities! All is emptiness and vexation of spirit!"

The lift of Solomon presents a striking contrast to his father's in its uneventful character. His great work was the building of the HOUSE OF GOD, commonly called the *Temple* at Jerusalem. The rest of the history of his reign is chiefly occupied with the description of his magnificence and wealth, as the sovereign of what was then the greatest monarchy of Western Asia

---

Solomon is Famous for His
1. **Wisdom**
2. **Wealth**
3. **Wives**
4. **Temple**

We have already related his birth as the son of Bathsheba, his proclamation as king at the time of the rebellion of Adonijah, his second and more solemn anointing at the last assembly held by David and the measures of severity forced upon him by the new conspiracy of Joab and Abiathar with Adonijah after his father's death, as well as the punishment of Shimei, though this was full three years after his ascension. We now return to the narrative of his reign.

2. The date of Solomon's accession as sole king can be fixed with precision to the year 970 B.C. Jewish tradition makes him eighteen years old at this epoch which agrees with the date of the Scripture narrative. He reigned forty years, or more precisely,

thirty-nine years and a half, the sum of his own and his father's reign being eighty years.

The first act of the foreign policy of the new reign must have been to most Israelites a very startling one. Solomon showed the desire to strengthen his throne by foreign alliances in a manner which marks the great difference of spirit between the new monarchy and the ancient theocracy. He made an alliance with Pharaoh, king of Egypt, and took his daughter to be his wife. This Pharaoh was probably Hor-Psibkhannu, the last king of the XXIst dynasty, for the eminent head of the XXIInd dynasty, Sheshonk I (Shishak), belongs to the latter part of the reign of Solomon and to that of Rehoboam (I Kings 3:1).[1] That this flagrant breach, not only of a general principle but of the specific law against intercourse with Egypt (Lev. 18:3), passed unpunished for the time, is an example of that great system of forbearance which lies at the basis of each new dispensation of God's moral government. But the law of retribution for sinful actions by their natural effects was working from the very first and this marriage of Solomon was the first step toward his fall into idolatry. Meanwhile "Solomon loved Jehovah, walking in the statutes of David his father," and "God was with him, and magnified him exceedingly"; and the only blot upon the outward purity as well as prosperity of the kingdom was the retention of the "high places," which had been the seats of the ancient worship, for sacrifice, in the absence of any house of God. The hill of Gibeon, where stood the tabernacle and the altar of burnt-offering, seems only to have been regarded as the chief of these high places; and it was probably in the course of a series of sacrifices at the different sacred heights that Solomon visited Gibeon, "the great high place," and there in the midst of a great convocation of the people, sacrificed a tenfold hecatomb — a thousand burnt-offerings — upon the altar (I Kings 3:2-4; I Chron. 1:1-6).

This was the occasion chosen by Jehovah for His first personal revelation to Solomon. In the following night God appeared to him in a dream and asked him to choose what He should give him. After a thanksgiving for the mercies shown to David and a prayer that the promise made to him might be established, Solomon, confessing himself to be but a little child in comparison to the great work committed him in governing and judging the people,

---

1. As Rehoboam was forty-one years old at his accession, Solomon must have married his mother — Naamah of Ammon — before his father's death, and therefore before he married the daughter of Pharaoh.

asked for the wisdom and knowledge that might fit him for the office — "an understanding heart to judge Thy people, to discern between good and bad." The desire, thus expressed in Solomon's own words, does not seem to have so high a meaning as is often assigned to it. He does not ask that profound spiritual wisdom, which would teach him to know God and his own heart; in this he was always far inferior to David. His prayer is for practical sagacity, clear intelligence, quick discernment, to see the right from the wrong amid the mazes of duplicity and doubt which beset the judge, especially among an Oriental people. And this gift he received. His aspirations, if not for the highest spiritual excellence, were for usefulness to his subjects and fellow-men, not for long life, riches and victory for himself; and because he had not selfishly asked these things, they were freely granted to him in addition to the gift he had chosen. Assured of God's favor, he returned to Jerusalem and renewed his sacrifices before the ark, and made a feast to all his servants (I Kings 3:5-15; II Chron. 1:7-13).

An occasion soon arose to prove his divine gift of sagacity. Two women appeared before his judgment-seat with a dead and a living infant. The one who appealed to the king for justice alleged that they had both been delivered in the same house, the other woman three days after herself, that the other had overlaid her child in the night and had exchanged its corpse for the living child of the first while she slept. The second declared that the living child was hers and both were alike clamorous in demanding it. The king resolved to appeal to the maternal instinct, as a sure test even in the degraded class to which both the women belonged. Calling for a sword, he bade one of his guards divide the living child in two and give half to one woman and half to the other. It is a strange proof of the progress of the monarchy toward despotic power that the command should have been taken in earnest but so it seems to have been. The woman who had borne the living child now prayed that it might be given to the other to save its life, while the latter consented to the cruel partition, and the king had now no difficulty in deciding the dispute. The fame of the decision spread through all Israel, inspiring fear of the king's justice and a conviction that God had given him that wise discernment which is prized in the East as a ruler's highest quality (I Kings 3:16-28).

3. Solomon arranged his court on the same general basis as his father's but on a scale of much greater magnificence. Among the

names of his chief officers we find several of his father's most distinguished servants and their sons. There were "princes" or chief governors, two "scribes" or secretaries, a "recorder," a "captain of the host," "officers" of the court, the chief of whom had, like Hushai under David, the title of "the king's friend"; there was a chief over the household and another over the tribute. The priests were Zadok and Abiathar though, as we have seen, the latter was deposed (I Kings 4:1-6). The supplies needed for the court were levied throughout the whole land by twelve officers, to each of whom was allotted a particular district to supply one month's provisions (I Kings 4:7-19). But these contributions were increased by the subject kingdoms between the Euphrates, which was the eastern border of Solomon's dominions, from Tiphsah on the Euphrates river to Azzah (or Gaza) in the land of the Philistines. The provision for each day consisted of thirty measures of fine flour and seventy measures of meal, ten fat oxen and twenty from the pastures and 100 sheep, besides venison and fowl (I Kings 4:21-24). Judah and Israel, increasing rapidly in numbers, gave themselves up to festivity and mirth, and "dwelt safely, every man under his vine and under his fig-tree, from Dan even to Beersheba, all the days of Solomon" (I Kings 4:20,25). In the great military establishment, which Solomon maintained for state as well as for defense, he set at naught the law against keeping up a force of cavalry. He had four thousand stalls for horses and twelve thousand horsemen (II Chron. 9:25), and their supplies of straw and provender were furnished by the twelve officers just mentioned. The horses and chariots were brought from Egypt, whence also the kings of the Hittites and the kings of Syria obtained theirs. A chariot cost 600 shekels of silver and a horse 150. The chariots and cavalry were placed in garrison in certain cities, called "chariot cities," and partly with the king at Jerusalem. The commerce with Egypt supplied also linen yarn, which was made a royal monopoly. As the result of this and other commerce (to be spoken of presently), silver and gold are said in the hyperbolical language of the East to have been as stones at Jerusalem, and the cedars of Lebanon as abundant as the sycamore, the common timber of Palestine (II Chron. 1:14-17).

But all this magnificence was transcended by the personal qualities of Solomon himself. We have, it is true, no direct description of his personal appearance, but the wonderful impression he made upon all who came near him may well lead us to believe that with him as with Saul and David, Absalom and Adonijah, as with most other favorite princes of Eastern peoples, there must have been the fascination and the grace of a noble presence. Whatever higher mystic meaning may be latent in Psalm 45 or the Song of Songs, we are all but compelled to think of them as having had, at least, a historical starting point. They tell us of one who was, in the eyes of the men of his own time, "fairer than the children of men," the face "bright and ruddy" as his father's (Song 5:10; I Sam. 17:42); bushy locks, dark as the raven's wing, yet not without a golden glow, the eyes soft as "the eyes of doves," the "countenance as Lebanon, excellent as the cedars," "the chiefest among ten thousand, the altogether lovely" (Song 5:9-16). Add to this all gifts of a noble, far-reaching intellect, large and ready sympathies, a playful and genial humor, the lips "full of grace," the soul "anointed" as "with the oil of gladness" (Psalm 45), and we may form some notion of what the king was like in this dawn of his golden prime. He used these gifts not only for the government of his people but for the acquisition and the embodiment in writing of all the learning of the age. He gave equal attention to the lessons of practical morals and to the facts of natural science. "He spake 3000 proverbs, and his songs were a thousand and five." "And he spake of trees, from the cedar-tree that is in Lebanon, even unto the hyssop that springeth out of the wall: he spake also of beasts, and of fowl, and of creeping things, and of fishes"; in short, of the whole cycle of natural history (I Kings 4:32-33). We must, however, avoid misconceptions, both as to the matter of Solomon's knowledge and as to the form of its utterance. Solomon's natural science, like that of Oriental philosophers in general, consisted rather in the observation of the obvious facts in the common life and habits of God's creatures, with an especial view to use them for the poetical illustration of moral lessons: and in this way we find such knowledge used, not only in the Proverbs ascribed to him, but in many of the Psalms and throughout the Book of Job. The discourses in the latter part of that book about Behemoth and Leviathan are probably a type of the manner in which "Solomon spake of beasts." His 3000 proverbs and 1005 songs probably contained nearly all that he wrote upon such matters in the form of poetical illustration. For the rest, it should be remembered that instruction in his time and long after, was chiefly oral. The tents of the patriarchs and the abodes of their descendants witnessed many an hour when the ancient father would discourse to his descendants on the lessons of his experience and the traditions handed down by his fathers; and such we conceive to have been the converse held by Solomon in the midst of his splendid court, only on a much grander scale and covering a much wider field. Thus, amid the public life of an Eastern monarch, not in the seclusion of the retired student, he poured out the knowledge which attracted the subjects of other kings from all nations of the earth, to hear for themselves that wisdom the fame of which had reached them in their distant countries (I Kings 4:34). In one celebrated instance the attraction proved sufficient to bring one of those sovereigns themselves from the remotest regions, but this visit of the Queen of Sheba belongs to a later period of Solomon's reign.

Solomon Wrote the Books of
1. Proverbs
2. Song of Solomon (Canticles)
3. Ecclesiastes (Koheleth)

---

4. The king was meanwhile occupied with three great works — the building of the house of God, of his own house and of the wall of Jerusalem. We have seen the vast preparations that David had made for the erection of the Temple, the designs for which he had given into the hands of Solomon and how he had been aided by Hiram, king of Tyre. That faithful ally sent an embassy of congratulation on his son's accession (I Kings 5; II Chron. 2), and Solomon sent back an answer informing Hiram of his prosperity, declaring his intention of building a house for God and requesting his assistance, which Hiram gladly promised in a letter (II Chron. 2:11).

An arrangement was made by which Hiram gave cedars and fir-trees out of Lebanon, which his servants felled, while those of Solomon squared and fitted them for their places in the building. The provisions for both parties were supplied by Solomon, for then as in the time of Herod Agrippa, the maritime region of Phoenicia derived its supplies of food from Palestine (Acts 12:20). The prepared timber was brought down to the sea and floated round to Joppa, under the care of the Tyrian sailors, whence Solomon undertook the thirty miles' transport to Jerusalem. He raised the laborers required for this great work by a levy of the strangers who lived in various parts of the land. All the remnant of these had been finally subdued by David, who instead of exterminating them, retained them in a condition similar to that to which Joshua had reduced the Gibeonites. Solomon found their number to be 153,600; he appointed 70,000 for the work of transport, 80,000 as hewers in Lebanon, and the remaining 3600 as overseers (I Kings 5:15-16; II Chron. 2:17-18). In addition to these, he raised a levy of 30,000 men out of all Israel, whom he sent to work in Lebanon by relays of 10,000, each relay serving for one month and returning home for two (I Kings 5:13-14). Besides the timber, they hewed the great stones which were to form the foundation of the house, stones which by the time they reached Jerusalem must have well earned the name of "costly stones," which is applied to them in the narrative (I Kings 5:17).

Besides these contributions of materials and labor, Hiram supplied Solomon with a chief architect, a namesake of his own, for whom the King of Tyre expressed the reverence of a disciple for an artist by calling him "Hiram, my father" (II Chron. 2:13; 4:16).[1] This Hiram was the son of a widow of Naphtali (or Dan), and his father had been a Tyrian artist. He devoted his hereditary skill to the service of the God whom his mother had doubtless taught him to reverence, in the spirit of Bezaleel, whom he resembled in the great variety of his accomplishments. Besides his principal profession as a worker in brass, he wrought in gold, silver and iron, in stone and timber, in purple, blue, fine linen and crimson; in short, his great gift seems to have been that of *design* in all its branches. The master-pieces of his art were the two pillars of cast brass, called Jachin and Boaz, which stood on each side of the porch in front of the Holy Place (I Kings 7:13ff; II Chron. 2:13-14). The workmen under him had already been provided by David, who as we have seen secured the services of all the foreign artists residing in the land.

5. The actual building of the Temple was commenced in the fourth year of Solomon's reign and the four hundred and eightieth year from the Exodus, on the second day of the month Zif (afterward Iyar = April and May), the second of the ecclesiastical year (I Kings 6:1; II Chron. 3:2). So complete were the preparations that no sound of axe or hammer was heard about the building during its whole erection and it was completed in seven and a half years, in the eighth month (Bul, afterward Marcheshvan = Oct. and Nov.) of the eleventh year of Solomon. It occupied the site prepared for it by David, which had formerly been the threshing-floor of the Jebusite Ornan or Araunah on MOUNT MORIAH. The whole area enclosed by the outer walls

---

1. "Huram" is only another form of "Hiram," and is applied to the king as well as to the artist in the original text (I Chron. 14:1; II Chron. 2:3, 11, 12; 8:2, 18; 9:10, 21).

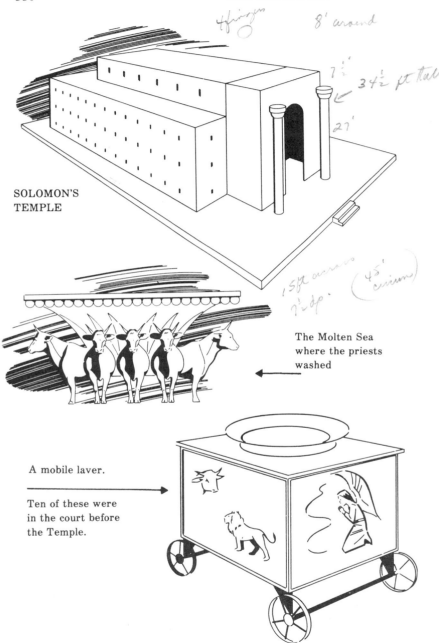

SOLOMON'S
TEMPLE

The Molten Sea
where the priests
washed

A mobile laver.

Ten of these were
in the court before
the Temple.

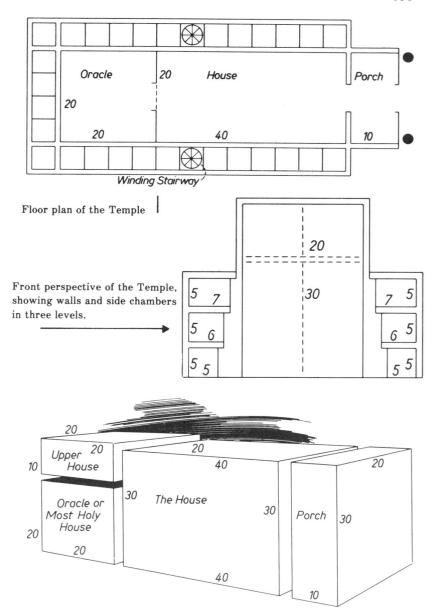

Floor plan of the Temple

Front perspective of the Temple, showing walls and side chambers in three levels.

Principal compartment of the Temple — side chambers not shown

The House, or holy place.

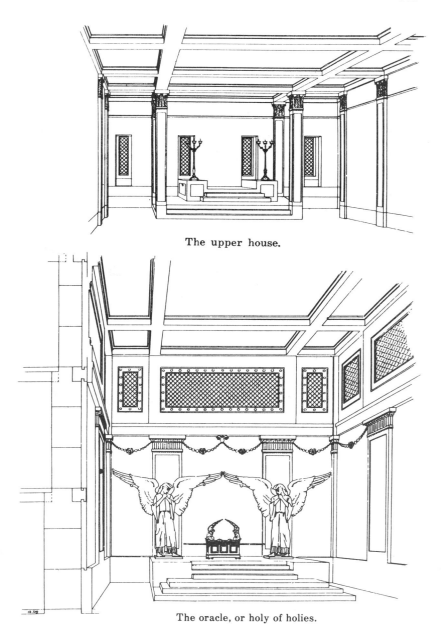

The upper house.

The oracle, or holy of holies.

formed a square of about 600 feet but the sanctuary itself was comparatively small, inasmuch as it was intended only for the ministrations of the priests, the congregation of the people assembling in the courts. In this and all other essential points, the Temple followed the model of the Tabernacle, from which it differed chiefly by having chambers built about the sanctuary for the abode of the priests and attendants and the keeping of treasures and stores. In most of its dimensions the Temple was double those of the Tabernacle, the ground-plan measuring 80 cubits by 40, while that of the Tabernacle was 40 by 20, and the height of the Temple being 30 cubits, while that of the Tabernacle was 10.

The Temple consisted of three principal parts: the Porch, the House (or Holy Place) and the Oracle (or Holy of Holies). The *House* or Holy Place was 40 cubits long by 20 wide by 30 high. The *Oracle* or Holy of Holies was a cube of 20 cubits. The place of the two "veils" of the Tabernacle were occupied in the Temple by partitions in which were folding doors. The floor dimensions of the House and Oracle together were exactly double the floor dimensions of the Holy Place and the Most Holy Place of the Tabernacle. The height of the House was, however, triple that of the Tabernacle Holy Place, being 30 cubits high. The whole interior was lined with woodwork richly carved and overlaid with gold.

The Porch of the Temple was ten cubits deep and 20 cubits wide, the same width as the House. Two gigantic brazen pillars stood before the porch. They were 18 cubits high with capitals of 5 cubits more, adorned with lily-work and pomegranates. The exact use of these pillars is obscure. Numerous scholars have contended that they were gigantic cressets or fire altars.[1] Free-standing pillars of this type are known to have been erected in temples of Syria, Phoenicia and Cyprus during this period (I Kings 7:15-22). The pillars were named Jachin *(He shall establish)* and Boaz *(In it is strength)*.

Around the sides and back of the Temple side chambers were built three stories high (I Kings 6:5-6). All of these side chambers were five cubits in height. Those on the bottom floor were five cubits in width; those on the middle floor were six; those on the third floor were seven. Apparently the walls of the Temple were built thinner in the upper portions; ledges in the walls at the ceiling levels of side chambers provided support for the ceiling

---

1. Unger, *Arch. & O.T.* p. 231.

beams and also made the next floor above a cubit wider (I Kings 6:5-7). The chambers did not reach to the top of the House and Oracle. This left space for windows in the Temple walls above the chambers.

Besides the three principal parts of Solomon's Temple, it appears to have had an *Upper House* or upper chambers (II Chron. 3:9; I Chron. 28:11). We presume that these were built above the Oracle, so that its ceiling would be level with that of the House. These upper chambers were also overlaid with gold. Josephus and the Talmud tell that there was a superstructure on the Temple equal in height to the lower part. Information from these sources cannot, however, be accepted as equal in authority with that from the Scriptures.

Within the Oracle was placed the same ark of the covenant that had been in the Tabernacle of Moses. Above the sacred ark were made two huge new cherubim, one pair of whose wings met above the ark and another pair reached to the walls. In the Holy Place, besides the Altar of Incense, which was made of cedar overlaid with gold, there were ten golden candlesticks instead of one, and the table of shew-bread was replaced by ten golden tables bearing, besides the shew-bread, the innumerable golden vessels for the service of the sanctuary.

The entire Temple complex, consisting of the Temple, Solomon's palace and other buildings, was surrounded by a great court made of three courses of stone and a course of cedar beams (I Kings 7:9-12). The Temple building itself was surrounded by a wall forming a smaller inner court of priests within the great court (II Chron. 3:9). Within this court of the priests, which corresponded to the court of the Tabernacle and contained similar equipment, a new altar of burnt-offering was made. It was much larger than the old one. Like the latter, it was square but the length and breadth were now twenty cubits and the height ten (II Chron. 4:1). It differed, too, in the material of which it was made, being entirely of brass (I Kings 8:64; II Chron. 7:7). Instead of the brazen laver, there was "a molten sea" of brass, a masterpiece of Hiram's skill for the ablution of the priests. It was called a "sea" from its great size, being five cubits in height, ten in diameter and thirty in circumference and containing 2000 baths.[1] It stood on twelve oxen, three toward each quarter of the heavens and all looking outward. The brim itself or lip was wrought "like the brim of a cup, with flowers of lilies," *i.e.,* carved outward like a

---

1. A *bath* is about six gallons, making the capacity of the molten sea about 12,000 gallons.

lily or lotus flower. There were besides ten smaller lavers for the washing of the burnt-offerings. These held forty baths each or 240 gallons (I Kings 7:38-39). They were on wheels and had an ornamented brass panel on each of their four sides (I Kings 7:27-37).

6. The dedication of Solomon's Temple was the grandest ceremony ever performed under the Mosaic dispensation, for the giving of the law from Sinai was too solemn to be called a ceremony. Solomon appeared in that priestly character which we have seen borne by his father to perform this great act on behalf of the people, leaving to the priests and Levites the care of the ark and the details of the service, especially the psalmody. The time chosen was the most joyous festival of the Jews, the Feast of Tabernacles, in the seventh month (Tishri or Ethanim = September and October) of the sacred year. Having done the labors of the field and gathered in the vintage, the people assembled at Jerusalem from all parts of Solomon's wide territories. The full body of the priests attended, the usual courses being suspended and they brought the ark in a grand and joyous procession from the city of David to the rest prepared for it in the Holy of Holies. There they placed it beneath the spreading wings of the cherubim and drew out the ends of the staves, that they might be seen as in the Tabernacle, behind the veil. Amid all the new splendors of its dwelling, the ark of the covenant was the same as of old; it contained nothing but the two tables of the law, which Moses had placed in it at Sinai. As the priests retired from within the veil, the Levites and their sons, arranged in their three courses of psalmody with all instruments of music and clad in white linen robes, burst forth with the sacred chorus praising Jehovah, "For He is good; for His mercy endureth forever." It was at this very moment, "just as the trumpeters and singers were as one, to make one sound to be heard in praising and thanking Jehovah," that He gave the sign of His coming to take possession of His house: "The house was filled with a cloud, even the house of Jehovah, so that the priests could not stand to minister because of the cloud; for the GLORY OF JEHOVAH had filled the HOUSE OF JEHOVAH" (I Kings 8:1-11; II Chron. 5). As that sacred cloud spread through the open doors over the sanctuary, the voice of Solomon was heard recognizing the presence of the God who had said that he would dwell in the thick darkness and for whom he had now built a habitation forever. Then turning to the people

from the great platform of brass, which he had erected in the midst of the court in front of the brazen altar, the king blessed Jehovah the God of Israel, who had chosen Jerusalem as the place sacred to His name and had performed His promises to David and fulfilled his desire to build him a house. And now kneeling down before the whole congregation, with his face toward the sanctuary, Solomon poured forth a prayer, unequaled for sublimity and comprehensiveness, in which the leading thought, repeated with beautiful variety and minuteness, is this: that the abode which Jehovah had now deigned to sanctify with His presence might prove the center of blessing and forgiveness to His people, that whatever prayer for help, whatever penitent confession in the time of suffering and exile they might offer toward that house, God would hear it from His true dwelling-place in heaven and forgive His people who had sinned against Him. The prayer is, indeed, a prophecy of the history of Israel and of God's chastisements of their sins, even to the Captivity. We see it still answered when Daniel opened his window at Babylon and prayed toward the site of the ruined Temple and at this hour its repetition by the people of Israel awaits a better restoration. He concluded with a blessing and exhortation to the people (I Kings 8; II Chron. 6).

The prayer of Solomon was followed by another sign of God's presence. The fire came down from heaven as on the first altar of burnt-offering and consumed the sacrifices, while the Shekinah again filled the house, preventing the entrance of the priests, as if, for that one day, God claimed the sanctuary as His very own to the exclusion of all mere creatures. Then Solomon and all the people offered their sacrifices on the altar: 22,000 oxen and 120,000 sheep, the priests executing their office while the Levites played and sang in the order and to the words of David. A great feast followed for twice seven days, seven for the Feast of Tabernacles and seven for the dedication, and on the twenty-third day of the month Solomon dismissed the people. They returned to their homes, "glad and merry in heart for all the goodness that Jehovah had shewed unto David, and to Solomon, and to Israel His people" (I Kings 7:62-66; II Chron. 7).

7. Four years more were occupied in the completion of the king's "own house," and of his other great works at Jerusalem. His palace consisted of a number of magnificent buildings serving

several purposes but grouped together under one roof or within one enclosure.[1]

The principal section within the palace was, as in all Eastern palaces, the great hall of state and audience, called "The House of the Forest of Lebanon," apparently from the four rows of cedar pillars by which it was supported. It was 100 cubits long, 50 wide and 30 high. Next in importance was the Hall or "Porch of Judgment," a guadrangular building supported by columns,[2] which possibly stood on the other side of a great court, opposite the House of the Forest of Lebanon. The third edifice is merely called a "Porch of Pillars." Its dimensions were 50 by 30 cubits. Its use cannot be considered as doubtful as it was an indispensable adjunct to an Eastern palace. It was the ordinary place of business of the palace and the reception-room when the king received ordinary visitors, and sat, except on great state occasions, to transact the business of the kingdom. Behind this, we are told, was the inner court, adorned with gardens and fountains and surrounded by cloisters for shade, and there were other courts for the residence of the attendants and guards and for the women of his harem.

Apart from this palace but attached, as Josephus tells us, to the Hall of Judgment, was the palace of Pharaoh's daughter: too proud and important a personage to be grouped with the ladies of the harem and requiring a residence of her own. On the completion of this palace, he conducted her to it in state from the city of David (I Kings 7:1-12). The palace of Solomon was below the platform of the Temple and he constructed an ascent from his own house "to the house of Jehovah" (I Kings 10:5). Among his other buildings may be mentioned a summer palace in Lebanon (I Kings 9:19; Song of Sol. 7:4), stately gardens at Etham, *paradises* like those of the great Eastern kings, the foundation of something like a stately school or college, costly aqueducts bringing water, it may be, from the well of Bethlehem, dear to David's heart to supply his palace in Jerusalem. It was about the same time that Solomon undertook the repair of the walls of the fortress of Zion, which David had "built round about from Millo[3] and inward" (II Sam. 5:9), as well as of Millo itself. These works

---

1. It appears to be an error to regard the House of the Forest of Lebanon and the Porch of Judgment as separate buildings from Solomon's palace. I Kings 9:1 and II Chron. 8:1 speak only of two buildings as comprising Solomon's building activities.

2. Josephus. *Ant.* viii, 5, 2.

3. Millo may have been a filled-in area behind stone terraces along the east side of Mt. Zion (Ophel). King Hezekiah later strengthened and fortified the area (II Chron. 32:5).

were under the superintendence of Jeroboam, the son of Nebat, of whom more will be heard presently (I Kings 9:15,24; 11:27).

After the completion of these works, God appeared a second time to Solomon as at Gibeon by night and assured him that the prayers he had offered at the dedication of the Temple were accepted, while the renewal of the covenant with David and his house was accompanied with the most impressive warnings of the ruin which disobedience would bring upon king, people and the sanctuary itself, which would be made as it has indeed become, "a proverb and a by-word among all nations" (I Kings 9:1-9, 24; II Chron. 7:12-22). Solomon arranged the Temple service according to the courses appointed by David and he set the example of sacrifice to the people by his own stated offerings on the brazen altar daily and on the Sabbaths and new moons, and at the three great festivals (I Kings 9:23; II Chron. 8:12-16).

These great works, all connected with the establishment of God's house and of his own royal state at Jerusalem, to which city they added an entirely new quarter, occupied the first half of Solomon's reign, a period of twenty years, 970-951 B.C. The services of the King of Tyre were acknowledged by the cession of twenty cities along the sea-coast of Galilee, a gift at which Hiram expressed his discontent by a play upon the name of one of them, *Cabul* (I Kings 9:11-14). The exact etymology of this name is uncertain but it was popularly associated with a similar word meaning "as nothing," and this well described Hiram's opinion of the cities. Notwithstanding his displeasure, Hiram returned the present, according to the custom of the East and a gift of 120 talents of gold and the alliance of the two kings remained unimpaired. The cities seem to have been restored by Hiram and fortified by Solomon (II Chron. 8:2).

8. The second half of Solomon's reign was inaugurated by magnificent works in other parts of his dominion and by enterprises of foreign commerce. In the southwest, he rebuilt Gezer, a city in the Shephelah 18 miles northwest of Jerusalem, which the King of Egypt had taken from the Canaanites and destroyed but which he gave to Solomon as his wife's dowry. He also fortified Baalath, Beth-horon (the upper and the lower), as well as all the cities where he kept his stores and chariots (I Kings 9:15-19; II Chron. 8:5). On the north he made a new conquest, the only one recorded in his reign of Hamath-Zobah. It is not clear whether this was the same or distinct from the capital of Hamath, the kingdom of Toi, who was an ally and probably

afterward a subject of David; but at all events this Hamath, which appears to include the valley of the Oronte as far as the defile above Antioch, belonged to the kingdom of Solomon, who built in it several of his "store-cities" (II Chron. 8:3-4), which formed depots for commerce. In the midst of the great Syrian desert, half-way between Damascus and Thapsacus (Tiphsah), where his kingdom reached the Euphrates and where was the great passage of that river, afterward called the "fatal ford," here in a beautiful oasis, he built the city of TADMOR, which became long after, under the name of PALMYRA, the seat of Zenobia's brief empire and whose ruins are among the most striking in the world. While thus linking his dominions with the great highways of commerce to the north and northeast, he opened the path of maritime enterprise, both in the Mediterranean and the Indian Ocean, in conjunction with the Tyrian fleets of Hiram. On the one side, it seems to be implied in *Kings,* and is expressly stated in *Chronicles* (I Kings 10:22; II Chron. 9:21), that the king sent a navy every three years, probably by way of Joppa, to trade with the distant regions of the west which were vaguely described by the name of Tharshish.[1] The phrase "ships of Tharshish" is however not confined to ships that actually went to those regions; but like the old British "East-Indiamen," it rather describes a class of vessels fit for the most distant and difficult voyages and the products which that navy brought seem rather to have come from Solomon's Oriental traffic. This was conducted from the two ports of Elath and Ezion-geber, at the head of the eastern gulf of the Red Sea *(Gulf of Akabah),* which the conquest of Edom had added to the kingdom and which were visited by Solomon in person. From these ports the fleet built by Solomon and navigated by the skilled sailors of Hiram, sailed to OPHIR, a place in the Indian Ocean, probably on the southwest coast of Arabia and returned after a three years' voyage, bringing gold, silver, ivory and precious stones for wealth and ornament, almug (or algum) trees, the rare wood of which was used for terraces (or verandas) to the Temple and lastly (for Solomon added to his magnificence the whims of luxury) apes and peacocks (I Kings 9:26-28; 10:22; II Chron. 8:17-18; Eccl. 2:4-6).

The amount of gold brought to Solomon by this navy is variously stated at 420, 450 and in one year as much as 666 talents,

---

1. Tharshish or Tarshish represents Tartessus, a city and emporium of the Phoenicians in the south of Spain. The articles which Tarshish is stated by the prophet Ezekiel (27:12) to have supplied to Tyre — silver, iron, lead and tin — are precisely such as we know through classical writers to have been productions of the Spanish peninsula.

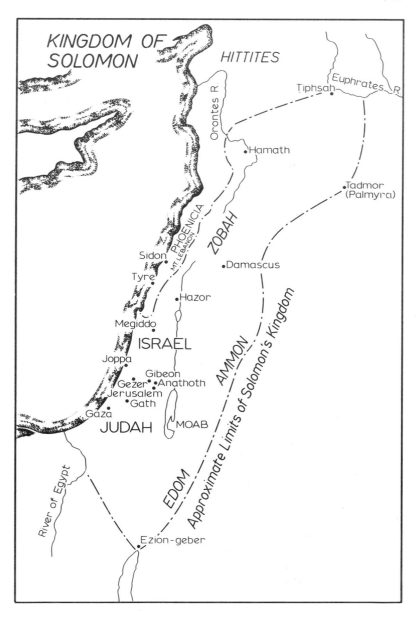

KINGDOM OF SOLOMON

HITTITES

Euphrates R.

Tiphsah

Orontes R.

Hamath

Tadmor
(Palmyra)

PHOENICIA

ZOBAH

MT. LEBANON

Sidon

Damascus

Tyre

Hazor

Megiddo

ISRAEL

Joppa

AMMON

Gibeon

Gezer • Anathoth

Jerusalem

Gath

Gaza

MOAB

JUDAH

Approximate Limits of Solomon's Kingdom

River of Egypt

EDOM

Ezion-geber

besides what was brought by merchants and the tribute of gold and silver from the chieftains of Arabia. Silver was so abundant as scarcely to be esteemed a precious metal and all the king's drinking-vessels were of gold. The "House of the Forest of Lebanon" too had all its vessels of pure gold, and in it were hung 200 targets of beaten gold, each weighing 600 shekels and 300 shields of three pounds each. But the most magnificent work made from these precious things was Solomon's throne of ivory and gold. It was a chair of state, such as we still see in the Assyrian thrones, with a round back and two lions supporting the arms and was elevated on six steps, each flanked by a pair of lions, the symbols of the tribe of Judah. The chair seems to have been made of ivory inlaid with gold, the steps of plates of ivory and the lions of beaten gold (I Kings 9:26-28; 10:11-27; II Chron. 8:17-18; 9:10, 13-22).

9. Seated "high on this throne of royal state," and "exceeding all the kings of the earth for riches and for wisdom," Solomon dispensed justice and received the visitors from all parts of the world, who came to hear his wisdom, bringing their presents of vessels of gold and silver, garments, armor, spices, horses and mules (I Kings 10:23-25). Among them came one, whose visit has been rendered doubly memorable by the allusion made to it by Christ. Far to the south, on the shores of the Arabian Gulf, the country of SHEBA (probably the modern *Yemen)* was ruled by a queen, who seems to have enjoyed among the tribes of Arabia a reputation like Solomon's for wisdom. His fame reached her ears and she determined to judge for herself. With an immense caravan of camels, bearing gold and precious stones and spices, she came to Jerusalem to try Solomon with those "hard questions," which have always formed the favorite exercise of Oriental ingenuity. "She communed with him of all that was in her heart." The perfect wisdom of the king's replies in this conflict of wit and learning, the magnificence of his buildings, the splendor of his royal state, the order of his court, completely overwhelmed the queen: "there was no more spirit in her." She confessed that all was true which she had heard and refused to believe in her own country; nay, the half had not been told her: and she blessed Jehovah, and the people to whom He had given such a king. Having given and received magnificent presents, she departed to her own country and the odor of her visit was long preserved by such an abundance of spices as was never known at Jerusalem before or since (I Kings 10:1-13; II Chron. 9:1-12).

Whether she went back a convert to the true faith, as her praises of Jehovah seem partly to imply, and how far her visit tended to the planting of the numerous proselytes whom we afterward find in Arabia, can only be matter of conjecture; and the traditions by which the simple narrative of her visit is overlaid, scarcely deserve notice. But the zeal with which she journeyed from the ends of the earth to prove for herself the wisdom of which she had heard so much, stands recorded by "One greater than Solomon," for the eternal shame of those who neglect to hear HIM, when he stands in their very midst; Him who is the incarnate WISDOM that formed the noblest subject of Solomon's discourse (Prov. 8; Matt. 12:42; Luke 11:31). The visit of the Queen of Sheba marks the culminating point of Solomon's glory. It remains for us to relate the lesson which his later years give of the vanity of all human splendor and the inherent defects of despotism, even when based on the recognition of the true religion.

10. The faults of Solomon were both personal and political. The fruit of the latter scarcely appeared till the reign of his son but that reign commenced with a protest against "the heavy yoke" of Solomon, and the whips with which he chastised the people (I Kings 12:4,9,10,11,14) and, as we shall presently see, the discontent had begun to show itself before his death. His personal faults were the natural result of unbounded wealth and luxury. He began, as we have seen, by taking a foreign and heathen wife, the daughter of Pharaoh; to her he added wives from the Moabites, Ammonites, Edomites, Sidonians and Hittites, in short, from all the nations with whom God had expressly forbidden intermarriages (Ex. 34:11-16); and in defiance of the charge of Moses to the king (Deut. 17:17), he had 700 wives and 300 concubines, with the result which Moses had foretold. In his old age, his wives turned away his heart from Jehovah to their gods and induced him to provide places for their worship. He served Ashtoreth (pl. Ashtaroth), the fertility goddess of the ancient Near East and Moloch (or Milcolm), the "horrid king" whom the Ammonites worshiped with human sacrifices. The Mount of Offense, forming the south summit of the Mount of Olives, which rises directly opposite to Mount Moriah on the east, was made the sanctuary of this deity. A high place for Chemosh, the abominable god of Moab, was built in the same area. Similar shrines were erected for other gods, at which his wives burned incense and offered sacrifice (I Kings 11:1-8).

11. These outrages, the more flagrant in the king who had

himself built the Temple and to whom Jehovah had twice given solemn warnings mingled with His promises, called down the wrath of God, whose covenant with David alone saved Solomon from the fate of Saul (I Kings 11:9-13; Comp. II Sam. 7:14-15). The judgment was denounced upon him, that his kingdom should be "rent" from him and given to his servant, and his last years were troubled with the beginnings of the revolution. He had already some formidable enemies. One of these was HADAD, prince of Edom, who had escaped to Egypt from the massacre of Joab and had married the sister-in-law of Pharaoh, who at last gave a reluctant consent to Hadad's return to his own country, where he began a harassing war against Solomon (I Kings 11:14-22). A still more formidable adversary was raised up in the person of REZON, who had been a servant of Hadadezer, the Syrian king of Zobah, upon whose defeat by David, Rezon gathered a band of outlaws, maintained himself against the whole power of Solomon and finally succeeded in founding the Syrian kingdom of Damascus, the relations of which to Israel were afterward so important (I Kings 11:23-25).

But the great danger denounced on Solomon for his sin arose from one of his own servants, JEROBOAM, the son of Nebat, an Ephraimite of Zereda, whose mother, Zeruah, was early left a widow. He grew up to be "a mighty man of valor" and was employed as a young man upon the fortifications of Millo. His energy attracted the notice of Solomon, who made him overseer of the works imposed upon the tribe of Joseph (Ephraim). However, on one occasion as Jeroboam went out of Jerusalem, he was met on the road by the prophet Ahijah the Shilonite, who snatched the new garment off his own back and tearing it in twelve pieces, gave ten of them to Jeroboam, telling him the word of God that He would rend the kingdom out of the hand of Solomon except one tribe, which should remain for the sake of David and to preserve God's worship at Jerusalem, while the other ten should be given to Jeroboam but only after the death of Solomon. The matter reached the ears of Solomon who sought the life of Jeroboam, but the latter fled to Egypt and remained there with Shishak (whose name is now mentioned for the first time) till the death of Solomon (I Kings 11:26-40). According to the LXX, Shishak gave him the sister of his wife and of Hadad's wife as an inducement to his remaining in Egypt.

12. Amid such beginnings of impending trouble, Solomon approached the end of his course. The history says nothing of his

repentance nor indeed of any result produced by God's warnings and chastisements. His whole character had probably become too worldly for the heartfelt penitence of his father. But yet we have in the Book of *Ecclesiastes* a review of the whole experience of his life based on the recognition of the fear of God, the review of a religious philosopher rather than of a spiritual believer. It gives the experience of a man who has tasted every form of pleasure and pronounces all to end in disappointment, and from this restless search after excitement — in which every supposed novelty is found to be the same thing over and over again, generation after generation, the Royal Preacher comes back to this simple result — that true life consists in the discharge of duty from religious motives: "Fear God, and keep his commandments; for this is the whole [life] of man" (Eccl. 12:13).

Solomon died at Jerusalem in the 40th year of his reign and was buried in the royal sepulchre in the city of David. The history of his reign was written by the prophets Nathan and Ahijah, by Iddo the seer in his "Visions against Jeroboam," and in the "Book of the Acts of Solomon" (I Kings 11:41-43; II Chron. 9:29-31). The first three works probably formed the basis of the narrative in the *First Book of Kings,* while the substance of the last is preserved in epitome in the *Second Book of Chronicles.* Notwithstanding his immense harem, we only read of his having one son, his successor REHOBOAM, the son of Naamah, a princess of Ammon.

Questions Over Section V
The Reign of Solomon

1. Whom did Adonijah request for his wife (I Kings 2:17)?
2. Who made the request for him (2:13)?
3. What punishment was inflicted upon Adonijah (2:25)?
4. Who carried out the punishment (2:25)?
5. What was the punishment given Abiathar because of his support of Adonijah (2:26,27)?
6. What punishment was given to Joab (2:34)?
7. Who was put in charge of Solomon's army at this time (2:35)?
8. Who became priest in Abiathar's place (2:35)?
9. What prophecy was fulfilled by the replacement of Abiathar (I Sam. 2:27ff)?
10. Under what condition did Solomon promise to allow Shimei to live (2:36-37)?
11. To what place did Shimei go in disobedience to the condition (2:40)?

12. Solomon married the daughter of what king (3:1)?
13. At what town did the Lord first appear to Solomon (3:5)?
14. What request did Solomon make of the Lord (3:9)?
15. What two other things did the Lord promise to give Solomon because of the request he had made (3:13)?
16. What was the condition of God's continual blessing upon Solomon and his family (3:14)?
17. What event is recorded in the Scripture which led the people to respect highly Solomon's wisdom (3:16-28)? Briefly relate.
18. What are the four things for which Solomon is famous?
19. Who was Solomon's recorder (4:3)?
20. Who was in charge of conscript labor (4:6)?
21. How many overseers were in charge of all Israel (4:7)?
22. Which books of the O.T. did Solomon write?
23. Of how many proverbs was Solomon originator (4:32)?
24. How many songs?
25. Who was the king of Tyre who befriended Solomon (5:1)?
26. How many years had elapsed between the Exodus and the building of the Temple (6:1)?
27. How long was the Temple (6:2)?
28. How wide was the Temple (6:2)?
29. How high was the Temple (6:2)?
30. What were the three principal compartments of the Temple (6:3, 8-9, 17-19)?
31. Of what basic material was the Temple constructed (6:7)?
32. How many years did it take to construct the Temple (6:38)?
33. How many years did it take to construct the royal palace (7:1)?
34. For which of his wives did Solomon build a special house (7:8)?
35. What was the name of the bronze worker brought from Tyre by Solomon (7:13)?
36. Of what tribe was his mother (7:14)?
37. What were the names of the pillars set up at the porch of the Temple (7:21)?
38. How many lavers were provided for the Temple (7:38)?
39. Of what were the altar and the table of shew-bread made (7:48)?
40. How many lampstands were in the Temple (7:49)?
41. What was in the ark when it was transferred from Zion to the Temple (8:9)?

42. Why were the priests unable to keep ministering in the house of the Lord (8:10,11)?

43. For what specific times (name seven) did Solomon invoke God's favor in his dedicatory prayer (8:22-53)?

44. What did God tell Solomon in His second appearance (summarize) (9:2-9)?

45. What name did the king of Tyre give the twenty cities presented to him by Solomon (9:13)?

46. What was the Millo (9:24)?

47. How many times each year did Solomon offer burnt-offerings and peace offerings at the altar (9:25)?

48. Where did Solomon build his naval fleet (9:26)?

49. From where was the queen who came to test Solomon with perplexing questions (10:1)?

50. What were her words after her inspection (10:6)?

51. How great were Solomon's wealth and wisdom in comparison with that of others of his day (10:23)?

52. Who was the goddess of the Sidonians (11:5)?

53. Who was the god of Moab (11:7)?

54. Who was the god of the Ammonites (11:7)?

55. How many wives did Solomon have (11:3)?

56. How many concubines did Solomon have (11:3)?

57. What *sins* of Solomon caused Jehovah's displeasure with him (11:2,4)?

58. Why did God not immediately take the kingdom from Solomon (11:12)?

59. Who were the three opponents with whom the Lord confronted Solomon (11:14,23,26)?

60. What did the prophet Ahijah give to one of Solomon's adversaries? What did this act prophesy symbolically (11:29-31)?

61. Of what tribe was the son of Nebat to whom Ahijah promised ten tribes (11:26)?

62. To whom did the son of Nebat escape when Solomon attempted to kill him (11:40)?

63. For how long did Solomon rule Israel (11:42)?

64. What son of Solomon became king upon the death of his father (11:43)?

Period IX
The Divided Kingdom

Section I
Neighbors of Israel and Judah

A. Amalekites. B. Ammonites. C. Aramcans (Syrians).
D. Assyrians. E. Babylonians. F. Edomites. G. Hittites.
H. Moabites. I. Philistines. J. Phoenicians.

A. Amalekites

1. Ancestry — Descendants of Esau (Gen. 36:12,16). (The reference to Amalek in Gen. 14:7 seems to be proleptic, that is, the name Amalek was applied to the territory later occupied by the Amalekites when Moses wrote of events that took place there long before the Amalekites lived there.)
2. Location
   a. The Amalekites wandered in the Sinaitic peninsula, west of Edom toward Egypt (Ex. 17:8; I Sam. 27:8).
   b. Also they dwelt in the Negev or southern part of Canaan (Num. 13:29).
   c. Sometimes they invaded Palestine itself (Judges 3:13; 6:33; 12:15).
3. Character — Warlike (Num. 14:45; Deut. 25:17-18).

4. History
   a. They made an unprovoked attack on Israel at Rephidim near Mt. Sinai (Ex. 17:8-13).
   b. God determined that they would be utterly destroyed (Ex. 17:14; Num. 24:20; Deut. 25:17-19).
   c. They and the Canaanites repulsed the Israelites when they attempted to enter Canaan from the south after the spies' report (Num. 14:45).
   d. Saul was told to destroy them (I Sam. 15).
   e. Amalekites destroyed David's city, Ziklag, and took its inhabitants captive (I Sam. 27:6).
   f. A remnant remained until the days of King Hezekiah (I Chron. 4:43).
5. No archaeological discoveries have been made relating to the Amalekites.

Questions

1. Where did the Amalekites live?
2. What was their character?
3. When was Israel's first contact with Amalek?
4. What did God determine to do with the Amalekites?
5. Who was sent to destroy them?

B. Ammonites

1. Descendants of Ben-Ammi, offspring of Lot (Gen. 19:38). A semi-nomadic people.
2. Situated east of the tribes of Gad and Rueben (former kingdom of Sihon) and north of Moab, from the Arnon River in the south to the Jabbok Brook in the north.
3. Historical notes:
   a. Israelites were commanded to leave Ammonites unmolested (Deut. 2:19) as they entered the Promised Land.
   b. The Ammonites fought against Israel during the period of the Judges (Judges 11:13); Israel delivered by Jephthah.
   c. Attempted war against Israel again at the beginning of Saul's reign (I Samuel 11) but were soundly defeated.
   d. David conquered their capital city (II Samuel 12) and relegated them to a very unimportant place from that time forward in the Kingdom Period.
4. Other scriptures referring to the Ammonites: Jeremiah 40:14; 41:5-7; Amos 1:14; Nehemiah 2:10,19; Ezekiel 25:1-7.

5. Worshipped Molech (also spelled Moloch, Milcom or Milcam) with human sacrifices ("children passed through fire") (Deut. 18:10; II Chron. 33:6; II Kings 21:6).

Questions

1. Of whom were the Ammonites descended?
2. Where was Ammon?
3. How did Ammon and Israel get along?
4. Who was the god of Ammon? How was he worshipped?

C. Aramaeans (or Syrians)

1. Descendants of Shem (Gen. 10:22,23; I Chron. 1:17).
2. Aram is the name of Syria (Num. 23:7) and it is translated Syria very often. (See II Sam. 8:5, I Kings 20:20, Amos 1:5.)
3. Situated widely from Lebanon mountains to east side of the Euphrates river and from the Taurus range to Damascus and northern Palestine.
4. Historical notes
   a. The Aramaeans were grouped into various centers of power.
      1. Aram-Naharim (Aram of the two rivers) — Mesopotamia, around Haran (Genesis 11:31, 24:10, 31:47).
      2. Aram-Damascus (I Kings 11:23,24). Constant enemy of the northern kingdom. Destroyed by Assyria in 732 B.C.
      3. Aram-Zobah, north of Damascus. Hadadezer was most powerful ruler (II Sam. 8:3-9). He also ruled Maacah, Geshur and Tob.
      4. Aram-Maacah, east of Jordan, near Mt. Hermon.
      5. Geshur, east of Jordan, in Manasseh's territory. Absalom's mother was from this area (II Sam. 3:3; 13:37).
      6. Tob, east of Jordan.
   b. Religiously, the people were idolaters (II Kings 5:18).
   c. David conquered these states and Solomon extended the kingdom far into these areas.
   d. "Rezon, the son of Eliada, of Damascus" was raised up to chasten Solomon (I Kings 11:23-25) and captured Damascus preparing the way for the rise of the Aramean kingdom.
   e. Kings of Syria (at Damascus)

1. Hezion (same as Rezon?) (I Kings 15:18).
2. Tabrimmon
3. Benhadad I (approx. 890-843 B.C.) Note: Benhadad I, hired by Asa (II Chron. 16:2) about 875 B.C., seems to have been the same person as the Benhadad (formerly called Benhadad II) who fought Ahab about 856 B.C. (I Kings 20:1).
4. Hazael (II Kings 8:15; 843-801 B.C.)
5. Benhadad II (II Kings 13:24-25; Duration of reign uncertain).
6. Rezin (II Kings 15:37; approx. 750-732 B.C.).

f. After the division of the kingdom, the Aramaeans of Damascus gained strength and became the foremost Syrian kingdom and Israel's chief enemy.

g. Asa, king of Judah, by sending gifts to Benhadad formed an alliance with him, and he in turn invaded Northern Israel under Baasha (I Kings 15:20-22).

h. Benhadad was kept at abeyance during the reign of Omri in Israel (c. 885), who greatly strengthened his position by alliances with various foreign neighbors.

i. During Ahab's reign (874-853), the northern Kingdom became stronger (I Kings 16:34; 22:39; II Kings 8·18,26), and Benhadad, leading a coalition of thirty-two other kings was soundly defeated around 856 at the Battle of Samaria (I Kings 20:1), and again in 855 (I Kings 20:26-43). During this time, the rise of the Assyrian power checked Syrian advancement also.

j. Ahab was killed by the Aramaeans, under Benhadad in the battle at Ramoth-gilead (I Kings 22:1-40).

k. Hazael became king of Damascus about 840 B.C. and because of Jehu's failure to aid in war against Assyria, he began to fight constantly against Israel (II Kings 10:32,33).

l. During Jehoahaz's reign in Israel (814-798), Hazael reduced Israel's territory to a very small area (II Kings 13:1-9,22,25). As Hazael advanced further south, he was kept out of Jerusalem only by the payment of a large amount of money obtained by using temple furnishings, etc. (II Kings 12:17,18).

m. The Aramaeans were weakened substantially by the Assyrians around 800 B.C. Jehoash reclaimed much of the territory taken by Hazael and during the days of Jeroboam II, Damascus was taken by Israel and the northern boundaries were restored as they had been in the days of Solomon (II Sam. 8:5-11).

n. When Jeroboam II died in 753, Rezin, king of the Aramaeans, regained independence, but in 732, in the days of King Ahaz of Judah, Tiglath-Pileser III, king of Assyria, captured Damascus, executed Rezin and ended Aramean power permanently.

Questions

1. What is another name for the Arameans?
2. Where was Aram?
3. Name four Aramean centers of power?
4. Name the six Aramean kings of Damascus.
5. When did the Arameans become Israel's chief enemy?
6. When did Damascus fall? To what king?

D. The Assyrians

1. The Assyrians were of Semitic origin (Gen. 10:22).
2. Assyria is sometimes referred to as *Asshur* or Assur in the Bible (Ezra 4:2; Ezek. 27:23).
3. Assyria was originally a small tract of land between the upper Tigris river and its tributary, the Zab river.
4. Nineveh on the upper Tigris was the capital of Assyria. Ruins of several palaces of Assyrian kings have been found at Nineveh and nearby.
5. Numerous Bible prophets preached concerning or in Assyria and Nineveh. Among these were Isaiah, Jeremiah, Ezekiel, Hosea, Micah, Zephaniah, Zechariah and Jonah. Nahum prophesied the destruction of Nineveh (Nahum 3:8-15).
6. Historical notes[1]
   a. After numerous periods of strength and weakness, the Assyrians reached the Mediterranean Sea about 1100 B.C. under *Tiglath-pileser I* (1115-1077 B.C.).
   b. The Aramean kingdom of Zobah became strong about 1000 B.C. and stopped the westward advance of Assyria.
   c. King David's defeat of Zobah (II Sam. 8:3) made it possible for the Assyrians to resume expansionist policies.
   d. During the tenth century B.C. Assyria began its rise to greatest power and it became the dominating power of the ancient world from the ninth to the seventh centuries.
   e. The kings of Assyria during its greatest strength:

---

1. See Schwantes, S.J. *A Short History of the Ancient Near East*, pp. 110-133.

1. *Assurnasirpal II* (883-859 B.C.). Unspeakably cruel. Conquered territory all the way to the Mediterranean.
2. *Shalmaneser III* (858-824). At the battle of Karkar (853 B.C.), he clashed in an indecisive battle with an alliance of the king of Syria, Ahab of Israel and other kings. Ahab apparently joined with the king of Syria to resist the encroachments of mighty Assyria (I Kings 20:34). King Jehu of Israel paid tribute to Shalmaneser. This is illustrated on the famous black obelisk of Shalmaneser.
3. *Shamsi-Adad V* (823-811).
4. *Adad-nirari II* (810-783). He subdued and collected tribute from Tyre, Sidon, Israel, Edom, Philistia and Damascus. Jehoahaz of Israel paid him tribute. He defeated Benhadad II (III) of Damascus. He is probably the "savior" referred to in II Kings 13:5. By defeating Syria he saved Israel from attacks from that source.
5. *Shalmaneser IV* (782-773). Weak king. Probably Jonah the prophet preached in Nineveh during his reign.
6. *Assur-dan III* (772-755). Weak king.
7. *Asshur-nirari V* (754-745). Weak king.
8. *Tiglath-pileser III* (744-727). Also called Pul. The greatest Assyrian of all. He took Gaza (734 B.C.). He took Damascus and slew Rezin (732). He took tribute from both Judah and Israel (II Kings 15:19,29). His monuments mention the Hebrew kings Azariah, Hoshea, Pekah, Menahem, Omri and Ahab. He took Israel's eastern and northern tribes. He conquered Babylon in his last year (727).
9. *Shalmaneser V* (726-722). He took tribute from Hoshea, king of Israel (II Kings 17:3-5). He besieged Samaria for three years (II Kings 17:5, 18:9).
10. *Sargon II* (or III) (721-705). Sargon claims to have captured Samaria and to have deported 27,000 Israelites (II Kings 17:6). He crushed the last stronghold of Hittite power, Carchemish (717). He took Ashdod in Philistia (711) (Isaiah 20:1).
11. *Sennacherib* (704-681). He recaptured the western part of Assyria's empire, Ammon, Moab, Edom and 46 cities of Judah (including Lachish). He threatened to take Jerusalem in Hezekiah's time, but the Lord's

angel slew 185,000 of his troops in one night (II Kings 18:13-19:36). He destroyed Babylon in 689.

12. *Esarhaddon* (680-669). He restored Babylon, destroyed Sidon, took King Manasseh of Judah to Babylon as a captive (II Chron. 3:11; Ezra 4:2). He defeated Tirkahah, king of Egypt, and occupied Memphis and lower Egypt (II Kings 19:9).

13. *Asshurbanipal* (668-631). Called *Asnappar* in Ezra 4:10. He was the last great king of Assyria. He took Thebes in Egypt, 663 B.C. He was a lover of learning and collected a library of over 20,000 cuneiform tablets, which have been discovered by archaeologists.

f. Nineveh was captured and destroyed in 612 B.C. by a confederation of Medes and Babylonians (under Nabopolassar). The power of Assyria was broken forever.

7. The Assyrians were an extremely cruel people. This fact is indicated both in the Bible and on Assyrian monuments.

a. The Bible calls Nineveh a "bloody city" (Nahum 3:1-3; compare 2:8-9; Isaiah 10:5-7).

b. It was the policy of the Assyrian kings to remove conquered peoples from the homelands and deport them to other areas. Most of the people of the kingdom of Israel were thus deported by the Assyrians and then conquered peoples from other areas were imported into Israel (II Kings 17:6,24).

c. The Assyrian monuments picture such things as men being impaled on sharp posts, people beheaded, captives being deported and vultures eating enemies.[1]

Questions

1. Where was the land of Assyria?
2. What was its capital city?
3. What was the character of the Assyrian kings?
4. To what Assyrian king did Jehu pay tribute?
5. Who was the probable Assyrian king in the time of Jonah the prophet?
6. Who was the greatest Assyrian king of all?
7. What Assyrian king besieged Samaria?
8. What Assyrian king threatened Jerusalem in the time of King Hezekiah?
9. When did Assyria fall? To whom?

---

1. W. Keller, *The Bible as History in Pictures*, pp. 210-227.

E. The Babylonians

1. The city of Babylon (Babel) was established by Nimrod not long after the flood (Gen. 10:8-10). It was located by the Euphrates river in a fertile area within easy reach of the Persian Gulf. It was an important city throughout its history. Many battles were fought for control of it and the city was destroyed and rebuilt a number of times.

2. Under *Hammurabi* (1728-1686 B.C.), Babylon ruled a great empire from the Persian Gulf to the middle Euphrates and upper Tigris. After the time of Hammurabi, Babylon was controlled by various peoples for nearly a thousand years: by Hittites, Kassites, Elamites and Assyrians.

3. During this time various Babylonian rulers tried to assert their independence without much success. *Merodach-baladan* (II Kings 20:12ff) tried to revolt from Assyria, and made Babylon independent twice briefly (722-710, 703-702 B.C.). He visited King Hezekiah probably around 712 B.C. Sargon II of Assyria crushed this rebellion and his son Sennaherib devastated Babylon in 689 B.C.

4. Sennacherib's son, Esarhaddon, rebuilt Babylon and took King Manasseh of Judah to Babylon as a captive (II Chron. 33:11).

5. In 626 B.C. *Nabopolassar* founded an independent dynasty at Babylon and started the great Neo-Babylonian or Chaldean empire. Nabopolassar, in alliance with the Medes and other peoples, defeated and utterly destroyed Nineveh in 612 B.C. He defeated the remnants of the Assyrian army at Haran in 610. In 605 he and his son Nebuchadnezzar defeated an alliance of the Egyptians under Pharaoh-Necho and remnants of the Assyrian army at Carchemish. This forever ended the existence of Assyria, and Egypt has never since been a powerful empire.

6. *Nebuchadnezzar* (605-562 B.C.) was the greatest king of the Neo-Babylonian empire. He was both a great conqueror and a great builder. He captured all the territory that had once been held by the king of Egypt from the brook of Egypt to the river Euphrates (II Kings 24:7). Nebuchadnezzar invaded Judah in 605 B.C. (Daniel 1:1), 597 B.C. (II Kings 24:1), and again in 586 B.C. (II Kings 25:1) when he destroyed Jerusalem. He besieged Tyre for thirteen years (598-585 B.C.).

Nebuchadnezzar built structures in Babylon until it became the most glorious city on earth. Massive double walls with bronze gates protected the city. Its famous tower or ziggurat was enlarged and repaired. The Hanging Gardens os Babylon became one of the seven wonders of the ancient world (Dan. 4:30).

7. After Nebuchadnezzar's time the Neo-Babylonian empire declined rapidly. His son *Evil-Merodach* or Amel-Marduk (II Kings 25:27) reigned 562-560 and was assassinated by a son-in-law of Nebuchadnezzar, *Neriglissar* (called Nergal-Sharezer in Jer. 39:13), who reigned 560-556. Neriglissar's son *Labashi-Marduk* succeeded him in 556 but was deposed by a popular uprising. One of Nebuchadnezzar's generals, *Nebonidus,* who was probably also a son-in-law of Nebuchadnezzar, was made king (556-539). Nabonidus appointed his son *Belshazzar* as co-regent in 553, and both ruled until Babylon was taken by the Persians and Medes in 539. Nabonidus spent a great deal of time in the Arabian city of Teima. The fall of Babylon is related in Daniel 5 and on the cylinder inscription of Cyrus the Persian, whose forces took the city.

8. Babylon declined in importance after this. It still existed in New Testament times (I Peter 5:13 — if the name Babylon is there to be taken literally). In the sixth to ninth centuries A.D. the Jewish rabbis had a notable center of learning there. Today Babylon is in total desolation and the ancient prophecy in Isaiah 13:17-22 has been fulfilled to the letter.

Questions

1. Who founded Babylon?
2. By what river was it located?
3. What man ruled a great empire from Babylon in the 17th century B.C.?
4. What Babylonian king visited King Hezekiah?
5. Who started the Neo-Babylonian empire?
6. Who was the greatest king of the Neo-Babylonian empire?
7. What contact did he have with Judah and Jerusalem?
8. Who were the last two kings of the Babylonians? What was their blood relationship and their relationship as far as ruling the country was concerned?

F. Edomites (or Idumeans)

1. Descendants of Esau (Gen. 25:30; 36:1,8,9, 31ff.).

2. The Edomites dwelt in Mt. Seir, the mountainous area south
   of the Dead Sea (Gen. 32:3; 36:8).
   a. Seir was named from Seir, the progenitor of the Horites
      (Gen. 36:20-22; 14:6).
   b. The original inhabitants of the country were called
      Horites. (See special study, *Canaanites and Rephaim.*)
      Immediately after the death of Isaac, Esau left Canaan
      and took possession of Mount Seir (Gen. 35:28; 36:6,7,8).
      When his descendants increased, they drove out the
      Horites and adopted their habits as well as their country
      (Deut. 2:12).
   c. On the south, Edom reached as far as Elath, which stood at
      the northern end of the gulf of Akabah and was the
      sea-port of the Edomites. On the north of Edom lay the
      territory of Moab, from which it was divided by the "brook
      Zered" (Deut. 2:13,14,18).
3. The ancient capital of Edom was Bozrah (Isaiah 63:1;
   34:5-6). But Sela, better known by its Greek name Petra,
   appears to have been the principal stronghold in the days of
   Amaziah (II Kings 14:7).
4. The Edomites were idolaters.
5. Edom refused passage to Moses and Israel (Num. 20:14-21).
6. King Saul fought Edomites (I Sam. 14:47).
7. David subdued them (II Sam. 8:13-14) and thus became heir
   to such natural resources as copper and iron from Edom.
8. Solomon made Ezion-geber and Elath his seaports
   (II Chron. 8:17,18). Hadad the Edomite was Solomon's
   adversary (I Kings 11:14-23).
9. Jehoshaphat defeated Edom (II Chron. 20:22).
10. Edom revolted in time of Jehoram of Judah (II Chron.
    21:8-10). Their hostility at this time may have called forth
    Obadiah's prophecy against them (II Chron. 21:16-17;
    Obadiah 1-16).
11. King Amaziah smote Edom (II Chron. 25:11-12).
12. Edom smote Judah in time of Ahaz (II Chron. 28:17).
13. The perpetual anger of Edom against Judah all the way
    down to the time of Jerusalem's destruction called forth
    condemnations by God's prophets (Amos 1:11-12; Jer.
    49:7-22; Ezek. 25:12-14; Psalm 137:7).
14. The Edomites took over the southern part of Palestine as far
    north as Hebron after Jerusalem was destroyed and Judah
    depopulated by Babylon 586 B.C.

15. About 325 B.C. an Arab tribe known as the Nabateans occupied much of Edom's territory. The Nabateans developed a prosperous society and built many spectacular buildings in the stone cliffs of Petra.

Questions

1. Of whom were the Edomites descendants?
2. Where did the Edomites dwell?
3. What was the name of the original inhabitants of the area?
4. What was the capital of Edom?
5. How did the Edomites get along with Israel?

G. The Hittites

1. The Hittites were descendants of Ham through Heth (Gen. 10:15). They are often called in archaeological inscriptions the Hatti or Khatti.
2. The main centers of the Hittites were in Asia Minor, with Boghaz-Koi as capital and Syria with Carchemish as a center.
3. They lived as far south as Canaan in Abraham's time (Gen. 15:20; 23:3-20). Esau married Hittite women (Gen. 26:34).
4. They were so dominant in Joshua's time that he speaks of all Palestine and Syria as "the land of the Hittites" (Josh. 1:4).
5. Critics of the Bible formerly contended that the many references to the Hittites in the Bible were mythological. However, archaeological discoveries in the 20th century have abundantly confirmed the biblical notations about the Hittites. Their hieroglyphic writing has been deciphered and read on thousands of tablets.
6. There were two main periods of Hittite power:
   a. The Old Kingdom, 1850-1550 B.C.
      1. The Hittites took Aleppo in 1570 and sacked Babylon in 1550.
      2. In the 15th century B.C. the Egyptians swept north into Hittite territory to the Euphrates under such kings as Thutmose III. Joshua and the Israelites defeated the Palestinian Hittites.
   b. The New Kingdom, 1450-1200 B.C.
      1. The Hittites regained supremacy by the use of horse-drawn war chariots (I Kings 10:29; IIK Kings 7:6).
      2. Their greatest monarch was Suppliluliuma (1385-1345 B.C.). He subdued the Hurrian kingdom of Mittani and

extended his borders to Lebanon. He brought order to the entire area. This was contemporary with the 40 years of Israel's peace under Othniel (Judges 3:11).

3. The Egyptian kings, Seti I and Rameses II, fought the Hittites and took Palestine and much of Syria from them.

4. The Sea peoples (of whom the Philistines were part), invading from the Mediterranean, overcame the Hittites about 1200 B.C.

7. The Hittites still held a few centers of strength after the fall of their empire, such as those at Hamath and Carchemish. (Carchemish fell to the Assyrians in 717 B.C.) David had Hittite soldiers in his army after 1000 B.C. (II Sam. 11:3).

8. The Hittites had codes of law with considerable humanitarianism expressed.[1] They built sturdy stone buildings of large stone blocks. They were fond of massive statuary. The Hittites were known for immorality (Ezek. 16:3, 45-46).

Question

1. Where were the two main centers of the Hittites?
2. How common were the Hittites in Palestine?
3. What contention of the critics about the Hittites has been refuted?
4. Give dates for the two main periods of Hittite power.
5. What battle equipment made the Hittites gain supremacy?
6. Who was the greatest Hittite king?
7. What peoples finally overcame the Hittites?

H. Moabites

1. Descendants of Lot (Gen. 19:39-38).
2. Located east of the Dead Sea and south of the Arnon river.
3. Historical notes
   a. Sihon, king of the Amorites, took much of Moab "even unto Arnon" (Num. 21:26), before the arrival of the Israelites around 1406 B.C.
   b. Israelites were forbidden by God to molest the Moabites (Deut. 2:9).
   c. Because of the fear of the Israelites who camped in the plains of Moab, Balak, the king of Moab, sent for the prophet Balaam, who seems to have advised Balak to

---

1. Robinson, G.L., *The Bearing of Archaelogy on the O.T.*, pp. 141-145.

seduce Israel to immorality (Numbers 22:1-25:5; Deut. 23:4).

  d. Moab oppressed Israel for eighteen years and was repulsed by Ehud (Judges 3:12-30).

  e. Ruth, a Moabitess, became an ancestor of Christ (Ruth 1:4). The book of Ruth seems to indicate that a friendly relationship existed between Moab and Israel at this time.

  f. Saul fought against the Moabites (I Sam. 14:47).

  g. David defeated the Moabites and brought them under subjection (II Sam. 8:2).

  h. During the reign of Jehoshaphat from 872-848 B.C., Moab confederated with the Ammonites, Edomites and others, but Jehovah delivered Judah (II Chron. 20:1-25, cf. II Kings 3:6-27).

  i. Moab was subservient to Israel for nearly 200 years but in the days of Isaiah (c. 700 B.C.) she seems to have regained much of her previous power and prosperity. (See Isaiah 15, 16, Jeremiah 48:47.)

  j. The national deity of Moab was *Chemosh* (Num. 21:29, Judges 11:24).

4. Archaeology uncovered Moabite Stone in 1868.

  a. Had been set up c. 850 B.C.

  b. Is record of Mesha, king of Moab, and his revolt from Israel in the days of King Jehoram (II Kings 3:24-27).

  c. Gives praise to Chemosh for successful revolt.

Questions

1. From whom were the Moabites descended?
2. Where was Moab?
3. What was the name of the national deity (god) of Moab?
4. Were the Moabites friendly toward the Israelites?

I. Philistines (Israel's Arch-enemy)

1. The country of Philistia was located on the Mediterranean shore extending from Joppa southward to south of Gaza.
2. Philistines were a non-Semitic people; some believe them to have been from the Isle of Crete or from the islands of the Aegean Sea.
3. Philistia had a strong political organization composed of five city-states ruled by city lords, independent, but cooperative in major military campaigns. The cities were: 1. Gaza, 2. Gath, 3. Ashdod, 4. Ashkelon, 5. Ekron.

4. The Philistines knew the secret of smelting iron and thus were at a great military advantage, even forcing their Israelite neighbors to buy and to maintain their farm implements at exorbitant prices (I Sam. 13:19-22).
5. Historical notes:
   a. The major Philistine influx seems to have occurred around 1200 B.C., although some Philistines lived in Palestine centuries before then (Gen. 21:32; 26:1).[1]
   b. The Philistines were used by God to prove (test) Israel (Judges 3:3).
   c. Shamgar killed 600 Philistines (Judges 3:31) and Samson slowed down the Philistine oppression considerably during his judgeship (Judges 13:16).
   d. Around 1070 B.C., the Philistines destroyed Shiloh and removed the ark to their own country (I Sam. 4:4; Jer. 7:12).
   e. By the time of Samuel and Saul, they held many cities within the territory of Israel. They occupied all the Mediterranean coast to Mt. Carmel and the valley of Esdraelon eastward as far as Bethshean (II Sam. 31:10), almost encircling Israel.
   f. Jonathan, son of Saul, defeated the Philistines (I Sam. 14) at Michmash.
   g. David experienced victories over the Philistines (I Sam. 17,18).
   h. David was probably oppressed by Philistia during his 7½ years at Hebron.
   i. When David united all of Israel under his control (c. 1003 B.C.), he soundly defeated the Philistines and they never again exerted powerful control in Palestine.
6. Other scriptures referring to Philistia: Joel 3:4-8, Amos 1:6-8, II Chron. 17:11; 21:16,17.

Questions

1. Where was Philistia?
2. Where did the people perhaps come from?
3. What were the five chief cities of the Philistines?
4. What skill gave the Philistines a military advantage?
5. When was the major Philistine influx into Palestine?
6. How much of Israel did the Philistines occupy?
7. Who permanently broke the Philistine control in Palestine?

---

1. *Biblical Archaeologist*, Sept. 1966, pp. 73-75.

J. Phoenicians

1. Phoenicia was a narrow strip of land along the east Mediterranean coast, north of Mt. Carmel and the Bay of Accho.
2. There never was a nation of Phoenicia. The power rested with the cities, primarily Tyre and Sidon. Sidon was stronger up to the time of King Ahab when all of Phoenicia was spoken of as the land of the "Sidonians" (I Kings 16:31). Later Tyre became more prominent (Ezek. 28:2).
3. The original Sidonians were Hamites (Gen. 10:15). However the Hamites, if any remained, were so absorbed by the Semitic immigrants that came in with the Amorite invasion of the Fertile Crescent (about 2000 B.C.) that the Phoenicians are considered Semites.   •
4. Phoenicians were famous for their maritime interests.
    a. Were noted as the most accurate sailors of the ancient world.
    b. Were noted, also, for their colonization which gave them seaports throughout the Mediterranean world.
5. The Phoenician (Canaanite) religion was very immoral and cruel. Some Canaanite gods and rituals are mentioned in the Old Testament — Baal, Ashtoreth, Anath, El and Dagon. Archaeological discoveries at Ras Shamra have revealed much about the Canaanite religion.
6. A number of Phoenician kings were named Hiram (or Ahiram).
7. Friendship existed between Phoenicia and Israel during the reign of David and Solomon (II Sam. 5:11, I Kings 5:1).
8. Ahab married the daughter of the king of Tyre and idolatrous practices of Canaan were introduced into the Israelite religion by Queen Jezebel (I Kings 16:31-33).
9. Several Assyrian kings besieged Tyre without taking it. Nebuchadnezzar of Babylon invaded Tyre for 13 years (598-585), taking the mainland portion of the city but not the island portion one-half mile out in the Mediterranean. Alexander the Great built a causeway of earth out to the island city, making it part of a peninsula and capturing the city (332 B.C.).

Questions

1. Where was Phoenicia?
2. What were its two chief cities?

3. What were the main business interests of the Phoenicians?
4. What was the nature of the Phoenicians religion?
5. What name did a number of Phoenician kings have?

Section II
Divided Kingdom — to Fall of House of Ahab (I Kings 12 — II Kings 11; II Chronicles 10-23)

1. Facts about the Divided Kingdom — Character of the two kingdoms — Superiority of Judah — Three periods of the history — Kings of Judah and Israel — Chronology of the Divided Kingdom. 2. Accession of Rehoboam — Assembly of Shechem — Revolt of the ten tribes under Jeroboam — Judah and Benjamin adhere to Rehoboam — War forbidden by the prophet Shemaiah — Government of Rehoboam — Religious declension — Jerusalem taken by Shishak — Death of Rehoboam. 3. Reign of Abijah, second king of Judah — Defeat of Jeroboam — Prosperity of Judah. 4. Jeroboam I, king of Israel — Extent of the kingdom — Idolatry of the golden calves — The prophet at Bethel — Abijah, son of Jeroboam — The prophet Ahijah. 5. Nadab, second king of Israel — His murder and extinction of the house of Jeroboam. 6. Baasha, third king of Israel — The prophet Jehu — War with Judah and Syria — Elah, fourth king of Israel — Murdered by Zimri — Extinction of the house of Baasha. 7. Zimri, fifth king of Israel, reigns only seven days — Deaths of Zimri and Tibni, his competitor — Omri, sixth king of Israel — Building of the new capital Samaria — Dependence of Israel on Syria — Wickedness and death of Omri. 8. Asa, third king of Judah — Reformation of religion — Asa's great army — Defeat of Zerah the Ethiopian — The prophet Azariah — Second reformation — War with Baasha and alliance with Benhadad I — The prophet Hanani reproves Asa — Religious persecution — Death of Asa. 9. Ahab, seventh king of Israel, and his wife Jezebel — Worship of Baal and persecution of Jehovah's worshipers — Elijah the Tishbite announces a three years' drought — Elijah nourished at Cherith, at

Zarephath by a widow — His appearance to Ahab and contest with the prophets of Baal at Mount Carmel — Victory of Elijah — The prophets of Baal slain — Elijah's prayer for rain — Fury of Jezebel — Flight of Elijah to the wilderness — His vision of Jehovah's glory at Horeb — His mission to anoint Hazael, Jehu and Elisha. 10. Wars of Ahab with Syria — Benhadad defeated at Samaria and Aphek. 11. The murder of Naboth and the judgment pronounced by Elijah. 12. Expedition of Ahab and Jehoshaphat to recover Ramoth in Gilead — The prophet Micaiah — Defeat of the two kings and death of Ahab. 13. Jehoshaphat, seventh king of Judah — His piety and prosperity — Alliance with Ahab — Jehoshaphat reproved by Jehu — His great reformation of justice — War with Moab and Ammon — The prophet Jahaziel — Great victory of Berachah — Alliances with Ahaziah and Jehoram — Maritime enterprise of Jehoshaphat, denounced by the prophet Eliezer — Death of Jehoshaphat. 14. Ahaziah, eighth king of Israel — Last appearance of Elijah — His translation — Elisha succeeds Elijah. 15. Jehoram, ninth king of Israel — Allies with Jehoshaphat against the revolt of the Moabites — Miracle of Elisha and defeat of Moab — Siege of Kir-haraseth and human sacrifice by the king of Moab — Elisha and the widow — The Shunammite woman — The healing of Naaman's leprosy — War with Syria — Elisha and the Syrians — The siege of Samaria miraculously raised. 16. Jehoram, fifth king of Judah — Marriage with Athaliah, daughter of Ahab — Idolatry and wickedness — Revolts of Edom, Libnah, the Philistines and Arabians. 17. Ahaziah, sixth king of Judah — Elisha anoints Hazael, who murders Benhadad II — Anointing and revolt of Jehu — Slaughter of Jehoram, Jezebel, Ahab's seventy sons, the princess of Judah, the worshipers of Baal and Ahaziah. 18. Usurpation of Athaliah, and murder of the royal family of Judah, except Joash, who is saved by Jehoiada — Restoration of Joash and death of Athaliah — Extinction of the house of Ahab in both its branches of Israel and Judah.

1. *Facts about the Divided Kingdom.* Very shortly after the death of Solomon, the prophecy of Ahijah was fulfilled; his kingdom

MEMORIZE THIS CHART

	Israel	Judah
Names of the two kingdoms	Israel	Judah
Number of tribes in each kingdom	Ten	Two (Judah and Benjamin)
Area included	Northern & eastern	Southern
First kings	Jeroboam	Rehoboam
Total number of kings	19	19 plus 1 usurper
Number of dynasties	Nine	One (House of David)
Character of the kings	All bad; some worse	Some good, some bad
Capitals of the kingdoms	Samaria (earlier Shechem; II Kings 12:25; and Tirzah, II Kings 14:17)	Jerusalem
Fate of the kingdoms	Conquered and deported by Assyria, 722 B.C.	Conquered and deported to Babylon, 586 B.C.

was rent in twain and the parts, both greatly weakened by the disruption, formed the separate kingdoms of JUDAH and of ISRAEL. It may be well to take a preliminary view of the somewhat intricate annals of those kingdoms and of the very different character which marked each. To a superficial observer, the northern kingdom including ten tribes, about two-thirds of the population and, with the region east of Jordan more than the same proportion of the land and that much the best in quality, would seem to have had all the elements of greater strength. The areas of the two kingdoms were, respectively, Israel about 9375 square miles and Judah about 3435. But on the other hand, Judah retained the capital, the center of the organized system of government and of the material interests of the nation, together with the accumulated treasures of Solomon. And to say nothing of the energy of the tribe of Judah, which was perhaps equaled by Ephraim, Zebulon and Naphtali, all the moral and religious elements of greatness were on the side of the southern kingdom.

From the very first, the blot of rebellion clung to the cause of Israel, the divine selection of Jeroboam to punish the sins of Solomon was not held to justify his rebellion. He was indeed assured that obedience to God's law would be rewarded by the establishment of his kingdom and his dynasty (I Kings 11:38), but his very first acts severed every religious bond to Jehovah and his worship and his course was followed by his successors, of whom with scarcely an exception we read the emphatic sentence, "he did evil in the sight of Jehovah, and walked in the way of Jeroboam, who made Israel to sin."

On the other hand, the kingdom of Judah was preserved from the defection of the other tribes, expressly for the sake of God's covenant with David and to maintain His worship at its chosen seat, and the immediate consequence of Jeroboam's *religious* revolt was to drive all the priests and Levites to Jerusalem (II Chron. 11:13-14). With the line of David remained God's promise of a permanent kingdom, made doubly sure by its ultimate reference to the Messiah, in that family the crown was handed on, generally from father to son while in Israel the dynasty of Jeroboam ended with his son; and there followed a series of murders and usurpations amid which the longest dynasties, those of Omri and Jeho, only numbered four and five kings each. From the disruption to the epoch at which Ahaziah, king of Judah, and Jehoram, king of Israel, were killed at the same time by Jehu, a period of ninety years (931-841 B.C.), Judah had only six kings (though Ahaziah reigned but one year) while Israel had nine; and in the whole period of 255 years, from the disruption to the captivity of Israel (931-722 B.C.), twelve kings of Judah occupy the same space as nineteen kings of Israel, a striking indication of the greater stability of the former dynasty. The moral superiority is equally striking, not only in the preservation of the worship of Jehovah at Jerusalem, while Israel was sunk in idolatry, but even on the comparatively weak ground of the personal character of the kings. It is true that the house of David was deeply corrupted, chiefly by its connection with the wicked house of Ahab, but it boasts the names of Asa, Jehoshaphat, Uzziah, Jotham, the godly Hezekiah, the penitent Manasseh, the pure Josiah, while not one of the kings of Israel is free from the blot of foul wickedness. Even the fierce zeal of Jehu had no purity of motive. The two kingdoms were equally distinguished in their final fate. The sentence of captivity was executed upon Israel about 130 years sooner than on Judah and while the ten tribes never returned to their land and only a scattered remnant of them shared the restoration of Judah, the latter became once more a small but powerful nation, not free from the faults of their fathers, but worshiping God with a purity and serving Him with a heroic zeal unequaled since the days of Joshua, and preparing for the restoration of the true spiritual kingdom under the last great son of David.

The part of the history thus reviewed down to the captivity at

Babylon, may be marked out into three great periods: a. From the disruption to the simultaneous deaths of the kings of Judah and Israel by the hand of Jehu in 841 B.C.; b. To the captivity of Israel by Shalmaneser (or Sargon) in 722 B.C.; c. The remaining history of Judah down to the captivity at Babylon in 586 B.C.

The Kings of Israel and Judah

(As the various kings are studied students should refer to the following outline and memorize the names of the kings and the principal events associated with each. Roman numerals along the margin indicate dynasties. The outline shows which kings were contemporary in Judah and Israel.)

ISRAEL

JUDAH

I
1. *Jeroboam*
   a. Golden calves.
   b. His altar denounced by a prophet.
2. *Nadab*
   a. Assassinated by Baasha.

II
3. *Baasha*
   a. Destroyed the house of Jeroboam.
   b. Fortified Ramah against Asa.
   c. Denounced by the prophet Jehu.
4. *Elah*
   a. Assassinated by Zimri.

III
5. *Zimri*
   a. Destroyed the house of Baasha.
   b. Seven-day rule.

IV
6. *Omri*
   a. Mighty
   b. Made Samaria the capital.
7. *Ahab*
   a. Jezebel and Baal worship.
   b. Contest with Elijah.
   c. Two victories over Benhadad.
   d. Naboth slain.
   e. Battle of Ramoth-gilead.
8. *Ahaziah*
   a. Accident and sickness.
   b. Elijah's prediction of his death.
9. *Jehoram*
   a. Mesha of Moab revolted.
   b. Ministry of Elisha.
   c. Seige and famine at Samaria.
   d. Wounded at Ramoth-Gilead.
   e. Slain by Jehu.

1. *Rehoboam* (Evil)
   a. Split the kingdom.
   b. Invaded by Shishak.
2. *Abijam* (Evil)
   a. Victory over Jeroboam.
3. *Asa* (Good)
   a. Beat a million Ethiopians.
   b. Religious reforms.
   c. Backslid a mile (hired Benhadad)

4. *Jehoshaphat* (Good)
   a. Religious teachers sent out.
   b. Alliance with Ahab.
   c. Victory over Moab and Ammon.
   d. Shipwreck.
   e. Goes with Jehoram to fight Moab.
5. *Jehoram* (One of the worst!)
   a. Married Athaliah.
   b. Slew his six brothers.
   c. Edom and Libnah revolted.
   d. Letter from Elijah.
   e. Hideous death.
6. *Ahaziah* (Evil)
   a. Visited Uncle Jehoram of Israel.
   b. Slain by Jehu.

10. *Jehu*
    a. Killed the house of Ahab and
       Ahaziah of Judah.
    b. Destroyed Baal worshippers.
11. *Jehoahaz*
    a. Lost most of his kingdom to
       Syria.
12. *Jehoash*
    a. Smote Syria three times.
    b. Conquered Amaziah and
       Judah.
13. *Jeroboam II* (The "Napoleon of
the Northern Kingdom")
    a. Restored territory to Israel.
    b. Conquered Damascus and
       Hamath.
    c. Amos announced the end of
       the kingdom (Amos 7:11).
14. *Zechariah*
    a. Slain by Shallum after 6
       months.

V

15. *Shallum*
    a. Slain by Menahem after 1
       month.

VI

16. *Menahem*
    a. Cruel in war.
    b. Invaded by Pul of Assyria.
17. *Pekahiah*
    a. Slain by Pekah.

VII

18. *Pekah*
    a. Joined Rezin in attacking
       Ahaz.
    b. Invaded by Tiglath-pileser.
    c. Slain by Hoshea.

VIII

7. *Athaliah* (Evil)
    a. Slew all but one of the house
       of David.
    b. Slain in a plot by Jehoiada.
8. *Joash* (Good and bad)
    a. The boy king.
    b. Repaired the temple.
    c. Forgot the kindness shown to
       him.
9. *Amaziah* (Good and bad)
    a. Conquered Edom and took
       its gods.
    b. Defeated by Jehoash.
10. *Uzziah* (or Azariah) (Good)
    a. Mighty.
    b. Became a leper.

11. *Jotham* (Good)
    a. Mighty.
    b. Threatened by Rezin and
       Pekah.
12. *Ahaz* (One of the worst)
    a. Introduced idolatry.
    b. Attacked by Rezin and Pekah.
    c. Hired Tiglath-Pileser to attack
       Israel.
    d. Made an altar like one in
       Damascus.
    e. Damaged the temple
       willfully.

IX

19. *Hoshea*
    a. Tribute to Shalmaneser.
    b. Conspiracy with Egypt.
    c. Siege of Samaria and fall of
       Israel.
END OF ISRAEL!

13. *Hezekiah* (One of the best)
    a. Temple reopened and cleansed.
    b. Great Passover.
    c. Sennacherib's invasion.
    d. Life extended.
    e. Visitors from Babylon.
14. *Manasseh* (The worst!)
    a. Idolatry unlimited.
    b. Cruelty unlimited.
    c. Announcement of Judah's end.
    d. Captive in Babylon.
    e. Repentance and reformation.
15. *Amon* (Evil)
    a. Continued his father's evils.
    b. Assassinated.
16. *Josiah* (The best!)
    a. Temple repaired.
    b. Book of the law found.
    c. Idolatry purged and true religion enforced.
    d. Altar at Bethel defiled.
    e. Slain by Pharaoh-Necho.
17. *Jehoahaz* (or Shallum) (Evil)
    a. Three months' reign.
    b. Deposed and taken to Egypt.
18. *Jehoiakim* (Evil)
    a. Enthroned by Pharaoh.
    b. Servitude to Babylon.
    c. Cut up Jeremiah's roll.
    d. First deportation to Babylon.

19. *Jehoiachin* (Evil) (Called Jeconiah and Joniah; I Ch. 3:16; Jer. 22:24,28; 24:1)
    a. Three months' reign.
    b. Captured and taken to Babylon.
    c. Second deportation to Babylon.
20. *Zedekiah* (Evil)
    a. Rebelled against Babylon.
    b. Siege and destruction of Jerusalem.
    c. Third deportation to Babylon.
END OF JUDAH!

Chronology of the Divided Kingdom

a. *Dates of the Kings*

ISRAEL	B.C.	JUDAH	B.C.
1. Jeroboam	931-910	1. Rehoboam	931-913
		2. Abijah	913-911
		3. Asa	911-870
2. Nadab	910-909		
3. Baasha	909-886		
4. Elah	886-885		
5. Zimri	885		
6. Omri	885-874		
7. Ahab	874-853		
		4. Jehoshaphat	873-848
8. Ahaziah	853-852		
9. Jehoram	852-841		
		5. Jehoram	848-841
		6. Ahaziah	841

(Jehu slays Jehoram and Ahaziah) — 841 B.C.

ISRAEL	B.C.	JUDAH	B.C.
10. Jehu	841-814	7. Athaliah	841-835
		8. Joash	835-796
11. Jehoahaz	814-798		
12. Jehoash	798-782		
		9. Amaziah	796-767
13. Jeroboam II	793-753		
		10. Uzziah	790-739
14. Zechariah	753-752		
15. Shallum	752		
16. Menahem	752-742		
		11. Jotham	751-736
17. Pekahiah	742-740		
18. Pekah	752-732		
		12. Ahaz	743-728
19. Hoshea	732-722		
		13. Hezekiah	728-695
End of Israel	722		
		14. Manasseh	695-642
		15. Amon	642-640
		16. Josiah	640-609
		17. Jehoahaz	609
		18. Jehoakim	609-597
		19. Jehoiachin	597
		20. Zedekiah	597-586

b. *Data concerning the chronology*

    1. The history of the divided kingdom contains dozens of chronological notations, such as: "Now in the eighteenth year of King Jeroboam, the son of Nebat, reigned Abijam over Judah. Three years reigned he in Jerusalem" (I Kings 15:1-2). It would therefore seem that the chronology of this period would be the most clearly defined and easily reckoned of all periods.

    2. However, upon serious study these chronological notes give no end of difficulty. The difficulties are of two main types:

        a. The total numbers of years at various points in the history of the kings do not seem to agree with the synchronisms given. For example, the total of Israel's first four kings — Jeroboam 22, Nadab 2, Baasha 24, Elah 2: total 50 — is synchronized with King Asa's 27th year (I Kings 16:10,15). However, Rehoboam's 17, plus Abijam's 3 and 27 of Asa equal 47, not 50.

        b. Also the years apparently indicated in the Hebrew scriptures do not agree with the carefully recorded dates preserved in the records of the Assyrians and Babylonians.

    3. These difficulties have seemed impossible to solve until recent years. With increased knowledge of Assyrian and Babylonian records and more careful study of the Bible, we now know that the biblical numbers of years are precisely correct. Our understanding has been faulty, not the Bible.

    A most helpful book on the chronology of the Hebrew kings has been issued in recent years. It is *The Mysterious Numbers of the Hebrew Kings*, by Edwin R. Thiele (Grand Rapids: Eerdmans, 1951; Rev. ed. 1965). We have followed the dates of Thiele on all the kings except Uzziah, Jotham, Ahaz and Hezekiah, where we prefer the dates proposed by Gleason Archer and J.B. Payne. Thiele's dates for these kings are affected by his dubious dating of Hezekiah.

    4. Absolute dates[1] for the Babylonian and Assyrian kings are known to us, as previously stated. These are most helpful in dating many biblical events, such as the reigns of Ahab and Jehu, the fall of Israel, the attack on Judah by Sennacherib,

---

1. Thiele, *op. cit.*, pp. 39-52.

the fall of Judah and the fall of Babylon. These events are related in the Bible and also in the Babylonian records.

    a. Several Assyrian lists, called eponym lists, give year by year records of Assyrian kings and their activities from 911 to 649 B.C. These lists mention an eclipse of the sun, which can be precisely dated in 763 B.C.

    b. A king list found at Khorsabad near Nineveh in 1932/33 lists all the kings of Assyria from the very earliest until 745 B.C.

    c. Another important document is the Canon of Ptolemy, which lists the kings of Babylon, Persia, Greece and Egypt from 747 B.C. to A.D. 161. This list notes several solar eclipses also.

  By the help of these lists we can precisely date the division of the Hebrew kingdom at 931 B.C. From this date we can compute the dates of Solomon, David, Saul and the Exodus (from I Kings 6:1).

5. Thiele has shown, conclusively, we feel, that the biblical numbers of the Hebrew kings harmonize with the Assyrian and Babylonian dates when we take into consideration the following data:

    a. Many kings of Judah and Israel had overlapping reigns with their predecessors and successors. Careful calculation of the numbers in the text makes this apparent in most cases even when the coregencies are not plainly stated. Because of these coregencies the total length of the reigns of the kings is considerably less than may at first appear.

      The fact of coregencies itself, however, raises problems. If a king in Israel is dated from a certain year in the reign of a king in Judah who was coregent with his father, is the date of the king of Israel calculated from the first year of the coregency of the king of Judah or from his first year as sole ruler? Such questions can be solved one by one, but lie outside the scope of this book.

    b. Different ways of counting the first year of a king's reign were employed. These different methods can make the enumeration of the years appear in error. Two systems were used, the accession-year system and the non-accession-year system. In the accession-year system that part of any year following the death of a king until the start of the next new year was not counted as the first year of the new king, but as his accession year. His first year began with the start of the new year following his accession. By the non-accession-year system the remaining portion of a year following the death of a king was spoken as the first year of the new king, and that portion of the year before the king died was the last year of the preceding king.

A comparison of dates from two kingdoms using the different systems of dating would make it appear that the kingdom using the non-accession-year system gained one year on the other kingdom each time a new king came to the throne.

   c. The time of the start of the years, whether Nisan to Nisan or Tishri to Tishri, makes a difference in the apparent length of the king's reigns. If two kingdoms started their years in different months and one used a non-accession-year system and the other the accession year system, two kings could start ruling on the same day and the one could be in his "second" year before the other was even in his first official year.

   d. The kingdoms of Judah and Israel apparently did not consistently stick with either the accession-year system or the other throughout their history. The switching back and forth must be accounted for.

6. For reasons too lengthy to give here Thiele concludes that:

   a. Judah counted its years from Tishri to Tishri (March), and Israel from Nisan to Nisan (September).

   b. Israel started with a non-accession-year system of reckoning, and Judah an accession-year system.[1]

   c. From the time of Jehoram of Judah to Joash (inclusive), Judah switched over to the non-accession year system of Israel. From the time of Amaziah on to its end Judah went back to the accession-year system.

   d. Israel seems to have shifted to the accession year system of Judah from the time of Jehoash to its end as a kingdom.

7. The most difficult part of the chronology of the divided kingdom is the date of Hezekiah. Two dates involving

---

1. Thiele, *op. cit.* 25, 27, 36.

Hezekiah are known from Assyrian sources: a. The fall of Israel, 722 B.C.; b. Sennacherib's invasion of Judah, 701 B.C.

The fall of Israel occurred in Hezekiah's sixth year (II Kings 18:9,10). Sennacherib's invasion occurred in Hezekiah's "fourteenth" year (II Kings 18:13). Now from 722 to 701 is much longer than fourteen years. Thiele avoids this difficulty by dating the start of Hezekiah's reign in 715, and alleging that the Hebrew historian committed an error in dating the fall of Israel in Hezekiah's sixth year. Such a conclusion would make it necessary to conclude that the original biblical manuscripts contained an error. The logical consequences of this are too grave; if there was one error in the originals, there could have been thousands of errors; if there was error, then Christ's evaluation of the O.T. Scriptures must be rejected and His omniscience questioned. Copies of the originals are not inerrant; the originals must have been so.

We prefer the suggestion of Gleason Archer[1] that there has been a scribal error in copying a single letter in I Kings 18:13 (substituting a *he* for a *mem*), which caused "twenty-four" to become "fourteen." If the twenty-fourth year (according to the emended reading just suggested) is reckoned from 725, the year of the death of Ahaz (with whom Hezekiah had been coregent for three years — cf. II Chron. 27:1,8), the result is 701 B.C., the date of Sennacherib's invasion. We therefore date Hezekiah 728-695, with his sole rule beginning at 725.

8. The twenty years of Pekah's reign is also a difficult feature of the chronology (II Kings 15:27). Menahem paid tribute to Tiglath-pileser of Assyria, as is known both from the Bible and Tiglath-pileser's inscriptions. T-P is dated 745-727. Reckoning backward from the fall of Israel in 722, we add nine years of Hoshea to 20 of Pekah, and this brings us to 752 B.C., a date *before* the time of Tiglath-pileser. How then could Menahem, who is listed as a predecessor to Pekah, have paid tribute to T-P?

The solution seems to be (as Thiele suggests) that Pekah set up a rival dynasty over Israel in Gilead (see II Kings 15:25) at the time when Menahem ascended to the throne

---

1. G.L. Archer, "Books in Review," *Christianity Today* (April 15, 1966), p. 35.

in Samaria. Thus Menahem's reign of ten years was at the same time as the first ten years of Pekah. When Pekah finally came into full power over Israel, it was quite natural that he should maintain that he had always been the only true king of Israel even from 752. This explanation seems to remove some of the difficulties.

Ahab's Wars with the Syrians
I Kings 20, 22

1. At Samaria (I Kings 20:1-25) — Result: Victory for Ahab.
2. At Aphek (I Kings 20:26-43) — Results: Victory for Ahab. King Ben-hadad spared.
3. At Ramoth-Gilead (I Kings 22:1-40) — Results: King Jehoshaphat almost killed. Ahab killed.

---

2. REHOBOAM (931-913 B.C.; I Kings 12:1-24; 14:21-31; II Chron. 10:1-12:16) was the son of Solomon by Naamah, an Ammonite princess. As he was forty-one at his accession, he must have been born about the time of his father's association with David in the kingdom. The luxury in which he was trained seems to have given him a light and headstrong character, on which his father's precepts were thrown away; he was quite unequal to the difficulties bequeathed to him by Solomon, and he was scarcely seated on the throne before the old jealousy between Judah and the other tribes broke out anew. It was probably to conciliate such feelings, as well as to comply with the form of popular recognition which had been observed in the case of Solomon, that not content with his accession to the throne at Jerusalem, he held an assembly of all Israel at the ancient sanctuary of Shechem, unless indeed that assemblage were rather the act of the Israelites themselves and of Ephraim in particular, with a view to resist his claims (I Kings 12:1; II Chron. 10:1). At all events, such an opposition seems to have been prepared from the first convocation of the assembly, and JEROBOAM was sent for out of Egypt by the malcontents (I Kings 12:2,20). His appearance at the head of the congregation may be taken as a proof that their demand for the redress of the grievances they had suffered under Solomon was a pretext for revolt. Rehoboam took three days for deliberation.

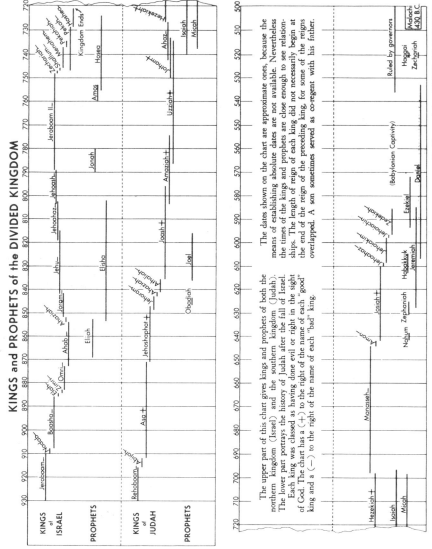

KINGS and PROPHETS of the DIVIDED KINGDOM

The upper part of this chart gives kings and prophets of both the northern kingdom (Israel) and the southern kingdom (Judah). The lower part portrays the history of Judah after the fall of Israel.

Each king was classed as having done evil or right in the sight of God. The chart has a (+) to the right of the name of each "good" king and a (−) to the right of the name of each "bad" king.

The dates shown on the chart are approximate ones, because the means of establishing absolute dates are not available. Nevertheless the times of the kings and prophets are close enough to see relationships. The length of reign of each king did not necessarily begin at the end of the reign of the preceding king, for some of the reigns overlapped. A son sometimes served as co-regent with his father.

Used by permission of STANDARD PUBLISHING

He was advised by his father's old counselors to take away the pretext by a conciliatory answer. This step, they thought, would have satisfied the majority of the people with whom the names of David and Solomon had not yet lost their prestige. But the king would not yield a jot and he took counsel with the younger men, who had grown up with him at the court. Urged on by them, he refused the petition with reckless insolence. "You complain of my father's heavy yoke; I will add to its weight! my little finger shall be thicker than his loins! He chastised you with whips; I will chastise you with scorpions!" Then Ephraim and all Israel raised again the old cry of Sheba (II Sam. 20:1), disclaiming all part in the house of David and calling Israel to their tents. Adoram, the chief officer of the tribute, being sent to appease the tumult, was stoned to death and Rehoboam only escaped by fleeing in his chariot to Jerusalem (I Kings 12:1-15; II Chron. 10).

The rebellion was complete and Jeroboam was proclaimed king over all Israel at Shechem. The cities of Judah, however, adhered to Rehoboam and the tribe of Benjamin soon espoused his cause. Ever since the great blow inflicted on that tribe, it seems to have been more or less subordinate to Judah. The appearances to the contrary are rather proofs of the impatience with which the yoke was borne. The capture of Jerusalem, which lay within the bounds of Benjamin, from the Jebusites, by the great king of Judah, gave his house a powerful hold upon the feelings of the tribe; and it is not improbable, from the similar course afterward taken by Rehoboam (II Chron. 11:23), that David may have established his sons in the fortified cities of Benjamin. Perhaps too, Jeroboam's profanation of their sacred city of Bethel may have offended the tribe. At all events, we find them answering the summons of Rehoboam to a war for the subjugation of the rebels, with all their military force. The united army of Judah and Benjamin amounted to 180,000 warriors; but the enterprise was forbidden by the prophet Shemaiah, as God had willed the separation of the kingdoms (I Kings 11:21-24; II Chron. 11:1-4). A desultory warfare was, however, kept up between the two kingdoms, under Rehoboam and his two successors, for a period of sixty years, and its cessation was followed by a most disastrous alliance with the house of Ahab. Meanwhile, Rehoboam made every effort to strengthen his diminished kingdom, fortifying several of the most important cities of Judah and Benjamin and

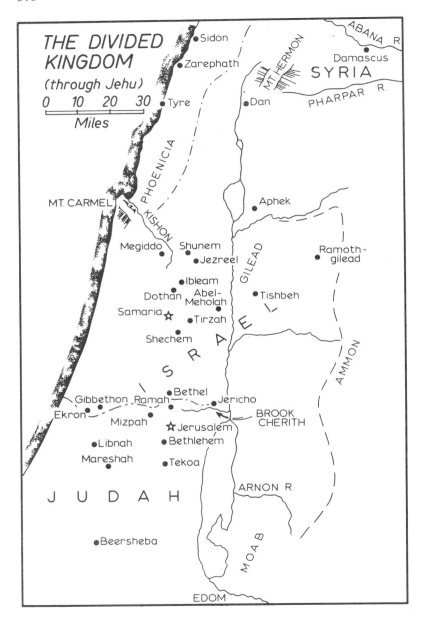

THE DIVIDED
KINGDOM
(through Jehu)

0   10   20   30
Miles

Sidon
Zarephath
Tyre
Dan
PHOENICIA
MT. HERMON
ABANA R.
Damascus
SYRIA
PHARPAR R.

MT. CARMEL
KISHON
Megiddo
Shunem
Jezreel
Ibleam
Dothan
Abel-
Meholah
Samaria
Tirzah
Shechem
Aphek
GILEAD
Ramoth-
gilead
Tishbeh
AMMON

I
S
R
A
E
L

Gibbethon Ramah
Ekron
Mizpah
Bethel
Jericho
BROOK
CHERITH
Jerusalem
Libnah
Bethlehem
Mareshah
Tekoa

J   U   D   A   H

ARNON R.

Beersheba

MOAB

EDOM

furnishing them with arms and provisions (II Chron. 11:1-12). When the boundaries of the kingdom of Judah became settled, they embraced the territories of Dan and Simeon, which were originally included in the lot of Judah and ultimately even a part of Ephraim (II Chron. 13:19; 15:8; 17:2). On the south, Edom was still retained till the reign of Jehoram, the fifth king, but we are not told whether Hadad was defeated or made tributary. The cause of Rehoboam was strengthened by the resort to him of the great body of priests and Levites from all parts of Israel whom Jeroboam had deposed from their functions, and the first three years of his reign were exceedingly prosperous. But he was corrupted, like his father, by his numerous harem which was composed of 18 wives and 60 concubines; he had 28 sons and 60 daughters. His three chief wives were all of his own family: Mahalath, the grand-daughter; and Abihail, the niece of David; and Maachah, the daughter of Absalom. The last was his favorite wife and the mother of Abijah, his successor. He provided for his other sons and guarded Abijah from their rivalry by giving them splendid establishments in the fortified cities of Judah and Benjamin (II Chron. 11). Meanwhile both king and people declined into idolatry and practiced the most abominable vices of the nations around (I Kings 14:21-24; II Chron. 12:1), and their punishment was speedy.

In the fifth year of Rehoboam (927 B.C.), Shishak (Sheshonk I), king of Egypt, whom we have already seen as the protector of Hadad and Jeroboam, made an expedition against Jerusalem with all the forces of his empire. He took the strong cities of Judah and had reached Jerusalem when the king and people, reproved by the prophet Shemaiah, humbled themselves before Jehovah, who saved them from captivity. Shishak, however, spoiled the Temple and the king's palace of their treasures and carried off the celebrated golden shields of Solomon, which Rehoboam replaced by shields of brass to keep up the old display when they were carried before him in processions (I Kings 14:25-28; II Chron. 12:2-11). The kingdom of Judah became for a time tributary to Shishak, that the people might learn the difference between the service of God and the service of heathen kings (II Chron. 12:8). The expedition of Shishak is one of the chief points of contact between sacred history and the records of the Egyptian monuments. On the wall of the great temple of Karnak are the sculptured figures of captains with features clearly Jewish, and the appended inscription contains, among a long list of conquests, the name of "Yuda Melchi" *(the kingdom of Judah)*.

The lesson seems not to have been lost on Rehoboam and his people. "There were yet good things in Judah"; but the sum of the king's character is this: "He did evil, because he fixed not his heart to seek Jehovah" (II Chron. 12:12,24). He died after a reign of seventeen years and was buried in the city of David. His acts were recorded by the prophet Shemaiah, by the seer Iddo in his book of genealogies and in the Chronicles of the kings of Judah (I Kings 14:29-31; II Chron. 12:13-16).

3. ABIJAH (913-911 B.C.; I Kings 15:1-8; II Chron. 13), the son of Rehoboam, was the second king of Judah. He succeeded his father in the eighteenth year of Jeroboam's reign and reigned three years at Jerusalem (II Chron. 13:1-2; I Kings 15:1-2). He continued the war with Jeroboam and gathered the whole force of Judah and Benjamin for the subjugation of the ten tribes. He brought into the field 400,000 chosen warriors and Jeroboam met him with 800,000 of whom 500,000 fell in the rout at Zemaraim in Mount Ephraim, where the favor of God prevailed against the skillful tactics which Jeroboam imitated from Joshua. The loss of the men of Judah is not stated. In consequence of this victory, Abijah took Bethel, Jeshanah and Ephrain, with their dependent towns; and Jeroboam never again prevailed against him (II Chron. 13:3-20; I Kings 15:6). This success, granted to the arms of Judah "because they relied upon Jehovah, the God of their fathers," proved His forbearance with the sins of Abijah for David's sake (II Chron. 13:18; II Kings 15:3-5). The fact that Abijah upbraids the men of Israel with their rebellion and idolatry and relies on the goodness of the cause of Judah, who had Jehovah for their God and the priests keeping His charge (II Chron. 13:4-12), is no proof that his personal vices are exaggerated in the *Book of Kings*. Abijah followed the example of his predecessors in his numerous harem. He had fourteen wives and was the father of twenty-two sons and fifteen daughters. His history was written by the prophet Iddo and in the Chronicles of the kings of Judah. He died and was buried in the city of David, leaving the kingdom to his son Asa in such a state of strength and prosperity that Jeroboam did not venture to resume the war, and the confusion which soon ensued in the royal family of Israel insured Judah a ten years' peace (I Kings 15:8; II Chron. 14:1). Abijah's death was followed in less than two years by that of Jeroboam to whose history we now return.

4. JEROBOAM I (931-910 B.C.; I Kings 12:20,25; 14:20), the first king of the separate kingdom of Israel was inaugurated (like Abimelech) at Shechem by the choice of the men of Israel. He fortified that city[1] and Penuel for his two capitals, west and east of Jordan, but fixed his own residence at the beautiful town of Tirzah (I Kings 14:17). The ten tribes which adhered to him are probably to be reckoned by taking Joseph (Ephraim and Manasseh) as *one*, and excluding Levi and Judah. The secession of Benjamin still left the number *ten*, by counting Ephraim and Manasseh separately. Dan remained in the number in virtue of its possessions in the north. Simeon was actually included in the kingdom of Judah, but the tribe seems to have sunk into such insignificance as to be numbered among the ten only by a sort of negative computation. Beyond the old limits of Palestine, Moab was attached to Israel (II Kings 3:4), and Ammon would naturally preserve its family alliance with Rehoboam, to whom, as we have seen, Edom was also subject, but a common interest soon prompted these tribes to union against both the kingdoms (II Chron. 20:1). As for the allies and tributaries of Solomon in Phoenicia and Syria, though now cut off from Judah, they are not at all likely to have submitted to the king of Israel. We hear of no further connection with Phoenicia and Lebanon and we soon find the Syrian kingdom of Damascus, whose rise we have already noticed, a most formidable enemy of Israel.

After all these deductions, Jeroboam was at the head of a fine kingdom, populous, powerful and fertile and abounding in the resources which Solomon had developed. The prophet Ahijah had promised the establishment of his kingdom on the condition of obedience to Jehovah. But Jeroboam had no faith in his political security so long as his subjects continued to resort to the capital of his rival as their religious home. There were ancient sanctuaries within his dominions and the erection of one of these into a new center of worship, though illegal, might not perhaps have been altogether inexcusable. Or he might have allowed the priests to continue their domestic ministrations and the people would only have been too ready to break off their visits to Jerusalem. But his fear prompted a more violent and fatal course, which added a religious schism to the political disruption and brought down the divine wrath on his house and kingdom. Resorting to the idolatry which he had witnessed in Egypt and

---

1. Shechem had been destroyed by Abimelech after its revolt.

following the example of Aaron, whose very words he used (I Kings 12:28; Comp. Ex. 32:4,8),

> "The rebel king
> Doubled that sin in Bethel and in Dan,
> Likening his Maker to the grazed ox,"

he set up two golden calves, possibly similar to the Apis bulls worshipped in Egypt at Memphis, in the extreme north and south parts of his kingdom. Dan was probably chosen as having been the sanctuary of the northern tribes, ever since the Danites had set up there the images of Micah, Bethel as the "house of God" for all Israel since its consecretion by Jacob. The latter was the chief seat of the new worship, which the king himself inaugurated on the 15th day of the 8th month, in imitation of the dedication of the Temple at the Feast of Tabernacles, but a month later, "in the month which he had *devised of his own heart*" (I Kings 12:26-33; 13:33; II Chron. 13:9). Having appointed priests "from the lowest of the people," in place of the Levites, whom he deposed and drove from their cities to Jerusalem, he erected an altar at Bethel, upon which he burned incense in the feast he had appointed. In the very midst of the ceremony, a man of God, sent by the word of Jehovah out of Judah, confronted Jeroboam at his altar, on which he prophesied that a son of David, named Josiah, should one day offer the bones of the idolatrous priests who sacrificed upon it; and he added a sign, that the altar should be rent and the ashes on it poured out upon the ground (I Kings 13:1-6).[1] The enraged king called on his guards to seize the prophet and put out his own hand to lay hold of him, but the hand was withered and fell helpless, and an earthquake rent the altar. On the prophet's prayer, entreated by the king, his hand was restored and he begged the man of God to accept his hospitality and a reward, which he refused and departed by another way as he had been commanded. How he yielded to an aged brother prophet the consent he had refused the king, how he was slain by a lion for his disobedience and buried by the old prophet, who entreated that his bones might be laid beside him to preserve them from the fate denounced on the idol priests, is one of those beautiful episodes of Scripture familiar to our earliest recollections (I Kings 13:7-32; Comp. II Kings 23:17-18). But the warning had no permanent effect on Jeroboam, who persisted in his idolatrous worship and consecrated any one as a priest who

---

1. Jewish tradition identified him with the prophet Iddo. For the fulfillment of the prophecy, see II K. 23:15,16.

could afford to bring the prescribed offering of a young bullock and seven rams (I Kings 13:23; Comp. II Chron. 13:9; Ex. 29:1,35; Lev. 8:2).

So another chastisement befell him in his own family. His son Abijah, the only one of his house "in whom there was found some good thing toward Jehovah the God of Israel," was mercifully removed by death from the wickedness around him. On his falling ill, Jeroboam sought help secretly from the God whom he had openly forsaken. It is an interesting point in the history of the kingdom of Israel, and one which most impressively teaches God's longsuffering, that in spite of the apostasy under Jeroboam, there were never wanting prophets to testify for Jehovah; and while the chief prophetic writers of a later age belong to Judah, those most distinguished for their actions, as Elijah and Elisha, prophesied in Israel. Thus Ahijah, the Shilonite, who had designated Jeroboam to the kingdom, was still at Shiloh, and to him the king's wife resorted in disguise with a present of bread and honey. The prophet was blind but God had warned him of her coming and given him a terrible answer for her. At the sound of her feet upon the threshold, Ahijah addressed her by name and recounting all the sins of Jeroboam, foretold the speedy extinction of his race and the coming captivity of Israel. The child was to die but as the reward of his piety, he alone of all his house should be buried in peace; the rest should be the food of dogs and vultures. The queen returned to Tirzah and the child expired as she crossed the threshold. He was buried and lamented by all Israel as their last hope amid the vices of the royal house and the calamitous defeat in the great battle with Judah. Not long after, Jeroboam died and was buried in the sepulchre of his fathers after a reign of twenty-two years. He was succeeded by his son Nadab (I Kings 14:1-20).

5. NADAB[1] (910-909 B.C.; I Kings 15:25-32), the second and last king of the dynasty of Jeroboam, succeeded his father in the second year of Asa, king of Judah, and reigned for parts of two years, imitating the sins of Jeroboam. The only recorded action of his reign is the siege of Gibbethon, a city in the territory of Dan, which having been abandoned by the Levites to whom it belonged when they were driven out by Jeroboam, had been occupied by the Philistines. Its possession was eagerly contested by the kings of Israel, who besieged it again and again (I Kings 16:15-17). Nadab

---

1. The name is identical with that of Aaron's eldest son.

here fell the victim to a military conspiracy under Baasha, his captain of the host, who killed the king and all the house of Jeroboam and so fulfilled the prophecy of Ahijah (I Kings 15:25-30).

6. With the extinction of the first dynasty, the crown of Israel passed from the tribe of Ephraim to that of Issachar, but the second dynasty also lasted for only two generations. BAASHA, the son of Ahijah, became the third king of Israel in the third year of Asa, king of Judah, and reigned at Tirzah four-and-twenty years (909-886 B.C.; I Kings 15:33, 16:7). From I Kings 16:2 it may be inferred that Baasha was of low extraction. His entire addiction to the sins of Jeroboam brought upon his house the same fate as theirs, which was denounced upon him by the prophet Jehu, son of Hanani (I Kings 16:1-7). His whole efforts seem to have been devoted to the war with Judah. In the thirteenth year of his reign (the fifteenth of Asa),[1] alarmed by the defection of the worshipers of Jehovah to the pious king of Judah, he attempted to blockade the frontier by fortifying Ramah; but Asa called in the help of Benhadad I, the Syrian king of Damascus, who invaded the north of Israel and took Ijon, Dan, Abel-maim, and the store-cities of Naphtali (I Kings 15:19-20; II Chron. 16:3). This diversion recalled Baasha from Judah, against which he seems to have made no more serious attempts. He died and was buried at Tirzah in the twenty-sixth year of Asa, leaving the kingdom to his son ELAH, the fourth king of Israel, who reigned for only parts of two years (886-885 B.C.) and was then killed at Tirzah in a state of intoxication by Zimri, the commander of half his force of chariots. With him perished all the house of Baasha, who were massacred by Zimri as Jehu had foretold (I Kings 16:8-14).

7. ZIMRI (885 B.C.; I Kings 16:8-20), the fifth king of Israel, enjoyed his usurpation at Tirzah only seven days. The whole military array of Israel were now engaged in the siege of Gibbethon and having elected Omri, the captain of the host, as king, they marched to besiege Tirzah. The walls were soon taken and Zimri shut himself up in the palace which he burned over his head. Another competitor for the crown appeared in the person of TIBNI, son of Ginath, who was followed by half the people. He was defeated and killed after a civil war of four years, from the twenty-seventh to the thirty-first of Asa (885-881 B.C.; I Kings 16:15-22).

---

1. II Chron. 16:1. The thirty-six years of this passage are evidently dated from the disruption of the kingdoms: "In the thirty-sixth year (Asa being king)."

OMRI (885-874 B.C.; I Kings 16:23-28) was the sixth king of Israel and the founder of the fourth dynasty which lasted for three generations and four kings. His father's name and tribe are unknown. The twelve years of his reign are probably to be dated from the death of Elah, as his full recognition is placed in the thirty-first year of Asa and the accession of his son Ahab in the thirty-eighth of Asa (874 B.C.), so that his six years' reign at Tirzah would include the civil war (I Kings 16:23,29). He abandoned that residence which (besides that the palace was burned) had proved indefensible in a siege and built the new and long-famous capital of SAMARIA, which remained the seat of government to the end of the kingdom. The dynasty which he founded surpassed all that had gone before in wickedness, to that "the statues of Omri" became a by-word for a course opposed to the law of Jehovah (Micah 6:16). Of the particular events of Omri's reign, we are only able to infer from a subsequent allusion, that the Syrian king of Damascus, Benhadad I, continued the war with Israel and forced his own terms on Omri, who consented to receive a resident envoy in his new capital of Samaria (I Kings 20:34). Israel was fast losing the power of an independent state but the kingdom was still adorned with much wealth and luxury when Omri left it to his son AHAB, in the thirty-eighth year of Asa, king of Judah.

8. ASA (911-870 B.C.; I Kings 15:9-24; II Chron. 14, 15, 16), the third king of Judah, succeeded his father Abijah in the twentieth year of Jeroboam I, king of Israel, and reigned for the long period of forty-one years. His name, which signifies *curing* or *physician*, was significant of his work. Himself a worthy son of David and having "his heart perfect with Jehovah all his days," he reformed the religious and moral abuses of the three preceding reigns. He put down the unnatural vices which had grown up under Rehoboam and destroyed the idols. Even his mother Maacah was deposed from the rank of "queen-mother" — which was reckoned a great dignity in the East (Comp. I Kings 2:19; II Kings 24:12; Jer. 29:2) — because she had set up an *Asherah,* that is, an image of the Canaanite goddess Asherah, who was associated with Baal. Asa cut down and burned her *Asherah,* and strewed its ashes on the brook Kidron just as Moses had treated the golden calf. Still, however, the old hill-sanctuaries were retained as places of worship. They were in later years partially suppressed by Jehoshaphat and again long after by the zeal of Josiah (I Kings 17:6; II Kings 12:8,13). Asa repaired Shishak's

plunder of the temple by rich offerings of gold and silver, in addition to those dedicated by his father, probably in the early part of his reign but since transferred to the heathen shrines. It is indeed curious to observe how soon the treasures of which the Temple was repeatedly stripped — by Shishak, by Asa himself at a later time, and by other kings — were again supplied. The commerce established by Solomon with Arabia and the East and with the silver-producing regions of Western Europe must have continued to flourish. The great victory of Abijah over Jeroboam secured peace to Judah for the first ten years of Asa's reign and he used it in building new fortifications to his cities.[1] He raised an army of 580,000 men, of whom 300,000 were men of Judah, armed with spear and shield, and 280,000 Benjamite archers (II Chron. 14:1-8). This military preparation was probably connected with an attempt to throw off the tributary yoke which Shishak had imposed upon Rehoboam, and it brought upon Asa the whole force of the Egyptian monarchy. At least it is probable that "Zerah, the Cushite" (or Ethiopian) was a king of Egypt (II Chron. 14:9).[2] He invaded Judah at the head of a million of men but Asa encountered him at Mareshah in the southwest of Judah, and after a fervent prayer to God, he routed the Ethiopian host and pursued them to Gerar. He returned to Jerusalem with the spoil of the cities round Gerar and with innumerable sheep and cattle (II Chron. 14:9-15). A solemn appeal was made by God to king and people, while their hearts were still warm with the victory. The prophet AZARIAH, son of Oded (II Chron. 15:1), met Asa on his return and exhorted him and his subjects to be strong, heart and hand, in seeking God. He gave an affecting description of the former state of Israel: "For a long season Israel hath been (or was) without the true God and without a teaching priest, and without law." His words roused the hearers to a new and more thorough reformation. The idols were removed from all the cities of Judah and Benjamin and those which had been won from Ephraim. The altar of burnt-offering, which had probably been polluted, was renewed and Asa called a great convocation at Jerusalem in the third month of the fifteenth year of his reign (896 B.C.). It was attended not only by all Judah and Benjamin, but by many of Ephraim, Manasseh and other tribes, and a covenant was made with solemn oaths and joyful shouts and music to serve God with all their hearts and to punish all idolatry

---

1. At the beginning, however, of his reign, Asa seems to have taken from Jeroboam some cities of Mount Ephraim. See II Chron. 15:8; 17:2.

2. Some scholars identify Zerah with one of the several Egyptian kings named Osarkon of the 22nd dynasty. Soldiers of this dynasty were in a great measure Ethiopian (II Chron. 12:3).

with death (II Chron. 15). This general defection to Asa of the
worshipers of Jehovah throughout the kingdom of Israel must
have added great strength, especially moral strength, to Judah. It
alarmed Baasha, the king of Israel, who renewed the war with all
his forces and, as we have seen, fortified Ramah as a sort of
blockading station on the frontier of Judah to prevent his subjects
from going over to Asa. It was then that the good king of Judah
committed the one great error of his life. He not only resorted to
the heathen king of Damascus, Benhadad I, but he took the
treasures of the house of God to purchase his alliance.
Benhadad's invasion of Northern Israel recalled Baasha from
Ramah and the stones and timber which he had collected were
carried away by Asa to build the frontier forts of Geba (the *hill*)
and Mizpeh (the *watch-tower*) in Benjamin. The great well of
Mizpeh was still remembered as Asa's work in the time of
Jeremiah (II Chron. 16:1-6; I Kings 15:16-22; Jer. 41:9).

Asa's want of faith was reproved by the seer HANANI, the father
of that Jehu who prophesied both to Baasha and Jehoshaphat. He
told Asa that he had lost the honor of conquering Benhadad by
seeking his alliance and denounced against him constant war for
the rest of his days. It is a sign of the growing loss of reverence for
the supreme authority of Jehovah, that even in Judah the
discharge of a prophet's office had now come to involve danger to
his person. Hanani was imprisoned by Asa in his rage and others
of the people were oppressed for the same cause. The king's
conduct is to be ascribed partly to unbroken prosperity and partly
to the irritation of disease, for in his last years he suffered from
the gout. The censure cast on him for "seeking not to Jehovah,
but to the physicians," is founded on the principle on which the
whole retributive system of the Mosaic law is based, that every
form of temporal suffering was to be viewed as a chastisement
from God, and to be met first by humiliation and prayer to Him,
who would then permit the physician or any other secondary
agent to do his office with such success as it might be His will to
grant. Asa sank under the disease in the forty-first year of his
reign, having been contemporary with all the first seven kings of
Israel. His body was laid in a bed of spices (Comp. John 19:39,40)
in a sepulchre he had prepared for himself in the city of David,
and precious odors were burned for him in great abundance as
was the custom at the funerals of worthy kings (I Kings 15:23,24;
II Chron. 16:7-14; Comp. II Chron. 21:19; Jer. 34).

9. AHAB (874-853 B.C.; I Kings 16:29, 22:40), the seventh king

of Israel and the second of the dynasty of Omri, succeeded his father in the thirty-eighth year of Asa and reigned twenty-two years at Samaria. His name has attained an evil eminence in the world's history. He stands forth an example of the lengths of wickedness to which a weak selfishness may be driven by the influence of a stronger will. His fate was decided by his marriage with JEZEBEL, a name even more infamous than his own, the daughter of Ethbaal, king of the Sidonians. The very name of this prince (the *Man of Baal*) suggests the consequences of the alliance. In place of the worship of Jeroboam's calves, which monstrous idols as they were, yet professed to be symbols of Jehovah, the service of Baal was established throughout Israel. Ahab built him a temple and an altar at Samaria and made him a grove for the impure orgies of Ashtoreth. There was a great college of his priests or prophets, who numbered 450, besides 400 prophets of the groves, and all these were maintained at Jezebel's table. By her orders, the prophets of Jehovah were put to death, except a hundred, who were hid and fed in a cave by Obadiah, the governor of Ahab's house; for even at his court there was at least one servant of Jehovah, as there were Christians in Nero's household. The influence of the court and the force of persecution completed the apostasy of the people, so that it was an unexpected consolation for the great prophet of the age to be assured that Jehovah had 7000 left in Israel, whose knees had not bowed to Baal and their lips not kissed him (II Kings 16:28-33; 18:3,4,13,19; 19:18).

Among the events of Ahab's reign, the sacred historian specially records the rebuilding of Jericho by Hiel the Bethelite in such a manner as to show that the curse foretold by Joshua was fulfilled: "He laid the foundation thereof in Abiram his first-born, and set up the gates thereof in his youngest son Segub" (I Kings 16:34; Comp. Josh. 6:26).

This darkest night of Israel's spiritual declension was broken by the appearance of the greatest of all the prophets since Moses, and the type of that great preacher of repentance (John the Baptist) who was the forerunner of the Christ (Matt. 11:14).

ELIJAH THE TISHBITE has been well called "the grandest and the most romantic character that Israel ever produced." He meets us with a suddenness as startling as the first appearance of John the Baptist preaching repentance in the wilderness of Judaea. There is not a word of his parentage and of his birthplace we only know that it was at a village called Tishbeh, a little west of Mahanaim in

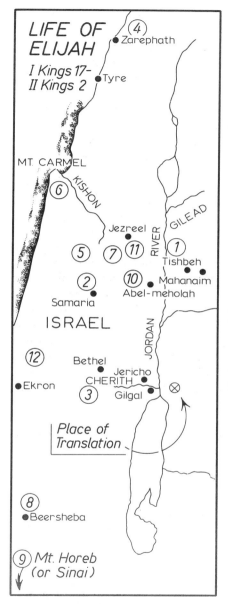

Life of Elijah

1. *Tishbeh* in Gilead (I Kings 17:1).
2. *Samaria.* Predicts drought (I K. 17:1).
3. *Cherith.* Fed by ravens (I K. 17:2-7).
4. *Zarephath.* At widow's house (I K. 17:8-24).
5. Somewhere in *Israel.* Meets Obadiah and Ahab (I K. 18:1-18).
6. *Mt. Carmel.* Fire on altar (I K. 18:19-45).
7. *Jezreel.* Flees from Jezebel (I K. 18:45; 19:1-2).
8. *Beersheba.* Fed by angel (I K. 19:3-7).
9. *Mt. Horeb.* Still small voice speaks (I K. 19:8-18).
10. *Abel-meholah.* Elisha called (I K. 19:19-21).
11. *Jezreel.* Ahab denounced in Naboth's vineyard (I K. 21:17-29).
12. Somewhere in *Israel.* Meets Ahaziah's messengers going to Ekron (II K. 1:1-16).
13. *Gilgal to Bethel to Jericho to Jordan.* Route of trip to Elijah's translation (II K. 2:1-12).

the land of Gilead east of Jordan. But this one fact accounts for the prophet's outward peculiarities. Like Jephthah among the judges, he came of a wild, uncultured, pastoral race, whose mode of life had become more and more assimilated to that of the Bedouins of the neighboring desert, and who retained great force of character and power of physical endurance. His only clothing was a girdle of skin round his loins, and the "mantle" or cape of sheepskin, the descent of which upon Elisha has passed into a proverb. Sheltered from Jezebel's persecution in the solitudes of Mount Gilead, he had been prepared by Jehovah for his mission to the apostate king and people.

It was probably about the tenth year of Ahab's reign that Elijah suddenly appeared before the king to declare as the word of Jehovah, confirmed by an awful oath, that there should be no rain in the land for three years but at his word (I Kings 17:1). From the New Testament we learn that the prophet was more than a mere messenger of the judgment. "He *prayed earnestly* that it might not rain: and it rained not on the land by the space of three years and six months. And *he prayed again,* and the heaven gave rain, and the earth brought forth her fruit" (James 5:17-18). This passage, introduced to show the power with God exerted by "men affected like ourselves," may help to guard us against too mechanical a view of the prophet's functions. In his agonizing prayer upon Mount Carmel, at the close of the drought, we see how his own desire went forth to meet the will of God; and though the history is silent as to all that preceded his message to Ahab, the words of James justify the supposition of a like scene when the prophet, brooding over the state of Israel, as we see him at a later period, and preparing to stand forth as the champion for God (like Luther in his cell) put up fervent prayers for the sign that might attest his mission. Like Luther again, he was saved from the immediate risk at which he discharged his mission by the command of God to hide himself by the brook Cherith (possibly the *Wady Kelt,* which flows from the west through a deep chasm into the Jordan about five miles north of the Dead Sea.)[1] The history leaves the court to follow the prophet, but it has been supposed that Jezebel's slaughter of the prophets was in revenge for the denunciation of Elijah. He remained in his hiding-place, fed by the ravens morning and evening with bread and meat, till the brook dried up and he had to seek another refuge (I Kings

1. McGarvey, *Lands of the Bible* 234, 483-484. Compare Nelson Glueck, *The River Jordan* (1968) pp. 138-142.

17:1-7). The word of Jehovah sent him, as our Lord Jesus emphatically declares, not to any of the secret worshipers of God in Israel nor to any city of Judah; but the honor of nourishing God's prophet was granted to a woman, a poor widow of the heathen city of Zarephath in the territory of Sidon (I Kings 17:8-9; Luke 4:25-26). Elijah went thither and found at the city gate a poor woman gathering a few sticks to bake a cake made of her last handful of meal and her last drop of oil, that she and her only son might share it and then die. We need not repeat the familiar story of the faith with which she consented to sustain Elijah, the miraculous replenishing of the barrel of meal and the cruse of oil, as long as the famine lasted, and the restoration of the widow's son to life at the prophet's prayer (I Kings 17:8-24).

In the third year, Elijah was bidden to leave his concealment and show himself to Ahab. The droubht had now become so disastrous that the greatest exertions were needed to find grass enough to save the lives of the king's horses and cattle. Ahab undertook the search in person, taking one way himself and sending his chief officer, Obadiah, by another. The latter, who has been mentioned as a zealous worshiper of Jehovah, was encountered by Elijah and reluctantly undertook the risk of announcing to Ahab the prophet's reappearance. The king met Elijah with the threatening question, "Art thou he that troubleth Israel?" — and the prophet retorted the charge upon himself for his apostasy and idolatry. He then challenged the king to a decisive trial between Baal and Jehovah and a scene ensued upon Mount Carmel which has no parallel in the history of the world. On the one side were Baal's prophets to the number of 450, supported by the court and followed by the people, for neither the few secret worshipers of Jehovah, nor the many whom His judgments had rendered dissatisfied with their idolatry, dared to show sympathy with the prophet. Elijah stood alone but God was with him. His challenge is all the bolder, considering the juggling tricks with which the heathen priests were familiar and which the king would be ready to abet. But it is on the side of Elijah that we find precautions taken against such tricks and taken by his own desire. He proposed a test of the simplest kind: that each party should prepare a bullock and wood and pray to their respective gods to send down fire upon the sacrifice, "And the god that answereth by fire, let him be God." All the people assented to so fair a trial. Elijah gave Baal's prophets the choice between the victim and the first trial. At early morn they prepared the sacrifice and the air resounded till high noon with their wild chorus, growing more and more excited, "O Baal, hear us! Baal, hear us! Hear us!" The stillness of the summer noon was unbroken by an answer and they leaped on their altar with frantic gesticulations. As the sun bent over the meridian, Elijah assailed both priests and god with that irony which the prophets often levelled at idolatry: "Cry aloud! for he is a god! He is only musing in his own thoughts! Or he has gone hunting, or upon a journey. Or perhaps he is asleep and must be awakened!" The priests renewed their cries, as if they half believed the last taunt, and cut their flesh with knives according to their custom, till their blood streamed down. But there was not a sign that their god so much as noticed them. And now the declining sun had reached the sacred hour of the evening sacrifice and the exhausted priests ceased their "vain repetitions" (Matt. 6:7). With the utmost deliberation Elijah repaired the broken altar of Jehovah and replaced the twelve unhewn stones that had formed it, for Carmel was a spot sure to have been a sanctuary though the fact is not previously recorded. Having made a trench round the altar and laid the bullock in pieces upon the wood, he for the first time commands the assistance of the people to exclude all possibility of fraud. Thrice they poured water over the victim, the wood and the altar, till the trench was full so that no fire could possibly be concealed. At the very moment of the evening sacrifice, Elijah invoked the God of the fathers to show His divinity, and to turn back the people's hearts; and the fire came down from heaven in sight of all the people consuming not only the sacrifice and the wood but the very stones and dust of the altar and licking up the water in the trench. All the people fell upon their face crying out, "JEHOVAH, HE IS THE GOD! JEHOVAH, HE IS THE GOD!" Their new-awakened zeal was at once turned by Elijah against the idolaters. "Take the prophets of Baal!" he exclaimed — "let not one of them escape!" He was obeyed and they were slain to a man on the bank of the river Kishon, a sacrifice to Baal in place of their vain offering. It must not be forgotten that these priests of Baal were, for the most part at least, apostate Israelites who had brought themselves under the penalties of the law against idolatry (Deut. 13:6ff).

Ahab, who seems to have been a passive spectator of the scene, now yields himself to the direction of the prophet, who assures him that he hears the sound of abundant rain and retires to his tent to eat and drink, while Kishon runs red with the blood of his priests. As he is thus engaged, Elijah withdraws to the summit of Carmel and sits with his head bowed down between his knees, while his servant looks out over the sea for the first sign of rain in the west. Six times the lad reports that the sky is clear and the prophet bids him look again, but at the seventh he brought back the message, which has ever since passed into a proverb: "Behold there ariseth a little cloud out of the sea, like a man's hand." At this sign the prophet sent the king word to prepare his chariot. The heaven grew black with clouds and amid the cataracts of a rain-storm in that climate, Elijah ran before the king's chariot to the gates of Jezreel, a distance of sixteen miles (I Kings 18).

The fierce spirit of Jezebel remained unsubdued and her threats drove Elijah again to flee for his life. He traversed all Israel and Judah to Beersheba and there he left his servant, while he himself went forward under the impulse of the same Spirit which long after drove Christ into the wilderness. After one day's journey, he was overcome by fatigue and despair and he sat down under a juniper-tree and prayed for death. His words betray that deep consciousness of individual weakness, to which the chosen servants of God have often yielded: "I am not better than my fathers." But an angel touched him and bade him arise and eat; he looked up and saw a fire with a cake of bread baked upon it and a cruse of water by his head, and in the strength of that food he passed 40 days and nights in the wilderness of Sinai. There, like Moses, he was favored with a vision of the glory of Jehovah. From that well-known scene of terrible convulsion, followed by an awful stillness, he learned the great lesson, that God's presence is to be felt, not so much in the grand displays of power which strike our senses as in the "still small voice" that speaks directly to the heart. He had seen the fire come down from heaven, heard the people confess their God and slain Baal's prophets and yet the work seemed all to be done again, but now he learned that the quiet power of God's spirit was working in the people's hearts and there were 7000 men who had not done homage to Baal. Thus reanimated for his remaining work, he was sent to prepare for three great changes affecting the state of Israel: to anoint Hazael as the future king of Syria in place of Benhadad; Jehu, the son of Nimshi, as king of Israel in place of Ahab's house; and Elisha, the son of Shaphat, to be prophet in succession to himself. These three were to follow each other in the destruction of the worshipers of Baal. Elijah only performed in person the last of the three acts, the designation of Elisha, leaving to him the other two, which he himself apparently found no opportunity to execute.

ELISHA's native place was at Abel-meholah (the *meadow of the dance*), a place in the valley of the Jordan near its junction with the plain of Jezreel (Judges 7:22; I Kings 4:12). He was plowing with twelve yoke of oxen, himself guiding the twelfth, a proof of the wealth he abandoned to "put his hand to the plow" of Jehovah, when Elijah arrived on his way up the valley toward Damascus, and without saying a word, cast his prophet's mantle upon Elisha as if claiming him for a son (Comp. Ruth 3:4-14). Elisha, with a heart prepared by God, only begged to give his father and mother a parting embrace and Elijah consented in words implying a keen feeling of Elisha's separation from the ties of affection. Elisha celebrated the sacrifice of himself by offering the yoke of oxen with which he had been plowing, the flesh of which he boiled with the wood of the yoke and the plow and made a parting feast for the people of the village. He then followed Elijah and became "his servant," for such was the relation between a prophet and his nearest comrade, as afterward in the case of Elisha and Gehazi. It was, indeed, an honor which the first minister of the greatest king might have coveted, to be known as "Elisha, the son of Shaphat, who poured water on the hands of Elijah." These events comprise the first period of Elijah's course. He disappears from the scene for a considerable time (I Kings 19).

10.   The last years of Ahab's reign were chiefly occupied by two great wars with Syria. Benhadad, king of Syria, had treated him as a vassal and the king of Israel had complied with his demands; but when Ahab was required to give up his wives and children, he saw that it was but a pretext for a final quarrel. He refused with spirit and it is to the mouth of this infamous king that we owe the noble proverb, "Let not him that girdeth on boast himself as he that putteth off" (I Kings 20:11). The king of Damascus received the message as he was carousing with the thirty-two confederate kings, who had followed him to the siege of Samaria, and he bade them set their immense forces in array against the city and returned to his cups secure of an easy victory. At this juncture a prophet came to tell Ahab that God had delivered these hosts into his hand. His little army of 7000 men went out of the city, preceded oy the 232 young princes of the tribes; and Benhadad, who was drinking in his tent at the noontide banquet with a contemptuous indifference as to whether they came out for a sally

or a surrender, ordered them to be taken alive. But each of the princes killed the man who laid hands upon him, their followers rushed to the attack, the panic-stricken Syrians were pursued with great slaughter, Benhadad hardly escaping on his horse. The same prophet warned Ahab to expect a new attack the following year. Benhadad's servants persuaded him to fight in the low country, as the gods of Israel were gods of the hills; but they added the good advice to replace the confederate kings by chosen captains. So the Syrians offered battle at Aphek, a walled city about five miles east of the Sea of Galilee, which they had taken from Israel. (Other battles with Syria were later fought there [II Kings 13:17].) Ahab divided the whole force of Israel into two bodies, which looked like two flocks of kids in presence of the vast armies of Syria, but a prophet announced to him that Jehovah would prove himself the God of the valleys as well as of the hills. After watching each other for seven days, the armies joined battle; the Syrians were routed with a slaughter of 100,000 men and 27,000 more were crushed by the fall (perhaps in an earthquake) of the wall of Aphek in which they had taken refuge. Benhadad now resolved to throw himself on the mercy of Ahab, whose impulsive nature was shown in a generosity which proved fatal to himself. Instead of seizing the opportunity to regain the frontier of Solomon on the northeast and to restore the kingdom of Israel in the fear of God, he was content with Benhadad's promise to give back the towns taken from Omri earlier and to receive a resident envoy in Damascus (I Kings 20:22-34). For the fourth time in this war, a prophet was sent to Ahab, and after obtaining the king's judgment against himself by the ingenious preparation of a supposed case, he told the king that God would take his life in place of the life of Benhadad. So Ahab returned to Samaria in displeasure (I Kings 20:35-43). See chart on p. 575.

11. Three years elapsed before war broke out again with Syria (I Kings 22:1). Elijah the prophet had not been seen for a long time at the palace of Samaria. The king of Israel, who no doubt supposed that he had got rid of his great "troubler," seized the opportunity to perpetrate a deed of enormous wickedness.

Ahab's capital was at Samaria but he had a favorite residence at the beautiful city of Jezreel, where we have already seen him. His regal lust of improving his fair domain was checked by a vineyard, the property of a man of Jezreel named Naboth, who clung like a true Israelite to his patrimony, though the king offered him its price in money or a better vineyard (I Kings 21:1-3; Comp. Lev.

25:23; Num. 36:7; Ezek. 46:18). With the petulance of a despot crossed in his will, Ahab took to his bed and refused to eat, but he was roused by Jezebel from despondency so unworthy of a king who had power to make law for himself. So abject was the degradation of the people, so shameless the tyranny of the crown, that the elders of Israel at once obeyed the written orders of Jezebel to proclaim a fast and, in the name of religion and loyalty, to put their fellow-citizen to death on the evidence of witnesses of their own suborning. Naboth was dragged out of the city and stoned as a blasphemer against God and the king, and at the call of Jezebel Ahab arose to take possession of the vineyard. But God sent Elijah to meet him there and the king's conscience betrayed itself in the cry, "Hast thou found me, oh mine enemy?" "I have found thee," answered the prophet and went on to mark the scene of this last crime as that of God's judgment for all his sins, "In the place where the dogs licked the blood of Naboth, shall dogs lick thy blood, even thine." Jezebel's fate was to be still more terrible; the dogs would eat her under the walls of Jezreel and the whole house of Ahab should be exterminated and their flesh given to the dogs and vultures (I Kings 21; Comp. II Kings 9:7, 26, 36, 37).[1] This was Elijah's last mission to Ahab and he does not appear again till the next reign. For once Ahab repented and humbled himself with fasting and sackcloth and God postponed the full execution of the sentence till after his death.

12. The peace with Syria lasted for three years (I Kings 22:1-3), but it does not appear that Benhadad restored the cities as he had promised. At length Ahab seized the opportunity of a visit from his ally, Jehoshaphat, king of Judah, whom he entertained sumptuously (II Chron. 18:2), to propose a joint expedition for the recovery of Ramoth-gilead. The pious king of Judah proposed to consult the word of Jehovah and Ahab tried to satisfy him by summoning his own 400 prophets, men who seem to have been trained as prophets of Jehovah and to have spoken His name, while prostituting their office to the king's pleasure.[2] With one voice they promised Ahab the victory in the name of Jehovah. Still Jehoshaphat asked if there were no more prophets of Jehovah and Ahab remembered a certain MICHAIAH, the son of Imlah, whom, however, he hated, as he was always a prophet of evil. He sent for him, apparently out of prison, and Micaiah went, declaring that he must speak the word which Jehovah should put

---

1. It is well worthy of notice that Jehu, the anointed avenger, was in the train of Ahab when he went to take possession of Naboth's vineyard (II Kings 9:25).

2. They can hardly be viewed as prophets of Baal, whose worship does not seem to have been publicly restored after its overthrow by Elijah.

into his mouth. He found the two kings upon their thrones in their robes of state and all the prophets before them, one of whom, Zedekiah, the son of Chenaanah, had placed horns of iron on his head, to show how Ahab should push the Syrians to destruction. Whether through fear or in irony, Micaiah at first chimed in with them; but adjured by Ahab to tell the truth, he foretold the king's death by likening Israel to a flock without a shepherd, and in the form of a vision like that at the opening of the Book of Job, he denounced the other prophets as possessed by a lying spirit sent by God to deceive Ahab. Upon this Zedekiah struck and taunted him, and the king sent him back to the dungeon while Micaiah warned both of their coming fate and called the people to witness his words (I Kings 22:1-28; II Chron. 18:1-27). The words of Micaiah induced Ahab to disguise himself in the ensuing battle at Ramoth-gilead, while Jehoshaphat wore his royal robes. Benhadad had commanded his chariots to direct all their force against the king, and Jehoshaphat was so hard pressed that he only escaped by crying out that he was not Ahab. In spite of his precautions, Ahab was mortally wounded by a chance shot from a bow. He was supported in his chariot, while the battle raged, till sunset and then he died. At his fall the cry went through the host, "Every man to his city and to his country." His body was brought to Samaria and there buried, but not till the words spoken by Elijah at Naboth's vineyard were fulfilled, for as his chariot was washed out at the pool of Samaria, the dogs licked up his blood. He was succeeded by his son Ahaziah (I Kings 22:29-40; II Chron. 19:28-34).

13. Following the order of the sacred narrative in I Kings 22, we go back to the start of the reign of JEHOSHAPHAT, king of Judah (872-848 B.C.; I Kings 22:41-50; II Chron. 17-20).

JEHOSHAPHAT, the fourth king of Judah, was the son of Asa and Azubah. At the age of thirty-five he succeeded his father in the fourth year of Ahab, king of Israel, and reigned at Jerusalem twenty-five years. He followed his father's piety and possessed an energy which makes him the most like David of all the other kings of Judah. He raised the kingdom to the highest point that it had reached since the disruption, but his unhappy alliance with Ahab went far to neutralize all his excellences and brought ruin upon his successors. He was contemporary with Ahab and his two sons, Ahaziah and Jehoram.

Jehoshaphat began his reign by fortifying the cities of Judah and Benjamin, as well as those taken by his father in Mount

Ephraim, while he became rich by the presents which attested the confidence of his subjects, and Jehovah was with him (II Chron. 17:1-6). He carried on his father's reformation by removing the groves and high places, but this was only imperfectly accomplished, "for as yet the people had not prepared their hearts unto the God of their fathers" (I Kings 22:43; II Chron. 19:3, 20:33). In the third year of his reign, he gave a commission to his chief princes, in conjunction with certain Levites and priests, to teach the people and to read the book of the Law in all the cities of Judah. His piety was rewarded with prosperity. He had peace with all the surrounding nations. Even the Philistines paid him tribute and the Arabians brought the immense flocks of rams and goats which David had described in the 72nd Psalm. He continued to fortify and garrison the cities; at Jerusalem he had a band of captains like those of David and under their command was a greater army than had yet been raised (II Chron. 17:13-19). His power had become too great for the king of Israel to hope for success in a new war and the growing strength of the Syrian kingdom of Damascus may have prompted the alliance which was now formed between Jehoshaphat and Ahab. The ensuing battle for Ramoth-gilead has been described previously.

After this battle Jehoshaphat returned to Jerusalem unmolested. The severe lesson of Ramoth-gilead was enforced by the prophet Jehu, who met him on the way, upbraiding him for his alliance with those who hated God but praising him for his piety. The king addressed himself with renewed zeal to the work of reformation. He went in person through his kingdom from Beersheba to Mount Ephraim, reclaiming the people to the God of their fathers. He appointed judges in all the fortified cities and in Jerusalem he established a court of priests and Levites and heads of houses, for the final decision of all cases relating to the law of Jehovah. At the head of the latter he set the high-priest Amariah for all religious causes, and Zebadiah, son of Ishmael, the prince of Judah, for matters relating to the king. To both he gave a charge worthy of his name.[1] The judges throughout the land were reminded that they judged not for man but for God and in the fear of Jehovah, with whom "there is no *iniquity,* nor *respect of persons,* nor *taking of gifts";* and the supreme court was admonished to "deal courageously and Jehovah shall be with the good" (II Chron. 19).

Meanwhile the disaster of Ramoth-gilead encouraged the old

---

1. Jehoshaphat = Jehovah-shaphat, "Jehovah is judge" or "the judgment of Jehovah."

enemies on the eastern frontier. The Moabites, the Ammonites, with the people of Mount Seir and the tribes of the neighboring desert, threw off the yoke which they had borne since the time of David. We read of two campaigns, the first against Jehoshaphat by a league of all these tribes and the second against Jehoram, king of Israel, and Jehoshaphat as his ally by the king of Moab, who was the vassal of Israel, as Ammon and Edom were of Judah (II Chron. 20; II Kings 3;, Comp. I Kings 22:47).

When word was brought that the hordes of the enemy were at En-gedi, on the west side of the Dead Sea, Jehoshaphat proclaimed a fast through all the land, and in a congregation of all Judah with their wives and children before the Temple, he offered a prayer which is the echo of Solomon's, appealing to God not to let the heathen whom he had driven out before His people cast them out of His possession; for so, in the true spirit of the covenant, he calls their land. The answer was at once given in a most striking and unusual form. In the midst of the congregation, the Spirit of Jehovah fell upon JAHAZIEL, the son of Zechariah, a Levite of the family of Asaph; and he cried out to the king with all Judah and Jerusalem to go forth on the morrow to a victory without a battle; their part would be only to "stand, and see the salvation of Jehovah." The king bowed his face to the ground while the Levites raised a lofty song of thanksgiving. With renewed sons of praise, they marched forth in the morning toward the wilderness of Tekoa, where at that very time a strange scene of slaughter was enacting. Confused by the ambuscades they had set for the men of Judah, the different nations fell one upon the other. The people of Moab and Ammon, having first cut to pieces the inhabitants of Mount Seir, turned to mutual slaughter, and when the men of Judah approached and their scouts looked out from the watch-tower over the wilderness, the whole face of the ground was covered with dead bodies. No less than three days were occupied in gathering the spoil, which was more than they could carry away and on the fourth they assembled to renew their songs of praise in the valley which was thence called Berachah *(blessing);* and they continued them as they marched back to Jerusalem and up to the house of God, with Jehoshaphat in their van (II Chron. 20:1-28). This great deliverance struck terror into all the nations and secured peace to Judah for the rest of his reign. The campaign in which he aided Jehoram against Moab had a very similar issue (II Kings 3:24-25). He also joined Ahaziah in an attempt to renew the maritime enterprises of Solomon by way of the Red Sea, but the fleet was wrecked at Ezion-geber as a punishment for his alliance with Ahaziah, according to the word of the prophet ELIEZER, son of Dodavah of Mareshah, and Jehoshaphat refused Ahaziah's proposal to renew the attempt. He died and was buried with his fathers in the city of David (about 848 B.C.; I Kings 22:41-50; II Chron. 20:31, 21:1), leaving his kingdom to his unworthy son Jehoram, who had already been associated in the government the last three years of his father's life (see II Kings 1:17; 8:16). His name is preserved in the "valley of Jehoshaphat," the deep ravine between Jerusalem and the Mount of Olives, also called the Kidron Valley. But is seems more than doubtful whether the name is derived from him and is not rather an appellative, signifying the great judgment of which the scene is laid by the prophet Joel in the "Valley of the Judgment of Jehovah."

14. AHAZIAH, the eighth king of Israel, began to reign in the 17th year of Jehoshaphat and reigned two years in Samaria (853-852 B.C.; I Kings 22:51-53; II Kings 1). He was the son of Ahab and Jezebel and his character is emphatically described by the words, "he walked in the way of his father and of his mother," as well as in the way of Jeroboam. Besides worshiping Baal, he sent to consult Baal-zebub, the god of Ekron, when he was dangerously ill from a fall through a lattice of his palace (II Kings 1:2). This brings Elijah again upon the scene. He was sent by God to meet the king's messengers and to announce their master's death, because he had inquired of an idol, as if there were not a god in Israel. The prophet was not personally known to the messengers but from their description of him as "a hairy man, gift with a girdle of leather about the loins," Ahaziah at once identified Elijah the Tishbite, whose wild form and sharp words had been the terror of his father's court. He sent a captain of fifty with his band to seize the prophet. They found him sitting on the top of the hill (possibly Carmel), and the captain, seemingly in a mocking tone, called to him, "Thou man of God, the king hath said, Come down." "If I be a man of God," said Elijah, "let fire come down from heaven, and consume thee and thy fifty": and it was done (Luke 9:24). A second captain of fifty went and repeated the order in a more peremptory form, "Come down *quickly*," and he had the same fate. The third implored the mercy of Elijah, who at God's command went with him and repeated to the king himself what he had already said to his messengers. This was Elijah's last appearance to the house of Ahab. As he had

predicted, Ahaziah never rose again from his bed but died, leaving his kingdom to his brother Jehoram (II Kings 1:17). His commercial league with Jehoshaphat has already been mentioned.

It is at this point that the sacred narrative introduces one of the greatest events of the old dispensation, the ascent of Elijah. The chronology is difficult but the event seems to have taken place about the time of Ahaziah's death. The chief difficulty arises from the letter which Elijah sent to Jehoram, king of Judah, prophesying his destruction because he followed the sins of the house of Ahab. This, by the way, is the only point of connection between Elijah and the house of David and the only mention of his name in the *Chronicles* (II Chron. 21:12-15). Now Jehoshaphat, the father of Jehoram, took part in the campaign which is related after Elijah's ascension, and in which too Elisha appears as the prophet. That Elisha ever left his attendance upon Elijah to act in public, before he received the prophet's mantle, is a supposition quite unwarranted by the history. That the letter of Elijah to Jehoram was written before but delivered after his ascension is an extreme assumption. The true and simple explanation is that Jehoram began to reign over Judah some years before his father's death, as we noted on p. 600. There is therefore no reason to depart from the order of the narrative in *Kings*.

When the time had come that God had appointed to "take up Elijah into heaven by a whirlwind," the prophet was with Elisha at Gilgal.[1] We know not what intimation he had received of the manner of his departure; but this much is clear, that he desired to end his life, as he had passed its greater portion, in solitude with God. But his devoted servant had also been forewarned of his loss and persisted in following him to Bethel (II Kings 2:2-3). There the sons of the prophets meet Elisha with the words, "Knowest thou that Jehovah will take away thy master from thy head to-day?" and he answers, "*I do know it:* hold ye your peace." The same scene is repeated at Jericho, where Elijah again fruitlessly asks Elisha to stay behind. They went on to Jordan while fifty of the sons of the prophets came out to gaze after them across the plain. Arriving at the river's edge, Elijah rolled up his sheepskin mantle and smote the water, which parted, as long ago before the ark and they walked through on dry ground. At the moment of

1. Probably not the famous place near Jordan, but one of the same name on the western edge of Mount Ephraim, fifteen miles north of Lydda.

passing the river, they exchanged their last words. Elisha desired to name a parting gift, asks that a double portion of Elijah's spirit may rest upon him, that is, that he may not only succeed to the prophetic office, but be made the true heir of the power to work miracles and turn the hearts of Israel to their forsaken God.[1] "Thou hast asked a hard (or bold) thing," said Elijah; "if thou see me taken from thee, it shall be so unto thee; but if not, it shall not be so." They were still talking as they walked forward, when Elisha found himself separated from his master by a chariot and horses of fire; and Elijah was borne up on the wings of the storm to the vault of heaven. Elisha saw him before he vanished in the sky, and rending his clothes uttered the bitter outcry of a bereaved son, "My father! my father! The chariot of Israel, and the horsemen thereof!" He saw the meaning of the chariot sent to convey him who had been the true strength of Israel against her own kings, who trusted in forbidden chariots and horses. He saw too that his last prayer to his master was granted: he took up the mantle which Elijah had let fall, and at once put his power to the proof by again dividing the waters of Jordan on his return to Jericho, where the prophets, who had remained watching, welcomed him as the successor of Elijah. The prophets sent fifty active men in search of Elijah, thinking that God might have carried him away to some lonely mountain, though Elisha warned them that it would be in vain; and his word was confirmed by the return of the messengers after three days. Elisha's stay at Jericho was marked by a miracle, which the local tradition commemorates to the present day, the cure of the bitter water of one of the two springs that rise at the foot of the hill east of the town by casting into it a new cruse of salt. Thence he returned by the way he had followed with Elijah to Bethel, and at this seat of the calf-worship of Jeroboam, he received an insult which is thus related by one familiar with the spot. The road to the town winds up the defile of the *Wady Suweinit* under the hill which still bears that in all probability are the ruins of Ai, and which even now, retaining some trees, was at that date shaded by a thick forest, the haunt of savage animals. To this place the young lads of the town came forth as Elisha was going forth by the way. Then they scoff at Elisha as he walks by, "Go up, thou baldhead; go up, thou baldhead." To call one a "baldhead" was an epithet of contempt, sometimes applied even to persons who were not naturally bald.

---

1. This seems to be the true meaning, according to the analogy of the ancient law of inheritance (Deut. 21:17).

For once Elisha assumed the sternness of his master. "He turned back, and looked on them, and cursed them in the name of Jehovah, and there came forth two she-bears out of the wood, and tore forty-and-two children of them" (II Kings 2:23-24). It is not said that they were killed; the bears clawed them. There is nothing to show that these "children" were too young to be responsible for their wantonness, which was probably meant to try whether the new prophet might be more safely insulted than his predecessor. From Bethel, Elisha returned to Carmel and thence he went to dwell at Samaria (II Kings 2:25), being fully recognized as the new prophet.

15. JEHORAM (abbreviated JORAM), the ninth king of Israel, was the son of Ahab and Jezebel and the successor of his brother Ahaziah (852-841 B.C.; II Kings 1:17, 9:26). His accession is marked by a twofold date — in the eighteenth year of Jehoshaphat, king of Judah, and the second year of Jehoram, the son of Jehoshaphat, that is, the second year of Jehoram's association with his father in the kingdom.[1] He reigned twelve years at Samaria. He maintained a close alliance with Judah and it was perhaps by the influence of Jehoshaphat that he was a shade better than his father and his brother. He removed Ahab's image of Baal but he still maintained the idolatries of Jeroboam (II Kings 3:2-3). The ministry of Elisha was very prominent during the reign of Jehoram.

The defeat of Ahab at Ramoth and the consequent dominion of the Syrians in the country east of Jordan had encouraged Mesha, the king of Moab, to revolt from Israel and to refuse his annual tribute of 100,000 lambs and 100,000 rams. Ahaziah's illness had prevented him from taking the field but Jehoram applied for help to Jehoshaphat, through whose territory it was now necessary to march to reach Moab on the east, by way of the wilderness of Edom. The king of Edom, the vassal of Judah, joined the expedition. After a seven days' march through the desert, the armies were without water. The pious Jehoshaphat longed to consult a prophet of Jehovah and it was found that Elisha, the son of Shaphat, "which poured water on the hands of Elijah," was in the camp of Israel. It was only after sternly bidding Jehoram to resort to the prophets of his father and mother that Elisha consented, for the sake of Jehoshaphat, to give an answer.

---

1. The occurrence of the same names (as again *Ahaziah*) marks the connection of the two families and the influence of Jehoshaphat is probably to be traced in the choice of such a name as Jehoram (*Exalted by Jehovah or Jehovah is exalted*). May it not be that the birth of Jehoram and the alliance of Ahab with Jehoshaphat, took place about the time of Elijah's victory over the prophets of Baal?

He called for a minstrel and as he played the Spirit of Jehovah came upon the prophet. Bidding them dig trenches all over the plain, he promised that God would give them not only water but a complete victory over Moab. In the night the trenches were dug and at the time of the morning sacrifice water flowed into them from the hills of Edom, so that the whole plain looked like a lake. As the Moabites advanced to meet the enemy, the red rays of the rising sun reflected from the water, threw a hue of blood on the whole plain. They remembered the recent slaughter which they had shared with the Ammonites and Edomites and thought that the allied armies had been destroyed by a like panic and raised the cry, "Now, therefore, Moab, to the spoil!" Rushing in disorder upon the camp, they were met by the whole army and were pursued into their own country with immense slaughter. The victory was followed up by an exterminating war. The cities of Moab were razed and their stones thrown into the corn-fields; the wells were filled and the fruit-trees were cut down. The only refuge left was the city of Kir-haraseth and even this was on the point of being taken by storm, when the king of Moab, with 700 chosen warriors, tried to cut his way through to reach the king of Edom, but he was driven back into the city. He resorted to the forlorn hope of his horrid superstition. Mounting the wall in sight of the besiegers, he offered his eldest son and heir as a burnt-offering to Moloch. It would seem that this act of despair roused the sympathy of the Edomites, as well as the horror of Jehoshaphat: "There was great indignation against Israel; and they departed from him, and returned to their own land"; and the next we hear of the relations between the allies is the revolt of Edom from the king of Judah (II Kings 3; Comp. 8:20).

To Elisha's aid in this war may probably be ascribed those friendly relations between Jehoram and the prophet which belong to the history of the latter. Indeed the deeds of Elisha filled the greater part of the annals of Israel under Jehoram. We need not repeat here the simple and familiar narrative of his multiplying the oil of a prophet's widow to save her and her two sons from the hard creditor; the hospitality he received from a great lady of Shenem, to whom a son was first granted at the prophet's prayer, and by the same prayer her dead son was brought to life again;[1] his healing of the poisoned pottage for the two sons of the prophets at Gilgal; his multiplication of the twenty

---

1. Three of Elisha's miracles foreshadowed those of Christ: raising the dead to life, multiplying food and healing the leper. Two of these had been performed also by Elijah but the last by Elisha only.

barley-loaves and ears of corn for the famished people of that place (II Kings 4); and his causing the iron axe-head that had fallen into the Jordan to swim to the surface (II Kings 6:1-7). The exquisite narrative of the healing of Naaman's leprosy and the punishment of Gehazi's covetousness brings us back to the affairs of the state and shows Israel harassed by predatory incursions from Damascus, and the king of Syria (Benhadad I) issuing his mandates in a tone which the king of Israel (Jehoram) bitterly resents (II Kings 5). During these incursions Jehoram was saved more than once by the warning of Elisha from being taken prisoner by the Syrian bands. Enraged at being thus baffled by the prophet, who, as a courtier told the king of Syria, could "tell the King of Israel the words that thou speakest in thy bed-chamber," Benhadad sent a great force to seize him at Dothan. During the night the Syrian chariots encompassed the base of the hill on which the ruins of the city still stand, and in the morning Elisha's terrified servant came to tell him that they were surrounded. The young man's eyes were opened at the prophet's prayer, and he saw the whole mountain full of chariots of fire and horses of fire, guarding his master; the oft-quoted emblem of those bands wherewith "the angel of Jehovah encampeth round about them that fear Him and delivereth them" (Psalm 34:7, 68:17; Gen. 32:1-2). As the Syrians drew near, they were struck blind and Elisha led them to Samaria, where he restored their sight. By his command the king of Israel fed them and sent them home again and the result was a cessation of the predatory attacks from Syria (I Kings 6:8-23; Rom. 12:20-21).

Thus far we see Jehoram, who had put down the worship of Baal, upheld against all his enemies by the power of Jehovah through the friendship of Elisha. But now comes a great change, which we cannot well be wrong in ascribing to his relapse into idolatry, which we find restored at the close of his reign. Not yet however is he forsaken by God. His great enemy presses him harder than ever: Samaria suffers a siege, unequaled in horror till the final catastrophe of Jerusalem (II Kings 6:25-29; Comp. Lev. 26:29); the king vents his rage upon Elisha, who had probably foretold the visitation; but the cruel purpose of "this son of a murderer," as the prophet terms him, is rebuked by Elisha's prophecy of the plenty that is to visit the famished city on the morrow — a prophecy fulfilled by the panic flight of the Syrian host during the night. No incident in Scripture history is more picturesque than the despairing visit of the four lepers to the deserted camp. "If we sit still here, we die! If they save us alive we shall live; and if they kill us, we shall but die!" (II Kings 7:4). The date of these events may be fixed, with great probability, to the fifth year of Jehoram's reign on the assumption that his last seven years coincided with the seven years' famine foretold by Elisha, probably as another visitation for the king's apostasy (II Kings 8:1-6). And now the time was come for the judgments, long since revealed by God to Elijah, to fall upon all the chief actors in the horrid drama of which the family of Ahab is the center and Jezebel their evil genius; on that house itself, on its enemy Benhadad and its allies of the apostate family of David, to whom we must now turn, to understand their share in the catastrophe.

16. JEHORAM, the fifth king of Judah, seems to have reigned in conjunction with his father for about three years (848-841 B.C.; II Kings 8:16-24; II Chron. 21). We have seen how the necessity of this supposition is involved in the date assigned to his namesake of Israel, and it is expressly stated that Jehoshaphat was still King of Judah when his son Joram began to reign at the age of thirty-two, in the fifth year of Joram, king of Israel. He reigned eight years at Jerusalem. Through his ill-fated marriage with ATHALIAH, the daughter of Ahab and Jezebel, he thoroughly imbibed the spirit of that evil house. He set up the worship of Baal in the high places and prostituted the daughters of Judah to the infamous rites of Ashtoreth. His reign would have been the last of the Jewish monarchy had not God remembered his covenant with David and forborne to cut off his house. But he was visited with judgments only short of such a catastrophe (II Chron. 21:16-18). Elijah's last public act was to send him the letter we have already mentioned, predicting his death by a loathsome disease and the destruction of his whole house. The latter was a fit retribution for his own atrocity to his father's house. Jehoshaphat had placed his six younger sons in fortified cities of Judah, besides giving them large presents in gold, silver and jewels, while he gave the kingdom to Jehoram (II Chron. 21:2). But as soon as Jehoshaphat was dead, Jehoram murdered all his brothers — the first example of that abominable mode of avoiding a disputed succession. The first calamity of his reign was the revolt of Edom. Marching with his whole force, he got hemmed in by the Edomites, and though he extricated himself by a successful night attack, the province was lost. Edom became again an independent state under its own king, as Isaac had predicted; and though fifty years later Amaziah overran the country, took Petra and

massacred many of the people, they were never again subjugated to Judah. Next came the revolt of Libnah, a fortified city of Judah, perhaps one of those that had belonged to the princes, rising to avenge their murder. Then the kingdom was nearly overthrown by a great invasion of the Philistines and Arabians, who had been tributary to Jehoshaphat (Comp. II Chron. 17:11), and who now stormed and plundered the king's palace and massacred or carried off all his wives and children except his youngest son Ahaziah.[1] The last infliction was a loathsome and incurable disease of the bowels of which he died, "and departed without being regretted." He was buried in the city of David but not in the sepulchre of the kings, and no odors were burned at his funeral. He died in the twelfth year of Joram, king of Israel, and was succeeded by his son Ahaziah (II Kings 8:16-24).

17. AHAZIAH, the sixth king of Judah, was twenty-two years old at his accession and reigned only one year (841 B.C.; II Kings 8:25-29, 9:27-29; II Chron. 22:1-9). Being the son of Athaliah, daughter of Ahab, he was nephew to Jehoram, king of Israel, a conjunction which threatened the establishment of idolatry in both kingdoms; for Ahaziah was addicted to all the evil practices of the house of Ahab.[2] But as if the presence of Ahab's grandson on the throne of David had filled up the measure of God's forbearance, both kings were cut off by one stroke. Toward the end of the seven years' famine already mentioned (843 B.C.), Elisha was sent to Damascus to designate Hazael, a high officer at the court of Benhadad I, as the future king of Syria (II Kings 8:7-15).[3] There is something strange in this appointment of a heathen king, the murderer of his master, and the cruel enemy of Israel by the prophet of Jehovah. Nor was Elisha himself insensible of this for he shed tears of grief and shame as he thought of the work to which Hazael was ordained. He was appointed by God the minister of his providence to execute His wrath on the house of Ahab; and so Cyrus, as the destroyer of Babylon and the restorer of Judah, is called "the anointed of Jehovah," though he knew him not. Benhadad was lying ill, when he heard of Elisha's coming; and he sent Hazael, with presents

---

1. The invasion of Judah in the time of Jehoram possibly was the historical setting of the book of Obadiah. Obadiah condemns Edom's violence to Israel in its time of disaster (Obad. 10-14).

2. Ahaziah had already reigned one year during his father's illness (II Kings 9:29; II Chron. 22:1-4). His age, 42, given in the latter passage appears to be a copyist's error, as it would make him older than his father. The names Azariah in II Chron. 22:6 and Jehoahaz in II Chron. 21:17 are variant forms of his name.

3. The question whether this was the long-deferred execution of the command to Elijah (I K. 19:15) or a second anointing, both in the case of Hazael and Jehu, can hardly be determined. An argument for the first view is the absence of any mention of anointing in this part of the narrative.

that loaded forty camels, to inquire of the man of God about his recovery. The reply was an enigma suited not to suggest, but to unveil the treacherous thoughts of Hazael. "Tell him he *may* recover" — his illness is not mortal — "but Jehovah hath showed me that he *shall* die," said the prophet, with a look that made Hazael blush for shame. Then with a burst of grief, the prophet foretold the cruelties that would be inflicted on God's people by Hazael, who exclaimed, "What, is thy servant a dog, that he should do these monstrous deeds?" "And yet he did them," says one of our old divines, pointing the moral lesson for all ages. Elisha replied by plainly announcing that Hazael should be king of Syria. Then followed the catastrophe of which history gives many other examples and which our great poet has idealized in the tragedy of Macbeth, when ambition plunges men into crime under the specious pretext of destiny. Hazael gave Benhadad the assurance that he should recover and the next day he suffocated him with a cloth dipped in water and usurped the kingdom.

It was probably amid the confusion of this change of dynasty that Jehoram, king of Israel, with Ahaziah as his ally, took possession of Ramoth-gilead, the scene of Ahab's death. Jehoram was wounded in a battle with the Syrians and returned to Jezreel to be healed, and Ahaziah soon afterward went to visit him. Their absence from the army gave the opportunity for their destruction. Elisha sent one of the sons of the prophets to Ramoth-gilead to anoint JEHU, son of Jehoshaphat son of Nimshi, one of the captains of the army to be king of Israel, according to the word of God to Elijah. Calling Jehu out of the court where the captains were assembled into an inner room, the prophet discharged his office and then fled. Jehu returned to his comrades, and after trying to pass off the visit as a madman's freak, he told them what had happened. This was the signal for revolt. The captains spread their cloaks as a carpet of state on the top of the stairs which mount from the inner court of an Eastern house to the roof; there they placed Jehu in sight of the army, blew the trumpets and shouted "Jehu is king." After taking precautions to prevent any one leaving Ramoth-gilead to carry the news, Jehu mounted his chariot and drove headlong to Jezreel. The approach of his party was announced by the watchman and Joram sent out a horseman to meet them. To the question, "Is it peace?" Jehu answered, "What hast thou to do with peace? turn thee behind me!" A second messenger was seen to follow Jehu in the same fashion. By this time they were near enough for the watchman to recognize Jehu by his furious driving, the sign of his impetuous character. Joram ordered his chariot in haste and went forth with Ahaziah. They met Jehu at a fatal spot, the field of Naboth the Jezreelite. Jehoram, who perhaps still thought that Jehu had come with tidings from the army, again asked, "Is it peace?" "What peace," retorted Jehu, "so long as the whoredoms of thy mother Jezebel and her witchcrafts are so many?" Crying to Ahaziah, "There is treachery," Joram fled, but an arrow from Jehu's bow entered his back and came out through his heart and he fell dead in his chariot. Then Jehu reminded Bidkar, his charioteer, how they had ridden together behind Ahab when Elijah laid upon him the burden of judgment at that spot, and bade him cast Joram's body into the plot which his father had seized by Naboth's murder, to be devoured by the dogs, while he himself rode on to Jezreel to execute vengeance upon Jezebel. Even then the spirit of the aged queen, who had defied Elijah in the hour of his triumph, did not quail. In her royal head-dress and with painted eyebrows, she looked down from the latticed window of her palace on the city wall and saluted Jehu with the taunt, "Had Zimri peace, who slew his lord?" But she too had traitors in her palace, and at the call of Jehu, two or three of her eunuchs dashed her down from the lattice. Her blood bespattered the city wall and Jehu drove his chariot over her mangled corpse, which was left in the space before the city into which offal is thrown from the walls to be devoured by the dogs. It was not till Jehu had sat down to feast with his comrades that he bade some of his soldiers to "go and see after the cursed woman and bury her, for she was a king's daughter." They went and found that the dogs had left nothing but her skull and feet, and the palms of her hands. Her fate recalled to Jehu's memory the words of Elijah concerning her, which he repeats with even greater minuteness than the original historian, so strong an impression had they made upon him (II Kings 9:30-37; Comp. I Kings 21:23). Thus perished this remarkable woman, distinguished above all the other monsters of her sex for never having betrayed a feeling of remorse. Her name is used by St. John as a type of the worst form of spiritual wickedness and after-ages have made it a proverb. There were still seventy sons of Ahab left at Samaria and Jehu sent letters to their governors and to the elders of Samaria, ironically challenging them to set up one of the seventy for king. On their promising submission, a second letter ordered them to bring him the heads of all the seventy to

Jezreel on the morrow. They were brought and piled in two heaps on each side of the gate and when the people assembled in the morning, Jehu appealed to them, "I conspired against my master and slew him, but who slew all these?" — thus committing them to a full share in the massacre. All that remained of the family of Ahab in Jezreel were hunted down and slain, with the officers of the court and the priests. Jehu then went to reside at Samaria. At the shearing-house beside the road he met forty-two of the kinsmen of Ahaziah coming on a visit to Jezreel, in evident ignorance of these events. All were seized by his order and slain at the well of the sheering-house. Proceeding on his way, Jehu met Jehonadab, the son of Rechab, who was afterward famous as the founder of the ascetic sect of the Rechabites. After mutual assurances that their hearts were "right," Jehu invited the zealot to mount the chariot and witness *his* zeal for Jehovah. Arrived at Samaria, he finished the slaughter of the house of Ahab, and then planned with Jehonadab one crowning act of zeal to destroy the worship of Baal at a stroke. He declared that "Ahab served Baal little, but Jehu shall serve him much," and proclaimed throughout Israel a solemn assembly for Baal in the temple which Ahab had built at Samaria. The worshipers of Baal took the bait and assembled to a man. As if to give more dignity to the festival but in reality to mark the votaries of Baal, he had them clothed in the sacred vestments and himself went into the temple with Jehonadab, to charge the Baalites to see that no servant of Jehovah remained to pollute the ceremony. Eighty men were stationed at the gates to prevent escape at the peril of their own lives. The sacrifices were offered and the orgies of the feast had begun, when Jehu gave the signal to the guards, who rushed in and slew the Baalites and cast out their bodies to the dogs and vultures. They then stormed the fortified sanctuary; they broke to pieces the great stone statue of Baal and burned the other images, razed the temple and made its remains into a latrine. Amid all the sins of the later kings of Israel, the worship of Baal was never openly restored.

18. The fate of Ahaziah, king of Judah, is somewhat differently related in *Chronicles* than in *Kings*. The exact details are obscure but the accounts are not irreconcilable. According to the account in the *Chronicles,* he fled to Samaria when Joram was killed, was found hidden there and was brought to Jehu, who put him to death, but granted him an honorable burial from respect to the memory of Jehoshaphat. The narrative in *Kings* conveys

the idea that Jehu, after mortally wounding Joram, turned to pursue the king of Judah, and that Ahaziah was mortally wounded at the pass of Gur near Ibleam (thirteen miles north of Samaria), and died when he reached Megiddo. This pursuit may have taken place in consequence of his being pointed out to Jehu while attempting to escape from Samaria. This much is clear, that his body was carried to Jerusalem and buried in the sepulchre of the kings.

One member of the house of Ahab was still left, his daughter Athaliah, the queen-mother of Judah and the heir to her mother's fierce and dauntless spirit. By her means it seemed as if the Baal-worship, destroyed in Israel, was to be restored in Judah. On hearing of her son's death, she slew all the royal seed of Judah except Joash, the youngest son of Ahaziah, a new-born infant, who was hidden by his aunt Jehoshabeath, the daughter of Jehoram (probably by another wife than Athaliah) and wife of the high-priest Jehoiada. Athaliah usurped the crown for six years (841-835 B.C.), but these may be passed over, for they are barren of events, to finish the story of the house of Ahab. While Athaliah herself was an active devotee of Baal (II Chron. 24:7, 23:17; II Kings 11:18), she does not seem to have brought over the people to idolatry; for it was the regular order of the Temple-service that enabled the high-priest to effect the revolution by which Joash was restored.

In the seventh year Jehoiada took counsel with five "captains of hundreds," by whose means the Levites and heads of houses were assembled from all the cities of Jerusalem to swear allegiance in the Temple, to the sole remaining scion of the house of David, a child seven years old. It was the custom on the Sabbath for the guard of priests and Levites to divide themselves into three bodies of whom one kept the doors of the Temple, another the gate called "Sur" (or "the gate of the foundation"), while the third were on duty at the royal palace. To avoid suspicion, the last occupied their usual post, but the other two-thirds formed a close line across the court of the altar round the person of Joash, armed with spears and David's sacred shields, with orders to cut down any who should attempt to enter, while the rest of the people were in the outer court. When all was prepared, Joash was brought forward and crowned with full ceremony.

The acclamations of the people reached the ears of Athaliah, who hastened to the Temple and found the king standing by the entrance amid the princes, the trumpets blowing and the singers praising God. She rent her clothes and cried out "Treason!" But Jehoiada commanded the five captains to carry her out of the Temple and to cut down any who tried to follow her, and they slew her at the entrance of "the horse-gate" by the royal palace. Jehoiada then renewed the covenant, as in the time of David, of the people and the king with each other and Jehovah. The Temple of Baal was razed, the idols destroyed and his priest Mattan slain before his own altar. The service of the Temple was arranged according to the order prescribed by David. The king was brought in solemn procession from the Temple through the great gate to the royal palace, and set upon the throne of Solomon. By the death of Athaliah the last member of Ahab's house had perished: "all the people of the land rejoiced, and the city was quiet."

Prophets and Contemporary Kings

Students should memorize the areas pertaining to each of the prophets listed below and the kings or events contemporary with each prophet.

Prophet and date of ministry[1]	Area involved	Contemporary kings or events
Elijah (Approx. 864-846)	Northern kingdom	Ahab, Ahaziah, Jehoram
Elisha (Approx. 846-796)	Northern kingdom	Jehoram to Jehoash
Isaiah (740-681)	Judah	Uzziah, Jotham, Ahaz Hezekiah
Jeremiah (627 till after 586)	Judah	Josiah, till after the fall of Judah
Ezekiel (597-570)	Jews in Babylon and in Judah	Babylonian captivity
Daniel (605-536)	Babylon	Babylonian captivity
Hosea (755-725)	Northern kingdom	Jeroboam II
Joel (830-?)	Judah	Joash of Judah (?)
Amos (760)	Northern kingdom	Jeroboam II
Obadiah (848-841?)	Edom	Jehoram of Judah (?)
Jonah (780?)	Nineveh	Jeroboam II
Micah (736-710)	Judah	Jotham, Ahaz, Hezekiah
Nahum (725-?)	Nineveh	Before fall of Nineveh, 612 B.C.
Habakkuk (605)	Judah	Jehoiakim; Battle of Carchemish, 605 B.C.
Zephaniah (627)	Judah	Josiah; Scythian invasion
Haggai (520)	Judah	Post-exilic period
Zechariah (520-480)	Judah	Post-exilic period
Malachi (430)	Judah	Post-exilic period

1. See G.L. Archer, *A Survey of O.T. Introduction,* for full information about the dates of these prophets.

Elijah, a Type of John the baptizer
(Malachi 4:5; Matthew 11:14; 17:10-13; John 1:21)

1. Both were rustic (II Kings 1:8; Matt. 3:4).
2. Both preached judgment (I K. 17:1; Matt. 3:7-10).
3. Both denounced a king (I K. 21:19; Matt. 14:4).
4. Both were brought down by a woman.
5. Both became discouraged (I K. 19:4,10; Matt. 11:2-3).
6. Both were followed by a greater prophet (I K. 19:19; Matt. 3:11-12).

Questions over Section II
The Divided Kingdom to Jehu

1. Give the names of the two kingdoms in the divided kingdom.
2. Which was northern in area? Which was southern?
3. What was the number of tribes in each kingdom?
4. Who were the first kings in each kingdom?
5. What was the total number of kings in each kingdom?
6. What was the number of dynasties in each kingdom?
7. What was the character of the kings in each kingdom?
8. What were the capitals of the two kingdoms?
9. What was the fate (with dates) of each kingdom?
10. Give approximate land area of each kingdom.
11. Why was the southern kingdom consistently superior?
12. Into what three periods may the divided kingdom be divided?

Rehoboam

1. Where did Rehoboam go to be made king (I Kings 12:1)?
2. What request did the people make to Rehoboam (I K. 12:4)?
3. Who was the spokesman of the people (I K. 12:3)?
4. What counsel did the old men give to Rehoboam? The young men (I K. 12:6-11)?
5. Whose counsel did he follow (I K. 12:13)?
6. Why did Rehoboam speak so foolishly (I K. 12:15)?
7. What was Israel's response to Rehoboam's speech (I K. 12:16,19)?
8. What happened to Adoram when Rehoboam sent him to Israel (I K. 12:18)?
9. Why did not Rehoboam fight Israel (I K. 14:21)?
10. Was Rehoboam a good king (I K. 14:21; II Chron. 12:14)?
11. Who was Rehoboam's mother (I K. 14:21)?
12. What defensive preparations did Rehoboam make in Judah (II Chron. 11:5-6)?

13. What religious people came into Rehoboam's kingdom? From where? Why (II Chron. 11:13-16)?
14. What effect did these religious people have on Rehoboam's kingdom (II Chron. 11:17)?
15. How many wives and concubines did Rehoboam have (II Chron. 11:21)?
16. What evils were practiced in Judah in Rehoboam's time (I K. 14:22-23)?
17. Who was Shishak (I K. 14:25)?
18. What did Shishak do to Rehoboam (I K. 14:26)?
19. What did the king and the princes do when Shishak invaded (II Chron. 12:6)?
20. What did God do when they humbled themselves (II Chron. 12:6-8)?
21. What substitute was made for golden shields (I K. 14:27)?
22. How did Rehoboam and Jeroboam get along (I K. 14:30)?

Abijah
1. Was Abijah a good king (K K. 15:3)?
2. Why did God not destroy the kingdom in Abijah's time (I K. 15:4)?
3. How did Abijah and Jeroboam get along (I K. 15:7)?
4. Where did Abijah deliver a speech against Jeroboam (II Chron. 13:4-5)?
5. What was the gist of Abijah's speech (II Chron. 13:4-12)?
6. How did Jeroboam try to defeat Abijah (II Chron. 13:13)?
7. What was the result of the battle between Abijah and Jeroboam (II Chron. 13:15)?

Jeroboam I
1. How many tribes were in Jeroboam's kingdom (I K. 11:31)?
2. Where was Jeroboam's capital (I K. 12:25)?
3. What idol did Jeroboam make? Why? Where (I K. 12:26-29)?
4. Whom did Jeroboam appoint as priests (I K. 12:31)?
5. What feast did Jeroboam ordain (I K. 12:32)?
6. Who denounced Jeroboam's altar (I K. 13:1-2)?
7. What was the name of the king who was to appear and defile the altar (I K. 13:2)?
8. How was Jeroboam's attempt to seize the prophet prevented (I K. 13:4)?
9. Would the prophet eat with the king? Why or why not (I K. 13:7-10)?
10. Who went to overtake the returning prophet (I K. 13:11-14)?
11. What lie was told to the prophet (I K. 13:18)?

12. What disturbing message was revealed as the prophets ate (I K. 13:20-22)?
13. What happened to the young prophet (I K. 13:24)?
14. Where was the prophet buried (I K. 13:29-30)?
15. What was the effect of Jeroboam's sin on his house (I K. 13:33-34)?
16. What was the name of Jeroboam's sick son (I K. 14:1)?
17. What was the son's character (I K. 14:13)?
18. Who was sent to Ahijah (I K. 14:2)?
19. What message about the son and about Jeroboam's house did Ahijah give (I K. 14:7-12)?

Nadab
1. What was Nadab's character (I K. 15:26)?
2. What city did Nadab besiege (I K. 15:27)?
3. Who assassinated Nadab (I K. 15:27)?

Baasha
1. Was Baasha good or bad (I K. 15:34)?
2. What did Baasha do to the house of Jeroboam (I K. 15:29)?
3. What prophet denounced Baasha (I K. 16:1)?
4. What prediction about the house of Baasha did the prophet make (I K. 16:2-3)?
5. What city did Baasha build and fortify against King Asa (I K. 15:17)?

Elah
1. Who conspired against Elah (I K. 16:9)?
2. What was Elah doing when he was assassinated (I K. 16:9)?

Zimri
1. What house (or family) did Zimri destroy (I K. 16:11)?
2. How long did Zimri reign (I K. 16:15)?
3. What city was under siege when Zimri became king (I K. 16:15)?
4. How did the people react to Zimri's being king (I K. 16:16)?
5. Who attacked the city where Zimri was (I K. 16:17)?
6. How did Zimri die (I K. 16:18)?

Omri
1. Who was a rival king to Omri (I K. 16:21)?
2. What hill did Omri buy for a capital? From whom (I K. 16:24)?
3. Was Omri strong or weak (I K. 16:27)?

Asa
1. Was Asa good or bad (I K. 15:11)?
2. What did Asa put out of the land (I K. 15:12)?

3. For how long did Asa have peace (II Chron. 14:1)?
4. Who attacked Asa? With how large a force (II Chron. 14:9)?
5. How did Asa get help for battle (II Chron. 14:11)?
6. What prophet encouraged Asa (II Chron. 15:1)?
7. When is the Lord with you (II Chron. 15:2)?
8. What covenant did Asa lead Judah to enter (II Chron. 15:12)?
9. Who was Maacah? What was done with her? Why (II Chron. 15:16)?
10. What king of Israel fortified a city against Asa and Judah (II Chron. 16:1)?
11. How did Asa stop the building of Ramah (II Chron. 16:2-4)?
12. What was done with the stones of Ramah (II Chron. 16:6)?
13. What prophet rebuked Asa (II Chron. 16:7)?
14. What was Asa's punishment (II Chron. 16:9)?
15. How did Asa react to the prophet's rebuke (II Chron. 16:10)?
16. What afflicted Asa in his old age (II Chron. 16:12)?

Ahab and Elijah
1. How did Ahab compare in character with Israel's other kings (I K. 16:30)?
2. Who was Ahab's wife (I K. 16:31)?
3. Who was Ahab's father-in-law (I K. 16:31)?
4. What religion was introduced into Israel by Ahab and his wife (I K. 16:32)?
5. Who rebuilt Jericho in Ahab's time (I K. 16:34)?
6. Where was Elijah from (I K. 17:1)?
7. What was Elijah's proclamation to Ahab (I K. 17:1)?
8. By what brook was Elijah fed (I K. 17:5)?
9. Where was Elijah sent after the brook dried up (I K. 17:9)?
10. What two things did Elijah ask the widow for (I K. 17:10-11)?
11. How much food did the widow have (I K. 17:12)?
12. How were Elijah and the widow fed (I K. 17:16)?
13. Whom did Elijah raise from the dead (I K. 17:17-22)?
14. What did Elijah pray about the boy's soul (I K. 17:21-22)?
15. Does every person have a soul that is distinct from the body (Compare Gen. 35:18; Matt. 10:28; II Peter 1:13-14; Eccl. 12:7)?
16. Who sent Elijah back to Ahab (I K. 18:1)?
17. Who was the overseer of Ahab's household and property? What sort of man was he (I K. 18:3)?
18. How had a hundred prophets been saved (I K. 18:4)?

19. What mission did Ahab and his servant go out on (I K. 18:5-6)?
20. Why did Ahab's servant fear to tell Ahab that he had met Elijah (I K. 18:8-12)?
21. What were Ahab's words when he met Elijah (I K. 18:17)?
22. How many prophets of Baal were there? How many of the Asherah (grove) (I K. 18:19)?
23. Where did Elijah call upon Ahab to go to prove who was God (I K. 18:19,21)?
24. What test did Elijah propose to prove who was God (I K. 18:23-24)?
25. How long did the prophets of Baal pray (I K. 18:26,29)?
26. How many containers of water did Elijah have poured on his altar (I K. 18:33-34)?
27. What did the fire from heaven burn up (I K. 18:38)?
28. What was done with the prophets of Baal? Where (I K. 18:40)?
29. Where did Elijah send his servant to go and look? How many times (I K. 18:43)?
30. How big was the cloud (I K. 18:44)?
31. Where did Elijah and Ahab hurry to? Who arrived first (I K. 18:45-46)?
32. How did Jezebel threaten Elijah (I K. 19:2)?
33. To what place did Elijah flee from Jezebel (I K. 19:3)?
34. Under what sort of tree did Elijah request to die (I K. 19:4)?
35. How did Elijah get food there (I K. 19:5-6)?
36. Where did Elijah go after eating the food (I K. 19:8)?
37. What question did God ask Elijah at Horeb (I K. 19:9)?
38. What three violent events occurred before Elijah (I K. 19:11-12)?
39. What sort of voice did Elijah hear (I K. 19:12)?
40. What three people was Elijah sent to anoint (I K. 19:15-17)?
41. How many people in Israel had not bowed to Baal (I K. 19:18)?
42. What was Elisha doing when Elijah found him (I K. 19:19)?
43. How did Elijah demonstrate his call to Elisha (I K. 19:19)?
44. What king of Syria besieged Samaria (I K. 20:1)?
45. What two demands did the king of Syria make (I K. 20:3-6)?
46. Did Ahab yield to these demands (I K. 20:9)?
47. Which men were to deliver the Syrians into Israel's hands (I K. 20:13-14)?

48. What was the king of Syria doing when Israel attacked (I K. 20:16-17)?
49. What was the outcome of the battle at Samaria (I K. 20:20-21)?
50. Why did the Syrians say they had been beaten (I K. 20:23)?
51. Where was Syria's next battle with Ahab (I K. 23:26)?
52. How did the armies of Israel look (I K. 20:27)?
53. How did the second battle with Syria turn out (I K. 20:29)?
54. Who suggested that the king of Syria ask for mercy (I K. 20:31)?
55. Did Ahab grant mercy to the Syrian king (I K. 20:32)?
56. What did Benhadad promise to give back to Ahab (I K. 20:34)?
57. What happened to a prophet when he would not smite his fellow-prophet (I K. 20:35-36)?
58. Where did the prophet wait after being smitten (I K. 20:38)?
59. How did the prophet say his prisoner had escaped (I K. 20:39-40)?
60. To whom was the story of the escaping prisoner applied (I K. 20:41-42)?
61. What penalty was pronounced on Ahab for letting Benhadad go (I K. 20:42)?
62. Whose vineyard did Ahab covet? Where was it (I K. 21:1)?
63. Would the owner of the vineyard give it to Ahab (I K. 21:3)?
64. Who volunteered to obtain the vineyard (I K. 21:7)?
65. How was the vineyard owner slain (I K. 21:8-10)?
66. Who met Ahab in the vineyard (I K. 21:17-18)?
67. What penalty was pronounced upon Ahab? Upon his house? Upon Jezebel (I K. 21:19-24)?
68. What did God say when Ahab humbled himself (I K. 21:29)?
69. What royal visitor came to see Ahab (I K. 22:2)?
70. What city did Ahab propose that they attack (I K. 22:3)?
71. Who requested that they ask the prophets about going to battle (I K. 22:5)?
72. How many prophets were gathered before the kings (I K. 22:6)?
73. What one prophet of Jehovah was brought (I K. 22:7-9)?
74. How did Ahab feel toward this prophet? Why (I K. 22:8)?
75. What prophet made iron horns? What were the horns supposed to demonstrate (I K. 22:11)?
76. What did Micaiah at first tell the kings to do? Was this message sincere (I K. 22:15-16)?

77. What vision of Israel's armies did Micaiah relate (I K. 22:17)?
78. What vision concerning the prophets did Micaiah relate (I K. 22:19-23)?
79. What did Zedekiah do to Micaiah (I K. 22:24-25)?
80. What disguise did Ahab put on for battle (I K. 22:30)?
81. What instructions had the king of Syria given his troops for the battle (I K. 22:31)?
82. How did Jehoshaphat nearly lose his life (I K. 22:32-33)?
83. How was Ahab killed (I K. 22:34-35)?
84. What prophecy was fulfilled when blood was washed from Ahab's chariot (I K. 22:38; 21:19)?
85. What was the material in Ahab's palace (I K. 22:39)?

Jehoshaphat

1. Was Jehoshaphat a good king (I K. 22:43)?
2. Whom did Jehoshaphat send throughout the cities of Judah? Why (II Chron. 17:7-9)?
3. What foreign nations sent tribute to Jehoshaphat (II Chron. 17:11)?
4. Was Jehoshaphat mighty or weak (II Chron. 17:12)?
5. What good thing did Jehoshaphat's captain Amasaiah do (II Chron. 17:16)?
6. How did Jehoshaphat become associated with the house of Ahab (II Chron. 21:6)?
7. With what words did the prophet rebuke Jehoshaphat for helping Ahab (II Chron. 19:2)?
8. What did Jehoshaphat instruct the judges whom he appointed to do (II Chron. 19:5,7,9)?
9. What peoples invaded Jehoshaphat's kingdom (II Chron. 20:1)?
10. What did Jehoshaphat do to prepare for battle (II Chron. 20:3-12)?
11. What prophet predicted deliverance for Jehoshaphat (II Chron. 20:14-15)?
12. Where did Jehoshaphat and his army go to face the enemy (II Chron. 20:20)?
13. What did Judah do as the battle began (II Chron. 20:21-22)?
14. How did the battle turn out (II Chron. 20:26)?
15. What was the place where the spoil was collected called? What does the name mean (II Chron. 20:26)?
16. Where did Jehoshaphat build ships? What were the ships designed to do (II Chron. 20:35-36; I K. 22:48)?
17. What happened to the ships (II Chron. 20:37)?

18. What offer of King Ahaziah did Jehoshaphat refuse (I Kings 22:49)?

Ahaziah of Israel

1. How did Ahaziah compare with his father in character (I K. 22:52-53)?
2. What kingdom rebelled against Israel after Ahab's death (II K. 1:1)?
3. How was Ahaziah injured (II K. 1:2)?
4. Where did Ahaziah send for information about his sickness (II K. 1:2)?
5. What message did Elijah send to Ahaziah (II K. 1:4)?
6. Whom did Ahaziah send to Elijah (II K. 1:9)?
7. What happened to two captains and two groups of fifty men (II K. 1:10-12)?
8. What did Elijah say to King Ahaziah (II K. 1:16)?
9. Name the four places Elijah and Elisha passed by on the way to Elijah's being taken up (II K. 2:1,2,4,6)?
10. What did the sons of the prophets tell Elisha on the way (II K. 2:3,5)?
11. How did Elijah and Elisha cross Jordan (II K. 2:8)?
12. What last request did Elisha make of Elijah (II K. 2:9)?
13. What divided Elisha from Elijah (II K. 2:11)?
14. How was Elijah taken into heaven (II K. 2:11)?
15. Why did the sons of the prophets want to search for Elijah (II K. 2:16)?
16. Where was the water bad (II K. 2:19,15)?
17. How did Elisha heal the waters (II K. 2:21)?
18. Where did youths mock Elisha (II K. 2:23)?
19. What punishment came upon the youths (II K. 2:24)?

Jehoram of Israel and Elisha

1. Who was Jehoram's father (II K. 3:1)?
2. What act of Jehoram shows he was a little better than his father (II K. 3:2)?
3. Who was king of Moab (II K. 3:4)?
4. Whom did Jehoram get to help in his battle against Moab (II K. 3:6-7)?
5. What dangers beset the armies as they marched (II K. 3:9)?
6. What prophet was with the armies (II K. 3:11)?
7. How did Elisha speak to Jehoram (II K. 3:14)?
8. What accompaniment did Elisha have as he prophesied (II K. 3:15)?

9. How was water obtained for the troops (II K. 3:16-20)?
10. What did the king of Moab think when he saw the water (II K. 3:22)?
11. What was done to the land of Moab (II K. 3:25)?
12. What desperate act saved Moab from total destruction (II K. 3:27)?
13. What complaint did a widow of one of the prophets bring to Elisha (II K. 4:1)?
14. How did the widow obtain money to pay her debts (II K. 4:2-7)?
15. Where did Elisha often stay and eat as he travelled (II K. 4:8)?
16. What did the woman and her husband make for Elisha (II K. 4:10)?
17. What did Elisha promise the woman (II K. 4:16)?
18. How did the woman's son die (II K. 4:18-20)?
19. Where did the woman go seeking Elisha (II K. 4:24-25)?
20. Who was Elisha's servant (II K. 4:25)?
21. Who rode back to the woman's house first (II K. 4:31)?
22. What did Elisha do in bringing the child back to life (II K. 4:33-35)?
23. What painful condition existed in the land in those days (II K. 4:38)?
24. What ingredient made the prophets' pottage deadly (II K. 4:39-40)?
25. How was the pottage made non-poisonous (II K. 4:41)?
26. From what place did a man come bringing food for the prophet (II K. 4:42)?
27. How much food was brought? How many men did it feed (II K. 4:43)?
28. Who was Naaman (II K. 5:1)?
29. What was Naaman's affliction (II K. 5:1)?
30. Who told about the prophet who could heal Naaman (II K. 5:2-3)?
31. Who sent Naaman to Israel? To what person in Israel was he sent (II K. 5:5)?
32. How did the king of Israel react to Naaman's arrival (II K. 5:7)?
33. What did Elisha tell Naaman to do to be healed (II K. 5:10)?
34. What were the two rivers of Damascus (II K. 5:12)?
35. How was Naaman persuaded to obey Elisha (II K. 5:13)?

36. What rewards did Elisha accept (II K. 5:16)?
37. What did Naaman ask to take back with him? Why (II K. 5:17)?
38. Who covetously overtook Naaman and asked for a gift (II K. 5:20)?
39. What excuse did he give for asking for the gift (II K. 5:22)?
40. How was Gehazi's act made known to Elisha (II K. 5:26)?
41. What was Gehazi's punishment (II K. 5:27)?
42. What complaint did the prophets have about their dwelling place (II K. 6:1)?
43. What happened to a borrowed axe (II K. 6:5)?
44. How did Elisha retrieve the axe head (II K. 6:6-7)?
45. What military secrets did Elisha reveal (II K. 6:8-10)?
46. Where did the king of Syria attempt to capture Elisha (II K. 6:13)?
47. How did Elisha's servant react upon seeing the city surrounded (II K. 6:15)?
48. What did Elisha pray the Lord would show his servant (II K. 6:17)?
49. Where did Elisha lead the blinded Syrians (II K. 6:19)?
50. What did Elisha tell the king to do to the Syrians (II K. 6:22)?
51. What was the effect of the kindness to the Syrians (II K. 6:22)?
52. What was the effect of the siege upon Samaria (II K. 6:25)?
53. How much was an ass's head sold for in Samaria (II K. 6:25)?
54. What most horrible act occurred during the famine (II K. 6:26-29; Comp. Lev. 26:29; Deut. 28:53)?
55. What was Jehoram wearing as an undershirt (II K. 6:30)?
56. What unreasonable decision did Jehoram make about Elisha (II K. 6:31)?
57. How was Jehoram the "son of a murderer" (II K. 6:32; I K. 21)?
58. What dramatic change in the famine did Elisha promise (II K. 7:1)?
59. What did Elisha tell Jehoram's captain would happen to him (II K. 7:2)?
60. Who discovered that the Syrians had fled (II K. 7:3)?
61. Why had the Syrians fled (II K. 7:6)?
62. What did the king think about the Syrians' departure (II K. 7:12)?
63. How was Elisha's prophecy about the captain seeing abundant food, but not eating of it, fulfilled (II K. 7:18-20)?

64. Where had Elisha sent the Shunnamite woman? For how long? Why (II K. 8:1)?
65. What remarkable coincidence occurred when the woman returned (II K. 8:4-5)?
66. What was returned to the woman (II K. 8:6)?
67. What foreign city did Elisha visit (II K. 8:7)?
68. Whom did Benhadad send to Elisha to inquire about his sickness (II K. 8:8)?
69. What did Elisha say about Benhadad's recovery (II K. 8:10)?
70. What did Elisha predict about Hazael's deeds (II K. 8:11-12)?
71. How did Benhadad die (II K. 8:15)?
72. Why had Jehoram been at Ramoth-gilead and what happened to him there (II K. 9:14-15)?
73. Whom did Elisha send to Ramoth-gilead? On what mission (II K. 9:1-3)?
74. Was Jehu anointed privately or publicly (II K. 9:5-6)?
75. What people was Jehu to smite and destroy (II K. 9:7-8)?
76. What did Jehu's servants call the anointing prophet (II K. 9:11)?
77. Where did Jehu go after leaving Ramoth-gilead (II K. 9:16)?
78. What did Jehu tell the horsemen from Jezreel who came out to ask him about his intentions (II K. 9:17-19)?
79. What was notable about Jehu's driving (II K. 9:20)?
80. Where did Jehoram meet Jehu? Who was with Jehoram (II K. 9:21)?
81. How was Jehoram slain (II K. 9:24)?
82. Where was Jehoram's body cast (II K. 9:25-26)?
83. What did Jezebel do when she heard that Jehu was coming (II K. 9:30)?
84. What king did Jezebel compare Jehu to (II K. 9:31)?
85. How was Jezebel slain (II K. 9:32-33)?
86. What happened to Jezebel's body (II K. 9:35)?
87. What prophecy did Jezebel's fate fulfill (II K. 9:36)?

Jehoram of Judah
1. Was Jehoram's life good or bad (II K. 8:18)?
2. Who was Jehoram's wife (II K. 8:18,26)?
3. What did Jehoram do to his brothers when he became king (II Chron. 21:4)?
4. What country and what city revolted in Jehoram's time (II K. 8:20,22)?
5. What prophet wrote Jehoram a letter (II Chron. 21:12)?

6. What did the letter predict concerning Jehoram (II Chron. 21:14-15)?
7. What peoples invaded Judah and Jerusalem in Jehoram's time and carried away all the goods (II Chron. 21:16-17)?
8. Which prophet (probably) wrote God's message against the Edomites for cruelty during Jehoram's reign?
9. How did Jehoram die (II Chron. 21:18-19)?
10. How did the people feel about Jehoram when he died (II Chron. 21:20)?

Ahaziah of Judah

1. Why was Ahaziah made king when he was his father's youngest son (II Chron. 21:17; 22:1)?
2. Who counselled Ahaziah to do wickedly (II Chron. 22:3)?
3. Whom did Ahaziah accompany to battle? To what place (II Chron. 22:5)?
4. Where did Ahaziah go to visit his sick uncle (II Chron. 22:6)?
5. Where did Jehoram of Israel and Ahaziah meet Jehu (II K. 9:21)?
6. Where did Ahaziah flee from Jehu (II K. 9:27)?
7. At what city did Ahaziah die (II K. 9:27)?
8. Where was Ahaziah buried (II K. 9:28)?

Jehu

(See questions 73-87 concerning Jehoram of Israel. These also concern Jehu.)

1. How many sons did Ahab have in Samaria (II K. 10:1)?
2. What challenge did Jehu make to those who cared for the sons of Ahab (II K. 10:2-3)?
3. How did Ahab's sons die (II K. 10:7)?
4. How thoroughly did Jehu destroy Ahab's house (II K. 10:11, 17)?
5. Whom did Jehu meet at the shearing-house in Samaria? How many were there (II K. 10:12-13)?
6. What happened to these men at the pit of the shearing-house (II K. 10:14)?
7. Who accompanied Jehu on his mission of massacre in Samaria (II K. 10:15-17)?
8. What pretence did Jehu make to the worshipers of Baal (II K. 10:18-19)?
9. How were the worshipers of Baal made obvious and distinct (II K. 10:22)?
10. What was done to the worshipers of Baal (II K. 10:25-28)?
11. Did Jehu serve Jehovah with his heart (II K. 10:31)?

12. What portion of Israel was lost to Syria in Jehu's time (II K. 10:32-33)?

Athaliah

1. Who had been Athaliah's husband (II K. 8:16,18)?
2. Who had been Athaliah's son (II K. 8:26)?
3. What did Athaliah do when her son was dead (II K. 11:1)?
4. How near did Athaliah come to destroying all the descendants of David (II K. 11:1-2)?
5. Who was saved? Whose son was he (II K. 11:2)?
6. Who hid the young prince (II Chron. 22:11)?
7. How long was he hidden (II K. 11:3)?
8. What did Athaliah do to the temple (II Chron. 24:7)?
9. Who was the leader of the plot against Athaliah (II Chron. 23:1)?
10. From where and at what place were Levites gathered to oppose Athaliah and appoint a new king (II Chron. 23:2-3)?
11. How many groups were the Levites gathered into for the revolt (II Chron. 23:4)?
12. Who was to be protected from all intruders (II K. 11:8)?
13. What was given to the boy when he was made king (II K. 11:12)?
14. What did Athaliah hear that aroused her (II K. 11:13)?
15. What did Athaliah say when she saw the new king (II K. 11:14)?
16. Where was Athaliah slain (II K. 11:15-16)?
17. Who led the people in making a covenant between the king, the people and God (II K. 11:17)?
18. What was done to Baal worship in Jerusalem (II K. 11:18)?

Section III
From Jehu to End of Israel

1. The dynasty of Jehu, Israel's tenth king — Jehu named on Assyrian monument — Jehoahaz, eleventh king — Israel brought low. 2. Joash, Judah's seventh king — Jehoiada, the priest — The prophet Joel — Restoration of the temple — Apostasy of Joash — Martyrdom of Zechariah — Syrian invasion of Judah. 3. Jehoash, twelfth king of Israel — Death of Elisha. 4. Amaziah, eighth king of Judah — Victory over Edom — Jerusalem taken by Jehoash. 5. Jeroboam II, Israel's

thirteenth king — Expansion of the kingdom — The prophets Jonah, Amos and Hosea — Zechariah, fourteenth king of Israel — End of Jehu's dynasty — Civil war. 6. Shallum, fifteenth king of Israel — Menahem, sixteenth king — Overlapping reign of Pekah — First invasion of Israel by Assyria — Tribute to Pul or Tiglath-pileser — Pekahiah, seventeenth king — Pekah, eighteenth king — His league with Rezin against Judah. 7. Uzziah, ninth king of Judah — His good reign and successful wars — Profanes the temple and dies a leper — Call of Isaiah. 8. Jotham, tenth king of Judah — His piety and prosperity. 9. Ahaz, eleventh king of Judah — His piety and prosperity. 9. Ahaz, eleventh king of Judah — War with Syria and Israel — Ahaz calls in Tiglath-pileser — Destruction of the kingdom of Damascus — Captivity of the Trans-jordanic and northern tribes — Ahaz goes to Damascus — His shameless idolatries. 10. Hezekiah, twelfth king of Judah — Reforms of religion — Great Passover — Brazen serpent destroyed — Defeats Philistines — Revolts from Assyria. 11. Hoshea, Israel's nineteenth and last king — Signs of a revival — Revolts from Shalmaneser — First Assyrian invasion — Hoshea's secret alliance with Egypt and imprisonment — Siege and capture of Samaria — End of Israel and captivity of the Ten Tribes — Summary of Israel's sins — Fate of the captives — Colonists later brought into the land.

1. *The dynasty of Jehu – Jehu named on an Assyrian monument – Jehoahaz, Israel's eleventh king – Israel brought low.* The fair promise of a new reign of religion in both kingdoms was soon overcast. The zeal of which Jehu so loudly boasted and which led him through such seas of blood was too hot to last and the character of Joash was yet to be formed. Turning first to Israel, JEHU (841-814 B.C.; II Kings 10:29-36), the tenth king, reigned twenty-eight years and founded the fourth dynasty, which consisted of five kings but lasted a much longer time than Omri's, namely 89 years.[1] This prolongation of his dynasty was expressly granted as the reward of his zeal against the house of Ahab. Nor was this all. Under the house of Jehu, Israel became almost as great as she had

---

1. Omri's dynasty of four kings lasted forty-four years.

been immediately after the disruption. Jehoash, the grandson of Jehu, entered Jerusalem as a conqueror. He also drove back the Syrians and his son Jeroboam II recovered the eastern frontier from Hamath to the Dead Sea. Jehu, however, became heedless of God's law and declined into the sins and idolatry of Jeroboam. From his reign began the loss of those territories which had been first occupied in the conquest of the land. "Jehovah began to cut Israel short." Hazael overran the whole land of the two and a half tribes in Gilead and Bashan, east of the Jordan as far south as the Arnon. Such are the few brief records of Jehu's long reign. He died and was buried at Samaria and was succeeded by his son Jehoahaz.

In Jehu's reign we are brought into contact for the first time with the great empire of Assyria which thereafter played so important a part in the history of Judah and Israel. An eight-foot obelisk of black stone was found at Nimrud in 1846 by Sir Henry A. Layard. This monument pictures Jehu kneeling before the Assyrian emperor. Following the prostrate king come Israelites bearing gifts. The inscription reads: "Tribute of Jehu, the son of Omri."[1] The fact that Jehu is wrongly called the son of Omri shows how mighty Omri had been. His name had become synonymous with Israel even after his dynasty had ended.

JEHOAHAZ (814-798 B.C.; II Kings 13:1-9), the eleventh king of Israel and the second of the house of Jehu, succeeded his father in the twenty-third year of Joash, king of Judah, and reigned seventeen years in Samaria. He followed the sins of Jeroboam and suffered from constant and unsuccessful wars with the kings of Syria, Hazael and his son Benhadad II. So low was Israel reduced that Jehoahaz was only suffered to maintain a force of fifty horsemen, ten chariots and 10,000 foot soldiers. "The King of Syria had destroyed them, and had made them like the dust by threshing" (II Kings 13:1-7; Comp. Amos 1:3). Still God did not withdraw all his compassion from them, for the sake of his covenant with Abraham; and in answer to the prayers of Jehoahaz, He raised up deliverers for them. The "savior" spoken of in II Kings 13:5 may have been the Assyrian King Adad-nirari III, who in 803 B.C. defeated Benhadad II of Syria and thus took the pressure of Syria from Israel. However, the "savior" may have been the succeeding king of Israel, Jehoash, who defeated the Syrians. Jehoash seems to have reigned two years in conjunction with his father. The death of Jehoahaz was near to that of Joash,

---

1. For details see M.F. Unger, *Arch. & O.T.* p. 246.

king of Judah (796), and shortly after that of Hazael, king of Damascus (801).

2. *Joash, Judah's seventh king – Jehoiada, the priest – The prophet Joel – Restoration of the temple – Apostasy – Martyrdom of Zechariah – Syrian invasion of Judah.* JOASH (abbreviated from JEHOASH)[1] (835-796 B.C.; II Kings 12; II Chron. 24), the eighth king of Judah, was the youngest son of Ahaziah, the sixth king, and of Zibiah of Beersheba. In the year 841 he was left apparently the sole survivor of the stem of David, lopped as it had been by repeated massacres. Jehoshaphat's sons were all slain by their eldest brother Jehoram. All Jehoram's sons were killed by the invading Philistines and Arabians except Ahaziah. Ahaziah's kindred were put to death by Jehu and his sons were all massacred by their grandmother Athaliah except Joash, whose escape and elevation to the kingdom we have already related. He was proclaimed in the seventh year of Jehu, being himself seven years old and he reigned forty years at Jerusalem (II Kings 12:1; II Chron. 24:1). For the first twenty-three years and more he kept his piety and enjoyed high prosperity under the guidance of his early guardian, the high-priest *Jehoiada.* His reign began, as we have seen, with the destruction of the idols and the renewal of the covenant of Jehovah, but the people still worshiped in the high places (II Kings 12:2-3).

The early period of the reign of Joash was probably the time of the prophet JOEL (about 830 B.C.). The background of his prophecy was a devastating locust plague (Joel 1:4,10). The Priests, elders and people are called upon to pray for deliverance (Joel 1:13-14). No mention is made of the king. This fits in well with the time when Joash was too young to have ruled except in name. The deliverance from the locust plague is presented as a type of future blessings, such as the pouring out of the Holy Spirit on all flesh (Joel 2:18-19, 27-28). This began to be fulfilled on the day of Pentecost after Christ ascended (Acts 2:1-17).

In conjunction with Jehoiada, Joash undertook the reparation of the Temple which had been severely damaged during the reign of Athaliah (II Chron. 24:7). The king's zeal was not satisfied with the progress made by Jehoiada and the priests in using the free contributions of the people, and there seems even to be a charge of stealing against the Levites. So the king

---

1. The abbreviated form is used in *Chronicles* and we keep it as a convenient distinction from Jehoash, king of Israel.

constructed the first "money-box" in the well-known form of a chest with a hole in the lid, which was placed at the gate of the Temple for offerings, and each day its contents were counted by the king's officers and handed over at once to the artificers. This was done in the twenty-third year of Joash; the repairs of the Temple were soon finished and there was enough money left to provide vessels for the service of the sanctuary. The money brought for trespass and sin offerings belonged to the priests (II Kings 12:4-16; II Chron. 24:4-14).

The order of the Temple-service was maintained during the life of Jehoiada, the high-priest, who died at the age of 130 and was buried among the kings, for his services to the house of God (II Chron. 24:15-16). A most unhappy change ensued. The princes of Judah, who had doubtless been jealous of the high-priest's unbounded influence, seem to have persuaded the king that it was time to be his own master, and the first use that he and they made of this new liberty was to neglect the house of Jehovah and to serve groves and idols (II Chron. 24:17-18). But not without warning and remonstrance, for though God was displeased with their wickedness: "Yet He sent prophets unto them, to bring them again unto Jehovah; and they testified against them: but they would not give ear" (II Chron. 24:19).

The Spirit of Jehovah came upon Zechariah the son of Jehoiada and probably high-priest, who told them that they could not prosper because they had forsaken God; and even in the court of the sanctuary, which they were perhaps attempting to profane by a sacrifice to Baal, they stoned him to death by the king's order, between the Temple and the altar.[1] This was the very space within which Joash had been guarded by Jehoiada and his line of Levites, and the narrative lays stress on the king's ingratitude to the son of the man who had saved his life. The dying cry of Zechariah, "Jehovah look upon it, and require it," never ceases to echo through the annals of the Jews till they "filled up the measure of their fathers" by invoking the guilt of Christ's blood upon their heads. Meanwhile it found an immediate response in the calamities of the last years of Joash (II Chron. 24:20-22).

---

1. The Zechariah, son of Barachiah, whom Christ mentions in Matt. 23:32,35 as the last of the O.T. martyrs, is almost certainly not the Zechariah, son of Jehoiada, whom Joash slew. Zechariah, son of Barachiah (520-480 B.C.), was the author of the book bearing his name. According to tradition he was martyred as Christ's words indicate. Only by affirming that Chronicles was the last book in the Jewish canon (which it was not in the familiar LXX), and that Matt. 23:35 erroneously has "Barachiah" for "Jehoiada," can anyone argue that Christ referred to the Zechariah whom Joash slew.

Hazael, the king of Syria, had overrun the trans-jordanic provinces of Israel during the disastrous reign of Jehoahaz, which began about the time that Joash finished the restoration of the Temple and was now drawing to a close. After a campaign against the Philistines, Hazael marched toward Jerusalem. His small force defeated the whole host of Judah, and the princes who had seduced Joash into idolatry were either killed in the battle or given up to Hazael and put to death as the ransom of the people from massacre. Jerusalem itself was only saved from the horrors of a sack by the surrender of all the consecrated vessels and treasures both of the Temple and the king's palace. Thus, within a year of the murder of Zechariah, "they executed judgment upon Joash" (II Kings 12:17-18; II Chron. 24:23-24). Scarcely had the Syrians retired, leaving Joash grievously ill in the fortress of Millo, whether from a wound or from vexation (for the cause is not stated), than he was slain in his bed by two of his servants of Ammonite and Moabite extraction at the age of forty-seven. Thus ended a reign that had promised to restore the purity of David's kingdom. Joash was buried with his fathers in the city of David and was succeeded by his son Amaziah (II Kings 12:19-21; II Chron. 24:25-27). It is noteworthy that Joash, though a king in name, was not buried in the tombs of the kings, whereas Jehoiada the priest, though not a king in name, was buried in the tombs of the kings (II Chron. 24:16,25).

And now it seemed as if God had sufficiently punished the personal faults of the first kings of both the restored monarchies for a new era of prosperity began for Israel and Judah under Jehoash and Amaziah, the histories of whose reigns are closely interwoven.

3. *Jehoash, twelfth king of Israel – Death of Elisha.* JEHOASH (or JOASH) (798-782 B.C.; II Kings 13:10-25; 14:15-16), the twelfth king of Israel and the third of the line of Jehu, began to reign in conjunction with his father Jehoahaz in the thirty-seventh year of Joash, king of Judah (798 B.C.), and alone two years later; his entire reign lasted sixteen years. There is an apparent discrepancy between his character and his actions. It would seem as if the calf-worship of Jeroboam had become so inveterate in Israel that a king who practiced it might yet be chosen as a deliverer from foreign oppression if he did not serve Baal; or it may be that God willed to give Israel a final opportunity of restoration, irrespective of the character of the king, "and would not destroy them, neither cast he them from his presence *as yet*"

(II Kings 13:23,5; 14:27). We find Jehoash received with favor when he visited Elisha upon his death-bed and he mourned over him in his own words when he lost Elijah, "O my father! my father! the chariot of Israel, and the horsemen thereof!" The prophet assured him of victory over the Syrians by significant actions. He bade him shoot an arrow from the open window toward Syria, and himself laid his hands with the king's upon the bow, as if to give divine power to the shot, which he called "the arrow of Jehovah's deliverance from the Syrians," who were to be smitten in Aphek. Then he bade the king strike the ground with the arrows. The three strokes signified three victories and the prophet was angry with the king for not striking five or six times, as he would then have consumed them utterly. The whole was a parable of the co-operation of human effort with the divine counsels. It was fulfilled by three great victories which Jehoash gained over Benhadad II, the son of Hazael, and by which he recovered the cities which Hazael had taken from his father. Meanwhile ELISHA died and a last miracle was wrought by his remains. A man was about to be buried in the same rock in which the prophet's sepulchre was hewn, when the bearers were alarmed by the approach of one of the predatory bands of Moabites that now infested Israel. They thrust the body hastily into the first open tomb in the face of the rock. It was that of Elisha and upon touching his remains, the dead man came to life and stood upon his feet. All these events happened in the early years of Jehoash. The other great event of his reign was the conquest of Jerusalem which is related under the reign of Amaziah. He died and was buried in the royal sepulchre at Samaria and was succeeded by his son JEROBOAM II, the greatest king of Israel (II Kings 14:15-16).

4. *Amaziah, eighth king of Judah – Victory over Edom – Jerusalem taken by Jehoash.* AMAZIAH (796-767 B.C.; II Kings 14:1-22; II Chron. 25), the eighth king of Judah, was twenty-five years old when he succeeded his father Joash, in the second year of Jehoash, king of Israel, and he reigned twenty-nine years at Jerusalem. His mother was Jehoaddan of Jerusalem. His was a mixed character like his father's: "He did that which was right in the sight of Jehovah, but not with a perfect heart" — "not like David his father"; and the people still sacrificed in the high places (II Kings 14:3-4; II Chron. 25:2). He put his father's murderers to death but spared their children in obedience to the law of Moses — an act of clemency which is recorded probably because it

was then unusual (II Kings 14:5-6; II Chron. 25:1-4). He prepared a great expedition for the recovery of Edom which had revolted from Jehoram. To the whole force of Judah and Benjamin, numbering 300,000 warriors of twenty years old and upward, he added 100,000 picked men of Israel whom he hired for 100 talents of silver. But at the command of a prophet, he dismissed these mercenaries who returned in anger and sacked several of the cities of Judah. Meanwhile Amaziah advanced into the "Valley of Salt" (the Ghor), south of the Dead Sea and there defeated the Edomites, with the slaughter of 10,000 men. Ten thousand more were dashed to pieces from the rocks of Sela (Petra), the Edomite capital, which Amaziah took and called Joktheel *(Possession of God)*. Then in a shocking display of stupidity and apostasy Amaziah sacrificed to the idols of Mount Seir; and he silenced the reproof of a prophet with threats and with the taunt, "Art thou made of the king's counsel?" "I know," rejoined the prophet, "that God hath determined to destroy thee"; and misfortune filled up the rest of Amaziah's reign. Whether urged on by arrogance or provoked by the conduct of the disbanded mercenaries, he sent a challenge to the king of Israel. Jehoash replied by a parable: "A thistle in Mount Lebanon demanded the daughter of the cedar in marriage; but a wild beast that was passing by trod on the thistle and crushed it: let not the King of Judah boast because he had smitten Edom, but stay quietly at home, lest he and Judah should perish together." Amaziah persisted and the armies met at Beth-shemesh. Judah was utterly defeated and Amaziah taken prisoner. Jehoash led him in triumph to Jerusalem, the north wall of which he broke down from the gate of Ephraim to the corner gate, a space of 400 cubits; and having taken all the treasures of the Temple and the palace, besides hostages, he returned to Samaria, where he died not long after. Amaziah survived Jehoash fifteen years, seemingly of continued declension, till his government became so hateful that he had to flee for his life from a conspiracy formed against him at Jerusalem. He was overtaken and killed at Lachish. His body was borne back by horses to Jerusalem and buried with the kings. He was succeeded by his son Uzziah. During much (23 or 24 years) of Amaziah's reign, his son Uzziah had been coregent. This is indicated by an analysis of data in II Kings 14:22-23; 15:1,8. Note the overlapping in the dates of Amaziah and Uzziah.

   5. *Jeroboam II, Israel's thirteenth king – Expansion of the kingdom –*

The prophets, Jonah, Amos and Hosea – Zechariah, fourteenth king of Israel – End of Jehu's dynasty – Civil war. JEROBOAM II (793-753 B.C.; II Kings 14:23-29), the thirteenth king of Israel and the fourth of the house of Jehu, succeeded his father Jehoash in the fifteenth year of Amaziah and reigned forty-one years at Samaria.[1] His reign is by far the most prosperous in the annals of Israel. To him even more than to his father is the statement applied that, in Israel's decline, God gave them a saviour, in remembrance of His covenant with their fathers; though he also followed the sins of Jeroboam, the son of Nebat. He not only recovered from Syria the whole district east of the Jordan, from Hamath to the Dead Sea, and reconquered Ammon and Moab, but he attacked Damascus itself; and if he did not actually take the city, he regained a large part of its territory for Israel (II Kings 14:23-29). The apparent ease of these conquests may be explained by the sufferings of Syria from the attacks of the great Assyrian empire during the early part of Jeroboam's reign, and then the fact that Assyria itself was weak in the latter part of his reign (II Kings 14:23).

This expansion of Israel in the time of Jeroboam was prophesied by JONAH (II Kings 14:25). This same prophet was sent by God to the great city of Nineveh. There is no more striking proof of the moral grandeur of the religion of Jehovah than this mission of a solitary prophet from the petty kingdom of Israel to warn the great monarch of Western Asia that he and his city should perish unless they repented before God (Jonah 1:1).

Jonah disliked the Assyrians so intensely that he did not want to preach to them lest they repent and God spare them (Jonah 3:10; 4:3). Perhaps the cruelty of the Assyrians accounts for Jonah's feelings. Whatever the cause, Jonah ran the opposite direction from Nineveh and only surrendered his resistance to God's commission after riding within the great fish three days. When Jonah went to Nineveh and preached, the men of Nineveh repented and Jonah himself learned the lesson that all peoples are valuable unto Jehovah, and He loves them all (Jonah 4:10-11). The story is simple and consistent: its truth is endorsed by the express testimony of our Saviour (Matt. 12:39-41; 16:4; Luke 11:29-32), and the objections simply resolve themselves into a disbelief in miracles at all. One needless difficulty has been raised by the use of the word "whale" in our version of the New

---

1. Jeroboam II began as co-regent with his father Jehoash about 12 years before Jehoash's death. (Comp. II K. 13:10; 14:1-2,23; 15:1.)

Testament in place of the "great fish," as it is correctly given in the Old (Jonah 1:17; Matt. 12:40). Cases of animals and men being swallowed by great fishes and surviving the experience even without miraculous help are on record.[1] The prophetic character of the book, though its form is narrative, is seen in the use made of it by our Lord, as an example of repentance in a heathen nation, and a sign of His own three days' abode in the earth. Nay, "the sign of the prophet Jonah" must have been, even without an interpretation, a striking emblem of the resurrection, the doctrine of which is clearly implied in one passage of Jonah's "prayer to God out of the fish's belly": "The earth with her bars was about me forever: yet hast thou brought up my life from corruption, O Jehovah, my God" (Jonah 2:6).

To this period of Jeroboam II belong also the prophets Amos and Hosea, whose writings aid us in filling up the brief narrative of *Kings* by the light they throw on the internal condition of the state, the prevalance of idolatry, the maintenance of "the king's sanctuary" at Bethel under its priest Amaziah, who tried to silence Amos, and the almost universal drunkenness, licentiousness and oppression.

Amos prophesied the judgments of God upon the surrounding nations and upon Israel itself, and in particular the destruction of the house of Jeroboam by the sword and the coming captivity of the people. Amaziah accused him of conspiring against Jeroboam and bade him to betake himself to Judah, his native country; but he did not shrink from predicting the full restoration of the house of David, while he promised the ultimate return of Israel from captivity and their final establishment in their land. His probable date is about 760 B.C. (Amos 7:10-17).

The prophecies of Hoshea are addressed almost equally to Israel and Judah, whose dissensions are deeply deplored, their captivity foretold and their final restoration promised. Hosea's experiences with Gomer, his unfaithful wife, illustrate God's painful experiences with unfaithful Israel. Hosea's children are given names signifying God's relationships with idolatrous Israel (Hosea 1-3). With respect to Israel, we are especially struck by the same tone of affectionate, nay, agonizing forbearance, which we have had occasion to notice repeatedly in the sacred narrative of the period. Like a father in the last struggle of nature against necessity, Jehovah dwells upon the good points in the character of Ephraim, the heir of Jacob's favorite son, before He will consent

---

1. See G.L. Archer, *A Survey of O.T. Intro.*, p. 314 (1974).

to cast him off as incorrigible, and the same spirit is shown to Judah: "O Ephraim, what shall I do unto thee? O Judah, what shall I do unto thee? for your goodness is as a morning cloud, and as the early dew it goeth away" (Hosea 6:4). "How shall I give thee up, Ephraim? how shall I deliver thee, Israel? How shall I make thee as Admah? how shall I set thee as Zeboim?[1] Mine heart is turned within me; my repentings are kindled together" (Hosea 11:8).

Jeroboam II died in 753 B.C. and was buried with the kings of Israel, and we are told, according to the usual formula, that "ZACHARIAH his son reigned in his stead" — the fourteenth king of Israel and the fifth and last of the dynasty of Jehu (II Kings 14:29; 15:8-9).

Of Zachariah himself we are only told that he walked, like his fathers, in the sins of Jeroboam, the son of Nebat. He died the victim to a conspiracy by Shallum, the son of Jabesh, who usurped the crown in the thirty-ninth year of Uzziah (752 B.C.; II Kings 15:9-13). Thus ended the dynasty of Jehu, having lasted 89 years and the promise was fulfilled, that his descendants should reign to the fourth generation; and so also was the prophecy of Amos against Jeroboam. A civil war now ensued as in the time of Omri and Shallum, the assassin of Zachariah, only reigned one month.

6. *Shallum, fifteenth king of Israel – Menahem, sixteenth king – Overlapping reign of Pekah – First invasions of Israel by Assyria – Tribute to Pul or Tiglath-pileser – Pekahiah, seventeenth king – Pekah, eighteenth king – His league with Rezin against Judah.* SHALLUM, the fifteenth king of Israel, had enjoyed his usurpation only a month when he was overthrown and killed, like Zimri, by another competitor, Menahem, the son of Gadi, who marched from Tirzah and took Samaria. It seems probable that, like Omri, Menahem was a general of the murdered king. Another incident of the civil war was the sack of Tiphsah, a city which refused to open its gates to Menahem, with the most horrid cruelties of war (II Kings 15:14-16).

The chronological data[2] make it appear that at the same time that Menahem began to reign in Samaria another soldier, PEKAH, began to rule over Israel in Gilead (752 B.C.; Comp. II Kings 15:25). Such an explanation accounts for the full twenty years of Pekah's reign (II Kings 15:27).

MENAHEM (752-742 B.C.; II Kings 15:17-22), the sixteenth

---

1. Cities of the plain destroyed with Sodom and Gomorrah.
2. Edwin Thiele, *The Mysterious Numbers of the Hebrew Kings*, pp. 123-124.

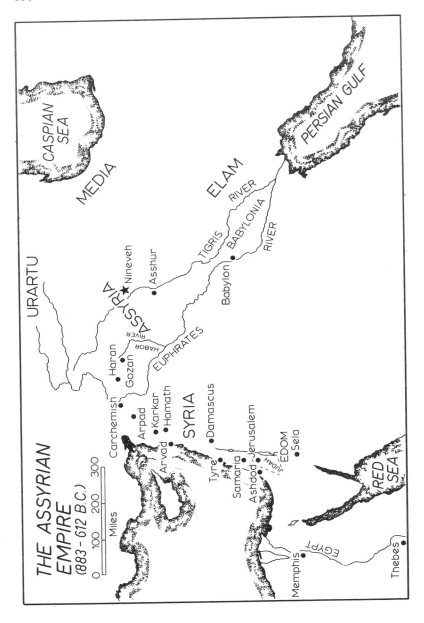

THE ASSYRIAN EMPIRE (883 – 612 B.C.)

Miles
0   100   200   300

king of Israel, and his son PEKAHIAH, the seventeenth king, compose the fifth dynasty, which lasted only twelve years. Of these, Menahem began to reign in the thirty-ninth year of Uzziah, and reigned ten years, with the character which now becomes a formula, "He departed not all his days from the sins of Jeroboam, the son of Nebat" (II Kings 15:17-18). The great point of interest in his reign is the first direct attack upon Israel by the Assyrians — a presage of the catastrophe which was finished thirty years later. The steps of the process have often been repeated in history. The first danger is averted by a bribe, which only serves as a temptation to new aggression. Each new attack leaves the doomed state weaker and weaker, till it is reduced to tribute, and at last a despairing effort to shake off the yoke brings down destruction. The king of Assyria who began the attack on Israel under Menahem is named PUL and is the first Assyrian king mentioned in Scripture. But there are indications that this was not the first contact[1] between Assyria and the kingdoms of Palestine. We have seen that Jehu appears as a tributary on the black obelisk of Shalmaneser III and it would seem that Menahem had neglected to apply to the king of Assyria for the usual "confirmation of his kingdom" (II Kings 15:19). Menahem submitted and paid Pul 1000 talents of silver as the price of his confirmation which he exacted by a forced contribution of fifty shekels apiece from the rich men of Israel (II Kings 15:17-22).

The Assyrian king called *Pul* was none other than the great Tiglath-pileser III, the greatest monarch in Assyrian history. He was called Pul (or Pulu) in Babylon (perhaps this was his original name), and took the name Tiglath-pileser from an earlier Assyrian conqueror. His nineteen-year reign (744-727 B.C.) was constant warfare and conquest. The name of Menahem appears in the annals of Tiglath-pileser.

PEKAHIAH (742-740 B.C.; II Kings 15:23-26), the son of Menahem, was killed after a reign of only two years by PEKAH, the son of Remaliah (752-732 B.C.; II Kings 15:27-31), and the eighteenth king of Israel, whose reign of twenty years is closely interwoven with the history of Judah. (It seems that Pekah began his reign over part of Israel in Gilead at the same time that Menahem began in Samaria.) Pekah's league with Rezin, king of Syria, against Judah and the consequent destruction of the kingdom of Damascus and captivity of a large part of Israel are

---

1. A monument of Shalmaneser III indicates that Shalmaneser in 853 B.C. fought a coalition of kings at Karkar, north of Hamath in the Orontes valley. Among the kings in the coalition were Benhadad of Syria and Ahab the Israelite. See M.F. Unger, *Arch. and O.T.*, p. 244.

related under the reign of Ahaz. He was put to death by Hoshea who succeeded him as the last king of Israel.

7. *Uzziah, ninth king of Judah – His good reign and successful wars – Profanes the temple and dies a leper – Call of Isaiah the prophet.* UZZIAH (or Azariah), the ninth king of Judah (790-739 B.C.; II Kings 15:1-7; II Chron. 26), was set on the throne by the people, after the murder of his father Amaziah, in the twenty-seventh year of Jeroboam II. He was then sixteen years old and reigned for the long period of fifty-two years. A study of II Kings 14:23 and 15:1, 8, indicates that Uzziah was co-regent with his father Amaziah 23 or 24 years. His mother was Jecholiah of Jerusalem (II Kings 15:2). He was contemporary with nearly half the reign of Jeroboam II, with Zachariah, Shallum, Menahem and Pekahiah, and the last year of his reign was the first of Pekah's. He was one of the ablest of the kings of Judah, serving Jehovah and enjoying unbroken prosperity, till he profaned the Temple, though still the high places were not removed. Like his grandfather Joash in relation to Jehoiada, he was at first under the influence of Zechariah, a prophet "who had understanding in the vision of God."[1] He began his reign by recovering and rebuilding Eloth (near Ezion-geber), the old port of Solomon and Jehoshaphat at the eastern head of the Red Sea (II Kings 14:22; II Chron. 26:2). His successful wars restored Judah nearly to the power she had possessed under the latter king. He received tribute from Ammon and subdued the Philistines, razing the fortifications of Gath and Ashdod, and building fortresses throughout their country. The Arabs of the southern desert, whom we have seen with the Philistines, first as tributaries and then as enemies of Judah, were reduced to the former condition. Towers were built and wells were dug, both in the maritime plain *(Shefelah)* and the Idumaean desert *(Arabah)* for the king's numerous flocks; and he had husbandmen and vine-dressers in the plains about Carmel (in the south) and in the mountains. While thus improving the resources of his country, Uzziah made preparations for its defense, whether against Israel, Syria or Assyria. He repaired the wall of Jerusalem, which had been broken down after his father's defeat by Jehoash, building towers at the corner gate and the valley gate, and the angle of the wall. He armed the fortifications with newly-invented military engines, the first of which we read in Jewish history, like the balista and catapult, for shooting arrows

---

1. II Chron. 26:4,5. This Zechariah must, of course, not be confounded with the priest martyred under Joash, nor with the prophet whose book is extant and who prophesied after the Captivity.

and great stones. He kept on foot an army of 307,500 men "that made war with mighty power," under 2600 captains, "the chief of the fathers of the mighty men of valor," with Hananiah as commander-in-chief. They went forth to war by bands, the roll of which was kept by the king's scribe, Jeiel, and the ruler of his house, Maaseiah. By the care of Uzziah, all the soldiers were armed with spears and shields, helmets and coats of mail, bows and slings. "And his name spread far abroad, for he was marvelously helped, till he was strong" (II Chron. 26:1-15). But he could not bear his prosperity. In his arrogance, he claimed the functions of the priests, not those which we have seen always exercised by judges and kings of offering burnt sacrifices, but those which belonged exclusively to the sons of Aaron. He entered into the Holy Place to burn incense on the golden altar. He was followed by the high-priest Azariah, with eighty of the most courageous of the priests, prepared to resist the profanation by force. The high-priest reproved the king with all the boldness of his office and warned him to leave the sanctuary, predicting that dishonor would befall him. What reply or deed Uzziah meditated in his rage we are not told, but as he stood, censer in hand, there rose with the flush of anger to his forehead the spot of leprosy, the sign of his exclusion even from the court of the house of God. When the priests saw it they thrust him out; nay, he himself was so struck with the judgment that he hastened from the sanctuary. He remained a leper to the day of his death, secluded in a separate house, according to the directions of the law, while the government was committed to his son, Jotham. When he died, he was not received into the sepulchre of the kings but buried in a field attached to it (II Kings 15:5-7; II Chron. 26:16-25). His life was written by the prophet Isaiah, as well as in the Chronicles of Judah.

In the year that King Uzziah died, the prophet ISAIAH saw the Lord in the temple in great glory. In that vision Isaiah was called to a life of high prophetic service (Isaiah 6). He preached and served as counsellor to kings for many years, during the reigns of Jotham, Ahaz and Hezekiah. According to tradition he was sawed in two in the time of King Manasseh (Heb. 11:37; II Kings 21:16).

8. *Jotham, tenth king of Judah – His piety and prosperity.* JOTHAM (751-736 B.C.; II Kings 15:32-38; II Chron. 27), the tenth king of Judah, was twenty-five years old when he succeeded his father Uzziah in the second year of Pekah, king of Israel, and he reigned sixteen years at Jerusalem. He was co-regent with his father about

twelve years of this period (II Kings 15:5,32). After the sixteen years of his reign, he continued on to a twentieth year, probably in retirement (II Kings 15:30). His mother was Jerushah, the daughter of Zadok. He was one of the most pious and most prosperous of the kings, but the people grew more and more corrupt. He carried on his father's works, both in peace and war. He built the high gate of the Temple and the tower called Ophel on the city wall, fortified cities in the mountains of Judah, and castles and towers in the forests. War was renewed with the Ammonites who were compelled to pay him an annual tribute of 100 talents of silver, 10,000 measures of wheat and 10,000 of barley. "So he became mighty, and established his ways before Jehovah his God." Toward the close of his reign, Rezin, king of Damascus, began, in alliance with Pekah, king of Israel, those attacks on Judah, which proved so disastrous under Jotham's weak successor Ahaz.

9. *Ahaz, eleventh king of Judah – War with Syria and Israel – Prophecy of Immanuel – Jewish captives restored by Israel – Ahaz calls in Tiglath-pileser – Destruction of kingdom of Damascus – Captivity of Trans-Jordanic and northern tribes – Ahaz goes to Damascus – His shameless idolatries.* AHAZ (743-728 B.C.; II Kings 16; II Chron. 28), the eleventh king of Judah, succeeded his father in the seventeenth year of Pekah, king of Israel, and reigned sixteen years at Jerusalem. He reigned about eight years as co-regent with his father Jotham (II Kings 15:27; 16:1; 17:1). He departed entirely from the virtues of the last three kings and plunged into all the idolatries of the surrounding nations, making molten images for Baal and sacrificing his children to Moloch in the valley of Hinnom, besides offering sacrifice in the high places, on every hill and under every green tree. His punishment quickly followed. The war already begun by Pekah and Rezin was vigorously prosecuted with a view to set on the throne of Judah a creature of their own, the son of Tabeal (Isaiah 7:6). The order of the events that followed is obscure. Most probably on the march to Jerusalem, the allies defeated Judah with the slaughter of 120,000 men in a great battle in which a champion of Ephraim, named Zichri, slew Maaseiah, the king's son, and two of his chief officers; and on their retreat they carried off 200,000 women and children from the cities which were now left undefended (II Chron. 28:5-8).

Their attack upon Jerusalem itself was unsuccessful, chiefly in consequence of the spirit infused into the people by ISAIAH. To this epoch belongs the celebrated prophecy in which the birth of the child IMMANUEL, whose very name, expressing the devout confidence, *"God is with us,"* was a sign of the speedy overthrow of both the hostile kings by Assyria (Isa. 7:10-14). A second sign was given by the birth of a child who received the significant name of Maher-shalal-hash-baz, "Make speed to the spoil! hasten to the prey!" (Isa. 8:1-4). And in that exalted style of pregnant meaning, which has given Isaiah the name of "the evangelic prophet," these passing wars are dignified by the most glowing prophecies of the Messiah's kingdom (Isa. 9:1-7).

It is a melancholy comment upon some of the grandest passages of Scripture that they seem to have made no lasting impression on the king to whom they were delivered. His persistence in sin insured the continuance of God's judgments. It would seem that Pekah and Rezin retired from Jerusalem by different routes. While the latter took from Judah the lately recovered port of Elath and gave it to the Edomites, the former returned toward Samaria with his miserable captives. The dying glory of Israel burns up with an expiring flame (Isa. 7:4) in the deed of mercy that followed. The prophet ODED went out to meet the army, reproved them for their purpose of enslaving the children of their brethren, and commanded them to restore the captives. The appeal touched the heart of the princes of the people and they refused to let the prisoners be brought within their borders. The soldiers left them in their hands and arrangements were at once made for their relief. They were fed and anointed, clothed and shod from the booty, the feeble were placed on asses and so they were conducted to Jericho and delivered to their brethren (II Chron. 28:6-15).

The retreat of Pekah and Rezin gave Ahaz no permanent relief. In the words of Isaiah, God had raised up against him the Syrians in front (the East), and the Philistines behind (the West). They overran the whole maritime plain *(Shefelah)* and the highlands that border it, taking Beth-shemesh, Aijalon and other cities. The Edomites, set free by the Syrians, invaded Judah and carried off many captives, while the Syrians and Israelites threatened to return. Ahaz now applied for help to TIGLATH-PILESER, king of Assyria, against Syria and Israel, declaring himself his vassal and sending him all the treasures that were left in the Temple, the royal palace and the houses of the princes. The "Tiger Lord of Asshur" marched first against Damascus, which he took, killing Rezin and transporting the inhabitants to Kir, as Amos had foretold (732 B.C.; II Kings 16:7-9; II Chron. 28:16-22; Amos 1:4-5). Thus ended the great Syrian kingdom of Damascus after a duration of about 235 years. Israel was stripped of the whole country east of the Jordan and the tribes of Reuben, Gad and half Manasseh at length reaped the fruit of their hasty desire to have the first settlement in the land by being the first who were carried into captivity. Their fate was shared by their brethren in Galilee but the captivity of these northern tribes was only partial (II Kings 15:29). Ahaz gained little by the intervention of his too powerful ally who, says the narrative, "helped him not." He went to meet the Assyrian king at Damascus; we know not what hard conditions were imposed upon him, but we are told that "in the time of his distress he trespassed yet more against Jehovah"; for he saw at Damascus an altar which incited him

> *"God's altar to disparage, and displace*
> *For one of Syrian mould, whereon to burn*
> *His odious offerings, and adore the gods*
> *Whom he had vanquished."*

He sent its pattern to Jerusalem, where Urijah the high-priest prepared an altar of the same form before the king's return from Damascus, when with a profanity on which Athaliah even had not ventured, Ahaz put it in the place of the brazen altar and commanded Urijah to offer on it all the burnt-offerings and other sacrifices. Superstition led him, however, to preserve the brazen altar for oracular uses and he placed it on the north of his great altar. The great brass sea of Solomon was dismounted from its supporting oxen and the lavers from their bases which were sent to the king of Assyria, together with the coverings which had been built for the king's entry to the house and for the shelter of the worshipers on the Sabbath. The golden vessels of the house of God were cut in pieces and sent with the rest and the sanctuary itself was shut up, while idol altars were erected in every corner of Jerusalem, and high places in every city of Judah (II Kings 16:10-18; II Chron. 28:22-25). It was not for want of provocation to Jehovah that Judah did not at once share the captivity of Israel; but for the sake of "the sure mercies of David" another respite was given, and a new era of godliness throws its light over the reign of Hezekiah, amid all the pressure of invasion and the threats of approaching captivity.

10. *Hezekiah, twelfth king of Judah – Reform of religion – Great Passover – Brazen serpent destroyed – Defeats Philistines – Revolts from*

Assyria. HEZEKIAH, the twelfth king of Judah (728-695 B.C.;[1] II Kings 18-20; II Chron. 29-32; Isa. 36-39), succeeded his father Ahaz in the third year of Hoshea, the nineteenth and last king of Israel. He was twenty-five years old and reigned twenty-nine years at Jerusalem. His mother was Abi (or Abijah), the daughter of Zechariah. His character is marked by the commendation which has not been repeated since Jehoshaphat, "He did that which was right in the sight of Jehovah, *according to all that David his father had done.*" The historian gives him this panegyric, "He trusted in Jehovah, God of Israel; so that after him was none like him among all the kings of Judah, nor any that were before him" (II Kings 18:5).

In the very first month of his reign (II Chron. 29:3), he began the reformation of religion by reopening and repairing the doors of the Temple, which had been closed by Ahaz, and cleansing the sacred edifice. The details of the work and of the sacrifices that followed, with the exhortations of the king to the priests and Levites, are related at length in the *Chronicles* (II Chron. 29). Then follows the account of the great Passover (the first recorded since the time of Joshua), which was kept in the second month for the reason expressly allowed in the law, the ceremonial impurity both of priests and people in the first month. The king had sent messengers through all Israel as well as Judah to invite the people to return to God, that He might return to the remnant who were escaped from the king of Assyria, and be merciful to those who had been carried captive.[2] The message was treated with general contempt; still, many came, not only from Ephraim and Manasseh but from the distant tribes of Issachar, Zebulun and Asher, to unite with their brethren of Judah to whom God had given one heart to obey Him. Several of these visitors being still unpurified, the paschal lambs were slain by the Levites for the people; and Hezekiah implored pardon for those who ate the Passover otherwise than according to the law, but whose *hearts* were prepared to seek the God of their fathers. The seven days of the feast were doubtless much interrupted through these causes,

---

1. See "Chronology of the Divided Kingdom" for information about the date of Hezekiah.
2. Eminent modern critics see here (especially in II Chron. 30:6-9; 31:1) a proof that this Passover was not kept till after the captivity of Israel in the sixth year of Hezekiah. But the language seems clearly to apply to a remnant still existing *as a people,* whose repentance might yet avert the fate that had befallen their brethren in the east and north. Nor is their general scorn of the message (30:10) credible immediately after such a judgment. Nor does the description at all correspond to the utter desolation described in II K. 17. See especially the mention of the Israelites returning "every man to his *possession, into their own cities.*" The chaotic conditions in Israel during its last years permitted the messengers of Hezekiah to circulate through the land without hindrance.

as well as by the occupation, to which the people zealously applied themselves, of destroying the idol altars throughout Jerusalem. By the spontaneous impulse of the worshipers, the feast was prolonged to fourteen days, amid such joy as had not been seen in Jerusalem since the time of Solomon and God heard their prayers. Departing to their homes, they broke to pieces the idols, cut down the Asherim and threw down the high places and altars through Ephraim and Manasseh, as well as through Judah and Benjamin, while the king arranged the service of the Temple (II Chron. 30, 31).

One instance of consummate wisdom, mingled with Hezekiah's zeal against idolatry, deserves to be especially mentioned. The brazen serpent, which Moses had lifted up in the wilderness, had long been an object of worship, not only as the memorial of a great deliverance but probably in connection with the serpent-worship prevalent in the East. No regard for so curious a relic of their early history prevented Hezekiah from breaking it in pieces like any other idol and speaking of it as only "a piece of brass" (Nehustan). We can well believe that this phrase was addressed to the "scornful men," certain rulers at Jerusalem, probably the old friends and counselors of Ahaz of whose opposition we learn from Isaiah, the king's great supporter and counselor by the word of Jehovah (Isa. 28:14-18). The head of this party was Shebna (probably a foreigner), who seems to have been degraded at the demand of Isaiah, from the office of treasurer to that of scribe (or secretary), the former post being conferred on Eliakim, the son of Hilkiah (Isa. 22:15-25; II Kings 18:18).

The reunion of the people in the fear of God infused new life into their national policy. The Philistines, who had made such inroads during the last reign, were beaten back again as far as Gaza with great slaughter.[1] Trusting in God's protection, Hezekiah even ventured to refuse the tribute which his father had paid to the king of Assyria (II Kings 18:7). The momentous character of such a step at the existing crisis will be seen by turning to the history of the kingdom of Israel. If it was taken after the overthrow of Samaria or even after the beginning of the siege, it might seem to have been the height of rashness. But it was more truly one of those acts of "considerate courage" by which nations are rescued in their extremity; and with prudence on the part of Hoshea, it might have proved the salvation of both

---

1. II Kings 18:8. According to Josephus all their cities were taken except Gath and Gaza (Ant. 9:13,3).

kingdoms. The revolt may be safely placed about the third year of Hezekiah.

11. *Hoshea, Israel's nineteenth and last king – Signs of a revival – Revolts from Shalmaneser – First Assyrian invasion – Hoshea's secret alliance with Egypt and imprisonment – Siege and capture of Samaria – End of Israel and captivity of the Ten Tribes – Summary of Israel's sins – Fate of the captives – Colonists later brought into the land.* HOSHEA (732-722 B.C.; II Kings 17), the son of Elah, the nineteenth and last king of the separate kingdom of Israel, had conspired against Pekah and killed him "in the twentieth year of Jotham, the son of Uzziah," by which we must understand the twentieth year from Jotham's accession, which is the fourth of Ahaz (II Kings 15:30). Calculating the reign of Hoshea from another starting point (as is evidently done in II Kings 17:1), from the time of Ahaz' co-regency with Jotham in 743, Hoshea's reign is reckoned as beginning in the twelfth year of Ahaz.

We are somewhat surprised to find that the character of Hoshea, Israel's final king, was not as evil as that of his predecessors. Though corrupted by the long prevalence of idolatry and wickedness, "he did evil in the sight of Jehovah," the record is qualified by the addition, *"but not as the kings of Israel that were before him"* (II Kings 17:2). We have seen the freedom with which the messengers of Hezekiah traversed his kingdom and with which the worshipers from Israel went up to Jerusalem; nor do we read of any opposition to their zealous destruction of the idols and altars in Ephraim and Manasseh. We read that Hoshea revolted from the king of Assyria (II Kings 17:4). Possibly Hoshea's revolt from Shalmaneser of Assyria was no less an act of patriotism than Hezekiah's, though not prompted by such purely religious motives. Hoshea was, in fact, the best king in the whole line from Jeroboam.

Nor ought we to be surprised that the final catastrophe came in his reign. Speaking humanly, the state was past redemption; the utter corruption and impenitence of the people are confirmed by their scornful rejection of Hezekiah's call to repentance and union. Even the king was only some shades better than his predecessors, and it was no partial reform that could save and renew the state. Viewing the case from the higher ground taken throughout the Scripture history — the inseparable connection between national prosperity or adversity and religious obedience or rebellion — we cannot say that it was too late for Israel to be saved; as Sodom would have been, if ten righteous men had been found in her: as Nineveh was, when her people repented at the preaching of Jonah. They had only forty days of grace; Hoshea and his people had six years: let us now see how they used them. In about the fifth year of Hoshea, Shalmaneser, who had succeeded Tiglath-pileser in 726 B.C., marched against Hoshea to enforce payment of the tribute. Hoshea submitted and became tributary to Assyria. We could plausibly argue that this revolt was politically and even morally justifiable. But in the religious point of view it was an utter wrong and failure. Had Hoshea made common cause with Hezekiah and thrown himself on the protection of Jehovah, we have a right to believe that the times of David might have returned. But Hoshea took the very course denounced by the law of Moses, reliance upon Egypt. The long contest had begun between the sovereigns of Egypt and Western Asia for the frontier province of Palestine and both had their partisans at the court of Samaria. The king of Egypt, who is called So in the Scripture narrative, was probably Shabaka or possibly Sib'e, who fought Sargon II in 720 B.C. He belonged to the warlike twenty-fifth (Ethiopian) dynasty, who opposed the progress of Assyria with all their force. Hoshea formed a secret league with him and withheld the accustomed tribute from Shalmaneser who, informed of the conspiracy, seized the king of Israel and shut him up in prison where he was bound with fetters and treated with cruel indignity (II Kings 17:4; Micah 5:1). His sudden destruction is compared prophetically by the prophet Hosea to the disappearance of the foam upon the water (Hosea 10:7). The imprisonment of Hoshea clearly preceded the siege of Samaria: it may be that he was seized on a visit to Nineveh for the purpose of excusing his conduct. Shalmaneser then marched against Israel and after overrunning the country, laid siege to Samaria in the seventh year of Hoshea, the fourth of Hezekiah (II Kings 17:5; 18:6). Then followed one of those memorable defenses, the despairing efforts of dying nations. We have no details of the siege but Isaiah gives a glowing description of the mighty instrument of Jehovah smiting like a hailstorm the glorious beauty of the city, which towered on its hill like a crown of pride, the head of the fat valleys of the drunkards of Ephraim (Isa. 28:1-4). Its strong position enabled the city to hold out for three years (II Kings 17:5), during which we learn from the Assyrian monuments that Shalmaneser died and was succeeded by Sargon II, a change not noticed in the Scripture narrative, which after the first mention of Shalmaneser (II Kings 17:3; Cf.

vss. 4-6), only speaks of the "King of Assyria." The city was taken in the ninth year of Hoshea, the sixth of Hezekiah (722 B.C.; II Kings 17:6; 18:10). Sargon himself claims (possibly falsely) the capture of Samaria in the following terms: "Samaria I looked at, I captured"; "27,280 men (or families) who dwelt in it I carried away." According to the Scripture narrative, he "carried *Israel* away into Assyria, and placed them in Halah and in Habor by the river of Gozan and the cities of the Medes." This deportation of the people extended to Samaria and its dependent towns, a region small in comparison to the original kingdom of the ten tribes. The region east of Jordan had already been so treated by Tiglath-pileser, who had also carried away the northern tribes, but not to the same extent; for a remnant were left who form the nucleus of the mixed population of the later GALILEE. The cities in the south of Ephraim, which had been attached to Judah by conquest or by the bond of religion under Hezekiah, probably shared the fortunes of the southern kingdom. The removal was of that complete character, which we have seen in the case of Damascus and which was frequently practiced by the conquerors of Western Asia. The process is compared to the act of "wiping out a dish and turning it upside down" (II Kings 21:13). Josephus states that the king of Assyria "transplanted all the people" *(Ant.* IX, 14, 1). These statements, which have the most important bearing on the national character of the later "Samaritans," are confirmed in various ways. Not a word is said of any remnant, as in the case of the captivity of Judah, when "the poor of the land were left to be vine-dressers and husbandmen" (II Kings 25:12); nor, if such a remnant had been left, could the new population have been so ignorant of "the manner of the God of the land" as to need one of the captive priests to be sent from Assyria to teach them to fear Jehovah (II Kings 17:25-28). The ten tribes never returned to their land as a distinct people: and the contrast between their fate and that of Judah in both these points marks the favor of God to the house of David, and to the people who never entirely cast off His worship.

Thus ended the kingdom of Israel after a duration of just 209 years (931-722 B.C.), under nineteen kings and nine dynasties. Four of these dynasties perished with their founders (Zimri, Shallum, Pekah and Hoshea) and hardly deserve to be called dynasties. Three dynasties — those of Jeroboam, Baasha and Mehanem had two kings each: the house of Omri numbered four kings in three generations: Jehu's, the longest of all, reigned for five generations from father to son and all its kings died a natural death except the last, Zachariah. Of the other kings, only Jeroboam I, Baasha, Omri, Ahaziah and Mehanem had the same lot; the rest were slain by traitors or in battle or died in captivity. Their character was even worse than their fate. Not one in the whole list is commended either for morality or piety: all were idolaters and traitors to Jehovah. Even the zeal of Jehu ended in idol-worship and the patriotism of Hoshea was marred by disloyalty to God. The sacred historian concludes their history with an impressive and affecting summary of their sins, in which they were followed by Judah, provoking the anger of Jehovah till "He removed them out of his sight." First, "there was none left but the tribe of Judah only"; but their sins had already caused Jehovah to "rend Israel from the house of David"; and at last "Jehovah rejected all the seed of Israel." But not till He had given them abundant invitations to return to God by the long line of PROPHETS, the preachers of repentance and reformation. Besides the many whose names are too often forgotten because their writings are not extant, ELIJAH and ELISHA shine amid the darkest night of Israel's idolatry; Zechariah, the son of Jehoiada, seals his testimony against the apostasy of Judah with his martyrdom; and the century before the fall of Samaria is glorified by the names of JONAH, AMOS and HOSEA in Israel; and JOEL, OBADIAH, ISAIAH and MICAH in Judah.

The end of the kingdom of Israel involves two questions of great interest — the fate of the captives who were carried away and the condition of the country after their removal. Respecting the first point, we have had the statement of their transplantation to certain districts of Assyria and Media, where we almost lose sight of them. Nor is this surprising. The gradual contraction of the limits of the Samaritan kingdom suggests, what the inscription of Sargon confirms, that the numbers carried captive at last were far less considerable than is commonly supposed. Their absorption in the surrounding population would be aided by their long addiction to the practices of idolatry, and the loss of reverence for their religion involved the absence of care for the records of their national existence. As they furnished no confessors and martyrs, like Daniel and "the three children," so neither did they preserve the genealogies on which Judah based the order of the restored commonwealth (Ezra 2; Neh. 7). But yet their traces are not utterly lost. The fact that a priest was found among them to teach the Samaritans to fear Jehovah, proves that

they maintained some form of worship in His name. The Book of
Tobit preserves the record of domestic piety among captives of
the tribe of Naphtali. The first Jewish exiles who were carried
away by Sennacherib, seem to have been settled in the same
districts as their brethren of Israel, on whom their influence
would be salutary, and after the great captivity of Judah, it is most
interesting to see how continually Ezekiel addresses the captives
by the name of *Israel*. The prophetic symbol of the rod of Judah
and "the rod of the children of Israel, his *companions*" being joined
into one, in order to their restoration as one nation, as Isaiah also
had predicted (Ezek. 37:15-28; Isa. 11:13,16), seems to imply that
all that was worth preserving in Israel became amalgamated with
Judah and either shared in the restoration or became a part of the
"dispersion," who were content to remain behind and who spread
the knowledge of the true God throughout the East. It is an
important fact that St. James addresses the "dispersion" as "the
twelve tribes." The edict of Cyrus, addressed to the servants of
Jehovah, God of *Israel*, would find a response beyond the tribe of
Judah, and though none of the ten tribes appear *as such* among
the returned exiles, there is room for many of their families in the
number of those who could not prove their predigrees.[1] As for
the rest, according to the very images of the prophet,

> "Like the *dew on the mountain*,
> Like the *foam on the river*,
> Like the bubble on the fountain,
> *They are gone and* FOREVER" (Hosea 13:3; 10:7).

The very wildness of the speculations of those who have sought
them at the foot of the Himalayas and on the coast of Malabar
among the Nestorians of Abyssinia and the Indians of North
America, or among the English-speaking people of Europe and
North America, proves sufficiently the hopelessness of the
attempt. Have then the promises of God concerning their
restoration failed? No! They were represented, as we have seen,
in the return of Judah; and for the rest, though they are lost to us,
"the Lord knoweth them that are His." We do not enter, in this
work, into the controversy respecting the return of Israel to their
own land. But of this there is no question, that when God shall
reveal, "out of every nation, those who have feared God, and
wrought righteousness," all the tribes of believers in Israel will be
owned, in some especial manner, as His people. That this

---

1. At the time of Christ there were Jews known to belong to other tribes than Judah, Benjamin and Levi; as
Anna, of the tribe of Asher (Luke 2:36). Such may have been descended either from returned captives or
from those left in the north beyond the limits of Samaria.

restoration will be not temporal but spiritual seems to be the plain teaching of St. Paul in the passage which forms the great New Testament authority on the whole subject (Romans 9-11).

We turn back to the condition of their deserted land, guarding first against the common error of confusing its limits with those of the old kingdom of the ten tribes. The final deportation by Shalmaneser (or Sargon), following upon that made by Tiglath-pileser, justifies our speaking of the captivity of the ten tribes, but the depopulation in the earlier captivity was much less complete than in the latter, at least on the west of Jordan. This has already been seen in the description of Hezekiah's reformation. It was only the region immediately round Samaria that was utterly depopulated. The description of its repeopling follows immediately upon the narrative of the Captivity in the *Second Book of Kings* (II Kings 17:24-41), but it is clear that at least most of the importation followed a very considerable interval. The new colonization is expressly ascribed to Esar-haddon, the grandson of Sargon, and "the great and noble Asnapper," a name for Asshurbanipal, king of Assyria 668-633 B.C. (Ezra 4:2,10). This is confirmed by the fact that some of the colonists came from Babylon, which only became subject to Assyria under Sennacherib, the father of Esar-haddon. It is probable that the colonization was suggested by Esar-haddon's observation of the state of the country during his campaign against Manasseh, about 675 B.C. It was effected by the usual Assyrian method of removing the whole population of other conquered cities or districts in a distant part of the empire, "from Babylon, Cuthah, Ava (or Ival), Hamath and Sepharvaim," the three last being places mentioned among the conquests of Sennacherib (II Kings 17:24; 18:3). The new inhabitants imported their idolatrous worship and God showed his jealousy for His own land by plaguing them with lions, which had doubtless multiplied during nearly half a century of desolation. They ascribed the infliction to their ignorance of "the manner of the God of the land," and the king of Assyria sent back one of the captive priests, who established himself at Bethel and "taught them how to fear Jehovah." His teaching was probably mixed with no little error but it seems to have been free from the old idolatry of Jeroboam. The worship thus established was regarded by the people as merely local and they none the less set up their own idols in the old high places of the Israelites: Succothbenoth, the god of

Babylon; Nergal, Ashima, Nibhaz and Tartak, the gods of Cuth, Hamath and the Arvites, while the Sepharvites burnt their children to Adram-melech. Priests were appointed for the high places from the lowest of the people. The compromise between their new religion and their old idolatries is thus summed up: "They feared Jehovah and served their own gods." The writer lays the greatest stress on their entire departure from the law of Moses, and concludes by stating that these practices were followed by "their children and their children's children: as did their fathers, so do they unto this day" (II Kings 17:41).

These facts explain that long course of mutual hostility which the subsequent history develops and which is summed up in the saying, "The Jews have no dealings with the Samaritans," not so much as to ask and receive a cup of cold water at a well-side in the noonday heat of travel (John 4:9).

Questions Over Section III
Jehu to End of Israel

Jehoahaz of Israel
1. What Syrian king had power over Israel continually during Jehoahaz' reign (II Kings 13:3)?
2. How did Jehoahaz obtain some deliverance (II Kings 13:4-5)?
3. How many troops, horsemen and chariots were left to Jehoahaz (II Kings 13:7)?

Joash of Judah
1. How old was Joash when he began to reign (II Kings 12:1)?
2. Was Joash good or evil (II Kings 12:2)?
3. Who was the good counsellor of Joash (II Chron. 24:2)?
4. What project did Joash undertake (II Chron. 24:4)?
5. How did Joash first try to raise money (II Chron. 24:5)?
6. How did this first financial drive work out (II Chron. 24:5-6)?
7. How was money finally raised (II Chron. 24:8,11; II Kings 12:9)?
8. How did the temple repair project progress (II Chron. 24:13)?
9. Who came appealing to Joash after Jehoiada's death (II Chron. 24:17)?
10. What prophet denounced Joash for backsliding (II Chron. 24:20)?

11. What happened to this prophet (II Chron. 24:21-22)?
12. What enemy army invaded Judah in Joash's time (II Chron. 24:23)?
13. What city did Hazael take (II Kings 12:17)?
14. Why did not Hazael take Jerusalem (II Kings 12:18)?
15. Who slew Joash and why (II Chron. 24:25; II Kings 12:20)?
16. Where was Joash buried (II Chron. 24:25)?

Jehoash of Israel
1. Was Jehoash a strong or weak king (II Kings 13:13)?
2. Who visited Elisha in his final sickness (II Kings 13:14)?
3. What did Elisha predict by the shooting of an arrow (II Kings 13:17)?
4. What miracle was done by Elisha after his death (II Kings 13:20-21)?
5. Why did not God permit Syria to wipe out Israel (II Kings 13:23)?
6. Who succeeded Hazael as king of Syria (II Kings 13:25)?
7. How many times did Jehoash smite Syria (II Kings 13:25)?

Amaziah
1. Was Amaziah a good king (II Kings 14:3)?
2. What did Amaziah do to the murderers of his father, Joash (II Kings 14:5)?
3. With what nations did Amaziah war (II Kings 14:7,11)?
4. What mercenary troops did Amaziah hire (II Chron. 25:6)?
5. Did he keep and use the mercenary troops (II Chron. 25:7)?
6. What did the Israelite troops do when dismissed (II Chron. 25:10,13)?
7. What people did Amaziah slaughter (II Chron. 25:11,14)?
8. How many did he throw off a rock cliff (II Chron. 25:12)?
9. What terrible thing did Amaziah do in Edom (II Chron. 25:14)?
10. How did Amaziah receive a prophet sent to reprove him (II Chron. 25:16)?
11. What challenge did Amaziah issue to Jehoash of Israel (II Kings 14:8)?
12. By what fable did Jehoash answer him (II Kings 14:9)?
13. Who won — Amaziah or Jehoash (II Kings 14:13)?
14. What did Jehoash do to Jerusalem (II Kings 14:13)?
15. How did Amaziah die? Where? Why (II Kings 14:19; II Chron. 25:27)?
16. Who succeeded Amaziah (II Kings 14:21)?

Jeroboam II
1. Was Jeroboam II strong or weak (II Kings 14:25)?
2. What territory and cities did Jeroboam recover and capture (II Kings 14:25,28)?
3. What three prophets prophesied in Israel in the time of Jeroboam II?
4. What prophet foretold Jeroboam's successes (II Kings 14:25)?

Zechariah
1. How long did Zechariah reign (II Kings 15:8)?
2. Who slew Zechariah? Where did the assassination occur (II Kings 15:10)?
3. Whose dynasty ended with the death of Zechariah (II Kings 15:12)?

Shallum of Israel, Menahem, Pekahiah and Pekah
1. How long did Shallum reign (II Kings 15:13)?
2. Who slew Shallum (II Kings 15:14)?
3. What did Menahem do to the city of Tiphsah (II Kings 15:16)?
4. What person seems to have begun to reign over Israel in Gilead at the same time that Menahem began to reign (II Kings 15:25)?
5. What foreign king came upon Menahem (II Kings 15:19)?
6. How much tribute did Menahem have to pay (II Kings 15:19)?
7. Who succeeded Menahem (II Kings 15:23)?
8. How long did Pekahiah reign (II Kings 15:23)?
9. Who slew Pekahiah (II Kings 15:25)?
10. What foreign king invaded Israel in the days of Pekah (II Kings 15:29)?
11. What area in Israel did the Assyrian king conquer (II Kings 15:29)?
12. Who slew Pekah (II Kings 15:30)?

Uzziah (Azariah)
1. How long did Uzziah reign (II Chron. 26:3)?
2. Was Uzziah good or bad (II Chron. 26:4-5)?
3. Was Uzziah strong or weak (II Chron. 26:6)?
4. What peoples did Uzziah conquer (II Chron. 26:6-8)?
5. What unusual weapons were devised in Uzziah's time (II Chron. 26:15)?
6. What presumptious act did Uzziah attempt to do (II Chron. 26:16; Cf. Num. 18:7)?

7. Who opposed Uzziah's presumptious act (II Chron. 26:17)?
8. What was Uzziah's punishment (II Chron. 26:19-21)?
9. What prophet wrote the acts of Uzziah (II Chron. 26:22)?
10. Who was co-regent with Uzziah (II Kings 15:5)?
11. What prophet saw the Lord in the year that King Uzziah died?

Jotham

1. Was Jotham a good or bad king (II Kings 15:32-34)?
2. Was Jotham a strong or weak king (II Chron. 27:6)?
3. What kings began to invade Judah during the time of Jotham (II Kings 15:37; Cf. Isaiah 7:1)?
4. How did the people live in Jotham's time (II Chron. 27:2)?
5. What nations did Jotham fight against (II Chron. 27:5)?

Ahaz

1. Was Ahaz good or bad (II Chron. 28:1)?
2. What idolatry did Ahaz practice (II Chron. 28:2-3)?
3. What nations smote Ahaz and Judah (II Chron. 28:5)?
4. What reassurance did Isaiah extend to Ahaz (Isa. 7:3-4, 10-11)?
5. What prevented many Judeans from being permanently enslaved in Israel (II Chron. 28:8-11)?
6. To whom did Ahaz send for help (II Chron. 28:16)?
7. What city did Tiglath-pileser conquer (II Kings 16:9)?
8. Did Assyria really help Judah (II Chron. 28:21)?
9. Why did Ahaz sacrifice to the gods of Damascus (II Chron. 28:33)?
10. What altar did Ahaz build (II Kings 16:10)?
11. Where did Ahaz erect altars in Jerusalem (II Chron. 28:24)?
12. What damage did Ahaz do to the temple (II Kings 16:17-18)?

Hezekiah (before Israel's fall)

1. Was Hezekiah good or bad (II Kings 18:3,5)?
2. What did Hezekiah reopen and repair (II Chron. 29:3)?
3. What did Hezekiah set the Levites in the temple to do (II Chron. 29:25)?
4. Where did the command to use instrumental music come from (II Chron. 29:25)?
5. Whom did Hezekiah invite to a great feast? What feast was it (II Chron. 30:1)?
6. How were Hezekiah's messengers treated in Israel? Did any Israelites respond favorably (II Chron. 30:10-11)?
7. What was done to permit those who were unclean to eat the passover (II Chron. 30:18-20)?

8. How great was Hezekiah's passover feast (II Chron. 30:26)?
9. What did the returning Israelites do after the Passover (II Chron. 31:1)?
10. How did Hezekiah provide for the priests (II Chron. 31:4-5)?
11. Were the priests adequately cared for by Hezekiah's system (II Chron. 31:10)?
12. What literary work did the men of Hezekiah do (Prov. 25:1)?
13. What brass object did Hezekiah destroy? What did he call it? What does this name mean (II Kings 18:4; Cf. Num. 21:8)?
14. What foreign nation did Hezekiah rebel against (II Kings 18:7)?
15. What people did Hezekiah smite (II Kings 18:8)?

Hoshea and Fall of Israel
1. Who was the last king of Israel (II Kings 17:1)?
2. What Assyrian king invaded Hoshea's kingdom (II Kings 17:3)?
3. With what other foreign king did Hoshea make a conspiracy (II Kings 17:4)?
4. How long did the king of Assyria besiege Samaria (II Kings 17:5)?
5. What was done with the people of Israel when Samaria was captured (II Kings 17:6)?
6. Name the places where the Israelites were taken (II Kings 17:6)?
7. What had caused Israel to be deported (II Kings 17:7)?
8. Had the Israelites lived better than the Canaanites that God had thrust out before them (II Kings 17:8)?
9. Whom had God sent to warn Israel of the consequences of their ungodliness (II Kings 17:13)?
10. How had Israel treated the prophets (II Kings 17:14)?
11. What gods and idolatrous practices had Israel taken up (II Kings 17:16-17)?
12. Had Judah kept the commandments of God (II Kings 17:19)?
13. What king of Israel had made Israel sin (II Kings 17:22)?
14. What people were imported into Samaria? By whom (II Kings 17:24)?
15. How did God show his displeasure to these imported peoples in Samaria (II Kings 17:25)?
16. How did the imported peoples react to God's punishment (II Kings 17:26-27)?

17. Who was brought back to Bethel to teach the law of Jehovah (II Kings 17:28)?
18. Did Jehovah become the exclusive God of Samaria (II Kings 17:29-32)?
19. Did God's chastening make Israel understand (II Kings 17:34,41)?
20. Who was king in Judah when Samaria and Israel fell (II Kings 18:9-10)?

Section IV
Judah after Israel's Fall

1. Assyrian wars after fall of Samaria — Sargon II and Sennacherib — Egypt, the principal opponent of Assyria. 2. Hezekiah's mortal sickness — Sign of retreating shadow — Visit of Merodachbaladan — Birth of Manasseh. 3. Sennacherib, successor to Sargon in Assyria — Invasion of Judah — Destruction of Sennacherib's host — Hezekiah's prosperity and death. 4. Manasseh, thirteenth king of Judah — Anti-religious reaction — Imprisonment of Manasseh in Babylon by Esarhaddon — His repentance and restoration — Possible alliance with revived Egypt. 5. Amon, fourteenth king of Judah — His wickedness and assassination. 6. Josiah, fifteenth king of Judah — Religious degradation in Judah — Josiah seeks the Lord — Book of the law discovered — Destruction of the idols — Great Passover — Important dates of the era. 7. Fall of Assyria and rise of Media and Babylon — Rivalry of Babylon and Egypt — Expedition of Necho — Death of Josiah — Revival of prophecy under Josiah: Nahum, Zephaniah and Jeremiah. 8. The successors of Josiah only nominal kings — Descendants of Josiah. 9. Jehoahaz, sixteenth king of Judah — Set up by the people but deposed by Pharaoh-Necho — Battle of Carchemish. 10. Jehoiakim, seventeenth king of Judah — Defeat of Necho by Nebuchadnezzar — Jeremiah prophesies captivity in Babylon — The Rechabites — Nebuchadnezzar takes Jerusalem — The first captivity of Judah: Daniel and his comrades — Public reading of Jeremiah's prophecies — The scroll burned —

1. *Assyrian wars after fall of Samaria – Sargon II and Sennacherib –
Egypt the principal opponent of Assyria.* There is a gap in the
Scripture narrative from the taking of Samaria in 722 to the
attack of Assyria upon Judah in the twenty-fourth year[1] of
Hezekiah (II Kings 18:13), 701 B.C. However, from an allusion in
Isaiah 20:1, from information in the history of Josephus and
from the records of the Assyrian kings Sargon II and
Shalmaneser, we know how the kings of Assyria employed
themselves after the fall of Samaria.

According to Josephus (Ant. IX, xiv, 2) Shalmaneser had been
besieging Tyre in Phoenicia since 724 B.C.; Sargon overran
Phoenicia shortly after Samaria fell. He was not, however, able to
capture Tyre.

In 721 there was a revolt in Babylon against Assyria led by
Merodach-baladan (II Kings 20:12); Babylon remained
independent until 710 when Sargon finally was sufficiently free
from warfare elsewhere to sweep southward into Babylon and
drive Merodach-baladan out and have himself crowned king at
Babylon. During the last portion of Merodach-baladan's
independence, probably about 712, he visited King Hezekiah of
Judah, probably attempting to line up a military alliance against
Assyria (Isaiah 39).

Sargon defeated the allied Egyptians and Philistines at Raphia
(in Philistia, south of Gaza) in 720. He had constant warfare with
northern portions of his empire (Ararat, Urartu, Lake Urumiah,

---

[1]. See Chronology of the Divided Kingdom, **p. 574**, for our reasons for changing "fourteenth" to
"twenty-fourth" in II Kings 18:13.

Medes, etc.) during the next few years. In 717 he defeated the Hittites and Mushki (Biblical Meshech) near Carchemish and took that city, ending forever the long Hittite influence there. Subsequent wars occupied all of Sargon's years.

In 711 Sargon made a sweep into Philistia, Edom, Moab and Judah; he took Ashdod (Isa. 20:1) and broke up the alliance against Assyria that had been formed by Merodach-baladan before this alliance had opportunity to trouble Assyria. This was followed in the next year by his drive into Babylon that drove out Merodach-baladan.

Sargon's last years are obscure. He was murdered in 705 and succeeded by his son Sennacherib (705-681 B.C.). Sennacherib was a capable but cruel king. He found it necessary to deal with revolts throughout his empire. In 701 he made the famous campaign into the West. He took Sidon, Ashkelon, Joppa, Lachish (II Chron. 32:9) and many other Judean cities (II Kings 18:13-19; II Chron. 32:1-22; Isaiah 36:1-37:38). Jerusalem was miraculously delivered from Sennacherib and Sennacherib returned to his own land.

Throughout all this period of conflict Assyria's great opponent was Egypt. Egypt was seeking to dominate Palestine and Syria just as Assyria was. Nations such as Phoenicia, Judah, Philistia, etc. were like small pawns in the larger contest between Egypt and Assyria. Isaiah the prophet warned Judah not to side with Egypt because it could not save them (Isa. 30:1-5; 31:1-3). True to this prediction Assyria did ultimately destroy Egypt. Esarhaddon of Assyria (681-669) took Lower Egypt and Memphis; Asshurbanipal (672-633) took Upper Egypt and Thebes, an event referred to in Nahum 3:8.

2. *Hezekiah's mortal sickness – Sign of retreating shadow – Visit of Merodach-baladan – Birth of Manasseh*. About this time must have occurred the mortal illness of Hezekiah: "In those days was Hezekiah sick unto death," and Isaiah was sent to warn him of his approaching end (II Kings 20:1-2; II Chron. 32:24; Isa. 38:1). The record of his feelings, written by his own hand when he recovered, is preserved for us by Isaiah in language highly poetical. In the same dismal tone as the patriarch Job, he deplores the end of life but chiefly as the end of all opportunities for serving God: "The grave can not praise Thee; death can not celebrate Thee; they that go down into the pit can not hope for Thy truth" (Isa. 38:18). He thought, doubtless, of his unfinished

work, of the danger still impending over Judah but, above all, of the Temple which he had restored and where he had hoped long to worship God (Isa. 38:22). He turned his face to the wall and prayed and wept sore. The prophet, who had but just left him, was sent back to promise that he should recover and go up to the house of God on the third day; at the same time he directed a poultice of figs to be laid upon the boil or carbuncle, for such was the king's disease (II Kings 20:7; Ida. 38:21). As was so usual with the Jews, Hezekiah asked for a sign and the shadow of the sun went back ten degrees upon the dial of Ahaz, signifying a proportionate addition to the days of his life (II Kings 20:8-11; Isa. 38:7-8).[1] But alas! For the weakness of our nature, this deliverance engendered a rash confidence, which brought new judgments on Judah and Jerusalem (II Chron. 33:25). The news of Hezekiah's recovery brought an embassy of congratulation from Merodach-baladan, king of Babylon, a power which now appears for the first time (II Kings 20:12; Isa. 39:1).[2] The ostensible object was to make inquiries respecting the astronomical marvel (II Chron. 32:31). But its real purpose was probably to form a league against Assyria. The kings of the lower Assyrian dynasty held Babylon by an insecure grasp and Merodach was at the head of the party of independence. From the records of Sargon and Sennacherib we learn that he was twice expelled from his kingdom, by the former in the twelfth year both of Sargon and of Merodach (710 B.C.), and by the latter in his first year (702 B.C.), when Merodach had only recovered his kingdom for six months. The embassy to Hezekiah falls during his first tenure of power, and if its object be rightly understood, the king of Judah's eagerness to show the ambassadors his treasures would have another motive besides mere ostentation, to prove his ability to enter on a great and dangerous war. Whatever the motive, the display was made in a spirit of self-glorification, which called down a divine judgment; and it must have been

---

1. The Heb. word translated by "dial" is the same as that rendered "steps" in A.V. (Ex. 20:26; I K. 10:19), and "degrees" in A.V. (II K. 20:9-11; Is. 38:8), where to give a consistent rendering we should read with the margin the "degrees" rather than the "dial" of Ahaz. In the absence of any materials for determining the shape and structure of the solar instrument, which certainly appears intended, the best course is to follow the most strictly natural meaning of the word and to consider that the dial was really stairs, and that the shadow (perhaps of some column or obelisk on the top) fell on a greater or smaller number of them according as the sun was low or high. The terrace of a palace might easily be thus ornamented. Ahaz's tastes seem to have led him in pursuit of foreign curiosities (II K. 6:10) and his intimacy with Tiglath-pileser gave him probably an opportunity of procuring from Assyria the pattern of some such structure.

2. The form "Berodach" is merely a dislectic variety. The name of the god Merodach has invariably the M. Merodach is the Hebrew equivalent of the Babylonian *Marduk*.

doubly bitter for Hezekiah to hear from Isaiah's lips that his kingdom was to fall prey, not to Assyria, but to the very power whose alliance he was courting. There had already been several predictions of the captivity of Judah, but this was the first distinct intimation of the quarter from which the judgment was to fall. Hezekiah humbled himself before God and he was comforted by the assurance that the sentence should not be executed in his days (II Chron. 32:31; II Kings 20:12-19; Isa. 39).

Up to the time of his mortal illness, Hezekiah seems to have been childless — a circumstance which would embitter his distress at the prospect of death. A son, named *Manasseh,* was born to him about three years later. Note the age of Manasseh at his accession (II Chron. 33:1). Manasseh's name never occurs elsewhere in the history of Judah. The adoption of the name of a rival tribe may be taken as a sign of the policy pursued by Hezekiah, from the time of the destruction of Samaria, to rally the remnant of the ten tribes in a religious union with Judah (II Chron. 30:6; 31:1).

3. *Sennacherib, successor of Sargon in Assyria – Invasion of Judah – Destruction of Sennacherib's host – Hezekiah's wealth and honor.* In 705 B.C. Sargon was succeeded by his son Sennacherib (or Sanherib), a monarch as warlike and able as himself. After crushing the revolt of Merodach and placing Belib, a creature of his own, on the throne of Babylon, he undertook a great expedition against Judah and Egypt. This was the crisis of the history of the men of Judah to prove whether the religious revival under Hezekiah would inspire them with faith in God or whether they would seek safety by forbidden means. There was a strong party in favor of an alliance with Egypt, the help of which they seem to have sought only to be repulsed with contempt (Isa. 30:1-5). Isaiah vehemently denounces this party and lays down the law — "Their strength is to sit still"; "In quietness and confidence shall be your strength" — in a series of his most magnificent prophecies, describing the destruction of the Assyrian by supernatural means when he should encamp against Ariel *(Lion of God),* the city of David, the establishment of Messiah's kingdom and the privileges of his people. These chapters stand in the Book of Isaiah immediately before the history of Sennacherib's invasion, for which they were evidently designed to prepare the minds of king and people (Isa. 29-35). The king proved worthy of such a prophet. Though he may have tampered with Egypt, a point on which we have no certain knowledge, and though he was driven to one act of disgraceful submission, his faith revived in the

supreme crisis. Encouraged by Isaiah, he committed his own and his people's safety to Jehovah, who wrought for them a deliverance as signal as the destruction of Pharaoh and his army in the Red Sea.

In anticipation of the Assyrian invasion Hezekiah covered over all the springs and cisterns near Jerusalem. He dug a tunnel from the spring Gihon, going under Mt. Ophel to a pool now known as the pool of Siloam. The tunnel, known as Hezekiah's tunnel, still carries water in Jerusalem (II Kings 20:20; II Chron. 32:2-4).[1]

The campaign was opened by an attack on the fortresses of Judah, of which several were taken (II Kings 18:13; Isa. 36:1; II Chron. 32:1). Isaiah describes the progress of Sennacherib through Benjamin and the distress of the cities on his route (Isa. 10:28-32). He was engaged in the siege of Lachish, a city in the southwest of Judah (apparently with the view of securing the whole country toward Egypt before attacking Jerusalem), when Hezekiah sent him a message of complete submission: "I have offended; return from me; what thou puttest upon me I will bear" (II Kings 18:14). The Assyrian exacted a contribution of 300 talents of silver and thirty talents of gold; to meet which, Hezekiah took all the silver vessels of the Temple and of his own palace, and cut off the gold with which he himself had overlaid the doors and pillars of the Temple, and sent it to Sennacherib (II Kings 18:15-16).

But this spoilation was only a preliminary to the intended extirpation of the Jewish people and the destruction of Jerusalem. Sennacherib sent an army against Jerusalem under a Tartan (or captain), Rabsaris (the chief eunuch), and Rabshakeh (the chief cup-bearer),[2] expecting apparently the surrender of the disheartened city without a siege. We are informed of the exact spot where the envoys stood to deliver their message, "the conduit of the upper pool in the highway of the fuller's field." Hezekiah sent to the conference the chief of his household, his secretary and recorder. Rabshakeh, who acted as spokesman, asked on whom the king of Judah relied. Was it on Egypt, a broken reed, that would pierce the hand of him who leaned on it? Was it on Jehovah? — the God, said the orator, with a strange confusion of ideas, whose high places and altars Hezekiah had

---

1. See M.F. Unger, *Arch. and O.T.*, pp. 373-375.
2. In the A.V., Tartan, Rabsaris and Rabshakeh are treated as proper names, but they are probably rather names of offices than of persons: Tartan signifying a "captain," Rabsaris "Chief eunuch" and Rabshakeh "chief cup-bearer." There are several other Assyrian and Babylonian names found with the prefix "Rab" in the sense of "chief."

taken away. Nay, his master even claimed to have been sent up against Jerusalem by the word of Jehovah, referring probably to the prophecies of Isaiah (Isa. 8, 10). Thus far he had spoken in Hebrew but now the officers of Hezekiah entreated him to speak in the Syrian language, so as not to be understood by the people on the wall. "They," rejoined Rabshakeh, "are the very persons to whom I am sent, to warn them of the consequences of resistance." Then, raising his voice, he cried to the men upon the wall to come forth to make their peace with him, promising that they should be unmolested till he came again to remove them to a land as good as their own. Let them not listen to Hezekiah, persuading them that Jehovah would deliver them, but look upon the nations subdued before Assyria, and see if the gods of Samaria and the rest had delivered them out of his master's hand. The people, as Hezekiah had bidden them, returned no answer, and the servants of Hezekiah reported to him the words of Rabshakeh. He sent them to Isaiah, while he betook himself to prayer. The prophet replied that God took the blasphemies of Rabshakeh as uttered against Him, and predicted that, in consequence of a "blast" sent upon him by God, and a "rumor" which he should hear, the king would retreat to his own land, and there perish by the sword.

Sennacherib had now left Lachish[1] and his messengers found him besieging Libnah, a city in the same vicinity. The news of the approach of Tirhakah, king of Ethiopia, compelled him to postpone his revenge for the defiance of Hezekiah, but he gave vent to his rage in a letter in the same tone as Rabshakeh's speech. Hezekiah spread the letter before God with a solemn prayer to Him to prove the difference between Jehovah, the only God, and the "no gods" whom the Assyrian had justly reproached; and the answer was given by the mouth of Isaiah in a sublime prophecy of the destruction of the Assyrian and the future glory of the remnant of Judah. On that very night the well-known catastrophe followed, not, as is too often supposed by cursory readers, before Jerusalem, which Sennacherib had never approached but only "shaken his fist at her" from the distance (Isa. 10:32). His army still lay before Libnah, not having even moved to meet Tirhakah, when in one night "the angel of Jehovah went out, and smote in the camp of the Assyrians 185,000 men." When the watchmen looked forth in the early morning, the plain was covered with their corpses:

---

1. For a picture of the stone relief of Sennacherib, showing the spoil of Lachish being exhibited before him, see W. Keller, *Bible As History in Pictures* (New York: Morrow & Co., 1964), p. 248.

"And the might of the Gentiles, untouched by the sword,
Had melted like snow at the 'blast' of the Lord."

(From "The Destruction of Sennacherib" by Lord Byron)

Sennacherib himself returned into Assyria and was there slain as Isaiah had foretold. But his death, which is mentioned at the end of the Scripture narrative, did not take place till some years later. He was murdered in the Temple of Nisroch by two of his sons, Adrammelech and Sharezer, who fled into Armenia, and was succeeded by another son, ESAR-HADDON, one of the most powerful of the Assyrian monarchs (681-669 B.C.) (II Kings 18, 19; Isa. 36, 37).

The fame of Hezekiah's deliverance brought him congratulations and presents from all the surrounding nations, and the remainder of the days, which God's special grace had added to his life, were spent in prosperity and wealth. Like Uzziah, he possessed numerous flocks and herds, in addition to the treasures that he collected at Jerusalem. When he died, he was honored with the chief place in the sepulchres of the kings (B.C. 698) (II Chron. 32:23-33). The glorious promise of his reign was terribly eclipsed under his successor.

4. *Manasseh, thirteenth king of Judah – Anti-religious reaction – Imprisonment of Manasseh in Babylon by Esarhaddon – His repentance and restoration – Possible alliance with revived Egypt.* MANASSEH, the thirteenth king of Judah (695-642 B.C.; II Kings 21:1-18; II Chron. 33:1-20), was only twelve years old when he succeeded his father Hezekiah and he reigned fifty-five years. But of this, the longest reign in the annals of Judah, our accounts are extremely scanty. In the *Second Book of Kings,* it fills only eighteen verses, which are occupied with a general description of the monstrous evils of the period, almost to the exclusion of particular incidents. It would seem as if the sacred writer abstained from recording more of a reign so disgraceful than was sufficient to point the lesson of retribution. The narrative in the *Chronicles* is scarcely longer, but it is distinguished from the other by one remarkable feature, the story of Manasseh's captivity, repentance and restoration.

The reign of Manasseh was a period of fatal reaction in the religious policy of the state. We have seen indications that the idolatrous party, who had been triumphant under Ahaz, did not yield without a struggle to Hezekiah. Such a reform as that king wrought must have been in a great degree superficial among a people so corrupted as the testimony of the prophets proves that the Jews had now become. The history of religious conflicts shows how well the losing party can succumb and bide their time, and the accession of a king too young to have had his character established by his father's teaching, but not too young to desire the gratification of his self-will, gave them a new opportunity. The princes of Judah, whose influence would naturally be great during the king's minority have been seen more than once on the side of idolatry, especially in the apostasy of Joash. It has been suggested that the policy which drew Hezekiah toward Babylon in the latter part of his reign may have had an evil influence over his young son. Certain it is that Babylonian superstitions are conspicuous among the religious errors of Manasseh, and his punishment came from the same quarter.

The description of Manasseh's idolatries includes every form of false religion and abominable vice that Israel had ever learned from the heathen nations. He restored the high places and groves which Hezekiah had removed, established the worship of Baal in a manner worthy of the house of Ahab and added to the obscene rites of Ashtoreth those unutterable abominations, which made princes and subjects "rulers of Sodom and people of Gomorrah" (Isa. 1:10). The Temple was profaned in a manner that even Ahaz had not attempted. An idol figure was set up in the sanctuary and altars for the worship of the heavenly bodies in the two courts of the Temple. The king made his son pass through the fire to Moloch in the valley of Hinnom. He dealt with wizards and necromancers, and in short "seduced the people to do *more* wickedness than the nations whom Jehovah destroyed before them" (II Kings 21:9).

The great apostasy was not consummated without warnings from the prophets who had flourished under Hezekiah. As the king and people had repeated the sins of Ahab, the prophets denounced the doom of Samaria on Judah and Jerusalem in the most striking figurative language (II Kings 21:10-15). The king attempted to silence them by the fiercest persecution recorded in the annals of Israel. We are only told in the sacred history that Manasseh "filled Jerusalem with innocent blood, which Jehovah would not pardon"; and that this was the crowning sin which doomed the nation to captivity (II Kings 21:16; 24:4). Fuller particulars of the persecution are preserved by Josephus who tells us that executions took place every day (*Ant.* X, iii, 1). Its effect is thus described by Jeremiah: "Your own sword hath devoured your prophets, like a destroying lion" (Jer. 2:30). After the death of Isaiah whom tradition makes the first victim of this persecution,[1] the prophetic voice was no more heard till the reign of Josiah.

These crimes were not long left unavenged. It is inferred from passages in the prophecies of the next age that the Philistines, Moabites and Ammonites, who had been tributary to Hezekiah, revolted from his son (Zeph. 2; Jer. 47, 48, 49). But the great blow came from Assyria. Sennacherib's successor, Esar-haddon, one of the most powerful of all the Assyrian kings, was God's agent to punish Manasseh. Esar-haddon is the only Assyrian monarch whom we find to have actually reigned at Babylon, where he built himself a palace, bricks from which have been recovered bearing his name. This fact accounts for Manasseh being taken to Babylon and not to Nineveh. To that city he carried Manasseh captive on a charge of rebellion and it would seem that Jerusalem was taken at the same time. Esar-haddon mentions Manasseh by name in his inscriptions.[2] The date of this event is placed by a Jewish tradition at the twenty-second year of Manasseh (673 B.C.), which agrees very well with the account of the new colonization of the country of Samaria by settlers whom Esar-haddon sent from *Babylon* and other places.

And now it seemed as if the time had come for the Babylonish captivity which Isaiah had foretold, but by a new proof of Jehovah's long-suffering with the house of David, the end was postponed for another century. The severity of Manasseh's imprisonment brought him to repentance. God heard his prayer,[3] and restored him to his kingdom at Jerusalem, where he again reigned long and prosperously. He removed the idols and their altars from the Temple and the city, repaired the altar and sacrificed upon it and commanded the people to serve Jehovah. There was, however, no thorough reformation of religion; the ark was not restored and the people still sacrificed in the high places. At the same time Manasseh put Jerusalem in a state of defense. He protected its weak side by a new wall "on the west side of Gihon, in the valley to the entrance of the 'fish-gate' ." He heightened the tower of Ophel, which Jotham had begun and he placed garrisons in the fortified cities of Judah. That these

---

1. Rabbinical tradition says that Isaiah was sawn asunder in a trunk of a tree by order of Manasseh, to which it is supposed that reference is made in Hebrews 11:37. But Isaiah must have been 80 or 90 years of age at Manasseh's accession.

2. M.F. Unger, *Arch. & O.T.*, p. 280.

3. The so-called "Prayer of Manasses" in the Apocrypha and Roman Catholic Bible is from a much later time, perhaps even in the Christian era, and is extant only in Greek. It is not to be regarded as the authentic prayer of Manasseh.

proceedings were permitted by Assyria can be easily understood from the less warlike character of Esar-haddon's successor, Asshurbanipal. But they were doubtless also connected with the new position of Egypt, the history of which now emerges from its long obscurity.

After the usurpation of the XXVth (Ethiopian) dynasty and the anarchy of the "Twelve Kings," Psamatek (663-609 B.C.) gained independence from Assyria, after Assyrian troops left Egypt in about 651. He founded a new native dynasty (XXVI) and slowly expanded toward Syria, finally sending his armies as far as southern Mesopotamia. He took Ashdod after a siege of twenty-nine years (Herodotus ii, 157). We have already seen that there was a powerful Egyptian party in Judah and the denunciations of the prophets, who began to prophesy under Josiah, prove that it had gained great strength. The name of Manasseh's son, Amon, who was born about the time of the accession of Psammetichus, though not incapable of explanation as a Hebrew word, points to a connection with Egypt. On these grounds it has been supposed that Manasseh sought the Egyptian alliance to strengthen him against Assyria. When he died, he was buried in the garden of Uzza attached to his own house, and not in the sepulchres of the kings, and his memory is held in detestation by the Jews (II Kings 21:17-18; II Chron. 33:20).

5. *Amon, fourteenth king of Judah – His wickedness and assassination.* AMON, the fourteenth king of Judah (642-640 B.C.; II Kings 21:19-26; II Chron. 33:21-25), succeeded his father at the age of twenty-two; and after a reign of two years, during which he followed Manasseh's idolatries without sharing his repentance, he fell the victim of a court conspiracy. The conspirators were slain by the people who raised Josiah, the infant son of Amon, to the throne. Amon was buried with his father in the garden of Uzza. His mother was Meshullemeth, the daughter of Haruz of Jotbah.

6. *Josiah, fifteenth king of Judah – Religious degradation of Judah – Josiah seeks the Lord – Book of the law discovered – Destruction of the idols – Great Passover – Important dates of the era.* JOSIAH, the fifteenth king of Judah (640-609 B.C.; II Kings 2:1-23:30; II Chron. 34-35), was eight years old at his accession and reigned thirty-one years at Jerusalem. His mother was Jediah, the daughter of Adaiah of Boscath. Though he fell in battle before he had completed his fortieth year, he left the brightest fame for piety and religious zeal among all the successors of David. He shares

with Hezekiah the praise of walking perfectly in the way of his father David. His reign marks the last dying glory of the earthly kingdom of David. It may, indeed, seem mysterious that a doom so often postponed by the repentance and faith of earlier kings should have followed so close upon the reign of the best and most zealous of them all and that he himself should have fallen by a premature and violent death. But we must look beyond the personal character of the king to the state of the people and their rulers. We have seen that the great reform of Hezekiah was probably superficial; the apostasy under Manasseh and Amon was the last and lowest stage in the long course of national degeneracy, and the deep corruption that prevailed during the minority of Josiah is drawn in the blackest colors by the prophets ZEPHANIAH and JEREMIAH. The very violence of Josiah's reformation indicates the absence of true and spontaneous sympathy among the people. In short, they were past purifying except by the fiercest fires of affliction.

Josiah must not be regarded as an example of the quiet growth of youthful piety under favorable culture. So evil were the influences about him that he "began to seek after the God of David his father" in his sixteenth year. His religion was his own decided choice as the first act of his opening manhood, a choice prompted by the loyalty to his high calling as the son of David, which marks every act of his reign. Doubtless he was aided and encouraged by some among the priests and by prophets, such as Zephaniah and Jeremiah, but it is a striking feature of his history that the king himself is the prime mover in every act of reformation. In the twelfth year of his reign at the age of twenty, he made a progress not only through Judah but through those parts of Israel which we have before seen recognizing Hezekiah as their religious head — Simeon, Ephraim, Manasseh and even as far as Naphtali — to put away all objects of idolatry. The altars, groves and statues were thrown down and destroyed, the molten and carved images were ground to powder and their dust sprinkled on the graves of their worshipers in the king's presence, and the bones of the idolatrous priests were disentombed and burned upon their own altars (II Chron. 34:3-7). These proceedings were continued for six years, during which the zeal of Josiah was quickened by a most important discovery. He had issued a commission to his chief officers to cooperate with the high-priest Hilkiah in a thorough renovation of the Temple (II Kings 22:3ff; II Chron. 34:8ff). Money had been collected by the priests from all the tribes that the king had visited, and it was delivered without reckoning to the workmen, who proved faithful to the trust — a striking contrast to the checks which were found necessary in the time of Joash. The ark, which appears to have been removed by Manasseh when he set up a carved image in the Holy of Holies, was restored to its place by Josiah (II Chron. 33:7; 35:3). During these repairs, the high-priest Hilkiah found the sacred copy of the book of the law and delivered it to Shaphan the scribe, who read it before the king. It is hard for us to realize the full force of this discovery. We can scarcely conceive of a state of things in which, during centuries of the nominal establishment of Christianity, the people should still observe solemn festivals to Buddha; the altars of the Aztec Indians should smoke with human sacrifices in every city, town and village; the statues of grotesque African gods should be set up in our church houses and the hills around our cities be crowned with temples to Jupiter and Venus: all this lasting for centuries, with an occasional and partial return to the purer form of worship, while the BIBLE, never multiplied by printing and only known in older and purer times through infrequent readings by the clergy, should have been utterly lost and forgotten! Add to this the supposition that the lost volume contained, not the dark symbols of the book of Revelation, but a clear warning of national destruction and captivity to befall us because of these idolatries, and then let us imagine our feelings on its sudden discovery! No wonder that Josiah rent his clothes and could not rest till he found a prophet to expound these terrible denunciations! For the first time since the days of Deborah, we meet with a prophetess, HULDAH, the wife of Shallum, keeper of the sacred vestments, who had her abode in the suburb of Jerusalem. Her reply to the high-priest and officers whom Josiah sent to consult her confirmed his worst fears for the fate of the city and the kingdom, but she added a message of comfort to the king. As he had shown a tender heart and had humbled himself before God when he heard His words of threatening, he should be gathered to his fathers in peace and not see the evil that was coming to Jerusalem (II Kings 22:3-20; II Chron. 34:8-28).

Josiah convened a solemn assembly at the Temple for the public reading of the law and the renewal of the nation's covenant with Jehovah. With new zeal the people set to the work of purging Jerusalem from idolatry. All the monuments of false worship were destroyed from the temples built by Solomon on the Mount of Olives, and the horses and chariots which successive kings had dedicated to the sun at the temple gates, to the altars set up by Ahaz and Manasseh. The images were brought out of the Temple and their dust strewn on the brook Kidron. The houses devoted to the orgies of Ashtoreth and the worser abominations of Sodom were pulled down. Tophet, the seat of the worship of Moloch in the valley of Hinnom was defiled with the bones of the idol-priests and the fire of the god was used for consuming the refuse of the city[1] (II Kings 23:1-14; II Chron. 34:29-33).

Jerusalem being thus purified, the king went to Bethel being now it would seem better informed of the events that had occurred there under Jeroboam. He broke down and burned the high place, the altar and the grove and fulfilled the word of the disobedient prophet by taking the bones of the priests out of the sepulchres and burning them upon the altar while he spared the remains of the prophet and of the other who was buried with him. The priests, who still dared to sacrifice in the high places, were put to death according to the law against idolatry. The wizards and necromancers shared their fate (II Kings 23:15-20; Comp. II Kings 13).

Returning to Jerusalem in the eighteenth year of his reign, Josiah kept the passover according to the directions of the newly-discovered Book of the Law. This passover was the greatest and the most exact that had been kept since the time of Moses. It is the last great united act of religion in the time preceding the Captivity (II Kings 23:21-23; II Chron. 35).

Important Dates of the Josianic Era

663 B.C. — Fall of Thebes to Asshurbanipal.

640—Accession of Josiah.

630(?)— Nahum's prophecy against Nineveh.

627—Scythian threat. (The Scythians were barbarians from the far north, around Ararat and the steppes of the Ukraine of modern Russia. They pressed westward and southward 650-620 B.C. The Scythian hordes passed through Philistia by Judah about 627, near the beginning of Jeremiah's prophetic ministry. The alarm indicated in Jeremiah 2-6

---

1. Because of this sickening defilement of Hinnom, it became the most abhorrent place imaginable to Jews, and Christ used it as a descriptive type of Hell. *"Gehenna"* (i.e., *Ge-Hinnom*, the *Valley of Hinnom),* with its carcasses consumed by worms and fire, became the type of the place of final punishment and destruction, "where their worm dieth not, and their fire is not quenched" (Matt. 5:22, 29, 30; 10:28; 18:9; 23:15,33; Mark 9:43, 45, 47; Luke 12:5; James 3:6).

and in Zephaniah may reflect the terror associated with this invasion. Judah, however, escaped and Psamatek of Egypt stopped the Scythians with Greek mercenaries.)

627—Zephaniah. Start of Jeremiah's ministry (Jer. 1:2).
626—Accession of Nabopolassar of Babylon.
621—Law found; Reforms introduced.
612—Fall of Nineveh to Babylonians and Medes.
609—Death of Josiah.
605—Battle of Carchemish. Accession of Nebuchadnezzar.
605(?)—Habakkuk.
597—Nebuchadnezzar takes Jerusalem.
586—Jerusalem destroyed.

7. *Fall of Assyria and rise of Media and Babylon – Rivalry of Babylon and Egypt – Expedition of Necho – Death of Josiah – Revival of prophecy under Josiah: Nahum, Zephaniah and Jeremiah.* The foreign relations of Judah were most favorable to Josiah's great reforms. Egypt was more interested in contesting the rising power of Babylon than in trifling with little Judah. The Assyrian empire was tottering to its fall which was consummated not long after Josiah had completed his reforms. It was about 612 B.C. that the allied forces of Media and Babylon finally laid siege to Nineveh, and after a long and obstinate resistance the last Assyrian king gathered his wives and treasures into his palace and perished with them in the fire kindled by his own hand. The fall of Assyria fulfilled the prophecies of Isaiah and the more recent predictions of NAHUM and ZEPHANIAH (Isa. 10:5-19; Nahum, the whole; Zeph. 2:13-15).

Upon its ruins rose two great empires, the one destined to overthrow and the other to restore the Jewish commonwealth. Speaking roughly, they were divided from each other by the highlands that bound the great valley of the Tigris and Euphrates on the east and north. While the MEDES sought the extension of their power beyond the mountains of Armenia and disputed with the Lydians the supremacy of Asia Minor, the king of BABYLON laid claim to the provinces that had owned the sovereignty of Assyria west of the Euphrates. NABOPOLASSAR (626-605) was the first king of the Neo-Babylonian empire. Psamatek of Egypt helped remnants of the Assyrian army at Haran against the Babylonians in 609 but lost. Psamatek's son PHARAOH-NECHO (609-593) then took up the struggle against Babylon. He won a victory over the Philistines and then advanced with a great army to Carchemish, which commanded a chief ford of the Euphrates. Contrary to the impression that might be conveyed by the common English Bible but not contrary to the permissible rendering of the Hebrew Bible, Necho went up to Carchemish (not "against"; II Chron. 35:20) to assist the remnant of the Assyrian army there against further encroachments from Babylon. Necho's line of march was through the great maritime plain and the valley of Esdraelon. Not only did he thus avoid Judah, but when Josiah showed signs of hostility, Necho sent him an emphatic but friendly warning to remain at peace. But the recollection of Assyrian oppressions in Judah was seemingly too strong for Josiah; he did not wish to see the Assyrians assisted by their one-time enemies the Egyptians. Marching down from the highlands of Manasseh into the plain of Esdraelon by the pass which issues near MEGIDDO, he encountered the whole force of the Egyptian army. He had so far deferred to the remonstrance of Necho as to try to conceal his being present in person but his disguise did not serve him. The Egyptian archers, shooting from their ranks as we still see them on the monuments, wounded Josiah mortally in his chariot. He was removed in his second chariot to Jerusalem (II Kings 23:30; II Chron. 35:24) and was buried among the sepulchres of the kings. His fall caused a universal mourning. Jeremiah wrote a lamentation for him, the spirit of which may be gathered from a passage in his larger *Book of Lamentations:* "The breath of our nostrils, the Anointed of Jehovah, was taken in their pits, of whom we said, under his shadow shall we live among the heathen (II Chron. 35:25; Lam. 4:20). His loss formed the burden of regular songs even after the captivity when "the mourning of Hadad-rimmon[1] in the valley of Megiddon" was still the type of the deepest national affliction (Zech. 12:11).

Well might such feelings be excited by the battle of Megiddo. That great valley of Esdraelon, the scene of the great victories of Barak and of Gideon, was now stained with a second defeat more disastrous than that in which Saul lost his life. Then it had witnessed the fall of the short-lived dynasty of the people's choice, but now it saw the virtual end of the earthly monarchy of the house of David. Hence may be traced the mystic significance which surrounds the name of this battlefield. The prophet Zechariah employs the mourning at Megiddo as a type of the more wholesome sorrow of Judah in the day when God shall pour out upon them the spirit of grace and prayer, as a preparation for

---

1. Hadad-rimmon seems to have been a sanctuary of the Syrian god, where the first mourning was made for Josiah on the spot where he fell.

his final destruction of all the nations that come up against Jerusalem; and his imagery is adopted in the visions of the Apocalypse. On the very scene of the two most signal defeats of Israel and Judah by their most inveterate enemies, the Philistines and Egypt, the seer beholds the mystic "Battle of Armageddon," which avenges all such defeats by the final overthrow of the kings of all the world in the great day of God Almighty[1] (Zech. 12:9-14; Rev. 16:14-16).

The reign of Josiah was marked by the revival of *prophecy,* which had long been silent under Manasseh and Amon. To this period belong Nahum, Zephaniah, Habakkuk and the greatest of all, Jeremiah. NAHUM's splendid prophecy of the destruction of Nineveh seems to have only preceded the event by a short time. The title of ZEPHANIAH's prophecy places him in the reign of Josiah; and though it has been inferred from one passage that he wrote after the restoration of Jehovah's worship, his vehement denunciations of the sins that prevailed in Judah seem rather applicable to an earlier period. JEREMIAH's long career began in the thirteenth year of Josiah (B.C. 627) with reproaches for sin and warnings of coming judgment, mingled with exhortations and encouragements to repentance and promises of restoration (Jer. 1:2). Since the start of his ministry coincides with the Scythian invasion through Philistia in 627, it has been supposed that the alarm reflected in the earlier chapters of Jeremiah reflects that threat. More probably Jeremiah's alarm concerned the more remote but more real threat of Babylonian invasion of Judah. Though Jeremiah is only once mentioned in the history of Josiah's reign, the language of his own book assures us that both as priest and prophet he animated the king and people in the work of reformation, and most vigorously denounced the policy of the Egyptian party. His final lamentation for the fate of Josiah must have been double embittered by seeing Israel again prostrate beneath her old oppressor (Jer. 2:18,36; II Chron. 35:24). In his prophecies we also trace that strange perplexity concerning the ultimate fate of the people, which even now weighs upon the student of their history and which must have been terribly felt while the event was still unknown. Was it possible for a state that had sunk so low, not only politically but morally, to be restored even by repentance and reformation? His only refuge from the despair involved in the true answer is in

---

1. "Armageddon" is the "fortress" or "height of Megiddo," according as we take the prefix for the Hebrew Ar or Har (=Hor).

contemplating the past proofs of Jehovah's goodness to the nation and uttering his inspired predictions of future glory.

8. *The successors of Josiah only nominal kings – Descendants of Josiah.* The death of Josiah in 609 B.C., marks the virtual end of the kingdom of Judah. The four kings who followed him were the mere puppets of Egypt and Babylon and the twenty-two years of their nominal reigns are occupied with successive conquests and deportations. These twenty-two years are divided into two equal parts by the captivity of Jehoiachin. To follow their events, we must first have a clear view of the family of Josiah, the stem of which is as follows:

Descendants of King Josiah

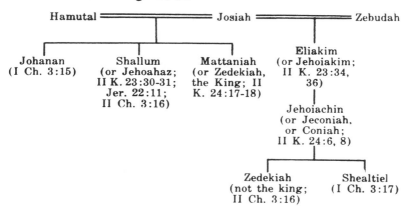

Josiah's son Jehoiakim had a different mother from Jehoahaz and Zedekiah; his mother's name was Zebudah, the daughter of Pedaiah or Ruma; theirs was Hamutal, the daughter of Jeremiah of Libnah.[1] When Josiah died in 609 B.C., Jehoahaz was 23 (II Kings 23:31) and Jehoiakim 25 (II Kings 23:36). If Hamutal was the first wife of Josiah, her eldest son would take precedence over the eldest son of the second wife, even though younger, in the succession to the kingdom. The absence of any mention of Johanan is accounted for by the supposition that he died before his father or fell with him at Megiddo, and the preference of Shallum to Eliakim may have been due to the superior rank of his mother.

The sons of Josiah are listed in *apparent* order in I Chron. 3:15 as Johanan, Jehoiakim, Zedekiah and Shallum. This makes it

---

1. This Jeremiah is a different person from the prophet.

appear that Johanan must have been the same as King Jehoahaz
(who is not mentioned in the list), who was made king after his
father Josiah. However, Jeremiah 22:11 expressly indicates that
Shallum was the same person as Jehoahaz. This information, plus
the fact that Zedekiah was only 21 years old when he began to
reign after the 11 years of Jehoiakim (II Kings 23:26; 24:18),
indicates that Jehoahaz, or Shallum, was Josiah's third son (after
Johanan and Jehoiakim) and Zedekiah was his fourth son rather
than the third as a first reading of I Chron. 3:15 suggests.

9. *Jehoahaz, sixteenth king of Judah – Set up by the people but deposed
by Pharaoh-Necho – Battle of Carchemish.* JEHOAHAZ, the sixteenth
king of Judah (609 B.C., II Kings 23:30-35; II Chron. 36:1-8),
was raised to the throne by the people after Josiah's death, while
Pharaoh-necho proceeded on his expedition toward Carchemish.
Very shortly thereafter Pharaoh's forces captured Jehoahaz and
brought him to Riblah by Hamath (on the Orontes) and there
kept him as a prisoner till his return to Egypt. Entering Jerusalem
as a conqueror, he placed on the throne Eliakim (the brother of
Jehoahaz), to whom he gave the name of Jehoiakim and imposed
a tribute of 100 talents of silver and a talent of gold (about two
million dollars), which Jehoiakim collected by a tax on the land.
Jehoahaz was carried by Pharaoh-necho to Egypt, where he died
soon afterward. His brief reign was characterized by wickedness
and oppression but he was lamented as the last king of the
people's choice. Jeremiah, who had mourned so bitterly for
Josiah, now says: "Weep ye not for the dead, neither honor him:
weep sore for him that goeth away; for he shall return no more,
nor see his native country" (Jer. 22:10-12). The fortunes of
Jehoahaz and his two successors are described in highly poetical
imagery by Ezekiel (Ezek. 19:1-9).

Four years elapsed before the battle of Carchemish was joined
between Pharaoh-necho with his Assyrian allies against the rising
Babylonian empire under Nabopolassar and Nebuchadnezzar.
In 605 B.C. the battle occurred; Egypt was utterly defeated;
Assyrian power ended forever; Babylon became the dominant
empire of the Near East.

10. *Jehoiakim, seventeenth king of Judah – Defeat of Necho by
Nebuchadnezzar – Jeremiah prophesies captivity in Babylon – The
Rechabites – Nebuchadnezzar takes Jerusalem – The first captivity of
Judah: Daniel and his comrades – Public reading of Jeremiah's
prophecies – The scroll burned – Rebellion and death of Jehoiakim –*

Habakkuk. JEHOIAKIM, the seventeenth king of Judah (609-597 B.C.; II Kings 23:34-24:7; II Chron. 36:1-8), was twenty-five years old when he was placed on the throne by Pharoah-necho, instead of his brother Jehoahaz; and he reigned eleven years at Jerusalem, doing evil in the sight of Jehovah. Jeremiah sternly rebukes his injustice and oppression, his cruelty and avarice and his reckless luxury in building himself a magnificent palace, and contrasts all this with his father's justice to the poor (Jer. 22:13-19): and in the *Chronicles* his name is dismissed with an allusion to "all the abominations that he did." From the very commencement of his reign, the voice of Jeremiah is heard plainly predicting and prefiguring by striking signs the captivity at Babylon as a judgment rendered inevitable by the people's sins, but adding the promise of their future restoration (Jer. 26, 13, 19). Attempts were made to silence him by the princes, priests and false prophets of the Egyptian party who represented him as a traitor. He often complains of these enemies and he expressly predicts the captivity of Pashur, the priest and governor of the Temple, who had beaten him and put him in the stocks (or pillory) (Jer. 20). Still he faithfully delivered the messages which Jehovah now gave him to the king of Judah by name, as plainly as Nathan had been sent to David. This directness of language is a striking character of the prophecies of Jeremiah and indeed of most of the historical prophecies. In one of these prophecies, after mourning the death of Josiah and the hopeless captivity of Jehoahaz, he predicts the fate of Jehoiakim to the very details of his dishonored end (Jer. 22:1-23). On another occasion the prophet took his stand in the court of the Temple, amid an assemblage from all the cities of Judah to proclaim that God would even yet repent him of the coming evil if they turned to Him, but if not that His house should be destroyed like the tabernacle at Shiloh and the city made a curse to all nations (Jer. 26:1-7). The priests and prophets now resolved on Jeremiah's death: and they had a precedent in the case of URIJAH, the son of Shemaiah of Kirjath-jearim, who having uttered prophecies like those of Jeremiah, had been pursued by the envoys of Jehoiakim into Egypt and brought back to suffer an ignominious death. The princes of Judah, however, before whom Jeremiah was arraigned, appealed to the better precedent of the times of Hezekiah, who allowed MICAH to prophesy with impunity, and Jeremiah's life was saved by the influence of Ahikam, the son of

Shaphan and other old counselors of Josiah (Jer. 26). These
warnings were given in the beginning of Jehoiakim's reign and
their fulfillment was soon begun by the overthrow of his Egyptian
protector.

The fourth year of Jehoiakim (605 B.C.) is a marked epoch
both in secular and sacred history. In this year we first meet with
NEBUCHADNEZZAR, the greatest of the Babylonian kings and the
destined destroyer of the Jewish monarchy. His father,
Nabopolassar, appears to have been still alive when he led a great
army against Carchemish, which was still held by the Assyrians
aided by the Egyptians, and inflicted a decisive defeat on
Pharaoh-necho. This blow put an end to the hopes of the
Egyptian party at Jerusalem as well as to all fears of subjugation
from that quarter, and left the city defenseless against
Nebuchadnezzar. "The King of Egypt came not again any more
out of his land; for the King of Babylon had taken from the river
of Egypt unto the River Euphrates all that pertained to the King
of Egypt" (II Kings 24:7). Meanwhile Jeremiah, having predicted
the overthrow of the Egyptians (Jer. 46:1-12), uttered that
memorable prophecy in which he fixes the duration of the
coming Captivity at seventy years and predicts the fall of Babylon
and the other nations hostile to the Jews. It was from this
prophecy that Daniel was enabled to calculate the time of the
promised restoration and it was fulfilled by the decree of Cyrus in
536 B.C. (Jer. 25; Dan. 9:1-2; II Chron. 36:22; Ezra 1:1).

The interesting episode of the flight of the RECHABITES to
Jerusalem also belongs to the time of Nebuchadnezzar's advance
from Carchemish to Jerusalem. Their fidelity to the patriarchal
laws of their ancestor, Jonadab the son of Rechab, is used by
Jeremiah as a powerful reproof of the faithlessness of the Jews
toward Jehovah (Jer. 35).

Nebuchadnezzar advanced to Jerusalem, which he took after a
brief siege (Dan. 1:1), dethroned Jehoiakim and put him in
fetters with a view to carry him to Babylon. For some reason this
intention was abandoned and Jehoiakim was restored to his
throne as a vassal. His treasures were carried off to Babylon,
where the vessels of the sanctuary were placed in the Temple. At
the same time Nebuchadnezzar commissioned Ashpenaz, the
chief of his eunuchs, to choose a number of royal and noble
Hebrew youths, excelling alike in beauty and mental
accomplishments to be brought up at his court and trained in the
learning of Chaldaea. Among those thus selected were DANIEL,

with his three companions, Hananiah, Mishael and Azariah, to whose well-known history we shall soon return (Dan. 1:3-7).[1]

The 70 years of Jer. 25:11-12 are dated from this deportation in 605 B.C. to the first return from captivity 536 B.C.

While the long train of Syrian, Jewish and Egyptian captives were led by the usual route, Nebuchadnezzar hastened back across the Syrian desert in consequence of his father's death and ascended the vacant throne without opposition. The state in which Jerusalem was left can be learned from Jeremiah, though there is great difficulty not only in determining the order of his prophecies, but in deciding among those that belong to this period which were delivered before and which after Nebuchadnezzar's first capture of the city. It seems to have been after his retreat that a great fast was appointed for the ninth month in the fifth year of Jehoiakim (Jer. 36:9). The occasion was seized by Jeremiah, at the command of God, to make a solemn appeal to the people to return from their evil way that they might even yet be forgiven. With the aid of his disciple and secretary, Baruch the son of Neriah, he had written in a volume the whole of the prophecies that he had uttered, from the days of Josiah downward, against Israel, Judah and other nations. Being prevented, perhaps by the command of God to insure his safety, from going up to the Temple himself, he commissioned Baruch to read the volume to the people assembled out of all the cities of Judah. Baruch took his station in a chamber above the new gate of the Temple, belonging to Michaiah the scribe, who was the grandson of Shaphan and a friend to Jeremiah. When Baruch had read the book to the people in the court below, Micaiah reported the whole to the princes who were assembled in the scribe's chamber at the palace. Having sent for Baruch and heard him read the volume, they advised him and Jeremiah to hide themselves while they laid the matter before the king. Jehoiakim was sitting in his winter palace with a fire burning in a brazier (for it was cold), and the prince Jehudi read the roll at his command. As fast as he read, the king cut off the leaves with a pen-knife and threw them into the fire till the whole volume was consumed in spite of the intercession of Gemaliah and others. Jeremiah and Baruch only escaped arrest through having followed the advice of the princes. But this earliest example of Bible-burning was as

---

1. A difficulty arises from the date in this passage, the *third* year of Jehoaikim, instead of the *fourth*, as in Jeremiah. The simple explanation is that Daniel followed the customary Babylonian practice of numbering the years of a king's reign *after* his accession year. Contrast Jer. 46:2 which speaks of this date as Jehoiakim's fourth year.

unsuccessful in suppressing the Word of God as later feats of the same kind. Jeremiah was bidden to take another roll and to write in it the same words with a further prophecy of the utter desolation of Judah and of the king's disgraceful end. So Baruch wrote in the next volume at the dictation of Jeremiah all the words of the book which the king had burned, "and there were added besides unto them many like words." Both king and people, however, remained obdurate (Jer. 36).

The failure of this last appeal can scarcely have surprised Jeremiah but it had a deep effect on his more youthful and ardent disciple. Baruch seems to have hoped that the people would have been stirred up by his words to a movement of new national religious life. Jeremiah reminded him of God's sovereign right to break down what He had built and to pluck up what He had planted, and adds: "Seekest thou great things for thyself? seek them not: for behold, I will bring evil upon all flesh, saith Jehovah: but *thy life* will I give thee for *a prey*" — as if snatched from the net of the destroyer — "In all places whither thou goest" (Jer. 45:1-5). The promise was fulfilled by Baruch's sharing with Jeremiah the protection of Nebuchadnezzar when Jerusalem was taken and by his afterward finding a refuge in Egypt with the remnant of the Jews (Jer. 43:6).

The burning of Jeremiah's prophecies indicates that spirit of defiance which led Jehoiakim to rebel against Nebuchadnezzar, after reigning for three years as a vassal of Babylon (II Kings 24:1). *The Chronicles of Chaldean Kings*[1] reveal that a battle occurred in 601 B.C. in which the Egyptians and Babylonians fought a standoff battle. This may explain why Jehoiakim ceased to pay tribute to Babylon (II K. 24:1), and, disregarding the advice of Jeremiah (37:6-11), turned for help to the "bruised reed" of Egypt (Isa. 36:6). The Lord sent against Jehoiakim groups of the Chaldeans, and Syrians, and Moabites, and Ammonites. King Nebuchadnezzar himself at last took the field in person and marched first against Tyre (besieged 598-585), which had rebelled about the same time as Judah. Having invested the city, he marched with a part of his forces against Jerusalem. Jehoiakim seems to have died in disgrace after the king of Babylon arrived at Jerusalem and his son Jehoiachin became king (II Kings 24:6; Jer. 22:18-19; 36:30; Ezek. 19:8-9).

The date of HABAKKUK, though far from certain, seems to have been within the reign of Jehoiakim, after the fall of Carchemish

---

[1]. D.J. Wiseman, *Chronicles of Chaldean Kings* (London: British Museum, 1961), p. 71.

(605 B.C.). Much to Habakkuk's surprise and dismay, God revealed to him that the violent Babylonians (or Chaldeans) would be used to punish the wickedness of Judah (Hab. 1:5-6). Habakkuk's strong reaction to this revelation shows that the character of the Babylonians was familiar to him, a circumstance more likely to have been true after 605 than before.

11. *Jehoiachin, eighteenth king of Judah – Deposed by Nebuchadnezzar – The second captivity of Judah – Subsequent history of Jehoiachin and the line of David.* JEHOIACHIN, JECONIAH or CONIAH, the eighteenth king of Judah (597 B.C.; II Kings 24:17-20; II Chron. 36:8-10), was eighteen[1] years old when he was placed on the throne and reigned only three months and ten days. Considering his youth "the evil which he did in the sight of Jehovah" must be understood of the policy pursued by those who ruled in his name, the old idolatrous and Egyptian party. The fate which they brought upon the young king is vividly described by Jeremiah, who compares Jehovah's rejection of "Coniah" to the plucking off and throwing away a signet ring and the king himself to a despised broken idol, foretells his captivity and his mother's, without hope of return and solemnly invokes the whole earth to hear the sentence of Jehovah, pronouncing this man childless and the last of his line who should sit upon the throne of David (Jer. 22:24-30). But even this terrible burden is accompanied with the promise of Messiah's kingdom and of the people's restoration (Jer. 23).

The machinations of the Egyptian party at Jerusalem were at once crushed by Nebuchadnezzar, who again turned from the siege of Tyre to Jerusalem, in the eighth year of his reign. The city was saved from a storm by the surrender of Jehoiachin, with his mother, Nehushta, and the royal harem, and all his princes and officers. They were all carried off to Babylon with all the mighty men of the country and all the skilled artisans, none being left behind but the poorest sort of the people. The total number of the captives was 10,000 of whom 7000 were soldiers and 1000 smiths and other craftsmen; it would seem that the royal family, the princes and the priests, made up the other 2000 (II Kings 24:10-16). Among the captives were Ezekiel (Ezek. 33:21; II Kings 24:18), who had not yet received his prophetic commission, and Shimei, the son of Kish (a Benjamite) and the grandfather of MORDECAI (Esther 2:5-6). At the same time all the remaining

---

1. II Chron. 36:9 has "eight." This is possibly an ancient copyist's error. II Kings 25:15 speaks of Jehoiachin as having wives, a thing most unlikely for an eight-year-old boy.

treasures of the Temple and palace were carried off and the golden vessels of the sanctuary were cut in pieces (II Kings 24:13; II Chron. 36:19). Mattaniah, the youngest son of Josiah and uncle[1] of Jehoiachin, was made king over the wretched remnant of Judah under the new name of Zedekiah (II Kings 24:7).

One of the most remarkable circumstances of this event is that Nebuchadnezzar abstained from the utter destruction of the rebellious city. We shall see that, in all probability, the king had already received the first of those great revelations of Jehovah's power and majesty which were made to him through David, and it seems impossible not to refer his moderation to this lesson. Ezekiel expressly states what was the policy of Nebuchadnezzar in thus continuing the existence of the state: "He hath taken away the mighty of the land, that the kingdom might be base, that it might not lift itself up, but that by keeping of his covenant it might stand" (Ezek. 17:13,14). The *covenant* referred to is the oath which Nebuchadnezzar exacted of the new king (II Chron. 36:13) and which Zedekiah shamefully broke.

Jehoiachin survived for many years after the fall of Zedekiah. For a long time his imprisonment at Babylon was rigorous; he was closely confined and clad in a prison dress. The plots of the Egyptian party and the hopes of his return held out by the false prophet Hananiah (B.C. 595) explain this severity as well as Hananiah's cruel execution (Jer. 28); but in the thirty-seventh year of his captivity (on the 25th or 27th day of the twelfth month, Adar = Feb. 562 B.C.) he was released by Evil-merodach, who had just succeeded to the throne of Babylon (II Kings 25:27-30;

The Deportations of the Jews to Babylon

1. 605 B.C. — Fourth year of Jehoiakim; Daniel and a few others were taken (Dan. 1:1,6).
2. 597 B.C. — Reign of Jehoiachin; King Jehoiachin, the prophet Ezekiel, and 10,000 captives were taken (II Kings 24:14-16; Ezek. 33:21).
3. 586 B.C. — Eleventh year of Zedekiah; all remaining people, except Jeremiah and a few of the poorest, were taken. Jerusalem was destroyed (II Kings 25:11-12; Jer. 40:6).
4. 582 B.C. — Minor deportation (Jer. 52:30).

---

1. In II Chron. 36:10 "brother" means "father's brother."

Jer. 52:31-34). He was received with kind words, was placed in the royal presence on a throne above all the other captive kings, received a robe of honor and a portion for his daily diet until his death.[1]

With Jeconiah the line of descendants from David who ruled on the throne in Jerusalem came to an end. Jeremiah prophesied of Jeconiah, "Write ye this man childless, a man that shall not prosper in his days; for no more shall a man of his seed prosper, sitting upon the throne of David, and ruling in Judah"[2] (Jer. 22:30). Zedekiah, who followed Jeconiah as king, was hardly a succeeding descendant but was an uncle of Jeconiah, appointed by the king of Babylon as a puppet ruler. Jehoiachin was still looked upon as king long after Zedekiah had fallen (II Kings 25:27). Zedekiah was called the king but he was not a further generation in David's line. To this day no merely human descendant of David has ever sat as king in Jerusalem. As governors they have, as kings never. The throne of David has been given to David's greater son, Jesus the Messiah (Luke 1:32-33; I Cor. 15:24-25; Rev. 3:21).

12. *Zedekiah, nineteenth king of Judah – Jeremiah advises submission. False prophets – Predictions of Restoration of Israel and fall of Babylon.* ZEDEKIAH, the nineteenth and last king of Judah (597-586 B.C.; II Kings 24:18-21; II Chron. 36:10-21) and the youngest son of Josiah and Hamutal, was twenty years old at his accession and reigned eleven years till the final destruction of Jerusalem. His proper name, Mattaniah, was changed to Zedekiah at his accession. The only events of his reign, except the brief record of the fall of Jerusalem, are those connected with the history of Jeremiah, from whose book we learn the spirit of the times. Zedekiah accepted his royalty over the impoverished remnant of the Jews as the vassal of Nebuchadnezzar, to whom he was bound by every principle of good faith. The fate of his brother and his nephew had proved the hopelessness of rebellion even before the whole strength of the nation had been carried

---

1. Clay tablets have been found which give a list of Jewish captives in Babylon to whom Evil-merodach granted daily rations. Among the names is that of Jehoiachin, king of Judah. M.F. Unger, *Arch. & O.T.* p. 293.

2. It might appear that Jeconiah did have sons after going into captivity — Shealtiel and Pedaiah among others. Pedaiah's son was Zerubbabel, the leader of the first return of Jews from Babylon (I Chron. 3:17-19). Matthew 1:12 lists Shealtiel and Zerubbabel as legal lineal descendants of Jeconiah. However, Luke 3:27 lists Shealtiel as the son of Neri in the line of David's son Nathan and Zerubbabel as his son. It appears that we have here two cases of adoption in two succeeding generations. Childless Jeconiah adopted Shealtiel, the son of Neri (and perhaps his brothers) as his heir. Then Shealtiel adopted (or obtained by Levirate reckoning) Zerubbabel, the son of his (Shealtiel's) brother Pedaiah.

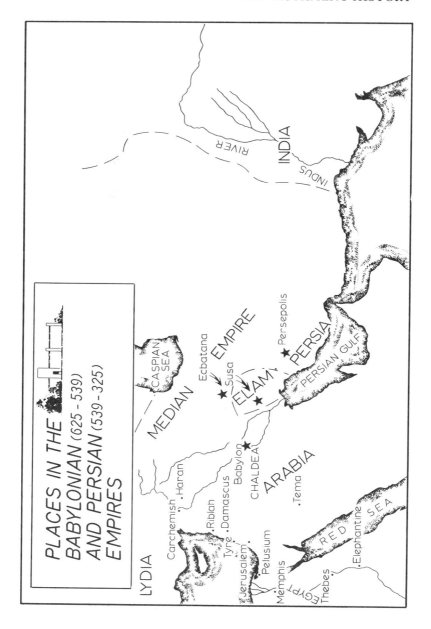

PLACES IN THE
BABYLONIAN (625 - 539)
AND PERSIAN (539 - 325)
EMPIRES

into captivity. The miserable remnant might well envy the condition of their captive brethren, and the time had at length come for piety and patriotism to show themselves in a wise submission to what was proved to be the will of God. Of such a course Jeremiah was the assiduous adviser. His parable of the two baskets of figs showed the goodness that God had in store for the captivity but the hopeless state of the remnant left behind (Jer. 24). His letter to the elders, priests and prophets at Babylon warned them, in opposition to the false prophets who promised their speedy restoration, to make all their arrangements for a prolonged residence there; and repeated the former statement that their captivity should last seventy years, adding that those left behind should, after suffering from the sword, the famine and the pestilence, be dispersed over all the world and became a by-word and reproach (Jer. 29:1-20). From what follows we learn more of the false prophets whom Jeremiah denounced. Two among them, Ahab, the son of Kolaiah, and Zedekiah, the son of Maaseiah, whose lives were as profligate as their principles, were seized by Nebuchadnezzar and "roasted in the fire," an example which must have been the more striking from its contrast with the deliverance of Shadrach, Meshach and Abednego (Jer. 29:21). Another of the same party, Shemaiah the Nehelamite (or the dreamer), dared to write, as if by the word of Jehovah, to Zephaniah and the other priests at Jerusalem, complaining of Jeremiah's letter and demanding his imprisonment (Jer. 29:21-32). Constant in his opposition to these false prophets, whether at Babylon or at home, Jeremiah uttered his grand prophecies of the restoration of Israel in God's own time but not till then (Jer. 30, 31), and of the judgments that awaited all her enemies (Jer. 48, 49). His great prophecy against Babylon, for the consolation of the exiles, was rendered the more impressive by the sign which followed it. Seraiah, the son of Neriah, who carried this prophecy to Babylon, was directed, after reading it, to tie a stone to the volume and sink it in the Euphrates, saying, "Thus shall Babylon sink, and shall not rise from the evil that I will bring upon her."[1] The occasion found for executing this commission was a visit which Zedekiah paid to Babylon in the fourth year of his reign (B.C. 594-3), probably to pay his tribute to Nebuchadnezzar, or perhaps to defend himself against the first suspicions of treasonable dealings with Egypt. For in the same year Pharaoh-necho, who seems never to have ventured to meet

---

1. The same symbol is used in Rev. 18:21 to predict the fall of spiritual Babylon.

Nebuchadnezzar after the defeat of Carchemish, was succeeded by his son Psammetichus II.

13. *Ezekiel prophesies in Babylon – Zedekiah conspires with Egypt.* From the Book of EZEKIEL, who began in this year to enforce upon the exiles at Babylon the same lessons that Jeremiah was teaching at Jerusalem, we learn that Zedekiah entered into a treasonable correspondence with the new king of Egypt, which the prophet denounces as a gross violation of his plighted faith, destined to end in the king's being brought to Babylon for punishment, while his people should fall by the sword or be scattered to the winds (Ezek. 17:11-21). The terms of the agreement with Egypt are expressly stated by the prophet: "He rebelled against him in sending his ambassadors into Egypt, that they might give him horses and much people"; and we are forbidden to give Zedekiah credit for a patriotic resistance by the declaration of the historian: "He rebelled against King Nebuchadnezzar, who had made him swear by God; but he stiffened his neck and hardened his heart from turning unto Jehovah, God of Israel" (II Chron. 36:13).

At Jerusalem the plot appeared so far ripe that the false prophet Hananiah promised the return of Jehiachin within two years and publicly broke off the neck of Jeremiah the yoke which he wore, as a sign of the hopeless subjection of Judah and the surrounding nations, who seem to have joined the Egyptian league. Jeremiah replied that the yoke of wood (the present vassalage of Babylon) should be replaced by a yoke of iron (the final destruction of the nation), and predicted the death of Hananiah, which happened within the year (Jer. 27, 28). We find further evidence of the progress of the conspiracy in the Book of Ezekiel. His vision of the Temple at Jerusalem in the fifth day of the sixth month of the sixth year of the Captivity (B.C. 594-3), reveals the idol abominations which would soon be punished by the destruction of all but a small chosen remnant, and other visions and types follow to the like effect (Ezek. 8, 9). The plainer language of Ezekiel, about a year later (on the tenth of the fifth month of the seventh year of Zedekiah) (Ezek. 10:12), when the elders of Judah came to him to inquire of Jehovah concerning the state of Jerusalem, serves to show that the rebellion had broken out (Ezek. 20, 22, 23). The utter corruption of the people at this time, their persecution of God's prophets and rejection of his word, so that his wrath came upon them "till *there was no remedy*"; the wickedness of Zedekiah in not humbling himself before the word of God by Jeremiah; his faithlessness to the oath he had sworn to Nebuchadnezzar, and that not from religious patriotism, for "he stiffened his neck and hardened his heart from turning unto Jehovah God of Israel"; and the result was the destruction of Jerusalem and the captivity of the people till the time of the Persian empire, so that the land kept her sabbaths for 70 years as Jeremiah had foretold; these outlines of the catastrophe are drawn by the writer of the Chronicles (II Chron. 36:11-21; Comp. Jer. 37:1-2).

It was still two years before Nebuchadnezzar laid siege to Jerusalem with the resolution to destroy it utterly for Zedekiah's treason. From this point the dates of Ezekiel's prophecies accompany the events at Jerusalem. The city was attacked in the ninth year of Zedekiah on the tenth day of the tenth month; and on the same day Ezekiel was commissioned to foretell its utter destruction by striking images to the exiles at Babylon (II Kings 25:1-2; Jer. 39:1; 52:4; Ezek. 24). The forces marshaled against Jerusalem comprised Nebuchadnezzar's whole army, all the vassal kings of his empire and all the nations around, Ammonites, Moabites, Edomites and others who came up to avenge the quarrels of a thousand years (Jer. 34:1). All the fortified cities of Judah had already been taken except Lachish and Azekah (Jer. 34:7).[1]

In this extremity Zedekiah proclaimed freedom to all Hebrew slaves and sent Zephaniah the priest with another messenger to entreat the prayers of Jeremiah. In reply, he announced the coming destruction of the city and the fate of the king himself (Jer. 37:1-4; 34:1-10). The king now attempted to silence him by a mild confinement in the court of the prison in the palace where he had the society of Baruch. While thus shut up and that in a city environed by a mighty enemy, Jeremiah purchased as the "Goel," a field at his native village of Anathoth in Benjamin, as a sign of that return which he went on to prophesy, together with the glories of Messiah's kingdom (Jer. 32, 33).

And now there broke forth a deceptive ray of hope. Pharaoh-hophra,[2] who had just succeeded to the throne of Egypt, led the forces which his father had collected to the relief of Zedekiah. His capture of Gaza (Jer. 47:1) caused Nebuchadnezzar to suspend the siege of Jerusalem and to march

---

1. Within the rubble of Lachish archaeologists have found twenty-one letters to the commander of the fort at Lachish from a number of military outposts nearby. They were written at this very time of invasion by Nebuchadnezzar (589 B.C.). One letter specifically mentions Lachish and Azekah as places not yet conquered. See M.F. Unger, *Arch. & O.T.*, pp. 285-288.

2. Also called Apries (588-569 B.C.).

against him. And now Jerusalem exulted with the joy of a city delivered from a hopeless siege. But Jeremiah forbade them to deceive themselves, while on the distant banks of the Euphrates Ezekiel also foretold the ruin of Egypt (Jer. 37:6-10; Ezek. 29, 30, 31).[1] The princes of Judah now broke their solemn covenant to release their Hebrew slaves, and Jeremiah, having denounced their conduct, left the city for his home in Benjamin. He was detained by one of his enemies, who happened to be captain of the gate. The princes accused him of deserting to the Chaldaeans, a course which had now become common; and he was imprisoned in the house of Jonathan the scribe, where he remained for some time (Jer. 34:11-22; 37:11-15). Meanwhile his warnings were fulfilled by the return of the army of Nebuchadnezzar, who according to Josephus, had defeated the Egyptians, though more probably the enemy retired without a battle[2] (See Josephus, *Antiquities* X, 7, 3).

14. *Jeremiah imprisoned – Fall and destruction of Jerusalem – Exultation of neighboring nations – The land not colonized.* Zedekiah now sent secretly for Jeremiah and asked him, "Is there any word from Jehovah?" "There is," replied the prophet, "thou shalt be delivered into the hand of the King of Babylon." Hoping, it would seem, for a more favorable answer, the king sent him back to the court of the prison, and ordered him to be fed while any bread was left in the city (Jer. 37:11-21). In reply to another request which the king sent to him by Pashur and Zephaniah to inquire of Jehovah, the prophet pointed out a surrender as the only hope of safety (Jer. 21). Upon this the princes demanded his death as a traitor and the king confessed himself too weak to withstand them. They threw Jeremiah to perish in a hideous pit of the prison, where he sank into the mire, but the better feelings of the king came to his rescue at the intercession of the Ethiopian eunuch Ebed-melech, to whom he promised his life "for a prey" in the destruction of the city (Jer. 38:1-13; 39:15-18). Once more adjured by Zedekiah, in private, to give him counsel from God, the prophet pressed him to surrender; but the king was afraid of falling into the hands of the Jews who had revolted to Nebuchadnezzar and who had doubtless many a wrong to avenge. So he entreated Jeremiah to keep the interview a secret

---

1. The dates of these prophecies are given: the twelfth day of the tenth month of the tenth year of Zedekiah = end of December, 588 B.C.; the seventh day of the first month of the eleventh year = April, 586 B.C.; and the first day of the third month = end of May, 586 B.C.

2. It is evident from Jer. 37:21 that the city was again besieged.

and sent him back to the court of the prison, where he remained till Jerusalem was taken (Jer. 37:14-28).

That catastrophe was now at hand: the ruin foreseen by Moses from the very birth of the nation, foretold by the prophets and postponed for the sake of pious kings, as often as it was provoked by their degenerate successors; held in suspense in remembrance of God's oath to David, but brought down at last by the shameless, persistent, inveterate violation of His covenant of piety and purity by the chosen people. Jehovah had done all he could by his prophets, whose words they despised and misused their persons, "until the wrath of Jehovah arose against his people *till there was no remedy*" (II Chron. 36:16).

In the nineteenth year of Nebuchadnezzar, as the eleventh year of Zedekiah drew to a close, Jerusalem, which had been besieged for two years and a half with no relief except the brief diversion made by Pharaoh-hophra, was reduced to the last extremities of famine. On the ninth day of the fourth month an entrance was effected at night through a breach in the city wall, probably on the northern side, and the great officers of Nebuchadnezzar entered the Temple and took their station in the middle court. Zedekiah, with all his men of war, fled by the garden gate of the royal palace on the south side, and took the road over the Mount of Olives to the valley of the Jordan. They were hotly pursued with the morning light. Zedekiah was overtaken in the plain of Jericho, his army dispersed and himself taken. He was carried to Nebuchadnezzar at Riblah in Hamath, whither the king had gone to watch the siege of Tyre. Zedekiah spoke with his conqueror face to face, as Jeremiah had predicted. Having seen the execution of all his sons and the princes of Judah, his eyes were put out and he was sent to Babylon, where he remained a close prisoner till his death. The pity, which might be felt for the sad fate of the last king who wore the crown of David at Jerusalem, must be withheld from the falsely-swearing vassal, who accepted his nephew's throne at the hand of a conqueror, only to prove a traitor alike to his earthly master and to his king, Jehovah.

Other victims were selected for the vengeance of Nebuchadnezzar. The high-priest Seraiah, the second priest Zephaniah, and three door-keepers of the Temple, the commander-in-chief, who was an eunuch, and five (or seven) of the principal courtiers, the scribe or mustering officer of the army — and sixty representatives of the people were carried by Nebuzar-adan, the captain of the guard to Riblah where

Nebuchadnezzar sentenced them to death, probably by impalement and even by worse tortures, if we may judge by the customs that still shock our eyes on the monuments of Assyria and Babylon. Amid all these horrors, there is something in the deliberate justice of the Eastern conqueror which bears a favorable contrast with the general massacre that attended the second great capture of Jerusalem by the virtuous Titus. Our involuntary respect for the grand king of Babylon is confirmed by the treatment which Jeremiah met with in obedience to his orders. As soon as the city was taken, Nebuzar-adan, with the other chief officers, sent for the prophet out of the prison and committed him to the care of GEDALIAH, the son of Ahikam, son of Shaphan, who plays a most important part in the subsequent transactions.

Meanwhile, the king of Babylon decided on the fate of the rebellious city which he had twice spared. On the seventh day of the following month (Ab, the fifth month), Nebuzar-adan returned to Jerusalem, charged to carry out the instructions of his master. Two clear days were occupied in collecting the booty that was still to be found in the Temple and the city after their former spoilations, including the ornaments of the Temple which had been considered too bulky for removal and the vessels which appear to have been left, out of religious respect, for the necessary service of the sanctuary. Among the former were the two great pillars of the Temple-porch, Jachin and Boaz, and the brazen sea, all of which were broken to pieces and their brass transported to Babylon. On the third day the Temple and city were committed to the flames, with the palaces of the king and princes, and all the chief house of Jerusalem and the walls were leveled with the ground. The day of the catastrophe was the tenth day of the fifth month (AB), in the nineteenth year of Nebuchadnezzar, just after the completion of the eleventh year of Zedekiah (July 586 B.C.).

While the work of destruction was carried on by the Chaldaean army, it was viewed with malignant exultation by the nations which had so long chafed beneath the yoke of their kinsman Israel. The Ammonites "cried Aha! against the sanctuary, when it was profaned; and against the land of Israel, when it was desolate; and against the house of Judah, when they went into captivity" (Ezek. 25:3). Moab and Seir said, "Behold, the house of Judah is like unto all the heathen" (Ezek. 25:8). The more active enmity, which was but natural in the Philistines who "took vengeance with a despiteful heart, to destroy it for the old hatred" (Ezek. 25:15) was emulated by Edom, the nearest kinsman and bitterest rival of his brother Israel. "Edom hath dealt against the house of Judah by taking vengeance, and hath greatly offended, and revenged himself upon them" (Ezek. 25). How deeply this blow was felt is seen in the well-known passage in which the Psalmist joins Edom with Babylon herself in a common imprecation, prefacing the most terrible words in which retribution was ever called down upon a cruel foe, with the indignant prayer: "Remember, O Lord, the children of Edom in the days of Jerusalem; who said, *Raze it! raze it! even to the foundation thereof!*" All these nations soon fell victims to the like fate which the prophets again and again denounce upon them (Psalm 137:7-9).[1]

The captives who were carried away on this occasion were but the gleanings of those who had been led off with Jehoiachin. After the escape of the warriors, the people left in the city and those who had deserted to the Chaldeans numbered only 832 persons fit to bear the march. A remnant of the very poorest class were left to till the ground and dress the vineyards; and to these must be added a few objects of the royal favor, as Jeremiah, and those of the fugitive soldiers and other roving bands, who had escaped pursuit in the fastnesses of Judaea and the desert. At the end of the Book of Jeremiah we have the following summary of the captivities under Nebuchadnezzar (Jer. 52:28-30):

1. In the *seventh* (eighth) year of his
   reign (597 B.C.)   3023 Jews
2. In the *eighteenth* (nineteenth) year
   of his reign (586 B.C.)   832 Jews
3. In the *twenty-third* (twenty-fourth)
   year of his reign (582 B.C.)   745 Jews
   Total   4600 Jews[2]

Those last mentioned were carried away by Nebuzar-adan at the time of the war with Egypt.

It deserves especial notice that the land which we may

---

1. Many scholars feel that this is the setting of Obadiah's prophecy against Edom. It seems more likely that this occurred during the invasion under Jehoram of Judah, for it appears that Jerusalem was still standing after Obadiah's prophecy (Obad. 13-14). This was not true after the Babylonian siege of 586. Comp. II Chron. 21:8, 16-17; 36:19.

2. The discrepancy of the numbers of the first captivity and the 10,000 reckoned in II Kings 24:14, seems to result from Jeremiah's not counting in the soldiers. The great difference between even the largest total and the number who returned from the Captivity, 42,360, seems to show how large an accession was received from previous captivities and especially from the Ten Tribes.

henceforth call JUDAEA,[1] to distinguish it from the other parts of
Palestine, was not subjected, like that of Samaria had been, to a
new colonization by heathen settlers. It lay ready to be occupied
by those to whom God had given it, after it had rested for the
sabbatic years of which it had been deprived and when they
themselves had been chastened by affliction. This hope sustained
those of the captives who, like Daniel, still had the faith to pray
with their faces turned toward Jerusalem: it is mingled with the
sad complaints of the pathetic Psalms that belong to the time of
the Captivity, and it even breathes through the more dismal
wailing of Jeremiah's *Lamentations*. These choice utterances of
Hebrew poetry may well excuse the vain attempt to point the
moral of a catastrophe, whose long-accumulating causes and sure
approach have been traced at every step of the history of the
Jewish people.

15. *The remnant in Judea – Gedaliah made governor – Ishmael
assassinates Gedaliah – Johanan – Flight into Egypt – Jeremiah's protests
– Nebuchadnezzar's further conquests*. Before pursuing the story of
the Jews at Babylon to the end of the Captivity, we may conclude
the history of Judaea itself during the last twenty-five years of
Nebuchadnezzar's reign (586-562 B.C.), comprising the fate of
the people left behind and the fortunes of Jeremiah. The
desolated land was not abandoned to anarchy. Nebuzar-adan
appointed GEDALIAH, the son of Ahakim, as governor at Mizpah,
and Jeremiah joined him having been left at liberty by
Nebuzar-adan to go to Babylon or wherever he pleased (II Kings
25:22; Jer. 40:1-6). The dispersed soldiers and people soon
gathered about the new governor, who prudently exhorted them
to live quietly as the subjects of the king of Babylon (II Kings
25:24). Many Jews appeared from the countries of Moab,
Ammon and Edom, and the people were soon peacefully
engaged in gathering the vintage and summer fruits throughout
their cities (Jer. 40:7-12). But the brief rest from trouble was cut
short by the envy of the king of Ammon and the ambition of a
Jewish prince of the royal blood, Ishmael, the son of Nethaniah.
They had the incredible audacity to attempt a new insurrection.
Ishmael and ten Jewish princes came to Mizpah as friendly
guests; and Gedaliah, who had refused to credit a warning of his
treachery, was murdered with the Jews and Chaldaeans who were

---

1. The name of *Jews* (i.e. men of Judah), which rarely occurs up to the time of the Captivity (II Kings 16:6;
Jer. 38:19; 40:11; 52:28), seems to have now become the common designation of the people by their
conquerors (Dan. 3:8,12; Ezra 4:12). Its gradual adoption by themselves is easily traced in the book of
Nehemiah.

with him at Mizpah, only two months after the departure of Nebuzar-adan. Two days later a band of eighty mourners appeared on the frontier, from Shechem, and Shiloh, and Samaria, bringing offerings for the desolated house of God, a touching proof of the religious patriotism which was still to be found even in the most heathenized part of Israel. By a treacherous artifice, Ishmael slew them all but ten, and cast their bodies with those of his former victims into a pit which Asa had dug at Mizpah for a hiding-place during his war with Baasha. He then collected the people who were at Mizpah, including the daughters of Zedekiah, who had been entrusted to Gedaliah's care, and carried them off as captives toward Ammon. He was pursued by the Jewish captains headed by Johanan, the son of Kareah, the same who had ineffectually warned Gedaliah. They overtook him by the great waters at Gibeon (II Sam. 2:13), and rescued the captives, while Ishmael, with eight comrades, fled to Ammon. Then instead of returning to Mizpah, they marched southward to Bethlehem, intending to take refuge in Egypt from Nebuchadnezzar's vengeance for the murder of his governor (Jer. 41). First, however, they asked Jeremiah for counsel from Jehovah. In ten days the answer came, forbidding them to go to Egypt, promising them the protection of God if they remained, and assuring them that, if they persisted in departing, the famine and sword and pestilence, from which they fled, would overtake them in their new refuge (Jer. 42). The prophet was faithful to the long-standing command that the people should never, under any pressure, seek to return by the way of Egypt. His warning only brought upon him a charge of conspiring with Baruch to speak falsely in God's name; and both he and Baruch were carried to Egypt against their will, with all the remnant who had been left under Gedaliah. Many of the Jews had already taken refuge there during the whole time that Egypt was regarded as their help against Assyria. They now formed a large community, living at Migdol, Tahpanhes, Noph and Pathros — a community which had afterward an important history of its own.[1] Meanwhile they fell into idolatry and Jeremiah denounced both on them and on Egypt itself the vengeance of Nebuchadnezzar — a prophecy echoed from the banks of the Euphrates by Ezekiel, whose warnings, promises and exhortations to the exiles at Babylon still kept pace with the current of events in Judaea.

---

1. Jews are known to have been living in Egypt on the island of Jeb (or Elephantine) about 408 B.C. Jeb is at the first cataract of the Nile. Numerous papyrus letters have been found at Elephantine, one of which makes a request to the Persian governor of Palestine for permission to rebuild the temple on the island.

The threatened blow soon fell. In 585 B.C. Nebuchadnezzar took the mainland portion of Tyre, after a siege of thirteen years. After a brief repose, Nebuchadnezzar led his victorious army into Egypt, probably on some new provocation by Apries. In the absence of his own annals or other direct testimony, we can only infer from the statements of Josephus *(Ant.* x 9, 7) and from the prophecies of Jeremiah and Ezekiel, that the chastisement he inflicted on Egypt reached the Jews who had taken refuge there. It was at this time, as we have already seen, that his general Nebuzar-adan carried off another remnant from Judaea, thereby probably almost completing the depopulation of the land (Jer. 52:30; 582 B.C.). There is evidence that Nebuchadnezzar invaded Egypt a second time (after 576) and this may be the occcasion of Ezekiel's last prophecy against the power.[1] At some time during the interval it is almost certain that the king of Babylon subdued the nations bordering upon Judah and for whose exultation in her destruction the prophets had denounced on them the heaviest woes, such as the Ammonites, Moabites and Edomites. There is a very remarkable passage in which Jeremiah comforts the Jews amid all these judgments by contrasting God's destruction of the other nations and of their present oppressors with His correction of themselves: "Fear thou not, O Jacob my servant, saith Jehovah: for I am with thee; for I will *make a full end* of all the nations whither I have driven thee: *but I will not make a full end of thee, but correct thee in measure;* yet will I not leave thee wholly unpunished" (Jer. 46:28). No words could express more fully the principle of Jehovah's dealings with the Jews as the type of his dealings with his own people in every age.

Questions on Section IV
Judah after Israel's Fall

Hezekiah (after Israel's Fall)

1. What Assyrian king attacked Judah in Hezekiah's time (II Chron. 32:1-2)?

2. What did Hezekiah do with the sources of water near Jerusalem (II Chron. 32:3)?

3. What did Hezekiah do to the walls of Jerusalem? Why (II Chron. 32:5; 25:23)?

4. What reassurance did Hezekiah give the men of Judah (II Chron. 32:6-8)?

---

1. Ezek. 29:17; 30:19. The date, the twenty-seventh year of the captivity of Jehoiachin, answers to the thirty-fourth of Nebuchadnezzar, 576 B.C.

5. How much success did the king of Assyria have in Judah (II Kings 18:13)?
6. To what place did Hezekiah send a message of submission to the king of Assyria (II Kings 18:14)?
7. What riches did Hezekiah send the king of Assyria (II Kings 18:15-16)?
8. What messengers did the king of Assyria send to Hezekiah? Who was their spokesman (II Kings 18:17,19)?
9. What two sources of help did the Assyrians urge the Judaeans not to trust in (II Kings 18:21-22)?
10. In what language did the Jewish leaders ask the Assyrians to speak? Why (II Kings 18:26-27)?
11. What did the Assyrians demand Judah and Jerusalem to do (II Kings 18:31-32)?
12. How did the Jews react to the Assyrians' demands (II Kings 18:37; 19:1-3)?
13. What prophet reassured Hezekiah (II Kings 19:6)?
14. What Egyptian (or Ethiopian) king caused the Assyrians to move (II Kings 19:8-9)?
15. What was sent to Hezekiah from the Assyrian king (II Kings 19:14)?
16. What did Hezekiah do with the item mentioned in question 15 (II Kings 19:14)?
17. Who sent word to Hezekiah that God would save Jerusalem (II Kings 19:20,34)?
18. How did many Assyrians die? How many? Where (II Kings 19:35,8)?
19. How did Sennacherib die (II Kings 19:36-37)?
20. Who succeeded Sennacherib (II Kings 19:37)?
21. What fearsome message came to Hezekiah while he was sick (II Kings 20:1)?
22. What did Hezekiah do when he heard this news (II Kings 20:2-3)?
23. How many years were added to Hezekiah's life (II Kings 20:5-6)?
24. What medication was prescribed for Hezekiah (II Kings 20:7)?
25. What miracle showed Hezekiah that he would be healed and go up to the house of the Lord (II Kings 20:8-11)?
26. What Babylonian king came to visit Hezekiah (Isa. 39:1-2)?
27. What did Hezekiah show his visitors (II Kings 20:13)?
28. What did Isaiah predict would happen because Hezekiah

showed all his precious things to the Babylonians (II Kings 20:14-17)?

29. Did Hezekiah seem to have been grieved over Isaiah's warnings (II Kings 20:19)?

Manasseh

1. How old was Manasseh when he began to reign (II Kings 21:1)?
2. What idolatry did Manasseh practice (II Kings 21:3,6)?
3. Where did Manasseh build altars (II Kings 21:4-5)?
4. Where did he set up idols (II Kings 21:7)?
5. How wicked was Manasseh (II Kings 21:11)?
6. What did God say he would do because of Manasseh's evils (II Kings 21:12-14)?
7. What cruelty did Manasseh practice (II Kings 21:16)?
8. Where was Manasseh taken captive? By whom (II Chron. 33:11)?
9. What change took place in Manasseh while he was a captive (II Chron. 33:12-13)?
10. What building projects did Manasseh undertake after his captivity (II Chron. 33:14-16)?

Amon

1. What evils did Amon practice (II Chron. 33:22-23)?
2. How did Amon die (II Chron. 33:24)?

Josiah

1. How old was Josiah when he began to reign (II Chron. 34:1)?
2. When in his reign did he begin to seek God (II Chron. 34:3)?
3. What did Josiah destroy (II Chron. 34:3-4)?
4. What did Josiah do with bones of priests? Why (II Chron. 34:5; Num. 19:11)?
5. What project did Josiah undertake in his 18th year (II Chron. 34:8,10)?
6. Who was priest in Josiah's time (II Chron. 34:14)?
7. Who was the scribe in Josiah's time (II Chron. 34:15)?
8. What was found in the temple (II Chron. 34:14)?
9. Who read the law to the king (II Chron. 34:18)?
10. How did Josiah react when he heard the reading (II Chron. 34:20)?
11. Why did Josiah send some people to go inquire of the Lord (II Chron. 34:21)?
12. What office did Huldah have (II Chron. 34:22)?
13. Summarize the message of Huldah to Josiah (II Chron. 34:24-28)?

14. What people did Josiah gather at the house of Jehovah (II Chron. 34:29-30)?
15. What did Josiah do at this gathering at the house of Jehovah (II Chron. 34:30)?
16. What did the king make before Jehovah (II Chron. 34:31)? What other people joined with him in making this (II Chron. 34:32)?
17. What did Josiah destroy in Jerusalem (II Kings 23:6, 12-14)?
18. What did Josiah destroy in Bethel (II Kings 23:15)?
19. What sepulchre and monument in Bethel did he spare? Why (II Kings 23:16-18; I Kings 13:1-2)?
20. What feast did Josiah keep (II Chron. 35:1)?
21. How great was this feast compared to other such feasts (II Chron. 35:18)?
22. How does Josiah compare in character to the other kings (II Kings 23:25)?
23. Why did not Josiah's goodness save Judah (II Kings 23:26-27)?
24. What king of Egypt went to fight? Where was he going? Through whose land did he pass (II Chron. 35:20; II Kings 23:29)?
25. Who were the opposing sides in the battle of Carchemish? Why is this battle one of the decisive battles of history?
26. What warning did the king of Egypt send to Josiah (II Chron. 35:21)?
27. What did Josiah do about his appearance before going to fight (II Chron. 35:22)?
28. How did Josiah die? Where (II Chron. 35:22-23; II Kings 23:29)?
29. What three prophets prophesied in Josiah's time (Jer. 1:1; Zeph. 1:1)?
30. What prophet lamented for Josiah (II Chron. 35:25)?

Jehoahaz of Judah
1. Who made Jehoahaz king (II Kings 23:30)?
2. How long did he reign (II Kings 23:31)?
3. Who put Jehoahaz in bonds (II Kings 23:33)?
4. Where was Jehoahaz taken and kept till his death (II Kings 23:34)?
5. Who was made king in place of Jeohahaz (II Kings 23:34)? What was his named changed to?
6. What was the relationship of the king that followed Jehoahaz to Jehoahaz (II Kings 23:34)?

Jehoiakim

1. What taxation did Jehoiakim impose on the people? Why (II Kings 23:33,35)?
2. What king took over Judah and other nearby lands from Egypt (II Kings 24:1,7)?
3. Who was taken captive in the fourth (or third) year of Jehoiakim (Dan. 1:1,6)?
4. Whom did Jehoiakim rebel against (II Kings 24:1)?
5. What peoples invaded Judah in Jehoiakim's time (II Kings 24:2)?
6. What did Jehoiakim do with the roll of Jeremiah's prophecy (Jer. 36:22-23)?
7. Who was Jeremiah's scribe (Jer. 36:4)?
8. Who came to Jerusalem to capture Jehoiakim (II Chron. 36:6)?
9. How did Jehoiakim die (Jer. 22:18-19)?

Jehoiachin

1. By what two other names is Jehoiachin known?
2. How long did Jehoiachin reign (II Kings 24:8)?
3. Who captured Jerusalem in the days of Jehoiachin (II Kings 24:10)?
4. How many people were deported (II Kings 24:14)?
5. What prophet was deported to Babylon at this time?
6. What was done with the temple in Jehoiachin's time (II Kings 24:13)?
7. What was done with Jehoiachin (II Kings 24:15)?
8. Who was made king in the place of Jehoiachin? To what was his name changed (II Kings 24:17)?
9. How long did Jehoiachin survive his captivity (II Kings 25:27)?
10. What Babylonian king released Jehoiachin (II Kings 25:27-30)?

Zedekiah

1. How old was Zedekiah when he began to reign and how long did he reign (II Kings 24:18)?
2. What had Zedekiah sworn to do which he did not do (II Chron. 36:13)?
3. What rebellion did Zedekiah make (II Kings 24:20-25:1)?
4. Who came and besieged Jerusalem (II Kings 25:1-2)?
5. How many years did the siege last (II Kings 25:1-2)?
6. What foreign army came to resist Babylon during the siege of Jerusalem (Jer. 37:5)?

7. What did Jeremiah predict about Pharoah's army and the fate of Judah (Jer. 37:7-10)?
8. Why did Zedekiah try to flee Jerusalem (II Kings 25:3-4)?
9. Where was Zedekiah captured (II Kings 25:5)?
10. What was the last thing Zedekiah ever saw (II Kings 25:7)?
11. Who was captain of the guard of the king of Babylon (II Kings 25:8)?
12. What was done with the valuables of the temple (II Kings 25:13-15)?
13. What was done to the temple? To Jerusalem (II Kings 25:9, 10)?
14. What was done with the people of Jerusalem (II Kings 25:11)?
15. What leaders of the Jews were executed (II Kings 25:18-21)?
16. How long was the land of Judah desolate and kept its Sabbaths (II Chron. 36:21)?
17. What privileges were granted to Jeremiah after Jerusalem fell (Jer. 39:11-12)?
18. What choices were given to Jeremiah by the Babylonians? Which choice did he make (Jer. 40:2-6)?

Judah after its Fall

1. Whom did the king of Babylon make governor over the land (Jer. 40:7)?
2. What did the governor urge the Judeans to do (Jer. 40:9)?
3. What agricultural produce did the people gather (Jer. 40:12)?
4. Who hired an assassin to kill the governor? Who was the assassin (Jer. 40:14)?
5. Whom did the assassins slay (Jer. 41:2-3)?
6. Where were the bodies cast (Jer. 41:9)?
7. Who fought the assassins (Jer. 41:11-12)?
8. Where did the Jews think they should go (Jer. 41:17)?
9. What did Jeremiah prophesy to the Jews about their proposed trip (Jer. 42:15-17,19)?
10. Did the Jews accept Jeremiah's prophecy (Jer. 43:2,7)?
11. What prophecy did Jeremiah make in Egypt (Jer. 43:10-11, 44:13-14)?
12. What did the Jews in Egypt say to Jeremiah in response to his prophecy (Jer. 44:16-19)?

Period X
Period of Exile

From the Destruction of the Kingdom of Judah to the Close of the Captivity at Babylon, 586-536 B.C.

1. Facts about the period of exile. 2. Nebuchadnezzar taught by the captives at Babylon — Daniel and his companions. 3. Nebuchadnezzar's dream — The imperial statue — The fiery furnace. 4. Nebuchadnezzar's humiliation — His death. 5. The successors of Nebuchadnezzar. 6. Rise of Cyrus the Great and foundation of the Persian Empire. 7. Cyris attacks Babylon — Defeat of Lydia and Nabonidus of Babylon — Belshazzar's feast — The city surprised and taken — End of the Babylonian Empire. 8. Reign of "Darius the Median," probably Gubaru. 9. Daniel under Darius — The den of lions. 10. Further prophecies of Daniel: a. Dream of the four beasts — b. Vision of the ram and he-goat — c. Prophecy of the seventy weeks — d. Vision of the Son of God and prophecy of the Last Days. 11. Subsequent history and final desolation of Babylon.

1. *Facts about the period of exile.*

a. The seventy years exile in Babylon may be calculated from the first deportation in 605 to the close of the captivity, 536 B.C., counting both the starting and closing years. Or it may be calculated from the fall of Jerusalem (586 B.C.) to the rebuilding of the temple (516 B.C.). See Zech. 7:5.

b. King Jehoiachin was released from imprisonment during the captivity (II Kings 25:27-30).

c. The Jews lived nearly normal lives in Babylon; they were not enslaved or persecuted. They had liberty to marry, build homes, plant gardens (Jer. 29:5-6), to assemble (Ezek. 20:1) and to rise to positions of prominence as Daniel did.

d. There were times of discouragement (Psalm 137), times when additional captives were brought into Babylon (Jer. 52:30) and times when idolatry was commanded (Daniel 3).

e. Some of the Jews were bitter against the Lord; some were indifferent; some doubtless lost faith (Ezek. 18:2,25; 33:31).

f. The prophets Ezekiel and Daniel guided and encouraged the captives. The books of Ezekiel and Daniel are our primary sources of information about life in this period. Psalm 137 is also from this time.

g. Tribal identity and genealogies were preserved by scribes during the period (Ezra 2:59,62).

h. Many of the Jews never forgot their homeland and were ready to return at the first opportunity (Psalm 137).

i. The dispersed Jews imparted to the peoples in whose lands they dwelt the knowledge of the true God and the hope of the Messiah (Matt. 2:1-2).

j. The *synagogue* came into existence. Since the Jews were far from Jerusalem and the temple was destroyed, meeting places were erected in the various Jewish settlements for the reading and teaching of the law. By New Testament times synagogues were to be found in every village of the Jews, even after the temple had been rebuilt.

k. The bitter experience of the exile in Babylon permanently cured the Jews of idolatry, at least those Jews who returned to Jerusalem after the exile.

2. *Nebuchadnezzar taught by the captives at Babylon – Daniel and his companions.* Of all historic figures, Nebuchadnezzar most strikingly represents the power of destruction. Like his own image on the plain of Dura, he towers over the ground he has cleared of every opponent from the Nile to the Euphrates. Above all, he had been the instrument in the hand of God to root out His people for their sins from the good land given to their fathers, but he had yet to learn that he himself was subject to their God. This

lesson was taught him while he enjoyed the fruit of his victories in the city of Babylon, which he had made the wonder of the world by his "hanging gardens" and other splendid works, and the appointed teacher was almost a repetition of that of Joseph at the court of Pharaoh.

We have seen that when Nebuchadnezzar first took Jerusalem in the third year of Jehoiakim (605 B.C.), he commissioned Ashpenaz, the master of his eunuchs, to select the most comely youths of royal and noble birth, possessed of natural grace and acquired learning, to be educated in the language and wisdom of the Chaldaeans. They were to receive their food and wine from the king's table and after three years' training they were to be brought before him. Among them were four belonging to the tribe of Judah, whose names were Daniel, Hananiah, Mishael and Azariah, which according to oriental custom (as in the case of Joseph), were changed by the prince of the eunuchs into Belteshazzar, Shadrach, Meshach and Abednego. In sacred history, however, Daniel has retained his own name, while the other three, being only mentioned on one important occasion, are known by their Babylonian appellations. Daniel resolved that he would not defile himself with the king's food and wine, and through the tender regard with which he had inspired the prince of the eunuchs, he obtained the favor of an experiment on himself and his three friends. After being fed for ten days with pulse (things sown, like grain and vegetables) and water, they were found in better condition than their comrades who had been nourished on the king's dainties; so this diet was continued to the end. Meanwhile God endowed them with all knowledge and wisdom and to Daniel, in particular, he granted the same insight into dreams and visions that had distinguished Joseph. When the time came for them to appear before the king, he found them the fairest of all their fellow-captives and ten times better in wisdom and discernment than all the magicians and astrologers of Chaldaea. So they stood before him among the courtiers (Dan. 1). We must not fail to notice that law of God's providence by which at every crisis of His people's history He raised up for them a leader skilled in all the accomplishments of their adversaries: Abraham, the stately prince, among the Arab sheiks; Joseph, the diviner and statesman; Moses, the warrior and learned in all the wisdom of the Egyptians; Daniel, the most learned sage and faultless governor in the realm of Chaldaea. Well might South reply to the flippant objection that God has no need of our learning — "Much less has He need of your ignorance."

3. *Nebuchadnezzar's dream – The imperial statue – The fiery furnace.* The great opportunity for the use of Daniel's power as an interpreter of dreams for the glory of God occurred in a manner very similar to the case of Joseph. The date assigned to this event is the second year of the reign of Nebuchadnezzar (604 B.C.). This dream experience throws a flood of light on the career of Nebuchadnezzar and especially on his repeated forbearance toward Jerusalem and his kindness to Jeremiah. It is needless to recount in detail those pictures which are so vividly impressed on our earliest recollections: the king's troubled sleep and dreams, which he forgot when he awoke in the morning; his despotic demand of the Chaldaean soothsayers, scarcely too severe a test of their extravagant pretensions, to tell him the dream itself, as well as the interpretation; the simplicity with which, for once in their lives, they confess their impotence to discover what was not first told them, instead of boldly avowing, like Daniel, that God would not conceal from the man divinely inspired to reveal His counsels the far lesser knowledge of the signs chosen to exhibit them. When their failure had all but involved in their sentence of death the Hebrew men of learning too, Daniel obtained from the king a respite, which he and his companions spent in prayer; and he received the revelation with one of those grand utterances of praise and prayer that form the great charm of his book. The vision, which he was inspired to expound to Nebuchadnezzar, is one of several by which, at this epoch, when the great monarchies of Asia were about to come into collision with the powers of the West, God revealed the steps by which the successive empires were to give way before His kingdom. The various empires were represented by different segments of a colossal statue:

a. Golden head — Babylonian empire (625-539 B.C.)
b. Silver breast and arms — Medo-Persian empire (539-331)
c. Brass belly and thighs — Grecian empire of Alexander the Great and his successors (331-63 B.C.)[1]
d. Iron legs and feet — Roman empire (63 B.C. - A.D. 476)

A stone cut out of a mountain without human hands struck the image of its feet and destroyed it. This depicted the establishment of the Kingdom of Christ, the church, in the days of the Roman

---

1. 63 B.C. is the date of the capture of Jerusalem by Pompey the Roman. As far as the Jews were concerned the domination of Rome dates from that time, although the Roman empire existed considerably before that time.

empire, on the Day of Pentecost, A.D. 34 (A.D. 30 by our calendar) (Acts 2).

The lesson was the same as that which was taught to the first Babel-builders on that very spot — that all attempts to build a universal human kingdom are futile, for the kingdoms of the world are reserved to be the kingdoms of our God and of His Christ (Rev. 11:15).

The confession which Daniel's exposition of his dream drew from Nebuchadnezzar is scarcely the language of a convert to the true religion but rather of a heathen yielding to the God of the Jews an exalted place among the gods. According to his promise (Dan. 2:4), he loaded Daniel with rewards, made him ruler over the province of Babylon and master of the Chaldaean sages; and appointed his three companions, at his request, to high offices in the province of Babylon.

Their fidelity to Jehovah soon underwent a terrible trial but came out as unscathed as their persons from the fiery furnace (Dan. 3). That Nebuchadnezzar should have condemned them for such a reason so soon after the lesson he had learned is a more striking than surprising example of a despot's impatience of opposition and readiness to take the bait of flattery. Daniel seems to have been away from Babylon when this crisis occurred, perhaps on government business elsewhere in the province.

There has been much discussion respecting the vision of the "Son of God" with the three Hebrews in the fiery furnace. His walking with them there seems to imply that they were conscious of His presence and sustained by His comfort, like Stephen in the agony of his martyrdom, and they would doubtless recognize in him the "Angel Jehovah," who had so often shown himself to their fathers and who had promised, "When thou walkest through the fire, thou shalt not be burned; neither shall the flame kindle upon thee." But we must not ascribe such divine knowledge to Nebuchadnezzar. To him the vision was that of some unknown deity, "a Son of the Gods" — but it was enough first to petrify him with astonishment and then to extort from him a warmer acknowledgment of the God of the Hebrews. Their enemies were silenced by a terrible decree and they themselves were promoted to higher stations in the province of Babylon.

4. *Nebuchadnezzar's humiliation – His death.* A third lesson, by which the king of Babylon was finally bowed in submission to Jehovah, is recorded in his own rescript to all the province of his empire (Dan. 4). Another dream, which Daniel again interpreted

when the Chaldaean soothsayers had failed, warned the king that his reason should depart and he should be driven from among men to herd with the beast of the field till "seven times"[1] had passed over his head. The judgment came upon him at the expiration of a year. His enemies had been subdued on every side, his great works of art and power had been completed and as he surveyed them from the roof of his palace, he forgot God of whose might he had had such proofs and exclaimed, "Is not this great Babylon that I have built for the house of the kingdom, by the might of my power, and for the honor of my majesty?" The words had scarcely mounted toward the vault of heaven when a voice replied, "O King Nebuchadnezzar, to thee it is spoken; THE KINGDOM IS DEPARTED FROM THEE;" adding the details of his exile from among men, all which were fulfilled for a space of seven years. Assuredly Nebuchadnezzar is the grandest of all despots but the climax of his grandeur is seen in his publishing the history of his own humiliation, in order to give glory to the most high God (Dan. 4:34-35).

After a reign of forty-three years he was succeeded in 562 B.C. by his son EVIL-MERODACH, whose release of Jehoiachin from prison is the last event mentioned in the books of Kings (II Kings 25:27-30).

5. *The successors of Nebuchadnezzar.* For the twenty-three years between the accession of Evil-merodach and the fall of Babylon (562-539 B.C.) there is a gap in the Scripture history. The Book of Daniel passes at once to the capture of the city and the death of Belshazzar, who is called the son of Nebuchadnezzar; but this word need not signify an immediate successor, as in Scripture it often refers to grandsons or more distant descendants. Many scholars now think that Belshazzar was the son of Nabonidus, one of Nebuchadnezzar's nobles, and his wife Nitocris, a daughter of Nebuchadnezzar.[2] Thus Belshazzar would have been the grandson of Nebuchadnezzar. The succession of kings seems to have been as follows:[3]

   a. Nebuchadnezzar (605-562 B.C.)
   b. Evil-merodach (562-560)
   c. Neriglissar (560-556)
   d. Labashi-marduk (556)
   e. Nabonidus (556-539)
   f. Belshazzar (coregent with Nabonidus, 553-539)

1. The term *times* seems to signify complete revolutions of the seasons or years. However, the term may refer to some shorter "time."
2. R.P. Doughtery, *Nabonidus and Belshazzar* (New Haven: Yale Univ., 1929), pp. 59ff, 194.
3. See Neighbors of Israel and Judah in this book, pp. 555-556.

Jeremiah, whose prophecies of this period are as detailed and definite as histories, predicts that all nations should serve Nebuchadnezzar, and *his son* and *his son's son,* until the very time of the land came; and the *Chronicles* state that the Jews were servants to him *and his sons* until the reign of the kingdom of Persia (Jer. 27:7; II Chron. 36:20).

6. *Rise of Cyrus the Great and foundation of the Persian empire.* During the latter years of the Babylonian empire, a great revolution was developing in the highlands of Persia and Media. Previously the Medes had been the dominant power in the area, but now under the leadership of the Persian CYRUS THE GREAT (559-530) the old dynasty in Media was overthrown and the resulting combined Medo-Persian empire was rapidly rising.

The triumph of Cyrus over Babylon and his work of restoring the Jews to their homeland make Cyrus of greatest importance in sacred history. So important was he, in fact, that God foretold his coming *by name* through the prophet Isaiah, over 150 years before he took Babylon (Isa. 44:28; 45:1 and other allusions in Isa. 41-45).

Although Cyrus was used by God for a high purpose, he nonetheless did not know God and possessed some of the barbaric traits of all great conquerors (Isa. 45:4).

Of the many conflicting versions of his history which were derived from the romantic stories of the Persian poets, that of Herodotus is the most probable and consistent. Passing over the fables of his exposure and preservation, we come to the fact in which all his historians concur that he dethroned Astyages, the last king of Media, and transferred the rule over the Medo-Persian empire to the royal family of Persia. This revolution transferred the Medo-Persian empire from an effete dynasty to a family of hardy mountaineers, both being of that Aryan race which had not yet occupied a leading place in history. The capital was fixed at Ecbatana.

Cyrus' conquest of Media was followed by victory over the kingdom of Lydia in Asia Minor under rich, powerful King CROESUS (546 B.C.).

The interval of nearly fifteen years before the final conflict with Babylon was probably occupied by Cyrus in finishing the conquest of the tribes of Asia Minor, strengthening his power in Media and subduing the more distant portion of the Babylonian empire in Upper Assyria. King Nabonidus of Babylon seems to have been heedless of the danger to his kingdom. After his third year he turned over the actual governing of the kingdom to his son BELSHAZZAR, while he spent much time searching for and studying ancient Sumerian and Akkadian (Babylonian) writings. During many of his years he resided at the Arabian oasis city of Teima.

When he finally came back to Babylon it was too late. Nabonidus seems to have fought one futile battle with Cyrus' forces and upon his defeat retired to the sacred Chaldean city of Borshippa, a short distance south of Babylon. Here he surrendered after the capture of Babylon. Cyrus spared his life and gave him a principality in Carmania, where he died.

7. *Cyrus attacks Babylon – Belshazzar's feast – The city surprised and taken – End of the Babylonian empire.* Meanwhile the people of Babylon remained in fancied security behind their immense fortifications. The city formed a vast square divided by the Euphrates. The city was about two and one-half miles long on each side. Its walls (altogether about eleven miles of them) were eighty-five feet thick in places and (according to Herodotus' probably exaggerated report) 300 feet high. The walls were pierced by eight gates, the most famous being the highly decorated Ishtar gate opening onto a broad Processional Street. The gates were made of brass. A moat fed by the Euphrates encircled the city. These walls and gates are particularly referred to in that striking prophecy of Jeremiah which is almost like a history of the siege (Jer. 50:15; 51:53,58). Little wonder that Belshazzar could feast with a thousand of his lords in contemptuous security while the Persians advanced upon his city (Dan 5:1).

The details of the siege of Babylon are uncertain. Herodotus indicates that Cyrus diverted the stream of the Euphrates and entered the city by its bed. Cyrus' own inscriptions mention no such actions. Rather he indicates that he entered the city without any battle, sparing Babylon any calamity.[1]

With the foolishness of impenitent reprobates, Belshazzar chose this time for a colossal feast (Dan. 5). A thousand of his lords were assembled at the banquet; and the prince inflamed with wine and flattery ordered the gold and silver vessels of the temple to be brought that he and his wives and concubines and courtiers might drink in them to the praise of their gods. At that moment a hand was seen writing upon the wall in the full light of the candelabra. Belshazzar, his joints unnerved by fear, cried out

---

1. Charles Pfeiffer, *Biblical World* (Grand Rapids, Baker, 1966), p. 178.

for the Chaldaean astrologers and soothsayers to be brought
before him and proclaimed that the man who could read the
writing should be invested with the insignia of royalty and made
third ruler in the kingdom.[1] While the hand moved slowly on
from letter to letter, they confessed their inability to read the
unknown characters. The king was beside himself with terror
when a new personage appeared upon the scene. The "queen,"
who addresses Belshazzar in the tone of authority was probably
his mother, Nitocris. She alone of all the court remembered the
wonders that had been revealed to Nebuchadnezzar by Daniel,
who seems to have been deposed from his post as master of the
soothsayers. By her advice the king sent for him and repeated his
offers of reward. Rejecting them with disdain, Daniel reproached
Belshazzar for not learning from the example of
Nebuchadnezzar and for the crowning insult of that night against
God. By this time the hand, which had been slowly moving over
the wall had completed its awful inscription—

MENE, MENE, TEKEL, UPHARSIN

Numbered! numbered! Weight! and Divisions (or *the Persians*).[2]
"The days of thy kingdom are *numbered* and *finished,*
Thou art *weighed* in the balances, and found wanting:
Thy kingdom is *divided,* and given to the Medes and *Persians.*"
Belshazzar's last act of sovereignty was to confer the promised
reward on Daniel. All that is added in the Scripture narrative is
this: "In that night was Belshazzar the king of the Chaldaeans
slain."

Seemingly an advance guard of the troops of Cyrus under the
command of one Darius the Mede, came that night upon Babylon
and in the midst of the great drunken feast entered it without
battle and raced to the palace where Belshazzar was slain. Cyrus
soon came to Babylon but gave control to Darius the Mede for a
brief time (Dan. 5:30-31; 9:1; 10:1; 11:1).

Belshazzar's father, Nabonidus, was taken as we have seen at
Borsippa, and thus fell the empire of Babylon little more than
twenty years after the height of its splendor under
Nebuchadnezzar. Its fate furnished not only a great example of
the fulfillment of ancient and recent prophecies, especially those
of Isaiah, Jeremiah and Ezekiel, but also a type of the worldly
splendor and power, the unbridled insolence and the

---

1. Daniel's being made third ruler is a confirmation of the Bible's accuracy. It is now known that Belshazzar
was co-regent with Nabonidus, and therefore Daniel could only occupy third place in the kingdom. Critics
formerly denied that such a person as Belshazzar ever existed.

2. The last word has this double meaning.

conspicuous ruin of the future oppressors of the Church of God, and especially of that one which is called in the Apocalypse "Babylon the Great, Mystery of Iniquity, Mother of Harlots" (Rev. 17:5).

8. *Reign of Darius the Mede, probably Gubaru.* Instead of following the progress of Cyrus, the sacred history remains with the Jews at Babylon, where we read, simultaneously with the death of Belshazzar, that "DARIUS THE MEDIAN took (or received) the kingdom, being about sixty-two years old" (Dan. 5:31; 9:1).

This Darius seems to have been the same person as Gubaru, who according to Persian inscriptions was an officer in Cyrus' army and who seems to have been made governor of the Persian province north of Babylon.[1] Darius' rule seems to have been contemporary with Cyrus' rule. The two years of Darius are included in the nine years which are assigned to Cyrus in the Babylonian annals (538-529 B.C.), as his real position was known to the scribes, while the close relations of Darius with the captive Jews account for their speaking of him as the king and dating the year of his death as the *first year* of Cyrus. This was the glorious year of their own restoration to their land. But before opening that new page of their history, we must glance at the last days of Daniel and the final fate of Babylon.

9. *Daniel under Darius – the den of lions.* We read that Daniel continued "even unto the first year of King Cyrus." Thus as the margin of our Bible formerly puts it, "he lived to see that glorious time of the return of his people from the Babylonian captivity, though he did not die then" (Dan. 1:21). Again we read, "This Daniel prospered in the reign of Darius, and in the reign of Cyrus the Persian" (Dan. 6:28). After the death of Nebuchadnezzar or in the dynastic contests which followed the reign of Evil-merodach, he seems to have retired into obscurity till he was called forth to interpret the handwriting on the wall. That proof of prophetic power would insure him respect from the conquerors who seem also to have recognized the rank conferred on him by Belshazzar. Shortly after the capture of Babylon we find him employed by the king in some commission to Susa (Shushan), one of the Median capitals (Dan. 8:1,2). When Darius made a settlement of the provinces in which we trace the germ of the satrapies of Darius, the son of Hystaspes, Daniel was made the first of the three "presidents" who were placed over the 120 "princes" of the provinces. The Medo-Persian princes were

1. John Whitcomb, *Darius the Mede* (Grand Rapids: Eerdmans 1959).

doubly offended at being placed under a Jew by birth and a servant of the late dynasty. His administration was too faultless to give an opening to their envy, so they set one of those ingenious traps in which religious persecution is concealed under the guise of loyalty. Two of the grandest pictures in the Bible are the faithful servant of Jehovah continuing his prayers thrice a day, neither diminishing their number nor withdrawing from his open window which looked toward Jerusalem, and the confessor calmly sitting in the den of lions, whose mouths God had shut while the king, who had consented to his death, remains restless and fasting. It is superfluous to relate his deliverance from the lions, the punishment of his enemies and the proclamation of Darius in honor of Daniel's God.

10. *Further prophecies of Daniel.* After this Daniel enjoyed unbroken prosperity under Darius and Cyrus and doubtless had a share in advising the restoration of the Jews. His last vision is dated in the *third year* of Cyrus, 534 B.C. (Dan. 10:1). The following is a summary of his visions, dreams and prophecies after the time of Nebuchadnezzar:

a. In the *first year of Belshazzar* (Dan. 7). Daniel's dream-vision of the *Four Beasts* pictures the rise of the same four empires of Nebuchadnezzar's image in Dan. 2. The four heads of the leopard (7:6) picture the four divisions into which Alexander's empire fell after his death. The unnameable beast is the Roman empire. Its ten horns are the divisions into which it was divided. The "little horn" (7:8, 20-21) may refer to the Roman Catholic religion which arose out of the ruins of the Roman empire, and had a mouth making great claims and was a persecuting power (e.g., the Inquisition).

b. In the *third year of Belshazzar* (Dan. 8). The vision which Daniel saw at Shushan of a conflict between a ram and he-goat, symbolized the Medo-Persian and Macedonian conflicts. The peculiar character of the former is represented by its two horns of which *the higher came up last.* Alexander is plainly represented by the "notable horn" of the he-goat and his successors by the four horns which replaced it. The "little horn" springing out of one of the others and representing "a king of fierce countenance and understanding dark sentences," prospering, persecuting and opposing the Prince of princes, till he is broken without hand, can be none other than the Syrian (Seleucid) King Antiochus Epiphanes, who persecuted and corrupted the Jews (175-163 B.C.) with such outrages that the Jews revolted and defeated him by the hand of Judas Maccabeus. (See the book of I Maccabees.)

c. In the *first year of Darius*, 538 B.C. (Dan. 9). This famous prophecy of the *seventy weeks* was given to Daniel following an intense prayer of confession. It was given as the seventy years' captivity drew near an end. God reassured Daniel that Israel would return and restore their land and the Messiah would come. All these events would occur during a period of "seventy weeks,"[1] or 490 days. Taking a year for each day as is often done in prophecy and starting at the time of the decree to Ezra to return to Jerusalem (457 B.C.), and going down through 69 of the 70 weeks (483 years), we come down to 26 A.D.,[2] the very year Christ Jesus began His ministry (Dan. 9:25). During these 483 years Jerusalem was rebuilt in troublous times. In the middle of the seventieth week (3½ years), the Messiah was to be cut off (Dan. 9:26), and indeed Christ was crucified after a ministry of 3½ years. But by that time He had brought in everlasting righteousness and taken away burnt offerings and sacrifices by the sacrifice of Himself (Dan. 9:27; Heb. 10:12). Following this would come an "abomination of desolation" (a hateful person who makes desolate): this refers to the Romans, who came and destroyed Jerusalem in A.D. 70 (Dan. 9:27; Matt. 24:15).

d. *In the third year of Cyrus*. The vision of the Son of God to Daniel on the banks of the Hiddekel (Tigris), in the same glorious form in which he appeared to St. John in Patmos and the prophecy that followed (Dan. 10-12). Throughout this prophecy both the imagery and the substance bear a close analogy to the Apocalypse. There can be little doubt that the earlier part relates to the contests between the two Greek kingdoms of Syria and Egypt which disputed the mastery of Judaea, but it is clear that at some point a transition is made to the final mysteries of God's government and judgment. How the study of those mysteries ought to be approached we learn from the prophecy itself. Daniel is bidden to "*shut up* the words and *seal* the book, even to the time of the end." When that time is so near that God reveals his purposes to his people, as he did

---

1. Literally, *Seventy Sevens*. It must not be supposed that the exposition rests on the general assumption that a *day* stands for a *year* in the symbolical language of prophecy. It is rather a plain inference from the whole bearing of the prophecy that the *sevens* spoken of are *sevens of years*, just as the word *Sabbath* is often used for the *Sabbatic year*. In fact, the phrase seems best interpreted as seventy cycles of Sabbatic years — 490 years.

2. Our present calendars are four or five years in error. By our calendars Christ was actually born 4 or 5 B.C. and was about 30 years old in A.D. 26 (Luke 3:23).

to Daniel from the books of Jeremiah, the Lamb in the midst of the throne will open the volume, seal by seal and page by page. Then all conflicting guesses will cease respecting the "time and times and dividing of a time," the 1290 and the 1335 days. "None of the wicked shall understand, but the wise shall understand." Meanwhile "Blessed is he that *waiteth,*" and blessed especially the man who is distinguished above all others by the assurance in God's own word of his personal salvation. The final word to Daniel was, "But thou, go thy way to the end; for thou shalt rest, and stand in thy lot at the end of the days."

11. *Subsequent history and final desolation of Babylon.* How different was the end of Babylon where Daniel delivered his testimony for God! Its fall was delayed for many years. Babylon remained the second city of the Persian empire and the residence of the king during the greater part of the year. Alexander ended his career in the city which he had designed to renovate for his capital. The Seleucid kings of Syria transferred the capital to Antioch, while they chose a more eligible site on the Tigris for the frontier city of Seleucia, to which most of the inhabitants of Babylon removed. The houses were deserted and the walls became quarries for building-materials. The site of the city was gradually swept over by the neglected river, while the mounds around it crumbled into the moat from which they were dug. "Babylon became heaps, a dwelling-place for 'dragons,' an astonishment and a hissing, without an inhabitant" (Jer. 51:37,43; Isa. 13:19-20), fulfilling to the very letter the prophetic visions of its utter desolation and presenting a lively image of the fate reserved for the mystic Babylon of later days. Only in our own days have those "heaps" given up the monuments of the city's grandeur and the records from which we have gained confirmations and illustrations of the Biblical record of its former kings and glory.

Questions Over the Period of Exile

1. Where were the Jews taken into exile (Jer. 25:11)?
2. For how long?
3. Which Bible books are our main sources of information about this period? Which Psalm tells of the period?
4. What dates mark the start and end of the period of exile?
5. Did the Jews have freedom or slavery in exile?

6. What meeting places for reading and teaching the law came into existence during this period?

7. What effect did the captivity of the Jews have on their chronic idolatry?

8. Who was the greatest king of Babylon (Jer. 25:9)?

9. What dream did Daniel interpret for Nebuchadnezzar (Dan. 2)?

10. Who were Shadrach, Meshech and Abednego (Dan. 1:7; 2:49; 3:12)?

11. Why were they thrown into a fiery furnace (Dan. 3:13-23)?

12. What Judean king was released by Evil-merodach (Jer. 52:31)?

13. Which Babylonian king made a feast for a thousand of his nobles? Who was this king's father? Grandfather?

14. Explain the handwriting, *Mene, Mene, Tekel, Upharsin* (Dan. 5:25-28).

15. Why was Daniel made *third* ruler in the kingdom?

16. Who was the king of Persia who conquered Babylon (Dan. 10:1)?

17. Who was the Mede who governed Babylon (Dan. 5:31)?

18. Which prophet had foretold the coming of Cyrus by name?

Period XI
Period of Return and Restoration
From the Decree of Cyrus to the Close of
the Old Testament Canon. 536-423 B.C.

Section I
Introduction to Ezra, Nehemiah and Esther

1. The three historical books — Ezra, Nehemiah and Esther and three books of prophecy — Haggai, Zechariah and Malachi — were written during the *period of return and restoration* after Babylonian captivity, after 536 B.C. During this period the Jews *returned* to their land and *restored* their temple, city and society.

2. These books were written during the time when the *Persian empire* ruled the world. The Medes and Persians conquered Babylon in 539 B.C.

3. Here is a list of the kings of Persia (after fall of Babylon):
a. Cyrus (the Great) ....539-530 B.C.
b. Cambyses II ....530-522 B.C.
c. Gomates (Pseudo-Smerdis) ....522-521 B.C.
d. Darius I (The Great, son of Hystaspes)......521-486 B.C.
e. Xerxes I (Ahasuerus) ....486-465 B.C.
f. Artaxerxes I (Longimanus) ....465-424 B.C.
g. Xerxes II...............................424-423 B.C.
h. Darius II (Nothus) ....423-404 B.C.

i. Artaxerxes II (Mnemon) . . . . .404-359 B.C.
j. Artaxerxes III (Ochos) . . . . .359-338 B.C.
k. Arses . . . . .338-335 B.C.
l. Darius III (Codomannus) . . . . .335-331 B.C.
(Alexander the Great overthrew Darius III at the battle of Arbela
in 331 B.C. ending the Persian empire.)

    4. Chronology of Biblical events during the period:

a. First return of the Jews to Jerusalem, 536 B.C. (Ezra 1:1-3)
b. Foundation of the temple laid, 535 B.C. (Ezra 3:8,10)
c. Ministries of Haggai and Zechariah, 521 B.C. (Haggai 1:1;
    Zech. 1:1)
d. Temple completed, 516 B.C. (Ezra 6:15)
e. Esther saves her people, 479 B.C. (Esther 2:16)
f. Ezra returns to Jerusalem, 458 B.C. (Ezra 7:1,7)
g. Ezra deals with mixed marriages, 458 B.C. (Ezra 9:1,2)
h. Possible abortive attempt by Ezra to build walls (Ezra 4:7,
    12-13; 9:9)
i. Nehemiah's return and first governorship, 444-433 B.C.
    (Neh. 1:1; 13:6)
    Walls rebuilt, 444 B.C. (Neh. 6:15)
    Ezra reads law, 444 B.C. (Neh. 7:73-8:1)
    Second separation from foreign marriages (Neh. 9:1; 13:3)
j. Nehemiah returns to Persia, 433 B.C. (Neh. 13:6)
k. Ministry of Malachi, around 430 B.C.
l. Nehemiah's second governorship, 428-423 B.C.(?) (Neh.
    13:6-7)
m. Accession of Darius II, 423 B.C. (Neh. 12:22). This is the last
    contemporary event referred to in the Old Testament. The
    close of the Old Testament canon came shortly thereafter.

    5. *Outline of the book of Ezra.* (Memorize the two main parts.)

Part I. Restoration under Zerubbabel, Chs. 1-6
    Ch. 1 — Cyrus' proclamation and the first return.
    Ch. 2 — List of those who returned from Babylon.
    Ch. 3 — Altar built, temple foundation laid.
    Ch. 4 — Temple hindered by adversaries.
    Ch. 5 — Temple resumed, letter to Darius.
    Ch. 6 — Temple finished and dedicated.
Part II. Reforms under Ezra, Chs. 7-10
    Ch. 7 — Ezra authorized to lead a return.
    Ch. 8 — Ezra's return.
    Ch. 9 — Grief over mixed marriages.
    Ch. 10 — Foreign wives put away.

6. *Points about Ezra.*

a. Portions of the book of Ezra are written in Aramaic (Syriac) rather than in Hebrew as in most of the Old Testament (Aramaic portions are Ezra 4:8-6:18; 7:12-26).

b. There is a long time gap between the two parts of Ezra's history. Part I (see outline) deals with events from about 536-516 B.C. Part II deals with events around seventy years later. See Sec. 4. above.

c. Ezra 4:6-23 is out of chronological order with the rest of the book. In Ezra 4:5 information is given about the opposition to the rebuilding program in the time of Darius II. Then in 4:6-23 a summary of later oppositions to the rebuilding is given. Then in 4:24 the discussion returns to events in the time of Darius II.

d. It appears that there was an abortive attempt in the time of Ezra to rebuild the walls of Jerusalem (Ezra 4:7, 12-13; 9:9). Ezra's failure to accomplish this may account for the lack of references to him in the early parts of Nehemiah's book.

7. *Outline of Nehemiah.* (Memorize the two main parts.)

Part I — Restoration of the walls by Nehemiah, Chs. 1-7

   Ch. 1 — Nehemiah's grief over Jerusalem's desolation.

   Ch. 2 — Nehemiah returns to rebuild Jerusalem.

   Ch. 3 — Details of rebuilding the walls.

   Ch. 4 — Oppositions during the rebuilding.

   Ch. 5 — Usury abolished.

   Ch. 6 — Walls finished.

   Ch. 7 — Those who returned from Babylon.

Part II — Reforms by Ezra and Nehemiah, Chs. 8-13.

   Ch. 8 — Ezra reads the law, feast of tabernacles.

   Ch. 9 — Public confession of sin.

   Ch. 10 — Public covenant to keep the law.

   Ch. 11 — Residents of Jerusalem and other cities.

   Ch. 12 — List of priests, dedication of the walls.

   Ch. 13 — Reforms of Nehemiah's second governorship.

8. *Outline of Esther.* (Memorize the two main parts.)

Part I. The danger of the Jews, Chs. 1-3

   A. Esther made queen instead of Vashti, Chs. 1-2.

   B. Haman's conspiracy against the Jews, Ch. 3.

Part II. The deliverance of the Jews, Chs. 4-10.

   A. Esther's courage brings deliverance, Chs. 4-7

   B. Vengeance on the Jews' enemies, 8:1-9:19.

   C. The feast of Purim, 9:20-32.

D. Mordecai's exaltation at court, Ch. 10.

9. *Points about Esther*

a. King Ahasuerus in the book of Esther is the same person as Xerxes I, the king famous for his wars with Greece. The events in the book pertaining to Esther took place in Xerxes' seventh year (4:16), after he returned from his defeat at Salamis. According to Herodotus (ix, 108) Xerxes sought consolation with his harem after this disaster.[1]

b. The book of Esther is peculiar in that it does not mention God's name. However, it does refer to fasting (4:16), to prayer (9:31) and to providence (4:14). 4:14 is a remarkable verse worthy of being memorized.

Questions

1. What three historical books and what three books of prophecy were written in the period after return from Babylonian captivity?
2. What do we call this period of time?
3. What empire ruled the world at that time?
4. Give the dates of (1) the first return of the Jews to Jerusalem; (2) Ezra's return to Jerusalem; and (3) Nehemiah's first return and governorship.
5. Write from memory the headings of Parts I and II of the outlines of Ezra, Nehemiah and Esther.
6. In what language was Ezra partly written?
7. By what other name was King Ahasuerus known?
8. What is peculiar about the book of Esther? Does this mean that the book is not a spiritual book?
9. Write from memory Esther 4:14.

Section II
Return and Restoration under Zerubbabel (Ezra 1-6)

1. The decree of Cyrus — Moral gains of the Captivity — Cessation of idolatry — More spiritual worship — Germs of new declension. 2. Numbers of the first caravan — The new nation composed of all the tribes — Arrival at Jerusalem and foundation of the Temple. 3. Opposition to the building — Later oppositions to

---

1. See G.L. Archer, *A Survey of O.T. Intro.* p. 419 (1974).

rebuilding the walls — The prophets, Haggai and
Zechariah — Temple finished under Darius —
Dedication of temple.

1. *The decree of Cyrus – Moral gains of the Captivity – Cessation of
idolatry*. In the first year of his sole reign at Babylon (536 B.C.),
Cyrus issued a decree for the rebuilding of the temple in
Jerusalem. We know from Cyrus inscriptions[1] that it was his
policy to let various conquered peoples who had been deported
by Babylon and Assyria return home and to replace in their
original cities gods and idols that had been removed. However,
his decree to the Jews included a recognition that Jehovah was
God of heaven and uniquely God (Ezra 1:1,3). Cyrus'
proclamation fulfilled the word spoken by Jeremiah (Jer.
25:12-14). Cyrus promptly invited the people of God throughout his empire to go up to the work and charged those among
whom they dwelt to help them with gold and goods and cattle.

The response to this act of noble generosity — for such is its
true character, whatever secondary motives may have been
mixed up with it — was the more easy, as the captive Jews had
preserved their genealogies and their patriarchal constitution
under their princes. It is even said that they had a kind of ruler,
called the "Head of the Captivity" or "Captain of the people" (II
Esdras 5:16 and the Talmud), but this is very doubtful. So the
chief of the fathers of Judah and Benjamin with the priests and
Levites, whose families are enumerated by Ezra, rose up to the
work. Their neighbors made them liberal presents, beside
freewill offerings for the Temple; and Cyrus caused his treasurer
Mithredath to deliver the vessels of the Temple which
Nebuchadnezzar had carried away, 5400 in number, to
Sheshbazzar or ZERUBBABEL,[2] the prince of Judah who was the
leader of the migration. Thus, as the Israelites had gone forth
from the first captivity laden with the spoils of Egypt, so now they
returned from the second enriched with the freewill offerings of
Persia, to be consecrated to the service of Jehovah (II Chron.
36:22,23; Ezra 1,2; Ps. 126).

But they carried greater riches than all the treasures of Persia,
in the moral gains of their captivity. Throughout the history of
the monarchy we have never lost sight of the fact that that form of
government was itself a departure from the will of God. Though

---

1. M.F. Unger, *Arch. & O.T.*, p. 304.
2. Though conclusive proof is lacking, it seems much more likely than not that Zerubbabel and
Sheshbazzar are the same person.

on the great principle of condescension and forbearance, God made this defection the occasion of His new covenant with David, the inherent vices of the monarchy broke out into that long course of idolatry and worldly pride, which was cut short by the captivities of both branches of the nation. After the captivity we hear no more of these forms of evil. Too soon, indeed, we find the commencement of other corruptions natural to fallen man, the spiritual pride and moral iniquity, which had utterly corrupted the people before the coming of Christ. But the seeds of those vices were as yet hidden in individual hearts. The people again presented as in the wilderness the outward aspect of the Kingdom of the living God. Owing their revived political existence to the will of Persia, they could not at first establish a new monarchy; nor was the attempt ever made till the usurpation of an alien — Herod the Idumaean — seemed to challenge their true King, the CHRIST, to assert His rights. The people seem to have learned to wait for His kingdom and their political dependence gave freer scope to their religious organization. Religion had shared the evils of the kingdom. Our admiration for the magnificence of Solomon's Temple is not unmingled with a misgiving of some loss of spirituality, and its destruction broke through a tradition which leaned toward an undue reliance upon ceremonies. The second Temple, so strikingly inferior in outward splendor, nay, wanting even the visible sign of Jehovah's presence in the Shekinah, became the centre of a more spiritual worship.[1] While the great festivals, like the other Mosaic institutions, were for the first time punctually observed, the experience of the captivity and the examples of such men as Daniel had taught the people that God might be worshiped not at Jerusalem only; and their local meetings in the SYNAGOGUES, which some suppose to have begun during the captivity, became a regular institution. The Scriptures, collected into a "Canon" soon after the return, superseded the prophetic office; their regular reading in the synagogues prevented that ignorance which had been so fatal under the monarchy; and the "scribes," who devoted themselves to their exposition, shared the respect paid to the priests and Levites. *Prayer,* private as well as public, regained that supreme place in God's worship, which had been usurped by rites and ceremonies. The *Sabbath,* which the prophets never cease to represent as the keystone both of religion and of the charities of

---

1. The return of only four out of the twenty-four courses of priests must have placed a great check on pomp in the Temple service.

social life, was firmly established, after a sharp contrast with worldly selfishness. Idolatry was henceforth unknown and the attempt of the Syrian kings to impose its practice adorned the Jewish Church with a cloud of martyrs, whose constancy confirms the many other proofs that the people had attained to a more spiritual faith. The shades of this fair picture were as yet in the background but the current of the history brought them into prominence very soon — such things as spiritual pride, perverted worship, oppression and immorality.

2. *The first caravan to Jerusalem – Altar rebuilt – Temple foundations laid.* The number of the people forming the first caravan, whom Ezra reckons, not only by their families, but by the cities of Judah and Benjamin and other tribes, to which they belonged with the priests and Levites amounted in all to 42,360 (Ezra 2:64-65), besides 7337 men-servants and maid-servants.[1] They had 736 horses, 245 mules, 435 camels and 6720 asses. These numbers may seem small, in contrast to the former population of Judaea, but they are large as compared with the enumeration given above of the several captivities. They no doubt included many of the Ten Tribes, for Cyrus addressed his proclamation to all the servants of God throughout the empire, and it was responded to not only by the fathers of Judah and Benjamin but "by all whose spirit God had raised," (Ezra 1:5). In fact, though the new nation are called *Jews,* the distinction of the tribes disappears (except in their pedigrees), and subsequent jealousies are religious and local, as those against Samaria and Nazareth. Those, however, who undertook the journey were doubtless a considerable minority of the captives, who as directed by Jeremiah had settled down quietly in the land of their captivity, built houses and planted vineyards. Some followed at a later period. Others remained behind forming what was called the "Dispersion," and how numerous these were in all the provinces of the empire we see in the Book of Esther.

The little band of 50,000, so few and weak in comparison of the host that crossed the Jordan under Joshua, were led by ZERUBBABEL, prince of Judah and grandson of Jehoiachin, who was appointed *Tirshatha* or governor of Judaea (Ezra 2:63). With him were associated the high-priest JESHUA (or Joshua) and ten of the chief elders. We have no record of the journey but the

---

1. The *Nethinum* who returned (Ezra 2:43) were temple slaves. Their name means "the given ones." They were probably descendants of the Canaanites, who had not been driven out of the land but who had been subjected to perpetual servitude to Israel and the temple (Num. 31:40, 42, 47; Josh. 9:21, 27; Ezra 8:20).

prophecy of Isaiah (48:20-21) indicates that they had a joyful trip with all needs supplied. After visiting their desolate cities, they assembled in the seventh month (Tisri = Sept.-Oct.) at Jerusalem, to rebuild the altar and offer their first sacrifices at the Feast of Tabernacles. Though dreading the hostility of the surrounding nations, they prepared to build the Temple, hiring masons and carpenters with the money they had brought and preparing provisions for the Tyrians and Sidonians, who had been commanded by Cyrus to bring cedar-trees from Lebanon by sea to Joppa, as Hiram had done for Solomon (Ezra 3:1-7).

In the second month of the following year (Iyar = Apr.-May, 535 B.C.), the foundations of the Temple was laid with great solemnities amid the sound of trumpets and the chorus of the sons of Asaph, "praising and giving thanks unto Jehovah, because he is good, for his mercy endureth forever toward Israel." But the shouts of the people were mingled with the weeping of the priests and elders who had seen the glory of the first house, so that the cries of joy could hardly be distinguished from those of sorrow (Ezra 3:8-13).[1]

3. *Opposition to the building – Later oppositions to rebuilding the walls – The prophets, Haggai and Zechariah – Temple finished under Darius – Temple dedicated.* The work was not long permitted to proceed in quiet. The descendants of the colonists whom Esar-haddon and Asshur-banipal (Asnappar) had settled in Samaria and whose strange mixture of idolatry with the worship of Jehovah has already been related, were not slow to claim affinity with the people so favored by Cyrus. Their request to join in building the Temple was indignantly rejected by the Jews who regarded them as idolaters and "adversaries," and they used all their efforts to earn the latter title. By hired influence at the court, as well as by their opposition on the spot, the building of the Temple was hindered till the reign of Darius, the son of Hystaspes.

A further record of later opposition to the rebuilding of Jerusalem is given in Ezra 4:6-23. The enemies of the Jews accused them falsely to Ahasuerus (Xerxes I — See Sec. I, Intro. to Ezra, Neh., and Est.), and later wrote a slanderous letter to Artaxerxes I (465-424), which caused Artaxerxes to stop the building of the walls. This section (4:6-23) makes no reference to the building of the Temple which had been completed long

---

1. Though it was seventy years from the first beginning of the Captivity, it was only fifty since the destruction of Jerusalem.

before the time of Artaxerxes, but to the *wall* (4:12-13). Apparently someone started the project of rebuilding the walls (Comp. Ezra 9:9), but the enemies got it stopped before any real progress was made. At Ezra 4:24 the discussion of the rebuilding of the Temple in the time of Darius is resumed.

The restoration of order under Darius, the son of Hystaspes, after a brief usurpation by one Gomates, was the signal for new hopes and efforts. In the second year of his reign (520 B.C.), the prophets HAGGAI and ZECHARIAH, the son of Iddo, commenced the exhortations and promises, mingled with reproofs and warnings, which we read in their books.[1] The rebuilding of the Temple was resumed by Zerubbabel and Jeshua, who appear in the prophecies of Zechariah as types of the great Prince and Priest of the approaching reign of Christ (Zech. 6:9-13). They had to deal, not with malignant adversaries, but with the just authorities of a settled government. Being called to account for their conduct by Tattenai, the Persian governor west of the Euphrates, they appealed to the edict of Cyrus, which was found among the records at Ecbatana; and the discovery brought a new edict from Darius, not only permitting the work, but bidding his officers to aid them with supplies and threatening all who hindered them with the severest penalties. So the work went on and prospered under the constant encouragement of the prophets Haggai and Zechariah; and the house was finished on the third of the twelfth month (Adar=Feb.-March) in the sixth year of Darius (516 B.C.), twenty-one years after its commencement.

The Feast of Dedication of the Temple was kept with great joy. Besides the 700 victims offered for a burnt-offering, twelve goats were offered for a sin-offering *"for all Israel,"* one for each tribe — a decisive proof that the returned "children of the captivity" regarded themselves as the representatives of all Israel. The courses of the priests and Levites were set in order, according to the law of Moses and the institutions of David. It was found that only four of the original courses of priests were represented, but by the division of each into six, the number of twenty-four was restored and the old names were adopted. The solemnities were concluded by the keeping of the Passover on the fourteenth day of the first month and of the seven days of the unleavened bread (Ezra 6). Psalms 146-150 may also pertain to the dedication of the second temple.

---

1. The reproofs of Haggai for the people's slowness in building the house of God, while making haste to build their own, are among the most impressive passages of the Hebrew prophets (Haggai 1:1-2:9).

4. *Zerubbabel's temple.* We must note here a few facts about Zerubbabel's temple, the second Jewish temple built on Mt. Moriah. While the height and breadth of Zerubbabel's temple were greater than those of Solomon's (Ezra 6:3; I Kings 6:2), the comparative overall appearance of the two made the second temple appear as nothing (Haggai 2:2). It lacked the elegant materials and workmanship of Solomon's. Probably it lacked the accessory buildings, porches and courts that enhanced the glory of Solomon's temple. Most of all the glory cloud of Jehovah's presence never entered into the temple of Zerubbabel as it did into Solomon's (I Kings 8:11). Herod the Great began in 19 B.C. to remodel, enlarge and renovate the temple of Zerubbabel until it became practically a new structure, more elegant by worldly standards than even Solomon's.

The Three Returns of the Jews from Babylon

1. 536 B.C. — Under Zerubbabel. About 50,000 returned.
2. 458 B.C. — Under Ezra. About 1,800 (Ezra 8).
3. 444 B.C. — Nehemiah.

Memory aid: "444 for fortification."
(Nehemiah returned in 444 to fortify and rebuild the walls of Jerusalem.)

Questions over Section II
Return Under Zerubbabel

1. Give the headings of the two parts of the outline of Ezra.
2. What Persian king let the Jews return to Judah (Ezra 1:1)?
3. To whom did the Persian king give credit for his being king (Ezra 1:2)?
4. What did the king declare that God had charged him to do (Ezra 1:2)?
5. What was to be given to assist the Jews who returned (1:4)?
6. What vessels were brought forth to the Jews to take back with them (1:7)?
7. Who was the prince of Judah (1:8)?
8. How many vessels altogether were given to the Jews (1:11)?
9. From what city to what city did the Jews return (1:11)?
10. Whose name heads the list of returning Jews (2:2)?
11. What were the Nethinim (2:43)?

12. Why were some Jews who returned excluded from the priesthood (2:62)?

13. How many returned with Zerubbabel (2:64-65)?

14. What was given by some of the Israelites for the house of God (2:68-69)?

15. What item of temple equipment was built first (3:2)?

16. What feast was kept by the returned Jews (Ezra 3:4)?

17. Where were cedar trees for the new temple sought (Ezra 3:7)?

18. Who led in the work of rebuilding the temple (3:8)?

19. How was the laying of the foundation celebrated (3:10-11)?

20. What mixed sounds were heard when the temple foundation was laid (Ezra 3:13)?

21. What did the adversaries of Judah request (Ezra 4:1-2)?

22. What did the adversaries do when their request was refused (4:4-5)?

23. How does Ezra 4:6-23 fit (or not fit) into the narrative of Ezra?

24. Who was Asnappar (Osnappar) (Ezra 4:10)?

25. How did the enemies stop the building of Jerusalem in the days of Artaxerxes (4:7,11,23)?

26. What two prophets stirred up the people to resume building the temple (Ezra 5:1)?

27. Who questioned the Jews' right to rebuild the temple (5:3)?

28. What did the governor request Darius to search for in his records (5:17)?

29. Where was the decree of Cyrus found (6:1-2)?

30. What order about the rebuilding of the temple did Darius give (6:7-11)?

31. During the reign of what king was the temple completed (Ezra 6:15)?

32. How long had it taken to build the temple?

33. What feeling did the Israelites have at the temple dedication (6:16)?

34. How many goats were offered as sin-offerings at the dedication? Why was this number offered (6:17; Comp. 8:35)?

35. What feast was kept after the temple was completed (Ezra 6:19)?

36. How did Zerubbabel's temple compare with Solomon's?

Section III
Esther

1. Ahasuerus (Xerxes) succeeds Darius — Queen Vashti deposed. 2. Xerxes' defeats in Greece — Esther added to his harem — Esther is not Amestris — Mordecai reports a plot. 3. Haman honored — Haman obtains a decree to destroy Jews. 4. Mordecai sends Esther unto Ahasuerus — Esther received by the king — Esther's banquet — Haman plots to hang Mordecai. 5. The chronicles read to Ahasuerus — Mordecai honored and Haman humiliated — Haman's plot exposed — Haman hung. 6. The Jews defend themselves — The feast of Purim. 7. Ahasuerus' taxation — Mordecai's greatness.

1. *Ahasuerus succeeds – Darius – Queen Vashti deposed.* During the interval between the first return of the Jews under Zerubbabel (536 B.C.) and the second return under Ezra (458 B.C.), incidents with far-reaching effects occurred in Shushan (or Susa), the winter-time capital of the Persian kings.

In 486 B.C. Darius I was succeeded by his son Xerxes, whose repulse from Greece fills so notable a page in the history of Europe. He is called Ahasuerus in the book of Esther.

During Xerxes' third year before his campaign in Greece he made a great feast in Shushan, lasting 180 days. During this feast he demanded that his queen, Vashti, come before the assembled princes and display her beauty. When she refused, she was deposed at the suggestion of the king's wisemen, who feared that other women would follow her example and disobey their husbands (Esther 1).

2. *Xerxes' defeats in Greece – Esther added to his harem – Esther is not Amestris – Mordecai reports a plot.* During the years that followed, Xerxes made a trip to Greece with a great navy. He was stopped at Thermopylae, defeated at the naval battle of Salamis and nearly annihilated at Plataea (479 B.C.). He returned to Persia and in his seventh year he sought consolation with his harem according to Herodotus (ix. 108).

Many fair virgins were brought to him, among them one Hadassah *(Myrtle)*, a Hebrew maiden better known by the name Esther (Akkad. *Ishtar* or *Venus)*, who had been brought up by an older cousin named *Mordecai.* Esther won such favor both with the king and his servants that she was made queen in the place of Vashti (Est. 2:1-18).

Greek historians tell that Xerxes had an infamous wife named Amestris as his queen at that time. On one occasion Amestris had fourteen noble Persian youths buried alive as a thank-offering to the god of the underworld (Herodotus vii. 113). Esther is not the same as Amestris. It is not surprising that the Greek historians do not mention Esther; they mention only those people connected with their own history. Xerxes was notably polygamous. Considering these things it is not surprising that the Greeks mentioned two wives of Xerxes not mentioned in the Bible and the Bible mentions Vashti and Esther, who are not mentioned by the Greeks.

In those times Mordecai at the king's gate overheard a plot on the king's life and reported it through Esther. The plotters were executed and a record made of Mordecai's deed (Est. 2:21-23).

3. *Haman honored – Haman obtains a decree to destroy Jews.* A prince of Ahasuerus named Haman was promoted to a high position. Haman was greatly disturbed by Mordecai, however, because Mordecai would not bow down to him. Haman obtained a decree from the king to destroy all Jews, including Mordecai. The day for this massacre was selected by casting lots (dice) called (in Assyrian) PUR (Heb. pl. *purim*). This decree was circulated throughout the vast empire of Ahasuerus from India to Ethiopia, including Judah (Esther 3).

If this decree had been carried out, all of God's promises to Abraham, to Moses, to David — all the promises of the Messiah — would have failed. But the word of the LORD shall stand forever (Isa. 40:8).

4. *Mordecai sends Esther unto Ahasuerus – Esther received by the king – Esther's banquet – Haman plots to hang Mordecai.* Mordecai, in great weeping over the decree, sent word to Esther in the palace, asking her to petition the king about the decree. In words of great eloquence he declared that she may have come to the kingdom "for such a time as this" (4:14). Esther bravely accepted this duty, knowing that if she approached the king without an invitation, she would be put to death unless the king extended his scepter in acceptance of her visit (Esther 4).

Esther's faith was rewarded. The king received her warmly and accepted an invitation to a banquet prepared by her that day. To this banquet Haman also was invited. At the banquet Esther requested their presence at a similar banquet the next day. Haughty Haman was exultant at the supposed honor to him but upon seeing Mordecai as he went home he was again angered. At the suggestion of his wife, Zeresh, he prepared that day a high gallows, and that night went to the king to obtain permission to hang Mordecai upon them (Esther 5).

5. *The chronicles read to Ahasuerus – Mordecai honored and Haman humiliated – Haman's plot exposed – Haman hung.* That night insomnia struck Ahasuerus and he requested that the chronicles of his kingdom be read to him. He heard of Mordecai's report of the assassins and learned that no reward had been given Mordecai. At that moment Haman came in to ask to execute Mordecai. The king asked Haman what should be done to one whom the king wished to honor. Supposing that it was he himself, Haman proposed that the honored one be royally paraded through the city on a horse led by a most noble prince. Haman was assigned the job of leading the horse as Mordecai was royally honored. Upon returning home in humiliation, his wife expressed her fear that Haman has started an irreversible fall before Mordecai the Jew. The unique power of the Jews was hated but recognized (Esther 6).

At that hour Haman was summoned to the second banquet. At this banquet Esther revealed to Ahasuerus that she was a Jewess and that Haman's plot would destroy her and her people. Ahasuerus stalked out in anger. Haman fell before Esther, pleading. Mistaking this for an attack upon her, Ahasuerus condemned Haman and he was hung upon the gallows that had been prepared for Mordecai (Esther 7).

6. *The Jews defend themselves – The feast of Purim.* While the laws of the Medes and Persians could not be altered or taken away, other laws could be added to them. Therefore Esther and Mordecai, who had been appointed to Haman's position, obtained from Ahasuerus a further decree permitting Jews to assemble to fight and defend themselves on the day that Haman had chosen for their extermination. This decree brought joy to the Jews and caused many Gentiles to become proselytes to the Jewish faith (Esther 8).

On the fearsome day scheduled for the slaughter of Jews and on the day after, the Jews throughout the empire gathered and defended themselves. They slew 800 enemies in Shushan and 75,000 throughout the empire. (Esther 9:12,15)

To commemorate this deliverance Mordecai sent out letters to

Jews everywhere to keep a holiday on the fourteenth and fifteenth days of the twelfth month, a feast called PURIM, after the name of the lots cast by Haman (Esther 9).

7. *Ahasuerus' taxation – Mordecai's greatness.* After this Ahasuerus laid a tax on the lands and islands of his empire, perhaps to pay for the expenses of his disastrous Grecian wars.

Mordecai became very great in the kingdom of Ahasuerus. His name has been found on a clay tablet verifying before all people his place in the history of Persia and of Israel.[1]

Questions Over Esther

1. What were the limits of Ahasuerus' kingdom (1:1)?
2. By what other name is Ahasuerus known?
3. In what city was his palace (1:2)?
4. In what year of his reign did he make a great feast (1:3)?
5. How long did the feast last (1:4-5)?
6. Does 1:6-7 sound like an eyewitness account of the feast?
7. Who was Vashti (1:9)?
8. What did Vashti refuse to do (1:11-12)?
9. Why did the wise men urge that Vashti be deposed (1:18,20)?
10. What did the king afterwards seek for himself (2:2)?
11. Who was Mordecai (2:5-6)?
12. Who was Hadassah (2:7)?
13. What did Esther not tell the Persians (2:10)?
14. How was Esther received by the king (2:17)?
15. What plot did Mordecai overhear (2:21)?
16. Where was a record made of Mordecai's report (2:23)?
17. Who was Haman (3:1)?
18. What honor did Haman receive (3:2)?
19. What made Haman angry (3:5)?
20. What did Haman decide to do with the Jews (3:6)?
21. What is Pur (3:7)?
22. What law did Haman get passed (3:13)?
23. How did Mordecai react to the decree (4:1)?
24. How did Esther find out about the plot against the Jews (4:7-8)?
25. What request did Mordecai send to Esther (4:8)?
26. What danger was there in Esther's entering the king's court (4:11)?
27. What confidence did Mordecai have about the future of the Jews (4:14)?

---

1. G.L. Archer, *A Survey of O.T. Intro.*, p. 420 (1974).

28. What preparation did Esther make for going in to see Ahasuerus (4:16)?
29. What was the king's reaction to Esther's visit (5:2)?
30. What did Esther ask of the king (5:4)?
31. What did Esther ask for at the first banquet (5:8)?
32. How did Haman feel about being invited to the banquet (5:9,12)?
33. What made Haman angry after the banquet (5:9)?
34. Who was Zeresh (5:10)?
35. How did Haman's wife propose that Mordecai be slain (5:14)?
36. How did the king occupy his mind when he could not sleep (6:1)?
37. About whom did the reader read to Ahasuerus (6:2-3)?
38. Who appeared and for what purpose at that moment (6:4)?
39. What question did Ahasuerus ask Haman (6:6)?
40. What suggestion for honoring a man did Haman offer (6:8-9)?
41. How was Haman humiliated (6:10-12)?
42. What prophetic word was uttered by Haman's wife (6:13)?
43. How did Ahasuerus react to Esther's accusation of Haman (7:6-7)?
44. What was Haman's fate (7:9-10)?
45. Who took the office of Haman (8:2)?
46. What did Mordecai write to the Jews after Esther had obtained the king's consent (8:11)?
47. How was this decree spread abroad (8:14)?
48. Why did many Gentiles become Jews (8:17)?
49. What happened on the day the Jews were to be slain (9:2)?
50. How many enemies of the Jews were slain in Shushan (9:6,15)?
51. How many were slain throughout the kingdom (9:16)?
52. What happened to Haman's ten sons (9:10, 13-14)?
53. How was the deliverance of the Jews commemorated (9:21)?
54. What is PURIM (9:26)?
55. What did Ahasuerus lay upon the land (10:1)?
56. Who became great in the kingdom of Ahasuerus (10:2-3)?

Section IV
Returns of Ezra and Nehemiah
(Ezra 7-10, Nehemiah)

1. Ezra and Artaxerxes — Ezra authorized to lead a return — Ezra's character — The king's commission. 2. Arrival in Jerusalem. 3. Marriages with foreigners — Ezra's grief — Foreign wives put away. 4. Grievous conditions reported in Jerusalem — Nehemiah's return — Rebuilding of walls commenced. 5. Oppositions to rebuilding of walls. 6. Religious celebrations — Ezra reads the law — Feast of Tabernacles — Covenant to keep the law. 7. The peopling of Jerusalem. 8. Dedication of the walls — Levites and singers appointed — Separation from foreigners. 9. Nehemiah returns to Persia — Apostasy in Judah — The prophet Malachi. 10. Nehemiah's second return from Persia — Purification of the priesthood — Sabbath violations stopped. 11. Collection of Old Testament books by Ezra — The Great Synagogue. 12. Samaritan temple built on Mt. Gerezim. Special Study, Between the Testaments.

1. *Ezra and Artaxerxes – Ezra authorized to lead a return – Ezra's character – The king's commission.* We have no further details of the history of the Jews after the experiences of Esther (479 B.C.) until Ezra appears on the scene in the seventh year of Artaxerxes I (Longimanus), 458 B.C. Artaxerxes gained the throne by putting down revolts. This may explain his early opposition to the restored Jews when they were accused of possible revolts (Ezra 4:7,15, 20-21). Unless perchance the Artaxerxes of Ezra 4 is an earlier king usually known by another name, it appears that Artaxerxes I stopped an attempt to rebuild Jerusalem's walls early in his reign.

In Artaxerxes' seventh year Ezra, a Jewish scribe[1] in Babylon, achieved great favor with Artaxerxes (Ezra 7:1-7) and Artaxerxes authorized him to lead a return of Jews up from Babylon to Jerusalem.

Ezra occupies a place toward the end of the history of the Old

---

1. The scribes were men who made copies of the law and taught the law. Because of their education and intelligence, they came to occupy one of the most influential positions among the Jews.

Covenant, resembling in many respects that of Moses at the beginning. He was a priest descended from the line of the later high-priests. His father Seraiah was the grandson of Hilkiah, high-priest in the reign of Josiah. Ezra was especially distinguished for his knowledge of the Scriptures, "a ready scribe in the law of Moses." Living at Babylon, he gained the favor of Artaxerxes and obtained from him a commission to go up to Jerusalem. The restored Jews had already fallen into great declension. Ezra's study in God's law had stirred him up to a work of reformation: "For Ezra had prepared his heart to seek the law of Jehovah, and to do it, and to teach in Israel statutes and judgments" (Ezra 7:10). No more praiseworthy description is applied to anyone in the Scriptures than this and indeed no finer resolutions could fill the heart of any son of God than the purposes of Ezra. Every step he takes is marked by some devout acknowledgment of the help of God "according to the good hand of his God upon him" (Ezra 7:6, 9, 27, 28; 8:22, 31).

The king's commission invited all the Israelites and priests and Levites in the whole empire who so wished to go with Ezra, who was sent by the king and his seven councilors to inquire concerning Judah and Jerusalem, bearing offerings from the king and his councilors and freewill-offerings from the people, to buy sacrifices and to decorate the Temple, besides vessels for its service. All the treasures beyond the Euphrates were commanded to supply his wants and the priests and ministers of the temple were exempted from taxation. Ezra was commanded to appoint and instruct magistrates and judges over the people beyond the river, with authority to punish, even to death, all who broke the law of God and the king (Ezra 7). The language of Artaxerxes' letter authorizing Ezra to return gave him authority to do almost anything he desired with the silver and gold they received (Ezra 7:10).

Ezra's exultation over the favor of Artaxerxes is understandable (Ezra 7:27-28); more especially is this so if indeed Artaxerxes had previously stopped the Jews' attempts to rebuild the walls of Jerusalem (Ezra 4:11-12, 21).

2. *Arrival in Jerusalem.* Ezra set out from Babylon with his companions to the number of about 1800 including many children on the first day of the first month (end of March, 458 B.C.). The journey occupied exactly four months, including a halt for three days at Ahava, where he collected his caravan and obtained an accession of two hundred and twenty Nethinim from

Iddo, the chief of the Levites at Casiphia. Ashamed to ask a guard from the king, whom he had assured of God's power to protect them, Ezra kept a fast at Ahava to pray for a prosperous journey; and this second caravan arrived safe at Jerusalem on the first day of the fifth month (end of July, 458 B.C.). After resting three days the treasure and vessels were delivered to the priests, burnt sacrifices were offered by the returned exiles, and the king's commissions were delivered to all the satraps west of the Euphrates (Ezra 8).

3. *Marriages with foreigners – Ezra's grief – Foreign wives put away.* On applying himself to the work of reformation, Ezra found the people already infected with the evil that had proved the root of all former mischief, intermarriage with the idolatrous nations around them. His first care was to impress them with the enormity of the sin. The example of his public mourning and prayer led some of the chief persons to come forward, and at their suggestion the whole people were summoned to Jerusalem on penalty of forfeiture and expulsion from the congregation. They assembled on the twentieth day of the ninth month (December, 458 B.C.) amid a storm of rain and, having confessed their sin, they proceeded to the remedy with order and deliberation. All the strange wives were put away, including even those who had borne children, by the beginning of the new year (end of March, 457 B.C. — Ezra 10:44). The divorcing took over two months to complete. At this point the account of Ezra's proceedings ends abruptly with the book that bears his name and he does not appear again till thirteen years later, as the associate of Nehemiah (Neh. 8:1). To the period of Ezra's reform should probably be referred the later prophecies of Zechariah, which relate to the declension, rejection and ultimate restoration of the Jews, and to the glories of the kingdom of Christ (Zech. 9-14).

4. *Grievous condition of Jerusalem – Nehemiah's return – Rebuilding of walls commenced.* In the twentieth year of Artaxerxes (445 B.C.) grievous tidings from Jerusalem reached the royal winter residence at Shushan. Whether Ezra had returned after executing his commission or whether the instability of the Jews and the malice of their enemies had been too much for him, things were in a worse state than at any time since the Captivity. (The reference to the "wall" in Ezra 9:9 and the absence of any reference to Ezra in the early part of Nehemiah causes us to suspect that Ezra may have tried and failed to get a wall-building project underway.)

The people of Judaea were in affliction and reproach; the wall of Jerusalem was still broken down and the gates burned as they had been left by Nebuchadnezzar. This news was brought by Hanani[1] and other Jews of Judaea to NEHEMIAH, the son of Hachaliah, who appears to have belonged to the tribe of Judah and who held the office of cup-bearer to Artaxerxes. Overwhelmed with the tidings, he fasted and prayed to God to incline the king's heart to grant his desire to help his brethren (Nehemiah 1).

Nehemiah was a man of prayer. His book contains many spontaneous (ejaculatory) prayers, offered at times of difficulty and of rejoicing in all places and circumstances (Neh. 1:11; 2:4; 4:4; 5:19; 6:9,14; 13:14,22,29,31). Nehemiah was one of the best rulers Israel ever had — God-fearing, courageous, wise, self-sacrificing, able.

. In Babylon at the end of four months (Chisleu to Nisan, November to March, 444 B.C.) an opportunity offered itself for Nehemiah to go to Jerusalem on the king's observing his cup-bearer's sadness. Nehemiah explained its cause and obtained leave of absence for a fixed time with letters to the governors west of Euphrates to aid his journey, and to Asaph, the keeper of the king's forest, to supply him with timber. Already before his arrival at Jerusalem he became aware of the hostility of Sanballat the Horonite and Tobiah the Ammonite, but he only resolved to do his work with the greater speed. After the usual three days of rest or purification, he took a private view of the city by night and then summoned the rulers to the work (Neh. 2). Led on by the high-priest Eliashib, all of them except the nobles of the Tekoites labored with heart and hand at their regularly appointed stations. The wall soon rose and the gateways were rebuilt (Neh. 3).

5. *Oppositions to rebuilding the walls.* But now Sanballat and Geshem and Tobiah, who had at first scorned the idea of the feeble Jews fortifying their city and had mocked at their wall as too weak for a fence against dogs (or jackals), became seriously alarmed. These three opponents of Nehemiah are now known from extra-biblical sources to have been governors or high officials in Samaria, Ammon and northwest Arabia respectively. A conspiracy was formed of the Arabians and Ammonites and the Philistines of Ashdod for an attack upon Jerusalem before the fortification was complete. Warned by the Jews who dwelt among them, Nehemiah called the people to arms behind the

---

1. Hanani was a brother of Nehemiah (Neh. 1:2; 7:2).

half-finished bulwarks. This attitude of resistance warded off the plot but henceforth half of the people remained under arms while the other half labored at the work, girded with their swords. Nehemiah kept a trumpeter always by his side to sound the alarm and neither he nor his guard put off their clothes except for washing (Neh. 4).

The oppositions by Sanballat, Geshem and Tobiah developed in several stages: (1) Laughter and scorn (Neh. 2:19); (2) Mockery (4:1); (3) Conspiracy and threats (4:8,11); (4) Request for a conference (6:2,7); (5) Attempts to "frame" and "smear" Nehemiah (6:10,13). The same techniques have been used by the enemies of God's successful servants throughout the ages.

Amid all this anxiety he found time for internal reform. The unsettled state of the nation and the pressure of the king's tribute had reduced the poorer citizens to destitution. They had mortgaged their lands and vineyards to their brethren, who moreover exacted usury from them contrary to the law, and many of them were sinking with their families into slavery through their debts. In a solemn assembly Nehemiah rebuked the unmerciful creditors and usurers and bound them by an oath to release the persons and lands of their debtors. He himself set the example of disinterestedness, keeping a table for one hundred and fifty Jews, besides any who returned from exile from time to time, and yet declining to draw the allowance which had been paid to previous governors during the whole twelve years of his rule (445-433 B.C., Neh. 5).

When Sanballat, Tobiah and Geshem saw that the walls were finished, the breaches repaired and that only the gates remained to be hung, they began new plots. Unhappily they were aided by a party of the nobles of Judah, turbulent and rebellious as ever, with whom Tobiah and his son Johanan were connected by family alliances. Their scheme was to frighten Nehemiah with a charge of suspected treason. They invited him to a conference in the plain of Ono, about 30 miles from Jerusalem near Joppa. But they really sought only a chance to harm Nehemiah, and he replied in wise words, "I am doing a great work . . . why should I leave it and come down to you?" (Neh. 6:3). Having failed to entrap him by the proposal of a conference, they wrote to him four times and the fifth time they sent an open letter, that the charge might be made public, declaring that it was reported among the heathen nations round about that the Jews intended to rebel and that Nehemiah was fortifying the city with the intention of making himself king. They charged him with appointing prophets to preach the news, "There is a king in Judah," and threatened to report the whole matter to the king unless Nehemiah would grant them a conference. The prophet Shemaiah was hired to frighten Nehemiah into a step for his own protection, which would have amounted to an act of treason. He contented himself with an indignant denial of the charge made in the letters and with appealing to the judgment of God against Shemaiah, the prophetess Noadiah and the others who tried to frighten him (Neh. 6:10-14).

The walls being finished and the gates hung and the porters and singers and Levites appointed to their stations, Nehemiah committed the charge of the city to his brother Hanani and to Hananiah, the ruler of the palace. The gates were kept barred till the sun was hot and the people were arranged in watches. Such care was the more needful as the city was still much too large for its inhabitants and few houses were yet built. By the seventh month (Tishri = September-October, 444 B.C.), that is, the beginning of the civil new year, the people were settled in their city and Nehemiah had completed the register of their genealogies (Neh. 7; Comp. Ezra 2, where a similar list of names is given. Nehemiah probably used this list as a basis for checking later arrivals and births.).

6. *Religious celebrations – Ezra reads the law – Feast of Tabernacles – Confession of sins – Covenant to keep the law.* The ensuing month, the one especially allotted by Moses to joyful religious celebrations, was celebrated as an inauguration of the people into their new life. If not according to the calendar "the year of release," in which the law was to be read before all the people (Deut. 31:10), it well deserved that title in their annals. Now, for the first time since the decree of Cyrus for their return, they could meet to worship God under the protection of their ramparts, with their new liberties, nay, their very existence as a nation, no longer at the mercy of their inveterate enemies. On the first day of the month the people were gathered as one man in the street before the water-gate and Ezra again appears among them. At their desire he produced the *Book of the Law* and having opened it amid marks of the deepest reverence from all the people, he read it to an audience wrapped in attention from morning to midday. The manner of reading was this: Ezra stood on a pulpit (Heb., tower), with six Scribes or Levites on his right hand and seven on his left, who seem to have relieved him in the reading; for it is said, *"they*

read in the book of the law of God *distinctly*" (Neh. 8:1-8. The text seems to suggest choral reading.).

The people stood in their ranks in front of the pulpit and among them were thirteen other ministers who, with the assistance of the Levites, "caused the people to understand the law." There can be little doubt that this phrase refers to a translation of what Ezra read in Hebrew into the mixed Aramaic dialect, which had become vernacular tongue during the Captivity. The book which was thus read was probably not merely the Pentateuch, but the whole body of sacred writings which had been collected into one volume by the care of Ezra, the first great Scribe, and which formed in substance what we call the BOOK OF THE OLD COVENANT (or Old Testament).

The reading produced an impression like that made on Josiah. All the people wept at what they heard, not only, we may well believe, with regret at the past glories of their nation but at the recital of the sins for which that glory had departed, not unmixed with a penitent consciousness of their own guilt. But Nehemiah (who is now first mentioned in the transaction), supported by Ezra and the Levites, bade them cease their sorrow and go home to "eat the fat, and drink the sweet, and send portions to those for whom nothing was prepared, for the day was holy to Jehovah." The people went away to make great mirth because they understood the words that were declared unto them. When the reading was resumed on the following day, they came to the institution of the Feast of Tabernacles in this very month of Tisri. Their excited minds caught the signal for fresh rejoicing in Jehovah. They went forth into the mount to fetch branches of olive and pine and myrtle and palm and thick trees, and made booths on the roofs and in the courts of their houses, in the Temple court and along the streets to the city gates. Such a Feast of Tabernacles had not been kept since the days of Joshua. The reading of the law was continued for all the seven days of the feast and the eighth was a solemn assembly, as Moses had commanded (Neh. 8).

After the burst of joy for God's mercy in restoring them, they turned to the solemn duty of humiliation and repentance for their sins. The Day of Atonement ought to have been kept on the tenth of this month (Lev. 23:26). It had probably been passed over, as requiring more solemn preparation and a more orderly arrangement of the Temple-service than was yet possible. In its place a fast was held two days after the Feast of Tabernacles on the 24th day of Tisri. All who were of the seed of Israel, carefully separating themselves from the strangers, appeared in the deepest mourning, clad in sackcloth and with earth upon their heads. The day seems to have been divided into four equal parts, only broken by the intervals necessary for refreshment. The first three hours were devoted to the reading of the law. The morning sacrifice fitly introduced the second quarter, which was spent in silent confession and prayer. When the hour of noon was past, the Levites, arranged on the steps of the Temple porch or on a scaffold erected for the purpose, called upon the people to stand up and bless Jehovah. Then in a solemn hymn, the epitome of which is a fit model for all such services, they recited God's mercies from the first call of Abram; they confessed the sins of their forefathers and God's forbearance in punishing without utterly consuming them, and they acknowledged his justice in their present state of humiliation and great distress, as servants to the kings set over them for their sins, to whom their land yielded its increase and who had dominion over their bodies and cattle at their pleasure. Submissive to God's will, they ended by making a new covenant with Him, and before the sun set it was recorded in writing and sealed by the princes, priests and Levites, whose names are recorded by Nehemiah, while the rest of the people bound themselves by a curse and an oath to walk in the law which God had given by Moses. The chief points of this covenant were: to make no intermarriages with the heathen; to abstain from traffic on the Sabbath, and to keep the sabbatic year with its release of all debts; to pay a yearly tax of a third of a shekel for the services of the sanctuary, which are carefully enumerated; to offer the first-fruits and first-born and the tithes due to the Levites and the priests; and in one final word, "We will not forsake the house of our God" (Neh. 9, 10). To most points of this covenant they remained faithful in the *letter*. The sins of the Jewish nation took henceforth a direction altogether different from the open rebellion and apostasy of their fathers. The more scrupulous their observance of the law, the more did they make it void by their traditions and pervert it to serve their selfishness.

7. *The peopling of Jerusalem.* Before the people departed to their homes, it was necessary to decide who of them should fix their abode at Jerusalem, which would have been left almost without inhabitants, had all taken up their residence on their old family allotments about the several cities and villages. It is a striking proof of the attachment of the Jews to their patrimonial

possessions, that the safer residence behind the walls of Jerusalem should not have been the object of competition. But it was regarded as a sacrifice to live there: "And the people blessed all the men that willingly offered themselves to dwell at Jerusalem. The rulers took up their abode in the capital: and for the rest every tenth man was chosen by lot to live there" (Neh. 11:1-2). The language of Nehemiah would almost seem to imply that those of the people who belonged to *Israel* (the Ten Tribes) had their possessions assigned in the cities of Judah and that the inhabitants of Jerusalem were taken from the tribes of Judah and Benjamin. The priests and Levites were divided in due proportions between the city and the country (Neh. 11; 12:1-26).

8. *Dedication of the walls – Levites and singers appointed – Separation from foreigners.* On the completion of all these arrangements a great festival was held for the *Dedication of the Wall* of Jerusalem (Neh. 12:27, 43). Some interpreters have assumed that this festival was held immediately after the completion of the wall, but 12:27 proves that it was after the Levites had been distributed over the country, from which they had to be brought together again. Perhaps the reason for the delay in the dedication was to avoid stirring up further trouble after all the opposition during the rebuilding of the walls. The priests and Levites, called together from all the cities of Judah, purified the walls and the people. The rulers were divided into two parts, which went round the walls in procession to the right and to the left, the one headed by Ezra and the other by Nehemiah, each with his train of priests and Levites blowing trumpets and singing thanks to God. The day was crowned with great sacrifices and their shouts of joy sounded from the rock of Zion far and wide over the hills of Judah (Neh. 12:43). The only remaining records of Nehemiah's first twelve years' government relate to the provision made for the priests and Levites and singers (Neh. 12:44-47); and the separation of the Ammonites and Moabites from the congregation, according to the sentence pronounced on them by Moses (Neh. 13:1-3).

9. *Nehemiah returns to Persia – Apostasy in Judah – The prophet Malachi.* In the thirty-second year of Artaxerxes Longimanus, 433 B.C., Nehemiah returned to the Persian court. During his absence many shocking evils erupted into view in Judah, evils that required Nehemiah to return again and employ drastic correction.

It appears that during his absence, around 430 B.C., that the prophet MALACHI was sent to testify against Judah. His book ends the Scriptures of the old covenant and he is therefore called by the Jews "the *seal* of the prophets." MALACHI (the *angel* or *messenger of Jehovah,* or *my messenger),* closes the canon of the Jewish Scriptures with words rendered doubly impressive by our entire ignorance of his personal history. Like the first prophet of the New Covenant, John the Baptist, whose preaching is an echo of his warnings, he is simply "the *voice* of one crying in the *wilderness,*" and preaching repentance from flagrant sin as the one indispensable preliminary to the reception of the expected Messiah. In this view his prophecy links the Old Covenant with the New, and the connection is made closer by his prediction of the coming of John the Baptist, as the Elijah of the new dispensation and the forerunner of the Angel-Jehovah, the messenger of the Covenant (Mal. 3:1; 4:5-6). Already was the Jewish Church groaning under the dissolution of the homes, the first and most sacred bonds of social life, and the new Elijah was needed to "turn the heart of the fathers to the children, and the heart of the children to their fathers," lest the expected Messiah should come only "to smite the earth with a curse." We have only to read the prophet's denunciation of rulers, priests and people to see that he is describing present evils and not merely predicting some future declension. These descriptions serve to fix the date of the prophecy. They agree so exactly with the state of things which Nehemiah found on the occasion of his last visit to Jerusalem, that the prophecy may be safely referred to the period just before Nehemiah returned to Jerusalem the second time. If Nehemiah had already visited Jerusalem the second time and made the strong reforms described in Neh. 13 before Malachi appeared, it seems unlikely that the evils described by Malachi would have been present. Therefore it seems preferable to date Malachi about 430 B.C., shortly before Nehemiah's second return.

The evils denounced by Malachi are the same as those dealt with forthrightly by Nehemiah: (1) Pollution of the priesthood (Neh. 13:22, 28; Mal. 1:6-8); (2) Marrying heathen wives (Neh. 13:23-24; Mal. 2:11); (3) Neglect of tithes (Neh. 13:10-12; Mal. 3:8-10); (4) Sabbath violations (Neh. 13:15-21; Mal. 3:14).

The fact that Nehemiah does not mention Malachi in his book suggests that Malachi was not preaching during Nehemiah's

second visit to Jerusalem. But this fact does not disprove the
probability that Malachi had preached for a brief period before
Nehemiah's return.

It is most probable that Ezra, the collector of the canonical
Scriptures, lived long enough to include in the Canon the book of
Malachi, as well as that of Nehemiah.

10. *Nehemiah's second return from Persia – Purification of the
priesthood – Sabbath violations abolished.* After an interval in Persia,
of what length we know not,[1] Nehemiah obtained the king's
permission to go and visit Jerusalem again in order to reform
serious abuses which had grown up through the weakness of the
high-priest Eliashib and the rapacity of the princes. Eliashib had
yielded the claims of Tobiah, which Nehemiah had so firmly
resisted; his grandson had married a daughter of the other
adversary, Sanballat (Neh. 13:28); Eliashib had prepared for
Tobiah a large chamber in the court of the Temple which had
been used as a store-house for the sacred vessels, the
meat-offerings and frankincense, and the tithes of corn, wine and
oil for the Levites, all of which had been removed to make room
for the furniture of Tobiah. Nehemiah cleared out the furniture
and caused the chambers of the Temple to be purified and
restored to their uses (Neh. 13:4-9). The Levites, defrauded of
their tithes, had betaken themselves to the Levitical cities, so that
the Temple was deserted. Nehemiah gathered them together
again, compelled the rulers to do them justice and the people to
bring the tithes, and appointed faithful treasurers (Neh.
13:10-14). He most indignantly reproved the nobles for the
profanation of the Sabbath, as the sin which had brought the
wrath of God upon their fathers. In the cities of Judah
wine-presses were trodden on the holy day and the gates of
Jerusalem were crowded with Tyrian and other merchants, who
carried in the supplies of luxury for a great city (Neh. 13:16).
Nehemiah had the city gates shut from dusk till the end of the
Sabbath and guarded by his servants. At first the merchants
pitched their tents round the wall, but Nehemiah called the
Levites to guard the gates and the Sabbath trading was abolished.
His last reform dealt with the old evil of the mixed marriages,
which had again been contracted with women of Ammon, Moab

---

1. Neh. 13:6. "After the end of days," is the only note of the time, but the phrase "all this time," as well as the
extent of the abuses, would seem to imply a considerable interval. The inference is still stronger from the
allusion in 13:24 to the children of the mixed marriages. Probably five to ten years were necessary to fulfill
these conditions. We suppose he returned about 428 B.C.

and Ashdod to such an extent that children were heard talking in a dialect half Jewish and half the language of Ashdod (Neh. 13:23-24). By the most energetic measures, Nehemiah exacted an oath of the offenders to abstain from all such alliances, and he expelled from the priesthood a son of Joiada, the son of the high-priest Eliashib, for his marriage with the daughter of Sanballat the Horonite (Neh. 13:28-29).

Nehemiah's narrative of these reforms is interspersed with the frequent appeal, "Remember me, O my God, for good, and spare me according to the greatness of thy mercy; wipe not out my good deeds that I have done for the house of my God, and for the observances thereof" (Neh. 13:14, 22, 31). His prayer has been answered ever since in the preservation of his book as a part of Holy Scriptures: the record of pure religious zeal tempered with that prudence, which is one of the highest duties of a governor, of unbending fidelity and self-denying liberality, all for the glory and in the fear of God.

11. *Collection of Old Testament books by Ezra – The great synagogue.* We must make note of the final collection of the Old Testament books, an act that was most probably done by Ezra. According to Josephus *(Ant.* XI, v. 5) Ezra died an old man. He lived long enough after the last people and events referred to in the Old Testament[1] to have collected all the books that are in the Old Testament. Ezra appears to have written the books of Chronicles, for his own book begins with the ending of II Chronicles (II Chron. 36:22-23; Ezra 1:1-3). He made the complete collection and arrangement of the Jewish Scriptures into one canon.[2] This did not involve any decision by Ezra as to which books of the many ancient Hebrew religious writings were inspired of God, for the true books had either been recognized by God-fearing men as divine from their very first appearance (note Jer. 36:16), or had been certified by fulfilled prophecies and miracles.

---

1. The last people and events would include: (1) the reign of Darius (Nothus) the Persian (423-404 B.C.); (2) Jaddua the priest (Neh. 12:11, 22), who was alive when Alexander the Great took Jerusalem (322 B.C.), but died shortly thereafter (Josephus, *Ant.* XI, 8:4-5, 7); he could have been a young man in the time of Ezra; (3) Pelatiah, the grandson of Zerubbabel, who led the first return of Jews from captivity (I Chron. 3:19-21). Ezra and Nehemiah could have written about all of these as early as 420. The completed canon need be dated no later than this.

2. The word *Canon* in classical Greek signifies properly a *straight rod,* as a carpenter's rule; and hence is applied metaphorically to a *testing rule* in ethics, or in art, or in language (the *Canons* of Grammar). As applied to Scripture, the word indicates the rule by which the contents of the Bible must be determined and thus secondarily a list of the constituent books. The Canon of Scripture may be generally described as "the collection of books which forms the original and authoritative written rule of the faith and practice of the Church."

There was every reason for the complete canon of Scripture to be collected and made known as early as possible after the return from Babylonian captivity. For this great work no other man was as well qualified as Ezra, in fact no other person is known who might have done this work (see Josephus, *Against Apion*, 1.8). That the work was performed by an inspired man is an axiom lying at the foundation of the whole question; unless we believe, on the one hand, that the Church is endowed in every age with power to decide what Scriptures are canonical or useless; on the other hand, we give up a *canon* in the proper sense of the word and reduce the authority of Scripture to that which literary criticism can establish for its separate books. If we do this we fly in the face of the authority of the Lord Jesus Christ, who spoke of the Scriptures as being a finished and settled collection of books (John 5:39; Luke 24:27), and said that the Scriptures cannot be broken (John 10:35), and that not one word of the law would pass away till all things be accomplished (Matt. 5:18).

To Ezra also is ascribed by Jewish tradition the establishment of the Great Synagogue, a council appointed to reorganize the religious life of the people. It consisted of 120 members with Ezra as president. While Neh. 8:13 implies the existence of a body of men acting as counsellors under the direction of Ezra, further details about this body are not known with any certainty.

12. *Samaritan temple built on Mt. Gerezim*. Sometime after 423 B.C., Manasseh, a grandson of the high-priest Eliashib, fled to his father-in-law Sanballat in Samaria after his banishment by Nehemiah because of his marriage (Neh. 13:28). Sanballat then built a rival temple on Mt. Gerezim. The Samaritans rejected the prophets and writings of the Old Testament, but kept a corrupted form of the Pentateuch. Their temple was destroyed by a Jewish leader named John Hyrcanus about 109 B.C. It was to this sanctuary, as well as to the ancient sacrifices of the patriarchs at Shechem, that the Samaritan woman referred in the words — "Our fathers worshipped in this mountain" (John 4:20).

Questions Over Section IV
Returns of Ezra and Nehemiah

Questions over Ezra 7-10
1. During the reign of what king did Ezra return (7:1,8)?
2. What was the date of his return?
3. What was Ezra's office (7:6)?

4. What three things had Ezra set his heart to do (7:10)?
5. What did the king give to Ezra that authorized his return (7:11)?
6. How much money was given to Ezra (7:15-16)?
7. How did Ezra react to the king's generosity and help (7:27-28)?
8. Approximately how many came back with Ezra?
9. By what river did the returnees gather as they started their journey home (8:15)?
10. Why was a fast proclaimed by the river (8:21-22)?
11. How was the safe delivery of the silver and gold checked (8:26,33)?
12. Did the returnees have a safe journey (8:31-32)?
13. What evil in Judah was reported to Ezra (9:1-2)?
14. How did Ezra react to this news (9:3)?
15. What did Ezra confess in prayer (9:6-7,12)?
16. Who gathered as Ezra prayed (10:1)?
17. How did the people show their guilt (10:1)?
18. What did Israel make a covenant with God to do (10:3)?
19. Where were the people to assemble to put away foreign wives (10:7)? What would happen to them if they did not come (10:8)?
20. What was the weather like when the people assembled (10:9)?
21. Did the people agree to put away the foreign wives (10:12-13)? Did all agree (10:15)?
22. How long did the divorce proceedings require (10:9,17)?
23. What groups of Israelites had married foreign women (10:18, 23, 24, 25)?

Questions on Nehemiah
1. Give the headings of the two parts of the outline of Nehemiah.
2. At what city did Nehemiah serve the king of Persia (Neh. 1:1)?
3. Under what king did Nehemiah serve (2:1)?
4. What was Nehemiah's office for the king (2:1)?
5. Who was Hanani (1:2; 7:2)?
6. What report about Jerusalem was given to Nehemiah (1:3)?
7. What did Nehemiah confess to God (1:6-7)?
8. For what did Nehemiah pray when he heard the bad news about Jerusalem (1:11)?

9. What did the king observe about Nehemiah (2:2)?
10. How prominent was prayer in Nehemiah's life (2:4; 4:4; et al)?
11. What did Nehemiah ask of the king (2:5)?
12. Who were Nehemiah's three adversaries (2:10, 19)?
13. When did Nehemiah inspect Jerusalem (2:12-13)?
14. What did Nehemiah challenge the Jews to do (2:17-18)?
15. What was the first reaction of the enemies to the wall-building project (2:19)?
16. Does Nehemiah 3 sound to you like an eye-witness account?
17. Name the seven gates of Jerusalem mentioned in Nehemiah 3.
18. What very unnoble behavior is reported about some nobles (3:5)?
19. How was Sanballat's opposition to the wall-building project expressed (4:1)?
20. What was stated about a fox and the wall (4:3)?
21. Why was the wall soon builded to half its height (4:6)?
22. What violent plot did the enemies make (4:8,11)?
23. How was the plot prevented (4:9, 13)?
24. What did half the workmen do as the work progressed (4:16)?
25. What did Nehemiah use as an alarm system (4:20)?
26. What were the working hours as they built the wall (4:21)?
27. What did the people cry to Nehemiah about (5:1-2)?
28. What had the people borrowed money to pay (5:4)?
29. What is usury (5:7)?
30. What demand did Nehemiah make of the nobles and rulers (5:7-10)?
31. How did Nehemiah dramatize his insistence that the nobles stop taking usury (5:13)?
32. How much salary had Nehemiah collected as governor? How much money for food allowance had he received (5:14, 18)?
33. How many people did Nehemiah feed each day (5:17)?
34. What did Nehemiah's enemies request when they saw the walls completed (6:1-2)?
35. Where was Ono?
36. What did one of the Jews urge Nehemiah to do? Why did he urge him to do this (6:10-13)?
37. How long did it take to build the wall (6:15)?
38. Why were many in Judah sympathetic to their enemies (6:17-19)?

39. Whom did Nehemiah appoint over Jerusalem (7:2)?
40. What precaution was taken about opening the gates (7:3)?
41. What was lacking in Jerusalem after the walls were built (7:4)?
42. What came into Nehemiah's heart to do after the walls were built (7:5)?
43. Who requested that the law be read (8:1)?
44. How long did Ezra read (8:3)?
45. Who assisted Ezra in the reading (8:7)?
46. In what manner was the law read (8:8)?
47. What was spoken during the reading besides the words of the law (8:8)?
48. How were the people told to feel when the law was read (8:9)?
49. What feast was observed after the law was read (8:14-15; Lev. 23:42)?
50. In what frame of mind did Israel assemble later that month (9:1-2)?
51. From what did the Israelites separate themselves (9:2)?
52. What history was narrated in the prayer of the Levites (9:6-37)?
53. When was the Sabbath day made known to man (9:13-14)?
54. How far did Israel's rebellion go in the time of Moses (9:17)?
55. How did Israel have clothing during the wilderness wanderings (9:21)?
56. What did the people promise God that they would make with Him (9:38; 10:28-29)?
57. Who was the first one to seal the covenant to obey God (10:1)?
58. What things did those who sealed the covenant promise to do (10:29-32, 35, 37)?
59. How was the population of Jerusalem increased (11:1-2)?
60. How many generations of priests does Neh. 12:10-11 trace?
61. Who were brought to Jerusalem for the dedication of the walls (12:27)?
62. Who led the two companies that marched around the walls of Jerusalem on opposite sides of town (12:31, 36)?
63. How loud was the praise when the two groups converged (12:40, 43)?
64. What nations were excluded from the house of God? Why (13:1-2; Deut. 23:3-5)?
65. What prophet probably prophesied during Nehemiah's absence after his first governorship (13:6)?
66. Who was Eliashib (13:4)?

67. For whom had Eliashib prepared a great chamber (or apartment) (13:5)?
68. What did Nehemiah do with Tobiah's stuff (13:8)?
69. How did Nehemiah provide the living for the priests (13:10-12)?
70. What was being done on the Sabbath days (13:15-16)?
71. How did Nehemiah stop the Sabbath activity (13:15-22)?
72. How did the children of mixed marriages speak (13:23-24)?
73. Whom had Eliashib's grandson married (13:28)?
74. What did Nehemiah do to Eliashib's grandson (13:28)?
75. Who collected the books of the Old Testament into one canon?
76. Where did the Samaritans build a temple?

Special Study
Between the Testaments
By Seth Wilson

History of the Interval

Although no Old Testament books record the history of this period, there were Jewish writings during the time. Some of these are the "Apocrypha," about 14 books or portions to be added to the Old Testament books, which have been "canonized" as a part of the Old Testament by the Roman Catholic Church. Of these, the first Book of Maccabees is the most valuable as history. Josephus, a Jewish historian who was born in the decade after Jesus' crucifixion, wrote two important works — "The Antiquities of the Jews" and "The Jewish Wars" — which give an account of the Jews from 170 B.C., through the destruction of Jerusalem by Titus in 70 A.D. The history of the empires of the world during this period between the Old and New Testaments is well covered by Greek and Roman historians. Moreover, this period is pictured with amazing accuracy, prophetically, in the Book of Daniel (Dan. 2:36-45; 7:3-8, 17; 8:3-22; 11:2-45). The history of the Jews in these times may be divided into six periods:

1. *The Persian Period* (538-332 B.C.). The return from Babylon took place under Persian rule (Ezra 1). Under the Persians, the Jews were usually governed by their own high priest, subject to the Syrian satrap or governor. Persian rule was usually mild and often very favorable toward the Jews (e.g., the stories of

Zerubbabel, Ezra, Nehemiah, Esther, Daniel). The Samaritans and renegade Jews caused the most trouble in this period. The Samaritan temple on Mt. Gerizin was built about 423 B.C., a seat of degenerate Judaism that continues until today.

2. *The Greek or Macedonian Period* (332-323 B.C.). The Persian rule was broken by the world-sweeping conquests of Alexander the Great, out of Macedonia. Alexander showed consideration for the Jews and did not destroy or plunder Jerusalem. His short but brilliant career had far-reaching results in the introduction of Greek language over Palestine and all the Mediterranean area.

3. *The Egyptian Period* (323-198 B.C.). On the death of Alexander, his empire was divided among four of his generals. Seleucus ruled Syria and Ptolemy ruled Egypt. Palestine, between them, was claimed by both of them. The Ptolmies early attached Palestine to Egypt. "They extended such privileges to Jewish settlers on the Nile, that Alexandria became the center of a large Jewish population and a celebrated seat of Jewish learning." It was, for the most part, a century of prosperity for the Jews. The most important event was the translation of the Old Testament into Greek at Alexandria. The Greek version is known as the Septuagint (meaning "seventy"), from the traditional number of translators.

4. *The Syrian Period* (198-167 B.C.). The Seleucidae (Greek kings of Syria) finally recovered Palestine from Egypt. "The period of Syrian rule was the darkest yet most glorious in the whole four hundred years. The Seleucidae were dissolute tyrants. Antiochus Epiphanes (175-164 B.C.) was the most notorious of them all. Returning on one occasion from defeat in Egypt, he vented his vengeance on Jerusalem. He massacred forty thousand of its population, stripped the temple of its treasures and outraged the religious sense of the Jews by sacrificing a sow on the altar and sprinkling the interior of the temple with the liquor in which a portion of the unclean beast had been boiled. He sought by every means to stamp out the Hebrew religion and spirit and transform the nation into Greeks. He shut up the temple and, on pain of death, prohibited the Jewish religion. Multitudes heroically sacrificed their lives rather than their faith." — B.S. Dean

5. *The Maccabean Period* (167-63 B.C.). A heroic revolt against such violence and sacrilege was led by a family of priest-patriots known as the Maccabees. An old priest, named Mattathias, and his five sons, in turn, led the Jews in a war for independence,

which was finally gained after thirty years of struggle. Judas Maccabeus (166-161 B.C.) led in a remarkable series of victories and re-opened, cleansed and rededicated the temple in honor of which the Feast of Dedication continued to be kept (John 10:22). Judas fell in battle but his brothers (first Jonathan, then Simon) fought on, and taking advantage of political deals with rivals for the Syrian throne, obtained in turn the dual office of governor and high priest recognized by Syria. Simon lived his last days in peace and made a league with Rome. He was succeeded by his son, John Hyrcanus, who was subdued by the Syrian ruler for a time, but found opportunity to throw off the yoke and went on to conquer much additional territory. His change from the Pharisee party to the Sadducees caused much bitter strife at home. His son was ambitious and murderous, took the title of king, ended the glory of a great family, started it on its decline, a period of 60 years filled with intrigue and barbarous civil war.

6. *The Roman Period* (63 B.C., through the New Testament period). Pompey captured Jerusalem in 63 B.C. The plots and murders of the different members of the Maccabee family continued to curse the land. Antipater, of Idumea (Edom), and his famous infamous son Herod, took part in the rivalries and the deals with Rome until Herod finally conquered Judea, amidst shocking atrocities in 37 B.C. He destroyed the rest of the Maccabee family, including his wife, Mariamne. This Herod rebuilt the temple (larger than Solomon's and much richer than Zerubbabel's), and slaughtered the babies of Bethlehem in an attempt to murder the Messiah (Matthew 2). He gave to the kingdom the greatest external splendor it ever knew, save in the reigns of David and Solomon. Yet the moral and religious quality of his reign was deplorable. Despite the outward splendor, Israel chafed under the yoke of subjection to Rome and under the crimes of Herod's regime. "The tabernacle of David was, indeed, fallen, and the elect spirits of the nation, the 'Israel within Israel,' looked and longed for him who should raise it up again and build it as in the days of old (Amos 9:12)." — B.S. Dean

There arose a party of *Herodians* who favored the rulers of the Herod family and their collaboration with Rome. An opposite party of *Zealots* worked "underground" to bring violent action against all such. The *Sadducees,* a small but influential party mostly of priests, became political opportunists, conniving at wrongs and losing faith in the scriptures. The *Pharisees,* who began as faithful upholders of the law against all Gentile influences, became self-righteous and hypocritical formalists, seeking public acclaim and political influence. Even devout believers among the common folk became political-minded and materialistic and found it hard to accept the spiritual nature of the kingdom of Christ as the fulfillment of Israel's hopes.

Preparations for the Coming of Christ

Throughout this dark period God was working His own plan for Israel. Several developments in these centuries helped to bring about the "fulness of time" for the Messiah to come.

1. *The Dispersion of the Jews.* Many more were scattered abroad throughout the empire than lived in the homeland, yet everywhere they remained Jews. Thus they became world-wide missionaries of the knowledge of the true God and of a message of hope in a hopeless world.

2. *The Synagogue,* which probably arose to meet the needs of the exiles in Babylon, became the center of worship for many of them who were too far separated from the temple and the place of instruction for all. The reading in the synagogue every Sabbath fixed the eyes of Israel more firmly on their Scriptures and the promised Messiah. Thus the synagogue everywhere became the great missionary institute, imparting to the world Israel's exalted Messianic hopes. Then after the gospel of Christ was given, synagogues became key places to begin its proclamation, and they furnished prepared persons for leadership and oversight in the new church.

3. *The Spread of the Greek language* prepared the world for the Word of God.

4. *The Septuagint Translation of the Old Testament,* spread throughout the world by the Jews and their synagogues, prepared the world for the gift of God in His Son. The Septuagint thus is a distinct forward movement in the fulfillment of the Abrahamic promise (Gen. 12:3; 18:18).

5. *Rome made of the world one empire* and Roman roads made all parts of it accessible, while Roman stress on law and order maintained a comparatively high degree of peace and safety, which encouraged travel and communication.

6. "The Jews themselves, embittered by long-continued martyrdoms and suffering, utterly carnalized this Messianic expectation in an increasing ratio as the yoke of the oppressor grew heavier and the hope of deliverance grew fainter. And thus when their Messiah came, Israel recognized Him not, while the

heart-hungry heathen humbly received Him (John 1:9-14). The eyes of Israel were blinded for a season, 'till the fulness of the Gentiles shall be gathered in' (Rom. 9:32; 11:25)." — H.E. Dosker

7. *The Silence of Prophecy for Four Hundred Years,* immediately preceded by the clear prediction of the coming of a great messenger like Elijah (Mal. 3:1; 4:5,6), put dramatic emphasis upon the message of John the Baptist. It strongly accented every inspired utterance that announced the coming of the Christ.

Bibliography on the Period Between the Testaments

Dana, H.E., *The New Testament World* pp. 7-106.
Free, Joseph P., *Archaeology and Bible History* pp. 255-282.
International Standard Bible Encyclopedia, art. "Between the Testaments."
Payne, J. Barton, *An Outline of Hebrew History* pp. 162-219.
Pfeiffer, Charles F., *Between the Testaments.*

INDEX

INDEX

INDEX

Machpelah, 96, 97, 138, 139
Mahanaim, 110, 464, 465, 502, 503
Malachi, 737, 738
Manasseh, King, 377, 663-665
  Son of Joseph, 128, 133
  Tribe, 319, 320, 321, 322
Manna, 181, 182, 214, 254, 307
Marah, 181
Marriage, 14
Mattaniah, See Zedekiah.
Measures, See Weights & Measures.
Media, 25, 670, 704
Megiddo, 61, 611, 671
Melchizedek, 78, 79
Memphis, 118, 119, 122
Menahem, 635, 637
Mephibosheth, 464, 466, 467, 485, 486, 501, 505
Merarites, See Levites.
Merodach-baladan, 555, 659
Merom, Waters of, 64, 313, 344
Mesha, 603
Messiah (Christ), 8, 21, 73, 135, 475, 476, 747
Methuselah, 30, 32
Micah, idolater, 377-378
Micah, prophet, 612
Micaiah, 596-597
Michal, 412, 430, 431, 465, 466, 472
Michmash, 409-412
Middle Kingdom of Egypt, 120, 126
Midian (Midianites), 125, 126, 153, 154, 173, 277, 350-353, 355-358
Midwives, 151
Millo, 469, 538
Miriam, 151, 152, 260, 267
Mizpah, 395, 396, 406, 587, 690-691
Moab (Moabites), 25, 65, 84, 271-272, 273-274, 277, 286, 381-383, 433, 476-477, 543, 559-560, 581, 599, 603-604, 631
Molech, 490, 543, 625, 664
Months, See Calendar.
Mordecai, 679, 724-726
Moriah, 89, 457, 458, 509, 529
Moses, 6, 140, 141, 148-149, 151-165, 180-184, 187-192, 201, 227, 233, 253, 256-271, 278, 286-294
Mountains, See also
  names of individual mtns.

N

Naaman, 605
Nabal, 435, 438-439

Nabonidus, 556, 703, 704, 705
Nabopolassar, 555, 670, 676
Naboth, 595, 596, 597, 609
Nadab, king of Israel, 583
  Priest, 213, 227, 256
Nahor, 69, 70
Nahum, 612, 669, 670
Naomi, 381-382
Naphtali, 109, 137, 323
Nathan, 421, 475, 478, 485, 488, 489, 511, 513
Nazirite, 231, 255, 370, 391
Nebo, Mt., 271, 276, 291
Nebuchadnezzar, 555, 556, 676, 677, 678, 679, 680, 683-688, 690-692, 699-704
Necho (Pharaoh), 121, 670, 671, 674, 684
Nehemiah, 714, 730-739
Nethinim, 219, 311, 718
New Kingdom of Egypt, 120-121
New Moon, Feast. See Feasts.
Nile River, 116, 117-118, 159
Nimrod, 54
Nineveh, See Assyria.
No (No Amon, or Thebes), 119, 120, 122
Noah, 36-40, 44-47
Numbers, 251-252

O

Obadiah, Book, 557, 607, 689
  Servant of Ahab, 588, 591
Obed-edom, 471, 474
Offerings, Burnt, 212, 228-230, 537, 720
  Meal, 230-231
  Peace, 228-231
  Sin, 228, 231-232
  Trespass, 228, 232
Og, 94, 272-273
Old Kingdom of Egypt, 119-120
Omri, 585
Oppression of Israel, 150-151, 152, 153, 156-157
Osiris, 122-123
Othniel, 321, 336, 341, 342

P

Palestine, 57-67
Paran, Wilderness, 172, 173
Passover, See Feasts.
Patriarchal dispensation, 3, 149
Patriarchs, 29, 30
Peace offerings, See Offerings.

INDEX

The seed of the woman...shall bruise the serpent's he[ad] Gen. 3:15

The Lord will raise up unto thee a prophet like unto me (Moses). Deut. 18:15